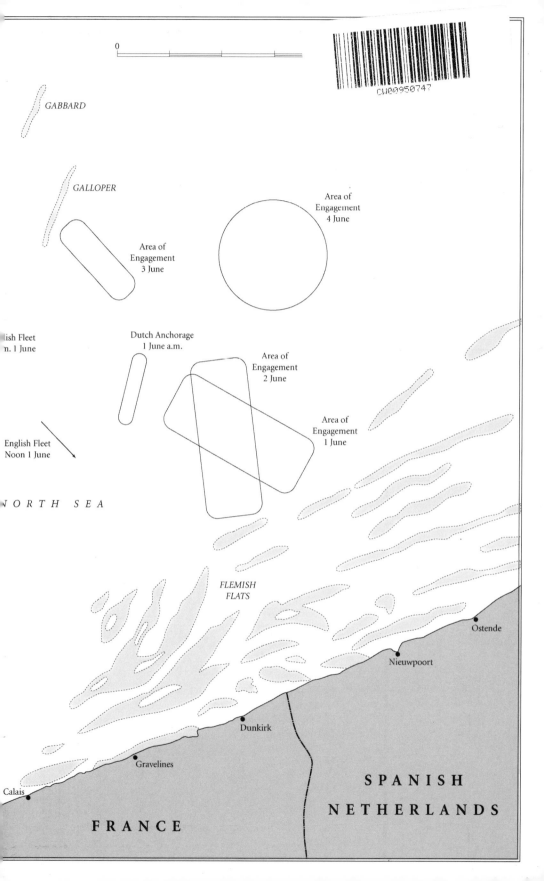

0

GABBARD

GALLOPER

Area of
Engagement
4 June

Area of
Engagement
3 June

ish Fleet
n. 1 June

Dutch Anchorage
1 June a.m.

Area of
Engagement
2 June

English Fleet
Noon 1 June

Area of
Engagement
1 June

NORTH SEA

*FLEMISH
FLATS*

Ostende

Nieuwpoort

Dunkirk

Gravelines

Calais

SPANISH

NETHERLANDS

FRANCE

THE
Four Days' Battle
of 1666

THE
Four Days' Battle
of 1666

*The Greatest Sea Fight
of the Age of Sail*

FRANK L FOX

Seaforth
PUBLISHING

Copyright © Frank L. Fox 1996 & 2009

First published 1996 as *A Distant Storm*

This edition first published in Great Britain in 2009 by
Seaforth Publishing,
Pen & Sword Books Ltd,
47 Church Street,
Barnsley S70 2AS

www.seaforthpublishing.com

British Library Cataloguing in Publication Data
A catalogue record for this book is available from the British Library

ISBN 978-1-84832-044-4

Designed and typeset by M.A.T.S. Typesetting, Southend-on-Sea, Essex
Printed and bound in Great Britain by the Cromwell Press Group, Trowbridge

Contents

List of Illustrations

Preface

On Friday, 1 June 1666, a large English fleet met a larger Dutch fleet in battle off the mouth of the Thames. A victor not being declared by nightfall, the contest resumed on Saturday. The antagonists pounded away all that day, sparred intermittently on Sunday, and then on Monday practically knocked each other to pieces. That afternoon, the outnumbered English at length abandoned the 'field' to conclude what had been the greatest engagement fought on the seas in all the age of sail. This tremendous encounter has long fascinated naval specialists, partly because of the sheer length and magnitude of the battle and partly because of the colossal mistake that led up to it. In view of the considerable controversy and speculation surrounding the affair, it is perhaps surprising that this is the first English-language book to be written about it.

Many readers will already be familiar with the rough outline of the campaign: the English, at war with both France and the Netherlands, heard incorrectly that a French fleet was approaching to join the Dutch. Prince Rupert, one of the English commanders, sailed with a strong squadron to meet the French, only to have the Royal Navy's weakened remainder under the Duke of Albemarle encounter Michiel de Ruyter's Dutch fleet. Recalled shortly before the battle, Prince Rupert returned in time to take part in the final day's fighting but could not reverse the outcome. Beyond that basic sequence of events, questions abound. What intelligence made the English think the French were near? What, precisely, was Rupert expected to do, and what prompted his recall? Why did the Duke of Albemarle choose to give battle at a disadvantage? Was he simply overconfident? Published accounts in English say little about the French fleet. Where was it, and why did it not join the Dutch? Did Louis XIV betray his allies? As for the fighting itself, historians are much at odds over tactics and manoeuvres. Even such fundamentals as where the action took place and the strength of the opposing forces have been matters of dispute.

Most of these questions are answered here with reasonable certainty. There are several surprises, especially the hitherto little-suspected role of Ireland in the division of the fleet. But much remains in doubt. The Four Days' Battle was an event of such overwhelming complexity that for some witnesses it literally defied description. The classic case (though unfortunately not unique) is a lieutenant's log in which day-to-day activities were normally set forth in minute detail; but for the battle, there is no information other than the infuriating excuse that 'ye particulars are too long for a journall'. Those mariners (including admirals) who did write down their recollections were seldom noted for their graceful articulation with the pen. Their wording is often bewilderingly ambiguous. Comparing several such halting accounts of a given incident frequently yields a reasonable explanation of events – but not always. Some stages of the battle such as the opening manoeuvres of the fourth day are very much subject to interpretation and undoubtedly will remain so.

The Four Days' Battle was the most spectacular event of the Second Anglo-Dutch War, but not the only one. Of the other important actions, the raid on the Vlie is admirably described by Richard Ollard in *Man of War, Sir Robert Holmes and the Restoration Navy*, and the attack on the English fleet at Chatham is fully dissected by P.G. Rogers in *The Dutch in the Medway*. But the battles of Lowestoft, Bergen, and St. James's Day have not been so thoroughly studied from the English viewpoint and are therefore covered here in somewhat greater detail than strict necessity demands for such peripheral subjects. Really proper treatment, however, would require a fairly thick volume for each.

Anyone writing on seventeenth-century naval subjects inevitably encounters language difficulties. Some familiar nautical terms of today had not yet appeared, others common at the time have since disappeared, and still others have changed meaning. For example, a *convoy* in the 1600s was not a group of escorted merchant-men, but the escort itself. Such expressions have generally been used here in their modern sense, or avoided entirely if a suitable substitute presented itself. But some long-lost terms that appear frequently in quotations may require explanation. *Grain* meant the water directly ahead of a ship along its projected course, the opposite of the familiar *wake*. *Tack*, the modern word meaning to change or reverse a ship's course by swinging the head into the wind, was already in use. But one as often finds the seventeenth-century captain writing that 'We hauled our larboard tacks on board', meaning that they tacked to port. *Port* was not used as the opposite of *starboard* (though I have employed it as such in the text); *larboard* was preferred instead, and *port* was restricted to its original meaning of an opening in a ship's hull. A greater potential pitfall is that the modern opposite of *tack*, to *wear* (or change course by swinging a ship's head downwind), was not in the mid-seventeenth century vocabulary; its meaning was expressed by the phrase *bear up*, which can cause untold confusion for the unwary. To reduce the likelihood of misunderstanding I have occasionally given it in the text as 'bear up to leeward', though pedants among Restoration seamen would have cringed in horror at such redundancy. Incidentally, the most lubberly readers will probably be the most accurate in pronouncing seventeenth-century nautical terms. Phonetic spellings in letters and journals show that many of the familiar seaman's contractions of today were yet to evolve. Thus, a forecastle was not a 'fo'c's'le', but a 'fore kastell', and *topgallant* was spoken just as it looks. *Tampion*, however, was already pronounced 'tomkin' and was often so spelled.

England in the 1600s was still using the Julian (Old Style) calendar in which the year began on 25 March and in which all the dates were ten days behind the modern Gregorian (New Style) calendar already adopted elsewhere in Europe. Following the conventional compromise of British historians, all dates in this book including those in quotations have been adjusted to Old Style except that the year is taken to begin on 1 January. A very few exceptions have been clearly labelled.

The text is as thoroughly documented as possible, but since the notes give no information other than sources and historiography, they have been banished to a separate page-referenced appendix to avoid the distractions of superscriptions and footnotes. The verses at the chapter heads are from Dryden's intensely patriotic *Annus Mirabilis*, published in November 1666. I have taken some of them outrageously out of context.

This book was produced over a period of twelve years, during which I was graciously assisted by more people than I could possibly name. I must offer special acknowledgement to Dr R.E.J. Weber of the Koninklijke Nederlandse Akademie van Wettenschapen for supplying invaluable data on the Dutch fleet, to the late G.C. Dik for his help with Dutch shipbuilding, to Brian Lavery for sharing his discovery of many useful documents, to Elsbee Hurst for translating Dutch sources, to Mary Malloy for grammatical and stylistic advice, to Peter Wilkinson (after an original by Nathan Glick) for the map on the endpapers, and to Amy Miller for accurately and patiently typing successive versions of the text. Thanks are also due to Richard Ollard, Dr P.J. Le Fevre, Adrian Caruana, and M.S. Robinson, all of whom uncovered errors in the manuscript and suggested important revisions (though they are in no way responsible for mistakes which undoubtedly remain). Robinson also made available his extensive research on seventeenth-century marine art, transcribed innumerable documents, and gave encouragement without which the whole enterprise might have foundered. I am also eternally grateful to David Roberts for having enough faith in the project to publish it, and for the unfailing cooperation, tact, and good humour with which he guided it to fruition.

The second edition contains some revisions to correct errors which have been uncovered in the thirteen years since the original version appeared. The revised edition came about largely through the interest, encouragement, and direct assistance of Bruce Twickler, to whom I am deeply grateful. Finally, thanks are due to my patient, good-humoured, and thoroughly professional editor at Seaforth Publishing, Rob Gardiner.

Chapter I

The Generals

To see this fleet upon the ocean move,
Angels drew wide the curtains of the skies;
And Heav'n, as if there wanted lights above,
For tapers made two glaring comets rise.

A battle is more than just a brief flurry of madness. The clash itself is only the most memorable occurrence – an emphatic punctuation – in a long train of interlocking decisions, actions, and coincidences which always begin long before the decisive moment. This was particularly true of the Four Days' Battle. The great engagement was shaped and influenced by over a decade of events, all of which have a place in the story. It seems appropriate, however, to select a starting point somewhat nearer the battle, and a convenient beginning can be found in a minor administrative ritual which took place on a winter day in the year 1666. It was such a mundane and everyday proceeding that the details of the scene are not even recorded; but on that day, somewhere in the rambling palace of Whitehall, a luxuriantly bewigged gentleman in his early thirties flourished a freshly inked quill over the foot of a handwritten document and scribbled his signature: 'James'.

With that short stroke of the pen, the chief sea command of the Royal Navy of England instantly changed hands. The heading of the document, written in a beautiful clerkly script, identified its author as 'James, Duke of York and Albany, Earle of Ulster, Lord High Admirall of England and Ireland & Constable of Dover Castle, Lord Warden of ye Cinque Ports and Governour of Portsmouth &c'. It was addressed 'To my most dear and entirely beloved Cousin Prince Rupert and George Duke of Albemarle'. The paper contained a single wordy paragraph written in the flowing, convoluted style so dear to seventeenth-century officialdom. It began:

> Whereas ye King my Soveraigne Lord and Brother hath thought fitt and expedient for his service, that ye chief Command of his Majs. Fleet should be exercised by Joint Commission, that so ye affaires thereof maybe carryed on by Joint Councill & advice and also in regard of ye accidents of warr, and ye distraction which many times happened by the loss of ye Chiefe Commander when ye same is entrusted on a single person. And whereas through ye long experience which his Maj. as well as myself hath had of your affection Courage and Knowledge in maritime affaires, His Maj. hath been pleased to approove of ye choice of you for ye Chief command of his Majs. Fleet for this present expedition . . .

The paragraph went on windily, finally closing with the standard phrase for official commissions, 'Given under my hand and seal at Whitehall the 22nd of Feb. 1666'.

The document was in fact only a formality. The men to whom it was addressed had been apprised of their appointment some three months earlier. But with the Duke of York's signature, Prince Rupert and the Duke of Albemarle officially took charge of the greatest battle-fleet then afloat in the world, consisting of over 150 men-of-war and some 28,000 officers, seamen, and marines. The vessels ranged from unarmed hoys with humble names like *Black Dog*, up to mighty three-decked floating fortresses of 70, 80, even 100 guns with names like *Royal Oak* that fairly thundered off the tongue.

The proprietor of this mighty force was Charles Stuart, King of Great Britain, the second of that name to occupy the throne. Thirty-five years old in 1666, the 'Merry Monarch' of the Restoration sat in amiable judgement over the sprightliest court in Europe. This most charming, lovable, and approachable of all English rulers thoroughly enjoyed his reign. His deliciously uninhibited amorous escapades need no embellishment, nor do his athletic prowess, his love of the theatre, or his enthusiastic patronage of painters, poets, composers, scientists, and architects. But beneath the affable façade was a soul scarred by an adolescence and early manhood which had known civil war, the execution of his father Charles I, and fourteen years of humiliating and penurious exile. This made him a cynical, wary, and deadly serious politician, determined never again to 'go on his travels'. He was nevertheless an able, fair-minded, and innovative administrator; he had to be innovative, for the machinery of his government ran on an exceedingly lean financial fuel which was grudgingly provided by one of the most parsimonious Parliaments ever to sit in England. Yet Charles somehow managed.

Among the multifarious interests of this remarkable ruler, none was closer to his heart than the Royal Navy. In his youth he had been irresistibly attracted to the sea, and all his life he maintained a special fascination for all things nautical. An avid yachtsman, he audaciously but appropriately named several of his pleasure boats after favourite mistresses. He understood seamanship and navigation as well as any 'tar', and was at ease with his shipwrights, knowledgeably debating the finer points of hull forms and ship-timbers. At least one observer, that grumpy chronicler Bishop Burnet, carped that Charles 'knew the architecture of ships so perfectly, that in that respect he was exact rather more than became a prince'. In fact, his encouragement of new ideas was a significant factor in the breathtaking growth and improvement of the Royal Navy that took place during the reign.

Charles also understood the uses of his navy. It was at once the country's principal line of defence, the chief instrument of foreign policy, the guarantor of commerce, the progenitor of empire, and a natural rallying point of national pride. On a more mundane level the fleet and its supporting industries – shipbuilding, timber production, ordnance manufacture – was England's largest employer and thus an important element in the nation's economic health. The navy's administration was technically the responsibility of the Duke of York as Lord High Admiral. In practice little that went on in the fleet escaped the King's notice. He constantly inspected dockyards, interviewed captains, visited ships and observed their sea-trials. He directly involved himself in operational planning and was a frequent participant in the flag-officers' councils-of-war. He also hand-picked the principal commanders; Rupert and Albemarle, for instance, were his selection and not James's; James would sooner have chosen himself.

England was then engaged in the second of three wars against the Seven Provinces of the United Netherlands, the other great sea power of the time. The struggle had opened with a smashing English success at the Battle of Lowestoft in June 1665, when the Dutch fleet had been driven from the seas in panic flight. But for the most part the spoils had eluded the victors, as every attempt to exploit the victory had come to nought for one reason or another. The enemy's merchant convoys had slipped through largely unmolested, and when the October gales had finally put an end to the campaign the battered Dutch fleet was still intact. Through the autumn there were rumours, though the details were sparse, that their arsenals were turning out men-of-war at a furious pace. The campaign of 1666 did not promise to be an easy one.

The English had already replaced two commanders-in-chief. The great victory of the previous June had been gained under the Lord High Admiral himself. But James was Charles's only heir, and the sobering casualties among other senior officers had made the King fear for his brother's life. James's replacement, the Earl of Sandwich, had performed competently, but had been put out owing to public displeasure over certain liberties which he had taken with the perquisites of his position. Prince Rupert and the Duke of Albemarle were thus the third and fourth commanders-in-chief within a single year.

The two men had much in common. Though both had commanded at sea, neither was a seaman. They were first and foremost soldiers; indeed the most famous soldiers then alive in England.

Rupert von Simmern, Count Palatine of the Rhine, Duke of Lusatia, Duke of Cumberland, and Earl of Holderness, was a first cousin to Charles II. Born in Prague in 1619, he was the third son of Elizabeth, sister of Charles I of England, and Frederick V, the luckless dispossessed Elector Palatine and deposed 'Winter King' of Bohemia. Prince Rupert was among the most renowned soldiers of the age; a masterful heavy cavalry specialist, fearless in action, and by far the greatest Cavalier hero of the Civil War. Tall, handsome, of sinewy build, and 'always very sparkish in his dress', he had a proud and commanding presence. He was an expert horseman, a superb athlete (said by Samuel Pepys to have been one of the finest tennis players in England) and a master of all kinds of weaponry.

Rupert lived at a breathless pace, his energy seemingly inexhaustible. When not campaigning with his troopers or pacing a quarterdeck, he delighted in grandiose overseas colonial and commercial adventures. These ranged from a dubious plan to settle Madagascar, to a far-fetched scheme based on a fabled mountain of gold in West Africa. He was a founder of the Royal Africa Company, and later formed the Hudson's Bay Company to seek the Northwest Passage. Rupert was in the forefront of the avant-garde intelligentsia of Restoration England. He was a frequent participant in the proceedings of the newly founded Royal Society and was himself a draughtsman, amateur scientist, and inventor of some note. Among other interests, he was a pioneer of mezzotint engraving and a recognized expert in metallurgy, foundry techniques, and all aspects of ordnance manufacture.

Though Rupert was the great defender of the English monarchy, and by extension of the Book of Common Prayer, he was, ironically, a Calvinist. Not much need be made of that, however, for he seems to have been little bound by the strictures of any religion. He played hard, drank hard, and cursed (in a German accent) as profanely as the roughest corporal. Rupert never married and was not notoriously promiscuous, but he sired at least two illegitimate children. Like his cousin Charles, he found actresses especially attractive, and his favourite, the beautiful Margaret Hughes, was the mother of a daughter named Ruperta.

Prince Rupert was unquestionably one of the most fascinating denizens of Charles II's court. But despite his undoubted talents and achievements, many people had mixed feelings about him. This was because, in addition to being brave, dashing, and generally brilliant, Rupert also happened to be opinionated, abrasive, tactless, insensitive, and insufferably arrogant. 'A man of no government', wrote Pepys, 'and severe in council, that no ordinary man can offer any advice against his'. It perhaps hardly needs saying that such an ego regarded few men as being more than 'ordinary'; the King, the Duke of York, and possibly Albemarle would easily complete the list. The Prince seemed to take pleasure in roguish behaviour. He scandalized the court with his mockery of protocol, using the foulest barracks language even in state councils. Pepys described a meeting of the Committee for Tangier in which 'Prince Rupert do nothing but swear and laugh a little, with an oathe or two, and that's all he do'. On another occasion he was reported as 'swearing bloodily to the King'.

There were other dark sides of Prince Rupert's character, some of them not so harmless. His sense of humour was decidedly twisted, and he had shown an unmistakable streak of cruelty on his campaigns. He was a dangerous man to have as an enemy. He was quick to take offence and his skill at arms made him a formidable duellist; but when Lord Culpepper challenged him at The Hague in 1648, Rupert's only response was to compound the original insult by sending a young tough to beat up Culpepper in the street.

One of the Prince's more laudable qualities was the consistent loyalty which he showed his chosen companions. They were mostly fellow men-at-arms such as Sir Robert Holmes, Sir Edward Spragge, and Sir Frescheville Holles; and Rupert also had the confidence, though not the friendship, of the King and the Duke of York. Throughout the country the picture of the dashing cavalier was generally accepted at face value, and in 1666 Prince Rupert basked in the warmth of public esteem, the beau-ideal of thousands of Englishmen.

Rupert's fame had been gained on land, where his thundering charges had produced glowing litanies of victories. His one sea campaign had produced little to indicate that he would become a successful fleet commander. After the Stuart defeat in the Civil War, a disgruntled portion of the Parliamentary navy revolted and delivered itself over to the exiled Royalists at the Dutch port of Hellevoetsluis. Taking command of this fleet (through an unseemly slander campaign against the incumbent, Sir William Batten) the Prince sailed with seven ships in January 1649 on an adventure-filled odyssey that was not to end for four years. With him went several men who were later to achieve prominence in the Restoration navy: Thomas Allin, Robert Holmes, possibly Edward Spragge (all destined to become flag-officers) and old Sir John Mennes, who would become the charming but incompetent colleague of Samuel Pepys on the Navy Board.

Rupert's cruise, though remembered as one of the most romantic episodes of the age, was an endless nightmare for the participants. It was hard enough in those days to keep even a regular national fleet repaired and manned, and its seamen paid, fed, and clothed. A government in exile could supply nothing at all; no dockyards, no arsenals, no pool of seamen to be impressed, and above all no money. Rupert's squadron survived on what it could catch, which meant English merchantmen. When prizes were scarce there was a very real threat of mutiny from the unpaid seamen. Add to this Atlantic gales, tropical hurricanes, and vengeful Parliamentary fleets which always seemed to be just over the horizon, and it becomes astonishing that Rupert was able to remain at large. But so he did.

The Prince's squadron was hunted relentlessly by a Parliamentary fleet under the General-at-Sea Robert Blake, who chased the Royalists from Irish waters, blockaded them at Lisbon, and hounded them into the Mediterranean. With most of his ships and their prizes destroyed or captured, Rupert finally escaped to the open Atlantic. In the Azores his semi-piratical seamen mutinied, and afterwards his ship, the *Constant Reformation*, opened her seams in a storm and foundered with most of her crew. Rupert was plucked from the sinking vessel at the last moment in a daring rescue by a boat from one of the other ships. It might be noted that the familiar custom of the captain going down with his ship was most emphatically not a part of the chivalric code of the seventeenth-century cavalier.

In the spring of 1652 Prince Rupert, needing money in any form, visited the West African coast for a gold-seeking expedition up the Gambia River. Predictably, the Englishmen so antagonized the local populace that they were fortunate to get out alive. From there the fugitive squadron made its way to the Cape Verde Islands and thence to the West Indies. There, the last Royalist strongholds had already submitted to Parliament, and the Prince found no friendly haven. The culminating catastrophe occurred in September, when a hurricane off the Virgin Islands wrecked the ship commanded by Rupert's brother Prince Maurice, who was never seen again. Six months later the sole remaining warship, the *Swallow*, staggered into the French port of Paimboeuf, leaking and rotten to the last frame.

This extended, disastrous cruise was the Prince's only sea experience until 1664. Charles II nevertheless had great confidence in him, and appointed him second-in-command of the fleet at the outbreak of the Second Anglo-Dutch War. In the fight off Lowestoft, Rupert lived up to the King's expectations, fighting with conspicuous bravery. Afterwards, he went ashore in disappointment at not being named sole commander-in-chief and took no further part until Charles offered him the joint commission with Albemarle.

Ostensibly, the reason for the King's insistence on a dual command was to ensure a continuity of leadership in case one of the admirals was killed. The real reason was that a steadying hand was felt necessary to offset the rashness and impetuosity which had often marked the Prince's land campaigns. But Charles need not have worried on that score, for Rupert the admiral was never as reckless as Rupert the general. He had a deeper respect for the weather than most landsmen; the loss of Prince Maurice and his own experience in the *Constant Reformation* made sure of that. On the whole, Rupert was not very comfortable at sea. He found the difficulty of ship-to-ship communications especially frustrating; in land warfare, if he disliked some disposition of troops, it was easy enough to gallop over, bark a crisp order or two, and set things straight. At sea it was not so simple. 'God damn me', he said, 'I can answer for but one ship, and in that I will do my part; for it is not in that as in an army, where a man can command everything'. Furthermore, as a dilettante seafarer he was subjected to constant advice from 'Ordinary Men' – mere captains, admirals, and the like – and for Rupert of the Rhine that was hard to swallow. There were muttered complaints that 'if a sober man give his opinion otherwise than the Prince would have it the Prince would cry "Damn him, do you follow your orders, and that is enough for you"'.

Harsh though his demeanour may have been, Rupert was a thorough professional at the art of war; he could fight, and that counted for more than manners with the seamen. Even so, most of the sea-officers must have been relieved that he had not been given the command alone. And to them, the King could not have chosen a better co-commander than the Duke of Albemarle.

George Monck was born in 1608. His parents were sturdy Devonshire gentry related to the Grenville family which had produced a long line of celebrated generals and admirals, and he was steered towards a martial career from an early age. He learned the ropes in the disastrous expeditions to Cadiz in 1625 and La Rochelle in 1627, afterwards joining the thousands of professional mercenaries who in those days filled the ranks of European armies. He slogged for nine years through the siegeworks of the Low Countries and fought in the Bishops' War in Scotland. The early years of the Civil War found him leading his own Royalist regiment. In 1644, he had the bad luck to be taken prisoner in the Parliamentary relief of Nantwich. His captors made every effort to convert such an experienced officer to their cause, and though he at first refused indignantly, two years' imprisonment in the Tower finally convinced him of the wisdom of 'taking the Covenant'.

Monck was posted to Ireland, where his cool-headed leadership caught the eye of Oliver Cromwell. When the future Lord Protector invaded Scotland in 1650, he raised a new regiment for Monck (the famous Coldstream) and made him one of his principal lieutenants. After a brilliant performance in the campaign Monck was left in command in Scotland, where his success in subduing the last pockets of resistance later led to his appointment as military governor under the Protectorate. Though ruling with an iron firmness, he maintained a good-natured tolerance of Scottish customs and religion which was most unusual in that age of fanaticism.

When Cromwell's death in 1658 plunged England into anarchy, Monck's army in Scotland – unswervingly loyal to him personally – became the only force capable of restoring order. With the nation's future in his hands, Monck resolutely marched his troops to London, where, after correctly gauging the public sentiment, he forced the election of a new Parliament favourable to the Royalists. When Charles II responded with conciliatory promises, Monck's 'Free Parliament' sent a fleet to the Netherlands in 1660 to escort the King on his triumphant return.

It would have been only natural for Charles II to wonder about the reliability of a man who had twice made complete about-faces in his allegiance. The Earl of Clarendon, the King's Chancellor and a keen observer of events, noted that Monck's twisting loyalties had been much eased by the fact that unlike most men of the time, 'he had no fumes of religion, which turned his head'. This was a perceptive remark, for the general often made ostentatious displays of religious fervour. He surrounded himself with chaplains, and throughout Commonwealth and Protectorate times his correspondence was heavily laced with pious expressions; but that was largely for the consumption of the Puritans. His true feelings were better revealed by the un-Puritan lack of bigotry in his dealings with the Irish and the Scots. Monck's loyalty was not to persons or religions, but to whatever appeared most likely to ensure peace and order. It might be noted that the Protectorate could well have been within his grasp had he chosen to reach for it in 1658. Fortunately for Charles II, Monck was not politically ambitious. At the time of the Restoration, however, that was not so clear, and the general's loyalty was a crucially important matter for his newly adopted master. It must have seemed all too obvious that if Monck could make a king, he could also unmake one. His power rested on his perceived reputation with the common people, it being believed that he had the means to conjure up legions of veteran Roundhead soldiers at the drop of a hat. Thus the Stuarts' attitude towards their deliverer was at first an odd mixture of deep gratitude and lurking fear.

The King spared nothing to satisfy his chief subject. In addition to granting an outright annuity of £7,000, Charles installed him as Master of the Horse, Gentleman of the Bedchamber, Privy Councillor, Knight of the Garter, and Captain-General at Land and Sea. Monck was also confirmed as Lord Lieutenant of Ireland, a post he soon relinquished with the public-spirited declaration that he thought it improper for the country to have an absentee governor. His penultimate honours came in July 1660 when Charles named him Duke of Albemarle and Earl of Torrington, titles which brought enormous estates and income.

Monck's influence seemed boundless. To be brought under his wing meant certain good fortune; no one, not even the Duke of York, had as much control over appointments to public offices. According to Clarendon, the Duke of Albemarle 'was an immoderate lover of money', and the sale of the offices at his disposal vastly enriched his already swollen coffers. But in most respects he proved to be an excellent bargain for Charles II. He worked tirelessly to fortify the position of the monarchy, his sheer competence at every aspect of administration fully justifying the powers granted him. He became, said Clarendon, 'the sole pillar of the King's confidence'.

The Duke of Albemarle's lofty status was maintained despite a continuous and vicious barrage of sniping from his jealous rivals. He made an extremely vulnerable target owing to a number of rather glaring social handicaps. Not the least of these was his amazingly coarse duchess, a former seamstress named Anne Clarges who had been a daughter of his regimental farrier. She had married him in 1652 after several years as his mistress; it was rumoured that an undivorced previous husband was still alive. The caustic tongue and gross manners of the 'Monkey Duchess' were ludicrously out of place beside the witty sophistication of the great ladies of the court. Samuel Pepys's descriptions of her range from the merely contemptuous ('ever a plain homely dowdy' and 'a damned ill-looking woman'), to the downright vituperative: 'the veryest slut and drudge and the foulest worde that can be spoke of a woman almost'.

Albemarle suffered ridicule for his own appearance and manner, which completely belied the seventeenth-century conception of the dashing man of action. In 1666 he was fifty-eight years old, gouty, myopic, asthmatic, and immensely fat. Little educated, he wrote clumsily and spelled atrociously even in an age of phonetic spelling. To make things worse, 'he was not a man of graceful elocution', and the resulting bluntness in his speech was little appreciated by the effete dandies of the court. Invitations to his table were desperately avoided; 'the dirty dishes, the bad meat, and the ill dinner' that one could expect were universally dreaded. Refined courtiers were further repulsed by the massive wad of tobacco that usually bulged his cheek. Monck's superficial shortcomings tended to hide what was actually a complex personality and a powerful intellect. Such concealment was enhanced by a dour, impassive – almost bovine – facial expression that led many of his contemporaries to underestimate him. Petty officials like the snobbish young Pepys assiduously cultivated his friendship for the patronage it could bring, all the while mocking him behind his back as 'a dull heavy man'. The Earl of Sandwich, a frequent enemy, wrote him off as 'a thick-skulled fool'; even Cromwell, a true friend who really knew better, described him as 'your honest General Monck who is a simple hearted man'. These were ill-considered things to say about one of the few who had found a safe course through the dangerous shoals of the interregnum. When half the nation's great men were cringing from Cromwell's executioners, there was Monck in splendour at Edinburgh; later, when the other half were cringing from the King's executioners, there was Monck in splendour at Whitehall. A heavy man he was, but not a dull one.

In the right company the Duke of Albemarle actually seems to have been a fairly genial fellow. He could smile like the rest at his wife's rages, displaying a sense of humour that would have escaped most men in the same situation. His habits were ordinarily sober and abstemious, but when one occasion called for a drinking contest his enormous bulk made him virtually immune to the effects; he was the last one standing.

It is difficult to be certain of anyone's true character from a distance of three centuries, but one gets the distinct impression that many of Monck's eccentricities were part of a conscious façade. Though he seemed as thick-skinned as an ox, he knew quite well who his enemies were, and what they were saying. His deadpan face was often a potent weapon; when he felt threatened he could prevaricate as shamelessly as any man alive. There were, of course, many who knew the real Monck. The King knew, and he never took him for granted. The Scots also knew. Above all, his soldiers knew. Without the unquestioning trust of his veteran regiments, a bloodless Restoration could never have happened. The soldiers knew from long experience that the mettle of their seemingly stolid general would always show best in the worst emergencies.

One of the worst emergencies imaginable arose in 1665, when the bubonic plague appeared in London and began its merciless march across the city. The nobles, the merchants, even the King and court, fled to the country, leaving the helpless poor to face the scourge by themselves. Of all the 'great men', only the Duke of Albemarle, the Earl of Craven, and Gilbert Sheldon, Archbishop of Canterbury, stayed behind to organize the defence at the risk of a miserable death. Unfortunately, the cause of the disease was not understood, so there was little they could do beyond bolstering morale. Monck did impose a series of commonsense rules of sanitation, some of which may have been helpful. The general was already held in high esteem by the English commercial and working classes, and such truly selfless concern for the public good earned him and his brave colleagues the everlasting gratitude of the people.

There was yet another group of men who knew and respected the Duke of Albemarle. They were the 'tarpaulin' officers and seamen of the Royal Navy, for Monck was not without experience of command at sea. It had been for only a few months, but those few months had seen a glittering succession of victories. His success had a marked effect on the conduct of the Four Days' Battle, and indeed on nearly every major sea-fight right up to the time of Trafalgar.

Monck's sea appointment had come in late 1652, at the height of the First Anglo-Dutch War. He was ordered to take joint command of the fleet with Robert Blake and Richard Deane, both of whom were army officers already serving as Generals-at-Sea. Deane had been mostly concerned with the shore establishment, but Blake was a seasoned commander. He had held the chief sea command since the later years of the Civil War, and had already fought three major engagements with the Dutch. Two of these had been stirring if rather indecisive victories; but in the third engagement, off Dungeness, he had been caught with his fleet divided and had suffered a discouraging reverse. It was then that Monck and Deane were sent to join him.

It seems astonishing that a navy would be entrusted to a committee of infantry generals, but at the time many European fleets were led by soldiers. On the Continent such men were usually selected simply because they came from aristocratic backgrounds. Something as important as a national fleet could not, it was felt, be left to the low-born; and nobles were notably scarce among the hardy ranks of professional seamen. Pedigree, however, was not a consideration in Commonwealth England. The Parliament's Generals-at-Sea were selected because they were known to be hard fighters and politically reliable leaders. It might seem remarkable that the joint command did not lead to serious rivalries, but the three commanders were good friends and their correspondence gives no evidence of discord.

That the Generals had little sea experience (Blake had served in merchantmen) was not viewed as a significant impediment. The well-rounded seventeenth-century man-at-arms was expected to be proficient in warfare no matter what the element, and anyway, the fighting functions of a fleet were regarded as quite distinct from mere navigation. It was presumed that there would be enough seamen with the fleet to take the ships where the soldiers wanted to go. A General-at-Sea could always keep an experienced officer close at hand to advise on nautical matters. Monck, for instance, took as his flag-captain the brilliant John Mildmay, one of the most skilful professional seamen in the fleet. Besides, the basic limitations of a sailing warship were not all that difficult to understand. One could not sail directly into the wind, and it was advisable to keep some water between the keel and the seafloor. Once those simple rules were mastered, there was no reason why a land officer could not command at sea as well as anyone else. At least that was the way most seventeenth-century politicians saw it; amazingly, they were sometimes right.

Monck was by any standards one of the most lubberly admirals that ever sailed the seas. He often amused the seamen by bellowing infantry commands such as 'Wheel to the right!' when he wanted the fleet to tack. But his inexperience was actually a valuable asset; lacking preconceived notions, he could bring fresh approaches to the thorny problems of naval tactics. He was hardly afloat when he saw his first action, the Battle of Portland in February 1653. The fleets were engaged for three days, though the issue was decided in a tremendous pell-mell mêlée on the first day. The Dutch under their great leader Maarten Tromp were defeated with heavy losses, and Monck's bravery was universally acclaimed. But while the Generals gave public thanks for their triumph, they were privately disappointed that they had not won more over-whelmingly. The fleets had been well matched in numbers, but the English ships had been larger and much more powerfully armed. Even so, the outcome on the decisive first day had been in doubt until the very end, and at times defeat had seemed dangerously near. While the ships refitted, the commanders held a series of councils-of-war to determine what had gone wrong. These conferences resulted in a radical revision of the fleet's tactical doctrine.

At Portland and earlier actions, each side had divided its fleet into groups, usually three on the English side and five or six on the Dutch. These squadrons had been assigned rough positions such as van, centre, and rear, or left wing and right wing; but individual ships had been in no particular formation. The English fighting instructions had directed merely 'that each ship shall take the best advantage they can to engage with the enemy next unto him'. Battles fought in those circumstances invariably became free-for-alls beyond the control of the commanders. Ships were unable to properly support each other, and boarding tactics (at which the Dutch excelled) always figured prominently. Worst of all, with the ships sailing in clumps only a few could engage at one time; the batteries of the rest were masked by their friends. That was why the English firepower superiority had not made itself more evident at Portland. The Generals accordingly resolved to eschew the mêlée and to rely in future on gunnery alone.

The fundamental problem was that a sailing warship, unlike an infantry battalion or a cavalry squadron, could not fight effectively to its 'front'. Its guns were arrayed along its sides, so the principal firepower was directed always towards the 'flank'. Thus, for a naval artillery duel to be successful, the enemy had to be kept at a right angle to the direction of advance. In addition, to avoid wasting firepower it was important for each ship to have an unobstructed field of fire. To the Generals, this meant that the English fleet would have to adopt a more orderly, disciplined, and formal method of fighting than it had previously employed.

The assessments of the councils-of-war undoubtedly provoked objections from some of the seamen. English fighting instructions of the sixteenth century had often called for an organized line, but thereafter experienced sea-dogs had consistently resisted the imposition of formal tactics. When a system of prearranged formations was proposed in 1625, the seamen complained

> that it intended to enjoin our fleet to advance and fight at sea, much after the manner of an army at land, assigning every ship to a particular division, rank, file, and station; which order and regularity was not only improbable but almost impossible to be observed by so great a fleet in so uncertain a place as the sea.

Theorist Sir William Monson, writing about 1640, agreed entirely, making the further point that adherence to a formal order would undermine the navy's offensive spirit:

> Ships which must be carried by wind and sails, and the sea affording no firm or steadfast footing, cannot be commanded to take their ranks like soldiers in a battle by land. The weather at sea is never certain, the winds variable, ships unequal in sailing; and when they strictly keep their order, commonly they fall foul one of another, and in such cases they are more careful to observe their directions than to offend the enemy, whereby they will be brought into disorder amongst themselves.

But the commanders of 1653 were soldiers, not sailors. They flatly refused to believe that seamen of the calibre of their subordinates were incapable of at least rudimentary station keeping. They also realized that an excess of offensive zeal was actually playing into the hands of the Dutch. The Generals' tactical ideas were set forth on 29 March 1653 in an historic document entitled 'Instructions for the better ordering of the fleet in fighting'. The key provision, embodied by Article Three, stipulated that upon the signal for battle, 'each squadron shall take the best advantage they can to engage with the enemy next unto them; and in order thereunto all the ships of every squadron shall endeavor to keep in a line with the chief'. This was the first official formulation of the line-ahead system which was to dominate naval tactics for the next three centuries. A single-file line had many advantages: it gave every vessel a clear field of fire, it exposed only the broadsides and not the vulnerable bows and sterns, and it conferred excellent mutual support. Above all, it meant that naval battles would become artillery duels rather than boarding actions.

A further advantage of the line was that it allowed the flag-officers to maintain some control over the proceedings. To strengthen this advantage the Generals made it clear that they intended to keep the line formed throughout the battle. Article Ten decreed that captains would not even be allowed to take possession of surrendered enemy vessels. The men should be saved, but the ships were to be immediately destroyed, 'and this we require all commanders to be more than mindful of'.

Another important provision was Article Seven, which required that if the flagship were to windward of the enemy – the attacking position – 'then upon hoisting up a blue flag at the mizen yard or the mizen topmast', any ship to windward of the admiral 'is to bear up into his wake and grain upon severest punishment'. The Generals apparently intended this partly as a means of restoring a disordered line and partly as a disciplinary warning to be directed at captains who were not doing their part. It was not long, however, before someone noticed that its wording could also be interpreted to mean 'conform to my actions', or more simply, 'follow me!' In that more or less accidental guise it was later to become one of the most useful of all the instructions.

The line-ahead was by no means a new tactical invention. Blake, for instance, had formed line in the fight off Dover in 1652, but only as a defensive measure in the face of superior numbers. The significance of the 1653 instructions was that the line was adopted not merely as an occasional arrangement, but as the standard battle formation.

No one knows who among the Generals first suggested the new instructions. Though Blake had fought in line at Dover, he had not leaned towards formal tactics in his other battles. He had in any event been seriously wounded at Portland and cannot have taken much part in the councils-of-war. Deane, on the other hand, was an artillery specialist who would certainly have supported anything to make better use of the fleet's broadsides. It is hard to imagine the Generals making such sweeping tactical reforms without the advice of Admiral Sir William Penn, the leading professional seaman. Nevertheless, most historians agree that only Monck, the new-comer, is likely to have demanded changes in a long-established system which had just produced a major victory. Monck too was an artillerist; in land warfare he had a reputation as one of the most scientific officers of the day. At Portland his squadron had been far to leeward at the beginning of the fight, and the two hours he had needed to beat into action had given him ample opportunity to study the developing battle unobstructed by the clouds of smoke which so confused the other participants. Seen through the critical eyes of a practised land tactician, the milling masses of ships would have seemed utterly chaotic. If there was one theme that ran through George Monck's public career, it was a love of order. The absence of it invariably offended him, and it is only natural that he would have sought improvements. Whether or not he was responsible, the introduction of the line of battle was the greatest single tactical advance of the entire age of sail.

For the next cruise the convalescent Blake initially remained behind, leaving Monck and Deane in charge. They jointly commanded the centre squadron and Penn led the van, while the rear was under Sir John Lawson, another seasoned professional. The Dutch were still confident after Portland, for Tromp knew full well how near victory had been. The fleets (over a hundred ships each) met off the mouth of the Thames on 2 June in an all-out trial of strength which is remembered as the Battle of the Gabbard. True to the new instructions, the Generals carefully arranged their fleet. 'They stayed upon a tack', ran a Dutch account, 'having the wind, within twice cannon shot about half an hour, to put themselves in their order they intended to fight in, which was in file at half cannon shot'.

At 11 o'clock the Generals made the signal to engage, whereupon the massed broadsides of the English line spoke with an awesome roar. The Dutch instantly replied; at the first exchange a 'cannon bullet' struck Richard Deane, killing him instantly and splattering Monck with gore. In the face of this unnerving experience, Monck calmly laid his cloak over the remains of his friend and quietly ordered the body taken below out of sight. But in this battle few other misfortunes befell the

English. Having the weather gage, Monck refused to close for boarding, and the Dutch soon found themselves at a disadvantage. Their groups of massed overlapping ships made excellent targets for their powerfully armed opponents and further hampered their own already inferior firepower. After five hours of unprecedented pounding, a change in the wind allowed the Dutch rear under Michiel de Ruyter to close with Lawson, at which Tromp tacked in hopes of isolating Sir John's squadron. By then, however, the cannonade had done its work. The other Dutch squadrons were too shattered to follow their chief's example, and Monck and Penn soon drove him back. The Dutch fell off towards Dunkirk, the English following through the night.

At dawn Monck called his flag-officers aboard to report Deane's death and to review the fleet's performance. Though Richard Lyons, a member of Monck's staff, later reported that 'our fleet did work in better order than heretofore, and seconded one another', his perfectionist general was angry that Lawson's squadron had 'by reason divers shew'd too much timorosity the day before'; but Monck assured everyone that he would forget the past if they would do their best in the present. The flag-officers returned to their ships, and shortly before noon the fleets were again in combat.

The English 'still battered them in file' at 'half cannon distance', but the Dutch were in no condition to receive further punishment; after briefly and vainly manoeuvring for the weather gage they retreated along the coast. Though encumbered by damaged ships, Tromp at first put up a creditable running fight. Then Blake unexpectedly appeared with a fresh squadron and the English swooped in, as one participant put it, to reap 'the harvest and the gleaning of the vintage'. The Dutch retreat became a disorderly rout; ships collided and disabled vessels were left to their fate. By nightfall some twenty ships had been burned, sunk, or captured, and the survivors that reached the safety of their ports were themselves 'in a lamentable tottered and distracted condition'.

The battle had been so one-sided that Monck was not even obliged to refit. He kept the sea and imposed a vice-like blockade on the Netherlands. But the indomitable Tromp mustered his weary nation's last reserves of strength and sallied forth for one final effort. It came on 31 July, off Scheveningen and Ter Heide. The Gabbard had made so profound an impression, however, that discipline among the Dutch was decidedly shaky; many captains had little stomach for the fight, and the result was only too predictable.

Blake was again sick ashore, so this was entirely Monck's battle. The English formed in line-ahead, while the Dutch once again drew up in a line of amorphous squadrons. The Gabbard had been a stand-up gun duel with both sides on the same tack, but Scheveningen became a gruesome ballet of grand manoeuvre. It was fought in a series of tremendous passes, or 'charges', as the participants called them, in which the fleets swept past each other from end to end on opposite courses. Once clear, both tacked and converged again like medieval knights jousting in the lists. The Dutch had the wind for much of the action, and took advantage of it to use their fireships with some success. Unfortunately, they sustained a grievous loss early on when their beloved Maarten Tromp was killed by a musket ball in the chest. Despite the loss of their commander, many of the Dutch fought with desperate courage, but as the hours passed ominous numbers of ships were observed stealing away from the fight and slinking off out of range.

Monck was at his best. In the first pass his line beat up from leeward and sliced through the Dutch centre, 'leaving part on one side and part on the other side of us'. In the third and again in the fourth pass he succeeded in cutting off the tail end of the Dutch fleet, and in both cases the vessels so isolated went away to leeward with no attempt to rejoin their friends. With each 'bout' the English artillery took its toll, but the fourth pass was incredibly destructive. Fought 'almost at push of pike', it left the sea littered with helpless, dismasted vessels. The terrible violence of this final encounter appalled participants on both sides; in one particularly ghastly incident, the men of the *Victory* repelled boarders with axes. Such horrors snapped the last bonds of discipline among the Dutch. They scattered in ones, twos, and small groups to any port they could reach, the English following all the way to the shoals.

Monck's fleet maintained its discipline throughout. The temptation to chase Dutch ships forced to leeward was resisted, and the prohibition against taking possession of surrendered vessels was strictly observed; the Dutch cripples, fourteen of them, were remorselessly burned or sunk, not a single prize being brought in. Contrary to some allegations, it was not true that Monck had forbidden his captains from giving quarter. As required by the Fighting Instructions, some 600–700 seamen were in fact rescued and taken to England.

The Battle of Scheveningen all but destroyed the sea power of the Netherlands, and the United Provinces accepted a humiliating peace the following April. George Monck had made a lasting impact on the English navy. His new way of fighting had been thoroughly vindicated, and in one short six-month span this doughty landsman had garnered a place for himself among the greatest of sea commanders. Though in 1666 he had not been afloat for thirteen years, the old tarpaulins had never forgotten their stout-hearted chief. In every respect the Duke of Albemarle appeared to be an eminently sound choice to command Charles II's fleet.

These then, were the commanders who were to play the leading English roles in the Four Days' Battle: the one a swashbuckling cavalier, the other a stern infantry soldier. Before passing straight to their fortunes at the helm of the Royal Navy – and the fortunes of the intrepid Dutchmen who would oppose them – it may be useful to browse for several chapters through the momentous events that led up to their appointment, to tour the stage on which the action occurred, and to visit the gilded engines of destruction with which the battle was fought: the ships, and the men who lived and died on their decks.

Chapter II

The Royal Navy

Of every size an hundred fighting sail,
So vast the navy now at anchor rides,
That underneath it the press'd waters fail,
And with its weight it shoulders off the tides.

The British navy which would one day rule the waves was still in its infancy in the mid-seventeenth century. Its pre-eminence was yet to be established, its traditions uncrystallized, its proverbial iron discipline little in evidence. Though a powerful force, it was small by later standards both in the number of ships and in the number of people needed to man and administer it. Most of the naval institutions of the eighteenth and nineteenth centuries were already in existence by Restoration times, but everything was in embryonic form. One did not speak of the Lords of the Admiralty, because the Duke of York *was* the Admiralty. The Lord High Admiral was personally vested with complete control of the navy's operations and administration, answerable only to the King. Charles II, to a greater extent than later monarchs, preferred to exercise his oversight through the Privy Council, which maintained a permanent Committee for the Navy. Its members included James, Rupert, Albemarle, the Earl of Sandwich, the Secretaries of State, and other ministers with interests in maritime affairs. Parliament had no authority over the workings of the navy other than the ultimate power to grant or withhold money for extraordinary expenses such as warfare or shipbuilding. The navy's ordinary administrative expenses were supposed to be covered by the Crown's fixed revenues, especially Customs receipts, though these were never sufficient.

The daily affairs of the Admiralty were directed by James's hard-working secretary Sir William Coventry and a small staff whose office adjoined the Duke of York's personal apartments in Whitehall Palace. Some administrative aspects were managed by more or less independent organizations: the Ordnance Office in the Tower; the Prize Office; the Commission for Sick, Wounded, and Prisoners; and Trinity House, which trained pilots and provided navigation aids. Some of the navy's basic needs were placed in the hands of private contractors, notably victualling and seamen's clothing. All other administrative matters came under the direct control of the Navy Board, whose 'nerve centre' was the Navy Office in Seething Lane. The Navy Board was in charge of the building and maintenance of ships, the royal dockyards, financial accounts, appointments of non-commissioned officers, and procurement of supplies and commodities for the fleet.

The members of the Navy Board were appointed by the Lord High Admiral. In 1666 they included four Principal Officers (the Treasurer, Comptroller, Surveyor, and Clerk of the Acts) along with seven commissioners. There were also clerks, messengers, and miscellaneous employees, though the staff of the Seething Lane office numbered no more than twenty even during the war years. The Treasurer of the Navy, who had a separate office in Broad Street, was Charles II's Vice-Chamberlain Sir George Carteret. A good man with figures, he was responsible for maintaining accounts and supervising the payment of seamen and contracts. He also ran the Ticket Office in Seething Lane where the seamen cashed their pay 'tickets'. The Comptroller, Sir John Mennes, was the official auditor of all accounts and transactions. The Surveyor, Sir William Batten, was in charge of shipbuilding and repairs, with roughly the same duties as a nineteenth- or twentieth-century Chief Constructor. The Clerk of the Acts was the ubiquitous Samuel Pepys, who in theory was supposed to be little more than a secretary and recorder. Of the seven commissioners, Coventry, Sir William Penn, Sir Thomas Hervey, and William, Viscount Brouncker (president of the Royal Society), served at large, while the remaining three were resident overseers of the royal dockyards: Sir Thomas Middleton for Portsmouth, Captain John Taylor for Harwich, and the famous shipbuilder Peter Pett for Chatham and Sheerness. The dockyards at Woolwich and Deptford had no resident commissioners since they were close enough to London to be supervised from the Navy Office.

That, officially, was the organization. In fact, Carteret worked in almost complete isolation from the rest and attended few meetings, Hervey was a political appointee who did essentially nothing, and Mennes and Batten were former sea-officers who were hopelessly out of their element as administrators. In practice Pepys assumed most of the Comptroller's functions and also negotiated many of Batten's contracts, while nearly all shipbuilding questions were referred to Peter Pett. Of the rest, Brouncker helped with shipbuilding and accounts, and Penn proved useful as a roving 'troubleshooter'. Coventry, who had daily contact with the Duke of York, coordinated the efforts of the others.

The most striking feature of the naval administration of the 1660s was that the whole edifice was 'ript and ransackt' by corruption. It ranged from accountants who embezzled, officials who demanded bribes for any service, contractors whose products did not match the samples, admirals who rifled prizes, captains who carried private cargo in the King's ships, and pursers who kept dead men alive on the books to get their pay, all the way down to the lowly dockyard labourer who brazenly walked home 'with a chip on his shoulder'; chips were supposedly waste timber, but whole towns were built from them. Underhanded dealings constituted the principal income of most office holders. On a modest salary, Commissioner Peter Pett lived in a mansion 'resembling some villa about Rome', complete with 'a pretty garden and banqueting house, potts, statues, cypresses', and a marvelous collection of ship models and nautical curiosities. Samuel Pepys performed valuable service in exposing and reducing the extent of embezzlement and theft of the King's property. Yet Pepys himself saw no harm in accepting 'gifts' from prospective contractors. These made him a wealthy man. He had counted his total worth in 1660 at £40. But despite a visible income thereafter averaging about £625 per annum – and a wife who knew how to spend it – Mr. Pepys could reckon his fortune by the end of 1666 at 'above £6,200'. On the occasion of that accounting he found to his 'great discontent' that 'my gettings this year have been £573 less than my last: it being this year in all but £2,986; whereas the last, I got £3,560'. For the modern value of that money one should multiply by about sixty!

The trouble was not with the navy, but with the whole society. It was an age in which judges and juries routinely accepted bribes from plaintiffs and defendants, sometimes from both in the same case. Corruption other than outright stealing was often regarded as no corruption at all. The property of the state was assumed to be there for the taking; the rake-off and the greased palm were universally looked upon as normal perquisites of office, by precedents from the dim past beyond anyone's memory. The attitudes that made it acceptable went to the very top. When the unusually honest Captain Sir John Berry reported fellow Captain William Poole for having profited illegally from carriage of merchants' money, the King merely responded 'that he was a fool for not doing as Poole did'. The extent to which public wealth was siphoned off into private hands cannot even be estimated, but it could hardly have been trivial. Fortunately for England, her enemies on the Continent conducted their business in precisely the same manner.

The commissioned officers of the mid-seventeenth-century navy do not compare readily with modern counterparts. The concept of the professional naval officer of today or even of Nelson's time did not exist in the 1660s. The idea of a man progressing by examination from midshipman to lieutenant, then by selection to commander, captain, and thence by inexorable seniority to flag rank and eventual retirement was completely unknown. The very term *naval officer* was not even in the seventeenth-century vocabulary. There were 'Officers of the Navy', but that referred to Samuel Pepys and his colleagues on the Navy Board; the men who commanded the ships were *sea-officers*, in lower case. A commissioned officer was anyone who through merit, influence, or otherwise was able to convince the King, the Lord High Admiral, or the commander-in-chief of the fleet to grant him a strictly temporary commission as captain or lieutenant of a ship. There were no stated qualifications, and no examination was required for any commissioned rank until 1677. Commissions carried no promise of future advancement or even of subsequent employment at the same level. Men could and sometimes did serve as captains one year and lieutenants the next, or admirals one year and captains the next. Since there was no half-pay in peacetime, the vocation of officer in the King's ships was necessarily a part-time occupation. Even the concept of seniority (one spoke of the 'eldest' captain to distinguish the holder of the earliest commission) applied only to determine which among a group of officers was in charge in the absence of a designated commander. It had no bearing on promotion.

Aside from the greatest flagships, Restoration warships had only one lieutenant as opposed to six or more in Nelson's day. Fifth- and sixth-rates had none at all. Admirals other than commanders-in-chief were usually the captains of their own ships; flag rank was a temporary *office* in a given fleet and not a permanent grade. Because of the few posts available, fleets of the period carried a number of supernumerary officers who served without formal commissions. These so-called 'reformadoes' were often elderly former captains, but also included qualified younger men for whom suitable positions had not been found. Berthed mainly in the flagships, reformadoes formed a convenient pool for replacements in the event of deaths or other unexpected vacancies among the commissioned captains and lieutenants.

The overwhelming majority of the sea-officers in the 1660s were 'tarpaulin' professional seamen. Most were veteran salts who had served the Commonwealth in the First Anglo-Dutch War and the Spanish War under the Protectorate, some having commanded Parliamentary ships and squadrons even in the Civil War. A few who were outspokenly hostile to the monarchy were quickly dismissed at the Restoration, but the rest wisely kept quiet and were forgiven their past 'disloyalties'. Many flag-officers of the Second Anglo-Dutch War were ex-Cromwellian tarpaulins; Penn, Lawson, Ayscue, Teddiman, Jordan, Smith, Myngs, Harman, Utber, and Sansum were all mariners of proven ability. Most former Commonwealth officers were from moderately affluent mercantile families, though a few had risen from the lower deck. Even those from middle-class backgrounds were often handicapped by coarse manners and lack of education, and some were incurably corrupt; nevertheless, they were experienced, disciplined, and accustomed to victory under Monck and Blake.

A second, very small, class of tarpaulin commanders had been Royalists in the Civil War and interregnum. They included James Ley, Earl of Marlborough, Admiral Sir Thomas Allin, and Captain Richard Beach. The elderly Marlborough was a nobleman who had taken to the sea in his youth when his family lost its estates; he had spent most of his adult life afloat all over the world and had served as a flag-officer under both Charles I and Charles II. Another group of professional seamen consisted of the captains of the trading ships hired for conversion to men-of-war in 1664–65. Although at first mistrusted, some merchant officers performed well enough in 1665 to be offered King's ships in 1666. In a class by himself was John (later Admiral Sir John) Kempthorne, flag-captain under Rupert and Albemarle. A former merchant captain, he was a wealthy, influential shipowner and respected brother of Trinity House who volunteered his services in 1664. He had never before served in men-of-war, but he proved to be a fighting mariner of great energy and skill.

Several sea-officers were primarily soldiers. The most prominent (aside from the fleet commanders) were Prince Rupert's protégés Robert Holmes, Frescheville Holles, and the Irishman Edward Spragge. They were not without sea experience; Holmes had sailed with Rupert in the Civil War, Spragge had commanded a Royalist cruiser in the 1650s, and Holles had established a brilliant reputation as captain of the Prince's privateer *Panther* in 1665. All were boisterous cavaliers in the mould of their patron: fun-loving, hard-drinking, profane, arrogant, and quarrelsome. Nevertheless, they were undeniably born leaders, adored by their crews. Though no seamen, all were good men to have on one's side in a fight. It is revealing that while serving as ship captains, Holmes and Holles preferred to be styled *Major* Holmes and *Major* Holles, which gives some impression of the degree of prestige attached to the sea-captain's rank in those days.

A final, and controversial, class of sea-officers were the 'gentlemen' commanders who began to enter the fleet with the resurgence of Royalist fortunes. Gentlemen competed with the tarpaulins for control of the navy and later dominated the service, but in the 1660s they were still a small minority. Their rise was assisted by powerful support from the nobility, who argued that the concept of command had nothing to do with seamanship. Their advocates recognized that it was advantageous for an officer to know something about ships, but felt that this qualification was dispensable if one were otherwise suitable in leadership, courage, manners, and social standing. A gentleman, 'naturally' accustomed to command by generations of breeding, could awe and inspire the men more effectively than a mere seaman. The captain's sole duties, they said, were to provide discipline and direction in battle and to uphold the honour of the Crown. To ensure proper advice in nautical matters it was only necessary that the gentleman surround himself with seamen of known ability in their humble calling.

The opposite view was put forward by Pepys, Coventry, Penn, and others in the naval administration. They contended that the gentlemen were unruly, often beyond discipline, and contemptuous of orders from superiors of inferior social background. They further pointed out that an officer who did not know his subordinates' duties could hardly be expected to govern their performance. Even worse, no captain unacquainted with the limitations and functions of the various pieces of rigging and equipment, or the significance of weather conditions, could ever evaluate the risks and dangers of possible courses of action. He would always be at the mercy of advisers who did not share his accountability.

The attitudes of the King and the Duke of York were somewhat ambivalent. With their usual common sense they suggested that sons of the nobility should be trained for the sea from an early age. In 1661 James made provision for young gentlemen volunteers, one per ship, who were to be prepared for command in the proper shipboard environment. Later known as King's Letter Boys, they were rated as midshipmen, a rank which previously had been filled by older petty officers of long experience. Although Charles and James introduced this important step in the development of a professional officer corps, they also contributed to the problem by giving commissions to their own friends, the Queen's and the Duchess's favourites, and other courtiers to whom debts were owed. The King often found it expedient to make places in the navy for sons of politically influential nobles, and in some cases for the nobles themselves.

The gentlemen officers of the mid-1660s were mostly well-to-do adventurers seeking glory and excitement. Fleet commanders often found them difficult to handle, and real trouble could arise when a high-spirited young courtier was placed under a stern old Commonwealth man. One such 'blade', Lieutenant Phillip Mansell, was hastily drummed out by the Duke of York in 1665 for his 'disobedience, unruliness, and reproachful language' to his superiors and for 'taunting them with their having been rebels and served under Cromwell's commission'. Tarpaulins were even more infuriated by the meteoric pace at which gentlemen with the right connections could ascend the ladder of command. Sir William Berkeley, whose brother happened to be a companion of the King, was first a lieutenant at age twenty-two, a captain at twenty-three, and a vice-admiral at twenty-six! The Duke of York's protégé Sir John Chicheley was commissioned a lieutenant in 1662, had his first command in 1663, and was a vice-admiral seven years later. But both these men had exceptional patronage; during the Second Anglo-Dutch War, most members of the gentry found their advancement retarded by the opposition of Penn and Coventry, and even more by the attitudes of Sandwich, Rupert, and Albemarle. The Generals had no use for silly, strutting popinjays in 'ribbons and feathers', and excluded them from important positions as far as possible. At the time of the Four Days' Battle, only Chicheley and Berkeley commanded major warships, and only a handful of others had anything greater than light frigates.

Although the gentlemen were inexperienced and sometimes enjoyed unfair advantages, it would be an injustice to condemn all of them indiscriminately. Certainly the worst were very bad, lacking in every quality of leadership and often profoundly ignorant of ships and the sea. Pepys was told of a new gentleman captain who, on the first inspection of his vessel, ordered the riding bitts removed as an unnecessary encumbrance! Yet some proved to be excellent commanders; conscientious, resourceful, eager to learn, and fearless in action. Chicheley performed creditably throughout his career, as did John Holmes, younger brother of the soldier Robert Holmes and eventually commander-in-chief of the fleet.

Despite the differences in background, training, and ability among the officers, they had certain qualities in common. Nearly all were violent men who were extremely sensitive of their personal honour. They were as yet little bound by tradition, and there was consequently a certain freshness of spirit that was sometimes lacking in the officers of later times. Most were courageous fighters, steady under fire. Victory was not unconditionally demanded as in Nelson's day; the Dutch were far too formidable to make that a practical requirement. Charles II was willing to accept a well-fought defeat and to overlook corruption, drunkenness, and debauchery among his officers, but the honour of the Crown was a sacred trust. Whether tarpaulins or gentlemen, few who violated that trust received another chance.

The Restoration navy depended heavily on skilled non-commissioned officers to support the sometimes inexperienced captains and lieutenants. All of a warship's operational functions were managed by five warrant 'standing officers': the master, responsible for navigation; the gunner, for weaponry; the boatswain, for the physical condition of sails, rigging, deck equipment, and boats; the carpenter, for hull maintenance; and the purser, for pay accounts, victuals, and other stores. Each was assisted by mates and a team of specialist ratings. All standing officers were appointed by the Navy Board, usually on the captains' recommendations. In practice, positions were open to purchase, for many captains expected something of value in return for their endorsements. The Principal Officers of the Navy were themselves open to such blandishments. Pepys found one Bagwell a succession of carpenter's posts to ensure the continued reception of his own blandishments by *Mrs.* Bagwell.

With most ships having only the one lieutenant, warrant posts carried more prestige and much greater responsibility than in later periods. This applied especially to the master. Next in command after the commissioned officers, he had roughly the same shipboard privileges as the lieutenant and was paid considerably more. It was the master who determined what sails to set, what course to steer to reach a given destination, how much rudder was needed for a given evolution, and other such decisions. He was held strictly to account for the safe navigation of the ship; if she were wrecked or in a collision it was not the captain but the master who was almost invariably blamed in the seventeenth century. The captain's career rarely suffered even for repeated mishaps. It was this fact which made it possible for ship commands to go to soldiers, courtiers, and even outright fools, for there was virtually no risk of disgrace except for cowardice or other misbehaviour in battle. Those who wanted a professional officer corps strove throughout Restoration times to shift greater responsibility on to the captains, but without success. The gentlemen and soldiers were outspokenly selfish about it. In 1683 gentleman-admiral George Legge, Baron Dartmouth, candidly admitted to Pepys regarding navigation 'that no commander ought to meddle with or command anything in it out of hand of the master, but at the hazard of being made accountable for the success of it'. As a young captain, Dartmouth himself had been gravely admonished by Sir Edward Spragge that 'while you live keep yourself as free from answering anything for the navigation of your ship as you can, for soon or late it may prove dangerous to you to do otherwise'. Regrettably, this was an attitude to which even the tarpaulin captains subscribed.

By the time of the Second Anglo-Dutch War the post of master was already a dead-end for seamen without influence. It was a position only a genuine blue-water sailor could fill, and though a very few were promoted to captain during the war, most new commands went to lieutenants and 'men of quality'. When gentlemen later gained full control, some prominent tarpaulin captains were reduced to accepting masters' posts or nothing at all. A particularly sad case was John Swanley, an able officer who commanded the third-rate *York* in all the great battles of the war. Afterwards, he could only find employment as a warrant master under Dartmouth, who had not been born when Swanley had gained his first command.

It should be noted that the post of master in the flagship of the commander-in-chief was a special case. This was a highly sought office of great prestige which was usually reserved for an experienced captain of high standing. The master of the Duke of York's *Royal Charles* at the Battle of Lowestoft, for example, was John Cox, a future knight and Navy Commissioner who commanded the first-rate *Royal Sovereign* the year following. During his tenure as master those who addressed him as anything other than *Captain* Cox would have done so at their peril.

The King and the Duke of York did not neglect the spiritual needs of the navy. Each ship above the fifth rate was assigned a supposedly accredited chaplain, and captains were bound by regulation to enforce regular observance of services. Most of the chaplains were undoubtedly conscientious, and many of the captains scrupulously encouraged their work. On the other hand, in view of the less-than-stringent moral tenor of Restoration society, it was perhaps inevitable that some chaplains who found their way into the fleet would 'swear, drink, and talk bawdily, as freely as any man'. One fairly rough-edged chaplain, a country parson named Henry Teonge who went to sea in 1675 to escape his creditors, left a spirited journal which is one of the best sources for day-to-day life in the King's ships. Teonge was as jealous of his prerogatives as any other officer. He thought nothing of subjecting the visiting Lord Mordaunt, a powerful politician, to a withering blast of invective for daring to preach a sermon aboard *his* ship.

Throughout the age of sail, the life of the common seaman was one of hardship and deprivation. In many ways things were better for the men in the Restoration navy than in other times, because for once a King and a Lord High Admiral took a sincere interest in their welfare. The navy's worst problem with its seamen was that there rarely seemed to be enough of them. Charles II never had the resources to make his service very rewarding either financially or otherwise, and even in a popular war, patriotism was not enough to attract free subjects to an existence not much different from slavery. Men did volunteer; some captains were accompanied from ship to ship by bands of faithful followers, and warships employed as commerce raiders seldom had difficulty filling their complements. There were as yet no enlistment bounties for volunteers, but they did receive special considerations such as occasional shore leave and exemption from winter service. Despite these inducements, a large majority of the navy's seamen found themselves aboard the men-of-war through impressment, the ancient quasi-legal form of conscription under which all the mariners in the kingdom were liable for service upon payment by the Crown of a one-shilling imprest bounty.

Impressment took several forms. Best remembered today are the press gangs which came from the fleet into the seaport towns to carry off all the able-bodied men they could catch. There were also shore-based gangs centred on the dockyards, and other seamen were gathered by private contractors hired for the purpose. In addition, chartered companies and guilds such as the Thames Watermen could usually be induced to turn over certain numbers of men in return for 'protections' for the rest. Though the pressmasters of the Restoration period were always prepared to use force if necessary, there was little of the senseless brutality that marked impressment in later eras. Recruits in the Anglo-Dutch Wars were customarily sent home to set their affairs in order, with instructions to report by a specified date. This humane policy was typical of the Duke of York's administration, but it was a disastrous failure. Men nonchalantly abused the privilege, and in November 1664 James was forced to write that

> Those who being pressed either do not appear, or run away, must be apprehended and punished, for it is grown so common that pressing of men is of little effect except to expend treasure; . . . their punishment is so important, that if the assizes or sessions be not very near, a commission of Oyer and Terminer should be ordered for their trial.

Seafarers did not evade service out of disloyalty, nor because of the hard living conditions in the King's ships; merchant seamen were equally ill-treated and their victuals reportedly abominable. It was just that the merchants and privateers offered a better wage, at least on paper. Men consequently signed aboard the trading ships in great numbers, but unless they were fortunate enough to find work in the press-exempt colliers they had scant prospect of avoiding the navy. Men-of-war stopped all the incoming merchantmen they could catch and routinely stripped them of every soul aboard except the officers. In such cases the navy provided trusted skeleton crews to take the ships into port and then return to the fleet. This was the most useful method of impressment, since it could be assumed that practically everyone taken was a trained seaman.

Press gangs ashore were notoriously subject to corruption. The possibility of bribery was obvious, and a man could often purchase his freedom. Seamen also escaped through the connivance of merchant shipping interests and town authorities who had no wish to see the most productive members of their labour force taken away. Rupert and Albemarle reported that the mayors, bailiffs, and constables of Yarmouth and Ipswich were especially 'refractory and backward'. Private pressmasters were assigned quotas, and they were often not too particular about the 'seamen' they gathered. In November 1664 Commissioner Peter Pett indignantly complained of one group 'lately sent in by Capt. Stoakes; they are in no way fit for the service, being made up of all sorts of country trades, and such a ragged crew as never was seen'. The Restoration navy's commissioners and sea-captains often refused to accept men who obviously did not belong in a man-of-war. Commissioner Pett angrily sent home Captain Stoakes's contingent with the comment that they were 'clothed with rags, full of vermin, and one of them even now ill with the smallpox'.

Some influx of landsmen could not be avoided owing to the shortage of proper seamen. It was also acceptable up to a point, for many important shipboard tasks required no prior experience. The crew of a first-rate with a complement of about six hundred included some seventy officers, mates, and specialists such as quartermasters, coxswain, cook, blacksmith, etc. Fifty more were marines, thirty were young boys and teenaged 'gromets' to run ammunition to the guns, and there had to be about one hundred true 'tars' to manage the sails in battle. Perhaps ten other reliable hands were required for powder handling in the magazines, and it was desirable for each piece of ordnance to have a gun captain and a loader who knew their business. The remaining 180 men, over a quarter of the crew, were little more than human beasts of burden who hauled on this or that rope on command, sweated at the capstan, or struggled with the gun tackles. The only requirement was that they be in sound physical condition. Thus, a man-of-war could sail into action in a reasonable state of efficiency even though a fair percentage of the ship's company had been tilling cornfields a few weeks before.

From the moment a new recruit climbed through a warship's gunport, he found himself in a regimented and rigidly structured environment. Ahead of him lay gruelling toil, endless drudgery, ever-present danger, and painful punishments which could be inflicted at the whim of his officers for the slightest infraction. With two-section watches, a full night's sleep was an uncommon luxury. Accounts of life afloat on the lower deck are scarce prior to the nineteenth century, for most seamen were illiterate. There is, however, a most entertaining journal kept by a young sailor named Edward Barlow who served in both merchantmen and men-of-war as a master's mate's apprentice during the 1660s. With the aid of his lively 'worm's eye view' and Chaplain Teonge's equally informative writings, it is possible to get a reasonably complete picture of the daily existence of the seventeenth-century mariner.

The savagery of naval discipline in the age of sail is proverbial. Parliament promulgated formal Articles of War in 1661 'for the Regulating and better Government of His Majesty's Navies, Ships of War, and Forces by Sea'. These dealt with behaviour in action and capital crimes such as mutiny, striking an officer, desertion, and murder. The Articles granted the accused in such cases the right of trial by a court-martial of at least five captains. A permanently appointed Judge Advocate (John Fowler in the war years) accompanied the fleet to conduct the trials, and all death sentences required the approval of the Lord High Admiral except in the case of mutiny.

Lesser shipboard offences were left to the discretion of the captain, who employed a broad range of penalties. Among the most common were ducking from the yardarm and watery variants such as towing from a boat. Somewhat more serious was the 'bilboes', iron stocks in which the miscreant was confined for hours by 'neck and heels' in unpleasant positions. For heinous offences the dreaded 'cat of 9 tayles' was already much in evidence in the 1660s. The terrible ordeal of 'flogging 'round the fleet' was just beginning in those years. The journal of Admiral Sir Thomas Allin mentions an early but not very severe example in 1678. Two men were given five to ten lashes apiece alongside each of three ships for stealing poultry from a farmer and 'a parcel of beans' from a poor woman ashore. It should be pointed out that the seventeenth-century cat was a lighter and less damaging implement than the fearsome scourge of later days.

How frequently punishments were applied is hard to determine; probably not very often, to judge from the little evidence available. Allin, whose journal recorded even minor sentences, mentions an average of only one per year during his almost continuous service from 1660 to 1668. They were mostly duckings or the bilboes for transgressions as serious as 'seditious and mutinous words' and 'striking over right my lieutenant', both of which were capital offences under the Articles of War. Significantly, two of the bilboes victims were merchant officers Allin felt were insufficiently respectful to the King's captain. There were only two major sentences, both floggings for thievery. One was 'a rogue who stole my salmon' – a singularly audacious larceny – and the other a foretopman caught red-handed looting a shipmate's seachest: 'He had twenty lashes, but never shed a tear, a graceless rogue and an old thief'. While commanding a squadron in 1670, Allin also punished a gunner 'for his beastly actions with boys', but the sentence was not described.

Teonge's diary confirms the relative infrequency of punishments, though his captains sometimes employed startlingly original sentences:

> This day 2 seamen that had stolen a peice or two of beife, were thus shamed: they had their hands tyd behind them, and themselves tyd to the maine mast, each of them a peice of raw beife tyd about their necks in a coard, and the beife bobbing before them like the knott of a crevatt; and the rest of the seamen cam one by one, and rubd them over the mouth with the raw beife; and in this posture they stood 2 howers.

Teonge witnessed two other imaginative oral treatments administered as a 'cure for swearers'. Otherwise, in nearly four years of sea service he reported a single ducking for absence without leave and one flogging for thievery. Barlow hardly mentions punishments at all except to note that men who complained about anything were likely to be beaten. He did, however, have one revealing experience himself. Purely through his own negligence he was once away visiting friends in another vessel when his ship sailed, forcing him to make an overland passage to rejoin at another port. In the eighteenth century his 'desertion' would undoubtedly have merited merciless retribution even though he returned. In 1664 he was welcomed back without a word of reproach.

If the Restoration sea-captain tended to be tolerant by later standards, part of the reason was that most disciplinary matters were handled on an unofficial basis by the ship's designated constable and justice of the peace, the boatswain. In Dutch warships this authority was vested in the gunner, the eighteenth-century office of master-at-arms having yet to be instituted in either service. The English boatswain's instrument of justice was the legendary rattan cane, traditions of which went back beyond Elizabethan times. According to one observer in 1707, the rattan was imbued with wondrous properties:

> This little stick . . . seems little inferior to the rod of Moses. It has cured more of the scurvy than the doctor and made many a poor cripple take up his bed and walk. Sometimes it makes the lame to skip, and run up the shrouds like a monkey; but what's most wonderful, it makes heavy-ars'd fellows tumble up from below, contrary to the tendency of all heavy bodies, which tumble downward.

The boatswain was an object of unmitigated terror for the ship's boys. The 'nippers', as they were called, were regularly paraded forth *en masse* and thrashed at the capstan for their 'waggery and idleness'. This seems to have been done mainly for the entertainment of the crew. Captain Nathaniel Butler recorded in about 1635 that

> commonly this execution is done upon the Monday mornings, and is so frequently in use that some mere seamen and sailors believe in good earnest that they shall not have a fair wind until the poor boys be duly brought to the chest; that is, be whipped every Monday morning.

Occasional 'Black Mondays', as Teonge called them, were still routine occurrences in Restoration times. As disgusting as these sadistic spectacles seem, it should be remembered that it was an insensitive age both afloat and ashore. Apprentices on land had it no better, while crimes and misdemeanors by adults ashore were dealt with even more brutally than on shipboard.

Despite the formidable range of punishments, the overall disciplinary standards of the Restoration navy were decidedly lower than in later times. Men were infrequently allowed ashore owing to the likelihood of desertion, but when the fleet was in port they regularly visited friends aboard other ships (as Barlow did), apparently coming and going much as they pleased. Shipboard drunkenness was endemic throughout the period. Though clearly illegal under the Articles of War, it was significantly absent from the offences punished by Allin and by Teonge's captains. The reason is not hard to find: the officers were as often 'o'erguzzled' as the men. In the free-spirited Restoration society few thought this remarkable. Prince Rupert once swore, 'God damn me, if they will turn out every man that be drunk, they must turn out all the commanders in the fleet. What is the matter if he be drunk, so when he comes to fight he doth his work?'

Women were often present. Thomas Penrose, captain of the third-rate *Monck*, had Mrs. Penrose with him throughout a winter cruise in 1666–67. Barlow reported this so casually that it could hardly have been unusual. When the fleet was in harbour, vessels which had been recently paid could expect many visits from 'wives', as they were euphemistically known. The arrival of the 'maids' invariably precipitated sustained sessions of unbridled debauchery. Chaplain Teonge described such a scene in 1675:

> Hither many of our seamen's wives follow their husbands and severall other young women accompany theire sweetharts, and sing, *Loath to depart*, in punch and brandy; so that our ship was that night well furnished, but ill mand; few of them being well able to keepe watch, had there beene occasion. You would have wondered to see here a man and a woman creep into a hammock, the woman's legs to the hams hanging over the sides or out at the end of it. Another couple sleeping on a chest; others kissing and clipping; half drunk, half sober or rather half asleep; choosing rather (might they have been suffered) to go and die with them than stay and live without them.

When the ship sailed and 'our Delilahs and Myrmidons' had to leave, Teonge observed that their

> weeping eys bedewed the very sids of the ship, as they went over into the boate, and seemed to have chosen (might they have had their will) rather to have stuck to the syds of the ship like the barnacles, or shell-fish, then to have parted from us. But they were no sooner out of sight but they were more merry; and I could tell with who too, were I so minded.

Even so, the ship saluted them 'with 3 cheares, 7 gunns, and our trumpetts sounding'. When Rupert and Albemarle joined the fleet in April 1666, the first order listed in their letterbook was to 'turn all ye women to shore and suffer none to come abord'. This was intended more to avoid infectious disease than for any moral or disciplinary considerations. Their command was not fully obeyed and had to be repeated a month later when a 'wife' turned up with the plague in the fourth-rate *Princess*.

Regardless of the state of discipline, every aspect of shipboard society was highly stratified. This was nowhere more obvious than in the berthing customs. The captain lived in the lap of luxury in the great cabin at the after end of the upper deck. In the *Greenwich* of 1666, a mere fourth-rate, the great cabin was by contract the full breadth of the stern and twenty-four feet long, with 'a studdy at one end thereof'. It had 'great panells and Pillasters on the sides, and spring panells with an Ovall panell overhead'. A painter's contract for two second-rates in 1656 called for the great cabin to be stained 'walnut tree colour in oil, grained and revailed, and what is proper to be gilded to be laid gold colour'. In a first-rate the commander enjoyed truly palatial surroundings. His accommodations were often 'very curiously wrought and gilded with divers histories' and 'wrought overhead and on each side with sundry figures in oil colours'. The carvings in the great cabin of the *Charles* of 1668 included 'thirty-four foot of raffled leaves, . . . four roses, . . . one hundred forty-four foot of laurell leaves, . . . ten lyons heads, . . . six pieces of folledge [foliage], . . . forty seaven foot of little eggs', and other wonders too numerous to mention. Often there was an elaborately decorated wash-stand and sometimes a fireplace.

The lieutenant and the master inhabited the roundhouse under the poop in fairly comfortable cabins, which were painted a pleasant 'stone colour and green'. Warrant officers, midshipmen, and petty officers had small 'standing cabins' in the gunroom at the after end of the lower deck, in the cockpit beneath the waterline, and others tucked between the guns everywhere possible above the gundeck. These claustrophobic compartments, by regulation no more than six feet by five, were of sturdy wooden construction until 1666. In that year the Lord High Admiral approved a more easily collapsible type devised by shipwright Sir Phineas Pett in which canvas was stretched over thin frames.

Accommodations became increasingly humble as one descended the social scale. Trumpeters and officers' servants lived in low, box-like cabins at the after end of the poop and between the guns of the quarterdeck. Barlow was once assigned to such a structure in the *Royal Charles*, commenting that it was 'a thing much like to some gentleman's dog-kennel, for I was forced to creep in on all fours, and when I was in and set upon my breech, I could not hold my head upright'. The rank and file of the crew slept in crowded conditions in hammocks slung from the overhead. These 'hammacoes' had been introduced in the Royal Navy earlier in the century. As comfortable a resting place as a hammock seemed in comparison with a ship's unyielding deck, it brought the sailor a whole range of back pains and spinal disorders; this long-suspected fact was not confirmed until the 1930s.

Sanitary facilities gave other clear marks of social distinction. The captain and sometimes the inhabitants of the roundhouse had access to the 'houses of office' in the quarter-galleries. Lesser officers used an enclosed latrine projecting over the side from the starboard main channel. Anyone else not fortunate enough to possess a chamber pot was restricted to the open-air 'seats of easement' on the structure of the head. To avoid the boatswain's wrath, seamen took scrupulous care to use the lee side only.

Dining habits were also socially revealing. Commissioned officers and senior warrant officers usually took over the coach beneath the forward end of the poop or the steerage under the quarterdeck as their mess, petty officers the gunroom. The crew simply squatted on the decks or used portable mess tables which could be slung overhead when not in use. A single meal was prepared at midday and was eaten with the fingers, as was usual for all Englishmen from the King on down. The captain, who had his own cook, and the officers, had tables set with pewter mugs and plates; the crew used wooden bowls and sheath-knives. As might be expected, the fare varied tremendously depending on one's status. Captains could usually afford to bring aboard pigs, lambs, poultry, and fine wines and delicacies. Teonge described a dinner given by Captain William Holden of the fourth-rate *Assistance* at sea off Portugal in July 1675:

> This day our noble Capt. feasted the officers of his small squadron with 4 dishes of meate, viz. 4 excellent henns and a peice of porke boyled, in a dish; a giggett of excellent mutton and turnips; a peice of beife of 8 ribs, well seasoned and roasted; and a couple of very fatt greene geese; last of all, a greate Chesshyre cheese: a rare feast at shoare. His liquors were answerable; viz. Canary, Sherry, Renish, Clarett, white wine, syder, ale, beare, all of the best sort; and punch like [as plentiful as] ditch water; with which wee conclude the day and weeke in drinking to the Kinge, and all that wee love; while the wind blowes fayre.

It is revealing to compare two shipboard Christmas dinners, both in port on foreign stations. One was enjoyed by Teonge and the officers of the fourth-rate *Bristol* at Port Mahon in 1678:

> . . . wee had to dinner, an excellent rice pudding in a greate charger, a speciall peice of Martinmas English beife, and a neat's tounge, and good cabbige, a charger full of excellent fresh fish fryde, a douzen of wood-cocks in a pye, which cost 15d., a couple of good henns roasted, 3 sorts of cheese; and last of all, a greate charger full of blew figgs, almonds, and raysings; and wine and punch gallore, and a douzen of English pippins.

One imagines such a bounty would have gladdened anyone's heart, but the chaplain grumbled that 'Wee had not so greate a dinner as was intended, for the whole fleete being in this harbour, beife could not be gott'. Seaman Barlow would have not complained. His Christmas of 1661, celebrated on the gundeck of the sixth-rate *Martin Galley* at Cadiz, was not so cheery:

> We had nothing but a little bit of Irish beef for four men, which had lain in pickle two or three years and was as rusty as the Devil, with a little stinking oil or butter, which was all colours of the rainbow, many men in England greasing their cartwheels with better.

The authorities who administered the Royal Navy were well aware of how far the seaman's victuals affected his morale. Samuel Pepys expressed it in memorable terms:

> Englishmen, and more especially seamen, love their bellies above anything else, and therefore it must always be remembered in the management of the victualling of the Navy that to make any abatement from them in the quantity or agreeableness of the victuals is to discourage and provoke them in the tenderest point, and will sooner render them disgusted with the King's service than any one other hardship that can be put upon them.

The King and the Lord High Admiral had the same attitude. Part-time seamen themselves, they knew how the men lived, were sensitive to their needs, and took their occasional petitions seriously. Actual rations lists from the 1660s are hard to find, but a victualling contract of 1677 (which differed hardly at all from a list of the 1650s) specified a generous daily allowance:

One pound avoirdupois of good, clean, sweet, sound, well-bolted with a horse cloth, well-baked, and well-conditioned wheaten biscuit; . . . one gallon, wine measure, of beer; . . . two pounds avoirdupois of beef, killed and made up with salt in England, of a well-fed ox . . . for Sundays, Mondays, Tuesdays, and Thursdays; or instead of beef, for two of those days one pound avoirdupois of bacon, or salted English pork of a well-fed hog . . . and a pint of pease (Winchester measure) therewith each of the said days; and for Wednesdays, Fridays, and Saturdays, every man, besides the aforesaid allowance of bread and beer, to have by the day the eighth part of a full-sized North Sea cod of 24 inches long, or a sixth part of a halberdine 22 inches long . . . or a pound avoirdupois of well-savoured Poor John, together with two ounces of butter, and four ounces of Suffolk cheese, or two-thirds of that weight of Cheshire.

In 1666 the Cheshire cheese was substituted in only half-measure rather than two-thirds, a sore point with the men. The total weekly allowance was thus seven pounds biscuit, seven gallons beer, four pounds beef, two pounds pork, one pound fish, one quart peas, six ounces butter and twelve ounces cheese. These quantities were for 'sea victuals' only. For long periods in port there was a reduced 'petty warrant' allowance which the seamen knew as 'Peter Warren'.

Whether sea victuals or petty warrant, the men never received the full allowance. As Barlow explained in 1661,

Our steward would oftentimes pinch something out of our 'lowance, and we had but 14 ounces to the pound, the other two being allowed to the purser of the ship for scraping of the cheese and butter and dust in the bread; yet it was always served out to us without scraping, the foul and the clean together, and the rotten with the sound, and mouldy and stinking and all together, and we had Hobson's choice, that or none, and the purser alleged that the waste was in the bread and butter and cheese, and that it would not hold out the same weight he had received it at. And so amongst them the poor seamen must suffer for it, going with many a hungry belly and a thirsty stomach.

Barlow's purser was not entirely candid with his victims. By long-established custom the one-eighth deduction would have been left ashore, the victualler having given the purser a cash rebate for its value. This so-called 'necessary money' was supposed to compensate for the candles, wood, and implements which the crew consumed gratis from the purser's stores. In practice it was one of the many means by which pursers supplemented their low salaries. Their corruption was built into the system, for they were also financially liable for shortages and losses. As Pepys put it, 'a purser without professed cheating is a professed loser, twice as much as he gets'.

Despite Barlow's experience, the Restoration navy's seamen could seldom be described as underfed. After deducting the purser's eighth (which did not apply to meat and fish), the victualling allowance was still ample, even for hard-working men in their prime. It was much more than they received in merchantmen and probably more than most of them could get ashore. The imbalance in the allowance is noticeable, particularly the absence of fruit and vegetables. Even at the time, many authorities believed that the emphasis on salt meat (which was already suspected of causing scurvy) should be reduced in favour of more healthful items. Most Continental navies had already taken this step, but the traditional meat diet was preferred by Englishmen both at sea and ashore. Captain Butler had explained the problem thirty years before:

> The difficulty consisteth in that our common seamen are so besotted in their beef and pork that they had rather adventure on all the calentures and scurvies in the world than to be weaned from their customary diet, or lose the least part of it. So that it may be doubted that any alteration this way would put them to a running away from the services of State as much as anything else whatsoever.

As for quality, it is noteworthy that Barlow's complaints came under the worst possible circumstances: on a foreign deployment where spoiled victuals could not be replaced, and in peacetime, when the small number of ships in commission allowed the victualler to build up his inventories so that provisions could sometimes lie in cask for long periods before being issued. In wartime things were different. Then, the victualler could barely keep up with the huge fleet's needs, so nothing stayed in the warehouses long enough to deteriorate. Abnormal contentment at the mess tables in 1665–66 is suggested by Barlow's uncharacteristic silence on the whole subject throughout the war. Some of his few comments were actually positive. In December 1665, for instance, he admitted that 'we had some fresh beef from Hull sent to us to keep our Christmas with, having fresh meat for three days, which was a good refreshing to us'. This made a sharp contrast with his miserable Christmas of four years before. The war did reveal problems. Both quantity and quality of beer fell short repeatedly, mainly because of preservation difficulties in summer weather. Water often had to be issued in its place, but that seems to have caused only minor grumbling. At times the fleet ran low on provisions at sea and had to go on two-thirds rations, but such periods of temporary deprivation were accompanied by an automatic 5s. per month wage augmentation.

What scanty evidence there is suggests that the English seaman of the Second Anglo-Dutch War devoured his allowance with less dissatisfaction than at any other time in the age of sail. Part of this was due to the fact that the Restoration navy's victualler was a strictly accountable private contractor and not, as in other periods, some formidable admiral or senior bureaucrat. Captains had no need to fear the contract-bound civilian and could take an aggressive stance towards him. They often refused to accept substandard provisions, unceremoniously heaving them over the side and imperiously demanding better. Much credit was also due to the victualler himself, a public-spirited entrepreneur named Dennis Gauden. Though his operations were disorganized and disastrously inefficient, he was undeniably honest, conscientious, and unusually self-sacrificing. In 1665 Coventry grudgingly acknowledged Gauden's standards. 'No fleete was ever soe ill-supplied for quantities of provision', he wrote, 'as, to do ye victualler right, none ever better for goodness, against which there is not one complaint'.

*

One matter on which there were many complaints was seamen's clothing. No one in the Royal Navy wore anything approaching a uniform in the seventeenth century. The only exceptions were the green coated marines, who came to be colloquially known as 'lobsters' almost from their inception. Officers dressed as gentlemen if they could afford it, while the common seamen purchased 'slops', or navy-issue clothing, in occasional 'fairs' held at the mainmast. Purchases were charged against the men's pay accounts at prices determined by a standing committee consisting of the captain, master, gunner, and boatswain. The maximum rates were established by the Duke of York in 1663:

Monmouth caps	2s.6d.	Cotton waistcoats	3s.0d.
Red caps	1s.1d.	" drawers p.	3s.0d.
Yarn stockings p.	3s.0d.	Neat leather shoes	3s.6d.
Irish "	1s.2d.	Blew neckcloathes	5d.
Blew shirts	3s.6d.	Rugs of one breadth	4s.0d.
White shirts	—	Canvas suits	5s.0d.
		Blew suits	5s.0d.

Unfortunately, the navy's contract slopsellers were of a more profiteering bent than the victualler; quality seldom matched the specified standards. Experienced men filled their seachests with private vendors' wares as far as their means would allow. Pictorial evidence shows that the floppy, broad-brimmed hats which were so fashionable ashore at the time were also popular afloat.

One aspect of sea life on which both officers and men placed great importance was their medical care. All ships above the fifth rate had a 'chyrurgeon' with a barber for a mate. The navy also fitted out fully-staffed hospital ships to transport sick and wounded men ashore. Their care on land was in the hands of a special Commission for Sick, Wounded, and Prisoners, of which the humanitarian diarist John Evelyn was a prominent member. Shipboard surgeons, mates, and the quality of their instruments were supposed to be certified by the Barber-Surgeons' Hall in London. As usual, there were abuses. The certifying authorities complained in particular of 'apothecaries getting acquainted with the commanders of ships, and recommending to them surgeons utterly unknown, who promise to fit their chests with them, and who are taken on board without the approbation of the Surgeons' Company'.

Seventeenth-century sea-surgeons were *not* physicians, though some did have a modicum of medical knowledge. They understood the efficacy of scalding baths and blistering poultices, knew how to bleed and purge a sick man practically to death, and how to cure respiratory ailments by making the patients breathe copious quantities of smoke. Men with such knowledge were highly sought, but mercifully most surgeons could do little more than treat injuries. They were in their proper element in probing for musket balls and splinters, suturing and dressing flesh wounds, setting broken bones, and carrying out quick and efficient amputations of badly damaged limbs. Despite the agonies of operations performed without anaesthetics, seamen thoroughly approved of the procedures. A man with a mangled arm or leg usually wanted it off, and the sooner the better. If one could withstand the shock of the operation, the chances of recovery were much improved. High mortality was inevitable, considering the total ignorance of hygiene and antisepsis; but men frequently survived the most astonishing injuries. A compassionate and well-trained surgeon was often a decisive element in a crew's morale. A good one was always revered, while a drunkard or an obvious incompetent could arouse indignation to the point of mutiny.

Health of seamen varied with the nature of their employment. Long voyages usually brought scurvy and other dietary maladies, and a cruise to mosquito-infested areas such as the Caribbean or West Africa could be tantamount to a death sentence for much of the crew. Surgeons in any seas were constantly occupied with shipboard accidents. Men fell from the rigging, tumbled down hatches, and were 'spoilt' in large numbers by hernias from bending over the yards. But except for these unavoidable troubles, all the evidence indicates that the Royal Navy in the Second Anglo-Dutch War provided a healthier environment than could be found ashore at the time. English seamen took pride in keeping their ships clean, and the fact that new recruits were often reported as 'infested with vermin' suggests that men on active service kept themselves relatively free of parasites. Raging epidemics sometimes swept through the fleet, but the deadly bubonic plague that ravaged England during the war years generally spared the navy. Inexplicable at the time, this was undoubtedly due to the relative cleanliness of the ships and to the fortuitous circumstance that the men-of-war rarely moored to a wharf or quay. The ships' indigenous populations of rats consequently had little opportunity to mingle with their shorebound cousins whose infected fleas were the unsuspected carriers.

Although the English seaman may have loved his belly above all else, gold in his pockets ran a close second. The monthly wage scale in effect in 1666 had been established under the Commonwealth. Based on a twenty-eight-day lunar month, earnings for officers and specialists varied with the rate of the ship:

Admiral of the Fleet	£112
Admiral of the White	70
Admiral of the Blue	56
Vice-Admiral of a Squadron	42
Rear-Admiral of a Squadron	28

Rate:	1st	2nd	3rd	4th	5th	6th
	£ s d	£ s d	£ s d	£ s d	£ s d	£ s d
Captain	21. 0. 0	16.18. 0	11. 0. 0	10. 0. 0	8. 8. 0	7. 0. 0
Lieutenant	4. 4. 0	4. 4. 0	3.10. 0	3.10. 0	No Lieutenant	
Warrant Master	7. 0. 0	6. 6. 0	4.13. 8	4. 6. 2	3.17. 0	Capt is Master
Master's Mate or Pilot	3. 6. 0	3. 0. 0	2.16. 2	2. 7.10	2. 2. 0	2. 0. 0
Midshipman	2. 5. 0	2. 0. 0	1.17. 0	1.13. 9	1.10. 0	1.10. 0
Warrant Boatswain	4. 0. 0	3.10. 0	3. 0. 0	2. 2. 0	2. 0. 0	2. 0. 0
Boatswain's Mate	1.15. 0	1.15. 0	1.12. 0	1.10. 0	1. 8. 0	1. 6. 0
Quartermaster	1.15. 0	1.15. 0	1.12. 0	1.10. 0	1. 8. 0	1. 6. 0
Quartermaster's Mate	1.10. 0	1.10. 0	1. 8. 0	1. 8. 0	1. 6. 0	1. 5. 0
Coxswain	1.12. 0	1.10. 0	1. 8. 0	1. 6. 0	1. 6. 0	
Warrant Carpenter	4. 0. 0	3.10. 0	3. 0. 0	2.10. 0	2. 5. 0	2. 0. 0
Carpenter's Mate	2. 0. 0	2. 0. 0	1.16. 0	1.14. 0	1.12. 0	1.10. 0
Warrant Master Gunner	4. 0. 0	3.10. 0	3. 0. 0	2.10. 0	2. 5. 0	2. 0. 0

Gunner's Mate	1.15. 0	1.15. 0	1.12. 0	1.10. 0	1. 8. 0	1. 6. 0
Quarter Gunner	1. 6. 0	1. 6. 0	1. 6. 0	1. 5. 0	1. 5. 0	1. 5. 0
Armourer	1.12. 0	1. 5. 0	1. 5. 0	1. 5. 0		
Gunsmith	1. 5. 0	1. 5. 0	1. 5. 0	1. 5. 0		
Warrant Surgeon	2.10. 0	2.10. 0	2.10. 0	2.10. 0		
Surgeon's Mate	1.10. 0	1.10. 0	1.10. 0	1.10. 0	1.10. 0	1.10. 0
Corporal	1.15. 0	1.12. 0	1.10. 0	1. 8. 0	1. 8. 0	1. 5. 0
Yeoman of Jeers, Shrouds, Hallihards, and Jacks	1.12. 0	1.10. 0	1.10. 0	1. 8. 0		
Warrant Purser	4. 0. 0	3.10. 0	3. 0. 0	2.10. 0	2. 5. 0	1. 5. 0
Steward	2. 0. 0	1.16. 0	1.10. 0	1.10. 0	1. 6. 0	1. 4. 0
Warrant Cook	1. 5. 0	1. 5. 0	1. 5. 0	1. 5. 0	1. 5. 0	1. 5. 0
Master Trumpeter	1.10. 0	1. 8. 0	1. 5. 0	1. 5. 0	1. 5. 0	1. 4. 0

Able Seaman		Ordinary Seaman	
Yeoman of the Powder		Shifter	
Steward's Mate		Barber	0.19. 0
Cook's Mate	1. 4. 0		
Swabber		Gromet	0.14. 3
Cooper		Boy	0. 9. 6
Ordinary Trumpeter			

These figures applied for 'sea pay' only. 'Rigging pay' for fitting-out periods and 'harbour pay' for in-port periods were somewhat lower. Under all circumstances each man's wages were reduced by 6d. per month to support the Chatham Chest, the ancient Elizabethan foundation for disabled mariners. Another 2d. was deducted for the surgeon's expenses, and 4d. for the chaplain. The chaplain's regular wages (19s. per month) did not appear in the navy's tables, for he was paid by the Bishop of London. Incidentally, an able seaman was one who had served seven years at sea and was over twenty-four years old.

The relative merits of the navy's pay can only be judged by the standards of the time. The Commonwealth had granted a twenty-five per cent increase; seamen did not receive another until 1797, by which time the average cost of living had quadrupled. In view of that, it can at least be said that the Restoration mariner was vastly better off than his great-great-grandchildren. How well he was paid in modern terms is difficult to say, because prices for the basic necessities of life have inflated unevenly. Clothing costs, for instance, have risen only eight to ten times, but food easily fifty to a hundred times. All in all, the £15 annual wage of the able seaman of 1666 was probably equivalent to about £1,000 in modern spending power, not counting the value of his free victuals and 'housing'. His overall income was somewhat less than a skilled London labourer's, but was two or three times more than an agricultural worker's. It was easily sufficient for a bachelor's needs, though a man with a wife and children would have been hard pressed to support them by himself. On the other hand, a bright professional seaman had better prospects for advancement than any tradesman ashore.

Unfortunately for the navy's recruitment efforts, most of the nation's seafarers were bedazzled by the much higher rates offered in merchantmen. These varied with the nature of the service, but normal monthly wages for a merchant able seaman in wartime averaged about 35 shillings. Barlow accepted 26s. as an ordinary seaman in a Guineaman in 1665. The glittering merchant rates, however, compared less favourably on close examination. The navy held out at least the possibility of prize money; though a seaman's share was usually small, some lucky ships' companies gained fabulous windfalls. The Chatham Chest also promised the naval seaman lifetime annuities for maiming injuries: £6 13s. 4d. for loss of a limb, £15 for both arms, £13 6s. 8d. for both legs, £5 for a disabled arm, and £4 for an eye. Merchants made no such promises, and seafarers often learned to their sorrow that private shipowners had dozens of ways of cheating them out of all but a fraction of their hard-earned wages. Especially vicious was the widespread practice of charging the crew for the value of spoiled cargo, and in leaky hulls on stormy passages losses could be ruinous. Similarly, if a merchantman were wrecked the men received nothing. Mean though the King's wages seemed, experienced mariners knew that they would at least get it all if they were willing to wait. Intervals between payments of months or even years were common in both trading vessels and men-of-war; merchantmen were paid off only at the end of a voyage, warships traditionally at the end of a commission.

The naval seaman was sometimes paid in hard money, but more often he received a voucher, or 'ticket', which could be cashed only at the Ticket Office in London. If as occasionally happened, the Ticket Office ran short of funds, the seaman might be left destitute for weeks. During the Second Anglo-Dutch War, this outrage was mostly confined to the autumn of 1666, when many crews were discharged simultaneously during a financial crisis. Before that time, the men were given no reason to mistrust their masters. When the fleet was laid up for the winter after the 1665 campaign, the crews were kept aboard on harbour pay. Those who were discharged (soldiers, volunteers, and sick or unfit men) had no difficulty cashing their tickets. The seamen's misplaced confidence in the pay system was further bolstered when the Duke of York (at Albemarle's urging) ordered a good faith payment to the whole fleet before the 1666 campaign. Ships were paid off a few at a time as money became available, beginning in January and ending in June when the last vessels were paid. In most cases crews received half their accumulated wages, the rest being kept on the books 'for fear', said Barlow, 'of our running away from the ship'. This payment came as a pleasant surprise to the men, and their morale at the time of the Four Days' Battle was consequently high.

The common seaman of the Restoration period unquestionably lived better in nearly all respects than his eighteenth- and early nineteenth-century descendants. But the difference was mainly one of degree; Jolly Jack Tar led a harsh existence under the best of circumstances. He was cheated, bullied, sometimes flogged, and even when he was not deliberately abused he was still exposed to storms, shipwreck, scurvy, and roundshot. Yet there must have been compelling compensations, for once a young man was impressed, entrapped, or enticed aboard either a merchantman or a man-of-war, there was an excellent chance that he would accept the sea as his permanent calling. Barlow was typical. His journal bristles for page after page with outraged accounts of maltreatment; at one point he despairs that 'whosoever putteth his child to get his living at sea had better a great deal bind him 'prentice to a hangman'. Yet he returned to the ships again and again for half a century, never staying ashore any longer than it took to spend his money. Evidently many were irresistibly attracted by the adventure, camaraderie, and sheer maleness of the mariner's life. Seamen swaggered about the seaport towns, boasted of their voyages, told wondrous lies, and undoubtedly considered themselves a special breed. For Barlow himself it was pure wanderlust:

> The hardships I endured made me think many times that I had better to have taken any other employment upon me than have come to sea; but I had always a mind to see strange countries and fashions, which made me bear these extremities with the more patience.

Chapter III

The Ships

With roomy decks, her guns of mighty strength,
Whose low-laid mouths each mounting billow laves:
Deep in her draught, and warlike in her length,
She seems a sea-wasp flying on the waves.

Warships of the Restoration period, like those of every age, ultimately determined naval strategy and tactics. Strategically, among the most fundamental considerations with seventeenth-century ships of war were the time and effort needed to acquire them. England and the Netherlands, the world's unchallenged leaders in the art (not yet science) of shipbuilding in the 1660s, kept huge battlefleets. Those fleets had been painstakingly accumulated over many years; no amount of money could buy a first-class navy overnight, as Louis XIV of France was disappointed to learn.

Shipbuilding was easily the most sophisticated of seventeenth-century enterprises. It required naval architects with special knowledge and experience, a large work-force expert in many unusual trades, and a broad range of often hard-to-find materials. Massive and naturally curved hardwood 'compass timbers' for hulls, straight-grained oak for decks, pine and fir for masts and spars, flax for sailmaking, hemp for ropemaking, iron for anchors and fittings, and miscellaneous substances such as pitch, tar, and tallow – all these were strategic commodities as important to the sea-powers of the age of sail as oil and steel are today. England had some iron and a barely adequate reserve of native oak and elm, but otherwise both sides had to procure nearly all their materials abroad. The Dutch drew on German oak forests along the Rhine and the English brought in pines from North America. Most of the other essential stores came from the steppes and pine-covered plains of Russia and the Baltic states. They could be obtained only from the Swedish-owned emporium at Riga on the southeastern shore of the Baltic, from the icy Russian port of Archangel on the White Sea, or at high prices from middlemen in Hamburg. Both the English and the Dutch suffered much anxiety over their precarious northern lifelines, but neither exhausted its supplies.

Most English warships were built in the royal dockyards at Woolwich, Deptford, Chatham, Portsmouth, and Harwich. There was also a fair amount of contract building at private yards in the Thames and to a lesser extent at Bristol and Yarmouth. In the Netherlands, the sprawling complex of slipways and docks lining the IJ at Amsterdam was the largest shipbuilding centre in the world. Nearly every Dutch seaport had at least some shipbuilding capacity; the Admiralties maintained major facilities at Amsterdam, Rotterdam, Hoorn, Medemblik, Enkhuizen, Harlingen, Middelburg, Vlissingen, and several minor sites. Contract building was infrequent, though de Ruyter's *Zeven Provinciën* was a notable exception.

Construction in England was invariably delayed by problems with labour and materials caused by lack of money. New English ships took fifteen to eighteen months from conception to delivery, including about two months at the start for design work and gathering of timber, and another month for fitting-out after launching. The Dutch were more efficient, often delivering new men-of-war within twelve months of the date of order, and that despite frequent delays in arming them brought on by an ailing gunfounding industry. Their wartime production of major fighting ships also far outstripped the English numerically – forty new vessels as opposed to only nine in England. In addition, Dutch shipwrights simultaneously found space, labour, and materials to build six large warships for the French.

The tremendous output from the Dutch dockyards did *not* translate into numerical growth for the States' Fleet. That was because of another strategically important characteristic of sailing men-of-war: they required large crews, typically over four hundred men for a 70-gun ship. The size of the fleets was rigidly tied to the number of seamen available, which was stretched to the limit in both countries throughout the war. Each found it virtually impossible to man many more ships than it already had, and beyond a certain point, new or captured ships could be added only by discarding other vessels. Still, the ease with which the Dutch could replace lost ships was a major advantage.

The Anglo-Dutch Wars took place just as the sailing warship was completing its evolution into the broadside artillery platform it was to remain for the following two hundred years. The pace of development had been quite rapid during the first half of the seventeenth century. Ships of the 1660s looked (and were) very different from the low-beaked, high-castled, broken-decked galleons which were still being built in all European dockyards as late as 1615. But except for gradual increases in size, the fundamental plan differed little from the middle of the seventeenth century until the coming of steam and the rifled gun in the middle of the nineteenth. With a few cosmetic changes, large warships of the Restoration period would not have seemed far out of place at Trafalgar. Such stagnation is easily explained: given the limitations of wind power, wood construction, and lack of significant gunnery advances, the standard ship design filled the requirements. When Samuel Pepys wrote in the 1690s of 'the little room that seems left for any improvement of naval architecture', he was quite close to the mark.

Large warships had two or three complete flush decks to carry the armament, a not quite complete orlop platform beneath the waterline, and partial decks in the upperworks including forecastle (sometimes omitted), quarterdeck, and poop. The internal layout remained the same for centuries. Hatches, ladders, ventilation gratings, capstans, pumps, and bitts and ranges for securing cables and rigging were lined up along the centre-line on each deck, leaving broad open spaces on either side for working the guns. Though the three-masted square rig varied in detail over the years, it too remained the same in principle. Many supposedly eighteenth-century characteristics such as staysails and studding sails were already in use in the 1660s, along with the more primitive spritsail topsail and lateen mizzen.

Despite the basic similarity of warships throughout the age of sail, those of every period displayed many idiosyncrasies. Of least importance (though not necessarily of least interest) were the fashions in the naming of ships. The naval powers of the seventeenth century were little attracted by the pantheons of mythological figures that populated European fleets from the mid-eighteenth century onwards. *Orions*, *Minotaurs, Auroras*, and *Endymions* were not to be found in the Four Days' Battle. Nor were the adjectival *Indefatigables, Powerfuls*, and *Valiants*; nouns were preferred. On the English side the King himself named or at least approved the names of all the ships. The greatest vessels glorified the kingdom itself, the person of the monarch, and the patron saints of the realm: *Royal Oak, Royal Charles, St. George*. Others honoured members of the royal family: *York, Anne, Royal Katherine, Henry, Gloucester, Henrietta*. Illegitimacy was no impediment: there was a *Monmouth* too. Famous Commanders such as *Fairfax* and *Essex* were mournfully commemorated, but it was not required that one be deceased; a *Monck* and a *Rupert* both fought in the Four Days' Battle, though the *Montagu* happened to be elsewhere. Traditional English ship names were as popular as ever (as they still are today): *Swiftsure, Triumph, Vanguard, Revenge, Dreadnought, Warspite*. For smaller warships towns, counties, gemstones, birds, and predatory beasts were most common, but older ships from Puritan days often displayed charitable sentiments like *Assurance, Amity, Assistance* and *Advice*. The English at this period were generally uninterested in palaces for ship names, though *Nonsuch* proved irresistible.

Dutch men-of-war were most often named after towns, provinces, and members of the nobility and the House of Orange, but many of the greatest ships expressed republican ideals: *Eendracht* (unity), *Vrijheid* (freedom), *Vrede* (peace), and *Liefde* (love). As one might expect from a Calvinist country, fleets often contained a smattering of *Jozuas, Gideons, Calebs*, and apostles. The Dutch were also fond of naming ships after notable buildings (*Raadhuis van Haarlem, Kasteel van Medemblik, Dom van Utrecht*) and after homes and estates belonging to admiralty directors and prominent citizens: *Huis te Zwieten, Huis te Kruijningen*.

The Dutch usually renamed prizes taken from the English, but the English preferred to retain the original names as trophies of sorts. No one thought it incongruous that an English fleet at war with the Netherlands could include a *Zealand* and a *Westfriesland*. The sternpiece of a Dutch ship usually bore decoration relating to the name. A vessel named after a town might show a panoramic view of the burg's skyline or its armorial symbol. When such a vessel was captured the English simply adopted the symbol as the new name whether or not its significance was understood. Thus the captured *Wapen van Edam* became the *Black Bull* and the *Groningen* the *Black Eagle*. Sometimes English seamen, mystified by a prize's sternpiece, could only ask the captive crew for the ship's name. The results could be amusing, for the universal English-speaker's penchant for butchering foreign phrases was already fully developed in the seventeenth century. The 60-gun Indiaman *Slot Hooningen*, taken in 1665, had been named after a castle belonging to an East India Company director. In the English service she became, incredibly, the *Slothany*.

Both sides duplicated names without the slightest hesitation. When Charles II renamed the former Protectorate flagship *Richard* the *Royal James*, another vessel already known as the *James* had to become the *Old James*. In 1666 the English fleet included a *Great Gift* and a *Little Gift*, a *Mary* and a *Little Mary*. There were also a *Victory* and a *Little Victory* (built from the 'chips', or leftover timber, from the bigger *Victory's* construction), along with a prize *French Victory* (ex-*Victoire*). The Dutch were even worse. Their ships were built by five separate regional Admiralties which thought nothing of pirating each others' favourite names. In the Four Days' Battle no less than nine sets of identical or closely related names were borne by two or more Dutch vessels. Sometimes there were duplicates even within one Admiralty's contingent. The Admiralty of the Maas, for example, had both a *Klein* (little) *Hollandia* and a *Groot* (great) *Hollandia*. These were not to be confused with Amsterdam's even greater *Hollandia* or the *Hollandia* belonging to Zeeland!

Mid-seventeenth-century warships were markedly distinctive in their decorative schemes. Instead of Elizabethan geometrical patterns or Georgian architectural motifs, vessels of the 1660s reflected their baroque context with carvings of human and animal forms. In England, the King's ships were an art form all their own. It was taken for granted that they should be beautiful; that the 'gilt' glinting from the carvings was only tar and white paint did not matter. Most of the nation's best wood carvers found employment in the dockyards. Since their works have not survived, they are mostly unremembered today. Nevertheless, Restoration masters such as John Leadman, Samuel Ive, Jonas Cord, Humphrey Bull, and whole generations of the Christmas family were respected in their day.

The seventeenth century is often regarded as a time of ridiculously ornate ship carving. Actually, the worst of the frothy rococo profusion was mostly confined to the last quarter of the century. At the time of the Four Days' Battle, decoration was not particularly extreme. Dutch warships were quite austere, with unwreathed gunports, simple quarter-galleries, and sternpieces usually painted rather than carved. Most of the English ships then afloat had been built or rebuilt under the Commonwealth, when excessive display was frowned upon. To be sure, some of the great flagships of the Protectorate had been given special treatment. In an earlier period Charles I had allowed real gilt for the spectacular carvings of the famous *Sovereign of the Seas* (known as the *Royal Sovereign* in Restoration times). It was this astounding expense, said diarist John Evelyn, which had 'cost his Majestie the Affection of his Subjects'. No doubt recalling his father's mistake, Charles II sharply restricted decoration, at least in the early years of his reign. Figureheads were simple lions except in rare cases, and gunport wreaths, commonly thought of as invariable features of Restoration warships, were far from universal in 1666. Many major vessels had none at all, and others only a few around the quarterdeck ports or those in the waist. Despite Charles's restrictions there were always a few Philistines who condemned all decoration as a prime example of the King's 'profligate' ways. In fact, when it cost £50,000 to build, arm, and equip a first-rate, £325 does not seem an extravagant expense for beauty. That was the charge for the carvings of the 96-gun *Charles* of 1668, the greatest warship of the decade.

Seventeenth-century men-of-war displayed characteristic structural details in the deep sweep of the headrails, the marked sheer in the rails and planking of the sides, the thin paired strakes of the wales, and the low position of the channels (only three or four feet above the gundeck ports). Paintwork on the hull was rather plain. The lower wales and the upper sides were usually black, the broad area between being 'paid' with a clear varnish. This took on a yellowish hue which inspired the poet Dryden's 'sea-wasp' analogy. The idea of sheathing a ship's bottom with copper or lead to protect against wood-boring marine worms had originated as early as the sixteenth century, but in 1666 problems arising from the electrolytic action of seawater were still unsolved. The underbodies of most seventeenth-century ships were covered with a mixture of tallow and hair. Inside the ship the practice of colouring everything but the decks bright red had not yet begun in the seventeenth century. In Restoration times the insides of the gunport lids were painted red, but the other surfaces were paid with a clear varnish.

Some internal fittings and equipment were unique to the seventeenth century. The familiar broad-headed capstan with radiating bars had not yet been invented in the 1660s; the earlier type was a tall drum in which the bars went all the way through one above the other. Ladders, especially those serving the officers' accommodations aft, were often twisting or spiral staircases as elaborate as anything that might be found in palatial homes ashore.

A seemingly minor problem that caused untold trouble for the seventeenth-century ship designer was the location of the cookroom. The fireplace was a brick furnace built around a pair of permanently installed copper kettles. In early Jacobean warships it had usually been found in the hold or on the lower deck forward of the mainmast. It filled the ship with smoke in either position, which was eventually found intolerable. A special naval reform commission in 1618 demanded that it be placed in the forecastle,

> because in the midship and in the hold the smoke and heat so search every corner and seam, that they make the oakum spew out, and the ships leaky, and soon decay. Besides the best room for stowage of victuals is thereby so taken up that transporters must be hired for every voyage of any time and which is worst, when all the weight must be cast before and abaft and the ships are left empty and light in the midst, it makes them apt to sway in the back, as the *Guardland*, and divers other have done.

Not everyone agreed; some authorities disapproved of heavy brickwork high in the forecastle, where it added topweight and was exposed to enemy shot. By Common-wealth times it was back in the hold; the specifications for the 'great frigate' *Speaker* of 1650 required that it be there. But the smoke was no less offensive than before. After coughing seamen with smarting eyes bravely endured the fumes for another decade, the cookroom at last found a permanent home under the forecastle, on the upper deck in two-deckers and the middle deck in three-deckers. Even then, some small two-deckers *had* no forecastle, so in those ships the hearth stayed below. A partial solution for such unfortunate vessels was found in 1665, when Captain Phineas Pett fitted his *Tiger* with a copper chimney to carry the smoke from the hold; with what success is not recorded. As late as 1675 a two-decker was built with the cookroom belowdecks, but it was unsatisfactory and the ship was soon modified.

English warships of the Restoration period were very fine-ended underwater. Though desirable for fast sailing, this limited their stowage capacity and hence endurance. Few English warships built before 1666 could stow more than three months' provisions, while double or triple that amount was deemed necessary later. This was not as serious an impediment as one might imagine. The day when the Royal Navy would have to fight its battles in distant oceans far from its bases was still well in the future; all the great actions of the Anglo-Dutch Wars were fought within a few days' sail of a friendly port. It might be argued that greater capacity would have allowed sustained close blockades such as were mounted against French ports in Napoleonic times. Unfortunately, that would still have been impossible, for Charles II's harried victualler was rarely able to provision the fleet for more than four or five weeks at a time.

Seventeenth-century warships were much more difficult to manage under sail than later vessels. The steering wheel was only invented about 1700; before then the rudder was swung by a vertical lever called a whipstaff attached to the end of the tiller. The tiller entered the hull beneath the overhead of the lower deck, and the helmsman stood on the deck above. This was satisfactory enough for two-decked ships (in some the helmsman had a small hatch above with a low companion through which he could keep an eye on the sails) but in large three-deckers one or two men at the whipstaff were incapable of controlling the enormous rudder. Their efforts often had to be supplemented or in some cases supplanted by gangs of seamen manning heavy tackles on the lower deck; helm orders had to be shouted down three levels. Handling also suffered from the inadequacy of the headsails prior to the introduction of the jib in the 1700s. It was difficult in some circumstances of wind and sea to tack or wear without using boats to tow the head around. The clumsiness of the ships explains why both English and Dutch seamen so long resisted adoption of the line-ahead and its concomitant coordinated manoeuvres. It also explains why eyewitness pictorial representations of the battles often show the lines in chaotic disarray, and why collisions were so common.

Like square-rigged ships of all periods, seventeenth-century men-of-war sailed best with the wind abeam or on the quarter, were sluggish close-hauled, and were hard to steer with the wind dead astern. Sailing qualities naturally varied from ship to ship. The fastest could make ten knots or more in ideal winds and with clean hull and proper trim, though six to eight was more usual. Few were very weatherly. The choice of headings was limited to about two-thirds of the compass in optimum conditions, as little as half the compass in crosswind swells or contrary currents. Some ships seemed balky no matter what, but not even the best could make upwind progress against a strong current. This had great importance in view of the racing North Sea tides.

Riding characteristics were largely determined by hull form and trim. With its relatively broad beam, deep keel, and great expanses of deadwood, the seventeenth-century hull gave excellent resistance to rolling. Less desirably, the fine-ended ships could pitch deeply and usually took on a steady heel to leeward. The amount of heel a vessel assumed under given conditions was mostly a matter of stability: the constant competition for displacement, stowage capacity, and low centre of gravity, in opposition to the need for fine lines and large sail area to give speed, for heavy armament mounted as high as possible, and for massive timbering above the waterline to resist enemy shot. Shipwrights understood this competition intuitively, but had no sound theory to go on other than rules of thumb from prior experience. Such rough and ready guidelines were generally reliable, though not always. Bafflingly, one vessel could ride proudly upright while a seemingly similar sister in identical circumstances wallowed along with her lee ports awash.

The uncertainty of navigation out of sight of land was an important element in the management of seventeenth-century ships under sail. Latitude could be determined within acceptable limits using a simple instrument such as the quadrant or the cross-staff; one merely measured the maximum altitude above the horizon reached by the sun or a given star, which varies predictably with every day of the year for each latitude. Unfortunately, longitude determination was impossible since it required an accounting of time beyond the capabilities of seventeenth-century instruments. A vessel on a long voyage could only adopt a course which would be certain of intercepting the latitude of the destination, and then stay on that latitude the rest of the way. Navigational problems were compounded even in sight of land by a lack of accurate charts, the poor precision of compasses, and the difficulty of estimating distances by unaided vision.

The system of rates, first through sixth, for classifying English warships was long established by Restoration times. Boundaries between the rates were subjective and rather elastic, the purpose being mainly to distinguish the officers' pay scales. Contrary to later practice, the number of guns was not particularly important. The fourth-rate *Leopard*, for example, had a greater numerical armament than the second-rate *Rainbow*. Though the members of a given rate were anything but homogeneous, they did have certain common characteristics. At the lowest end of the scale were about a dozen ship-rigged single-decked sixth-rates carrying 6 to 14 small guns. Seldom found with the main fleet, they were used mostly for commerce raiding, fishery protection, anti-smuggling work, and general coastal patrol. They were often assigned to Irish, Scottish, and overseas colonial waters. Also classed as sixth-rates were ketches, pinks, yachts, and other small craft. Ketches (mostly hired from private owners) *were* assigned to the main fleet. Their weatherly fore-and-aft rig made them excellent 'advice boats' for relaying messages within the fleet and communicating with the shore.

Fifth-rates were two-deckers of 250–300 tons and 20–36 guns. They had a complete lower tier, but the upper deck usually carried guns only under the forecastle and in the steerage beneath the quarterdeck; the waist was left unarmed. At the beginning of 1665 there were thirty-one such vessels in service, of which only seventeen were English-built. The rest were an assortment of prizes including former Royalist privateers, an Algerine corsair, and ships taken at various times from the Dutch, French, and Spanish. Although three were built during the war and four more acquired by capture, the inventory of light frigates diminished steadily through losses and conversion to fireships, for which the Navy Board appropriated nine mostly older prizes. Fifth-rates were wisely excluded from the battle-line because of their uniformly thin scantlings and light armament, few having anything better than 9-pounder 'demi-culverins'. Fleet commanders nevertheless found them useful for scouting, towing damaged vessels, defeating enemy fireships, and supporting their own fireships. Rupert and Albemarle repeatedly requested at least one fifth-rate for each flag-officer, but only two were on hand for either the Four Days' Battle or the St. James's Day Fight.

Warships larger than fifth-rates were unofficially regarded as ships-of-the-line, though that term had not yet been coined. All third-and fourth-rates were two-deckers, the rather arbitrary dividing line between them falling at about 650 tons with some overlap. The Royal Navy began the war with thirty-five English-built fourth-rates and seven old and somewhat decrepit prizes: four Dutch, two Royalist, and one Portuguese. Of the English-built ships, two were small and unimpressive 34-gun survivors of Charles I's Ship Money Fleet, and six were lightly timbered but exceptionally fast Parliamentary frigates from Civil War days ranging from 375 to 475 tons and carrying about 40 guns. All the rest had been laid down during the 1650s. These Commonwealth and Protectorate ships included the outsized *Leopard* (which really belonged with the third-rates), four imitations of the much-admired Parliamentary class, and twenty-two fairly normal vessels of 510–630 tons and 46–52 guns.

The navy completed only three new fourth-rates during the Second Anglo-Dutch War, none of them in time for the Four Days' Battle. A quicker and much cheaper means of acquiring warships was taking them from the enemy. Fifteen vessels of fourth-rate size were captured in the early stages of the war and another in 1667. The English chauvinistically disparaged their 'Flemish-built' ships as slow, weakly constructed, and very cramped with the gunports too close together. Actually, the English misunderstood the philosophy behind the ships' design and did not know how to get the best out of them. The Dutch concentrated on shallow draught and high freeboard for the lower-deck ports, deliberately using light timbers to save weight. They were restricted by both policy and ordnance shortages to relatively small guns, which is why the gunport intervals were so short.

The Royal Navy invariably re-armed its prizes with overly massive ordnance. This made them ride deeper than their designers had intended, thereby ruining their sailing qualities. Furthermore, there was often too little space to work the larger guns efficiently and, worst of all, the recoil shock of the heavy ordnance was too great for the slender Dutch frames. Scarfs and joints between the timbers worked loose and the ships wore out prematurely. Only a single Dutch two-decker taken during the war survived beyond 1668. Despite their short lifespans, the prizes made more important temporary contributions to the fleet's firepower than the English were willing to admit.

Also classed as fourth-rates were the many merchantmen hired during the war from trading companies and individuals. Such vessels were normally chartered for six months at a time at a rate of 9 or 10s. per ton per month. There was never any shortage of hulls for hire. With most overseas trading under wartime embargo, profitable risk-free leases to the Crown were attractive alternatives for the shipowners. Typical hired ships required certain modifications before they could be thrown into battle. A powder room, including a filling room, had to be installed, along with new bulkheads at the after end of the hold to form a bread room and steward room. Conversion also entailed substantial improvements in firepower. Sizeable English merchantmen had imposing numbers of gunports to discourage pirates and privateers, but that was mostly bluff. Owners, always balancing security against profits, were seldom inclined to squander money and weight otherwise available for cargo on full outfits of expensive guns which would demand unaffordably large crews anyway. Only about half the ports were filled in normal merchant guise, so for the King's service the rest of the armament had to be made up by the Ordnance Office. The Navy Board was at first not very discriminating in the ships it chose. Thirty-three were employed as men-of-war in 1664–65, some of them no larger than fifth-rates and as weakly armed; only three had more than 44 guns. A few originally designed with an eye to privateering must have been reasonably good sailers, but the rest were notoriously slow and unhandy. That made them unfit for any employment other than the battle-line, in which the smaller ones were soon recognized as liabilities. In 1666 standards became higher. Only seventeen merchantmen were hired that year: ten of the least objectionable from the original group and seven newly hired ships of the East India and Levant trades. The newly hired ships were sturdy vessels averaging over 500 tons and mounting 48–56 guns of respectable calibres. Unfortunately, they were not ready in time for the Four Days' Battle.

Though fourth-rates of all sizes were considered worthy of the line of battle, the faster ones were sometimes released for commerce-raiding. The lean Parliamentary frigates, typified by the speedy *Tiger*, *Elizabeth*, and *Adventure*, were particularly well suited for independent cruising and were highly sought commands by young officers hoping to make their fortunes from captured merchantmen. Fourth-rates assigned to the main fleet naturally made less impact than the first-, second-, and third-rates, and by the end of the century they were beginning to be excluded from the battle-line altogether. In the Anglo-Dutch Wars, however, there was still an important role for the versatile small battleship which could penetrate shoal waters where the great ships could not.

In 1665 there were fifteen third-rates measuring 650–800 tons, all built by the Commonwealth and Protectorate in the 1650s. During the war five larger ones were built and five more of various sizes obtained by capture. Most of the Commonwealth ships were armed (officially at least) with only 58 guns – not many more than a typical fourth-rate carried. But that was deceptive; few fourth-rates had anything larger than 18-pounder 'culverins', while third-rates were equipped with full lower-deck batteries of 32-pounder 'demi-cannon'. Stoutly timbered and generally excellent sailers, third-rates displayed an ideal combination of characteristics which eventually made them the standard ships-of-the-line in all navies. In the Restoration fleets they were the ships of choice of many captains even when larger vessels were available.

Above the third-rates were the 'great ships': the three-decked first- and second-rates. After 1669 new members of these two classes became essentially indistinguishable except in size, but during the Second Anglo-Dutch War there were noticeable structural differences. Unlike first-rates, second-rates in the 1660s were left without a forecastle to conserve topweight, the whole upper deck being uncovered forward of the quarterdeck. More obviously, second-rates had only two complete tiers of gunports. The upper deck had two or three ports on each side forward and five to seven on each side abaft the mainmast; in between there were no ports, the bulwarks in the waist dropping to only a foot or two above the deck. Two-tiered three-deckers were common in European fleets between 1625 and 1670, particularly in the 1660s when they seem to have been universally popular. The configuration went out of fashion thereafter, though the English briefly revived it near the end of the century with some of the despised third-rate '80s'. It should be noted that the lack of a complete upper tier of gunports did not preclude a complete third tier of guns. Pictorial evidence shows that some captains mounted ordnance in the waist despite the absence of ports, the barrels simply protruding over the low rail with canvas 'fights' rigged above for the safety of the gun crews.

At the beginning of the war the Royal Navy had thirteen second-rates which could be grouped in two distinct categories. Eight were elderly warships of between 800 and 900 tons dating from before the Civil War. Of these, the *Rainbow* and *Vanguard* were rebuilt versions of ancient Elizabethan galleons; both had fought the Spanish Armada. The *Triumph*, *St. George*, *St. Andrew*, and *Swiftsure* were survivors of a group of ten vessels built by shipwright William Burrell to the requirements of the landmark naval reform commission of 1618. Burrell, though overshadowed in history by his more flamboyant contemporary Phineas Pett, was actually among the most brilliant and influential of all English shipbuilders. His eminently successful 1618 classes were the earliest examples of large flush-decked warships and marked a sharp break with Elizabethan traditions. The remaining old second-rates were the *Unicorn* and *Old James*, members of Charles I's well-found but politically disastrous Ship Money Fleet of the 1630s.

Most of the Early Stuart men-of-war had originally been regarded as two-deckers and were so arranged internally; the great cabin, for instance, was on the second deck. But like other ships of their time they had been equipped with a light spar deck, actually little more than a grating, above the two principal battery decks for shelter and protection against boarders. During the 1630s and 1640s ordnance enthusiasts caused the spar deck to be strengthened for additional armament, thereby transforming the ships into three-deckers. They were evidently among the most strongly-built vessels the Royal Navy ever had; five were afloat until at least 1680, the *St. George* until 1694. By the time of the Second Anglo-Dutch War all had been repeatedly rebuilt or refitted, and though heavy sailers by Restoration standards they were still important warships. Armament ranged from the 56 guns of the *Rainbow* to the *Triumph*'s 72, all having 32-pounder demi-cannon in the lower tier.

The other second-rates were newer, larger men-of-war of over 1,000 tons and 72–80 guns. They included the *Henry* of 1656, the *Royal Oak* and *Royal Katherine* of 1664, and the *Victory*, one of Burrell's old Jacobean ships which was rebuilt in 1665–66 to the size of the other large second-rates. A sister-ship of the *Henry*, the 80-gun *London* of 1656, was destroyed by an accidental magazine explosion in March 1665. These vessels were important flagships. Moderately good sailers, they were also exceptionally well-armed for their size; all but the *Henry* had at least partial batteries of 42-pounder 'cannon-of-seven' on the lower deck. Construction of new second-rates was projected on several occasions during the war, but they proved beyond the navy's financial means. A single vessel was completed, paid for by public subscription.

At the top of the fleet list were the mighty first-rates. In size, strength of construction, firepower, and decoration they represented the ultimate expression of the shipbuilder's art. There were four of them: the 82-gun *Royal Charles* and *Royal James*, built (with other names) under the Protectorate; the 92-gun *Royal Prince* of 1610; and the 102-gun *Royal Sovereign* of 1637. The smallest, the *Royal James*, did not quite 'fit' with the others. At 1,108 tons she was not much bigger than the latest second-rates, with which she was originally classed, and her largest guns were only demi-cannon. On the other hand, she was reputedly one of the fastest and most weatherly ships in the fleet. The very old *Sovereign* and *Prince* were the most powerful; despite their age they were fully up-to-date warships, both having been recently rebuilt. Even so, the more modestly-sized *Royal Charles* was usually preferred as the fleet flagship by reason of superior accommodations. She had two spacious and sumptuously appointed great cabins, whereas in the *Prince* and *Sovereign* the middle-deck cabin was merely an unadorned 'upper gunroom' with neither stern windows nor access to the quarter-galleries.

The first-rates and the largest second-rates formed the core of the English battle-fleet. Their towering sides and populous complements made them less vulnerable to boarding than smaller vessels, and their value in a gunnery duel was self-evident. Such leviathans were never an English monopoly, but in the mid-1660s no Continental navy had more than one or two comparable vessels. Giant warships did have disadvantages. It was difficult to man and maintain them, and their construction required such a tremendous investment that the loss of even one was a national disaster. And in war, losses were inevitable; the great ships burned as readily as any vessel, their rigging could be shot away as easily, and their gunpowder was no less explosive. Their deep draught imposed serious limitations on the whole fleet. This proved particularly embarrassing in the Anglo-Dutch Wars, when most campaigns took place in or near coastal shallows and estuarine shoals.

The Dutch did not distinguish rates beyond the functional categories of 'ships', 'frigates', and lesser ship-rigged 'three-mast yachts'. Vessels classed as ships corresponded to English men-of-war of the fourth rate and larger, and were expected to do most of the serious fighting. Except for a single smallish experimental three-decker with the two-tiered configuration of the English second-rates (this was the 70-gun *Spiegel* of 1663) and an elderly prize (the 60-gun *Luipaard*, formerly the English *Leopard* of 1635), all large Dutch warships until late 1666 were conventional two-deckers. The greatest could carry as many as 80 guns, though calibres were relatively small by English standards. Dutch frigates were similar in arrangement and firepower to the English fifth-rates, and three-mast yachts bore the same relationship to sixth-rates. Both classes performed the same functions as their English equivalents.

Like the Royal Navy, the States' Fleet augmented its strength with merchant ships. Twenty were fitted out and loaned to the Admiralties in 1665 by the United East India Company (the *Vereenigde Oostindische Compagnie* or V.O.C. as it was popularly known). These ships varied widely in size and quality. Two were 18-gun yachts and fourteen were normal East India traders armed with 30 to 54 rather small guns and sharing in most respects the mediocrity of their enemy counterparts. But the remaining Company ships had no equals among the English merchantmen: four giants of 70–78 guns rivalling the best of the men-of-war in dimensions. At least two were originally intended as men-of-war themselves, having been built on contract for foreign navies but appropriated by the States and given to the V.O.C.

Even a cursory examination of pictorial sources reveals differences between English and Dutch warships. Decorative and stylistic preferences are fairly obvious. Closer examination shows a number of functional idiosyncrasies such as the location of catheads and associated anchor linings, the musketry loopholes in the Dutch waist bulwarks, and minor variations in rigging details. More significant was the construction of the stern, the Dutch (and all other Continental shipbuilders except the Portuguese and sometimes the Danes and Swedes) favouring flat transoms forming right angles with the sides, the English a 'round tuck' with bowed transoms. The English design was structurally superior but more expensive to build due to the requirement for curved timbers. The English system may also have conferred marginally better handling characteristics, though so many other factors were involved there that most seamen probably would not have noticed.

A difference of much greater tactical impact is not evident from paintings and drawings: the underwater hull form. The Dutch had to allow for the extensive shoals of their coastline, ships from some ports requiring very shallow draught merely to clear their own harbours. The midship section of the underbody of a Dutch man-of-war was consequently flat-bottomed and markedly rectangular, so much so that special pumps had to be installed near the sides because water in the lee bilge could not drain to the centre-line well. Their opponents' hulls were much deeper and had nearly semi-circular midship sections. English forms may have produced slightly faster and more weatherly ships on the average, but those qualities were of use mainly to solitary scouts and groups of specially selected cruisers. The speed of the individual vessel was of relatively small value in a major action since a fleet was inherently limited to the pace of its poorest sailers. The Dutch were left with the important advantage that their entire array could float in little more than three fathoms, a depth at which most English ships larger than fourth-rates would be hard aground. Because the English had to take particular care of their huge first-rates, which nearly scraped bottom in four fathoms, the Dutch fleet could enter waters some five feet shallower than their enemy could. Use of this more or less fortuitous circumstance became a fundamental element of Dutch strategy.

Though the opponents were roughly equal at the outset in both numbers of ships and numbers of guns, the English had the larger vessels and mounted ordnance of substantially greater calibre. This firepower deficit, an important factor throughout the Anglo-Dutch Wars, was not due to any notable failing on the part of the Dutch.

Despite their difficulties in manufacturing cannon, they always found enough guns by one means or another to arm their fleet at least as well as other Continental navies of the day. Their misfortune was that the English men-of-war were armed on a truly colossal scale, not only by the standards of their own time, but by later standards as well. For example, although the 80-gun *Victory* of 1666 (1,029 tons) was actually smaller than the 50-gun *Warwick* of 1765 (1,053 tons), she could throw over twice the *Warwick*'s weight of shot: 1,704 pounds as opposed to 828 pounds for the later ship. Dutch, French, Spanish, Scandinavian, and Venetian warships of the mid-seventeenth century were all armed on a tonnage to firepower ratio similar to the *Warwick*'s, which was typical for most of the age of sail prior to the coming of the carronade in the 1770s.

The remarkably disproportionate firepower of Charles II's fleet had several explanations. For one thing, his shipwrights felt comfortable with a deep-load waterline as little as three to three-and-a-half feet from the lower-deck ports, even though this rendered the largest guns unusable on the lee side in anything beyond moderate winds and seas. Foreign contemporaries (and English descendants) considered this inadvisable and mounted the guns some twelve to twenty-four inches higher. By forgoing that extra foot or two of freeboard, the Restoration navy obtained fully twenty to twenty-five per cent greater weight of ordnance. Like small stowage capacity, the willing sacrifice of heavy weather capability was largely a function of the fleet's expected employment: home waters, in mostly benign summer conditions. If inclement weather was more likely, as in winter or on foreign stations, the sacrifice became unacceptable and the armament was much reduced.

The whole question of freeboard versus firepower had been controversial in England for many years. In 1618, when Spain was the principal maritime rival and battles in the open Atlantic seemed likely, the Jacobean reform commission demanded that the lower deck be placed 'at such convenient height that the ports may bear out their whole tier of ordnance in all seas and weathers'. In Restoration times the King himself and some shipwrights still maintained that opinion. In December 1664 Charles personally directed shipwright William Castle to recast the design of a new ship to work in enough beam so the guns could be carried four-and-a-half feet from the water. But artillerists could argue persuasively that a deep-riding, heavily gunned English fleet would always have telling superiority in good weather, while in really bad weather neither side could fight effectively. There would admittedly be some range of wind and sea conditions in which the English could not run out their lower tier, while the enemy still could. However, that disability would apply only on the lee side, to the fleet with the weather gage – and the fleet with the weather gage had the option of declining or delaying action. This matter was to have direct bearing on the Four Days' Battle.

The King's wishes for improved height of battery were simply ignored. When a choice between firepower and freeboard presented itself, Restoration seamen took the guns every time. If a vessel was found to ride unusually high, they invariably regarded it as an opportunity to pack in more and bigger guns. Castle's ship, the *Defiance*, was a case in point. He did indeed add beam as the King had required, but when she was finished the Ordnance Office used up most of the extra freeboard by loading in some 110 tons of guns rather than the 88 tons originally intended, along with equivalent ballast to maintain stability. This presumably spoiled Castle's designed trim, for the *Defiance* was a disappointing sailer. The tendency to re-arm high-freeboard vessels was particularly noticeable in prizes taken from the enemy. The 70-gun Dutch ship *Huis te Zwieten* had a lower-deck armament of 18-pounders, with a few larger pieces, at the time of her capture in 1665. The English promptly replaced the Dutch guns with a complete lower battery of 32-pounder demi-cannon. It was the same with other captured Dutch vessels and also with the French ship *Rubis* taken in September 1666. The French had armed her with 60 guns, but under new ownership she eventually received 80, including a full tier of demi-cannon. The 'guns first' mentality in these years often went far beyond the bounds of good sense. Some particularly overloaded vessels such as the *Royal Katherine* of 1664 initially rode so deeply and were so topheavy that they could not be sent to sea without major modifications. The logical solution would have been to mount lighter ordnance. Instead, the authorities preferred to reduce the size of masts, spars, and sail area, and to 'girdle' the hull with extra planking at the waterline to improve stability. Speed and virtually everything else could be sacrificed, but not the guns.

Another reason for the extraordinary firepower of Restoration warships was the premium placed by English ordnance experts of the day on economy of weight in the guns themselves. This was evident in the extensive employment of several kinds of special lightweight weapons which will be described in the next chapter. Also important were the powerful brass guns which were favoured by the Restoration navy for the largest calibres. England had an advantage in those days of being a leader in brass founding technology, and the founders produced considerable numbers of the huge newly introduced 42-pounder 'cannon-of-7' for which the Dutch had few equivalents. Brass cannon, strong and relatively light weight, had a serious drawback: brass was very expensive, often several times the cost of iron, but the firepower advantage of the big guns seemed worth the expense.

The navy's quest for high-quality guns was much facilitated in those years by a lack of competing ordnance demands from the army. Charles II for all practical purposes had no army; his Parliament never trusted him enough to let him keep anything beyond Guards regiments, temporary militia, and garrisons for Ireland and foreign possessions. Indeed, when Oliver Cromwell's once-mighty siege train was mounted on ship-carriages, and when inland fortifications were left with empty gun embrasures, it seemed a source more of comfort than alarm to a generation of Englishmen for whom civil war and military dictatorship were still fresh memories. Such attitudes would have been utter folly for any warring nation other than an insular sea power. In England not even the soldiers objected; the generals, after all, were the admirals of the fleet! Consequently, nearly all the best ordnance in the kingdom went to the navy, which was an advantage Continental admiralties did not enjoy.

The extreme emphasis on naval firepower in Restoration times was actually a transient aberration for the Royal Navy even within the seventeenth century. One of the oldest ships to fight in the Four Days' Battle was the *Triumph* of 1622. Built by

Burrell to the high-freeboard requirements of the 1618 Commission, her original armament had been quite modest: 42 guns throwing 516 pounds of shot. This was proportionately very close to the scale of the eighteenth-century *Warwick*. But by 1666 the *Triumph*'s firepower had gone up *two-and-a-half times*, to 74 guns of 1,312 pounds' shot. The whole fleet's ratio of broadside weight to hull tonnage had risen steadily in the first half of the century, reaching its maximum in 1666. It remained high through the Third Anglo-Dutch War, but dropped sharply thereafter. In the late 1670s the growing maritime ambitions of France increased the likelihood of battles in rough Atlantic swells far from home. This gave higher freeboard renewed importance. At the same time, the cost of lightweight brass ordnance became prohibitive for the many new ships needed to counter the French threat. The navy, however reluctantly, had to accept bulkier iron guns and mount them farther from the water; both factors demanded reduced calibres. The twenty 70-gun ships built under the 1677 programme were nearly all greater in tonnage than the second-rate *Victory* of 1666. But instead of the brass cannon-of-7 which the older ship had carried on her lower deck, the new ones had to make do with iron 32-pounder 'demi-cannon' which weighed little less. Comparably sized vessels built in the 1690s had still smaller calibres. As late as 1750, ships of 90 guns had weaker broadsides than the old *Victory* despite hull tonnages greater by up to seventy per cent.

The ordnance policy of the early Restoration navy was thus unique. The economic, geographic, and political factors that came together in the 1660s had a powerful resonant effect which created a level of firepower for the size of the ships involved that had no parallel in any sailing navy. The special circumstances which produced that resonance did not persist for long. While they did, the English fleet enjoyed a decisive gunnery advantage over any opponent – at least as long as the seas were calm.

Chapter IV

Guns, Flags, and the River Thames

The distance judg'd for shot of every size,
The linstocks touch, the pond'rous ball expires:
The vig'rous seaman every porthole plies,
And adds his heart to every gun he fires.

Seventeenth-century sea tactics, like those of every age, were largely determined by the available weapons, the capabilities of communications, and frequently geography. Of these, the armaments are at the very least the most obvious.

The primary shipboard weapon of the 1600s was a smoothbore muzzle-loading cannon usually firing a solid iron ball. The gun was made of either cast bronze (always called 'brass'), or cast iron. Such pieces had been introduced as early as the fourteenth century, but were uncommon at sea until the early 1500s when they began to replace the untrustworthy wrought-iron breech-loaders previously favoured. The cast gun, though clearly superior to its predecessor, underwent a long and troubled evolution during the sixteenth century before it became a truly satisfactory sea-service weapon. As every gunner knew, brass cannons which were weak or contained defects quickly bulged out of shape, while those of iron burst without warning in the faces of their crews. Metallurgists of the Tudor period understood that the density and strength at the bottom of a casting increased with the mass above. The gun was cast in a vertical posture, muzzle up, to ensure that the metal be strongest at the breech where the greatest stresses would occur on firing. The highest fluid pressures and thus the best results were attained in very long guns which were unfortunately of limited utility afloat. Shorter cast guns made for service at sea had inherently lower density at the breech and were fortified with thicker metal. But the Tudor manufacturing process left guns of all lengths with inferior metal at the muzzles (exacerbated by the 'dross', or impurities, that rose to the top of the castings), while strength throughout the barrels fell far short of its natural potential. Consequently, for much of the sixteenth century guns could be charged only with weak 'serpentine' powder which produced unimpressive results by later standards. One variant, a short cast weapon known to the English as the 'cannon-perrier', combined the weak charge with a light but relatively large diameter stone ball. Though highly effective in action, the individually sculpted shot proved intolerably expensive. At last, a major technological breakthrough occurred during Elizabethan times when gunfounders realised that they could increase the density of a casting by pouring a massive conical 'gunhead' at the top which could afterwards be cut off. The gunhead also supplied a reservoir into which the dross could rise well clear of the muzzle. In the 1580s, gunners discovered that weapons of utilitarian lengths and weights manufactured by this method could withstand charges of vastly more powerful 'corned' powder. This granular propellant, long known but previously restricted to small arms, resulted in dramatically improved performance. With this great advance, the smoothbore muzzle-loader became a formidable weapon capable of inflicting fearsome destruction on ships and their crews. By 1666, several refinements and variations had been introduced, but the basic gun remained fundamentally unchanged.

The largest standard English naval gun in the 1660s was the 42-pdr 'cannon-of-seven', so-called because of its seven-inch bore. Found only in the most massively timbered ships, it weighed about three tons and was typically nine-and-a-half feet, or about sixteen calibres, in length. Other large- and medium-calibre guns (32-pdr 'demi-cannon', 24-pdrs, 18-pdr 'culverins', 12-pdrs, and 9-pdr 'demi-culverins') became slightly shorter but proportionately much longer with decreasing calibre. A demi-culverin with a four-and-a-quarter-inch bore was commonly about nine feet long, or twenty-five calibres. Lesser guns (8- and 6-pdrs, 5¼-pdr 'sakers', 4-pdr 'minions', 3-pdrs, and 2½-pdr 'falcons') were highly variable in proportion. The heaviest Dutch cannon was a 36-pdr, but there were very few pieces of that size; the next largest was only a 24-pdr. The Amsterdam pound, however, was some nine per cent heavier than the English, so the nominal Dutch 24-pdr actually threw a ball weighing about 26 English pounds. Both sides used numerous captured (and in the case of the Dutch, purchased) guns of foreign manufacture calibrated to different weight standards.

The English, in their almost obsessive striving for broadside power, were particularly attracted to lightweight weapons of large calibre. Two such types were adopted, neither of which was found in very great numbers outside of England. One was the 'drake', which had been common in the Royal Navy for many years. It was a relatively short, thin-bodied piece with a 'taper-bored' chamber much narrower than the ball diameter and intended for small charges. Use of these guns allowed some vessels as small as 600 tons to carry 32-pdr demi-cannon. Unfortunately, drakes had a vicious recoil, and could easily burst due to shot jamming in the mouth of the tapered chamber. The other lightweight weapon was the 'cutt' piece, a normal gun from which about three feet were sawn off. Many 9-pdr demi-culverins were so treated (or were manufactured in cutt condition from the beginning) and were then light enough to be mounted on quarterdecks and forecastles. This was a large calibre to be carried so far from the water, other navies of the time using only 6-, 4-, and 3-pdrs there. Cutts had an important advantage over drakes, which were virtually useless at distances beyond three hundred yards. True-bored cutts suffered far less in range from their mutilation than one might suppose; no more than about ten per cent. Their single drawback, one glaring enough to cause the eventual suppression of the type, was the extreme violence of the recoil; the guns all too often hurled themselves right out of their carriages. Despite the disadvantages, both drakes and cutts contributed considerably to the Restoration navy's overall firepower superiority.

There were also special guns expressing the opposite ideal. Most English ships above the fourth rate carried a few unusually long and massively fortified pieces meant for extra-heavy charges. They were thought (erroneously, as it was later discovered) to have inherently greater-than-normal range and were placed at the ends of the lower deck, in the stern ports and the luff ports forward. Abnormally bulky, these 'chasers' had to be of lesser calibre than the ordinary broadside guns. Most chasers assigned to second- and third-rates were 18-pdr culverins about eleven feet long, while the three largest first-rates (whose lower-deck broadside guns were cannon-of-seven) had huge demi-cannon chasers. The Dutch followed a different policy. Having perhaps learned from ballistics tests that increased barrel length did not improve range, they used chasers of ordinary proportions but *greater* calibre than the broadside pieces.

Shipwrights of the mid-1600s paid greater attention to end-on fire then their eighteenth-century descendants. Nelson's *Victory* could conveniently bring only two guns to bear aft, both on the lower deck. Restoration first- and second-rates had six to ten stern ports (the *Royal James* had *twelve*) disposed on up to four levels. But owing to the effects of recoil shock and blast on the fragile stern structure, chasers above the lower deck were used only in emergencies. In another uniquely seventeenth-century feature, the gracefully bowed sheer of the gundeck often ceased abruptly near the mizzenmast, the deck sloping slightly downwards from that point to the transom. This gave the stern chasers the benefit of an 'uphill' recoil. Ahead fire was obtained from the luffs and by as many as eight guns pointing through the forward bulkhead on at least two levels. The deep curve of the seventeenth-century headrails and much of the complexity of the bowsprit rigging were designed to allow clear arcs for these guns. Bow and stern chasers in both English and Dutch ships usually did double duty as broadside guns, pieces being shifted back and forth as necessary. The Dutch did the same with their lower-deck luffs, always leaving one of the two foremost ports on each side unarmed. The English, characteristically unwilling to let a gunport go to waste, generally filled both despite the sometimes convergent recoil paths of the guns.

Overall distribution of shipboard armament was still evolving in the seventeenth century. From the earliest days of broadside cannon, fundamental stability considerations had always demanded that the heaviest pieces be mounted low in the ship and the lightest higher. By the 1660s some ordnance authorities were beginning to realize that ammunition supply could be simplified if all the guns on a given deck had the same calibre. The English were somewhat ahead of their Continental rivals in that respect, most of the Royal Navy's ships deviating only in the special lower-deck chasers. In 1666 the principle was actually carried a step beyond later practice, for many vessels were assigned demi-culverins for the upper deck and cutts of the same calibre for the quarterdeck. The Dutch at the time still considered homogeneity relatively unimportant. For a fairly typical example, the *Zeven Provinciën* carried twelve 36-pdrs and sixteen 24-pdrs on the lower deck, and fourteen 18-pdrs and twelve 12-pdrs on the upper deck.

The seventeenth-century naval gun rested on a wooden carriage with four solid wooden wheels called 'trucks'. Preferably made of elm, the carriage was a boxlike affair open at front, rear, and top, with sides formed by heavy 'cheeks' stepped down at the rear to a solid horizontal bed. The gun's trunnions were secured with iron straps into semi-circular recesses in the carriage cheeks directly over the front trucks. Cannon and carriage were tethered to the ship's side by a thick breeching rope. The English ran the breeching to the cascabel behind the breech through rings in the cheeks; the Dutch preferred to pass it through holes in the cheeks. The gun was run out with smaller ropes using a pair of double-block tackles, one on each side, rigged between ringbolts in the cheeks and corresponding ringbolts in the ship's side. A similar 'train tackle' was rigged from the rear of the carriage bed to haul the gun in. Where this tackle's inboard block was secured is something of a mystery, as ringbolts in the decks are not mentioned until the 1690s.

The loading process for muzzle-loading cannon hardly varied for centuries. The first step after firing was to scour the barrel with a spiral iron prong, or 'worm', to dislodge any fragments from the previous powder cartridge that may have adhered to the cylinder wall. At the same time the gun captain scoured the narrow vent at the top of the breech. Next, a wet sponge cleaned and cooled the cylinder, and above all extinguished any still-smouldering particles. This operation was observed with more than casual interest by the man who would load the powder, for his life could depend on the sponger's thoroughness. For a large gun the charge consisted of coarse-grained corned powder weighing a little less than half as much as the shot; small guns used proportionately more powder, typically about three-quarters of the shot weight. The charge was contained in a sausage-shaped cartridge about three calibres long made of parchment or canvas; the Dutch preferred parchment, the English canvas. There were also paper cartridges, but as Rupert and Albemarle explained in April 1666,

> We finde that if we fill paper Cartridges with powder, that ye salt petre will make them moist, and so, when we come to charge our guns, they will be apt to break and be something dangerous at such a time when there are so many lighted matches about ye shipps besides ye disappointment, if they should break in ye Gunners hands, when they are to charge ye gunns.

The cartridge was placed intact on a long-handled ladle and deposited in the chamber. A rammer wielded by an experienced hand was then tamped against it to force it to the back wall of the breech, after which a wad was packed in to hold it in position. Wads were preferably made of 'junk' (old rope), but cloth and canvas were also used. The loader then placed a shot in the muzzle and rammed it home, followed by another wad. The gun captain now took centre stage. First he thrust a sharp instrument called a priming iron down the vent to puncture the cartridge, taking care not to cause any sparks in the process. Next, he filled the vent with fine-grained priming powder which he carried in a horn suspended from his belt. Loading completed, the crew manned the tackles to haul the carriage out to the ship's side. To fire the piece, the gunner simply stabbed the touch-hole with his linstock. Flame rushed down the vent, the charge went off with a mighty bang, and the ball was on its way. The gun reacted to its discharge with a powerful recoil; it rumbled inboard of its own accord until the carefully pre-adjusted breeching brought it to a halt at the proper loading position. The crew then secured it in place using either the train tackle or perhaps chocks inserted under the trucks. The time required for the whole cycle varied greatly depending on the size of the cannon and the expertise of the crew. By the late eighteenth century the best-drilled English gun crews could get off a round in under two minutes; in the mid-1600s ten minutes was not bad for the larger guns.

Shot were normally stowed in lockers in the hold, often clustered around the pump well at the mainmast. For battle they were brought topside and conveniently lined up along the centre-line coamings in rope-loop 'garlands'. Powder in barrels was kept in a magazine deep in the hold (forward in most English ships, aft in Dutch and French ships), with chests installed nearby for stowage of filled cartridges; a smaller powder room towards the other end of the hold was stocked with cartridges before going into battle. Ships typically carried enough powder for about forty rounds per gun, but the gunner generally kept only a few rounds in filled cartridges. This was because the constituents of the powder could begin to separate if the charges were not expended fairly soon, and the defective cartridges would have to be emptied and laboriously refilled. In battle, nimble ships' boys hurried charges to the guns in wooden cases, no more powder than absolutely necessary being allowed above the waterline at any given time. Powder supply could be troublesome for the guns on the quarterdeck, which in a three-decker was five levels above the powder rooms. Some captains permitted cartridges to be staged in the roundhouse under the poop. Such ready-use magazines were presumably protected by coils of cable or some such means, but the whole idea was most unwise and it was not unusual to hear of a ship having its entire aftercastle blown away.

How a seventeenth-century sea-captain controlled and directed his ship's gunfire is much in doubt. Full, simultaneous broadsides are described with awe in many eyewitness accounts, but were apparently infrequent because of the strain they imposed on a ship's timbers. Probably much more common was the simultaneous firing of partial batteries. Except in calm seas or at very close range, rippling or sequential broadsides cannot have been effective because the roll of the ship brought all the guns level at the same moment. When engaging a relatively distant target, the firing may have been left to the experts. English ships above the fifth rate had six or seven such professionals aboard: the gunner, one or two mates, and four quarter-gunners. Perhaps each was assigned half a tier. He could advance from gun to gun, aiming and discharging each in turn, and then return to his starting point before the first gun was ready again. Such a system would have been quite feasible in view of the time required for the loading cycle. Something like this was definitely done at the Battle of Lowestoft, when the Duke of York ordered the gunner of the *Royal Charles* 'to lay all the guns himself'.

Aiming a smoothbore cannon was no easy matter, even for professionals. The gun's only sighting aid was a small notch. The gunner peered along the top of the barrel, firing when the roll of the ship brought the 'line of metal' to the desired angle. Elevation was changed to compensate for a steady heel by adjusting the 'quoin', a sliding wedge under the breech. The gun could be traversed as far as the gunport width allowed by levering the carriage around with handspikes forced under the rear trucks. This was hard work, and if the tactical situation permitted, it was better to point the ship itself rather than the guns. As Sir William Monson explained in about 1635, 'a principal thing in a gunner at sea is to be a good helmsman, and to call to him at the helm to luff or bear up, to have his better level, and to observe the heaving and setting of the sea to take his aim at the enemy'.

The seventeenth-century cannon was extremely limited in both range and accuracy. When fired 'at random' (that is, with maximum elevation of about fifteen degrees) it could reach out well over two miles, but accuracy was so poor at such ranges that hardly anyone ever tried it. When Monson admonished, 'he that shooteth far off at a ship had as good not shoot at all', he was not exaggerating. Both English and Dutch had standing instructions forbidding such wastage of ammunition and promising violators certain retribution. The *effective* range of a normal gun was about five hundred yards, the distance the ball would carry with level 'line of metal' sighting. This was known as 'point blank'. It technically meant zero elevation, though in practice the line of metal produced two or three degrees' elevation due to the tapered external shape of the gun.

In modern parlance point blank is often interpreted to mean 'too close to miss'. That was anything but true in the seventeenth century, for even at five hundred yards a high percentage of hits could not be expected. To strike the hull of a sailing warship at that distance, the deflection error could be only three degrees, the elevation error one-half degree. That was a small margin considering the constant motion of the deck and the appreciable fraction of a second needed for the priming powder to burn its way down the vent to ignite the charge. Even if the gunner aimed his weapon accurately and timed his fire precisely, the odds were still against him. More often than not he was betrayed by the internal ballistics of the gun and the erratic aerodynamic characteristics of the projectile. It was impossible in those days to manufacture either a perfectly spherical shot or a perfectly bored cannon. Furthermore, brass barrels could 'droop' and cylinder walls could easily be fouled by cement-like powder residues. To avoid any possibility of a ball jamming and bursting the gun, one always took care to use shot of smaller diameter than the bore. Such 'windage' was customarily a quarter-inch in the seventeenth century. The unavoidable result was that the ball ricochetted violently off the walls as it flew down the barrel, emerging at the muzzle with some small but significant deviation from the axis of the bore. Once airborne, its behaviour was governed by an unpredictable rate and direction of spin. It could rise, dive, 'slice' or 'hook' like a golf ball, or on occasion even fly true. Other factors also contributed: differences in windage, great variations in strength of powder, and, not least, the level of training of the gunners. The Duke of York's 'General Instructions to Captains' of 1663 specified that

> for the first month the men be exercised twice every week to the end they may become good Fire Men, allowing six Shott to every exercising. That the 2nd month they may be exercised once every week, and after that only once in two months allowing six shott to each time of exercising.

With practice one could inflict punishing damage at the outer limits of point-blank range, as Monck's gunners proved at the Gabbard, but it took hours of sustained bombardment.

Guns could fire many kinds of projectiles. At five hundred yards nearly all the shooting was with the roundshot, which was the least inaccurate. In its larger sizes it could shatter the greatest ship timbers, leave hulls pocked with holes, and dismount the heaviest guns. It caused terrible casualties, both by itself and by the showers of splinters it created. With luck the roundshot could also bring down whole masts, but it was generally not very effective against sails and rigging. Those targets were better attacked by various ingeniously designed double-headed bar and chain shot, which could be used for best effect within about three hundred yards. For yardarm to yardarm duels the small-calibre guns on the upper deck and quarterdeck could spew an array of fearsome shrapnel ammunition: burr, bace, and case shot – cylindrical canisters filled with musket balls, nails, rocks, and other lethal missiles 'good to ply amongst men which stand naked'.

Both sides used all the varieties of shot, but there was a marked difference in emphasis. English ships carried only a few rounds per gun of bar and chain shot, and those only for medium- and small-calibre guns. The English preferred to fight with the roundshot. Gunners were trained to fire on the 'down roll' to ensure the maximum number of hits on hulls as opposed to rigging. Such roundshot assaults were not meant to sink the opponent, which was in fact quite difficult to do. Shot penetrating a hull underwater rarely made holes much larger than themselves, so the carpenter's crew could usually effect emergency repairs in a matter of minutes. Even if flooding could not be quickly stopped, it took a great deal of water to overwhelm the powerful suction pumps employed by the Dutch or the even more powerful chain pumps favoured by the English. There was also little chance of reaching an enemy's magazine, which was always far beneath the waterline; powder explosions of ships not already afire were nearly always accidental. The English intention was simply to force the opponent to surrender, by a merciless battering until the enemy captain and crew became too demoralized to carry on. The Dutch had different ideas. Knowing that they were overmatched in weight of broadside, they hoped to even the odds by cutting the opponent's rigging to shreds and immobilizing him. Dutch ships consequently carried large proportions of bar and chain shot for guns of all sizes. Abundant evidence indicates that Dutch gunners deliberately fired on the 'up roll'.

If the range closed to within a hundred yards, the character of the fighting could change completely. At such distances the great guns sometimes became secondary weapons. The lighter pieces in the upperworks began loading with case, and small arms came into play. Musketeers opened up from every conceivable topside vantage point, though the exceedingly heavy and clumsy muskets of the day were no more accurate than the cannon. One spoke of 'annoying' the enemy with musketry. Even so, with enough sharpshooters banging away a few would occasionally find the mark. Their fire was mostly directed at the enemy's own musketeers, but the officers striding the poop in their plumed finery also made inviting targets.

If the opposing ships actually locked together, boarding and entering became a distinct possibility. This was a particular speciality of the Dutch, the English being trained more for defence against boarding than for boarding itself. In 1665 each side established a special regiment of marines to be distributed among the ships purely for musketry and hand-to-hand fighting. These 'sea-soldiers' used exactly the same weaponry as shore-bound infantry of the period. The 'munitions and habiliaments of war' issued to the second-rate *Swiftsure* for a cruise to the Mediterranean in 1661 included eighty snaphance or matchlock muskets, twelve blunderbusses, twenty pairs of pistols, two hundred 'hand granadoes', six halberds, eighty pikes, twenty bills, and forty each of hatchets, swords, and hangers. With such equipment, a ship's marine company must have looked like the stalwarts in Rembrandt's 'Nightwatch'.

While most English victories were decided by heavy cannon, and Dutch victories by musket and sword, seventeenth-century fleets also employed another important weapon. This device, which influenced the sea tactics of the day out of all proportion to its effectiveness, was the fireship. Incendiary craft were by no means peculiar to the seventeenth century. They were used with success against fleets at anchor in both the sixteenth and eighteenth centuries, but it was only in the 1600s that they regularly took part in open-sea battles. Most fireships were converted merchantmen or old fifth- or sixth-rate warships. Their conversion involved strategic placement of great quantities of oil, gunpowder, rags, and other combustibles, extra ventilation for belowdecks spaces, grapnels suspended from the yards to snag the enemy's rigging, and a 'sally port' cut in each side near the stern through which the daredevil crew could escape at the last moment to a boat towed astern. In later periods it was usual to fit gunports with downward opening lids, but pictorial evidence suggests that this was not common in Restoration times. Fireships generally carried from four to twelve guns for their own defence. In addition, they were sometimes fitted with wooden dummy cannon barrels protruding from the ports to help disguise their identity.

Fireships were nearly always manned by volunteers, to whom most navies offered substantial rewards for successful service. In the English fleet the Lord High Admiral in 1665 established a standard bounty of £10 to each officer and crewman of any fireship which destroyed an enemy man-of-war of 40 guns or more. This was no mean amount; £10 at the time was over eight months' pay for an able seaman. James also gave assurances that the fireship's officers would be 'taken care of' and promoted to good ships 'before any persons whatsoever'. The fortunate captain would 'receive a meddal of golde to remaine as a token of honour to him and his posterity', and was promised 'such other incurradgement by preferrment and command as shall be fitt both to reward him and induce others to performe the like service'. Lastly, it was stipulated that if the victim were a flagship, all rewards would be doubled to 'expresse the eminency of the service'. This provision had an unwanted (but entirely predictable) result: incendiary captains began hopefully reporting everything they incinerated as 'flagships', and that regardless of size.

Whatever the amount of the bounty, it was usually well earned. One could hardly imagine a more hazardous duty. It took the steadiest nerves and more than a little skill to press home an attack in a veritable floating volcano through the midst of hostile forces with close-range cannon fire splintering the hull from every direction. Careful judgement was required to time the right moment for ignition: too early, and the fireship's own sails would be consumed before reaching the target; too late, and the entangled quarry could free itself before the flames took hold. Even after the attack was carried out, the danger for the fireship's crew was far from over. Fleeing in a small open boat from a vengeful enemy possibly not inclined to give quarter cannot have been a very enjoyable experience.

English fifth-rates and equivalent Dutch frigates (which, as noted earlier, were too small to take part in the great gun duels) were intimately associated with fireship tactics. Whenever possible they accompanied the fireships into action and took on any of the enemy's frigates that attempted to interfere. More importantly, as Rupert and Albemarle explained, the presence of a friendly fifth-rate 'would much countenance ye fireshipps to doe Execution, when they shall see themselves each aided with a small friggott to take up their Men'. Fifth-rates were also the main defence against fireships. English instructions from 1653 on specified that frigate captains were 'to know the fireshipps belonging to the enemy, and accordingly by observing their motion doe their uttmost to cutt off theire boates if possible, or if oppertunity be that they lay them on board, sieze and destroy them'. Cutting off the boat was the surest way of foiling a fireship, for it rendered the attack suicidal. The real test for a fifth-rate came when the deadly craft was already ignited. The Fighting Instructions sternly exhorted frigate captains to

> show themselves men in such an exigent and steere on board them, and with their boates, grapnelles, and other meanes cleere them from us, and destroy them; which service, if honourably done to itts merritt shall be rewarded, and the neglect thereof strictly and severely call'd to an accompt.

In April 1665 the Duke of York publicly set a reward for crews of frigates capturing or destroying enemy fireships at 40s. per man, 'besides the preferrment which shall be given to the commander and officers of such shipps performing such service answerable to theire merritt'.

That was perhaps asking too much. There was nothing a mariner feared more than fire. All around him were tier upon tier of seasoned hardwood with pitch and oakum filling the seams; above him were miles of tarred rope and vast canvas sails that could go up like torches; below were hundreds of barrels of gunpowder awaiting the tiniest spark to blow him to bits. The smallest shipboard blaze could become catastrophic. Fire-fighting gear consisted only of axes, hooks, and water buckets. Captains and crews of fifth-rates naturally considered themselves less expendable than the Fighting Instructions implied, so it need come as no surprise that in practice they seldom threw themselves in a burning fireship's path. Better suited for the sacrificial defensive role were a fleet's own fireships. They *were* expendable, and their small crews could more easily escape if necessary. When no such lesser vessels intervened, the great ships could only manoeuvre out of the way as best they could, using their firepoles (long booms extended from bows and quarters) to fend off the attacker.

Fireships were efficient predators of men-of-war caught at anchor, aground, dismasted, or otherwise helpless. In hard statistical terms, however, they achieved rather disappointing scores against vessels actually under sail. Even when grappled, ships with well-disciplined crews often broke away with nothing worse than superficial scorching. Only three warships in condition to defend themselves were successfully attacked and destroyed in the entire Second Anglo-Dutch War; in the Third only two succumbed. Fireships could also be counter-productive, endangering members of their own fleet or unwittingly burning enemy vessels which had already surrendered. This happened at Lowestoft and also in 1676 at the Battle of Öland between the Swedes and Danes. It was mostly the psychological effects – the disorder and sheer terror fireships inspired among the opponents – that accounted for their continued employment in battlefleets throughout the century despite the paucity of tangible results. Admirals of the Restoration period invariably wanted as many as they could get, and unanimously dreaded the enemy's. Thus, though fireships neither determined nor even very strongly affected the outcome of a single seventeenth-century sea-fight, they were never ignored. Among their many tactical influences, their presence in every fleet was one of the more compelling reasons why possession of the weather gage seemed so overwhelmingly important to the commanders of the time.

Communications is an important, though frequently overlooked, element of naval tactics. This could be troublesome even within an individual ship, for shouted commands were often inaudible above the clamour of battle. Most orders were signalled by trumpeters, usually four per ship, and often a kettle-drummer, all of whom were stationed on the poop near the captain. Ship-to-ship communications depended on the ability of commanders to make their intentions known to their subordinate captains under conditions likely to be encountered in action. The problem required a two-fold solution in that the admiral and his captains needed to be able to identify each other, even in fleets of a hundred quite similar ships, and instructions had to be transmitted clearly.

Identification was by flags and pendants. Seventeenth-century commanders realized that their huge and unwieldy fleets demanded subdivision and delegation of authority if there was to be any tactical flexibility at all. In 1653 the English devised a standard organization for large fleets that served well for the remainder of the century. The ships were grouped into three squadrons, designated Red, White, and Blue, each of which was further suborganized into three divisions. The Red Squadron, forming the centre, was personally directed by the commander-in-chief; the White (van) Squadron by the second-in-command, or Admiral of the White; and the Blue (rear) Squadron by the third-in-command, or Admiral of the Blue. Every squadron had three flag-officers in all, each in charge of one division. The admiral took the centre division, a vice-admiral the van division, and a rear-admiral the rear division, though the order was sometimes varied. Within each rank of flag-officers those of the Red were senior, those of the White next, and the Blue last. Thus, the Vice-Admiral of the Red was the most senior of the vice-admirals, and the Rear-Admiral of the Blue the junior flag-officer in the fleet. These were not permanent grades, as in later times, but merely temporary operational appointments for each campaign.

The English identification system was quite simple. An admiral flew a plain flag of the colour of his squadron at the main, his vice-admiral a flag of the same colour at the fore, and his rear-admiral the same flag at the mizzen. The only exception was the Admiral of the Red, who as commander-in-chief was usually authorized to display something more distinctive than the plain red flag. The Duke of York, the Lord High

Admiral and brother of the King, always used the royal standard. Other commanders-in-chief; including Rupert and Albemarle, normally substituted the Union. Alone among admirals-of-the-fleet, the Earl of Sandwich flew a plain red flag in 1665. Individual ships advertised their squadron membership by displaying ensign and masthead vanes of the colour of their squadron. Despite erroneous representations by some marine artists, the ensign in Restoration times was a red, white, or blue flag with the canton having only the red George's cross on a white field.

Smaller fleets used simpler arrangements. Those of middling size (say, twenty to forty ships) had only an admiral, vice-admiral, and rear-admiral, each commanding an unsubdivided squadron. The flagships in such cases nearly always flew the Union flag, at the main for the admiral, the fore for the vice-admiral, and the mizzen for the rear-admiral. In such cases all the ships wore the red ensign. In still smaller independent detachments, a lone flag-officer usually flew a Union at the main. The Union flag in the seventeenth century (as well as its smaller jack version) was identical to the modern British national colours except that the red diagonal Irish saltire had yet to make its appearance.

The Dutch used more complex arrangements. Their order of battle was not firmly established and changed with almost every campaign. The fleet could contain anywhere from three to seven squadrons which might or might not be further subdivided. Identification systems were complicated by the fact that the five Admiralties liked their respective contingents to be distinguishable even though fleet squadrons were not divided along strictly Admiralty lines. Admiralty affiliations were usually signified by combinations of different jacks and ensigns. Ships of Zeeland, for instance, might wear the Vlissingen standard (containing the silhouette of a ewer, the armorial symbol of the town) as a jack and the national tricolour as an ensign; ships of another admiralty might use the tricolour as a jack and the nine-striped 'triple prince' as an ensign. Squadron membership was indicated by masthead pendants. In a fleet with three squadrons, the ships of the commander-in-chief's squadron typically had a pendant at the main, the second squadron a pendant at the fore, and third a pendant at the mizzen. Any additional squadrons used shorter *vluegels* (vanes, sometimes swallow-tailed) of different colours, rather than pendants. Each squadron, whether further subdivided or not, usually had three flag-officers; there were sometimes more, but the extra ones were supernumerary. Flagships were nearly always indicated by the common tricolour, or prince's flag. It was flown at the main by the squadron commander, at the fore by a vice-admiral, and at the mizzen by a rear-admiral, though there were exceptions at times.

Both English and Dutch used a variety of signalling methods, including guns, lights at night, flags, and peculiar activities with rigging such as raising and lowering yards. Of the various signalling devices, flags were the most useful for passing tactical orders. In 1666, English battle instructions were transmitted with only nine flags: the Union, the royal standard, the three ensigns, the three admiral's flags, and the red and white striped merchant jack. The Sailing Instructions employed several others. The meaning of a signal was denoted not only by the flag itself; but by where it was displayed. For example, a royal standard at the ensign staff had a quite different meaning from the same flag flown from the mizzen shrouds (the former meant 'form line abreast', the latter called a council-of-war). Vocabulary could be multiplied by rapidly raising and lowering a flag, by making a 'weft' (binding a flag in the middle), or by combining it with a pendant. An English commander could also direct instructions to an individual ship. He merely preceded the order with a special address signal consisting of a red, white, or blue flag at a certain location and a pendant at a certain masthead. The colour of the flag indicated the addressee's squadron, the masthead at which the pendant was flown indicated the division, and the location of the flag was the private sign for the ship. The same sign could be shared by nine different vessels, one for each division. The English signalling system was so new in the 1660s that nearly every major action produced a round of changes and adjustments. It was nevertheless quite sophisticated for its time, the many permutations allowing a virtually limitless range of orders. On the other hand, the lack of an alphabetic code made it impossible to signal a message not previously agreed upon. If the Duke of Albemarle wished to encourage the fleet with a stirring 'England expects', he could only send ketches around to pass the word, or else call the captains aboard and inspire them personally.

Though the Dutch used the same fundamental methods as the English, they employed relatively few fleet-wide signals. They preferred instead to delegate wide authority to the squadron commanders, each of whom made his own arrangements. As confusing as this must have been, it at least gave the captains some reason to stay near their proper commanders.

The geographic setting of the Four Days' Battle, which took place at the mouth of the Thames, was a major element in the course of both the action itself and the campaign that led up to it. The estuary of the river of London is a drowned flood plain and delta created mostly during the ice ages when the sea level was lower. The resulting fossil topography presents the seaman with exceptionally complex navigational difficulties. Deep draught traffic was (and is) mostly confined to narrow channels by enormous migratory sandbanks. Passage through these obstacles is complicated by dense fogs that often shroud the area and by immense tides which sweep through twice a day.

The tides have always been a dominant factor in the navigation of the Thames. Magnified by the funnel-shaped North Sea and English Channel, tidal flows in the estuary regularly course through the shoals at well over two knots, in many places ranging over eighteen feet. This had important implications. Where at one point there might be water enough to float a seventeenth-century third-rate, six hours later could be drying mud. Ships ascended the river on the flood, descended on the ebb, and at low water were confined to deep pools and channels. There was greater freedom of movement at high water, but then the invisibility of the shoals called for extreme caution. Big ships did not venture over the sands without good reason.

The sands themselves are gigantic underwater dunes in a slow but constant state of motion. Some channels have become wider over the centuries, others narrower. Tide-scoured passes which were once well known are silted over today, while new ones have opened in their place. Great storms and occasional monster tides sometimes produce noticeable readjustments overnight. One consequently cannot reconstruct the configuration of the lower Thames in the seventeenth century in anything approaching exactitude. But the gross features are underlain by stable rock outcroppings, so most of the principal barriers to navigation in seventeenth-century charts and sailing directions are still recognizable in at least general terms.

The estuary forms a broad V opening to the east, with arms about thirty miles on a side. At the apex of the V, in midstream near the confluence of the River Medway, Trinity House maintained a buoy marking the little shoal known as the Nore Sand. The two-by-four-mile rectangle of deep water downstream from the buoy of the Nore was the traditional assembly point and main operating base of the English navy. From there the fleet had easy access to and from the royal dockyards at Woolwich and Deptford below London, and the great naval arsenal at Chatham in the Medway. The anchorage itself was directly served by a small new dockyard and supply centre at Sheerness near the northernmost point of the Isle of Sheppey.

On either side of the Nore anchorage and extending for many miles along both shores are vast shelves of shallow sand and silt. The bank to the north is the Maplin Sand which follows the curve of the Essex coast. It merges with the Foulness Sand, is briefly interrupted by a channel cut by the River Crouch, and then resumes to the north as the Buxey Sand. From the Buxey a prominent linear tongue known as the Gunfleet Sand extends northeastward into the estuary for a distance of about twenty miles. The shelf on the southern side of the estuary is called the Kentish Flats. From its northeastern corner a broad line of shoals known as Long Sand stretches off to the northeast roughly parallel to the Gunfleet for some twenty-five miles. These two enormous natural jetties lying seven to ten miles apart confine the main tidal flow of the Thames. Between them are three other parallel linear features. Beginning with the southernmost they are called Sunk Sand (with its inner extension, known as Knock John), the Barrow Sand, and the slender Middle Ground. These divide the estuary into four principal channels: the Black, Barrow, and Middle Deeps, and to the north the Swin or King's Channel. The Middle Deep was avoided in the seventeenth century and may have been narrower than it is today. The Barrow was surveyed for possible use by the fleet in 1666, and Trinity House is known to have employed pilots certified for the Black Deep since at least Elizabethan times. Being in the middle of the estuary, however, both the Barrow and the Black Deep kept the mariner too far from land to obtain useful bearings except in perfect weather, and they were consequently regarded as dangerous; this was especially true in wartime, with the buoys removed. The preferred route in the age of sail was the King's Channel, which is ironically obstructed and impassable for large ships today, parts of it lying within the modern navy's firing range. In the 1600s it evidently had a wide fairway, for the fleet routinely utilized anchorages all along its length. A particularly favoured spot was the area at the tip of the Gunfleet, from which the men-of-war could be served by the repair and supply facilities of the nearby royal dockyard at Harwich. The Gunfleet was the fleet's usual 'jumping off' point. It lay conveniently equidistant between the other two principal advanced bases for war against the Dutch, the open roadstead at Solebay to the north and the sheltered haven of the Downs to the south covering the Straits of Dover.

The King's Channel and its parallel alternatives had an important disadvantage in that they forced traffic to and from the Downs and the Channel to reach well out to sea to the northeast to ensure clearance of Long Sand Head. This more than doubled the straight-line distance from Dover to the Nore, and the loss in time could be even greater; a wind which was fair for the southwest–northeast axis of the King's Channel was frequently foul for the north–south axis of the Dover leg, or vice-versa. Since slow progress could often be expected on at least one leg, captains planning to use this route usually allowed at least two days for the passage even though the distance covered was only about seventy miles. This detour is worth remembering, for it was on its seaward segment that the English encountered the Dutch in June 1666.

Time-saving short-cuts between the Nore and the Downs had been known for decades. Queen Elizabeth's Channel (today known as Queen's Channel) and others had appeared on charts since the 1500s. Such routes crossed portions of the Kentish Flats or went through tortuous passages in the complex submerged hillocks near the southern end of Long Sand. Prince Rupert took the *Royal Sovereign* into the river by one of these routes in 1673; on being asked what the brothers of Trinity House would think, shipwright Sir Phineas Pett 'answered that he believed they would say his Highness was mad, whereto the Prince replied, "I believe so too."' This suggests that the channels were poorly surveyed, but it is also obvious that if the *Royal Sovereign* with her twenty-four-foot draught could get through, any ship could. Unfortunately, the southern passages were not suitable for fleets. The routes known at the time crossed areas of shallow water, requiring deep-going vessels to creep through near the end of the flood a little before high water (or at the start of the ebb for outgoing traffic). The channels were thus useful only for individual ships or small squadrons which could cross together on a single tide. That was not possible for a big fleet which in confined waters could require half a day to file past a given point even in ideal conditions. Negotiation of any of the channels of the Thames was strongly dependent on a fair wind. It was considered unwise to beat upwind through a fairway less than a mile wide, for a man-of-war that experienced the slightest delay in tacking was likely to go aground. This was a particularly important consideration when entering on the flood; a ship on a sandbank at high water was in serious danger of becoming a semi-permanent landmark of that stretch of the river.

In addition to the shoals of the Thames, there were other treacherous obstacles in the North Sea outside the confines of the estuary. Most prominent were four major sandbanks that lay within eight to fifteen miles of Long Sand Head. From that point the Shipwash bore to the north, the Kentish Knock to the south, the Gabbard to the northeast, and the Galloper to the east. All were linear features on N.N.E.–S.S.W. axes.

Shipping everywhere in the estuary was much hampered prior to the eighteenth century by a lack of accurate charts. Much to the embarrassment of the Royal Navy, the best guides to the river were to be found in navigational atlases published in the Netherlands. These were known as 'Waggoners' to the English because the most widely circulated set had been compiled by the Dutchman Wagenhaer in the late sixteenth century. None of the Waggoners in use in the 1660s were sufficiently up to date to be fully relied upon.

Trinity House carried out constant surveys and in peacetime maintained buoys marking the main channels. These aids were hurriedly removed at the onset of the war, partly to frustrate penetration by the Dutch but also to help enforce the merchant shipping embargo imposed while the navy sought men. The temporary absence of buoys left the fleet dependent on pilots to carry it in and out of the river. Trained, certified, and paid by Trinity House, the pilots were often unsung heroes. Not only did they have to be thoroughly familiar with the latest conditions of the shoals, they also had to be sober men of iron nerves and often great force of character; the safety of the fleet could depend on their willingness to hold to their navigational convictions in the face of opposition from high-ranking officers not accustomed to being contradicted. Pepys found it terrifying

> that the whole safety of the ship, men, officers, and the admiral himself, lie entirely in the hand, skill, diligence, courage, life, or goodwill of one man, the pilot, without having liberty safely to withstand him, though the admiral, even with the concurrence of every commander, master, mate, midshipman, and seaman also, be of a different mind.

Even with reliable pilots in attendance, a fleet on the move in the estuary was always preceded by flotillas of small craft taking soundings along the prospective route. The Thames could never be taken lightly.

Chapter V

Preparations

Both furl their sails, and strip them for the fight,
Their folded sheets dismiss the useless air:
Th' Elean plains could boast no nobler sight,
When struggling champions did their bodies bare.

The Second Anglo-Dutch War was part of the heroic three-century-long struggle for worldwide maritime supremacy waged by the sea powers of Western Europe. The great rivalry had begun with the commercial awakening which accompanied the electrifying discoveries of Columbus and da Gama. Portugal had won the early rounds but had been displaced by Spain, which had in turn been eclipsed by England and the Netherlands. In the middle of the seventeenth century the global ambitions of France had not yet become evident, so the two North Sea rivals were for the time being the only claimants.

Both countries were then at the height of prosperity and vitality. Every year each sent forth hundreds of ships to explore, to trade, and to colonize in the farthest reaches of the earth. They found themselves competing in every sea, but the contest was by no means confined to colonial areas. In home waters there were fierce disputes over coastal fishing rights and bitter jealousy over the European carrying trade. For that purpose Dutch shipwrights had devised utilitarian merchantmen which could be built and operated more cheaply than those of other nations. As the shipping firms of Holland and Zeeland gradually came to dominate this profitable business, English competitors began to demand protection from their government. The Parliament of the Commonwealth responded by passing the Navigation Act in October 1651. It required that English exports be carried only in English ships, while imports could be borne only by English ships or those belonging to the country of origin of the goods. When Dutch merchantmen began to be searched and confiscated, the First Anglo-Dutch War inevitably broke out. From this the English emerged victorious, forcing their enemy to swallow the Navigation Act and other humiliations. But much to the chagrin of the English merchants, the Netherlanders suffered little loss in their carrying trade. The shipping regulations were easily evaded, often with the connivance of English manufacturers and retailers who disliked high freight rates as much as anyone else. In distant oceans the Dutch remained as strong as ever.

After the Restoration, mercantile elements of the City of London, in alliance with the King and the nobles of the Court, began to take increased interest in overseas resources and markets; this meant direct and deliberate conflict with the Dutch. In December 1660 'The Royal Adventurers into Africa' (better known as the Africa

Company) were chartered to trade in gold, slaves, and hides in West Africa. The investors included the Duke of York, Prince Rupert, and the Duke of Albemarle. The mere formation of the company was a hostile act, for it intended to do business in areas regarded as private preserves by the Dutch West India Company. In March 1661 five royal warships which had been loaned to the new English firm descended on the African coast and proceeded to evict a small Dutch garrison from a dilapidated fort on an island in the mouth of the Gambia River. An English presence established, the squadron returned home and the company began its commercial operations. The commander of this first expedition was Major Robert Holmes, a swaggering Royalist soldier-sailor who had cruised with Prince Rupert in the Civil War. When word of his high-handed doings reached the Netherlands, the States-General protested vigorously and caused reprisals to be taken against the new company's ships and settlements. From there, relations steadily deteriorated. Holmes went back to Guinea in 1664, where he made open war on the Dutch by capturing their ships and driving them from their forts at Goree, Anta, and Cape Coast. These blatantly provocative attacks aroused such disapproval in Continental capitals that Charles II found it advisable to lock Holmes in the Tower on his return. He was released after a few months, however, and restored to his command with private congratulations for having stirred things up so thoroughly.

England also behaved aggressively in the New World. While Holmes rampaged in Africa, Charles thought it appropriate to bestow a huge tract of land in North America on his brother James, Duke of York. It was no coincidence that the grant included the valley of the Hudson River, where the Dutch had maintained a thriving and inoffensive colony for many years. A squadron under Captain Richard Nicholls sailed imperiously into the Hudson in July 1664. After a month's blockade the Dutch were forced to give up the New Netherlands, which was subsequently renamed New York in honour of James.

At home the English commercial classes actively fomented war. A wave of pamphlets denounced Dutch monopolies in the East Indies and their 'usurpation' of the North Sea herring fisheries. There was understandable resentment over the stubborn refusal of the Dutch East India Company to hand over the spice island of Pulo Run, which had been awarded to England by an Anglo-Dutch reparations committee after the previous war. With less justification, the pamphleteers also raked up such long-forgotten indignities as the Amboina massacre, an ugly incident which had taken place in Indonesia over forty years before.

On 20 April 1664 a group of City merchants petitioned the House of Commons for redress of 'grievances in respect of injuries inflicted by the Dutch nation in divers traffics and encounters in the course of thirty years'. For alleged losses of ships, trade, and settlements the Africa Company claimed damages of £330,000 and the East India Company £237,000. Parliament responded sympathetically by enjoining the Crown to take all necessary actions to protect English trade from further encroachments. This played directly into Charles's hands. As Pepys had earlier surmised, 'the King's design' from the beginning was 'getting underhand the merchants to bring in their complaints to the Parliament, to make them in honour begin a warr, which he cannot in honour declare first, for fear they should not second him with money'.

By now the Dutch were furious. Charles's nefariously unscrupulous ambassador to The Hague, Sir George Downing, had consistently answered their every protest with bland denials and specious counter-accusations. Downing's presentation of the English companies' demands for compensation, coming on top of the news from West Africa, threw the States-General into a frothing rage. This time they responded to Holmes's depredations with more than mere protests. Their Mediterranean fleet under Michiel Adriaanszoon de Ruyter, Lieutenant-Admiral of Amsterdam, was ordered to go to Guinea and hunt down Holmes. To hide this move from English spies, the orders were quietly and unconstitutionally issued by the provincial States of Holland rather than the States-General. But the English found out soon enough. As it happened, de Ruyter missed Holmes, though he did recover the Dutch forts and for good measure sacked the English post at Cormantyne. He then sailed across the Atlantic. In American waters he wreaked havoc with English shipping but found himself too weak to recapture the Hudson River colony.

De Ruyter's reprisal was the overt response for which Charles had been waiting. As soon as the States' Fleet was known to be on its way to Guinea, the Royal Navy was secretly ordered to begin hostilities. In December the Mediterranean squadron under Captain Thomas Allin surprised the Dutch Smyrna convoy off Cadiz; there was a spirited battle. In the Channel a group of frigates under Captain Thomas Teddiman attacked a Bordeaux wine convoy without provocation, capturing most of it. These insults were too much for the Dutch. They declared war in January 1665, the English following suit a month later.

Despite the various trumped-up causes, few in England made any attempt to conceal the true issue. As Captain George Cocke, a director of the Africa Company, explained to Samuel Pepys, 'the trade of the world is too little for us two, therefore one must down'. This was echoed by the Duke of Albemarle, who bluntly said that 'what we want is more of the trade the Dutch now have'. The war was popular in all segments of English society. One of the very few who had any reservations was the Duke of York's secretary, Sir William Coventry, who was more familiar than most with the government's all-but-bankrupt financial condition. In a private paper circulated among his closest friends he noted several facts which everyone had ignored. Even if the Dutch could be defeated, 'to which possibly some objections might be made from the posture of his Majesty's stores and treasure', he feared that 'the Crowne may pay too dear' for trade benefits that might turn out to be a 'vaine imagination'. In any event, he concluded, 'the enriching the people by beggaring the Crowne is not a good policy'.

Charles was playing a dangerous game in another respect. Despite intensive diplomatic efforts, England was able to recruit only one active Continiental ally – the Dutch-hating Bernhard van Galen, Bishop of Munster. 'Bombing Bernhard' caused the Netherlands some embarrassment by marching an army into the province of Gelderland, but this was a mere pinprick. The Dutch had treaties of friendship with the Elector of Brandenburg and with Frederik III of Denmark-Norway, but these were only minor threats to England. Brandenburg had no navy to speak of; and Charles was on reasonably friendly terms with Karl XI of Sweden, Frederik's mortal enemy, so the Baltic powers would presumably cancel each other out. The real danger was Louis XIV of France. In 1662 that immensely wealthy and inscrutably unpredictable young monarch had concluded a mutual defence pact with the Dutch. By its terms each signatory was to declare war within four months on any third party which attacked the other. As the English knew, Louis had regretted the agreement almost before the ink had dried. His primary objective had been to trick the Dutch into helping him in a land war which he intended to wage against the Spanish Habsburgs to obtain their Flemish provinces; he had not expected to be drawn into a naval fight with England for which he was poorly equipped. It was for that reason that Charles II took pains to ensure that the Dutch declared war first. This gave the King of France a flimsy pretext – which he eagerly grasped – to evade his obligations by claiming that the Dutch were legally the aggressors. Despite anguished protestations from The Hague, Louis sublimely ignored the English provocations. Nevertheless, he clearly favoured the Dutch, and no one could be sure that he would stay his hand indefinitely. The States-General's ambassador to the Court of St. Germain, Conrad van Beuningen, patiently and relentlessly pressed his arguments; if his diplomacy succeeded, England could be in deadly jeopardy.

The Second Anglo-Dutch War was in many ways a strange conflict. Neither side withdrew its ambassador until the contest was well into its second year, and mail service by regularly scheduled packet boats continued for the same period. Thereafter, correspondence had to go through neutral Spanish Flanders, but that caused little inconvenience. There was no land campaign other than brief coastal raids and the Bishop of Munster's march into Gelderland, and civilian populaces were unaffected except for rising prices, special taxes, and shortages of certain commodities caused by the interruption of shipping. The fighting throughout was seasonal. Neither side thought it wise to expose its fleet to the storms of winter; as if by mutual consent, both navies annually withdrew to their harbours as the cold months approached.

Seventeenth-century governments displayed an oddly differing attitude towards the desirability of battles on land as opposed to those at sea. Ashore, armies seldom met face to face. Many wars could have been settled in a single all-out encounter, but generals and politicians were reluctant to risk everything on one throw of the dice; land campaigns usually bogged down in marches, counter-marches, and tedious sieges. By contrast, the all but irreplaceable navies were committed to battle without the slightest hesitation. During the Anglo-Dutch wars the fighting assumed a frequently repeated pattern: the fleets would emerge from their winter hibernation in March, gather in April and May, and meet in early June to begin each year's campaign with a titanic struggle.

In 1665 both sides considered an early showdown especially desirable. The English wanted it because they knew their treasury could not stand the strain of a drawn-out stalemate. Goaded by the commercial classes, Charles II and his Privy Council embarked on the great adventure with little conception of how much it would cost. In February 1665 they congratulated themselves on having wrung from an exceptionally tight-fisted Parliament £2,500,000 to cover the charge of the war for three years. But the grant melted away at an astonishing rate; it was soon discovered that the first year's share would be gone in five months, and the second year's would obviously last little longer. In April, Pepys presented the facts to the Council, whereupon the ashen-faced ministers 'held up their hands crying, "what shall we do?"' Sir Philip Warwick, Secretary to the Treasurer, had already informed Pepys that it would be impossible to find additional revenue, 'unless the King can get some noblemen or rich money-gentlemen to lend him money, or to get the City to do it'. But Charles had long since exhausted his credit, and no one stepped forward. It was an incredible predicament. Having deliberately provoked a duel with the greatest maritime and financial force in Europe, England had discovered too late that she lacked the means to fight it. The navy did all it could to reduce expenses. The hiring of merchantmen for conversion to warships was curtailed, and new construction was cut back sharply. This was to have unfortunate long-term consequences. Charles II embarked on an ambitious shipbuilding programme as soon as war with the Dutch had been decided. On 26 October 1664, the King in council directed the royal shipwrights to undertake construction of two second-rates, three third-rates, and two fourth-rates, with another third-rate to be built in a private yard on contract. After passage of the Parliamentary grant in February, additional contracts were placed with private builders for a supplementary programme of one third-rate and three fourth-rates. Yet another project came about in March, when the aldermen and companies of the City of London generously offered to pay for a new ship to replace the second-rate *London* which had been blown up by accident. The King gratefully directed that the new man-of-war, also a second-rate, be named the *Loyal London*. This brought the number of major vessels authorized to thirteen: three second-rates and five each of the third and fourth rate. Then the April financial crisis forced a sudden re-examination of the entire shipbuilding effort. In the resulting holocaust two second-rates, one third-rate, and two fourth-rates were cancelled outright or deferred indefinitely. That left on the slips only four third-rates, three fourth-rates, and the donated *Loyal London*. As it turned out, even the abbreviated programme became discouragingly expensive and took an inordinate amount of time to complete. The prospect of long delays in payment caused suppliers of shipbuilding materials to charge abnormally high prices. Labourers who knew they would have to toil for months without their wages assiduously avoided employment in the royal dockyards. Forcibly impressed, they staged slowdowns, strikes, mutinies, and riots, and learned to make a living by stealing from the dockyard stores. Their officers, underpaid in the best of times, had long before become proficient at all the arts of graft and embezzlement. Their grand-scale corruption in turn made Parliament even less inclined to generosity.

Coventry, Pepys, and their colleagues on the Navy Board were fully aware in the spring of 1665 that the most remorseless economies would be to no avail. Simple arithmetic showed that the navy could afford only one summer's campaign. The situation would have been serious against any opponent, but against the Netherlands it appeared doubly dangerous. Dutch money seemed inexhaustible. The Seven Provinces had built their prosperity on the produce of the seas and the traffic of the oceanic highways: North Sea herrings, Arctic whales, West African slaves, the lucrative commerce of the Mediterranean, the carrying trade of every port in Europe, and above all, the cornucopia of riches from the faraway Indies. Although the war could be expected to disrupt the fisheries, the continuing transfusions of wealth from overseas would allow the Dutch to fight on indefinitely and outlast any maritime opponent. Their navy was large, and their imposing shipbuilding capacity seemed sure to make it larger; their dockyards already had no fewer than twenty-four new warships on the stocks. The best hope for the English was a total victory early in the conflict, before the money ran out and before the enemy reached his full potential. Unfortunately, the Dutch appeared to have nothing to gain by offering battle, and nothing to lose by waiting it out. Coventry glumly summed up the English fears in a private letter to the Earl of Arlington:

> The enemy will still build and increase, while by casualties, &c, the English fleet must decrease, and if one battle is lost, ten times the money that would have ensured victory will not bring it to equal terms again. The expense will tire the English before the Dutch, because the latter still carry on their East India, Straits, and Guinea trade, destroying that of the English there, and they would therefore be foolish to risk a battle without great advantage.

While the English were mulling over their troubles, the Dutch were equally worried. Their position was not as unassailable as Coventry believed. It was true that they had plenty of money and credit at the outset, but their whole vast economy was in fact a delicate and precarious structure. Their land offered few natural resources, so the loss of their fisheries was more punishing than the English knew. They did still have their foreign trade, and if the spices and the gold continued to flow they could indeed go on forever. But if trade was their strength it was also the fatal weakness; cut it off, and the *bourses* would fail even faster than Charles's treasury. Securing the lines of sea communications was therefore the central object of Dutch strategy – and there the English had an advantage. For if time was the enemy of England, the foe of the Dutch was simple geography: the British landmass blocked their path to the oceans. Whereas most English shipping could approach its ports from the 'rear' of the theatre of action, every Dutch merchantman from every corner of the world was condemned to march straight through the North Sea battleground, across the face of the enemy. There were no safe routes; the Dover bottleneck was out of the question, and the English fleet, if unopposed, would render the Scottish detour untenable as well. Thus, even when the Dutch might have preferred a waiting game, the need to protect the convoys forced their hand; it was fight, or face economic ruin.

Geography also dictated the nature of the fighting. Since all Dutch merchantmen had to funnel through the same waters, there was no need for the English to weaken their forces by dispersing commerce raiders to distant stations. The same object could be attained to better effect by massing the whole fleet in the North Sea shipping lanes. This forced the Dutch to concentrate as well, which meant that the battles would be very large ones.

The outlook for the Dutch was especially grim in the spring of 1665. The rich Smyrna trade numbering forty ships was on the way home from the Mediterranean, ten incoming East Indiamen were already in the Atlantic, and twelve warships under de Ruyter were expected from North America and would be vulnerable during their passage. The loss of any of these fleets would be a telling and demoralizing blow so early in the war, and it went without saying that the capture of the bloated Indiamen could transform the English finances overnight. Each government urged its admirals to hurry their preparations.

For Charles II, the first and most delicate decision of the war was selecting the fleet's principal leaders. There were five men who could make strong claims to the chief commands through either prestige or proven experience. At the top of the list was the King's brother, James, Duke of York, the Lord High Admiral. An able and conscientious administrator, James was no mere figurehead. He concerned himself with every aspect of the navy's management: improving shipbuilding and increasing timber resources, rooting out dockyard corruption and fighting abuses in the pay system, seamen's clothing, victualling, press gangs, prize agents, care of the sick and wounded, and every other problem imaginable. Though there was never enough money to fully implement his reforms, James was perhaps the best friend the English common seaman ever had. He was also enough of a yachtsman to understand the fundamentals of navigation and seamanship. But although James had performed commendably in warfare ashore, he had never commanded a fleet and had never seen a sea-fight. Moreover, he was the only legitimate Stuart heir; his untimely death would be a catastrophic dynastic disaster.

Prince Rupert's titles and prestige made him the next ranking alternative, but he was short on sea experience and his prudence was suspect. The remaining claimants were all battle-tried Generals-at-Sea of the Commonwealth and Protectorate: Albemarle, Sir William Penn, and Edward Montagu, Earl of Sandwich. Penn was the only pure seaman among the senior commanders and the only one with neither peerage nor royal blood. Forty-five years old, he was a corrupt, opinionated, and irascible professional who openly resented the intrusion of soldiers, cavaliers, and princes into what he considered his rightful province. At various times his jealous Navy Board rival Samuel Pepys called him 'a knave', 'a cowardly rogue', 'a counterfeit rogue', and 'the falsest rascal that ever was in the world'. But not even Pepys could deny his ability; along with Albemarle and Deane he was one of the original architects of the line-of-battle system, and he understood its uses and limitations perhaps better than anyone. Penn may have had a special claim on the King's affections. In 1654 Oliver Cromwell placed him in charge of a large fleet sent to attack Spanish possessions in the West Indies. According to the Earl of Clarendon, Penn communicated with the exiled Charles, declaring himself a secret Royalist and offering to deliver the fleet to the Stuarts. Charles, however, had no harbour available and in any event doubted that the plot could succeed. The offer was gracefully declined, but with assurances that such loyalty would not be forgotten. Clarendon's story is by no means impossible, though his contemporaries make no mention of it and documentary evidence has not come to light.

The Earl of Sandwich was one of the great Cromwellian soldier-admirals. Almost alone among the landsmen appointed to the navy, he had taken the trouble to learn his seamanship, and by 1665 he knew as much about it as many of the tarpaulins. At sea he maintained a journal in which he carefully recorded daily weather and position, based on his own sightings. He had an excellent grasp of line-of-battle tactics and had suggested several useful refinements in the Fighting Instructions. Sandwich had definitely earned the King's gratitude. In command of the Protectorate's sea-forces in 1660, it was he who had delivered the fleet to the Restoration.

The Royal Navy has rarely had such a glittering array of authority and talent available at one time, but finding worthy places for them all was no easy matter. Although the standard fleet organization made provision for nine flag-officers, vice- and rear-admirals' posts would be demeaning for men who had directed whole fleets; only full squadron commands would be acceptable. But how could three squadrons be divided among five men? As a prince of the blood Rupert could claim primacy over everyone but James, and Sandwich could expect an important post from his title as Vice-Admiral of England. At the same time Charles dared not slight Albemarle, and Penn was professionally the best qualified. Fortunately, an amicable solution was found when the Duke of Albemarle let it be known that he would forgo a sea commission if his prestige were otherwise maintained. Charles decided that James, despite the danger to the succession, would be risked at sea as commander-in-chief. Albemarle would remain ashore as acting Lord High Admiral, a position well befitting his administrative talents and august authority. Rupert would be Admiral of the White and Sandwich Admiral of the Blue, while Penn would serve aboard the flagship as adviser to the Duke of York. This was happily accepted by everyone – at least until Rupert and Sandwich belatedly discovered that Penn would actually be in charge, issuing his own orders under James's absolute authority.

On 23 March the Duke of York took leave of his royal brother at Whitehall. Accompanied by his nephew the Duke of Monmouth and by the Duchess, the Queen, Prince Rupert, and a horde of adventurous nobles, he boarded his yacht and sailed down the Thames. After a brief pause at the Hope to bid farewell to the ladies, he continued on to the Gunfleet anchorage near Harwich where the flagship *Royal Charles* received him with booming salutes. Built as the *Naseby* in 1654 to commemorate Cromwell's greatest victory, the *Royal Charles* was special to the Stuarts as the ship which had borne Charles II to his homecoming; he had changed the offending name on his first night aboard. She was a first-rate mounting 80 brass guns in three tiers and manned by 600 seamen and marines. The length of her keel was 131 feet, but from the gilded Stuart arms on her stern to the haughty Neptune guarding her prow was a distance of over 200 feet. The Neptune was a recent addition to the ship, having replaced the original effigy of 'Oliver on horseback, trampling six nations underfoot', which had been torn out and burned in a festive public bonfire in December 1663.

Four days after James and Rupert arrived at the Gunfleet, the Earl of Sandwich came down from the Nore in the *Royal Prince*. A very old ship freshly rebuilt, she was a first-rate even larger than the *Royal Charles*. Under the name of *Resolution*, the *Prince* had been Monck's flagship at the Gabbard and Scheveningen. Prince Rupert also had a first-rate, the smaller but unusually speedy *Royal James*. Lesser flagships and individual men-of-war came in over the next few days, and soon the King's Channel was choked for miles by a mighty assemblage of over eighty great warships. But though the ships were there, any hopes that James may have had for early action were quickly dispelled by the hard reality of logistics.

The navy had begun its preparations for war in the previous autumn. Initially the greatest need was the 28,000 seamen required to man the ships. At first the press gangs found the seamen flocking to the colours with carnival enthusiasm. At Norwich, 'a company of 40 marched through the town, with drums beating and other expressions of joy at their taking water', and at Yarmouth it was reported that 'throngs are mustering up and down the streets, frolicking away their press money, and saying, when their friends try to dissuade them from going, that they could not serve a better master'. But the supply of eager volunteers quickly ran out, and then the less willing candidates had to be flushed out of hiding in door-to-door searches. A 'hot press' also went on at sea. One large contingent of men was obtained in a body from the ships of the Africa Company. The seamen had crowded into these vessels following the announcement that they would be press-exempt. When de Ruyter's descent on the Guinea coast caused their voyage to be cancelled, the exemptions were revoked and all the men taken. Among those who found themselves in the navy's net by this means was young master's mate's apprentice Edward Barlow, pressed from the Africa Company's ship *Madras*. He appears to have been disappointed but not embittered at his fate; it was all part of a seaman's life. He merely noted in his journal that he was given a ticket for the pay he had accumulated in the merchantman, and that it was duly paid a few months later. 'And so it fell to my turn', he laconically wrote, 'to be put with forty men on board of a frigate called the *Monck*, having 58 pieces of ordnance'.

The press from the Company ships improved the manning situation greatly, but even when the seaports had been picked clean and merchant shipping brought to a standstill, the fleet was still shorthanded. The King had already tried sweetening the inducements. In an Order in Council of 28 October 1664 he had announced

that seamen, whether serving on the King's ships or on merchantmen, shall receive 10s. per ton on all prizes taken by them, £6.13s.4d. for each piece of ordnance, and £10 a gun for every man-of-war sunk or destroyed; also the pillage of all merchandise upon or above the gundeck.

He further promised that 'care is to be taken for the sick and wounded and widows, and medals to be given for eminent service'. The proclamation was greeted with rejoicing by the men already gathered, but it did little to attract others.

In desperation the Privy Council tried to supplement the navy's press with round-ups by civilian authorities. A quota was established for each maritime county, and the justices of the peace were directed 'to order the constables of each parish to leave tickets at the houses of seamen, ordering them to appear and enlist; those who fail to be apprehended and sent to common gaol, to remain till they engage in the service by taking imprest money'. This had discouraging results. Local officials regarded the order as a heaven-sent opportunity to rid their parishes of undesirables. They emptied the almshouses, and if any of the frail old men whom they sent to the fleet were mariners it was purely coincidental. To be sure, the navy's own pressmasters brought in quite a few tailors, shoemakers, and others 'fitter to keep sheep than to sail in such great ships'. But these were at least hale and hearty specimens who could reasonably be expected to strain at a capstan without falling dead. The parish derelicts ('those pitiful pressed creatures who are fit for nothing but to fill the ships full of vermin') could not be employed at all. From Portsmouth, Commissioner Thomas Middleton angrily complained of

> men utterly unfit for service, some 50, 60, and even 70 years of age. No man will admit them into his ship; they cannot return without pay, and no one has power to send them home again, so they wander up and down the streets, starving and spreading infection in the town; if they go home they will be put into gaol.

When unhappy wretches were herded into the ships, many ran away at the first opportunity, stealing boats and even swimming. Desertion reached alarming proportions. In February 1665 Middleton recommended drastic action:

> The only remedy for it is to set up a gallows in every town between Portsmouth and London, and out of every ten men taken, going away without leave, to hang one by lot. Captain Salmon misses 120 men, and every ship 20, 30, 50 and some 100.

The commanders must have despaired of ever manning the ships, but a late decision to fill out the crews with soldiers (who were soon found to make surprisingly good seamen), brought the fleet well above its war establishment by the time the fighting began.

As the number of men swelled, the matter of feeding them gradually assumed a higher priority. Roads all over southern England were soon trodden into quagmires by the endless processions of cattle and pigs shuffling to the waterside slaughterhouses, but the sheer size of the wartime fleet overwhelmed Dennis Gauden's victualling arrangements. Though he did his best, supplying meat and produce of a wholesomeness unheard of in later periods, Gauden found it almost impossible to meet the demands of a large operational fleet. The fundamental trouble was that he could not oversee operations in every port simultaneously. Corrupt agents and incompetent subordinates consistently overstated inventories, storeships always seemed to sail at the wrong times and to the wrong places, and shipboard pursers as always embezzled shamelessly. The inevitable lack of money aggravated everything. The navy fell behind in Gauden's payments; to meet obligations to his suppliers he was forced on to his own credit, which proved 'too much for any one man's purse'. He was eventually driven into bankruptcy, and only the Navy Board's intercession saved him from debtors' prison.

Victuals were by no means the only failing. When James assumed command he found many commodities wanting, including several seemingly mundane items without which a fleet could not function effectively. Boats, cables, shrouds, casks, hammocks, ammunition, ordnance stores, surgeon's 'medicaments', and colours were all in short supply. The lack of flags was particularly serious since signalling was impossible until they arrived. This problem was exacerbated when the second-rate

London carrying all the bunting for the Blue Squadron was blown up accidentally. The fleet also found itself without firepoles, the booms which ships in battle extended from their quarters to fend off fireships. When the poles finally came, they were too heavy and had to be reordered. Slops, or seamen's clothing, posed unexpected difficulties. The authorities had assumed that this need would not become urgent until the men had worn out the things they brought with them. Unfortunately, most of the recruits turned up in tatters and rags totally unsuitable for the usual North Sea weather. Despite belated efforts to rectify matters, the initial cruises were carried out with many men poorly clad.

The thankless task of managing supply problems fell mainly on Sir William Coventry, who with a few clerks constituted James's entire working staff. The Duke was fortunate in having the services of this dedicated and competent administrator. The fleet of the Restoration period is often spoken of with some justification as 'Mr. Pepys's Navy', but in the 1660s the true indispensable man was Coventry. During April and May of 1665 his desk produced an astonishing volume of correspondence. With Albemarle helpfully cutting the red tape in London, he resolved every problem one by one – with the notable exception of the victualling morass, which seemed hopeless.

James himself had much to do to ensure the fleet's discipline. The court-martial of Lt. Mansell on 6 April gave abundant warning that the commander-in-chief 'would severely reprehend any expressions of past divisions' between Royalists and ex-Cromwellians. Less official proceedings demonstrated that he would brook no insubordination from the gaggles of young gentlemen and great nobles who flocked to the fleet to get in on the excitement. Two of the most powerful nobles, the Duke of Buckingham and the Earl of Peterborough, showed up with commissions from the King granting them each command of a second-rate; Buckingham the *St. George* and Peterborough the *Unicorn*. To this James made no open objection, but he stiffened when Buckingham, citing his status as a Privy Councillor, demanded admission to the flag-officers' council-of-war. Finding himself 'not in the esteem a great man should be', Buckingham marched off to Whitehall to complain to the King. James's explanation, though, arrived first, and the unhappy lord found no redress. He returned to the Gunfleet, where he gave up his command and thrust himself as a volunteer into Sandwich's ship 'to show that he came not to seek safety'. As for Peterborough, he found 'little satisfaction and great mortifications on board', and was soon back ashore. James undoubtedly regretted having made enemies of such important politicians, but the challenges to his authority could not be tolerated.

Also of concern were a few unproven officers whose steadiness under fire was less than certain, especially the merchant captains of the hired ships. Seeking some dramatic way to 'make people take good heed to their actions', James found his chance just days before the first battle. The occasion was the spectacular court-martial of Captain Edward Nixon of the fourth-rate *Elizabeth*. On a cruise off Scilly in company with the fifth-rate *Eagle*, he had fled disgracefully from a pair of Dutch privateers while his plucky little consort had stood in gallantly to receive damage and casualties. On Nixon's return the Duke of Albemarle, who, said Coventry, 'hates a coward as ill as a toad', summarily ordered him to the Gunfleet for trial. James made the most of the opportunity, deliberately creating a sensational atmosphere and pointedly requiring every captain in the fleet to sit on the court. The proceedings convened in the great cabin of the *Royal Charles* on 25 May. Nixon at first mounted an eloquent if ineffectual defence based on bad weather, 'the evill councell of his shipp's officers', and other equally feeble obfuscations, but ultimately 'concluded with acknowledging he had greatly offended and begged the Duke's mercy'. At that James growled angrily of 'how much the honour of the King and the Nation was wounded in this miscarriage', noted the penalty demanded by the Articles of War, and then stalked out to leave the transgressor's fate in the hands of his fellow officers. The verdict was never in doubt; Captain Nixon was sentenced to be shot. The affair made a lasting and profound impression on the captains and, as it turned out, the timing could not have been better.

While Coventry wrestled with logistics and James with unruly nobles, Penn and the flag-officers worked out their tactical plans. They began with Monck's old Fighting Instructions, which they reissued on 10 April with a few minor changes. The stern prohibition against taking possession of surrendered enemy vessels was somewhat relaxed, and a new article was inserted for forming line on either tack from an initial abreast arrangement; Sandwich had introduced this technique a few months earlier. These basic regulations were then expanded by a remarkable set of 'Additional Instructions' containing many significant tactical advances. Among other things, they established the interval between ships at a half-cable (120 yards), specified a close-hauled line in defensive situations, and for attack required the headmost ship to steer for the headmost of the enemy's. Another article made it a matter of law that no ship could leave the line to assist damaged vessels that were not in danger of sinking, 'being that nothing but beating the body of the enemyes fleet can effectually secure the lame shipps'. Most importantly, provision was made for tacking 'from the rear' or together, so that the fleet could reverse its order in a single evolution. This manoeuvre gave the English an unprecedented degree of tactical flexibility.

Much attention was devoted to the fleet's organization. The ships were assigned to their respective squadrons and divisions on 7 April, the complete order of battle being issued two weeks later. As usual the White Squadron formed the van of the fleet, the Red the centre, and the Blue the rear. In the White Squadron Vice-Admiral Christopher Myngs had charge of the leading division, followed by Rupert and then the division of Rear-Admiral Robert Sansum. In the Red Squadron, Vice-Admiral Sir John Lawson was in the van, James and Penn in the centre, and Rear-Admiral Sir William Berkeley in the rear. The centre division of the Blue Squadron was under Sandwich, but the natural order of his other divisions was reversed. Rear-Admiral Thomas Teddiman had the van, whilst Vice-Admiral Sir George Ayscue took the rear. This was to ensure that a relatively senior flag-officer would have the prestigious position at the head of the line if the fleet reversed course together.

The order of battle was arranged with intelligent care down to the last detail. In the White and Blue Squadrons, the commanders of the van and rear divisions were placed respectively at the very head and tail of the line, so that in all circumstances a flagship would be the leading unit. Following one of Sandwich's innovations of the previous year, every vessel had a pre-ordained station in the line. The stations were assigned more or less at random, but the principal commanders took care to place specially trusted captains in the honoured position of 'second' next to themselves. In James's wake was his companion John Chicheley, followed by James Ley, Earl of Marlborough, who despite his title was a wizened old leatherback of decades' experience. Rupert's next ahead was his faithful protégé Robert Holmes, while Sandwich was flanked by Henry Fenne and John Hayward, friends from Protectorate times whose careers he fostered. Each flagship was to be attended in battle by a cluster of smaller vessels: two or three ketches and smacks to relay messages, and at least one fifth- or sixth-rate. These lightly armed scouts were not intended to be in the battle-line itself, but to hold themselves ready to deal with the enemy's fireships. As for the fleet's own fireships, they were under the direct control of the squadron commanders, and were expected to stay close by the flags until ordered into action.

A change in the order of battle was suggested by Sandwich on 31 May, just before the first engagement. The fleet at that time included twenty-four hired ships belonging to merchants and shipping syndicates. Their force was not inconsiderable (from 32 to 46 guns) but nearly everyone considered their value negligible. Sandwich's proposal, which was not adopted, was to remove them from the line entirely and group them as a separate reserve squadron for use in emergencies,

> by which means our ships of force of the King's would have had their strength contracted into a lesser room (by near a league) than when they are intermixed with the merchant ships. They would have been much stronger to make an impression on the enemy in any part, or to resist any combined force of the enemy attempting us. They would have had no impediment by bad sailors. And the commanders of the King's ships more entire and resolved to aid one another than it is to be feared the others are.

In spite of the reservations about the merchant captains, this English fleet was exceptionally well officered. Of the six subsidiary flag-officers, the only one who had not gained his position through merit was the courtier Sir William Berkeley, and he at least had four years' sea experience. The other five were all salty, well-tested Commonwealth men who had fought alongside Monck, Blake, and Deane in the glory days of the 1650s. The same was true of most of the captains. Coventry noted approvingly that 'there are only eight or ten of the good old commanders left on shore, and they either declined service or were unfit to be invited'.

The English fleet in the spring of 1665 was numerous and its ships well built, well armed, and – thanks to Coventry – well equipped for battle. Its victuals were good if not plentiful; its officers experienced, confident, and tactically well prepared; its seamen (most of them, anyway) in good health and high spirits. It was not without reason that the Earl of Falmouth, volunteer in the *Royal Charles*, could write with pride that 'there never was seen so brave, well-manned, and resolute a fleet as this'.

War preparations were no easier in the Netherlands than they were in England. Due to the virtual impossibility of coordinating the efforts of five independent and often competing Admiralties, many problems arose over stores and victuals. The States-

General made ample money available, but manning was still troublesome; no matter how much the navy offered, the merchants could always pay more. An embargo on outgoing shipping improved the situation, for the Companies discharged their crews and unemployment drove men to the fleet in substantial numbers. Even so, fourteen undermanned vessels had to be left behind when the fleet sailed.

The Dutch had ample numbers of ships, though few were the really large men-of-war that meant so much in a battle. The four big merchantmen from the V.O.C. were among the six most powerful vessels in the fleet, and if they performed poorly there would be little force to back them up. Good naval guns were in short supply, particularly the large-calibre pieces that made the English ships so formidable. Dutch foundry capacity was hopelessly inadequate to meet the needs, and the Admiralties desperately transferred artillery from land forces and purchased more abroad. Despite all efforts, some great ships initially went to sea with contemptibly small guns, while others had bewildering mixtures of eight and even nine calibres, often of antique vintage.

The Dutch had no trouble selecting their principal commander. The supreme post had been filled for twelve years by Jacob van Wassenaer, Baron van Obdam, Lieutenant-Admiral of Holland and Westfriesland. A distinguished old cavalry soldier, his chief qualifications for the job were his noble lineage and the fact that he was *not* a seaman. After the death of Maarten Tromp in 1653, the Admiralties had quarrelled over which of their mariners was the greatest, and Wassenaer had been the compromise choice. The seamen were never very happy under 'foggy Obdam', but his appointment at least left everyone *equally* dissatisfied.

Few sea commanders have ever had to put up with as much interference from their civilian governments as Wassenaer van Obdam. A delegation from the States-General, headed by Johan de Witt, Raadpensionaris of Holland and *de facto* prime minister, lodged itself in the fleet to oversee the preparations. De Witt was one of the greatest leaders the Netherlands ever produced, and one who worked tirelessly for the navy's improvement; still, his meddling was not well received. Relations between the politician and the admirals eventually became so bad that one leading flag-officer, Cornelis Tromp of Amsterdam, 'would not so much as stirre off from his bed to speake to him'. But the States-General was the law, and de Witt's will prevailed.

Among the matters which the States chose to dictate was the fleet's order of battle, and they determined its makeup on largely political grounds. In those days every Admiralty except Friesland had its own set of flag-officers whose prerogatives were jealously guarded. In 1665 a dispute arose because the lieutenant-admirals, or senior commanders, of the Admiralties of Amsterdam and the Noorderkwartier were away on foreign operations. These Admiralties therefore insisted that their vice-admirals temporarily be given the rights usually reserved for their absent seniors. This in turn caused the Admiralty of Zeeland, all of whose flag-officers were present, to demand that *their* vice-admiral be given the same status. To further complicate matters, the Admiralty of Amsterdam had more than twice as many ships as any of the others. The resulting compromise, worked out by politicians, was a uniquely Dutch solution. The States-General decided that there should be seven squadrons. These were not subdivided, but each was assigned three flag-officers anyway, trusted captains being given temporary appointments to fill out the twenty-one available spaces. The first squadron was under Obdam himself and consisted of predominately Amsterdam ships. The second, led by Lieutenant-Admiral Jan Evertsen of Zeeland, was a curious mixture of Rotterdam and Zeeland ships; the officers of those two Admiralties were never the best of friends. The third squadron was another mostly Amsterdam group, but its commander was the Lieutenant-Admiral of Rotterdam, Egbert Cortenaer. The fourth was composed mainly of Friesland ships under their own Lieutenant-Admiral Auke Stellingwerf. This squadron was originally designated the seventh, because the Friesland commanders did not have formal flag rank; when this was subsequently granted, Stellingwerf jumped to fourth place. The fifth was an all-Amsterdam squadron under the fiery young Amsterdam vice-admiral, Cornelis Tromp, the son of the great Maarten Tromp. Next came another ill-fitting Zeeland-Rotterdam combination, led by Vice-Admiral Cornelis Evertsen of Zeeland (Jan Evertsen's brother) – with a Noorderkwartier captain as rear-admiral. The last squadron consisted of the Noorderkwartier contingent under the Noorderkwartier vice-admiral, Volckert Schram.

The arrangment worked poorly because of the lack of a hierarchical chain of command. Obdam's squadron commanders all had the same level of responsibility, while the fourteen subsidiary flag-officers were entirely superfluous except as replacements for their chiefs. Even worse was the assignment of commanders to groups of ships from other Admiralties, whose captains they neither knew well nor trusted, and with whom they had no special bonds of loyalty. Since some captains were of questionable reliability from the outset, the weak organization was particularly ominous.

The order in which the squadrons were intended to fight is not very well documented. Wassenaer's squadron was to be in the centre and Cortenaer's in the van, with Tromp lying somewhere between them. Stellingwerf's squadron was to form the rear and Schram was to be between him and Obdam. Where the two Zeeland commanders belonged is not known; in the action Jan Evertsen lay towards the van and his brother Cornelis near the rear.

Individual ships were not assigned specific stations within their squadrons, for the Dutch had not yet adopted the line-ahead system. From the earliest times they had favoured boarding and mêlée actions. Such tactics demanded heavy concentrations of force at the points of attack, and in a large fleet an extended single-file line was incompatible with that requirement. Their preference for boarding came partly because it was what they did best, but also because artillery duels seemed somehow unsporting; one should, they felt, meet the enemy face to face. This is not to say that Dutch officers were unwilling to make use of the firepower advantages of the line when the situation called for it. If grappling was for some reason undesirable (as against shore fortifications or against opponents at sea too numerous or well-manned to be boarded) they had not hesitated to form line for gunnery. Some examples are Cornelis Jol against the Spanish silver fleet in 1638, Maarten Tromp's bombardment of Dunkirk in the same year, Tromp again in one stage of the Battle of the Downs in

1639, and Johan Lichthart versus the Portuguese at Tamandare in 1645. But barring special circumstances (and against the English there appeared to be none) the Dutch meant to fight in their traditional manner. In fact, the States-General made it a matter of law:

> The Lord Wassenaer and others of the Head Officers are to draw up and give orders for the chasing and attacking the enemy, either by laying aboard or entering or otherwise. Which said Boarding and Entering is most seriously recommended to them and to the respective Captains.

The Dutch formation was a column of distinctly separate groups, in each of which the ships gathered around their squadron commander in a compact mass. If the weather gage could be obtained, the fleet would draw up parallel to the enemy, and then all the squadrons would 'charge' simultaneously. The idea was for each group to gain a temporary local concentration over a few vessels which could be quickly carried by boarding. The initial advantage thereby won, a mêlée would ensue. If the enemy kept the weather gage, close bunching of ships was also felt to have defensive value since the assailants would find it difficult to cut off and isolate individual men-of-war. In all circumstances captains were expected to rush to the assistance of neighbours in distress, and any who failed to do so were to be 'punished without mercy'.

These were the doctrines that Maarten Tromp had developed in the First Anglo-Dutch War – and which had failed so wretchedly in the face of Monck's disciplined artillery pounding in 1653. The English introduction of the line, with its awesome offensive firepower and phalanx-like defensive order, instantly rendered Tromp's ideas obsolete. This fact had not penetrated to the Dutch commanders, much less to the armchair tacticians in The Hague. The débâcles of the Gabbard and Scheveningen had been universally attributed to inferior ships and cowardly captains, never tactics. The grappling ideal not only remained alive, but was actively promoted throughout Obdam's tenure. He undoubtedly felt comfortable with the principles of local concentration, mêlée action, and defensive clustering, which were all very much like his familiar cavalry tactics ashore. Indeed, squadrons were often spoken of as 'right wing' and 'left wing' rather than van and rear. Obdam had tested the group methods at the Battle of the Sound in 1658, and his partial success had given seamen and politicians alike renewed confidence in the system. Alas, their conclusions were deceptive, for the victory had been won over Swedish opponents who had fought in the very same way.

In the spring of 1665 the Dutch were in no condition to face the English. Their battle order was hopelessly unmanageable, their ships underarmed, the discipline of their captains uncertain, and the tactical ideas of their leaders fatally outmoded. Though the truth was realized by few, they were inferior in every respect save courage – and of that their opponents had an equal measure.

As the preparations drew to a close, all Europe looked on with macabre fascination. The war of words grew increasingly heated. For the ears of their wavering allies the Dutch denied all weaknesses, reporting that the English had '105 sail in all, among which are forty good vessels well mounted, but all the rest are small and there are more than thirty which do not carry more than twelve guns'. They insisted that Obdam had 'twelve ships which will make no difficulty about engaging *teste à teste* the greatest vessels of the English fleet', and that therefore the English would 'have at least half the fear'. Since the Duke of York had 'encouraged the rupture', the States publicly proclaimed that 'his flagship will be attacked, contrary to the laws of warfare on land, where the guns always respect the royal flag'. In England the talk was equally brave. Vice-Admiral Sir John Lawson declared himself 'so confident in the strength of the fleet' that he desired 'nothing from God but that He shall be neutral, to obtain victory over the Dutch'.

Chapter VI

Lowestoft

Victorious York did first, with fam'd success,
To his known valor make the Dutch give place:
Thus Heav'n our monarch's fortune did confess,
Beginning conquest from his royal race.

The English were the first at sea, but only because James tired of the delays and sailed on 20 April with victualling allowances half filled. As Coventry uncharitably put it, 'Mr. Gauden hath taken care wee shall not be able to stay long abroad'. The Dutch were not yet ready, and sure enough, dwindling supplies compelled the English to return to the Gunfleet after only three weeks. They brought nothing to show for their frustrating cruise except eight motley flyboats taken from a Bordeaux wine convoy. James's premature move temporarily left the Dutch the initiative. As soon as the English had gone, Obdam led his squadrons to the Dogger Bank and almost immediately had the good fortune to capture an important English convoy carrying naval stores from Hamburg. Consisting of nine merchantmen and the escorting hired man-of-war *Good Hope*, it mistook the Dutch fleet for the English and sailed right into it. Captain Anthony Archer of the *Good Hope* was said to have been 'so overtaken with drinck' that he was '2 hours aboard of the [Dutch] vice admirals ship before he knew wher he was'. The incident caused considerable consternation in England, but the admirals could only fume impotently at anchor while the victualler vainly struggled to make up the shortages. Replenishment was still incomplete when, on 29 May, authoritative intelligence was received from Holland that Obdam had 'orders to seek us out even to the mouth of the river of Thames'. At this James and his council-of-war prudently decided to move away from the shoals of the estuary, where the shallow-draught Dutch ships would have an advantage. The whole fleet including the storeships accordingly weighed the next day and sailed to the deep-water roadstead at Solebay a few miles south of Lowestoft.

On the morning of 1 June the English fleet lay in its new anchorage. A little before noon a London-bound collier convoy passed by offshore, upon which Captain Thomas Allin's *Plymouth* and James Lambert's *Happy Return* sailed out to press some of the colliermen, 'notwithstanding the Proclamation prohibiting it'. The *Plymouth* had chased some distance to sea when at 1 o'clock her men heard the boom of a cannon and noticed the *Happy Return* rushing towards them with her fore topgallant sheets loosed. This was the signal for 'enemy in sight'. Allin immediately had the *Plymouth* fire a gun as well and then stood into Solebay repeating Lambert's signal. By then the Dutch were visible as a forest of masts and sails on the horizon. In the anchorage Prince Rupert's *Royal James* quickly raised the alarm, and within an hour the whole array was under sail. For seaman Barlow it was an exciting moment. 'Our General firing a gun', he wrote, 'and making a sign that they saw them, the whole fleet presently weighed anchor, and making all things clear and ready and heaving all lumberment overboard to clear our decks and guns, so plied towards them, they being to windward of us'.

The adversaries were well matched in numbers. The Dutch had 107 men-of-war, of which 81 States' ships and eleven Indiamen were substantial vessels of more than 30 guns, nine were frigates of 24–30, and six were three-mast yachts of 14–21. There were in addition four lightly armed advice-yachts, eleven fireships, and twelve unarmed *galjoots*. Discounting fireships and small yachts, the fleet mounted 4,864 guns and was manned by slightly more than 21,500 seamen and marines. The English initially had only 95 ships, but five more joined after the action began. Of the 100 engaged, 64 men-of-war and 24 hired merchantmen were 'ships of force' of 30 guns or more, ten were fifth-rate frigates of 24–30, and two were sixth-rates of 12–14. There were also four 8-gun ketches, five fireships, and an indeterminate number of unarmed ketches, hoys, and smacks. Again discounting ketches and fireships (averaging about 8 guns and 40 men each), the fleet had a nominal strength of 4,542 guns and 22,055 men. These figures were somewhat understated. The English did not count guns smaller than 4-pounder minions (though the Dutch did) and the complements did not include the many supernumeraries known to have been embarked. The adjusted strength would have been approximately 4,800 guns and over 24,000 men.

The apparent equality of force was in fact deceptive. More meaningful than numbers was the size of the guns and the weight of the shot they could throw, and in that the Dutch suffered a crushing handicap. Adjusting for the different national weight standards of the time, the English had twenty-seven ships capable of firing over a thousand pounds of shot, the Dutch only one. That was Obdam's own *Eendracht*, on which no expense had been spared; but at least seven of the English ships were better armed than she, and Sandwich's *Prince* by half again. Overall, the English had a firepower superiority of some twenty per cent.

As the fleets drew up, the weather was fair and the breeze E.N.E., which was the direction from which the Dutch approached. The English emerged from their anchorage close-hauled to the S.E., the best heading they could make to close the range. At 4 o'clock the tide changed, and Penn anchored to allow the Dutch to come down on the flood. To everyone's surprise, Obdam declined the invitation; despite both wind and current at his back, he anchored as well. When the ebb began around 10 p.m. the English weighed and beat into the darkness to reach the position the Dutch had last occupied, but in the morning Obdam bore nine miles to the E.S.E. The wind on the 2nd continued to favour the Hollanders. During the day it gradually veered from E.N.E. to east to E.S.E., yet Obdam stubbornly refused to attack, remaining close-hauled and working farther out to sea. Just before sunset the tables turned. The wind swung south and then S.W., giving the English the weather gage.

Obdam's hesitation to take the offensive when he had the opportunity mystified his opponents. Dutch tactics were certainly more effective in attack than in defence, particularly in view of their preponderance of fireships, so it seemed that Obdam had thrown away his best chance for victory. Most of the English would have agreed with seaman Barlow: 'They loved not to fight too near our shore lest they should have too far to run home if they should be beaten, and we the less chase after them'. Dutch officers were equally perplexed; one of their captains wrote that 'God Almighty took away our admiral's brains, or else He never gave him any'. But neither of these often-quoted assessments was fair. Obdam was no fool, and he had not come to the English shore for a social call. He most assuredly meant to fight, hopefully from windward; but not with the easterly breeze barring his line of retreat. It appears that he intended to wait until the wind came south or north, then manoeuvre for the weather gage, attack, and hope for the best; if the worst happened he could still run for it. After all, a single victory would not win the war, and a single reverse would not lose it – unless an east wind trapped his defeated fleet on the field of battle, in which case *everything* could be lost. Obdam's much maligned delay was a gamble which did not pay off on the day of battle, but in the long run it may have saved his country from ruin.

During the night of the 2nd both fleets sailed close-hauled to the westward, the English wishing the breeze would swing more westerly, the Dutch that it would hold southerly. A little before sunset a Dutch ship caught fire and burned all night. The English optimistically identified it as a flagship, but it turned out to have been a fireship which was set ablaze 'by the imprudence of him that commanded it, who was got drunk'. On the morning of 3 June, the fleets were about forty miles southeast of Lowestoft, the Dutch lying E.S.E. of the English. The wind, 'a fine chasing gale', lay between S.W. and S.S.W., favouring the English but not by much. Just before dawn, at about 4 o'clock, Obdam made a sudden dash for the weather gage. Straining as close to the wind as their ships could lie, the Dutch crowded sail with their heads to the west in hopes of passing to the south of their enemy. The English instantly tacked to the southeast to foil the attempt, Vice-Admiral Christopher Myngs resolutely leading the way in the *Triumph*. The heads of the two fleets were on collision courses, the red lions on the beaks of the Dutch ships glaring balefully at the golden lions of the English. Flags and pendants fluttering, drums rumbling, trumpets shrieking, men cheering to hide their fears, the fleets rushed together. The English won the race for the weather gage. Myngs cut across the bows of the Dutch; the red 'bloody flag' broke out at the foretop of the *Royal Charles* – the signal to engage – and the broadside of the *Triumph* crashed out. The Battle of Lowestoft had begun.

After the initial contact the fleets swept majestically past each other on opposite tacks. Because the Dutch were initially sailing westward and their opponents southeasterly, Myngs presumably altered course to the east to keep in range. This produced a bow in the line and explains why it was afterwards reported that the English were 'drawn up in the formation of a half-moon'. The leading Dutch ships – Cortenaer's *Groot Hollandia* was the first – were forced by the English line to steer northwest, so that the initial encounter was fought in a vast arc. 'Both fleets', wrote Sandwich, 'passed their broadsides as they crossed one by the other, we to windward of the enemy. In which pass some hurt was done, but not much, neither did the ships pass at a very near distance'.

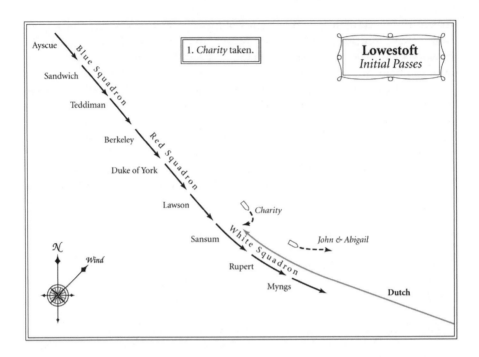

Obdam's sudden lunge surprised his own fleet as much as the enemy's. Flag-officers were not with their squadrons, the squadrons never properly formed, and leaderless ships simply milled in the stream 'in the last stages of confusion'. The English were much better sorted, but Sandwich nevertheless grumped that

> Whereas our order of battle was a line, that so every ship might have his part in fighting and be clear of his friends from doing them damage, yet many of our ships did not (even in this first pass) observe it, but luffed up to windward, that we were in ranks 3, 4 or 5 broad, and divers out of reach of the enemy fired over us and several into us and did us hurt.

Other ships were out of place to leeward. When the Dutch swerved to the northwest they weathered the hired merchantman *John & Abigail* and the 46-gun fourth-rate *Great Charity*. These two were beyond the help of their friends, and their fortunes made, said Barlow, 'the best sport' of the first pass. Perhaps to the surprise of the Duke of York, it was the merchant captain who kept his wits, and the King's captain who lost them. Joseph Sanders coolly kept his *John & Abigail* to leeward on the starboard tack; though given up for lost and 'much paid with their broadsides', she eventually passed to the rear of the Dutch and emerged safe and sound. Robert Wilkinson of the *Charity* foolishly tacked and threw his ship squarely in the path of the enemy. Trapped and alone, Wilkinson made a spirited defence, but nothing could undo his mistake; after enduring close-range broadsides from numerous opponents, the ship was finally boarded and carried by Jan de Haan's 56-gun *Stad en Lande* of

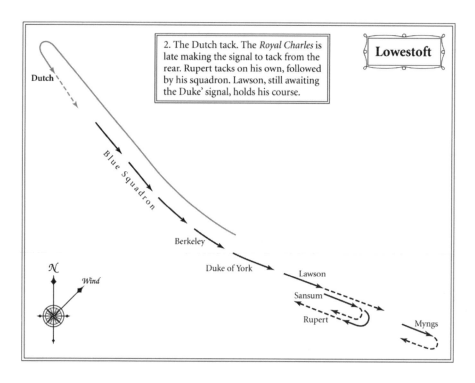

2. The Dutch tack. The *Royal Charles* is late making the signal to tack from the rear. Rupert tacks on his own, followed by his squadron. Lawson, still awaiting the Duke' signal, holds his course.

Lowestoft

Dutch

Blue Squadron

Berkeley

Duke of York

Lawson

Sansum

Rupert

Myngs

𝒩

Wind

Tromp's squadron. As de Haan led his prize to the Texel the *Charity*'s seamen (of whom many were Channel Islanders) proved so recalcitrant that the Dutch herded forty of them into the longboat, 'wounded and well alike', and left them without oars in the middle of the North Sea; they were later rescued by an English vessel. Seventy others, more than a third of the crew, had been killed in the fight. A merchant who saw the *Charity* at the Texel said 'that he never saw any ship so battered and torne, being as full of holes as a hony comb, and the whole ship within bespattered with blood'. She was originally a Dutch ship named *Liefde* taken in 1653. Her loss caused slight discouragement to the English, Barlow casually writing her off as 'old and rotten, and worth little'.

All sources agree that the first pass was otherwise fought at long range 'to little or no purpose'. When the van of each fleet drew clear of the other's rear, the leading ships and groups tacked to converge again for a second 'bout'. On the English side the operation of coming about did not go smoothly. Penn intended the fleet to tack from the rear according to the newly inserted article in the Fighting Instructions. Unfortunately, as James afterwards explained, 'the sailor, who had got up the mast to give the signal, was so long about it, that before he could let the flag fly, Obdam had, with the van, bore up round, ship after ship, and brought his starboard tacks on board'. Prince Rupert observed all this from a litter suspended on his quarterdeck, having been ill for some weeks. Realizing that something was wrong, he acted on his own without waiting for a signal from the flagship. In Sandwich's words,

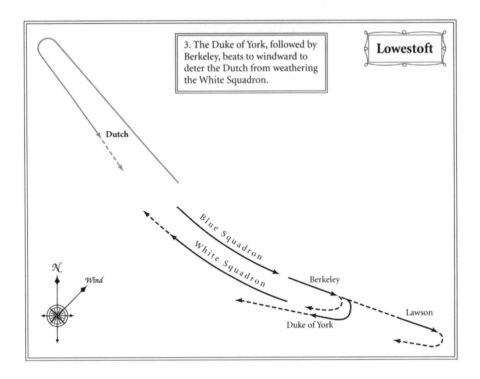

3. The Duke of York, followed by Berkeley, beats to windward to deter the Dutch from weathering the White Squadron.

Lowestoft

Prince Rupert very bravely after the enemy's fleet was passed by him tacked after them and was himself the headmost ship (his sails and hull was much torn the first pass). This was about 6 o'clock in the morning about which time there was an intermission of shooting near an hour, until Prince Rupert came up with Obdam's ship, who had now tacked upon us again with his head to the South-Eastward.

When Penn saw what Rupert was doing he quickly cancelled the original orders. Even so, there was further confusion, for when the White Squadron came about and headed back up the line, the Red Squadron's leading division under Sir John Lawson did not follow. Lawson was presumably expecting the rest of the fleet to begin tacking from the rear at any moment; but the signal (a Union flag at the mizzen) would not have been easily visible from ahead, so he might not have known whether it was flying or not. Whatever the reason, he made a potentially ruinous mistake in not conforming when Rupert tacked from the van. This was probably what Sandwich meant when he later told Pepys 'how poorly Sir John Lawson performed, notwithstanding all that was said of him'. The result of the mix-up was a rapidly widening gap in the wake of the White Squadron. If Obdam steered for that huge expanse of open water, he would divide the English fleet leaving his own to windward of the greater part. Strangely, James and Penn do not seem to have recognized this possibility, though Sandwich certainly did. According to the reports from those aboard the *Royal Charles*, the only fear was that the initial delay in tacking would give Obdam an opportunity to weather Prince Rupert and thereby get to windward of the whole fleet. Fortunately for the

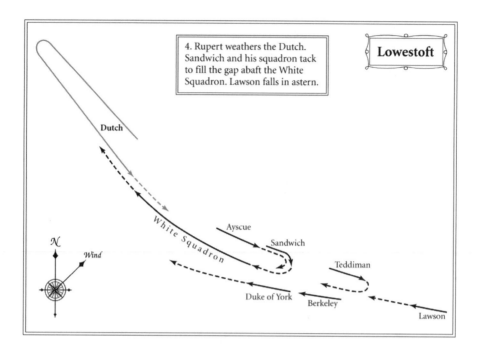

4. Rupert weathers the Dutch. Sandwich and his squadron tack to fill the gap abaft the White Squadron. Lawson falls in astern.

Lowestoft

English, Penn's remedy forestalled both dangers. In a daring move that few commanders of later eras would have attempted, he deliberately hauled the *Royal Charles* out of line, signalled Sandwich and the other ships to do the same, and beat far to the westward across the wake of the White Squadron. There he formed a second line, so that if the Dutch did weather Rupert they would find other English ships still to windward. As Coventry related, it appeared to achieve its object:

> Upon this tack the Dutch endeavoured to get the wind of us, which they hoped to have done; which His Royal Highness foreseeing they would endeavour, kept so close to the wind, that when the Dutch tacked, hoping to weather Prince Rupert, they found H.R.H. to weather them; and therefore, rather than pass between two lines of our fleet, they chose to bear to leeward of Prince Rupert.

Whether the Dutch passed to leeward of the White because of Penn's action is open to doubt. It is at least as likely that they were simply unable to work far enough to windward, or that Obdam had already decided to try to split the English by sailing into the gap astern of Rupert's squadron. That possibility was undoubtedly what worried Sandwich; by his description,

> His Royal Highness suspecting the enemy would weather our fleet, if we stood on and tacked in our proper berths to make good the line (though himself was in the middle of the fleet) tacked after the enemy and kept his luff all he could and commanded me to tack, which I did instantly (though in a great crowd of ships and not without danger of being entangled with them) and stood after the Duke within

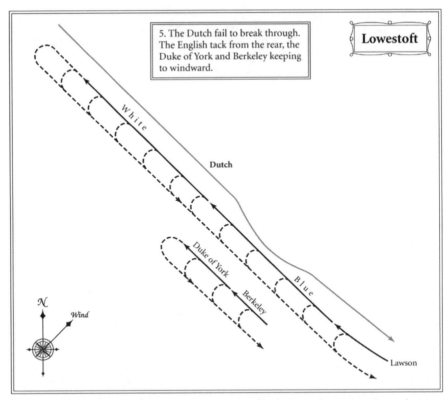

5. The Dutch fail to break through. The English tack from the rear, the Duke of York and Berkeley keeping to windward.

Lowestoft

one ship of him. The enemy, though designed to break through us upon this tack, yet by our timely tacking we had preserved our advantage and they not able to perform their intention.

It is clear from the subsequent positions of the squadrons that the Blue did not go as far to windward as James and Penn, but instead fell in immediately astern of the White. By Sandwich's presence of mind the leewardmost of the English lines again formed a continuous if somewhat disordered array. The White Squadron led, with Lawson's division of the Red now in the rear; in between lay Sandwich's squadron, the other two divisions of the Red lying parallel to the Blue and some distance to the west. When the manoeuvre was completed the vans were already exchanging broadsides to begin the second encounter. The English were on the port tack to the northwest, still to windward, their enemy on the opposite course. The fighting in this pass was at closer range than before. As Sandwich expected, Obdam made determined efforts to smash through and gain the wind, and several vessels succeeded in penetrating the English line. As a Dutch account admitted, these ships were turned back by the presence of the Red divisions to windward of the Blue: 'Because the Duke of York's squadron kept the Weather gage without engaging in Fight, it was impossible for the Dutch to win that Advantage'. Sandwich too referred to this incident, giving details of the action when the Dutch broke through:

Some of them, viz. Tromp and Evertsen (as Evertsen's own letter says) passed very near my ship between me and the Montagu and another frigate. They wounded me my master and divers others with musket shot, sorely paid my fireship, whom I commanded to lay one of them on board, which he bravely attempted and was within his ship's length of him, when his main topmast was shot by the board, 5 men killed and wounded upon the deck, torn sadly in the hull and the man at the helm killed, which made the ship sheer another way.

The brave fireship captain was Richard Cotton of the *Bryar*.

A few of the Dutch did gain the wind one way or another, for observers in the *Royal Charles* noticed a great Zeelander estimated at 'above eighty guns' and two smaller vessels to the west of both English lines. The English incorrectly assumed that they were late 'recruits' for the Dutch fleet brought out by Cornelis Evertsen the Youngest ('Devil Evertsen', the son of Vice-Admiral Cornelis Evertsen) who had been captured in a single-ship action earlier in the year but later exchanged. Cornelis the Youngest was in fact serving as his father's flag-captain. The only Zeeland ship within twenty guns of the reported force was the huge 76-gun East Indiaman *Oranje* (known to the English as the phonetically rendered *Urania*) commanded by Captain Bastiaan Senten. Whoever it was, he and his followers resolutely fell in amongst the two windward divisions of the Red. The Duke of York recorded that the big Zeelander attacked Allin's *Plymouth*, the two being 'so near that the yard-arms of both Ships touch'd'. Following an exchange of heavy broadsides the unsupported Dutch vessels eventually fought through the English fleet and rejoined their own.

After the Dutch failed to win the weather gage, the opponents continued to file past each other. As the fleets drew abreast, James and Penn again resolved to tack from the rear. Waiting until the Dutch van was opposite the English rear, the *Royal Charles* broke out the Union at the mizzen, this time promptly. As required by the Fighting Instructions, each flag-officer repeated the signal until the last ship in the line became aware of it and tacked, whereupon all the rest did the same more or less simultaneously. It was a complex operation requiring careful timing under the best of circumstances; in the smoke and confusion of battle it must have been a nightmare, with captains cursing, some ships tacking, others bearing up, some missing the signal entirely, all desperately trying to keep out of each others' way, and the broadsides never ceasing. Somehow it was accomplished; almost certainly the only time a whole fleet ever attempted it while under fire.

The English order was now reversed. 'Sir John Lawson', said Sandwich, 'then was the headmost ship of our fleet and with him some others and then my ship and squadron, the Duke making sail to run ahead of us, Prince Rupert and his squadron in the rear'. The reversal prevented the Dutch from tacking, so the fleets lay side by side, heads to the southeast. The first passes had cost the English the *Charity*, and the Dutch had lost two lieutenant-admirals. Auke Stellingwerf of Friesland had been cut in two by a cannonball, and Egbert Cortenaer of the Maas ('one of the best men they have' according to an English intelligence report) lay dying from a roundshot wound in the thigh. Otherwise casualties and damage had been generally light. But now the fighting began in earnest, for Penn had adroitly brought the English fleet into the attitude he wanted: to windward of the Dutch and alongside them on the same tack, the situation which had produced victory at the Gabbard. The lee position made it difficult for the Dutch to close for boarding, kept them from using their fireships, and limited their manoeuvres. The common heading had significant implications for gunnery. Instead of facing enemies which flitted past the gunports at a relative rate of ten or twelve knots, as they had in the two head-on passes, gunners could now aim carefully at targets of nearly constant bearing and range. The improved accuracy would increase the dominance of the heavier English guns.

Beginning at 8 o'clock, the cannonade rose in intensity; the opponents 'knocked it out' for eight hours without pause, 'sometimes at great distance and sometimes fair by'. Diagrams and dry discussions of tactics can give no hint of the confusion and horror of a great sea-fight. Captain Thomas Cubitt's description of the apocalyptic last pass at Scheveningen would have applied as well to Lowestoft: 'The very heavens were obscured by smoke, the air rent with the thundering noise, the sea all in a breach with the shot that fell, the ships even trembling, and we hearing everywhere the messengers of death flying'. The sound of the battle carried remarkably, shaking windows in Deal and Dunkirk and clearly audible in London. John Evelyn, in charge of wounded and prisoners, heard the noise at Rochester and told his surgeons and warders to make ready. For the grimy, sweating gunners serving the guns in the semi-darkness of the lower decks off Lowestoft, the roar of the guns was made even more terrifying by the hissing of shot, the shattering of wood, and the screams of the injured. When the range closed, muskets crackled. Dutch marines fired through loopholed wooden bulwarks, while the English crouched behind more sensible splinterproof canvas 'fights'.

In the *Royal Charles* there was one rather unlikely musketeer. It was the condemned Captain Nixon, still alive through a series of odd coincidences. At the time appointed for his execution a violent storm had arisen which lasted for two days, causing a postponement. This brought him additional grace, for the following day was a Sunday, and Monday was the King's birthday. Then on Tuesday and Wednesday the fleet was under sail in dense fog. On Thursday the weather was at last suitable for a public execution, and Nixon's time seemed to have run out. But that afternoon the Dutch were sighted, at which he begged the Duke to allow him to redeem himself in combat. James responded by giving him a musket, saying that

> while it is true that captains of the British crown are obliged to resist several enemies, he was satisfied, as a first example to spare his life, allowing him to pass the rest of his life in the royal service as a soldier, seeing that he had not the courage to fight more than one, when it was his duty to encourage and command others.

Whether or not Nixon survived is not recorded.

All reports of this stage of the battle are fragmentary; in the thick clouds of smoke no one could see clearly what was happening. The Dutch were in disarray from the start, and it is impossible to say with confidence where the various squadrons and flag-officers were engaged. It appears that Cortenaer's ships were matched against Lawson in the van, followed by Jan Evertsen and Obdam a little farther north. Ships under Tromp and Cornelis Evertsen were mostly in the centre and rear, while Schram's and Stellingwerf's squadrons seem to have been badly scattered. Sometime during this period the English received two separate small reinforcements. The fourth-rate *Amity* and two smaller frigates joined from Lowestoft, and from Harwich came the fourth-rate *Leopard* under Captain Richard Beach and the hired *Katherine*. Beach made a dramatic entry. Rather than search out his formal station, he simply 'ran into the thickest of the fight, and for an hour could not be seen for smoke'.

Around midday a minor crisis developed among the English when the headmost ship, Lawson's *Royal Oak*, luffed out of her station and crawled away to windward, 'which was universally wondered at and an opinion conceived that Sir John Lawson must be killed'. Lawson himself soon cleared up the situation by sending word to the flagship that he was 'sorely hurt' in the knee 'and his master killed also and the ship in some disorder for want of government'. Penn instantly drew the Duke's attention to the second-rate *St. George*, whose commander was his friend and former Commonwealth flag-officer Joseph Jordan. The *St. George* was lying disabled with sixty-two casualties; cartridges staged in her roundhouse had exploded, blowing away much of her stern. James accordingly ordered Jordan to take over Lawson's ship and lead the division. Quickly restoring discipline in the *Royal Oak*, Jordan 'ran in again very gallantly' and 'did brave things in her'.

Through most of the long artillery duel the Red Squadron's centre division and the rear division under Berkeley remained well to windward, to all intents and purposes out of the fight. Their sheltered position later led to some resentment from those more closely engaged. Berkeley was openly called a coward and Sandwich did not exaggerate when he privately told Pepys 'that the most the Duke did was almost out of gunshot'. Allin, one of James's captains, wrote of this stage that they 'fought very far off, that few shot reached, and those laid at random'. That these ships were so long out of action at first seems hardly credible; but their inaction is confirmed by James's own account, in which he blamed it on the seaman who spoiled the signal to tack from the rear at the end of the first pass. 'This little accident', he said, 'lost above six hours'. That gives an acceptable explanation for why they went to windward in the first place, but not why they stayed there. The story did not escape the vigilant pen of satirist Andrew Marvell. Under the pseudonym of a well-known lunatic, he published a vicious poetic attack on the fleet's commanders. After describing various fanciful means by which James's entourage might have kept themselves safe (including a diving bell suspended under the ship), Marvell wrote, '*But these the Duke rejected, only chose / To keep far off, and others interpose*'.

Coventry afterwards went to some pains to justify his master's lengthy idleness on the grounds of ensuring the weather gage:

His Royal Highness, who had observed in the beginning of the battle the endeavour of the Dutch to gain the wind, and by what means it was prevented, and also the great benefit we had by it, by securing us against the enemies' fireships, (in which they had placed a great part of their hopes), had always a regard to keeping that advantage which God had so favourably given us.

He found another, less convincing, excuse in Lawson's disablement:

> The continual smoke would not give us leave to see very far before us what the enemy
> did; and therefore the actions of others were in some measure to be the guide even
> to the admiral. H.R.H., therefore, having seen Sir John Lawson, with his accustomed
> valour, bear in towards the enemies' line, but soon after to edge off again to windward,
> concluded that Sir J. Lawson had seen some of the enemies' ships endeavouring to get
> the wind of us; and therefore, to prevent that, H.R.H. kept near the wind, which was
> a guide to the whole fleet.

From James's position to windward, in fact well clear of the smoke, he would have had
a good view of any Dutch ships reaching ahead of Lawson. There was, however, a
further explanation; one that might not have met the full approval of the public, but
tactically sound nevertheless. It may be that Penn, finding the two divisions fortuitously
positioned to give support anywhere along the line, deliberately held them back as a
reserve similar to what Sandwich had recommended for the hired merchantmen. This
would have had the unspoken advantage, perhaps discreetly whispered by the members
of the Duke's household, of preserving James's irreplaceable person from harm until the
last possible moment. At any rate, most of the Red Squadron certainly functioned as a
reserve, whether intentionally or otherwise.

In the temporary absence of so many English ships the Dutch held their own
throughout the morning, maintaining particularly heavy pressure against the Blue
Squadron. James and Penn kept a close watch on this part of the line, and a little before
noon they began to feed in reinforcements. One of the first was Allin of the *Plymouth*:

> His Highness sent me word to stand in and I presently stood in so near as not to
> shoot in vain and plied my guns very hard for 2 hours upon General Obdam, and
> another Flag-man and 2 ships lying on a line and a Vice Admiral and 4 more, 9 in all,
> but they paid me handsomely. I lost 4 good seamen and had six sorely wounded. My
> masts, yard, sail and hull very much torn and rigging ropes. And setting my mainsail
> to stretch ahead from the flagships came two new frigates or scouts fresh upon me.
> I was forced to take and receive all to get off, but paid the biggest frigate soundly.
> I went and mended what I could, but it was late, 3 oclock, before I was fit to fight.

The battle in the centre raged fiercely around the flagships. Sandwich reported that
'about 2 oclock in the afternoon Obdam and the *Oranje* and 3 or 4 more great ships
plied me hotly for 2 hours together'. Henry Fenne of the *Montagu* tried to relieve him
by taking on the *Oranje*, but Captain Bastiaan Senten crashed the giant merchantman
into Fenne's ship and sent his marines and seamen swarming over the gunwales. With
pistols, pikes, and cutlasses they hacked their way across the *Montagu*'s deck and drove
the Englishmen below. At that point, with Sandwich and his seconds in obvious distress,
James and Penn threw their full weight into the fight. The Earl of Marlborough in the
Old James made for Fenne's ship. Loosing his broadside into the *Oranje*, he forced
Senten to call back his boarders and haul away from the *Montagu*. At the same time the
Royal Charles and others rushed up to rescue the *Prince*. 'His Royal Highness', said
Sandwich, 'stretched it out ahead of me and most bravely himself entertained Obdam'.

With James and Berkeley entering the action the Blue Squadron was given a breathing space. In that interval the Earl of Sandwich observed that the Dutch fleet was in confusion and disorder. Far to the north, Prince Rupert reached the same conclusion. Acting independently, both simultaneously initiated what turned out to be the decisive moves of the day. By Sandwich's account,

> When his Royal Highness began the aforesaid close engagement, at the same time I let fall my mainsail and bore up upon the enemy (putting abroad my blue flag upon the mizzen peak, a sign for my squadron to follow me) and we pressed sore upon them . . . At the same time when I bore up, Prince Rupert and his squadron very bravely fell in upon the enemy.

Sandwich deliberately broke through the Dutch centre. Some ships gave way before him, but others more resolute luffed up to block his path; four of them (all from different squadrons) ran together and became entangled, 'into whom we poured our broadsides as we passed by and left them to the mercy of that part of our fleet that followed us'. In the rear, said Sandwich, the Dutch 'endeavored to have clapped by a wind the other way' in a desperate effort to weather the White Squadron, but Rupert matched them tack for tack and they could not evade his onslaught.

As these attacks developed, momentous events occurred near the van. There, the Duke of York headed for the *Eendracht* to 'have a bout with Obdam'. The two flagships drew near and greeted each other with thundering broadsides. It was a short, savage contest. A chain shot scythed across the quarterdeck of the *Royal Charles* and struck down at one blow the Earl of Falmouth (Lord Fitzharding, brother of Rear-Admiral Berkeley), Lord Muskerry, and Richard Boyle (son of the Earl of Burlington). These young gentlemen had been standing in a group next to the Duke; they were hurled across the deck, killed instantly, and James was splattered with gore and cut in the hand by a flying skull fragment. The unfortunate Falmouth, a confidant of the King, was an ambitious but untalented courtier. His sudden death evoked a brutal and unsympathetic epitaph from Andrew Marvell:

> *Falmouth was there, I know not what to act*
> *(Some say 'twas to grow Duke too by Contact).*
> *An untaught Bullet in its wanton Scope*
> *Quashes him all to pieces, and his Hope*
> *Such as his Rise such was his Fall, unprais'd:*
> *A Chance-shot sooner took than Chance him rais'd:*
> *His Shatterd Head the fearlesse Duke distains,*
> *And gave the last first proof that he had Brains.*

The scene in the *Eendracht* was equally gruesome; men fell by the dozen at every broadside. Wassenaer van Obdam, a victim of gout, directed the action from a chair on the poop. Wounded by a musket shot, he refused to leave the deck, and soon afterwards the commander-in-chief of the States' Fleet was literally 'carried away by a cannon ball from the royal flagship'. His followers had little time to grieve; minutes later, with no warning, the *Eendracht's* magazine detonated with a cataclysmic blast that broke windows in Dunkirk and was heard as far as The Hague. The ship disintegrated. Her sides blew out, masts crashing down in an awesome ball of fire, and only five men were saved out of 409 aboard. The cause of the disaster was never established. A ship's magazine was so far beneath the waterline that it was practically impossible for an enemy shot to reach it, so treachery was suspected. Some said that a disgruntled servant of Obdam's touched it off in revenge, another that it was 'an Englishman who had got on board, who was observed to throw himself into the sea without necessity, that is after, it is supposed, he had set the match lighted for this purpose'. A more likely cause was some accident among the powder handlers.

The explosion occurred while the Blue and White Squadrons were pressing home their attacks. It had a devastating effect on the already disordered Dutch, and their clumsy chain of command completed their confusion. Next in seniority after Obdam was Jan Evertsen, a Zeelander and therefore mistrusted by the political leaders of the Province of Holland. To prevent him from gaining command the Hollanders had forced a decree through the States-General naming Egbert Cortenaer of the Maas as Obdam's designated successor. But Cortenaer had been gasping in agony in the cockpit of the *Groot Hollandia* ever since the first pass; his flag-captain, Ate Stinstra, had nevertheless kept the admiral's flag flying all day without informing the other commanders. And Stinstra chose this moment to panic. His nerves shattered by the loss of the *Eendracht*, he put before the wind in headlong flight with many nearby ships following. Other officers could only assume that Cortenaer had unaccountably abdicated his responsibilities; taking matters into his own hands, Jan Evertsen boldly raised the pendant of command to the main beneath his flag. Cornelis Tromp of Amsterdam, however, would not accept the Zeelander's authority, and he too hoisted the pendant. Thus, in their hour of greatest distress the Dutch captains had to choose among three flagships; most chose the *Groot Hollandia*.

By then it made little difference, for Sandwich and Rupert were rampaging unchecked, spewing death and destruction. As Barlow quaintly expressed it, the Dutch 'began to turn their arses and run . . . with the English fleet firing at their breach'. Tromp and Evertsen valiantly rallied what ships they could, but the stampede could not be stemmed. In the rear, Prince Rupert 'made them downright bear up before the wind and run with studding sails, cutting off their boats and using all advantages of flight'. The White and Blue Squadrons sailing abreast of each other about nine miles apart pursued relentlessly.

Far to the south, Berkeley belied the charge of cowardice by chasing nine Dutch ships (possibly Cortenaer's) with six of his own. But most of the Red Squadron and Teddiman's division of the Blue were prevented from joining the pursuit largely by the noble heroics of a single Dutch vessel. It was the *Oranje*, seemingly everywhere. After the *Eendracht* blew up, Bastiaan Senten resolved to take on the *Royal Charles* himself. The great Indiaman approached with her guns quiet, holding her fire to the last moment. Mistaking her silence, the inexperienced gentlemen near the Duke cried excitedly that she was a fireship; but James, who had watched this ship with admiration all day long, gravely responded that 'they would quickly find their mistake, by the broadside she was preparing to give them'. Seconds later the *Oranje* spoke with an angry roar, and amid storms of shot and showers of splinters the two ships ground together. The English flagship was in imminent danger of being boarded, 'and actually was so by some desperate fellows who were killed in the attempt', according to one account 'by his Highness's own hand'. Senten had little chance to press his attack. Another ship of James's division, the third-rate *Mary* under Captain Jeremy Smith, had accompanied the *Royal Charles* into action. She bore in to fall upon the *Oranje*, and Senten sheered off to deal with his new assailant. Like Fenne before him, Smith found that he had a tiger by the tail. The *Mary* lost ninety-nine men in an hour, all her standing officers being killed except the master who lost a leg. Other English ships soon came up; Rear-Admiral of the Blue Thomas Teddiman joined in with the new second-rate *Royal Katherine*, as did Jordan in the *Royal Oak* and Teddiman's second, Richard Utber in the third-rate *Essex*. With the *Mary* clinging grimly to one side, the *Oranje* drove off opponent after opponent from the other, while Senten stomped about the poop, 'brandishing a two handed broad-sword'. Despite his obstinate defence, the beleaguered merchantman had not been designed to take such punishment; bit by bit she was torn to pieces. At length, with 'abundance of her men killed and the ship scarce able to swim', she yielded to the hardly less shattered *Mary*. This amazing duel awed even Marvell:

> The Dutch Urania *carelesse at us saild,*
> *And promises to do what Opdam faild.*
> *Smith to the Duke does intercept her Way*
> *And cleaves t' her closer than the Remora.*
> *The Captaine wonder'd, and withall disdain'd*
> *So strongly by a thing so small detain'd:*
> *And in a raging Brav'ry to him runs.*
> *They stab their Ships with one anothers Guns,*
> *They fight so near it seems to be on Ground,*
> *And ev'n the Bullets meeting bullets wound.*
> *The Noise, the Smoak, the Sweat, the Fire, the Blood*
> *is not to be exprest nor understood.*
> *Each Captaine from the Quarter-deck commands,*
> *They wave their bright Swords glitt'ring in their hands,*
> *All Luxury of Warre, all Man can do*
> *In a Sea-fight, did passe betwixt them two.*
> *But one must conquer whosoever fight;*
> *Smith took the Giant, and is since made Knight.*

As the *Oranje* was ruined beyond repair the English took out the survivors and set her afire. Bastiaan Senten, terribly wounded, was sent aboard the *Royal Charles*, where he irately condemned his fellow captains 'for having not seconded him according to an oath they had taken on board their admiral the day before'. The brave Senten died a half-hour later, 'to the great trouble of the Duke, who gave him a great testimony for a very gallant man, and much desired to preserve him'. He was said to have been an expatriate Scot.

Senten's sacrifice bought Jan Evertsen enough time to gather a few ships together to cover the flight of the Dutch van. Evertsen stood his ground against much of the Red Squadron for as long as he dared; but when the capture of the *Oranje* finally released so many other English ships, he could only fall back. All the Dutch were now in retreat, the English following. At 6 o'clock the Blue Squadron encountered the 78-gun Indiaman *Maarseveen* (the biggest ship in the Dutch fleet), the 46-gun *Ter Goes*, and the 30-gun *Zwanenburg*, all of which had luffed up to make a stand. Sandwich engaged the *Maarseveen*,

> and after some dispute made him bear up round and so sheer aboard his two consorts, and being fast together and well paid they struck their colours unto me and gave over shooting; but I left them to the ships in the rear who might have preserved and secured them, but one Gregory in a fireship of Prince Rupert's squadron went and set fire on them and they were all destroyed but 100 saved in a boat and some few taken up out of the water. This cruel fact was much detested by us as not beseeming Christians and his Royal Highness ordered the Judge Advocate to examine the matter, in order to have the judgement of a Court Martial thereupon.

With this tragic mistake Captain Gregory instantly went from hero to goat. Only minutes before, his little *Dolphin* had attacked and captured the 18-gun yacht *Ruyter*. Having no illusions on his chances before a court-martial, he prudently fled after the battle and was not heard from again.

When the Red Squadron entered the chase, the *Royal Charles* soon came upon the four ships which had run together when the Blue Squadron broke through. One was the 56-gun *Koevorden* under Gilles Thijssen Campen, Tromp's vice-admiral; the others were the *Prins Maurits*, 53, the *Elf Steden*, 54, and the *Stad Utrecht*, 48. As Sandwich related,

> His Royal Highness (as I am told) ordered a fireship to burn them if they would not yield, which was presently put into execution and all destroyed, not above 100 men saved, that were taken out of the sea by our ships' boats as they passed by. Here happened a strange accident, one of the 4 ships burning, when her powder took fire, blew up, and that same force struck away the mast and rigging of one of the rest (of about 40 guns). The hull of which ship not being much possessed by the fire, the men extinguished it and sheered off their ship and were towed away by another ship of theirs after our whole fleet had passed by. But whether the ship was towed into harbor or not, we know not.

The lucky vessel was the *Elf Steden* of Friesland under Captain Tjerk Hiddes de Vries, and she did indeed make it home. The fireship responsible for all this destruction was the *Fame* commanded by John Gethings, who was richly rewarded.

The Dutch were now approaching total disintegration. Sandwich had divided them in the middle, so the separate bodies of their fleet had to run for different ports. Tromp and Cornelis Evertsen retreated to the Texel before Rupert; Jan Evertsen sailed for the Maas with the rest of the English close astern, and still others made for the Scheldt. To this point Penn, Sandwich, and Rupert had directed the battle with admirable skill and resourcefulness, but the pursuit was not carried out with equal vigour. In the course of the evening one or two Dutch ships too damaged to keep up with the others were overtaken and captured. The English commanders, however, were for some reason unwilling to order the all-out general chase that might have brought the rest to heel. At about 9 o'clock Sandwich actually shortened sail to allow the Duke to come up and personally take the lead. This lost valuable distance, but was perhaps necessary in such protocol-conscious times.

A greater mistake – deliberate and reprehensible – was committed during the night by Henry Brouncker, master of the Duke's bedchamber and brother to Lord Brouncker of the Navy Board. This gentleman, 'who with wonderful confusion had sustained the terror of the day, resolved to prevent the like on the day succeeding'. When the weary Duke had gone to sleep Brouncker approached Penn and, reminding him of the consequences should the heir to the throne be lost, beseeched him 'to slacken the sails, that the Dutch might get what ground they could, to avoid a further encounter'. Penn indignantly replied that 'he durst give no such orders, except he had a mind to be hanged, for the Duke had himself given positive charge to the contrary'. But Brouncker was not to be denied. He waited until Penn had gone below and then took his request to John Harman, the ship's captain. This time he pretended that the orders were James's own, and after some protest Harman reluctantly obeyed. As the other ships were keeping station on the *Royal Charles*'s lantern, they too shortened sail, allowing the Dutch to pull far ahead. The Duke eventually learned that the courtier had acted on a promise to the Duchess to keep her husband safe. Since Brouncker was one of her favourites no immediate harm came to him, but when the story came out in the Parliamentary inquiry after the war, he had to flee for his life.

On the morning of the 4th the English commanders belatedly unleashed the fastest frigates to catch what they could, and these did have a few successes. The fireship *Bramble*, a speedy ex-sixth-rate under Captain Nepthali Ball, ran down the 60-gun *Hilversum* of Cortenaer's squadron. Undeterred by the punishing fire from the Dutchman's broadside and waiting to the last moment to take to his boat, Ball rammed the blazing *Bramble* into his quarry's side. The *Hilversum* luffed to disentangle herself from the fireship and extinguish the flames, but the delay allowed other English vessels to come up; her position hopeless, she struck to the fourth-rate *Bristol*. The *Plymouth* also had good luck. Overtaking the 54-gun East Indiaman *Carolus Quintus*, Allin fired a single challenging shot and was agreeably surprised to see the Dutch colours come down without further ado; her mutinous crew had betrayed their captain. Other opponents defended themselves honourably, but those too damaged aloft to keep pace with their friends had little hope of escape. The 38-gun *Wapen van Edam* put up furious resistance to the much larger *Anne* and *Ruby*, and only gave up after inflicting heavy damage on the *Ruby*. In the chasing action the fast-sailing fifth- and sixth-rates took a more prominent part than they had in the battle itself. The 28-gun *Colchester* received the surrender of the 52-gun Indiaman *Nagelboom*, and the 14-gun *Martin Galley* took the 36-gun *Jonge Prins*. The Dutch afterwards made much of the *Nagelboom*'s defence, though the English termed her behaviour 'disgraceful'. The 48-gun *Tromp* was also captured, and her captain, Adriaan van Rheede, taken prisoner to

England; but the ship was somehow 'lett goe' and escaped. In other incidents – one or two of which were probably the day before – the 36-gun *Delft* struck to the *Leopard* and *Breda*, the 50-gun Indiaman *Mars* to the *Assurance*, and the 34-gun *Zeelandia* to the *Centurion*. But that was all. The rest of the Dutch reached the security of the shoals, where the deep-going English ships could not get at them. A few more fireships might have made a difference, but no undamaged ones remained.

Thus, whilst Lowestoft had been one of the most brilliant actions in the history of the Royal Navy, marked by some of the most remarkable manoeuvres of the entire age of sail, the fruits of victory were decidedly disappointing. Though few realized it at the time, the escape of the Dutch was more significant in the long run than their losses. England had missed a chance to end the war at a single stroke, and the chance would not recur. For as Coventry had warned, the enemy would 'still build and increase'. The Dutch would lose other battles, but never again would they be so heavily outgunned or tactically outclassed, and never again would their discipline falter.

For the present, things looked very bad for the Dutch. Their losses had been staggering. Though official figures were not released, about five thousand men, over twenty per cent of those engaged, were killed, wounded, or captured. Eight ships were destroyed, including the fleet's three largest, and nine others captured for a total loss of seventeen vessels. Their opponents were sure two others sank, but this was not acknowledged by the Dutch. According to Sandwich the English had suffered a trifling 283 killed and 440 wounded not counting the casualties in the *Charity*, the only ship missing. The English did suffer heavy losses in senior officers and other 'great persons'. In addition to the three gentlemen who died next to the Duke, Rear-Admiral Robert Sansum was killed, as were Captains John Abelson of the *Guinea* and Robert Kirby of the *Breda*, plus Sir Edward Broughton, a volunteer. Sir John Lawson's injuries were not thought to be serious, but his wound turned gangrenous, and he died at Greenwich on 25 June. Another great loss was the gallant Earl of Marlborough, killed soon after the *Eendracht* blew up. By his side died the Earl of Portland, a young volunteer who had requested service in the *Old James* because of Marlborough's lifelong friendship with his father. Lawson and Marlborough were among the few who fared well at Marvell's hands. Of Lawson the poet wrote:

> He led our Fleet that Day, too short a Space,
> But lost his Knee (dy'd since) in Gloryes Race.
> Lawson, whose Valour beyond Fate did go
> And still fights Opdam through the Lakes below.

And of the Earl:

> Marleburgh, that knew and dar'd too more than all,
> Falls undistinguisht by an Iron Ball.
> Dear Lord, but born under a Starre ingrate!
> No Soule so clear, and no more gloomy Fate.
> Who would set up Warr's Trade that meant to thrive?
> Death picks the Valiant out, the Cow'rds survive.

Allin took over the *Old James* after the action, 'and found her much torn, her great cabin lying all open to the deck and stateroom much torn also'. She was one of a handful of English vessels which sustained damage of any consequence, the others being the *Mary*, *St. George*, *Royal Oak*, and to a lesser extent the *Prince* and the fourth-rate *Ruby*. The rest of the fleet was so little harmed that the English remained at sea without difficulty for ten days after the battle. Only when it became apparent that the Dutch would be out of action for some time did James lead the ships back to the Thames to refit and replenish.

The victorious fleet was welcomed home on 14 June with ecstatic rejoicing. On the 29th the King came to the buoy of the Nore to personally congratulate the officers and to honour those who had fought particularly well. Teddiman, Myngs, Smith, Allin, and Jordan were knighted, along with Edward Spragge of the *Lion* and Roger Cuttance of the *Prince*. Others were rewarded with promotions to better ships and promises of future favours; Coventry was granted a seat in the Privy Council for his fine staff work. Less pleasant was the matter of dealing with those who had performed poorly. Some two dozen captains were questioned closely as to why their ships were so little damaged; Jonas Poole of the *Vanguard* and Henry Hyde of the *Sapphire* were cashiered. Another offender was Edward Grove of the fifth-rate *Success*. In early May his ship along with three other men-of-war and a ketch had been detached to seek a Dutch naval stores convoy off Norway. On the return voyage his squadron had just put in at Lowestoft when the battle began. The other three ships immediately sailed to the sound of the guns and joined the action; but the *Success* did not, for which Grove was dismissed from the service as 'a prating coxcombe, and of no courage'. It was found that he had been dead drunk.

As with nearly every major seventeenth-century sea-fight, the Battle of Lowestoft was followed by a round of bickering among the officers. There were murmurings of Berkeley's supposed cowardice, and Sandwich became intensely jealous of the glowing praise accorded to Prince Rupert in the news accounts. Another squabble arose over the flag-officers' places made available by the deaths of Lawson and Sansum. Jordan was assured of one; for the other Prince Rupert recommended his friend Robert Holmes of the *Revenge*, but James instead offered the post to Captain Roger Cuttance. Surprisingly, Cuttance declined out of loyalty to Sandwich and asked to be left as flag-captain of the *Prince*. At that James selected his own flag-captain, John Harman, upon which Holmes angrily resigned his commission and went ashore.

Chapter VII

The Indian Prize

Like hunted castors, conscious of their store,
Their waylaid wealth to Norway's coasts they bring:
There first the North's cold bosom spices bore,
And winter brooded on the eastern spring.

As satisfied as Charles II was with the victory at Lowestoft, he was profoundly shaken by the casualties among the senior officers and gentlemen. Especially distressing was the loss of his companion, the Earl of Falmouth. Even more daunting, Falmouth had been struck down within an arm's length of the King's brother; that much difference in the Dutch gunner's aim, and the future of the House of Stuart could have been instantly ruined. Though James protested vociferously, Charles insisted that his brother command at sea no more. This was perhaps just as well, for the responsibility of protecting him had sometimes caused the flag-officers to advise more cautious courses of action than they might have otherwise. James's disappointment was to some extent assuaged by a gift of £120,000 which Parliament granted him in gratitude for his services.

The question of the chief command was thrown wide open again. In the spring, the King had found a solution which had satisfied everyone, but this time it could not be done. During his visit to the fleet at the end of June, Charles suggested to Prince Rupert that he and Sandwich command jointly. Rupert refused, 'saying, there could be no government, but that it would be better to have two fleetes, and neither under the command of the other, which he [the King] would not agree to'. At that Sandwich was called, and in the Earl's own words, the King 'expressed more value for me than I deserve (God knows) and told me I should be sure either to command jointly with the Prince or be trusted alone with the whole affair'. Faced with the choice of accepting the arrangement or going ashore, Rupert resigned.

The change at the top caused a major adjustment in the whole command organization, all the flag-officers shifting places. In later eras such rearrangements would have been based on strict seniority, with commanders of each rank advancing successively through ascending grades from Blue to White to Red and then on to the next rank. In Restoration times this rigid order did not exist; all appointments were temporary, and the reorganization was governed largely by a desire to preserve the pre-existing squadronal compositions as far as possible. Sandwich's squadron, formerly the Blue, became the Red with Ayscue and Teddiman as vice- and rear-admiral over the same captains they had commanded previously. The former Red Squadron became the White, with Penn in the *Royal Charles* as admiral, Berkeley the vice-admiral, and Jordan the rear-admiral. In like manner the former White Squadron became the Blue, with Myngs as vice-admiral and Harman taking Sansum's place as rear-admiral. An exception to the pattern was Sir Thomas Allin, who made a mighty leap from private captain to Admiral of the Blue, passing six other flag-officers in the process. This was not as surprising as it seems. Allin had served as a flag-officer in 1664, having commanded in the Mediterranean at the outbreak of the war. He would have received a division in the first campaign, but all the positions had been filled when he returned from the Straits. He now took over Rupert's former flagship, the *Royal James*.

Lowestoft left the English in undisputed control of the North Sea, and in the aftermath their principal objective was the capture of the convoys and squadrons which were approaching the Netherlands from overseas; in particular the East Indiamen and the warships under de Ruyter. On 2 July intelligence came that de Ruyter was crossing the Atlantic from Newfoundland, and the Duke of York ordered all the ships that were ready for sea to sail at once. Sandwich was then ashore at Groombridge visiting his ailing wife, so Penn took the fleet to sea. This nearly caused serious trouble, for Sandwich feared that Sir William might have thought himself in permanent command. The Earl 'did ruminate a little on this matter', but when the *Royal Prince* caught up with the fleet on the 6th, Penn came aboard and, said a very relieved Sandwich, 'without hesitation put all things to my dispose'.

After joining the fleet, Sandwich at first had to content himself with a passive search because many of his ships were still in port due to the inevitable victualling deficiencies. It was unsafe to begin offensive operations until the whole force was gathered, for the Dutch fleet might put to sea. He therefore waited on the eastern side of the Dogger Bank, hoping that de Ruyter or the Indiamen might blunder into him. When Sir Thomas Allin arrived with twenty more ships on the morning of 17 July, Sandwich called the flag-officers aboard the *Prince* for a council-of-war. In the course of its discussion the council recognized that if the fugitive convoys coming around Scotland 'should put it to the adventure to go home', they would find 'the flat coast along the shore of Jutland advantageous for them to escape by'. But the flag-officers thought it more likely that the Dutch would seek shelter in neutral Norwegian havens, probably Bergen or Flekkerö, 'until they had a fleet to protect them or the winter come on'. It was accordingly resolved to go there and 'attempt them in harbour if there were opportunity'.

In deciding to attack the Dutch in Norwegian ports, the council-of-war was acting with the blessings of Whitehall. From the outset of the war Charles II hoped to entice Frederik III of Denmark-Norway to the English side. Charles's envoy to Copenhagen, Sir Gilbert Talbot, found through private discussions with Frederik that his attachments to the Netherlands were actually very tenuous. Like the English, the Danes had seen their visions of overseas trading empires pre-empted by Dutch monopolies in Africa and the Far East. They also blamed the Dutch for having drawn them into a disastrous war with Sweden in 1658. Until Lowestoft Frederik honoured his treaties, but after the battle his attitude veered sharply. He realized that with the English ruling the North Sea, a great many Dutch merchantmen would take refuge in his ports. His treasury deeply in debt, he began to cast avaricious eyes upon the wealth he knew those ships would contain, and was finally overcome by visions of the huge East Indiamen labouring under their burdens of spices and jewels. Consequently, when Talbot approached him on 14 June with the suggestion that Danish forces seize the ships when they arrived, Frederik replied that nothing would make him happier, but that, alas, 'he wanted strength to do it'. Sir Gilbert responded guardedly that he might be able to persuade his master the King of England to send a fleet for the purpose, in return for half the profits. Frederik replied 'that he would be content with all his heart, to share equally with his Majesty'.

Three days later Talbot wrote in cypher to the Earl of Arlington, Principal Secretary of State, reporting that a deal had been struck: 'All is now well & ye King is now ready to dismiss ye Holland Extraord. [envoy] & declare his Treaty with Holland broken whensoever I desire it'. Since de Ruyter and the East Indiamen were soon expected in Norwegian ports, and

> since ye King of Denm. doth resolve to breake his Treaty with Holland, I would have it declared to ye Dutch Extraord. when it is too late for him to give advice thereof to that fleete to avoid their coast, which will somewhat justify ye honour of ye King of Denm. to ye world; and because ye King of Denm. hath not force to make himself master of those fleetes I propose that he should have some of his Majesty's ships to help him & to divide ye prize equally between them; but this must not be drawn into consequence that Denmark consenteth to ye violation of their ports, for it is to be understood but a connivance. This King catcheth at ye proposall & desireth me to propose it to his Majesty in his name, which I make choice to doe through yr. Lordship, humbly desiring that it may be managed with that secrecy which ye nature of ye thing requireth; & that I may have the King's speedy answers to it.

Charles II and his advisers must have puzzled over the unexplained 'connivance' in violating Frederik's ports, for Talbot's rather imprecise wording otherwise implied a simple joint operation following a sudden but proper Danish declaration of war. Talbot did not immediately offer clarification, an omission which was exacerbated in that messages between London and Copenhagen were usually some twelve days in passage. Before a more detailed account of the transactions reached Whitehall, the expedition had already been set in motion on the basis of the ambassador's original communication. Arlington apprised Sir Gilbert of Charles II's assent in a letter of 30 June, and on 2 July the Duke of York's orders to the fleet formally authorized assaults in Norwegian harbours. Four days later James sent Sandwich the further explanation

> that Sir Gilbert Talbott had written that the King of Denmarke was ready to declare his treaties broaken with Holland but would bee glad to take an advantageous time to say it, which would bee when any considerable substance of the Hollanders was lodged in their ports: that then if the English fleete would attempt them by sea, hee would assist and goe halfe shares in the prize.

This information reached the fleet before Sandwich's council-of-war of the 17th, and based on it the English started out for Norway at once.

Meanwhile, all was not as well in Copenhagen as Talbot had reported. The Danes backed away from a complete breach with the Netherlands, claiming uncertainty over the attitude of Sweden. In fact, the cowardly Frederik had deluded himself into believing that he could get his loot and still somehow avoid direct involvement in the war. He categorically forbade any Danish participation in the attack, insisting that 'for his honors sake he would not openly assent to the Seizure'. The best Talbot could obtain was a charade in which the Norwegian authorities 'to blind the world should storm high and pretend to be greatly offended' when the English entered their harbours. In the course of the protests a letter from Talbot would be 'slipt' to Sandwich or his representative saying 'That the English should boldly assault their Enemy's in Port for as much as the Danes would make no resistance against them under pretence of fear that the English if provoked might destroy their towns, and carry away all as their prize'. The captured merchantmen would then be taken out to sea for a clandestine division of spoils. Talbot tried to forward this information to Sandwich on the 20th and again on the 26th, but the first messenger was taken at sea by de Ruyter (who fortunately did not question him closely) and the second never found the fleet.

Even as the English sailed north, part of their quarry eluded them. De Ruyter had touched at Bergen for news on the 13th and then headed south, following the very course along the Danish coast that the English council-of-war had laid out for him. In addition to his twelve men-of-war, he had nineteen merchantmen in company, some of them prizes taken during the voyage. His foul-bottomed ships were slow and leaky after sixteen months at sea, his weary crews decimated by disease and attrition, his provisions nearly exhausted; had the English taken the precaution of tracing the Jutland route on their way north, they might have bagged the lot. Instead, they underestimated his resolve and complacently sailed direct to Norway, passing by him some sixty miles to seaward. De Ruyter made for the first available Dutch port, Delfzijl on the Ems River, where he anchored on the 27th with only six days' victuals left. His deliverance was regarded in the Netherlands as little short of miraculous.

There yet remained the East Indiamen. Sandwich had still heard nothing of them when his force arrived off Norway, but the fleet was too poorly victualled to allow much time to wait for them; any raid on Frederik's ports would have to be accomplished quickly or not at all. After considering Flekkerö, the English commanders decided to try for twenty-eight merchantmen which were reportedly at Bergen. A special squadron of twenty-two men-of-war and two fireships was selected under Rear-Admiral of the Red Sir Thomas Teddiman, who shifted from the *Royal Katherine* to the third-rate *Revenge* for the attempt. On the morning of the 30th the council-of-war resolved to send Teddiman in, despite the presumed absence of the Indiamen. This plan was adopted without enthusiasm, Penn in particular being in favour of calling off the whole thing and going to the Texel instead. Then, as the council was adjourning, a neutral vessel which had just left Bergen brought electrifying news: the East India fleet was in the port. Hopes soared, and Teddiman was detached that afternoon.

During the night and most of the next day the squadron encountered heavy southerly gales. When Teddiman reached the outlying islands on the morning of 1

August only fifteen men-of-war and two fireships remained, the rest having been driven out to sea. The fleet nevertheless pressed on and was within sight of Bergen by mid-afternoon. The inner harbour where the merchantmen rode was a U-shaped inlet opening to the north, less than a mile long and nowhere broader than five hundred yards. The neck of the bay was guarded on the eastern side by the formidable Bergenhus Castle, and there were other well-armed forts and batteries on both sides. The city, a picturesque wooden medieval town, skirted the southern shore. When the English peered into the harbour, they discovered that it contained more Dutch merchantmen than anyone had dared to imagine. They included some fifty deeply laden ships of the Smyrna, Spanish, Portuguese, and Biscayan trades, along with the ten East Indiamen, of which six were great ships of 48 to 60 guns. The Earl of Rochester, a volunteer in the *Revenge*, wrote that everyone was 'full of hopes and expectation, having allready shared amongst us the rich lading of the East India merchants, some for diamond some for spices others for rich silkes and I for shirts and gould which I had most neede of'.

What took place at Bergen over the next few days was described in detail by Sir Thomas Clifford, a diplomat accompanying the expedition as representative of the Earl of Arlington. Clifford recounted that a 'gentleman of quality' named Charles Harbord had gone ahead in a pinnace earlier in the day with letters from Sandwich and Teddiman advising the Danish governor of their intentions. Harbord met the fleet outside the harbour to deliver a noncommittal but courteous welcome from the Governor of Bergen, Johan Caspar von Cicignon. At this the English 'sailed merrily on' and entered the neck of the bay. Then, as the squadron laboriously warped up the inlet against the south breeze and began to take up berths facing the Dutch, an English-speaking official (the tax-collector of Norway, as it turned out) named Jens Toller came aboard the *Revenge*. Though Toller himself seemed friendly enough, he presented a surprisingly hostile message asking why the English had violated a long-standing treaty by bringing more than five warships into a neutral harbour. He politely but firmly warned that if the additional vessels did not depart at once, the forts would open fire. Somewhat nonplussed, Teddiman responded that the treaty to which Toller referred actually allowed six ships to enter at any time and any number more if safety demanded. It would be impossible for the rest of his ships to find safe anchorages before nightfall owing to the deep water and 'dismall rocks' outside the harbour. Thinking that Toller and perhaps even the governor might not have been privy to the secret plot, Teddiman decided to send Sandwich's cousin Edward Montagu to the Bergenhus to straighten things out with the highest-ranking Dane, the commander of land forces in Norway General Claus von Allefeldt. But Montagu found that Allefeldt too claimed ignorance of the agreement.

Amazing as it seemed, the general was telling the truth. The carefully concerted plans had been irrevocably spoiled by Frederik's fearful dithering: his orders had not been sent in time. The English afterwards spoke bitterly of the 'false Dane', charging the King of Denmark with everything from stupidity to betrayal. Although it is hard to have much sympathy for 'that blockhead', as Sandwich called him, a more charitable and possibly more accurate explanation of Frederik's hesitation is that he had simply thought it unwise to take action before the arrival of the Indiamen was reported; he did not know that Talbot's ill-phrased dispatches had already caused the English to launch the operation. Ironically, the situation was almost saved by accident, for Frederik's hand was forced on 20 July by the news that de Ruyter was on the Norway coast. Fearing that the Dutch admiral might convoy the merchantmen home, the King sent Allefeldt instructions 'to use all fair means to keep the Hollanders still in their harbours', and apparently explained that sufficient strength to capture them would soon be at hand, *but gave no details.* Additional orders, the message said, would be forthcoming in cypher. Since there was then no word of the Indiamen, Frederik did not bother to send out the vital cyphered follow-up (with which Talbot's letter was enclosed) until the 24th. This delay was fatal, for the overland passage to Bergen took at least ten days. A copy reached Gyldenlöve, the Viceroy of Norway at Christiania, but two ships which Gyldenlöve sent to give Sandwich the details never found the English fleet, and with that, the plot was doomed.

After Frederik's courier began the journey much happened at Bergen. De Ruyter sailed away, the Indiamen arrived, and so did the uncyphered but decidedly cryptic message telling Allefeldt to trap the Dutch in the harbour. Lacking other information, the general interpreted the orders to mean that *he* was to capture the merchantmen, and supposed that the force to do it would be supplied by a *Danish* fleet. Thus, when confronted with what Montagu claimed to be a firm pact with the English, Allefeldt found himself in an awkward situation. If such a treaty existed he certainly did not wish to violate it, but he hesitated to allow the division of what he supposed to be his own master's intended loot without authorization. He therefore took the only course available: he fought for time, hoping that either the Danish fleet or the promised cyphered instructions would arrive before the explosion.

A series of exceedingly complex negotiations dragged on through the night, with boats rowing back and forth between the *Revenge* and the castle in a steady procession. Allefeldt proved to be a slippery adversary; at each round of talks, said Clifford, he 'sung another song'. He at first recoiled from Montagu's overtures with lofty professions of outrage, seeming 'very tender not onely of his owne but his masters honour, and concluded that if we endeavoured to anchor within his castle he would shoote at us'. As the English emissary was delivering this unpalatable news to Teddiman a shot suddenly rang out from the castle, wounding a man in a boat from the *Foresight*. Though incensed, Teddiman continued to arrange his ships for battle without retaliating.

Allefeldt now had second thoughts. Seeing that the English were undeterred by threats and fearing that they might take all the prizes for themselves if no accommodation were reached, he sent Toller to invite Montagu back to the castle. On the Englishman's arrival the general disavowed the cannon shot, offering to have the man who had fired it hanged at once if Teddiman desired. He also conceded the probable authenticity of the English claims and declared that he would cooperate after all. The discussion now shifted to the rules of engagement. The Danes sought to limit the attacking force to the six ships legally allowed in the harbour and insisted that the assault be postponed until Sunday the 6th pending the arrival of the expected orders from Copenhagen. After a midnight consultation with Teddiman, Montagu accepted the six-ship limit (the small size of the harbour would impose similar restrictions anyway) but rejected the delay on the grounds that the Dutch fleet might appear in the meantime. In attempting to intimidate the English, the general had also 'let fall' that twenty-two Danish warships were expected at any time. This revelation considerably strengthened Teddiman's decision not to wait.

At dawn, which comes early at that latitude in summer, Allefeldt yielded a little, requesting two days' delay instead of four. But Teddiman had tired of negotiating. A man of action with little patience for the niceties of diplomacy, the admiral had concluded that the stalling by the Danes was only a ruse to give the Dutch time to prepare their defences; he had already been greatly angered to find that new batteries and fortifications had sprung up all around the bay during the night. Montagu was accordingly sent back to the Bergenhus to report that there would be no delay whatever. Realizing that Teddiman's attack was about to begin, Allefeldt tried a last, desperate ploy. Pretensions of honour forgotten, 'he confessed ingeniously that the greatest matter that troubled him was the parting with halfe the booty'. He admitted (and undoubtedly believed) that he had orders 'to secure the whole when he had strength enough to doe it', and he consequently could not allow it to be shared without further advice. If the English would not put off the assault, he pleaded, would they at least refrain from plundering the ships and instead keep their holds sealed until his orders arrived? Montagu responded that the English would be happy to comply, provided that half the prizes wait at sea with Sandwich's fleet. This being unsatisfactory to the Danes, negotiations ceased.

While the English and the Danes were snarling at each other like lions over a kill, they had both neglected something: their prey was not yet dead, and his claws were sharper than they knew. The Dutch were by no means quaking with fear. Though their ships were 'lying one on another, incapable of execution' when Teddiman first appeared, their leader, *Commandeur* Pieter de Bitter of the Indiaman *Walcheren*, had difficulty restraining his captains from rashly charging the English. When cooler heads prevailed, he proceeded to organize a masterful and well-conceived defence. Taking full advantage of the respite given him by the transparent treachery taking place in the castle, he moored the six largest Company ships in a line across the bay: the *Brederode* guarding the western side; in the centre the *Phoenix*, *Wapen van Hoorn*, *Jonge Prins*, and his own *Walcheren*, with the *Slot Hooningen* to the east beneath the southern end of the Bergenhus. The *Catherina*, a Lisbon trader of about 40 guns under Captain Ruth Maximiliaan, squeezed into the line between the *Walcheren* and *Slot Hooningen*. There being no room for additional ships, the Indiaman *Rijzende Zon* and three smaller vessels also belonging to the V.O.C. drew up inshore of the main line as a reserve.

Although the fifty-odd merchantmen huddling together along the southwestern shore were useless for fighting, they were still a valuable source of guns and men. Many of the seamen were ashore sampling the amenities of the town, but most of the celebrants were soon rounded up and herded to the waterfront. Some were rowed out to augment the crews of the Indiamen, while others were put to work hoisting seventy guns or so out of the smaller merchantmen and mounting them in hastily erected fieldworks ashore; these were the batteries that Teddiman observed with such concern. In another important measure, men were sent to reinforce the Bergenhus and the forts. The Danish garrisons were evidently unaware of their master's perfidy and consequently accepted the Dutch without question, particularly since they brought some of their portable treasure with them for safekeeping.

Soon after daybreak on the 2nd Teddiman completed his own dispositions. Moored opposite the Dutch in an arc stretching from the north end of the Bergenhus on the east to the toll-house on the west were the English fourth-rates *Prudent Mary* (hired), *Breda*, *Foresight*, *Bendish* (hired), *Happy Return*, *Sapphire*, and the fifth-rate *Pembroke*. These ships were almost touching each other, the space was so restricted. Behind them on the eastern side of the harbour the fifth-rate *Norwich* took position to engage a Dutch battery just north of the castle, while the fourth-rate *Golden Lion* and the hired *Society* anchored with their broadsides facing the palisaded Sverreborg battery on the hill above the castle and another fort to the north. On the other side of the bay the fifth-rate *Guernsey*, the *Revenge*, the hired *Coast Frigate*, and the fourth-rate *Guinea* formed a north–south line against the heavily-armed fortress of Nordnes which dominated the high ground of the western peninsula. The sixth-rate *Martin Galley* kept watch to seaward of Nordnes.

As soon as the morning mists cleared, at five o'clock, Teddiman gave the word. The English loosed their broadsides with a mighty roar, the Indiamen responding in kind. The vessels facing the forts were under strict orders to hold their fire if the Danes kept quiet. At the last moment Allefeldt decided not to intervene; Clifford wrote that 'for a little time the Castle and forts forbore, for near the space of a quarter of an houre, and our men shot low to the Shipps only without annoying the towne'. But the Danish commander was literally no longer the master of his own house. The hundreds of Dutchmen that de Bitter had poured into the forts had no intention of allowing the neutrality of the King of Denmark to be sullied with impunity. Shouldering the hesitant Danes aside, they took over some of the guns and opened up on the English. The English angrily returned the fire; Danish gunners began to join in, and soon torrents of shot came ripping into the English fleet from every direction. Aghast, Allefeldt vainly struggled to regain control. Having ordered his men to cease fire, at six o'clock he hung a white flag from the castle. Teddiman, however, could not see it; the *Revenge* was wreathed in smoke on the other side of the bay. Others did, but the Dutchmen serving the Danish guns never missed a salvo, and the English ships 'being constantly shot at from thence our men would not be hindered from answering them and therfore did not cease shooting at them or take any heed to give the Admirall Sr. Tho. Teddeman notice of the white flag out'. After fifteen minutes Allefeldt withdrew the flag and sullenly washed his hands of the affair.

The English would probably have had difficulty even with Danish collusion, because for once the Dutch had a firepower advantage. Only one of the vessels directly opposed to the Indiamen had more than 46 guns, while five of the Dutch were 50- and 60-gun giants. The English endured the hail of iron as long as they could, but finally slipped their cables and ignominiously limped away at about 8:30. As Teddiman sadly explained to Sandwich,

They had in ye Castle & Forts upward of 300 Gunns mounted beside ye East India shipps in ye port. The dispute lasted 3 houres & a halfe ye wind right out of ye Port, that for my heart I could not gett ye fireshipps in, their beinge soe many Gunns placed on mee that cutt to peeces our cables, for that wee had like to have drove foule one of another. Ye wind blew right out beinge at South; The worst place that ever men came to.

He added that his ships were 'much shattered & torne' with over four hundred men killed and wounded. The dead included the negotiator Edward Montagu and six captains: Seale of the *Breda*, Haward of the *Prudent Mary*, Lawson of the *Coast Frigate*, Utber of the *Guernsey*, Pierse of the fireship *Bryar*, and Cadman of the *Hambro' Merchant*. Cadman's ship was not present; he was shot down aboard the *Revenge*, having probably been temporarily assigned there owing to knowledge of Norwegian waters.

The English casualties fell unevenly. The eight ships which engaged the Indiamen and the Dutch battery to the east lost a startling 379 men – over a quarter of their complements – while only 41 were hit in the seven which fought the Danish works. One would expect the opposite in an engagement involving shore batteries, so apparently the Danes did not exert themselves too strenuously. De Bitter's fleet suffered 95 casualties. The only seriously damaged Dutch ship was Maximiliaan's *Catherina*, which was holed underwater and had to be run ashore. Danish losses were negligible, though Rochester noted with vengeful relish that the English had 'beate the towne all to peices'.

The battered squadron withdrew to a nearby fiord to repair what damage it could. Two days later Teddiman was astonished to receive an ingenuously conciliatory letter from Allefeldt inviting the English to reopen negotiations; the instructions from Copenhagen had arrived. With Montagu dead, diplomatic duties were assumed by Sir Thomas Clifford, who slipped ashore disguised as a seaman to meet the general and Governor von Cicignon. By then de Bitter had strengthened his defences immensely, having placed a boom of heavy spars across the harbour and having shifted additional men and guns into the Indiamen. In view of that and because of the damage Danish guns had caused, Clifford pressed for active assistance. Allefeldt replied that his orders told him to permit the attack but to do nothing that might be interpreted by the Netherlands as an act of war. He not only refused assistance, said Clifford, but now imposed 'such rules and conditions in the assaulting of the Dutch, that none but madmen would attempt it the second time; for if wee should drive them from their ships, yet wee must bee under the power of their Castles how wee are to dispose of them'. The English would not be allowed to cross the Dutch boom, were forbidden to put men ashore to attack from the rear, and could not use fireships (though de Bitter had prepared one). No Englishmen other than officers were to enter the Dutch ships under any circumstances. Allefeldt himself would govern the duration of the engagement, with the right to enforce an immediate cessation any time he wished by displaying a white flag from the castle. The English negotiator protested that such obstructions to the assault went well beyond neutrality, but Allefeldt was unbending.

When the general boasted that the Danes themselves were strong enough to keep the merchantmen from escaping, Clifford realized that Charles II would never see one penny of the prize money no matter what Teddiman did. The English sailed away in disgust.

The fiasco cost neither Teddiman nor his captains much loss of prestige; their casualty list proved that they had done their best. In Copenhagen, news of the battle 'so afflicted his Majesty of Denmarke that for a month he look't like Death, as well he might'. His fear, mistrust, and zealous secrecy had cost him 'a treasure more by much than all his Crowne was worth', and made war with his potential English allies unavoidable. Claus von Allefeldt, with whom Frederik cannot have been well pleased, seems to have been motivated throughout by pure greed. His deliberate discouragement of the English even with the King's orders in hand suggests that he still believed a Danish squadron was on the way. After the English retired he continued to keep the merchantmen trapped in the harbour, though it turned out that there was no Danish fleet. But Allefeldt was not one to be discouraged by a minor setback. Cheerfully determined to make the best of the situation, he demanded 100,000 Thalers from the Dutch as a reward for having so honourably defended them. He confiscated a small part of it from the goods de Bitter's captains had foolishly deposited in the castle before the battle, and he was still trying to extort the rest when the timely arrival of the Dutch fleet put a stop to it. After that the general had to be satisfied with a flowery letter of thanks which was substituted for the Thalers, but he never gave back the guns de Bitter had mounted ashore.

While Teddiman was at Bergen, the rest of the English fleet intended to lie offshore watching for de Ruyter, whose escape had not yet been discovered. But the weather deteriorated and the Bergen squadron took longer than expected; when provisions began to run dangerously low Sandwich made for the pre-arranged rendezvous at Bressay Sound in the Shetlands. After staying there for six days to take on water, the fleet sailed south, met Teddiman off Flamborough Head on 18 August, and finally put in at Solebay for revictualling on the 21st. The cruise had been a failure in every respect. Morale was at a low ebb and disease in the form of 'divers high spotted fevers' swept through the fleet. The ships were at least 3,000 men below their complements.

Sandwich could not afford to remain at Solebay for very long, for the Dutch were reported to have sent their fleet to bring home the merchantmen from Norway. He put 1,000 unhealthy men ashore, received new recruits as replacements (many of them sick themselves) and took others from those of Teddiman's ships that required dockyard repairs. As usual the victualling system was in chaos. He was able to get ample dry provisions and some meat, but so little beer that he would need extraordinary luck to find the Dutch before the casks ran dry. The fleet weighed on 30 August, still thinly manned, and made for its intended station between the Texel and the Dogger Bank.

The Dutch fleet had sailed in early August, seventy-seven ships strong, its spirits buoyed by de Ruyter's presence. He had been appointed Lieutenant-Admiral of Holland and Westfriesland, but on this voyage the real commander was the Raadpensionaris, Johan de Witt. Determined to prevent another Lowestoft, de Witt had taken quarters in de Ruyter's flagship, the *Delfland*, and personally involved himself in every decision. Fortunately, the politician and the admiral were of a like mind on most issues, and got along remarkably well. When the Dutch arrived at Bergen on the 19th, the winds had shifted to the northwest, and the merchantmen (now seventy-five in number) could get out of the bay only with difficulty. Ten days later about fifty of them including most of the Indiamen were clear of the harbour, whereupon the fleet's commanders decided that it would be foolhardy to linger any longer on that rocky coastline. They started south that day, but soon encountered a ferocious northwesterly gale. When the tempest abated two days later, men-of-war and merchantmen alike were hopelessly dispersed; de Ruyter gathered forty-seven vessels and could only hope the other eighty would somehow find their way safely.

Sandwich's haste to get to sea now paid valuable dividends, for on the morning of 3 September his scouts encountered an isolated group of Dutch ships about ninety miles northwest of the Texel. The English chased all day and came up with them in the afternoon. In a running fight, the 40-gun *Hoop* struck to the *Mary*, while the fourth-rates *Adventure*, *Assurance*, and *Antelope* took the 50-gun *Groningen*, the 50-gun *Westfriesland*, and the 56-gun *Zevenwolden* respectively. These last three had been flagships at Lowestoft, but bigger game still awaited. The *Adventure* and the fifth-rate *Hector* overtook a great ship of over 60 guns, and another of similar size was engaged by the *Plymouth* and the fifth-rate *Milford*. After a sharp fight both were taken, and to the unbounded joy of the English crews they proved to be deeply laden members of the elusive East India fleet. The *Adventure*'s prize was the *Phoenix* and the other was the *Slot Hooningen*, both having been subsidiary flagships at Bergen. The English lost a ship themselves; shortly after the *Phoenix* surrendered, the *Hector* suddenly foundered, drowning her captain and eighty men. It was believed that she had encountered a heavy sea with her gunports open. Following this action, English frigates spread out to see what else they could find. No more Indiamen were captured, but by the next afternoon seven smaller merchantmen had been brought in, including yet another taken by the ubiquitous *Adventure*.

For the next few days the English searched for the Dutch fleet along the eastern side of the Dogger Bank. De Ruyter was then south of the Dogger, seeking his scattered squadrons. On the 3rd he found Tjerk Hiddes de Vries, the new Lieutenant-Admiral of Friesland, with a few ships, and from him he learned that the enemy was in the area. Though heavily outnumbered, de Ruyter immediately prepared for battle and began to look for Sandwich. English scouts sighted the Dutch on the 6th, but the fleets crossed back and forth without meeting. On the 7th, de Ruyter went to Terschelling, where he met Tromp and Vice-Admiral Adriaan Banckert of Zeeland with fourteen ships. The next day the English discovered them all off Vlieland, shepherding the merchantmen into the Vlie, but Sandwich dared not venture after them into the shoals.

De Ruyter's main body had thus escaped, but many vessels were still at sea. During the night fifteen of the missing ships unknowingly wandered too close to the English; they were discovered at daybreak on the 9th, and by 9 o'clock in the morning seven or eight merchantmen had been captured along with four ships belonging to the V.O.C. These four had been serving as men-of-war with the main fleet and were not a part of de Bitter's squadron. They were the *Huis te Zwieten* of 70 guns, the *Geldersche Ruyter* of 46, and two separate 40-gun ships named *St. Paulus* (one from Enkhuizen and one from Middelburg). The *Huis te Zwieten* was probably the best ship taken from the Netherlands in all of the Anglo-Dutch wars. Not really a merchantman, she was a proper warship which had been built on contract for the navy of Genoa in 1653, but taken over by the States-General on completion. For some reason Van de Velde the Elder mistakenly called her the 'Great Venetian'.

The pursuit had drawn Sandwich near the shallows, and in the afternoon he tacked away from the coast, close-hauled on a southwest breeze. After the English had sailed a short distance to the west, yet another Dutch squadron hove into view from the north. This one contained some thirty sail which had been gathered by Aert van Nes, Vice-Admiral of Rotterdam. Holding a southerly course, Van Nes weathered the English in the late afternoon, but many ships came close enough to exchange broadsides; Captain Laughorne of the *Revenge* was wounded. When the Dutch had passed, Harman, Berkeley, and Jordan tacked to follow with their divisions. Another fight seemed likely, and the English burned the damaged prize *St. Paulus* of Middelburg in preparation. Sandwich, however, called them back. Little daylight remained, and the weather showed every sign of turning ugly; the fleet was badly undermanned and had twenty-three vulnerable prizes to guard with other Dutch warships possibly nearby. As he explained,

> To engage ships promiscuously in the night when neither friend nor foe can be distinguished, may occasion God knows how great damage to a Fleete of 150 sayle and upwards as we all were. Before daylight they would have been in port or have led us ashore to ye ruine of the whole Fleete if we had persued.

His caution drew criticism later, though it was in fact a fortunate decision; the wind rose sharply after sunset, eventually building to 'a powerful storm, so much as blew our foresail and fore topsail quite out of the bolt-ropes, and a great sea'.

The English commanders were now becoming anxious over the security of their prizes, and the fleet accordingly stood for home on the 10th. Sandwich at last had reason to be satisfied. This single two-week cruise, with the ships ill-manned and ill-provisioned, had accomplished more for England in material terms than even Lowestoft. He was undoubtedly confident that his reputation, slightly tarnished by the earlier failures, would revive with the news of the captured ships. As it happened, his trophies carried instead the seeds of his downfall.

In those days there was no official share system for the distribution of prize money. The only statutory regulation was the common seaman's monetary reward for captured warships and right of 'free pillage' of goods lying on or above the gundeck; in effect the personal possessions of the enemy crew and any cargo not stowed in the hold. But for the senior officers, all distributions were purely at the pleasure of the King and the Lord High Admiral, though neither had ever been miserly towards their sea-officers. Indeed, those who had done their duty in the past had always received fair and graciously bestowed portions. As the fleet sailed towards the Thames, however, some of the flag-officers began to be assailed by the fear that this time, in the kingdom's current condition of debt, their shares might be less generous than usual. Few of these men were wealthy, but they were expected to maintain outward displays of opulence, with servants, entertainments, and other trappings of authority. Their pay was barely enough to cover the expenses, and was almost always in arrears. And here, sailing right alongside, were the *Phoenix* and *Slot Hooningen* whose swollen bellies overflowed with costly spices and gleaming jewels and fine cloths beyond imagining. The value of the cargoes in the thirteen merchant prizes was eventually estimated at about £400,000; this at a time when a man could live in style on a salary of £100 per annum. Samuel Pepys later visited the Indiamen, and in their holds he saw

> the greatest wealth lie in confusion that a man can see in the world. Pepper scattered through every chink, you trod upon it; and in cloves and nutmegs, I walked above the knees – whole rooms full – and silks in bales, and boxes of Copperplate, one of which I saw opened.

The thought of these fabulous commodities preyed on the minds of the flag-officers, and they finally fell to temptation. At a council-of-war just after the fleet entered the Thames, Penn broached the subject. Claiming that the King had promised him favours, he suggested that they assign shares among themselves, dole them out immediately, and seek approval afterwards. As Sandwich subsequently explained to Pepys, it seemed 'easier to keepe money when got of the King than to get it when it is too late'. When other officers, notably Sir Roger Cuttance, supported Penn, Sandwich foolishly approved. He established shares of £4,000 each to himself and Penn, £2,000 to each of the other flag-officers, and like amounts to the three knighted private captains, Cuttance, Smith, and Spragge. Significantly, untitled captains were not allotted a share.

The prizes were brought up to the Nore, where the lucky men of the *Plymouth*, *Adventure*, *Milford*, and the survivors of the *Hector* were turned loose on the decks of the Indiamen. They plundered thoroughly, searching every conceivable hiding place for the contraband cargoes that the East India crews invariably smuggled aboard. Soon there were reports of common topmen festooned with jewels and hawking whole cartloads of cinnamon and cloves. When the seaman completed their allotted time, the hatches were opened, and the flag-officers greedily waded into the wonders below. There was an orgy of looting; some far exceeded their shares. 'They did toss and tumble and spoil and break things in hold', said Pepys, 'to a great loss and shame, to come at the fine goods, and did take a man that knew where the fine goods were, and did this over and over again for many days'. Pepys himself obtained a permit from Sandwich (his cousin) to buy spices from Cuttance for profitable resale. But the Duke of York soon learned of these proceedings. Furious that his prerogatives had been circumvented, he empowered the Prize Commissioners and Customs officials to confiscate all they could find. The affair became a public scandal; the jealous private captains talked openly. The guilt of the offenders was further magnified in the eyes of the public by the fact that some of the commanders refused their shares despite pressure from the others; Smith and Spragge out of respect for their untitled fellow captains, Sir Christopher Myngs because he had been caught looting prizes earlier and nearly ruined his career. Above all there was Sir George Ayscue, described long before by Coventry as 'a very honest, gallant man' and one who 'does not serve mercenarily, for he lives very handsomely and honourably in the fleet, beyond his pay'. Another, Sir William Berkeley, tried to claim innocence, but Pepys had heard him called 'the chief hand that did it'.

A storm of fury broke upon the Earl of Sandwich, who was blamed not only for the prize-goods fiasco, but for all the missed opportunities of the summer: the escape of de Ruyter, the disaster at Bergen, and the decision not to engage Van Nes at the end of the campaign. Just as the criticism was reaching its height, de Ruyter and the Dutch fleet suddenly appeared in the mouth of the Thames. The English were in no condition to return to sea. The government was out of money and could not afford to keep the fleet in sea pay. Crews were sick, ships needed repairs, and victualling arrangements were near complete collapse; there was no hope of provisioning another expedition. The whole country was in a pitiful state; 1665 was the year of the plague, and it was at its worst in September and October. Sandwich was in any event not very worried about the Dutch. There was little de Ruyter could accomplish, for few English merchantmen were abroad at that time of year. Experienced seamen knew that the howling autumn gales would soon drive him away, and they recognized that the blockade was mostly a show to raise morale in the Netherlands and convince Louis XIV that the Dutch were not defeated. Thinking it foolish to take the fleet back to sea, Sandwich laid up the great ships for the winter and went off to Oxford, where the Court was sitting because of the sickness in London. After a month, disease and weather did indeed force the Dutch back. Even so, powerful people including the Duke of Albemarle assailed the Earl's lack of concern. Exasperated by the criticism, he at last returned to sea with a poorly equipped squadron in late October, but by then the Dutch had gone.

Charles II loyally defended the admiral for as long as he could. The King knew that no serious wrong-doing had been intended in the matter of the prize-goods, for Sandwich had informed him of the distributions and had requested approval from the beginning. This Charles granted retroactively on 17 October. But when the storm did not die down, it became lamentably clear that Sandwich would have to go. To his credit the King removed his faithful commander gently and protected his reputation as far as possible. The admiral was chosen as a special ambassador to Spain to negotiate an end to the long war between that country and Portugal, a struggle which was causing England anxiety for a number of reasons. In faraway Madrid the Earl would be well removed from further harm.

Sandwich thus passed from the scene. It should be noted that his diplomacy succeeded after two years of patient and painstaking effort. When he returned to England in 1668, his prestige was as high as ever. He again went to sea on the outbreak of the Third Anglo-Dutch War, but was drowned in the Battle of Solebay in 1672. By then he had been rightly recognized as one of the greatest seamen of the age and a statesman of unusual ability.

*

Except for the initial victory and the captures of September, the sea campaign of 1665 was disappointing for the English. Dutch merchantmen had mostly escaped the traps set for them, their fleet had largely recovered from the effects of Lowestoft, and their enormous naval shipbuilding programme was beginning to bear fruit. The events at Bergen had added Frederik III to England's list of enemies, and now ominous rumblings began to be heard from Louis XIV. Worst of all, the expense of the war had 'beggared the crowne' even more severely than Coventry had predicted. On the other hand, the Royal Navy had shown itself superior to the Dutch in battle, and victory seemed well within reach if the ships could only be kept provisioned. For a while it was feared that it would be financially impossible to fit out the fleet for the following year, but on 31 October Parliament voted an 'Additional Aid' of £1,250,000. The amount was far short of requirements, and the plague had so debilitated the economy that only half the money could be collected in the time intended. Nevertheless, the expectation of future revenues temporarily improved credit just enough to permit a second summer's fighting; the unpaid contractors and creditors could be put off by empty promises.

With another campaign assured, Charles II turned his attention to replacing the fleet's commander. As before, the King wanted Prince Rupert at the helm – but not by himself. As the Earl of Clarendon explained, Charles

> had great confidence in the affection and unquestionable courage of Prince Rupert: but he was not sure, that the quickness of his spirit and the strength of his passion might not sometimes stand in need of the advice and assistance of a friend, who should be in equal authority with him; and had therefore thought of finding some fit person to be joined with him, and so make one admiral of two persons.

The only 'fit person' was the Duke of Albemarle, whose phlegmatic temperament appeared to make him the perfect foil for the Prince. Since Rupert's earlier rejection of a dual arrangement had caused such an unpleasant breach with Sandwich, Charles this time took careful precautions to avoid hard feelings if either candidate objected. The Prince, 'from whom the greatest difficulties were expected to arise', was approached privately at Oxford by the Earl of Clarendon. To everyone's relief Rupert accepted, though with the frank admission that 'he was much more willing to have gone alone'. As he had demanded on the proposed combination with Sandwich, he also expressed 'a great desire to go in a ship apart, and that they might not be both in one ship'. Fortunately, 'the Prince was persuaded not to be positive in that particular', since in a time of action the orders could not be the same, if they who gave them were not together and in the same place'.

There remained only to ask Albemarle, who was still at Whitehall fighting the plague. Though the general was not expected to pose any obstruction, it was decided – just in case – to follow the same confidential procedure that had been used with Rupert. Accordingly, as soon as the Prince had given his reluctant consent, Charles found a petty pretext for calling Monck to Oxford, where he duly appeared on the night of 28 November. At the first opportunity Clarendon drew him aside and informed him of the true reason for the summons. On hearing it 'the general appeared really surprised and full of thoughts'. He confessed 'that for his own part he should be willing to go out of London tomorrow, and think himself much safer in any action against the Dutch than he could be in the post he was, where every day men died about him and in his view'. Even so, he protested, he was sure 'that he had done the King better service by staying in London, than he could have done in any other place'. The Chancellor hastened to assure the general that His Majesty himself 'had suggested the other designation of him to the service of the fleet, upon the good conduct whereof his own and the kingdom's happiness so much depended'. At this Albemarle professed himself willing to do whatever was asked of him, magnanimously offering 'that if the King pleased, he would most readily serve under the command of Prince Rupert'. Clarendon hastened to respond that 'the King would never consent to that'.

The Lord Chancellor must have been brought almost to tears by the general's noble expressions; here surely was honest, simple-hearted George after all. In fact, Albemarle had carried off a performance which he must have been rehearsing in his coach all the way from London. The truth is that the Duke had guessed the reason for his summons the moment it arrived. Pepys had met him in London the day before his departure, and found that he knew perfectly well that his going to Oxford was 'upon putting the sea business into order', and that he was all 'agog to go to sea himself the next year'. He also understood the King's mind well enough to know that he would not let Rupert command alone.

Once Clarendon had at length 'convinced' the general to accept the appointment, he suggested that they see the King immediately. As they were on their way, Albemarle suddenly stopped the Chancellor and, with a sheepish grin, imposed a condition. It was, he said, that everything be kept temporarily secret, 'for if his wife should come to know it, before he had by degrees prepared her for it, she would break out into such passions as would be very uneasy to him; but he would in a short time dispose her well enough'.

Albemarle's attempts to dispose his wife failed dismally. As soon as she found out, Her Grace 'was all storm and fury; and, according to the wisdom and modesty of her nature, poured out a thousand full-mouthed curses against all those who had contributed to that counsel'. She swore that the whole thing was only a plot to get her husband away from the court, so that his enemies could ruin him in his absence. Her rage fell especially on poor Clarendon, who had been nothing more than a messenger. She 'threw all the ill words at him which she had been accustomed to hear, accompanied with all her good wishes of what she would have befall him'. Her wrath did not soon abate. The Duchess seized on Sandwich's appointment to Spain with a vengeance: 'If my Lord had been a coward he had gone to sea no more; it may be then he might have been excused, and made an Embassador'. She had the astonishing gall to say this across the dinner table from Samuel Pepys, who enjoyed Sandwich's special patronage. Pepys gave her such an icy glare that she actually blushed. Even that was not the end of it, for six months later she latched on to a new culprit in the person of Sir William Coventry. He had had little to do with it either, but she cursed him for it anyway. Fortunately, the Duchess's reputation was such that no harm was done; even so, one can appreciate the general's eagerness to get to sea.

In view of the formidable characters of Prince Rupert and the Duke of Albemarle, it is not unreasonable to wonder how they could possibly have tolerated each other on the same quarterdeck. That question occurred to many at the time, though none expressed it as well as Andrew Marvell:

> *United Gen'ralls! sure the only spell*
> *Wherewith United Provinces to quell.*
> *Alas, ev'n they, though shell'd in treble Oake,*
> *Will prove an addled Egge with double Yolke.*

Rupert, especially, was expected to cause trouble. The Prince had made it clear from the start that he would have preferred to command by himself, or failing that, to at least command from another ship. Yet Clarendon, who reported the Prince's reservations, said in almost the same breath that otherwise 'there appeared great unanimity and consent between them'. Clarendon's opinion was echoed by Thomas Gumble, Albemarle's biographer and one of his chaplains. Gumble emphatically asserted that 'the two Generals governed with that unity and agreement, as if they had been acted by one soul; and in all that service there was never the least appearance of so much as a strangeness between them, which was a certain presage of glory and victory'. The assurances of Gumble and Clarendon are well borne out by the available evidence. The worst that can be said about the co-commanders' relationship is that any 'strangenesses' that developed were kept strictly private.

There was certainly ample opportunity for strain. The Generals' dealings with their subordinates were particularly sensitive and almost sure to cause problems. Like all powerful men of the time, the Prince and the Duke were each at the apex of a pyramid of patronage in which substantial numbers of ambitious followers had to be kept satisfied. The rivalry between the jealous groups of disciples was often intense. The Generals handled this potential powder keg with extreme delicacy, doling out the available subsidiary commands in a carefully balanced manner. Here Rupert's 'creature' would be made vice-admiral of this squadron, there Albemarle's vice-admiral of that. Nevertheless, in July 1666 a noisy row boiled up between Sir Robert Holmes and Sir Jeremy Smith, respectively Rupert's and Albemarle's principal protégés. Their mutual loathing quickly became a major scandal; a duel was rumoured, and it took the King's personal intervention to unruffle the feathers. The uproar rocked the fleet for weeks. Pepys heard that

> Holmes commanded all on the Prince's side, and Sir Jeremy Smith on the Duke's, and every body that come did apply themselves to one side or the other; and when the Duke of Albemarle was gone away to come hither, then Sir Jeremy Smith did hang his head, and walked in the Generall's ship but like a private commander.

A dispute of this magnitude might have caused a breach between the Generals, but surprisingly, their correspondence remained 'business as usual' right through the troubles. It is difficult to find evidence of even minor discord. Near the end of their commission they disagreed in their estimates of the Dutch intentions, but found a perfectly amiable solution: 'The Generall thinks they will not come out again to fight this year; Prince Rupert is of a different opinion, and they have laid a wager of five pieces upon it'. When both were ashore afterwards, Pepys reported a definite falling out; 'the Duke of Albemarle and Prince Rupert do less agree', he wrote. Yet Pepys's own words give testimony to their prior harmony.

The fact is that Rupert and Albemarle were too intelligent to let anything come between them from beginning to end. They could be sure there were enemies ashore who were scrutinizing their every move, and the defence of their reputations demanded that they always present a common front. Even considering such imperatives, it is possible that they actually liked each other. After all, despite their undoubted differences in personality they had much in common: they both spoke the language of the soldier, they had the same standards of discipline and conduct for their juniors, and each had a capacity for hard work and attention to detail that the other would have admired. They shared a commonsense attitude towards administrative affairs which was especially evident in their mutual dislike for paper-shuffling bureaucrats like Samuel Pepys, whose accounts became a particular target of their ire.

Marvell's wit notwithstanding, the sea campaign of 1666 was to show the Generals better together than apart. Far from addling the egg, the double yolk had surprising strength.

Chapter VIII

The Other Side of the Hill

To nearest ports their shatter'd ships repair,
Where by our dreadful cannon they lay aw'd
So reverently men quit the open air,
When thunder speaks the angry gods abroad.

While the Earl of Sandwich roamed the North Sea at will in the summer of 1665, the Dutch desperately sought means to restore their once-mighty sea power. The Battle of Lowestoft was one of the most disappointing, humiliating, and demoralizing defeats ever suffered by the Netherlands. The sight of the shattered ruins of the fleet, on which so much effort had been expended, at first produced widespread incredulity and bewilderment. But the Dutch were a proud race. Their despondency soon changed to anger, and then to a firm determination that it would not happen again.

The navy's deficiencies were largely caused by the internal disunity of the nation. The Republic was a loose federation of seven independent Provinces, each jealous of its own rights and institutions. Government was by a hierarchy of oligarchic assemblies; town councils had above them provincial States, usually dominated by self-perpetuating exclusive cliques of prominent burgher families. At the highest level was the States-General at The Hague.

No governmental organ in Europe was quite like the States-General. Officially the ultimate authority in the land, it had no legal power over the internal affairs of the Provinces, but it did control foreign relations and national defence. Its members, individually or collectively, were distinguished by the titular prefix 'Hoogh Mogend', which translates into English as the rather pompous 'High and Mighty'. Englishmen loved to poke fun at the 'hogen-mogens', though the term was no more pretentious in Dutch than 'The Honourable' in modern English. The States-General was an extremely disputatious body. The Provinces were equally represented, and as they seldom agreed outright on anything, compromise was the usual order of business. More often than not, resolutions tended to be slanted in favour of the Province of Holland, which dwarfed the others in population and economic strength. The vibrant cities of Holland – Amsterdam especially, but also Rotterdam, Delft, Leiden, Gouda, Haarlem, The Hague, and others – were larger and more prosperous than those of the other Provinces. Their tax contributions and the credit offered by their bankers were so much greater than the rest that no decisions involving sizeable outlays of money (for the navy, for instance) were possible without the consent of the Hollanders. This sometimes amounted to an unofficial veto. Consequently, in order to determine the actual drift of national policy, one often looked first to the provincial States of Holland.

The dominance of the Hollanders was never complete. Their pre-eminence was much resented elsewhere, particularly by their natural commercial rivals in the second-strongest Province of Zeeland. Even when the two maritime Provinces agreed, they were often opposed by the other five, which were more agriculturally oriented. At times it seemed as though there were seven different countries, and the States-General a congress of ambassadors. It was not without reason that a contemporary English observer, Sir William Temple, called them the 'Disunited Provinces'.

There were also intense class and factional disputes. The ruling middle class often had to contend with a jealous and steadily declining landed nobility, mainly in Friesland and the eastern Provinces. Nobles and burghers alike were challenged by the rural peasantry and a large and volatile urban working class which shared few of the pleasures of their wealthy overlords. As elsewhere in Europe, there were serious religious differences. A narrow-minded Calvinist clergy stayed constantly at odds with a multiplicity of Protestant dissenters and a large proscribed Catholic minority.

Still further discord came from a burning, unresolved constitutional issue: the rights of the House of Orange, whose hereditary prince had formerly held the title of *Stadhouder* (chief of state) in most of the Provinces. This office had carried virtual control of the armed forces. In 1650, Stadhouder William II had died, leaving as his only heir a son still in the womb. A special Grand Assembly of all the provincial States had dealt with this crisis by abolishing the Stadhouderate and vesting its powers in the States-General. But a viable Orange party remained. It rallied around the infant William III, born a week after his father's death, and made the future of the young prince the principal political issue in the Netherlands for over twenty years. The debate produced a broad spectrum of views. At one extreme were the ruling republicans, who wished to exclude the House of Orange from politics forever. They were opposed by a moderate Orangist faction which accepted the States-General only as temporary regents, by a more conservative party which considered the abolition of the Stad-houderate illegal, and finally by an avowedly monarchist minority. The whole range of opinions could be found anywhere in the country, but there were definite provincial preferences; Holland in particular was strongly republican, Zeeland intensely Orangist. The dispute naturally spilled over into the fleet, where it added its poison to all the other rivalries.

Then there were the five Admiralties. These 'Colleges', as they were known, were civilian boards of directors responsible for administering the sea-forces of specific maritime regions. Each had its own flag-officers, its own men-of-war, its own logistical establishment, and its own dockyards. The Admiralties were not fully autonomous, for their decisions and appointments were subject to review by their respective provincial States and the States-General. They were also dependent on the States for extra-ordinary grants of money, though normal expenses were covered by taxes on merchant shipping. Furthermore, the Admiralties were purely administrative bodies with no authority over operational matters; that was the States-General's responsibility. Even with such limitations, the decentralized system complicated every aspect of the navy's management. The Admiralties bickered incessantly over disputed privileges, competed for allocations of funds, and bid against each other for scarce naval stores. But no one ever considered changing the arrangement. It was merely another manifestation of the ingrained Dutch respect for traditional rights; the Admiralties had preceded the union of the Provinces.

Two of the Admiralties represented the provincial navies of Zeeland and Friesland. Zeeland, the southernmost maritime Province, lay astride the estuary of the Scheldt. Its Admiralty was based at the busy port of Vlissingen, but also built ships at Zierikzee, Middelburg, and Kampveere. The Zeeland dockyards produced relatively few warships of the larger sizes and contributed fewer ships to the main fleet than the other Admiralties. Instead, the Zeelanders were by long habit great corsairs, regularly unleashing swarms of light commerce raiders which could cause extensive damage to an enemy's merchant fleets. The Province was immensely proud of its separate heritage. Its ships could be easily distinguished by the provincial arms (a lion rising from the sea) emblazoned across their sterns, and by the standard of Vlissingen which they often displayed as a jack in place of the normal Dutch tricolour. As with other Zeeland state institutions, the Admiralty bitterly resented the second-class status to which it was usually relegated by the Hollanders. A particular source of discontent was the post of commander-in-chief, from which Zeelanders were systematically excluded.

The Admiralty of Friesland, the Province on the north shore of the Zuiderzee, was located at Harlingen. In most respects it was the least important of the five. The Frisian towns never approached the prosperity of those of Holland and Zeeland, and their political power was slight. Though they had always contributed stout ships, it was only in 1665 that their commanders were granted formal flag rank.

The other three Admiralties all served the Province of Holland. Centred in Rotterdam at the southern end of the Province was the Admiralty of the Maas, the broad river forming the principal outlet of the Rhine. By reason of seniority the Admiralty of the Maas claimed precedence over the others. This was grudgingly recognized elsewhere; the commander-in-chief of the fleet traditionally sailed in a Rotterdam ship, and in battle the Admiralty's own senior flag-officer was usually the designated successor if the commander was killed. The central part of Holland was the territory of the powerful Admiralty of Amsterdam. Its vast dockyards produced about three times as many ships as any of the others. With political support in the States of Holland and the States-General, Amsterdam from time to time sought to dislodge the Admiralty of the Maas from its first-place position. But though the city's will prevailed in most disputes, it failed in this one; traditional rights were sacrosanct. The third Holland Admiralty was the College of the Noorderkwartier with jurisdiction in Westfriesland. Its administrative centre was at Hoorn, and it built ships there and also at Enkhuizen, Medemblik, and Monnikendam. Though the Noorderkwartier's contribution in ships was usually second only to Amsterdam's, its political influence was relatively weak.

With so many divisive influences and diverse loyalties, it is hard to see how the navy or even the Republic itself could have functioned effectively for long without the guidance of some unifying leadership. That need had formerly been filled by the Stadhouder; the suppression of his powers had carried the potential for disintegration.

Fortunately for the Netherlands, a great leader arose in the person of Johan de Witt. A lawyer from a leading oligarch family of Dordrecht, de Witt was named *Raadpensionaris* of Holland by the provincial States in 1653. He was aged only twenty-eight at the time. Literally 'Council Pensionary', the Raadpensionaris was the chief minister of the Province and its leading deputy in the States-General. De Witt fortified his position by marrying into a prominent regent family of Amsterdam and associating himself with the city's interests. With powerful backing from that quarter, he was able to impose his will on the Netherlands for two decades. De Witt was a master of persuasion and compromise, the consummate politician. Through every device of parliamentary arts, ethical and otherwise, he patiently pieced together coalitions which would support his aims. Over the years he became a wise administrator and a statesman of high ability.

In de Witt the Seven Provinces found not only the political leader they needed, but a leader who was also an unswerving advocate of sea power. Though this was evident from the first, he obtained few improvements in the fleet until 1664. Then, with an English war clearly unavoidable, de Witt became alarmed at the slow pace of naval reform and took personal charge of its direction. At The Hague he dunned the non-maritime Provinces to extract their share of financial support, brought about a vast shipbuilding programme, and saw to the appointment of deputies from the States-General to coordinate the operations of the Admiralties and suppress corruption. He founded a specialized regiment of marines. Though his attempt to institute conscription was unsuccessful (the concept was too foreign for the Dutch) he did obtain regular pay for the seamen and better conditions of life afloat. He also initiated new surveys of channels and anchorages to allow the fleet to take better advantage of the coastal shoals.

Not all of de Witt's ideas were useful. He was a strong-willed and rather overbearing man who mistrusted (and was mistrusted by) most of the sea-officers, who were generally Orangist sympathizers. He frequently involved himself in matters that would have been better left to the seamen, for despite his enthusiasm for the navy he understood seamanship and the mechanics of shipboard warfare much less perfectly than he thought he did. This led to the unfortunate seven-squadron fleet organization and the foolish official endorsement of the group-fighting tactics. For these errors, though, de Witt could hardly be held solely responsible. On the whole, his influence was highly beneficial. Indeed, without his resilience and resolve it is quite possible that the Second Anglo-Dutch War would have ended with the first battle.

In the immediate aftermath of Lowestoft all was confusion. Because the fleet had fled to at least four different havens, the extent of the disaster could not be determined for some time. At first, it was feared that it might have been catastrophic; in France, ambassador Van Beuningen publicly admitted the loss of twenty-four ships. But when the Admiralties finally counted survivors and found only seventeen vessels missing, de Witt realized that there was still hope. He grimly began preparations to set forth another fleet. Before it sailed, he meant to identify all the causes of the defeat and eliminate them.

The first and most immediate problem was finding a suitable commander-in-chief to replace Obdam. In those days each Admiralty had the right to appoint three permanent flag-officers for the fleet: a lieutenant-admiral as senior officer, a vice-admiral, and a *schout-bij-nacht* (rear-admiral). In addition, the States of Holland named the Lieutenant-Admiral of Holland and Westfriesland as admiralissimo of the three Holland Admiralties. This person was usually designated commander-in-chief, though the States-General could name someone else if it wished. In the wake of Lowestoft there was a serious difficulty. Three lieutenant-admirals had been killed: Obdam of Holland and Westfriesland, Cortenaer of the Maas (the intended heir-apparent), and Stellingwerf of Friesland. Of the remaining three, de Ruyter of Amsterdam and Meppel of the Noorderkwartier were in American waters along with the senior vice-admiral, Aert van Nes of the Maas. That left only Jan Evertsen of Zeeland. Though Evertsen was a distinguished officer of long experience, the Holland politicians regarded the prospect of his elevation with distaste. Being a Zeelander was enough in itself, but he was also a particularly outspoken Orangist, making him doubly unacceptable to the republicans. The Hollanders themselves suffered from a lamentable dearth of senior candidates. Johan de Witt favoured de Ruyter, a universally respected commander and moreover a staunch republican. Unfortunately, de Ruyter's chances of slipping through the English blockade seemed slim at best. In his (and Meppel's) absence, the only available Hollander worthy of notice was Cornelis Tromp of Amsterdam, a mere vice-admiral. With all seven Provinces having equal votes in the States-General, there seemed a greater than usual chance of the Zeelander getting the nod. This possibility the Holland deputies resolved to prevent by any means.

At the Battle of Lowestoft, the Earl of Sandwich's attack had split the Dutch in two. One fragment under Evertsen had entered the Maas, while a much larger part had gone with Tromp to the Texel and the Vlie. When it was reported ashore that Evertsen was not with Tromp, many Hollanders assumed that the Zeelander had abandoned the fleet. This convenient canard did not displease Johan de Witt. Reports of the admiral's supposed treachery were quickly disseminated throughout the Provinces and also in foreign capitals. In Paris, Venetian ambassador Alvise Sagredo was told that 'Admiral Everson of Zeeland, instead of succeeding to the command, as he should, and resisting the confusion beginning among his countrymen, spread all his sails to the wind and gave himself to a most disgraceful flight'. Sagredo was not sure what to make of this, for the English ambassador, Lord Holles, specifically praised Evertsen as one of the few who had fought to the last.

In Holland the most preposterous stories were believed. As the admiral journeyed to The Hague to report to the States-General, he encountered an angry mob at Den Briel. Amid shrieks of treason, the mindless rabble roughly dragged him from his carriage, flung him into the water, and pelted him with stones; he was finally rescued, half dead, by the burgomaster and the town garrison. Evertsen was subsequently escorted to The Hague, where the battered old mariner, incredulous at the attacks against him, addressed the States-General in his simple sailor's language. His account was raucously jeered by the Holland deputies as a 'feeble harangue'. Johan de Witt, in a perversion of justice that soiled his own reputation, demanded that Evertsen's name be added to the list of officers to be tried for cowardice. Despite the outraged protests of the Zeeland deputies, the admiral was forthwith borne to the Texel and clapped aboard ship in humiliating close confinement. The trial proved embarrassing to de Witt. The hatred for the Zeeland commander so evident among the republican burghers was not shared by the sea-officers. Captain after captain, Hollanders included, testified only to Evertsen's bravery. It came out that his flagship, the *Hof van Zeeland*, had staggered home with sixty men dead (the most of any surviving vessel) and 115 shot holes in her sides. Evertsen was completely exonerated, but too late. The States of Holland had made Tromp Lieutenant-Admiral of the Maas, and as senior officer of the senior Admiralty he was approved by the States-General as acting commander-in-chief.

Jan Evertsen resigned in disgust. Cornelis Evertsen replaced his brother as Lieutenant-Admiral of Zeeland, and Jan's own son Cornelis the Younger was made *schout-bij-nacht*. Friesland also named a new lieutenant-admiral to replace Stellingwerf. The Frisians had been unimpressed by the performance of their junior flag-officers, Rudolf Coenders and Hendrik Bruynsvelt. The provincial States passed over them and selected Captain Tjerk Hiddes de Vries; he had been one of the few who had made a stand against Sandwich's attack, and the one who had saved the *Elf Steden* from seemingly certain destruction.

The new commander-in-chief, Cornelis Maartenszoon Tromp, had much to recommend him. Born in 1622, he was the son of the great Maarten Tromp and had benefitted greatly from the connection; he had been made a captain at twenty-eight and a flag-officer at thirty-two. But he was also a highly-regarded seaman in his own right; his stern father had made him toil for years as a common seaman before granting his commission. The son was an extroverted, rather flamboyant officer, fond of fine clothes and the trappings of wealth. A natural leader, he was daring, fearless, and idolized by the seamen. Though undeniably headstrong and temperamental, he was an enlightened tactician and an early proponent of the line-ahead system.

Cornelis Tromp was undoubtedly proud to see his pendant of command fluttering from the masthead, but his position was anything but secure. Johan de Witt instinctively disliked his Orangist leanings and made it clear that he was a decidedly second choice. The States-General and the States of Holland accordingly provided for his supercession should de Ruyter somehow return before the fleet sailed; the title of Lieutenant-Admiral of Holland and Westfriesland was pointedly withheld. Despite the slight, Tromp set to work with great energy to reorganize the fleet and restore its discipline. In late July, with the ships nearly ready for sea, it was announced that three High and Mighty Gentlemen of the States-General would accompany the expedition aboard the flagship to give 'superintendence, direction, and guidance' to the commander. Inevitably, one was de Witt himself. The others were Johan Boreel of Zeeland, Burgomaster of Middelburg, and eighty-year-old Rutger Huygens of Gelderland; all three had identical attitudes towards the navy. Tromp understandably resented, as had Obdam before him, de Witt's condescending interference in 'a business so different from his vocation'.

The final blow for Cornelis Tromp came when de Ruyter's squadron unexpectedly arrived home on 27 July. The country greeted the long-lost admiral as if he had won a tremendous victory; crowds lined his anchorage in the Ems, cheering madly. Five days later the States of Holland appointed de Ruyter Lieutenant-Admiral of Holland and Westfriesland, whereupon the States-General named him commander-in-chief. Tromp was crushed. His fleet was practically ready to sail; in a few days he would have been loose in the North Sea, where a success of any degree would have fortified his position. He publicly declared that he would go ashore rather than serve under de Ruyter, but the States-General bluntly advised him to stay with the fleet or face trial for insubordination. When the new Admiral-General arrived at the Texel on 8 August, Tromp respectfully submitted. But the wounds were deep ones, and not to be healed easily. The affair had a depressing effect on the fleet, and discipline suffered. There was an ugly mutiny among the seamen, who preferred Tromp; one man was hanged, another flogged. For de Ruyter it was not an auspicious beginning.

Against this backdrop of unhappiness and dissension, the Dutch navy rose from the depths of defeat to contest anew the control of the seas. Throughout the months of its rebirth, the bickering, disagreements, and arguments among admirals and politicians never ceased for an instant. But this was simply the Dutch way. Underneath the surface turmoil, improvements were happening continuously, and they began almost before the smoke of the first battle had cleared.

In the wake of Lowestoft, the more realistic thinkers among the Dutch sea-officers identified three principal causes for the disaster. The most obvious, and the one which the politicians regarded as paramount, was the glaring absence of discipline among captains and admirals. Johan de Witt was particularly unhappy with the flag-officers, and the States-General reproached them collectively for neglecting the leadership of their squadrons. Even more disturbing were the many cases of disobedience and apparent cowardice among the captains, and the unprofessional attitude of officers throughout the fleet. The nation's traditions of independence had always made Dutchmen particularly indisposed to rules and regulations. Furthermore, most of the captains had come up through the merchant service, where the preservation of one's ship was everything.

The moment Cornelis Tromp's shattered flagship, the *Liefde*, returned from the battle, he stormed to The Hague to denounce the captains before the States as 'a parcel of rogues'. After some weeks of hesitation, the High and Mighty directed a council-of-war to try the malefactors and bring them to justice. At first Tromp asked to be excused from presidency of the tribunal because criminal trial procedures were beyond his ken, but also with the frank admission that he did 'not wish to incur the ill will and envy of many persons of rank, by being obliged to condemn their relatives'. He had no doubt of the verdicts. The States-General would not accede to his request, but did assign deputies and Admiralty commissioners to participate in the trials and relieve the acting commander of some of the onus. The trial commission inspected the ships minutely, and the captains of those which were undamaged were summoned to account. In due course a series of draconian sentences resulted; Cornelis Tromp was conveniently ill on the day they were announced. Three captains were dismissed, their swords broken by the public executioner, and three more were exiled, including

Stinstra, Cortenaer's flag-captain. The worst offenders were shot to death in view of the whole fleet: Captain Anthony Evertsen de Marre of the Amsterdam ship *Wakende Boei*, Jacob Bruynings of the Noorderkwartier's *Westfriesland*, and Jan Pieterszoon Onclaer of the Rotterdam East Indiaman *Nieuw Batavia*. Stinstra was forced to witness the executions with a noose around his neck.

If the Dutch leaders were determined to demonstrate that dereliction of duty would not go unpunished, they also took pains to demonstrate that success would not go unrewarded. Captain Jan de Haan, whose *Stad en Lande* had brought in the English *Charity*, found himself the proud recipient of an outright grant of 4,000 Guilders, plus the value of the prize and all its provisions and munitions. Few Dutch sea-officers of this period were wealthy, so de Haan's spectacular windfall may have had an even more salutary effect than the executions.

Discipline continued to improve under de Ruyter's vigilant eye. A few captains whose unreliability was suspected but not proven (or who had escaped trial because of powerful friends) still remained. The companies of sea-soldiers in their ships were pointedly assigned to marine officers of unimpeachable reputations who would be certain to report any misbehaviour among their seniors. Hand in hand with discipline went morale. This had suffered not only from defeat, but also from Jan Evertsen's farcical trial and the row between Tromp and de Ruyter. Under the new Admiral-General spirits slowly revived, though mainly from the surprising inability of the English to take advantage of their victory. The heavy Dutch losses to Sandwich's fleet in September could have caused further dismay, but the burghers were so relieved at the deliverance of most of the Indiamen and the other merchantmen from Bergen that they thanked the seamen instead of chiding them. Finally, de Ruyter's bold October cruise in the mouth of the Thames left everyone with a healthy renewed confidence.

The second great weakness of the Dutch fleet at Lowestoft was tactical. That the seven-squadron organization left something to be desired was self-evident. Even so, breaking away from the mêlée tradition was not easy, for the fleet's landsmen overseers did not immediately grasp what had happened. Far from embracing any changes, the shore-bound authorities reaffirmed the old system within a few weeks after the battle. A special commission including Johan de Witt stated that 'the greatest advantage for this nation lies in boarding and entering', and merely recommended that ships be more strongly manned. The Admiralty of Zeeland followed with advice that the English gunnery superiority could be overcome only if all efforts were

> directed so that promptly and at the first opportunity we may board, and so fight ship against ship, in which with God's blessing the best hope for a signal victory lies for this side because of the unusual address and animosity, which is found in our seamen on grappling and leaping into the enemy's ships, and that so much more because the English themselves try to avoid it, showing how and where they can and must be attacked in their weakness.

The politicians in The Hague took the view that the defeat had been due to the negligence of the commanders who had allowed the squadrons to become dis-organized. On 17 July the States-General issued instructions which admonished the flag-officers to stay with their squadrons, to keep the squadrons separate and distinct, and to ensure that individual ships did not interfere with each other. Above all, the commanders were to see to it that 'everyone shall do his duty to board, grapple, and conquer' the enemy's ships.

By then the sea-officers had seen enough of the group fighting methods. They realized that the battle had been decided by the gun, that their ships had been smashed to splinters while their carefully ordered enemy had gone almost unscathed. They knew that aside from the *Stad en Lande*, only the *Oranje* had succeeded in boarding anything, and she had been lost. Some officers had probably begun to think in terms of formal tactics long before. A few including Obdam himself had evidently imitated the English on an improvised basis even at Lowestoft, for Sir Thomas Allin mentioned having encountered the *Eendracht* and several other ships 'lying on a line'. When Johan de Witt and his two colleagues from the States-General journeyed to the Texel towards the end of July to oversee the fleet's operations, they were surprised to find all the flag-officers urging adoption of the hierarchical English organization of three squadrons of three divisions each – and with it the single-file line of battle. Indeed, Cornelis Tromp had already established the three squadrons. Faced with the united front presented by the admirals, de Witt for once deferred to their judgement. In a landmark for the Dutch navy, the line was officially introduced in a general instruction approved by the States-General's plenipotentiaries on 5 August 1665.

Even with this giant advance, the sea-service was unable to shake free from the influence of the politicians, for the new instructions contained a strange provision that had no counterpart in the English system. In testimony before the States of Holland shortly after the battle, Tromp had graphically described the disorder which had occurred with the early loss of Cortenaer and Stellingwerf, and the utter carnage following Obdam's demise. The provincial deputies had afterwards decided among themselves that such calamities could be best avoided if the principal commanders kept aloof from the fighting at the start of a battle, engaging only after the rest of the fleet was committed. Johan de Witt carried this view to the Texel and insisted that it be incorporated in the instructions. As applied to the three-squadron line of battle, it meant that the centre squadron under the commander-in-chief should initially place itself farther from the enemy than the other two, and within each squadron the admiral's division should do likewise. The result would be a wavy formation which eventually came to be known as the *slangvormige* (snake-shaped) line. It can be safely assumed that the sea-officers tolerated this curious concept only to placate the politicians. Such a formation would have been virtually impossible to maintain in action, while the very thought of holding back from the fray flew in the face of the traditional code of conduct of the seventeenth-century man of action. Though the *slangvormige* line remained official Dutch tactical doctrine for many years, admirals never paid it the slightest attention.

The new general instruction had hardly been issued when a major amendment was introduced. On 8 August de Ruyter arrived at the Texel to supersede Tromp as commander-in-chief. That day the two commanders and the three plenipotentiaries met in a private conference, during which de Witt suggested that a fourth squadron be created. This squadron would be under de Ruyter himself, and in action it would keep to windward of the battle-line as a reserve to be thrown in where needed. Just before Lowestoft the Earl of Sandwich had advocated a related scheme for the English fleet in which the extra squadron would have consisted of hired merchantmen which he regarded as unfit for the main line. De Ruyter too had experimented with reserves; during his return from North America he had set aside several ships from his little squadron for just such a purpose. But that the reserve should include the commander-in-chief was a new departure. Like the snake formation it originated in the States of Holland, in part as another manifestation of the desire to preserve the chief commander. The deputies were perhaps also influenced by reports of the Duke of York's actions at Lowestoft. There, James and Penn had kept much of their squadron well to windward of the rest of the fleet. Dutch seamen credited that move with having preserved the weather gage for the English, and undoubtedly reported how effective the fresh ships had been when finally brought into the fight. In addition, the always politically sensitive de Witt appears to have had the secondary motive of ensuring that all six lieutenant-admirals receive suitably prestigious positions; an inactive fifth squadron of the ships left in port had already been created for Meppel of the Noorderkwartier, while the Lieutenant-Admiral of the Maas (de Ruyter's designated understudy) would lie in the reserve squadron ready to take over command if necessary.

Whatever the origins, de Witt, Huygens, and Boreel forthwith added the reserve squadron to the general instruction with de Ruyter's blessing, but without bothering to obtain approval from the full council-of-war. The plenipotentiaries extracted twenty-one ships to form de Ruyter's contingent, and the two final cruises of 1665 were accordingly carried out in four squadrons. There matters stood until the following May, when the fleet gathered at the Texel for the 1666 campaign. This time de Witt left affairs in the hands of de Ruyter, who was still satisfied with the four-squadron arrangement. But when the question was laid before the council-of-war, which had not been previously consulted, the commander-in-chief found the flag-officers voicing objections to the reserve squadron. On 23 May representatives of the Admiralties presented a collective opinion supporting the flag-officers' arguments, and de Ruyter reluctantly acquiesced.

With acceptance of the three-squadron order the Dutch adopted the fundamentals of the English fighting method – nine days before going into action. There remained certain unique features in the Dutch expression of the system, even beyond the bizarre snake formation. For one thing, the Dutch gave unusual latitude to the squadron commanders in conducting their affairs. The signalling system was decentralized, each of the senior officers for the most part working out his own arrangements. Unlike the English, the Dutch never completely eschewed the grappling ideal; they still had every intention of fighting hand to hand should the opportunity present itself, and among the few general signals was a series ordering close action for boarding. In other respects the Dutch incorporated as many of the English ideas as they could. A close-hauled line was specified, provision was made for tacking from the rear, and small frigates were relegated to subsidiary duties. But the Dutch had not yet assimilated some of the more sophisticated English manoeuvres, and their line consequently had less flexibility. Nevertheless, despite the tentative and still experimental nature of the Dutch system, it was a far cry from the shambles of the old ways.

The third cause of the Dutch defeat at Lowestoft was the inferiority of their ships. There was nothing wrong with the fundamental designs; Dutch shipbuilders were renowned the world over, their dockyards regularly producing powerful warships for France, Spain, Venice, and other foreign customers. Sadly, the shipwrights had rarely been allowed to build such great vessels for their own fleet. Dutch men-of-war were simply too small, too weakly timbered, and too lightly armed to trade blows with the English. For this the Admiralty of Amsterdam was largely to blame.

In 1652, early in the First Anglo-Dutch War, Maarten Tromp warned the States-General that the English had better ships. He recommended immediate construction of a new class of men-of-war to be at least 150 feet long from stem to sternpost and proportionately broader and deeper than before; at the time the largest proper warship in the Dutch fleet measured 134 feet. Though Tromp's proposal was received enthusiastically by the Admiralty of the Maas, the Admiralty of Amsterdam was unwilling to build anything longer than 140 feet because of the difficulty of getting big ships across the bar in the approaches to their harbour. Fearing that Rotterdam's proposed great ships would enhance the prestige of the Admiralty of the Maas relative to their own, the Amsterdam authorities selfishly sought to limit new construction to the smaller sizes they themselves desired to build. Rotterdam's deputies pointed out in exasperation that huge Indiamen routinely passed the shallows twice a year, but the States-General as usual sided with Amsterdam. A series of 'charters' was imposed similar to the pernicious English 'establishments' of the eighteenth century. The charters specified three classes of ships, 130, 136, and 140 feet in length. Subsequently, Maarten Tromp won the Battle of Dungeness in November 1652. His influence enhanced by the victory, Tromp renewed his request for larger ships. The States-General thereupon reopened the matter, and after spirited debate a compromise was reached. The Maas was allowed to build the 150-foot *Eendracht* in 1653 to serve as the fleet flagship and the similar *Groot Hollandia* in 1654 as Rotterdam's own flagship, but all other Rotterdam ships were to be built to the smallest (130-foot) charter. Amsterdam would build to all the chartered dimensions up to 140 feet, while the Noorderkwartier, Zeeland, and Friesland would have 130- and 136-foot ships only. Though some shipwrights exceeded the specified lengths by up to three or four feet, the charters continued to be observed until after 1660. In all of the decade of the 1650s, the dockyards added only the two big Rotterdam ships (plus the 146-foot Genoese ship which Amsterdam appropriated in 1653) and about sixty vessels 130 to 140 feet long. The States-General was presumably satisfied with the ships, which did well enough against the Swedes in 1658, but all were decidedly mediocre by English standards.

Comparing the ships of the two navies is not a straightforward matter. For a given length and breadth, the displacement was about the same because the differences between the shallow flat-bottomed Dutch sections and the deep semi-circular English sections roughly cancelled each other out. But comparing dimensions is not straightforward either, for the opponents used different methods of measurement. The English took the keel as the basic length measure, though the more meaningful internal gundeck length is recorded for many ships. The Dutch employed an external stem-to-sternpost measurement and expressed it in the 283 mm. Amsterdam foot (as opposed to the 305 mm. English foot). Allowing for these variations, the 130- to 140-foot Dutch ships were about the same length as the small and medium-sized English fourth-rates of the 1650s. The *Eendracht* and *Groot Hollandia* were equivalent to ships with a gundeck length of about 135 English feet, barely within the size range of the English Commonwealth third-rates and the Early Stuart second-rates. Due to the limitations of the charters, the Dutch in effect built a whole fleet of fourth-rates with a pair of third-rates as flagships. There was nothing comparable to the English first-rates.

After 1660 the Dutch gradually broke away from the charters. Between 1661 and 1664 they built about ten ships on the old patterns, but finally produced three others which matched the *Eendracht* and one which exceeded her – the *Spiegel* of 1663. It was only at the outbreak of the war that the Dutch suddenly awakened to the inadequacy of their former policies. At de Witt's urging the States-General ordered construction of twenty-four large ships, adding a second group of twenty-four several months later. These vessels were far from completion at the time of Lowestoft. Furthermore, the *Spiegel* and most of the other big ships which had already been completed were for various reasons not available to Obdam. Thus Maarten Tromp's warning of thirteen years before had been effectively ignored, and Obdam and some 5,000 of his seamen paid the price for the short-sighted behaviour of the Admiralty of Amsterdam.

Through the summer of 1665 the Dutch had to make do with the old fleet. Beginning in September the new ships at last began to appear at a rate of two, three, and even four each month. By May most of the first group were ready and some of the second, twenty-seven in all. They included five ships of 50–56 guns, ten of 60–68, ten of 70–78, and two of 80. Because of the shallow-draught requirement the Dutch had made no attempt to equal the English first-rates; all the new ships were two-deckers. Attitudes on this were changing, however. In a complete reversal of policy, the Admiralty of Amsterdam had begun to espouse very big ships despite the sandbars, and three-decked two-tiered designs comparable to the English second-rates were already under construction. Even without the three-deckers, the vessels already completed were better than any the Dutch had ever had. The 70-gun ships were longer than the old *Eendracht* and considerably broader, the 60-gun ships only slightly smaller. Best of all were the great flagships. Amsterdam built the 80-gun *Hollandia*, 165 feet long, and the Noorderkwartier contributed the 78-gun *Westfriesland*. The Maas added two: a new *Eendracht* of 76 guns, and a powerful 80-gun flagship for the commander-in-chief named the *Zeven Provinciën*. This most famous of all Dutch warships was to serve de Ruyter in six great battles. Built on contract by a consortium of shipwrights at Delfshaven, she joined the fleet in October 1665. Though shorter than Amsterdam's *Hollandia*, the *Zeven Provinciën* was unusually beamy and could carry a much greater weight of ordnance.

With all the new construction the Dutch had more ships than they could man, so ten very old vessels of 34–40 guns were discarded during the winter. A further deletion came about through the worthless alliance with Denmark. Though the Dutch hoped Frederik might play an active role in the war, he was so afraid of the Swedes and of possible English reprisals that he clamoured for the Netherlands to help *him*. To placate their reluctant ally the States-General chartered eight elderly men-of-war to Denmark for the duration. Another noticeable difference in the fleet of 1666 was the absence of the once-proud East India Company contingent. Though the *Oranje* and some other Indiamen had fought well in 1665, the ships were too slow and too weakly timbered to combine properly with the men-of-war. In addition, they often drew more water than the greatest flagships and thereby wasted part of the tactical benefit of the warships' shallow hull forms. The remaining merchantmen were returned to their owners, and the V.O.C. was directed to make contributions in a different form. Accordingly, the Amsterdam chapter promised to pay the cost of fitting out twenty men-of-war already belonging to the Admiralty.

The effect of all this was a complete transformation of the Dutch fleet. The old, weak, and unfit ships had been mostly cast away and replaced by powerful new ones. The original core of medium-sized vessels still remained, but they now flew the pendants of junior captains rather than the admirals' flags they had flown at Lowestoft. The 1666 fleet was numerically weaker than before, but much more potent. There can be little doubt that the long and menacing rows of gunports in de Ruyter's reconstituted squadrons did much to restore the seamen's confidence.

None of this is meant to imply that the Dutch fleet had become in any way superior, or even equal, to the English. As impressive as the *Zeven Provinciën* and *Hollandia* seemed, the best English second-rates were still larger, the first-rates very much so. There was also the matter of ordnance. The biggest English ships had full lower-deck batteries of massive 42-pdr cannon-of-seven, while smaller three-deckers and all large two-deckers were equipped with 32-pdr demi-cannon. The whole Dutch fleet had only twenty guns larger than 24-pounders, mostly in the *Zeven Provinciën*. It was true that a Dutch ship typically mounted more guns than an English ship of the same dimensions, but the English ship invariably carried a greater weight of ordnance and had a much heavier broadside. For instance, the five largest Dutch 70-gun ships (*Pacificatie, Walcheren, Spiegel, Reiger,* and *Gouda*) were similar in size to the new 64-gun English third-rates *Rupert* and *Defiance*. The English ships could each throw 1,334* pounds of shot, while the best-armed of the Dutch could fire but 1,054 pounds (*English* pounds) and the least 924.

This difference was partly the result of deliberate policy. As noted earlier, firepower was everything for the English, who packed guns into their ships until the lower ports were as little as three feet from the water. The Dutch preferred greater freeboard, which

*According to the Establishment of 1666; in fact, both carried guns above their allowance.

significantly limited the allowable weight of ordnance. Broadsides also suffered from the relative scarcity of large-calibre brass guns and the less extensive employment of lightweight drakes and cutts. The Admiralties did all they could to obtain brass ordnance; English pieces were especially prized, and some were smuggled in through the connivance of profiteering manufacturers. Swedish guns were also highly regarded, though with Sweden on close terms with England their acquisition required a certain amount of sleight-of-hand. On 7 April 1666 an English-language newsletter from The Hague reported a notable success:

> We have made a shift to bye 60 brass guns which carries 24 pound bullet of the Swedes in English merchants names. A good part of our artillery carryes bullets of greater weight then wee were wont to doe. The English have had a great advantage in that over us, but wee will remedie it, as wee have done partly already.

But such windfalls were rare, and the shortage of ordnance continued. The *Zeven Provinciën* was delayed for months by want of guns; in Zeeland things were so bad that the Admiralty had to take the cannons from the walls of Middelburg and Kampveere to arm their new flagships.

The Dutch were thus still individually overmatched, but the margin had been significantly narrowed. The latest 'butter-boxes', as English seamen derisively termed their opponents' square-sterned ships, were not to be despised. By 1666 the States' Fleet had at least partially corrected every area of its former weakness. Discipline among the officers had been assured; shooting a few 'to encourage the rest' had taught everyone what was expected. The ships were much improved (eighteen were bigger than the best of Obdam's) and a better way of using them had at last been devised. The Dutch had in addition a final element which had been lacking the year before, one which may have outweighed all the rest: they now had Michiel Adriaanszoon de Ruyter.

The greatest seaman of the age was born in Vlissingen in 1607. Of humble origins, his father a brewer's drayman, he was at first known only as Michiel Adriaanszoon. Ruyter came later, a nickname meaning *horseman* derived from a cavalry soldier grandfather. As was typical of the sons of Zeeland, he was sent to sea at the age of eleven as a boatswain's apprentice. Most of his youth was spent 'before the mast' in merchantmen, privateers, and whalers. He gradually worked through the lower ranks – able seaman, boatswain, chief mate – until at the age of thirty he became a merchant captain and privateersman for the Lampsens, the great Zeeland shipping magnates. In a short time he evidently acquired a high reputation, for in 1641 he was nominated by the Admiralty of Zeeland and confirmed by the States-General as rear-admiral of a national fleet fitted out against Spain. The expedition met indifferent success, but de Ruyter distinguished himself in a violent fight with the Spaniards off Cape St. Vincent. When the fleet was disbanded at the end of the campaign he returned to the service of the Lampsens. A number of profitable trading cruises followed, and by 1651 he had saved enough money to retire. He married (for the third time, two earlier wives having died) and settled in to enjoy a life ashore.

The First Anglo-Dutch War ended de Ruyter's brief retirement. As a *commandeur*, or junior flag-officer, of the Admiralty of Zeeland, he served as a squadron commander with the main fleet in nearly all the great actions of the war. Though the Dutch lost most of the battles, de Ruyter performed consistently well. In the fleet reorganization following the death of Maarten Tromp at Scheveningen, the States of Holland invited him to become the chief sea commander of the Admiralty of Amsterdam. De Ruyter's appointment was remarkable in view of the strained relations between the Provinces of Holland and Zeeland. But he was respected by the Holland officers, and unlike most Zeelanders he was strongly republican, which carried much weight with Johan de Witt. As an adopted Hollander, de Ruyter saw successful and almost continuous sea service for the next eleven years, fighting the Portuguese, the Swedes, and the North African corsairs. He remained the senior Amsterdam officer until his appointment as commander-in-chief in 1665.

De Ruyter was not a willing man of action. He disliked warfare and preferred to be with his family tending the garden behind his gabled house in the sailors' quarter of Amsterdam. His portraits show a broad ruddy face, a sturdy neck, and the generous girth of a prosperous burgher. He followed a sober, simple existence according to strict Calvinist precepts. He wore 'the clothes of the commonest sea-captain', ate ordinary 'sailor's fare', kept only a single servant, and spent most of his free hours reading his Bible. Incurably domestic, he thought nothing of sweeping out his own cabin and kept flower-boxes in the stern window-sills. Though he had almost no formal education, he wrote with a graceful script, spoke French tolerably and English fluently. His normal manner was reassuringly calm, but he had a volcanic temper which could be vented with equal wrath at common seamen and flag-officers alike. He once 'tore out his hair with anger' at a Danish admiral, and on another occasion he blew up at Meppel, the Lieutenant-Admiral of the Noorderkwartier, 'uttering threats', said Meppel, 'and other things in such a way that it would seem he was the Pope of Rome and could not sin'. Trembling subordinates learned to steer clear when such a mood possessed him.

As a commander, de Ruyter had an excellent grasp of naval strategy, though he was not a particularly advanced tactician. Long after the introduction of the line-ahead, he continued to yearn for the old days of pistol and sword. More importantly, he brought the States' Fleet a standard of conduct and adherence to regulation which had long been lacking among the freedom-loving Dutch. He was a fair and even-handed disciplinarian, but inflexible when it came to obedience. During his Guinea and North American cruise in 1665, he fined Meppel for allowing his ships to stray apart. In 1666 he inflicted a similar sentence on his own flag-captain for going ashore without permission. Though at first resented, his firm authority gradually produced a more professional attitude among the officers.

De Ruyter proved adept at balancing the often conflicting demands of the various shore-based authorities: the States-General, the provincial States, the five Admiralties, and above all Johan de Witt, with whom he shared a warm friendship. Despite occasional outbursts of temper, his tactful handling of the flag-officers also gradually brought about some degree of unity in the fleet.

Above all other qualities, de Ruyter possessed prudent judgement. He never lost sight of the awesome responsibility entrusted to him, and unlike most commanders of his time, English and Dutch, he would never have risked his irreplaceable fleet merely through some misbegotten sense of honour. Perhaps alone among the great captains of history, de Ruyter never knew the satisfaction of a smashing, overwhelming victory at sea such as a Lepanto or a Trafalgar. He always faced skilful, well-trained opponents whose ships were usually stronger than his own. He learned to take advantage of the enemy's mistakes; the English later found, to their horror, that their ships were not safe from de Ruyter even in their own harbours. He became a master of the element of surprise, of the unexpected attack as at Solebay in 1672 and Schooneveld in 1673. In such uneven contests against superior numbers he seemed to have an uncanny ability, amid the indescribable pandemonium of battle, to sense the right moment to extract his fleet from harm. His seamen learned to trust his judgement completely. They could be certain that he would lead them into danger, but never into the impossibly hopeless situations they had so often faced in the past. There would be no Lowestofts under de Ruyter.

By the winter of 1666, all the Dutch – politicians, burghers, seamen – firmly believed that they now had a fleet and a commander worthy of the nation. As that fleet gathered for the coming storm, there was yet another cause for confidence: in Paris, ambassador Van Beuningen had at last wrought the diplomatic miracle for which everyone had prayed.

Chapter IX

The Division of the Fleet

Offended that we fought without his leave,
He takes this time his secret hate to show;
Which Charles does with a mind so calm receive,
As one that neither seeks nor shuns his foe.

On 16 January 1666, Louis XIV declared war on England. He had made every effort to evade his treaty obligations, for a naval campaign was sure to interfere with his military preparations against Spain. Nevertheless, he knew the destruction of the Dutch fleet would leave England unchallenged at sea and in a position to spoil his Spanish plans. He had therefore spent much of 1665 trying to mediate a settlement. At the same time, he had been unable to resist the opportunity of putting French troops into the Low Countries, thereby actively assisting the Dutch on land against the Bishop of Munster. This had angered the English and undermined his credibility as an impartial peacemaker. When his mediation failed, Louis still entertained hopes that the combined threat of France, Denmark, and the Netherlands would bring Charles II to terms without further hostilities. But the English showed no signs of backing down.

The navy of France was then in the midst of an ambitious expansion. Under the leadership of Louis' talented adviser Jean-Baptiste Colbert, the dockyards at Brest, Toulon, and Rochefort were rapidly being refurbished and enlarged. Scores of new men-of-war were planned, and throughout the country the forests rumbled and shook as oak trees were felled by the tens of thousands to provide their sturdy frames. While the French shipwrights were preparing their programme, Colbert arranged to have eight powerful vessels built in Dutch and Danish dockyards. The fruition of these efforts, though, lay well in the future; Colbert's reforms having followed a long period of dismal neglect, France could not be considered a first-class naval power in 1666. Even so, the forty-odd warships that Louis could dispose would, in combination with the Dutch, pose a serious threat to the English.

The larger part of the French fleet was in the Mediterranean, where it had for several years engaged in desultory punitive warfare against the corsairs of North Africa. This squadron, commanded by François de Vendôme, duc de Beaufort, was based at Toulon. The smaller Atlantic fleet lay at Brest. Louis' intention was for Beaufort to bring his squadron to the Atlantic, link up with the Brest contingent, and then join the Dutch. While these plans were still in their initial stages, the waters were muddied by an unanticipated development: Charles II sent a fleet to the Straits of Gibraltar. It was commanded by Sir Jeremy Smith, one of the heroes of Lowestoft, and Louis' agents heard that the squadron had twenty warships. The French understood that Smith had been sent to England's newly acquired colony at Tangier, a former Portuguese stronghold on the African side of the Straits, but they supposed he would enter the Mediterranean when he learned of the declaration of war. His presence seriously jeopardized the Franco-Dutch conjunction; the duc de Beaufort obviously could not sail away and leave the Mediterranean unprotected until the English force had been destroyed or driven away. Nonetheless, since the expedition had sailed nearly a month before Louis entered the war, the French were not sure what Smith was up to. As early as 22 December the King had advised Beaufort not to be alarmed:

It hardly seems likely that these twenty frigates have been ordered to remain in the Mediterranean; instead, having to sustain a vast war on the seas during the coming campaign, it is likely that they will decide to reassemble all their forces rather than keep them separated, and that this detachment was made only for the purpose of supplying Tangier.

Louis was by no means dismayed by Sir Jeremy's arrival. On the contrary, he viewed it as an excellent opportunity of striking a decisive blow at the very outset of the campaign. On 16 February the sea commanders were notified that the plan for uniting the Dutch and French forces was to be temporarily shelved, 'since it would be even more advantageous for the common cause to defeat this fleet'. It was accordingly ordered that Beaufort

use all diligence to obtain certain advice of the whereabouts of the aforesaid fleet and that he seek it out wherever it shall be, even though it may have sailed to the Levant beyond Sicily, and that he engage it in battle, inasmuch as it is impossible that he would not find the aforesaid fleet in the event it remains in the Mediterranean.

The instructions reassuringly added, 'one may logically assume that the Sieur duc will defeat the aforesaid fleet'. Despite such encouragement, it soon became apparent that Louis' orders could not be so easily carried out. The reported size of Smith's squadron meant that Beaufort would require a larger force than the eighteen ships originally envisaged. No other proper warships being available, the additional strength would have to be scraped up from undependable hired merchantmen and rickety Algerine prizes, all manned by captains and crews with little experience. Considering all factors, Beaufort felt that at least thirty men-of-war would be needed to defeat 'Capitaine Smid'. Unfortunately, it had been many years since France had sent out such an armada, and nearly everyone had forgotten how difficult it was. As in all navies of the day, manning was particularly troublesome. After the seaports were thoroughly scoured of men, the government paid exorbitant ransoms to the North African corsairs for French seamen held captive. Further delay came from the need for the dockyard at Toulon to repair and fit the fleet for the North Sea campaign, since the Atlantic Dockyards were still poorly equipped.

The problems of the French shore establishment were much aggravated by the fleet's commander. The duc de Beaufort was a scion of the royal family, which seems to have been his only qualification for the command. Though he had gained some degree of military repute during the Fronde, he knew next to nothing of warfare at sea, and still less of naval administration. From his correspondence it appears that no one was better intentioned and more eager for action, and he did show commendable energy. Nevertheless, his impulsive and constantly changing demands caused nothing but headaches for the local commissioners. Despite constant urging from Paris, the French fleet lay paralyzed for week after week and then month after month.

The stationing of Smith's squadron at Tangier was regarded by most European observers as a brilliant and clairvoyant stroke by the English. Actually, as Louis suspected, its presence was entirely fortuitous. Tangier had come to Charles II as a part of the dowry of Catherine of Braganza, his Portuguese queen. The Portuguese negotiators had thrown it in almost as an afterthought. The colony had caused constant ill feelings with Spain, which had never recognized Portugal's sovereignty over it, and defending it against the Spanish and the equally belligerent Moors had become an onerous drain on the Portuguese treasury. Though they could not afford to see it in the hands of an enemy, they were glad to get rid of it. The English were well aware of the strategic importance of the Straits, but Tangier was not a suitable base for supporting a permanent fleet. Its water supply was uncertain, and with hostile tribesmen controlling everything beyond the city gates, it was dependent on convoys from England for its sustenance. It was nevertheless a valuable acquisition as a commercial staging point and warehouse for English Mediterranean trade.

Smith had departed Plymouth on 19 December with no thought of blockading the French. The sole object of the expedition was to protect Tangier and the English shipping in the Straits from the depredations of a group of Dutch raiders operating from the Spanish port of Cadiz. Spain, though already fighting Portugal and on the brink of war with France, had made Cadiz available to the Dutch to express her displeasure over the English occupation of Tangier. Madrid was also in an uproar over a devastating raid on Central America which had been mounted from Jamaica by the English buccaneer Henry Morgan.

At least one account has it that after the French entered the war Smith was not eager for battle. Samuel Pepys, visiting Tangier some years later, wrote that

> Sir Jer. Smith was so observed to skulk (when he was here with a fleet) between this road of Tangier and that of the bay behind Cape Spartel to avoid the French as the wind was either East or West, that from thence to this day it is and ever will be called, by the English at least, Jeremy Bay.

The real reason the squadron lurked in 'Jeremy Bay' was because it made such a profitable blind, hidden by the cape, from which to ambush enemy shipping passing the Straits. But Smith would have been foolish in the extreme to have ignored the French fleet, since Beaufort was much the stronger in both numbers and force. The disparity was substantially greater than the French realized, for their intelligence reports had drastically overstated Sir Jeremy's strength. His original force comprised fourteen warships – not twenty – and four of the fourteen were dismasted in a gale a few days after their sailing and had to return to England for extensive repairs. Two others joined him in late January after escorting ambassador Sir Robert Southwell to Portugal, and three of the storm-damaged vessels finally arrived in March. These brought Smith to his maximum strength of only fifteen men-of-war, two fireships, and a ketch. Furthermore, the French Toulon fleet was itself reinforced by the Dutch squadron under Commandeur Jan Gideonsz. Verburgh which had fled Cadiz on Smith's approach. Verburgh brought three men-of-war, three converted merchantmen, and two English merchant prizes (both of which became fireships). Fortunately for Smith, the poor state of repair of the Dutch ships further set back the French departure.

The English had another unpleasant possibility to consider. Abraham Duquesne, the irascible sea-dog who commanded the French Atlantic fleet, had only eight (later twelve) ships, but he advised Louis to have the Dutch send twenty men-of-war to join his own. This combined force would sail south to meet Beaufort in the Straits – and Smith would be cornered between them. 'The English fleet which is in the Levant', wrote Duquesne, 'could not avoid battle, nor prevent the union of the King's naval forces'. His suggestion was not adopted, but from the possibilities it is obvious that Sir Jeremy was in no little danger. Thus it must have been with few regrets when he received orders in March to return to England for the summer campaign; the squadron sailed on the 26th. By his presence at Tangier, Smith had unwittingly delayed the French fleet's departure by two months.

Three weeks later, on 19 April, the duc de Beaufort at last nosed out of Toulon and set his course for the Straits, still expecting to meet the English squadron. With him were thirty-two French men-of-war, the Dutch refugees, nine fireships, and a swarm of merchantmen which had gathered to take advantage of the fleet's protection. Fog and foul winds retarded their progress, as did the need to shepherd the merchant convoy from port to port along the way. On 30 April Louis, having learned that Smith had returned to Plymouth, reported the fact to Beaufort and directed him to proceed with the conjunction of the fleets as originally planned. The squadron plodded doggedly onwards, but many of the ships were heavy sailers; accidents occurred frequently. When they reached Cadiz on 9 May, the English consul Martin Westcombe was not overly impressed: 'Ships that came in their convoy from Malaga, Genoveses, were ashamed to see how they handled their sails; twenty English frigates would rout them all to pieces'. Another observer wrote that 'Admiral Beaufort is in his old ship, which proves a mere slug in sailing'. But whatever the state of the French fleet, the campaign of 1666 had begun.

In England the Royal Navy's preparations were well advanced by mid-April. An imposing array of warships had assembled at the buoy of the Nore, and Prince Rupert and the Duke of Albemarle arrived there on the 23rd. The advent of the new commanders-in-chief caused another reshuffling of the flag-officers. The Generals took charge of the Red Squadron in the *Royal Charles*, appointing Sir Christopher Myngs and Sir Joseph Jordan as Vice- and Rear-Admiral of the Red. The White Squadron was assigned to Sir Thomas Allin, whose vice- and rear-admirals would be Smith (when he returned from Tangier) and Sir Thomas Teddiman. Sir George Ayscue was made Admiral of the Blue with Sir William Berkeley and John Harman as vice- and rear-admirals. The chief beneficiary of the new arrangement was Smith, who jumped all the way from private captain to vice-admiral through the support of Albemarle and the Duke of York. The scandal over the Dutch East Indiamen in the previous autumn apparently had much to do with the order of precedence of 1666. It was probably no coincidence that the most senior subsidiary posts went to Allin, who had been sick ashore when the looting occurred, and to Ayscue, Myngs, and Smith, all of whom had refused their shares. Berkeley, Jordan, Teddiman, and Harman had all been more or less guilty and were relegated to the junior posts, while the flagrant offenders, Penn and Sir Roger Cuttance, were excluded entirely.

Prince Rupert's return to sea brought Robert Holmes, now Sir Robert, out of his voluntary retirement. Though still without a flag, he was given command of a fine new third-rate. He and Rupert's other favourite, Sir Edward Spragge, were the senior private captains and would be in line for preferment when flag positions next fell vacant. Both were to take prominent parts in the forthcoming events. Most of the other captains were the same Commonwealth veterans who had won at Lowestoft, but several observers noted with distaste that the new class of ambitious young gentlemen was beginning to shoulder the tarpaulins aside. These high-spirited adventurers had previously been lieutenants in the flagships and captains of lucrative commerce-raiding fifth-rates; in 1666 a few moved up to command ships large enough to lie in the battle-line. They included John Holmes (Sir Robert's brother), Charles Talbot, and a Frenchman put forward by the Duke of York, Jean-Baptiste du Tiel. A few, Holmes among them, would distinguish themselves, but others less responsible would become a curse on the service.

The fleet differed somewhat in composition from that of the previous year. There were far fewer hired merchantmen, their numbers being made up mainly by the Dutch prizes of 1665. The shipbuilding programme was finally beginning to show results. The rebuilt second-rate *Victory* and two big third-rates were already launched and fitting out, while five other new vessels including the great *Loyal London* were nearing completion. The existing fleet was generally better equipped than before and even more heavily armed. Victualling was still a constant weakness, though the assignment of Samuel Pepys to coordinate Dennis Gauden's operations produced noticeable improvements. The overriding trouble in 1666 was manning. The press gangs marched without cease, but men ran away as fast as they could be brought aboard. The problem became so severe that many ships otherwise fully equipped could not be sent to sea, and this was to have serious consequences.

For the first week or so after joining the fleet, the new commanders were too immersed in administrative matters to pay much heed to strategic questions. When they did, it was Denmark rather than France that first drew their attention. There were reports that Frederik would send twenty men-of-war to help the Dutch, bringing the opposing fleet to about 110 ships even without the French. The Danish squadrons included three-deckers of the largest size, so the possibility of their participation was viewed with concern. Fortunately for England, nothing came of it. English diplomacy with Sweden succeeded sufficiently to alarm the King of Denmark; he was far too mistrustful of his hereditary enemy to send his fleet away, and his cooperation with the Dutch remained minimal.

The first suggestion of English interest in the French plans came in the first week of May when Charles II and the Duke of York conducted a three-day visit to the fleet at the buoy of the Nore. They spent most of their time conferring with the flag-officers and reviewing the ships, but before departing on the 5th they went aboard the old second-rate *Triumph* commanded by Sir Edward Spragge. Spragge was the only private captain to be so honoured. The reason, unexplained at the time, was that Sir Edward had a well-placed 'correspondent' in France whose activities were being closely monitored by the English high command. Then on 10 May Prince Rupert wrote to the Duke of York:

> Y^r Highness will understand that Monsieur de Beauford is for certaine expected on the west coast of France and is already sailed with his Fleet towards the Streights Mouth convoying many French & Dutch Merchants. I most humbly therefore offer whether this might not bee good time, & whilst the Dutch are not in a condition to come out, to attempt the intercepting of the aforesaid Mr. de Beauford.

This is the earliest known mention of an expedition against the French, though Rupert later indicated that he had previously discussed it with the King. In fact, the wheels were already turning. Spragge's agent had come to the fleet in person, reporting that the flagship of the French Atlantic squadron was lying off Belle-Île on the west Brittany coast with a few other frigates. This seemed to give the rendezvous for the French sea-forces, which presented obvious possibilities. The next day, the 11th, Rupert and Albemarle wrote jointly to the Earl of Arlington, one of the two Principal Secretaries of State, giving Spragge's intelligence and urging that an attempt on Beaufort's fleet be initiated at once. The letter was carried to London by Spragge himself, the spy going with him. The Generals had added an endorsement recommending that the informant 'bee well gratified, hee having taken much paines in this businesse'.

At Whitehall the news was considered important enough for the King to order a Privy Council session for 13 May, a Sunday. It convened at Worcester House, the London residence of the Earl of Clarendon, the Chancellor, who was then incapacitated by gout and could not have attended elsewhere. Although both Clarendon and Coventry left accounts of this fateful conference, important details are much in doubt. The King and Council first questioned Spragge and then sent him outside. Once he was out of earshot the Secretaries of State, Arlington and Sir William Morrice, gave their latest estimates of the situation in the Netherlands. According to Clarendon, Arlington reported 'that the Dutch were not yet well manned; and that the ships which were in the Texel, and were to join with the other under De Ruyter in the Weilings, were more unprovided'. This was flatly contradicted by Morrice who, said Clarendon, 'had always better intelligence from Holland'. Morrice had been informed 'that all the ships in both places were so ready that they would join within very few days'. The Chancellor's version of these transactions, however, is suspect because of the loathing he felt for Arlington, his principal political rival.

The ambitious Henry Bennet, Earl of Arlington, was a confidant of the King and a multi-lingual specialist in foreign relations. Although the Secretaries of State were supposed to have equal status, Arlington's vastly superior knowledge of international affairs not only assured his ascendancy over Morrice, but made him a threat to Clarendon's own primacy in the government. Arlington's climb was supported by Coventry, who assisted in undermining the Chancellor's influence. This had succeeded so far that in 1666 Arlington was granted private access to the King's apartments through a secret staircase, a privilege previously extended only to Clarendon.

Foreign intelligence was among the primary duties of the Secretaries of State. At the time there was no official secret service establishment, and the two secretaries instead maintained separate information offices in direct and often vicious competition with each other. Technically, Arlington was responsible for France and Spain, Morrice for Holland and Denmark; in practice Arlington poached on his rival's turf on a grand scale. Both had cloak-and-dagger spies on their payrolls, but the heart of each organization was an extensive reciprocal newsletter exchange with well-placed sub-scribers on the Continent. The subscribers, unaware that they were dealing with foreign espionage networks, naïvely gave away sensitive state secrets in return for watered-down and carefully censored English reports. These schemes were lubricated by elaborate clandestine postal arrangements through which messages from Holland and France could be received within three days. In this Arlington had an inestimable advantage: he was also Postmaster General, a position from which he could intercept and sabotage his competitor's communications. This opportunity he exploited to the fullest; in 1666 Morrice's system was in ruins.

The correspondence of Sir Joseph Williamson, Arlington's intelligence chief, and of Henry Muddiman, Williamson's opposite number in Morrice's office, gives a reasonably complete picture of the information available to the Secretaries of State at the time of the Council meeting. Clarendon's description of Morrice's estimate was apparently accurate, for a news summary written by Muddiman two days after the meeting announced that the Dutch preparations had been 'brought to that perfection as that they have 80 sayle ready and well mann'd'. But the Chancellor was undoubtedly misleading on his rival's reports. Williamson's sources did *not* dispute that the Dutch squadrons would soon unite; the Zeeland contingent, they said, would shortly sail to the Texel assembly point where the Holland squadrons under de Ruyter were already gathering. The informants, however, insisted that the Dutch were undermanned. Despite Clarendon's venomous evaluation, Arlington's intelligence from the Nether-lands was the more reliable, though that was not clear on 13 May.

With the Dutch question unresolved, the Privy Council turned its deliberations to the French. Clarendon's account contains at this point another curious passage: 'But the Lord Arlington, who thought he ought to be more believed, received as positive advertisement from France, "that the Duke of Beaufort set sail from Brest on such and such a day."' This makes Arlington appear a fool for offering such absurd intelli-gence. Actually, the Chancellor's context shows that it was he, and not Arlington, who had misapprehended the ocean from which Beaufort sailed. Clarendon displayed the same confusion in a description of the winter preparations, writing that 'the Duke of Beaufort, Admiral of France, was already gone to Brest, and had taken leave of the King at Paris, whither he was not to return till after the summer's service at sea'. A likely explanation for this strange mistake lies in Beaufort's name, François de

Vendôme. To someone not thoroughly familiar with the French naval dispositions (and distracted by gout), Spragge's news that 'the Vandosme [Vendôme] the Admiral of France' was at sea near Belle-Île could easily be construed to mean Beaufort. But in the seventeenth century the term *admiral* often meant a ship rather than a person; *Vendôme* also happened to be the name of a large man-of-war, and that man-of-war was by coincidence the flagship of Abraham Duquesne. *He* was the one who had sailed from Brest.

However Clarendon's confusion arose, it is probable that Arlington merely confirmed what Rupert had reported, that Beaufort was at sea and 'must be well advanced in his way'. Indeed, three days earlier an accurate account of the French fleet's departure from Toulon had appeared in Arlington's own *London Gazette*, of which Williamson was senior editor. At any rate, according to Coventry the King concluded after much debate that 'it seemed very desirable to crush the King of France's preparations in the beginning'. Nevertheless, in view of the uncertainty over the Dutch he wanted to hear from his admirals before the plans went any further. It was accordingly decided that Coventry and Vice-Chamberlain Sir George Carteret, who was also Treasurer of the Navy, should visit the fleet and confer with Rupert and Albemarle.

The next morning the Council's delegates sailed to the Nore in Sir Edward Spragge's pinnace, arriving aboard the *Royal Charles* in the afternoon. The details of the meeting were later recalled by Coventry. He and Carteret were greeted by Albemarle, the Prince having 'gone on shoare to divert himselfe in shooting'. The Duke ushered them into the great-cabin and ordered everyone else to leave. After relating what had transpired at Worcester House, the delegates explained that the only question in the King's mind was whether a detachment strong enough to defeat the French would leave the main fleet enough force to deal with the Dutch. According to Coventry, 'My Lord Generall replyed, "leave us 60 saile & wee shall doe well enough," whereupon wee desired to looke over the list of ships there, & finding 80 my Ld. Generall concurred that 20 should goe'. Coventry's recollection of this was probably somewhat faulty. Albemarle's correspondence subsequent to the conference consistently referred to seventy ships as his minimum requirement, while the fleet list on 14 May cannot have contained fewer than ninety vessels. It is known to have stood at ninety-one a week later; if anything it should have been stronger on the 14th, since in the meantime the hired merchantman *Society* and the fourth-rates *Westfriesland* and *Charles V* had been deleted. As early as 16 March the list had totalled seventy-nine ships, to which fourteen were added on Smith's return from Tangier on 21 April. It is also certain that the list Coventry saw included all the vessels assigned to the Generals and not merely those actually at the Nore, for several of the twenty ships picked for the expedition were elsewhere at the time of the conference. Thus, the Duke can be assumed with reasonable certainty to have said, 'leave us seventy sail'. This may seem a rather nitpicking point, but Coventry's quotation has often been used to make Albemarle appear foolishly overconfident. As will soon become obvious, he was anything but.

However the number was determined, the general did select twenty of the fastest ships to meet the French. He judged Vice-Admiral Sir Christopher Myngs 'a fitt man for such an expedition', so his vessel, the newly rebuilt second-rate *Victory*, became the sole three-decker assigned to the squadron. After a short interval Prince Rupert returned aboard and was informed of the arrangements. In general he 'liked very well of itt', but he objected to the inclusion of the *Victory* on the grounds that she was too new for her sailing qualities to be known. The second-rate *Henry* was suggested in her place, 'but the Prince did not like that neither, but proposed the *R. James*'. This surprised the delegates. The *Royal James* was a first-rate, and they questioned the wisdom of removing such an important vessel from the main fleet. The Duke, however, made no objection. Coventry and Carteret were probably unaware that the first-rate status of the *Royal James* was a mainly administrative classification. She was only marginally more heavily armed than the *Henry*, and the *Victory* was more powerful than either. But even Albemarle must have started when the Prince suddenly backtracked, saying that perhaps the *Victory* should go along after all, *in addition* to the *Royal James*. He then off-handedly asked who was to command the expedition. The delegates, by now mystified, replied guardedly

> that the King had given us noe instructions as to that, but was soe farr from resolving who should command, that hee had not resolved whether there should bee any ships sent untill hee heard their opinions of it, whereupon his H. replied that the King had promised it to an officer in that fleet (the word [was] very remarkable).

There was a brief pause, and then Rupert coolly announced that the King had promised the detachment to him. The dumbfounded delegates could only stammer back that they 'knew nothing of it, but doubtless whatever the King had promised would bee made good'. It at least explained the Prince's haggling over the ships, since it was well known that the *Royal James* was his favourite.

Through most of the foregoing discussion Albemarle remained silent. Rupert had never hidden his desire for an independent command, and it probably made no difference to the Duke whether the Prince was with him or not. Both commanders appeared satisfied. As the meeting ended, the Generals informed the Councillors that they intended to move the fleet from the buoy of the Nore to the Downs, from whence Rupert could conveniently depart. This seemingly innocuous decision was later to be regretted.

Carteret and Coventry returned to London the next day, the 15th, and presented the Generals' recommendations to the King. They also brought word from the fleet that the intelligence about the Dutch being not ready was 'confirmed to be the same that his Majesty had heard', while the information about Beaufort was considered 'very probable'. With this reassuring advice Charles tentatively approved the plans on the 16th. From that point there was a seemingly unaccountable hiatus of six days before the detachment's orders were drawn up. In the interval, contrary winds prevented the fleet from moving to the Downs as planned. Rupert and Albemarle found this unavoidable delay frustrating, but they became even more anxious over the non-arrival of the instructions. They began to bombard Whitehall with reminders, Albemarle directing his impatience at Coventry in a postscript to a routine letter: 'Wee have heard nothing as yett of the businesse you & Sr. Geo. Carteret came about'.

But there was a good reason for the King's hesitation. Unbeknown to the Generals, a new and most unwelcome development had drastically changed the situation. It began with a disturbing message which Williamson received from Paris on or about the 14th:

> The [French] King has ordered that the Companies in each Regiment shall be enlarged to 80 men a piece; and 'tis said, that he intends suddenly in person for Rochel, to see his fleet, which is to come about thither & on which, he intends to embarque 5 or 6000 men, besides those already taken in at Provence.

The embarkation of so many soldiers implied a landing in force at some weak point in the English defences. Scotland was a possibility, but there was another, far more vulnerable target: Ireland – downtrodden, unhappy, and sullenly resentful of English rule. On the 15th there was direct confirmation. A merchant seaman who had been captured and briefly interned on the Île de Ré had returned home to Warwickshire claiming that 'there are 15,000 French soldiers drawn into that island and about Rochell, which are destined for Ireland'. Still more confirmation came in from other sources. The number of troops varied, but the theme was the same: 'that M. Beaufort, Admiral, was ordered from the Straits to transport those regiments'.

Charles II and his strategic advisers were all too aware, as were successive British governments right through Napoleonic times, that Ireland was an Achilles' heel in any war with Catholic France. An uprising abetted by French troops was an ever-present spectre, the inevitable conflagration certain to require a disproportionate diversion of English forces from the main theatre. Threats of such disturbances never failed to generate reflexive responses. In this case it was taken very seriously, for it was a particularly opportune time for a French landing. News had just come from Ireland that the English garrison at Carrickfergus had openly rebelled over non-payment of its wages, and the insurrection was yet to be quelled. The atmosphere was tense throughout the island. One observer wrote from Lisburn as late as the 26th that 'the army is reduced to great straits and I fear that the spirit which animated the mutiny at Carrickfergus will spread'. With the English defenders temporarily incapacitated, and the Catholic populace as disgruntled as ever, the King had every reason to worry.

It appears that the full Privy Council was *not* aware of the invasion intelligence beyond the initial vague news from Paris. Of the subsequent confirmation Arlington seems to have informed only Charles, James, Coventry, and a few trusted allies. They kept it to themselves, and when it later proved false, no one was the wiser. Clarendon, sick at home with the gout, learned little if anything of it, which gives some indication of the degree to which his influence had waned. Arlington's other enemies on the Council were not told either, or they would surely have bandied it about afterwards to discredit him. Outside of the highest circles, no one knew. Pepys, usually so well informed by Coventry, never heard a word. Nor did Andrew Marvell, for whom it would have made deadly ammunition. He and most other critics automatically assumed Clarendon was behind every failure. Whoever knew, from the moment a French landing was recognized as a possibility, it became the principal element in the high command's thinking. All other considerations, including even the conjunction of the enemy fleets, seemed to pale by comparison. It was this problem that caused the delay in Prince Rupert's instructions; the King feared to commit himself until the French intentions were clarified.

After several days of inconclusive search for further intelligence, it was realized that a decision had to be made. Orders were finally drawn up and approved by the King on the evening of the 22nd. The rough draft was retained by Coventry for preparation of the official copies, but it was too late to do any more that night. For security's sake Sir William decided not to show the document to his clerks, so the following morning he began to copy it in his own hand. Meanwhile, the Generals at the Nore had resolved to send Sir Edward Spragge back to London to hurry things along. With him went an urgent plea from Prince Rupert to Arlington:

> Att present wee are as ignorant of his Majs or the Ducks comands as wee were when Sr W Coventry & Sir G Cartheright left us. Since which time we heard not one word from him concerning that businesse, how nesessary and precious time is for the pursuance of it yr L may judge. If I weere soe happie as to receave his Majs will concerning it alle should be in that reddynesse that wee should not stoppe in the Downes one minute if the wind served for to carrie us through. I hope in god that his Majs good fortune will attend me and make me an instrument to doe him the service my hart is full of. This bearer is in that hast that I can only adde in few words that I am faithfully yr Lor servant.

Spragge left the fleet on the 22nd. His mission was kept secret, the flag-officers being told only that he was going away 'to hasten our provisions'. He arrived in Westminster the next morning and was referred to Coventry's office, where he learned that Sir William needed an hour or two to finish the orders. At last Coventry took the instructions to Spragge 'at the Tennis Court next the Cockpitt & there delivered them to him before 11 of the clocke'.

At this point it is appropriate to interject a brief story which has caused much confusion concerning the division of the fleet. The facts are simple enough. In early May the young gentleman captain of the fourth-rate *Elizabeth*, Charles Talbot, was directed to take charge of four merchantmen bound for Lisbon. His orders called for him to escort the convoy only a short distance beyond the Channel. The seas all along their route, however, were known to be teeming with 'capers' (privateers) from Zeeland, so Talbot decided to ignore the orders and accompany his charges all the way to their destination. This proved fortunate, for two 'picaroons' shadowed the merchantmen for several days but were deterred by the *Elizabeth*'s bristling broadside. Then, as Talbot's little convoy neared Lisbon on the 14th, it stumbled on to a far greater danger: about three miles off the Tagus was a powerful fleet including a number of large men-of-war which Talbot quickly identified as French. This seemed confirmed when the nearest warships approached menacingly and tried to work between him and the shore, at which the merchantmen scuttled in panic for the harbour mouth. As soon as Talbot saw them safely into the Tagus, 'he flew homewards with Top & Top-gallant, and sent up Express to Whitehall of the French Fleets approach'. A few weeks afterwards, his report was found to have been a grotesque mistake (as will be explained later). That much is beyond doubt; but according to popular belief, it was the *Elizabeth*'s news that finally galvanized the King and Council into issuing the orders for the division of the fleet, and for that reason Captain Talbot has been held largely responsible for the resulting misadventures.

The timing, however, makes this theory impossible. The *London Gazette* for 31 May records that the *Elizabeth*'s landfall was at Falmouth on the 22nd, which was indeed the very day the orders to Prince Rupert were drawn up. But the connection was illusory, for Falmouth was fully three hundred miles or *three days* from London by road. Talbot's express reached Whitehall on the 25th, as Coventry mentioned in a letter to Albemarle that day. By then the instructions had been in Spragge's hands for some forty-eight hours. The news from Lisbon was therefore not in time to play a part in the decision to divide the fleet, and no one in the administration ever claimed it did. On the contrary, as will soon be evident its true effect was *precisely the opposite*! Thus the scapegoat's mantle can at last be lifted from the shoulders of Captain Talbot, though for other reasons his disgrace was still richly deserved.

The *Elizabeth*'s supposed blame for the division of the fleet found believers soon after the Four Days' Battle. How the rumour began and spread is mostly explained by the nature of the 'licenced news' regulations then in effect. In those days the public had no access to governmental deliberations and knew nothing of the actual dates of orders and decisions, particularly when a defeat was involved. Private citizens were limited for information to the heavily censored *London Gazette*, the sole official news organ. From that source one could find only that Captain Talbot had arrived home reporting a French fleet at Lisbon, and that soon afterwards Prince Rupert was detached. The public understandably concluded that those events were somehow related. The administration for its part neither advanced that conclusion nor denied it. The whole affair was merely one of a great many misconceptions that the King and his advisers afterwards found convenient to allow the public to believe in order to distract attention from more embarrassing blunders. As one anonymous observer (who did, incidentally, subscribe wholeheartedly to the *Elizabeth* story) sagely related, 'Since those who knew best where the fault lay were faulty themselves, it concerned them to let the Truth be disguised at any rate, that the blame being so divided & dispers'd, might divert, & not fall too heavy upon 'em'.

In Spragge's absence the wind at the Nore finally came around to the southwest, fair for sailing downstream. The fleet weighed on the 23rd. It reached the Gunfleet that day, stretched past Longsand Head on the next, and then beat south on the 25th. After anchoring outside the Goodwins for a day it entered the Downs on the 27th. Spragge, racing after in his pinnace, caught up with the fleet on the 25th and handed over the long-awaited instructions. They were enclosed with a letter of the 22nd which the Duke of York had addressed to both Generals:

> You will perceive by the Instructions sent by this conveyance to my Cousin Prince Rupert that the King hath entirely approved of the Resolutions taken by you, when Sr. George Carteret & Sr. William Coventry were with you, the Instructions being for the most part pursuant to the Report which they made to His Majty . . .

That, by the way, should be enough in itself to exonerate Captain Talbot. But despite James's assurances, Prince Rupert must have found some provisions of the orders very surprising. They began:

> Whereas his Maj. upon intelligence received of the French King's fleet putting to sea from Toulon & intending to come into the ocean seas & joyne with other ships of the French Kings, hath resolved to send a fleet to attend their motions & endeavor to destroy them. Of which fleet upon your owne desire whereof his Majesty hath thought fitt that the chiefe command bee given to you.

The Prince was told to take twenty ships from the main fleet and sail down the Channel to the Lizard, where other vessels already on the western station would join him. Then, the orders continued,

> you shall endeavor to find out & destroy the French fleet, especially that under the command of the Duke of Beaufort if it shall bee come into these seas; & if you shall not have any good intelligence of their being in some other place, you are to saile directly for Belle-Isle or to the Isle of Rhee & Rochelle where it is most probable their rendezvous will bee & where his Maj. hath been informed that some of the French Kings ships of warre were already some time hence.

If the enemy were not found at the places expected, the squadron was to remain on the French coast no more than eight days before sailing for England, and was forbidden to search south of the mouth of the Gironde. Rupert probably had no previous knowledge of the threatened Irish invasion, but now he learned that thwarting such an attempt was a primary object of the operation:

> You are to endeavor by all meanes you can to get intelligence from the French Coast what numbers of soldiers are in any places there, & what preparations they make for embarquing them, & if any thing considerable of that nature come to your knowledge you are to give notice by ketches or small vessells to his Maj. & likewise to the Lord Lt. of Ireland that soe in case of any attempt both kingdomes may bee in readinesse to oppose them.
>
>   In case the French shall ship any Land Forces in any port you are to use your utmost endeavors to keepe them from going out, or to intercept them in their passage, but if that cannot bee done you are to follow them, & endeavor to destroy them in their landing either their men or other necessities, & alsoe to hinder all recruits to come to them after their landing.
>
>   In case the french fleet shall [sail] without any Land army embarqued or them get the start of you & saile about by the North of Scotland, you shall then returne into the Channell the sooner to joyne his Majs. fleet soe that it may bee in a condition to encounter the united forces both of Dutch & French.*

That last paragraph is worthy of special notice, for it shows that the King regarded the conjunction of the enemy fleets as a decidedly secondary danger.

*The full text of the orders is given in Appendix A.

LEFT: Charles II, by Sir Peter Lely.

BELOW: Prince Rupert during the 1660s. Miniature after Lely.

BELOW: James, Duke of York, by Lely.

George Monck, 1st Duke of Albemarle,
painted about 1660 after S. Cooper.

Samuel Pepys in 1666, by Hayls.

Edward Montagu, 1st Earl of Sandwich, by Lely.

Sir William Penn, by Lely.

Royal Charles as she appeared at the Restoration in 1660, as portrayed by Willem Van de Velde the Elder.

Jacob van Wassenaer, Baron van Obdam.

Egbert Cortenaer, by Bartelemeus van der Helst.

Battle of Lowestoft: The *Eendracht*, engulfed in flame at centre, blows up under the guns of the *Royal Charles* (royal standard at the main and red flag at the fore). The English are in a ragged but recognizable line stretching from extreme left to centre background, with the Dutch in confusion on the right.

Sir Thomas Allin, by Lely.
The scar on his cheek was from
a wound sustained in the
St. James's Day Fight.

The second-rate *Old James*. Launched in 1634, she was a member of Charles I's 'Ship-Money' fleet.

THIS AND FOLLOWING FOUR PAGES: The Bergen action as viewed from the English side with the Bergenhus at the top right of this page. The artist, Van de Velde the Elder, arrived with the Dutch fleet after the battle. He drew the background on the spot, but the English ships were filled in a year or more later. Van de Velde mistakenly thought the second-rate *Swiftsure* (which was not present) had been Teddiman's flagship, and included an excellent portrait of the ship to the far right of the panorama.

The Friesland ship *Zevenwolden*, in which Lt.-Adm. Auke Stellingwerf had been slain at Lowestoft, was captured by the *Antelope* in the North Sea in September 1665. As the English fourth-rate *Seven Oaks*, she was retaken by the Dutch on the first day of the Four Days' Battle.

The third-rate *Montagu*.

he *Expedition*. Built in 1637, the *Expedition* and her sister-ship the *Providence* were the oldest fourth-rates in e fleet.

Few ship portraits of members of the French fleet of 1666 have been found, but the largest vessels were probably similar to *Le Terrible* of 1670, shown here.

ABOVE: Johan de Witt.

RIGHT: Engraving of Jan Evertsen.

JAN EVERTSEN,
Luitenant - Admiraal
van Zeeland.

A. Schouman del. naar't Origineel by den Haer N. Evertsen Schepen en Raad te Middelburg. J. Houbraken fecit.

Cornelis Tromp, by Abraham Willaerts.

Michiel Adriaenz. de Ruyter, after Hendrick Berchman.

Louis XIV, by le Brun.

Colbert, by le Brun.

FRANÇOIS DE VENDÔME DUC DE
BEAUFORT PAIR AMIRAL ᴅᴇ FRᶜᵉ

The Duc de Beaufort.

Abraham Duquesne, by Graincourt.

Jan Corneliszoon Meppel, by Rotius.

The *Hollandia*. The drawing is from an offset, and thus in reverse.

Visit of the deputies of the States-General to the Dutch fleet, May 1666, a grisaille by Van de Velde the Elder. At far left is Tromp's *Hollandia* and at left centre is a vice-admiral's flagship with no pendant, perhaps the

acificatie under Volckert Schram of the Noorderkwartier. In the foreground is the yacht of the States-General.

Isaac Sweers's *Gouda* (right) and Tromp's *Hollandia* (left) at sea before the Four Days' Battle. A grisaille by Van de Velde the Elder.

The *Royal Charles*, probably in 1667.

Interestingly, the planners had ignored a potentially ruinous possibility. There was a remote chance that the junction of de Ruyter and Beaufort might take place on the French coast and not in the North Sea. William Blunden, the English consul at Alicante, heard just such a plan when Beaufort's fleet touched there on 28 April: 'They report themselves that they are bound for Rochelle, where they are to join with a hundred and four sail of Dutch men-of-war, who are to come about by the north of Scotland'. Blunden's spurious intelligence did not reach Whitehall in time to affect decisions. Had it proved true, Rupert might have been facing annihilation.

The instructions left several questions unresolved. Some of the twenty ships selected to go with Rupert had not yet joined the fleet, and the high command had designated only two of the vessels which would meet him on the western station. Besides, he thought it safer to have the western ships rendezvous at Torbay rather than the storm-exposed waters off the Lizard required by the orders. The instructions also failed to specify the squadron's command flags – a matter of peculiar importance to seventeenth-century sea-officers. The Generals wrote on the 26th and 27th requesting clarification of these points, but the Prince sailed before the answers arrived. The question of the missing ships cleared up by itself when they were found to be waiting in the Downs when the fleet anchored there on the 27th. As for the flags, Rupert decided on his own to have the flagships fly the Union.

There was also the problem of the detachment's command structure, which proved rather complicated. It had been decided in advance that Sir Christopher Myngs would go as vice-admiral in the *Victory*, but the rear-admiral had not been named. All concerned felt that Sir Edward Spragge should be allowed to participate in some capacity in view of his role in creating the squadron. Unfortunately his ship, the second-rate *Triumph*, was a creaking 43-year-old relic from James I's reign; though still a formidable man-of-war, she was much too slow and clumsy to keep up with the elite greyhounds that had been hand-picked to sail with Rupert. Another difficulty was that the *Royal James*, which the Prince had insisted on taking, was already the flagship of Admiral of the White Sir Thomas Allin. In the covering letter which accompanied the orders, the Duke of York logically suggested that Spragge should become flag-captain of the *Royal James*, while Allin could retain command of the White Squadron by shifting to the *Triumph*. James, however, left the final decision up to Rupert, and Rupert wanted Spragge to have a flag of his own. The Generals accordingly reported on the 26th that they had decided to move Sir Edward into the third-rate *Dreadnought* to be the squadron's rear-admiral, with the former captain of the *Dreadnought*, Henry Terne, taking Spragge's place in the *Triumph*. Finally, in an unexpected decision, Allin was directed to remain in the *Royal James* as Rupert's flag-captain.

Prince Rupert's election to sail with Allin was not without reason. The Prince, still unsure of himself afloat, wanted a professional sea-officer close at hand, and Spragge was no more of a seaman than Rupert. Allin, on the other hand, was that great rarity in the Restoration navy, a life-long tarpaulin who had been a Royalist in the Civil War. He was a natural choice as the Prince's adviser, and Rupert probably intended it as a compliment. But Sir Thomas could hardly have been pleased. Aside from the loss of the White Squadron, his new position would offer little hope of distinction. If the French were defeated, the Prince would get the credit; if not, Sir Thomas would make a splendid scapegoat. Professional that he was, Allin nevertheless accepted the appointment without public complaint. His journal merely records that he was called to the *Royal Charles* to learn of his latest 'honour' on the 25th: 'I went aboard, where I received the news of his Highness going in the *Royal James* to the westward. The wind at S'.

After the orders were sent to the fleet, intelligence of many kinds continued to flow into Whitehall. Some of it involved the Irish invasion threat. Arlington had warned the Duke of Ormonde, Lord Lieutenant of Ireland, on the 15th. Ormonde had replied in a letter of the 22nd with evidence of his own:

> In August last one Choysin, a Frenchman, came to Kinsale and, though he is a Roman Catholic, yet to obtain freedom in that town he has taken the oathes prescribed by law, and this last season made extraordinary provisions of salt beef under colour of sending them to the Indies, yet neither salted the flesh for such a voyage, nor took many offered opportunities to send it away, but continues still in that harbour. I have been hitherto loth to discourage an exportation or person so profitable to our trade, but with my present knowledge and no security that this beef may not be intended for an enemy, I shall to-day order his ships to be brought up into Cork harbour to prevent any advantage to an enemy and, if occasion shall be, to make use of the provisions. At least those vessels shall be stayed till Monsieur Beaufort's intentions shall be known. In the meantime I think this fellow's courage gives some confirmation of the news.

Ormonde also reported rather depressingly on the state of his defences. Aside from the still raging mutiny at Carrickfergus, he had 'not enough money to repair the forts or put the army in a condition to march'. His letter passed in transit a second warning which Arlington posted on the 26th:

> Our intelligence still holds, that the rendezvous of the French fleet will be at Rochelle, and that they are to take in 6000 foot there, and that the King of France will give them a visit; by all computation we judge them there already, for letters of Tangier of the 6th said they expected them there, but without any fear of them, and from Lisbon on the 14th that they passed before the mouth of the river; if they should take in land men, everybody concludes they must have some design upon Ireland or Scotland if they should think of joining with the Dutch fleet by the north: wherefore it is time your Grace bethink yourself what you would do in case the former happens.

Most indications pointed to a French landing, but there was one small, troubling morsel of information that seemed to suggest the contrary. On the 11th an isolated report had come in from the master of the Dover–Calais packet boat saying that 'severall Dutch pilots' were 'gone to Marseilles and Toulon to fetch the French Fleet'. This had been lightly regarded, but now Williamson had received unexpected confirmation in a newsletter from Paris. The need for Dutch pilots seemed illogical if Beaufort meant to come up the Channel (French navigators knew that route themselves) so it seemed probable that, whatever he intended for Ireland, he would attempt to join the Dutch by sailing around Scotland through waters unfamiliar to his countrymen. But why were the pilots sent all the way to the Mediterranean and not to the much nearer rendezvous at Belle-Île or La Rochelle? Could this mean that Duquesne's ships would not be involved at all and that the Toulon fleet would not stop to embark an army? What if Beaufort simply dashed for the North Sea *via* Scotland without touching in France? Then there was Talbot's news from Lisbon. His story gained credence from a letter received about the same time from Colonel Henry Norwood, Lieutenant-Governor of Tangier, stating that the French had been observed approaching the Straits (only four or five days' sail from Lisbon) on the 6th.

The fog of war was thickening. Confronted with the first sightings of the French fleet, and with puzzling conflicts in the other intelligence, a worried Charles II summoned his advisers to re-evaluate the situation. On the 28th the Duke of York reported the results in a long letter to Prince Rupert. In the process he answered some of the Generals' queries of the 26th, naming eight ships which would join in the west (ten actually sailed) and approving Spragge's appointment as rear-admiral. As it happened, the letter was not written in time to arrive in the Downs before the squadron sailed. A copy sent to Portsmouth for forwarding did eventually reach the Prince, but at the same time as later orders negating it. The letter is nevertheless of great interest, for it included a detailed explanation of the high command's strategic thinking, and also significant additions to the original instructions:*

> His Maj. having received certaine intelligence that the Duke of Beaufort was come to this side of the Straights, did againe enter into consideration of the designe on which you are about to goe, & although the debate did not produce any alteration in the maine designe, yet I judge it may bee of use to acquaint you (as much as may bee at this distance) with some considerations as arose upon the debate. It was by some suggested that possibly the Duke of Beaufort (who was seene at Lisbon on the 14th instant) might saile directly to the North of Scotland soe to endeavor a conjunction with the Dutch, in which case his Majesty would encline not to send you from the fleet, if there should bee any certainty of it.

James explained that such a possibility was implied by the Dutch pilots having been sent to the Mediterranean. But that rather vague intelligence

> was over balanced by the probability of his touching in France to joyne with the Vandosme & other ships provided for him, which it was judged hee could not with certainty meet at sea, & very improbable hee would goe without them. Upon supposition that hee would touch in France the places most probable seemed Belle Isle or Rochelle, & upon that supposition the next consideration was what probability there might bee of your finding him there, for that supposing him to have already been there some days, if hee had no other businesse but to joyne the Vandosme & not to stay, it is probable hee may bee gone before you get thither, & then you will bee wanting from the body of the fleet, whilst they joyne the Dutch, and the rather because of the depth of the Bay into which you goe.

*The complete letter is reproduced in Appendix A.

On the other hand, in case the D. of Beaufort have any army to embarque in order to an invasion (which if intended must bee for Ireland) it is conceived that soe much time will bee required for his embarquing as may give you opportunity of falling upon him, which would bee most desirable.

Rupert was accordingly urged to gather as much intelligence as possible from French shipping near Brest before entering the Bay of Biscay, and

When you shall find cause to conclude the D. of Beaufort sailes from the Coast of France without a land army & other necessaries for invasion, his Maj. would have you make all possible haste to the Body of the fleet by returning into the Channell, but if there bee ground to believe in invasion, then to follow him as farr as the Blasquets on ye west of Ireland, but not past them, which if hee passes without endeavoring landing there will bee noe danger of it & therefore the businesse of the sea is wholly to bee intended by uniting his Majs. fleets againe.

In all of this the high command made two fundamental points. The first was that Prince Rupert was not to risk a battle with the French unless they could be caught at anchor, or if they intended an invasion. In any other circumstance he was to return to the main fleet at once. The reason, unstated, involved a basic fact of which the Prince was well aware: Beaufort and Duquesne together would outnumber him as heavily as de Ruyter outnumbered Albemarle. That was recognized even by lowly seaman Barlow. Describing the squadron's mission, he cynically added, 'which you may well think would be a wise engagement, twenty against sixty'. The true odds would have been thirty against forty-two, still daunting enough. Unless the French were taken by surprise or encumbered with transports, there was little likelihood of defeating them. It would be better to gather the English fleet in home waters, where additional hired ships and long-overdue new construction would soon augment its strength. The second point was that if the French did not intend an invasion, the high command feared it was already too late to intercept them. Captain Talbot had reported them at Lisbon on the 14th. With a fair wind the *Elizabeth* had made it home on the 22nd – eight days. But the French would have had the same wind. In those eight days and the six days since, Beaufort could easily have covered a much greater distance than the *Elizabeth*, even stopping to pick up Duquesne. By the 28th it was quite feasible for him to have sailed far to the north and out of Rupert's reach. *That* was the true import of Talbot's intelligence. James's letter implies that the news from Lisbon would have caused the King to call off the division of the fleet then and there had it not been for the dreaded Irish invasion. That danger had now become the expedition's *only* justification.

In London, also on the 28th, the King appointed the 31st a fast day to pray for the success of the fleet. Samuel Pepys did not know what had prompted this, but 'I suppose', he wrote, it must be 'upon some sudden news of the Dutch being come out'. That had not been the reason for the fast, but it was all too true.

Chapter X

Rupert's Expedition

The Prince long time had courted Fortune's love,
But once possess'd did absolutely reign:
Thus with their Amazons the heroes strove,
And conquer'd first those beauties they would gain.

When the English fleet entered the Downs on the 27th, the commanders were greeted by two unpleasant revelations. One involved a security breach. Three gentlemen visiting the fleet from London, 'the two Seymours & Mr. Trelawney', were found to know all about the plans, 'though wee would nott acknowledge anything of itt, nor noe Flag officers knew of itt till such time as wee gave out orders for the shippes'. The prospect of the enemy also getting wind of it was unspeakable, so the Generals prudently stopped the Dover packet boat. Albemarle also recommended a temporary foreign shipping embargo, which was so ordered. Despite the precautions, confused accounts of the division of the fleet somehow reached both France and the Netherlands, though not in time for de Ruyter to be notified. In Paris the Venetian ambassador, Marc Antonio Giustinian, heard about it on the 29th:

> The English have decided to make two bodies of their fleet, one destined to fight the Dutch fleet and prevent them from advancing to unite with that of France, if the latter should attempt this; the other bound to the waters of Brittany, each of them, according to report, having more than seventy powerful ships.

At The Hague it was rumoured on the 27th that 'the King of England has detached part of his Fleet to join Smith' (whose Tangier squadron was thought to be at Plymouth) but the Comte d'Estrades, the French ambassador, assured Louis XIV 'that this advice has not been found true'. The source of the 'leak' was never determined with certainty; Coventry afterwards told Albemarle that it was believed to have involved an indiscretion by John Hayes, Prince Rupert's secretary.

The Generals' other discovery on the 27th was equally disturbing. As soon as the ships had wet their anchors, a boat from Deal bearing Major John Miller of the Duke of Albemarle's regiment of Guards was rowed alongside the *Royal Charles*. Major Miller climbed through the entry port and, no doubt beaming at being reunited with his chief, handed the Generals a letter. But whatever smiles the commanders may have worn were instantly erased when they read its contents. It was from Coventry, dated the 25th. It began: 'The letters out of Holland say that the Dutch will very suddenly bee out, and it is said so confidently that I doe believe it'. Surprisingly, Coventry did not seem unduly perturbed. He reassuringly suggested that the Dutch, instead of giving battle immediately, would likely sail north to await the French coming around Scotland and to cover the incoming East Indiamen. He also informed the Generals of the other late development: 'This day Capt. Talbott of the *Elizabeth* sends me an Expresse to tell me that on the 14th instant the French Fleet was plyeing before Lisbone; an irregular Voyage of his gave him the opportunity of learning this newes'. The express itself was enclosed. On the 28th the commanders received another letter, this one written by Arlington on the 24th, repeating that the Dutch were ready. The Secretary of State agreed that the Dutch would go north, but thought they meant to meet the Danes as well as the French, as suggested by an intelligence report from Holland. Albemarle rightly discounted the Danish combination: 'For ye Danes I beleive if ye Dutch had set out ships to joyn with them they would not have done it for fear of ye Sweeds'. The admirals in any case could not afford to make assumptions about what de Ruyter would do. They detached scouts at once: the new fifth-rate *Sweepstakes* to observe the Texel and the Vlie, the fourth-rate *Kent* to watch the Ostend–Calais region, and the fourth-rate *Bristol* to cruise the waters off the North Foreland.

Astonishingly, the Dutch coast had not been scouted for nearly a week. A squadron under Captain Robert Clark, consisting of the third-rate *Gloucester* and five fourth-rates,* had roamed off the Texel from the 14th to the 21st, rejoining the fleet on the 24th with a veritable bonanza of merchant prizes. Clark had observed the Zeeland squadron sailing northwards from the Scheldt, but had found nothing to indicate that the Holland and Friesland squadrons were ready for sea. This agreed with the earlier intelligence from The Hague, so Rupert and Albemarle had not bothered to follow up Clark's cruise. This omission, damaging enough in itself, was compounded by bad luck. The latest news of de Ruyter's fleet had arrived in London on the 25th, but thereafter the previously copious flow of intelligence from Williamson's agents in the Netherlands suddenly dried up. The cause was a westerly wind which detained the packet boats from Flanders, and the result was that letters written in Holland after the 22nd only reached Whitehall on the 30th.

Their own scouting failures aside, the Generals must have found it odd that the high command in London seemed so blasé about de Ruyter. Coventry later explained that Rupert's instructions had never been contingent on the movements of the Dutch. 'The expedition was not grounded upon that', he wrote, 'if it had it would have changed upon new intelligence'. It was impossible to argue with such flawless *a priori* reasoning; the plans obviously had not changed upon the new intelligence, for the supplementary orders confirming the Prince's detachment went out on the 28th. But something was nevertheless very wrong.

In the beginning, the Duke of Albemarle had confidently advised the Council that he would be perfectly safe with seventy ships, 'though I suppose they will be about 20 more shippes than wee shall bee'. As late as 23 May some ninety-three men-of-war appeared to be available for the two Generals' use, not counting those on the western station. The list of 21 May actually showed only ninety-one, but the fifth-rate *Guernsey*

Centurion, Crown, Diamond, Dover and *Jersey*, plus the hired ketch *Bachelor*.

was subsequently added, and the fourth-rate *Guinea* returned from Lisbon and was ordered to join from Portsmouth. Thus, even after subtracting Rupert's twenty, there should have been seventy-three remaining to face the Dutch; just enough to satisfy Albemarle's needs. Admittedly, many of the vessels were scattered from Plymouth to the North Sea, but all were optimistically expected to be in hand by the time the Prince sailed. As it happened, since the 23rd there had been a rash – indeed a full-scale epidemic – of unforeseen delays, reassignments, and minor calamities, causing ship after ship to be struck from the list.

Things went amiss right from the start, with four vessels left behind when the fleet sailed from the buoy of the Nore. The third-rate *Slothany* (formerly the Dutch East Indiaman *Slot Hooningen*) and the fourth-rates *Sancta Maria* and *Convertine* had been refitting at Chatham; though launched and moved to Sheerness, they were not fully manned and victualled. The fourth vessel left in the river, also at Sheerness, was the mighty *Royal Sovereign*, then the largest ship in the world. The Generals had already sacrificed the fourth-rates *Charles V* and *Westfriesland* to allow their crews to help fill the *Sovereign*'s 700-man complement, but she was still 300 men short when the fleet sailed.

There was further disappointment when the dockyards unexpectedly failed to complete the powerful new vessels under construction. The second-rate *Loyal London*, the third-rates *Warspite* and *Cambridge*, and the large fourth-rates *Greenwich* and *St. Patrick* had been expected to join the fleet by late May. Albemarle had entertained particularly high hopes for the *Warspite* and had confidently included her among his projected seventy ships, but all five suffered last-minute delays. The general's troubles began to multiply on the 25th. On that day the fourth-rate *Centurion*, freshly returned from Captain Clark's cruise on the Dutch coast, had to be sent up to Sheerness to repair a leak which her carpenter could not control. Soon afterwards the fireship *Happy Entrance* developed a similar problem and was ordered to Harwich. Then the Prince's instructions arrived, and the accompanying letter from the Duke of York announced that two ships which had been expected to join the main fleet from Plymouth, the third-rate *Resolution* and the fourth-rate *Foresight*, were instead to be among those to wait for Rupert in the west. Albemarle had earlier agreed to their reassignment when he had thought he would have more than seventy ships. Now that things had changed, he became visibly upset at losing them, lamenting to Coventry that 'wee had better hopes of getting upon 70 shippes speedily, and besides Pr. Rupert having taken away all the best sailing Frigotts from us has left us butt few'. Despite his complaints, strength continued to drain away: the *Eagle* and *Guernsey* were ordered to convoy duty; the *Fountain* was needed at Jersey. Though these last three were only fifth-rates, their loss was still serious since the fleet had only two remaining light frigates, and one of them was still victualling at Harwich. That was why it was necessary to use the *Bristol* and *Kent*, both fourth-rates, for scouting when lesser vessels would have been preferable. The *Eagle* and *Guernsey* might have been lost to Albemarle anyway, for the Duke of York had contemplated sending them with Rupert.

Yet another disheartening blow fell when it became known that a contingent from Portsmouth under Sir Jeremy Smith, the Vice-Admiral of the White, would be delayed.

His ships had required revictualling and minor repairs after their return from Tangier on 21 April. Still with him were the third-rates *Mary* (his flagship) and *Montagu*, along with the fourth-rates *Guinea* and *Hampshire* which had come home from other voyages. Coventry wrote to Albemarle on 31 May that the Portsmouth ships would 'bee with you with the first wind'. In fact, only the *Hampshire* sailed, the others being delayed until the 5th. Ironically, the *Hampshire* had not been expected to help. Her hold contained a consignment of silver from the merchants of Tangier, and she had orders to take the money to the buoy of the Nore before joining the fleet. The orders, however, were disregarded. In addition to the known deletions from Albemarle's forces, others seemed likely. The *Dover* and *Oxford* were victualling at Harwich, and the *Bristol*, *Kent*, and *Sweepstakes* were 'upon the scout'; it was uncertain when any of these would rejoin. Fortunately, all but the *Kent* did come in before the battle, but that still left a depressing total of eighteen ships which could otherwise have been on hand, sixteen having been struck since Rupert's orders were issued.

Even as the situation deteriorated, the high command continually promised reinforcements. The *Convertine* and *Sancta Maria* were ready to start down the river, and the dockyards were fitting out eleven hired merchantmen of which several were quite large vessels with over 50 guns.* Although some were already victualled and prepared for action, Coventry regretfully reported that there did not seem to be enough men to fill their complements. To this the Generals fired off a blistering retort: 'If the Captains doe butt bestirre themselves there are men now about London that may bee impressed for the purpose'. But the manpower shortage was only too real. In some exasperation the Lord High Admiral finally consented to send the *Sovereign*, *Slothany*, and the hired ships *Turkey Merchant*, *East India Merchant*, *Castle Frigate*, and *Coronation* down to the fleet despite their shorthanded condition. Coventry assured Albemarle on the 31st that the six ships

> shall all saile toward the Gunfleet by Saturday or Sunday if the weather permitt. I cannot say they are well manned, but I think I may say their staying here will not mend them, and if they come not to bee engaged on both sides, they are very well, and if they were not, the number & Countenance of such shipps is better than lying in the River.

James wrote the same day, reiterating that the ships would sail 'by Saturday or Sunday if the Wind favour'. He further explained that 'The Soldiers you desired for the fleet I have been forced to use for sending out these shipps which I could not have gotten out without them, Seamen being more scarce here, than can be imagined'. Regrettably, no one in Whitehall realized how urgently the ships were needed; the troops were still in London on Saturday. That afternoon, Pepys finally went 'down to Blackewall and there saw the soldiers (who were by this time gotten most of them drunk) shipped off'. These besotted levies would presumably have arrived in time for the vessels at

---

* *Turkey Merchant*, *Coronation*, *Richard & Martha*, *East India London*, *London Merchant*, *Charles Merchant*, *Albemarle*, *East India Merchant*, *Castle Frigate*, *George*, *Loyal Merchant*. The last four named had served in 1665 but had been released after the campaign.

Sheerness to start downstream on Sunday; but perversely, an east wind that day made it impossible. A letter from Captain Cox of the *Royal Sovereign* shows that the ships actually sailed on Monday the 4th, expecting only 'to get this evening below the Buoy off the spites'. By then it was much too late.

The Duke of Albemarle thus found himself far short of his seventy-ship minimum, clearly removing one of his original pre-conditions for the division of the fleet. In view of this and the known preparedness of the Dutch, why was Rupert allowed to proceed? The main reason was the Irish invasion, but the planners in Whitehall had also undergone a subtle transformation in their thinking about de Ruyter. His actions had previously seemed irrelevant because it had been supposed that he was not ready for sea and that Albemarle would in any event have enough force to contain him. Neither condition had been met, but the high command now convinced itself that there was little to fear anyway. After all, most of the missing English ships were nearly ready and would be arriving in a few days, maybe a week at the most. In the meantime it was assumed that the fleet could simply wait in the Downs; that was a dangerously false assumption which no one yet realized. As for the Dutch, while the unanticipated word of their preparedness was disconcerting, they were not viewed as an immediate threat. Arlington in particular seemed amazingly complacent and overconfident. His letter of the 24th warning Albemarle that the Dutch were ready for sea had also insisted that they were 'very poorly manned & as poorly spirited', and on the same day he had written to the Earl of Sandwich that 'all conclude they are weakly manned, & with little courage to fight us'. Besides, the King's advisers had no evidence that de Ruyter had actually come out; if he had, they reasoned, English scouts would surely have found him. But Albemarle had had no scouts for a week, and of that the politicians were blissfully unaware.

There was yet another reason for the high command's euphoria. The leading strategists, Coventry and Arlington, had become transfixed by the likelihood that de Ruyter, when he sailed, would proceed not towards the Thames or the Channel, but to the north to meet the French rounding Scotland after their Irish adventures. At first this had seemed a mere possibility. As the days passed it was gradually rationalized into a probability, and finally into an established fact. The northern theory did receive support from some of Arlington's agents in the enemy countries, but in accepting it the councillors ignored other spies who consistently gave advice to the contrary. As early as 21 May Williamson had received intelligence of the 18th from The Hague that the Dutch fleet's 'design will be ye same in generall as before, to come before or into ye River of London, to block it up or fight'. This might have been of more than passing interest to the Duke of Albemarle, but it was so lightly regarded that no one even bothered to show it to him until after Rupert had sailed. There were other letters to the same effect. A particularly alarming one came in on the 30th reporting that de Ruyter intended 'to go find the English in their dunes'; this meant the Downs. Another which arrived the same day mentioned the Scottish course as a possibility, but held it 'most likliest' that the Dutch would 'goe & venture a battle with ye English fleet'. This too was discounted. The King's ministers were convinced de Ruyter would go north and were indisposed to accept anything else. On the day after those last two messages were received, with the Dutch by then *known* to be at sea, Arlington was confident enough in the northern conjunction to allow Williamson to publish intelligence for it in the *London Gazette*: 'The discourse of the Town [Paris] is, that Monsieur de Beaufort is to pass round Scotland, and to joyn the Dutch Fleet & in order to which, the Hollanders have furnished him with several pilates over land'. Coventry was equally certain. On the same day, the 31st, he soothingly advised Albemarle that there was nothing to fear from the Dutch:

> I cannot think they have any intention of seeking yr. Grace, though without the P., much less could that bee their intention, when they went out, and your fleet not divided, so certainely their designe must bee Norward, though wee have no intelligence but of their beeing before the Texell. . . . I suppose their Aime must bee a Conjunction with the French, because the Danes I cannot conceive to bee yet ready, and under the same Expedicion to secure their E. India men, which never the lesse is but my conjecture.

Conjecture or not, he was so sure of it that he declared it unsafe for the colliers in the Thames to sail for Newcastle. The mariners in the coal trade were supposed to be exempt from impressment. However, noted Sir William, since the colliers could not sail anyway, there was no reason why Albemarle should not 'borrow some of their men to recruit these shipps which come thinly manned to you'. This letter must have given the general a bitter laugh. By the time he read it he *knew* the Dutch had not gone north, for he was locked in battle with them against long odds.

In the Downs, on 28 May, Prince Rupert prepared to sail. He moved his 'furniture' to the *Royal James* and the ships completed their victuals, but contrary winds delayed their departure. In the afternoon the Generals held a final conference, during which the Prince suggested that if the Dutch appeared the Duke could bring the fleet into the Channel and rejoin the detached squadron in the west. This would have been unwise, since Albemarle's absence from the Thames would have left every port north of Dover at de Ruyter's mercy. It was in fact negated by a subsequent order from the King, but it does indicate that Rupert himself was not convinced that the Dutch would sail harmlessly off to Denmark and Scotland. He had his secretary, John Hayes, leave word for Coventry that the squadron would call at Portsmouth, 'where ye Prince expects to heare from you'.

The early morning of the 29th brought no improvement in the winds, but Rupert's squadron weighed at 3 o'clock and took advantage of the tide to beat out of the Downs to the south. The detachment was hardly clear of the anchorage when a mishap occurred. The fourth-rate *Advice* failed to allow room for the *Bonaventure* to tack; they collided, and the *Advice*, 'having broken her head', had to be sent back to Sheerness. At this Rupert blithely scribbled off a note asking Albemarle for a comparable replacement. Despite his own desperate shortage of ships, the general unhesitatingly selected the fourth-rate *Expedition* and sent her off to follow Rupert.

As the Prince's squadron disappeared around the South Foreland, the Duke of

Albemarle was worried. Even before the news had come that the Dutch were ready for sea, he had shown unmistakable signs of uneasiness. On the 26th he had expressed his concerns to Coventry:

> I doubt wee shall nott make upon 70 shippes these 3 weekes. I desire you will acquaint his Royal Highness this much, & to know his Highnesses commands what I shall doe in case the Dutch come upon us before wee can make upon 70 shippes; whether I shall fight them or noe.

When word of the Dutch readiness arrived the next day, he again wrote to Coventry, this time in a more emphatic vein:

> In my opinion I thinke itt would doe well to hasten all the shippes to us you can: as the *Hampshire*, the Merchant Men, & all other shippes that are behind. I should bee loath (though I have little force heere) to retreate from the Dutch, and therefore I desire you to hasten those shippes, and that I may receive his Majs. Commands what to doe in case ye Dutch come upon us before any more shippes come to us. Of the shippes heere there will bee butt 54.

Yet a third plea went out on the 28th, this time to Arlington:

> I have received yours of the 24th instant whereby I understand the Holland Fleet will bee suddainly out. I could heartily wish his Majesty would hasten away those ships that are to come out to us for at present wee shall not bee here above 56 ships. If wee could make up 70 sayle I should bee very confident to meet ye Dutch any where & on the other side I should bee Loath to retreat from them being it goes agst my stomach to doe it.

These passages hardly show the picture of the smug, overconfident commander that most historians have painted of Albemarle. He was obviously downright pessimistic. He flatly reported that he was too weak to defeat the Dutch; in view of that, the strong hints that he would not decline battle without specific instructions should have sounded an alarm in London. Though he would never have expressed it openly, there can be little doubt that he was begging, urgently, for the King to order him not to fight. Otherwise, why would he have written at all?

A weakness common to many of Charles II's sea-officers was an extreme sensitivity to even the slightest aspersions on their courage. It was undeniable that the public often interpreted any behaviour much short of sheer bravado as faint-heartedness; note Pepys's sarcastic remarks about Smith's Tangier cruise. A few years later Clowdisley Shovell, captain of a small fourth-rate, nearly had his career ruined when he was accused of cowardice for having understandably declined to attack a whole Spanish fleet in their own harbour in a peacetime disagreement over a salute. To avoid such charges some officers felt obliged to stand and fight even in suicidally hopeless situations. Albemarle understood this attitude, and to prevent needless catastrophes he regularly took it into account in dealing with his own subordinates. The orders to Clark's scouting squadron, for instance, had contained instructions 'to be very careful to avoid fighting with any Enemy, that is stronger than yourselfe'. But Albemarle was even more subject to such pressures than the rest. For one thing, he could be absolutely certain that the most terrible critic of all was waiting at home in the form of his rough-hewn duchess. That formidable valkyrie had been overheard to hope that 'the King would send her husband to sea with the old plain sea Captains, that he served with formerly, that would make their ships swim with blood, though they could not make legs as Captains now-a-days can'. He also had enemies who would stretch every inch of political mileage out of the spectacle of his fleeing before de Ruyter. The true circumstances would make no difference, *unless* he acted under express command. In this respect it is probably significant that he requested orders not only from the Lord High Admiral, but from the King himself. Aside from that, he had his own considerable pride.

The Duke of York's reply arrived on the night of the 29th. He and the King had misunderstood the point of the general's request; they did not forbid him to fight:

> My secretary haveing also shewed me your letter to him in which you desire directions, whether you should fight the Dutch with lesse than 70 saile. I spake also with His Majesty about it, who conceived it best to leave it to your prudence, to doe what you shall think best for His Majesty's Service.

It is usually considered desirable to allow a commander enough freedom of action to take advantage of unexpected opportunities, but in this case Charles made a grave mistake. To Albemarle the order was, as he had tried to warn, exactly the same as an unconditional command to give battle. The general's fatalistic attitude in the subsequent days has marked parallels in Blake before Dungeness, Torrington before Beachy Head, and Tourville before Barfleur. In each instance a normally prudent commander hurled himself against a vastly superior opponent mainly on a point of honour. Albemarle's case had a special element of tragedy. The very letter by which the King unwittingly condemned him to defeat contained another passage which made it clear that Charles was anxious to avoid an uneven battle:

> Nevertheless, in reguard Pr. Rupert's sailing will so much weaken the Fleet, & that diverse ships are yet to goe out of the River, His Majesty judged that it might be expedient to change your station to the Gunfleet, where the Great Shipps remaineing may come securely to joine with you, and where you cannot bee forced to doe anything but what you choose, which in the Downes you cannot.

This move, which, noted James, 'I think cannot bee done too soone', was a belated recognition of a serious error in dispositions. The Downs was a deadly trap for an outnumbered fleet. The long barrier of the Goodwins prevented egress to the eastward, and the shoal-strewn Gulls passage to the northeast was negotiable for deep-draught vessels only within narrow limits of tide and weather. Though frequently used by single ships and small groups, the Gulls was not suitable for fleets. Since there was a clear opening only to the south, the anchorage was a cul-de-sac made to order for de Ruyter's fireships, a fact well known to the Dutch. In 1639 Maarten Tromp had annihilated a great Spanish fleet which had foolishly anchored there; in one of the most one-sided naval actions of all time, a few more than a dozen ships escaped out of seventy. In 1652 Tromp had tried to spring the same trap on the Commonwealth fleet, but his quarry had been lucky enough to be absent. As if to underscore the gravity of Albemarle's situation, it was also on the 29th that he was at last shown the eleven-day-old intelligence from Holland that de Ruyter would seek a battle at the mouth of the Thames.

The decision to go to the Downs had been made for sound strategic reasons; there, the English fleet would be in a position to guard the Straits of Dover against passage by either of the enemy forces. But it was pointless if Albemarle was not strong enough to defeat the greater opponent. Rupert could just as well have parted company from one of the sheltered anchorages in the northern parts of the estuary. Once the under-strength squadrons rounded Longsand Head, every inch of ground they covered to the south took them that much farther from safety. Albemarle had crawled out on a limb, and the Downs was at the end of it. He was now faced with climbing back in along the same very exposed limb, and in much diminished strength.

The mistake might have been avoided had the professional seamen been involved in the planning. Any of the tarpaulin commanders – Ayscue, Myngs, Jordan, Teddiman, Harman – could have explained the problem from the beginning had they been consulted. Teddiman had grown up in Dover, almost in sight of the Downs, and might well have witnessed the demise of the Spaniards in 1639. Unfortunately, the Generals' intentions had been kept from the flag-officers for security purposes. The only people in the know were Rupert, Albemarle, and Spragge (all soldiers) plus Charles, James, the Generals' secretaries, and some of the politicians on the Council. It is noteworthy that it was Charles, the yachtsman, who first perceived the danger. He knew the charts almost as well as the seamen, and he acted quickly when he became aware of the rapid reduction of the fleet's strength which had occurred in the four preceding days.

In all justice it should be noted that the Downs was so frequently used as a fleet anchorage that its vulnerability was not readily obvious even to some seamen. No less eminent a mariner than Sir William Penn later said that Monck would have been perfectly safe had he stayed there. Penn's opinion, though, was not unbiased; he was rabidly jealous of Albemarle and routinely condemned everything he did on general principles. Penn did not know of the King's orders. Another seaman, Sir Thomas Allin, heard the plans on the 25th but apparently said nothing about the anchorage. But then, Allin learned at the same time that he would be losing the White Squadron, so he could be excused if his thoughts were elsewhere. Regardless of such assessments, one thing was certain: in May of 1666 the English needed to vacate the Downs without delay.

Albemarle's new instructions were received too late on the 29th for anything to be done that day. On the following morning the general called his flag-men aboard the *Royal Charles*, issued a revised squadronal organization necessitated by the Prince's departure, and disclosed the King's order to return to the Gunfleet. A spirited debate ensued; everyone agreed emphatically that the Downs was unsafe, but the flag-officers were not much happier with the Gunfleet. They pointed out 'that if there should bee an Easterly winde and the Dutch fleete should come out, wee should nott bee able to stirre and they might send in fireshippes, and putt us into disorder, besides itts an ill place to take in victualls'. By this they meant that there was too much sea room off the Gunfleet; the Dutch could easily work around to the south and trap the English against the sand. The flag-officers preferred to go instead 'to the Swin betweene the Gunfleet & the Middle Ground'. This is the anchorage known today as the East Swin, a strip of deep water lying only a few miles from the buoy of the Gunfleet. Its advantage lay in the narrow sandspit of the Middle Ground, which would bar attacks from the south and also give calm waters for victualling. If necessary, the King's Channel provided a safe escape route to the Nore. At the conclusion of the council-of-war Albemarle wrote to the Duke of York that, unless overruled, the Swin was where he intended to go. There he would wait until seventy ships were collected. He would then move the fleet to Southwold Bay (Solebay), from whence he could await the Dutch or actively seek them out if he chose. The commanders were ordered to recall any men that were ashore and to be ready to sail on the next morning, the 31st.

But events were rapidly overtaking the general's intentions. His letter concerning the new anchorage was hardly on its way when an unidentified ketch sailed into the Downs and ran alongside the flagship. She proved to be a prize taken by the *Kent*, and she was bearing an urgent message written on the 26th by the *Kent*'s captain, Thomas Ewens:

> May it please your Grace:
> This morning being off Gravelines in chase of a small ship and a ketch belonging to Newport as they pretended whom I have sent into the Downes to your Grace. I mett with a Sweed who came from Amsterdam on Sunday last in his ballast bound for Bordeaux who relates that 75 sayle of the Flemish fleet sett sayle out of the Texcell the 21st present and 18 more from Zeeland, leaving 6 ships behind them whose men they took out to man the rest of the fleet & stood away to the Northwest, which as my duty binds me I thought fitt to acquaint your Grace, & humbly kissing your hands.

Albemarle immediately dispatched Ewens's letter to Coventry, dashing off a covering endorsement of his own saying that 'Wee had the like intelligence from another shippe yesterday and therefore I desire you will hasten out the shippes to us'. The word 'yesterday' in the General's note gives reason for pause. After the war, when Coventry was under attack for his part in the campaign, he assembled a battery of evidence to prove that the division of the fleet was not predicated on the actions of the Dutch. One of his peripheral arguments came

> From the D. of Albemarle's letter of May 30th enclosing Capt. Ewen his letter informing the Dutch were abroad. The D. of Albemarle's letter saith they had the same information the 29th, which was the day the Prince sailed, yet he sent not to the Prince (who was then noe farther than Folkestone).

Coventry did not mean this as criticism, but Albemarle's inaction on the 29th nevertheless demands an explanation. It should first be noted that two of the general's other letters, both written on the 30th before Ewens's message was received, contained conditional language such as '*if* . . . the Dutch fleet should come out', and 'wee should

... bee ready to meet the Dutch *against* they come out'. This indicates that the source on the 29th (presumably the *Sweepstakes*, which returned early from her scouting expedition) did not seem reliable. But even if he believed it, Albemarle had no authority to recall the squadron; the King himself had ordered the expedition to forestall a possible invasion of Ireland, and had confirmed it with Rupert's supplementary orders of the 28th. Coventry also noted that one of his own letters previously 'told [the] Ld. Gen. the Dutch would very suddainly bee out; yett, that altered not P. Ruperts sailing'. The whole plan was based on the assumption that Monck could take care of himself. He reported his weakness in ships, and in response he was merely advised to shelter in a safer anchorage until his strength was sufficient. Thus, the news that de Ruyter was at sea only caused him to redouble his demands for the ships still in the river to be rushed down at once and prompted him to hasten his retreat to the Swin. As for Rupert, the word that the Dutch were out would not have been especially worrisome; nor was it when he did find out. Surely no one expected him to sail to La Rochelle and then perhaps all the way to Ireland, where he might have to fight a pitched battle, and weeks later return to the fleet; all of this with de Ruyter obligingly waiting in port!

Captain Ewens's intelligence reached London in the afternoon of the 31st. While it was in transit on the evening of the 30th, Williamson at last received a long-delayed mail delivery from his agents in the Netherlands. From this source the King learned that de Ruyter had come out of the Texel on the 22nd with '51 great shipps, and joined with 14 which came from Zealand. There were 7 more to goe out the next day, which in all would make 72 shipps of warre'. When this report had been posted parts of the Friesland and Noorderkwartier contingents had not yet arrived, thereby accounting for the numerical discrepancy with Ewens's note. At nearly the same time, an interesting message came in from the north: a Dutch warship of 50 guns had come inshore at Scarborough on the 27th, capturing a flyboat and scattering the colliers.

The King's advisers were quickly summoned. After considering the latest intelligence Charles decided that Rupert's detachment should be recalled. Seen with the pristine clarity of retrospect, the position of every squadron and every ship clearly known, the recall appears to have been so obviously necessary that it hardly seems to require comment. Few authorities have questioned it, and it is generally presumed that the King had at last somehow 'come to his senses'. Actually, in view of the assumptions under which the high command was operating, it was one of the more complex decisions of the campaign. As noted repeatedly, the politicians did not regard Rupert's expedition as dependent on de Ruyter's actions. That the Dutch were ready for sea was known in London five days before the Prince sailed. Nor was the main fleet thought to be in danger. True, a mistake had been made in the choice of its anchorage, but the King had already acted to set things right. As far as he knew, the fleet would soon be in a secure haven in the northern shoals of the estuary, where the ships still in the river would soon be joining it.

What, then, changed the King's mind? The reason was, as Coventry later explained, 'Because it was beleaved the Dutch & French were about a conjunction by the North, having not heard of them in 10 days from their coming out, & letters having said it was soe intended, in which case the Prince must have made a fruitless if not a hazardous voyage'. The reasoning here was rather complicated. As long as intelligence reports merely said de Ruyter was *ready* to sail, all was well. But the news that the Dutch had actually been at sea for ten days *without being seen* was another matter entirely. Had they stayed in the vicinity of the Texel, or advanced towards the Thames, it seemed inconceivable that they could have gone undiscovered for so long. But Monck's (non-existent) scouts had reported nothing, so it was assumed that de Ruyter must have sailed north; there was nowhere else he could have gone. Also important was that the Dutch had come out while Rupert and Albemarle were still together. Arlington's correspondence shows that no one in Whitehall thought de Ruyter would chance a battle with the combined English forces, when joining the French could give him an overwhelming advantage.

The Scarborough incident may have been the decisive evidence. It was supposed, in the Duke of York's words, that the marauder 'might be some shipp ye Dutch had sent to make land', implying that their fleet was nearby. That was a clever guess, but unfortunately wrong. The raider was probably one of several independent cruisers operating from the Elbe and other northern bases; de Ruyter's array had stayed near the Texel. To the council, though, the 'fact' that the Dutch fleet could be placed in the latitude of Scarborough was taken as solid confirmation that the enemy forces would meet somewhere in the north – which was already suspected. That was why Arlington felt secure in printing intelligence for it in the *London Gazette* on the 31st, and why Coventry wrote to assure Albemarle of it the same day.

When combined with other factors, the assumption that the Dutch had gone north inexorably led to further conclusions. It could be assumed that de Ruyter would not leave his own coastline and harbours unprotected any longer than necessary, while the *Elizabeth*'s news that the French were off Lisbon on the 14th made it quite possible that Beaufort too was now in Scottish waters. The conjunction therefore seemed imminent. In that case, the French would not have had time either to embark troops or support their landing, so the Irish fears could at last be put to rest. Rupert, then, was recalled because his principal mission was no longer a concern, and because it was believed he was too late to intercept the French anyway. He was *not* recalled to save Albemarle.

The King's decision was made on the night of the 30th. His orders were for the Prince to return to the Downs, and if the fleet had departed he was to rejoin at the buoy of the Gunfleet (Albemarle's intention to go to the Swin having not yet reached Whitehall). It is important to realize that no one in London felt any sense of emergency, which was later misunderstood; the recall was only another chesspiece move to counter an imagined enemy gambit. There was nonetheless a very real urgency in transmitting the change of plans to Prince Rupert, and it was this hurry that so deceived the critics. According to the Duke of York the reason for the urgency was simply that the wind in London that night was hard from the east, and it was feared that if Rupert had the same breeze he would rapidly be carried out of range of communication. To increase the chance of finding him it was decided to send copies of the orders to Portsmouth, Plymouth, and Weymouth.

Coventry stayed up late copying the instructions, and at midnight awakened the Lord High Admiral for the necessary signatures. He then had one of his clerks carry the papers to Arlington, who as Postmaster General was responsible for obtaining special couriers. When the messenger reached Arlington's lodgings, he found that His Lordship had gone to bed. Incredibly, his servants were afraid to disturb him; 'a tenderness', Clarendon acidly noted, 'not to be in the family of a secretary'. The clerk trudged back to Whitehall and returned the orders. Having no idea how to find couriers in the middle of the night, Coventry finally sent the instructions by post express at about 1 a.m. on the 31st. For this Sir William afterwards found himself 'under the lash of people's discourse'; it was alleged that his 'negligence' prevented the message from reaching Rupert in time. Actually, though an express may have been marginally less secure than a special courier, it was nevertheless the most rapid and reliable means of public communication then available in England. As Coventry himself put it, no doubt correctly, whatever gentlemen couriers he might have found 'would at least have lost more time in fitting themselves out, than any diligence of theirs beyond that of the regular post'. In fact no time was lost at all. The story of how the recall came to the Prince's hands was given by Sir Thomas Allin and Sir Phillip Honeywood, Lieutenant-Governor of Portsmouth, in depositions written after the war specifically to dispel the charges against Coventry.

Prince Rupert had not benefitted from the east wind in London. Except for one brief interlude the breeze in the Channel had had a steady westerly component, and on the 31st the squadron had not even reached Portsmouth. As he had promised, however, the Prince sent the *Bachelor* ketch on ahead to inquire for dispatches from Whitehall. At Portsmouth, Honeywood was already holding a message for Rupert which Coventry had sent down a few days earlier; this was the Duke of York's supplementary instructions of the 28th. When Sir Phillip saw the ketch approaching on the morning of the 31st, he wrote a brief note to the Prince and enclosed Coventry's packet. Just as he was finishing the note he saw the *Bachelor* come into the harbour and somehow run herself aground at Portsmouth Point. This accident was also noticed by Admiral Sir Jeremy Smith, who was still struggling to get the *Mary* and *Montagu* ready for sea. Smith and Honeywood both hurried to the Point, finding the *Bachelor* stuck fast. Until the tide changed all efforts to refloat her were fruitless, and it was only about 4 p.m. that the hapless vessel got off with the help of Sir Jeremy's pinnace. The *Bachelor* must have been somewhat leaky after her brush with the land, and her master apparently saw no urgency in his mission; to the astonishment of Smith and Honeywood, the ketch headed not out to sea, but towards the dockyard. The admiral, no doubt muttering whatever expletives his Puritan upbringing allowed, sent the pinnace after her. When the *Bachelor* was at length seen to be pointed in the right direction, Sir Jeremy and Sir Phillip walked back to the Governor's house. There, as Honeywood afterwards assured Coventry, 'about five of ye clock of afternoon an expresse came to my hand from yourself dated at one of ye Clock of morning with an inclosed for ye Prince (part of which Laybell is yett by me)'. He added that the postmark showed it to have been only 'about 16 houres on ye way'. Considering the rutted tracks that passed for roads in seventeenth-century England, that was good time indeed. On receiving the express, Smith and Honeywood dashed back to the waterside. Finding Lieutenant Henry Lake of the *Montagu*, they shoved the orders into his hands and sent him in Sir Jeremy's ubiquitous pinnace to overtake the ketch, which he did.

With the instructions in hand, the master of the *Bachelor* was now faced with the problem of finding Prince Rupert. Hailing some merchantmen newly arrived at Spithead, he was told that the Prince had already passed Portsmouth. The ketch accordingly started off down the Solent to the west, but the wind was dead foul and the *Bachelor*'s master soon realized he could clear the Isle of Wight more easily by working around to the east. Rupert actually had passed Portsmouth, but he too had tired of battling the winds and had decided to retrace his course for a short distance to wait out the weather at St. Helens. There, by sheer luck, the *Bachelor* stumbled on to the Prince's squadron lying at anchor at about 10 a.m. on 1 June.

Prince Rupert was not alarmed by the news. Allin's journal records that after receiving the orders the detachment delayed sailing for six hours to have the benefit of the tide 'to get about the Owers'. While they were still waiting, the *Hampshire* under Captain George Batts came out with the cargo of silver and met the squadron. It seems likely that Rupert told Captain Batts that it would be prudent, with the Dutch at sea, not to take the silver to the Nore, but to offload it in the Downs into the custody of Deal Castle and then join the squadron. The *Hampshire* spread her sails and raced ahead. The squadron itself was under way about an hour later; it passed Beachy Head around 5 a.m. on the 2nd but only reached Dover in the early afternoon. The Prince was later reproached for having taken an inordinate amount of time on the voyage. That the *Hampshire* reached the Downs many hours sooner was taken as evidence of some negligence on Rupert's part, though in fact the *Hampshire* had good winds all the way while the squadron encountered very light airs near Dover; Allin's journal mentions that 'we had all our small sails abroad' for a considerable period. Even so, Rupert's pace does seem to have been rather leisurely. Individual ships even detached themselves to chase unidentified merchantmen, as though nothing were wrong. But as far as Rupert knew, there *was* nothing wrong. The recall gave no information other than 'that ye Dutch fleet is come forth', and as noted earlier that was no cause for panic.

The first indication that something might be awry came in the afternoon of the 2nd, when a boat from the Downs brought news that the English and Dutch fleets had been seen in close proximity on the 31st. The observer, 'one Ralph Fell of Newcastle', had 'judged they might engage that day'. On receipt of this information the squadron quickly increased sail and tried to reach beyond the Goodwins. Perversely, the wind chose this moment to fall completely calm and then come easterly, forcing the detachment to fret all night at anchor. At 4 a.m. on the 3rd, a ketch came out of the Downs (having been sent in the previous day to see if the fleet was still there) reporting that the fifth-rate *Colchester* had also seen the Dutch on the 31st, off Ostend. As soon as the tide was favourable, about 5 o'clock, the squadron weighed and continued to beat around the Goodwins. The weatherly little *Bachelor* was sent ahead to the Gunfleet, where the instructions said the fleet would be, to inform Albemarle of the Prince's approach. Shortly afterwards one of the Duke's scouts, the fourth-rate *Kent*, emerged from the Downs and joined the squadron. She was found, according to Allin, 'plying out to the South Head of the Goodwin, when she might have been through the Gulls and met us sooner by three hours'. The *Hampshire* had presumably come out earlier. The wind was still light and easterly, forcing the detachment to tack to the south before finally rounding the sands.

Prince Rupert had no inkling of what might lie ahead. He prudently ordered his captains to clear their decks for action and then headed north, steering for the broad pass between the Kentish Knock and the Galloper Sand. About 2 o'clock the lookouts reported many sail on the horizon to the northeast. All eyes strained anxiously in that direction, but it was another hour before the scene could be resolved. It was a shocking sight: Albemarle's ships were in headlong retreat, the triumphant Dutch hot on their heels.

Chapter XI

The French

Till now, alone the mighty nations strove;
The rest, at gaze, without the lists did stand:
And threat'ning France, plac'd like a painted Jove,
Kept idle thunder in his lifted hand.

As Prince Rupert beheld de Ruyter's fleet, stretching off into the distance as far as the eye could see, he must have wondered about the duc de Beaufort. Where were the French? The answer to that question did not become known in England for several weeks, but when it did it caused an anguished outcry. Beaufort was in fact lying peacefully in port more than a thousand miles away; Prince Rupert's voyage had been a fool's errand. All over England people asked, and have often asked ever since, how such a thing could have happened.

The truth was that the whole English campaign had been built around non-existent threats. Nearly every piece of intelligence the high command had received about the French was false, out of date, or had been misinterpreted. Louis had little thought of sending his fleet around Scotland; Beaufort had meant to come straight up the Channel. Furthermore, though Duquesne was indeed lying off Belle-Île, he was no longer expecting Beaufort at the time Spragge's correspondent found him. He was only awaiting the remainder of his own squadron, which had orders to escort a French princess to Lisbon to be the new Queen of Portugal. Her wedding, a proxy affair, was to take place at La Rochelle; the supposed Irish invasion forces were merely the regiments sent there for the grand review which would accompany the ceremony. There were no plans to invade Ireland or anywhere else; Jean Choisin, the Frenchman at Kinsale, was a perfectly legitimate Barbados beef merchant. And to top it all, the fleet that Captain Talbot of the *Elizabeth* had seen off Lisbon was not French, but Spanish! Spain was at war with Portugal and had dispatched eighteen warships under Almirante Mateo Maes to blockade the Tagus. Maes had no compunction against attacking English ships which ignored his blockade (he had captured one the week before) and that explained his hostile behaviour. Talbot's error nevertheless seems downright incredible, for French and Spanish warships of this period were distinctly different in appearance. It becomes a little easier to understand when it is realized that the *Elizabeth*'s captain was a gentleman commander of the very worst kind. He was later to disgrace himself by cravenly abandoning a great battle with his ship scarcely damaged, 'walking the deck in his silk morning gown and powdered hair'. Such a fool probably could not have told a French man-of-war from a Chinese junk. It would be interesting to know if his officers were equally deceived; one wonders if they were the same men who had given Captain Nixon such 'evill councell' aboard the *Elizabeth* in 1665.

Almost as soon as the division of the fleet was discovered to have been a mistake, an angry public began seeking the identity of the villains responsible for it. The search for a scapegoat has continued down to the present. Almost everyone concerned has been indicted at some time or other: Spragge and Talbot for the intelligence they produced, Rupert and Albemarle for proposing the plan, Coventry and Carteret for presenting it, and Charles and James for approving it. Some had darker thoughts; seaman Barlow was sure it was 'papists and traitors'. By an anonymous account,

> Some said, that the Lord Chancellor [Clarendon], envying the glory of the Generall, had purposely devised this way to ecclipse it. Others said, that the Lord Arlington, having married a Dutch Lady, she held private correspondency with some of her great kindred, who sat at the Helm in Holland, and by that means, all the Councills in Whitehall were discover'd, and betray'd; that the Dutch knew the English Fleet was to be divided, before wee knew it our selves, for which great summs of money were paid, to I know not who . . . and upon the whole matter wee were merely bought & sold.

But the writer added, 'there was no sence at all, nor shadow of reason in those surmises', and he was right.

The fact is that the decision to attack the French was by no means unsound, given the available intelligence. The English could hardly stand by idly while forty men-of-war reinforced the enemy and stirred up the Irish hornets' nest; that would have had incalculably grave consequences. Even so, the glaring and incontrovertible futility of the expedition has always tended to obscure the many other failings which were equally necessary to create the disaster. The division of the fleet was not the worst mistake. The Prince's squadron could have been gone for weeks without any ill effects had the proper precautions been taken at home. The error was not so much that Rupert was detached, but that Rupert was detached while the main fleet was in an untenable anchorage, with insufficient force, with no knowledge of the true whereabouts or intentions of the Dutch, and with its commander in a dangerously fatalistic mood.

Some of the most damaging lapses were the fault of the Generals themselves. One was the decision to go to the Downs before the fleet was at full strength, and another was the inexplicable failure to maintain a constant watch on the Dutch coast. The one serious scouting effort, Captain Clark's, was completed on the 21st and was not repeated. By cruel coincidence, de Ruyter chose the next day to begin coming out. His enormous armada, over ninety sail strong by the 26th, cruised in plain view for a full week, conducting exercises and holding councils-of-war; but no English scouts were there to see it. Only on the 27th, when word came *from London* that de Ruyter might be ready, did the Generals belatedly think it necessary to order further reconnaissance. Thus at the very time accurate news of the Dutch was most desperately needed, none whatever was forthcoming. This did not go entirely unnoticed. The anonymous observer quoted above saw it clearly:

Upon [Clark's] intelligence, the Admiralls depended too much; when it would have
been more adviseable, to send three or four frigatts once a weeke, alternatively, on so
important an Errand, to continue their station untill they should be releev'd, or have
made a discovery of the Enemies motion. No danger of the surprize of such scouts
can excuse the omission of sending them, for there were always in our Fleet, many
frigats nimble enough to outsaile the best of the Enemy's. The Dutch were abroad 2,
or 3 days before the English sail'd from the Buoy of the Nore. And therefore, if any
English ships had been upon the scout, to give the Admiralls timely notice, no
intelligence from the Westward, whether false, or true, would have tempted a Division
of the Fleet. On the contrary, they would have sail'd directly to fight the Dutch, before
their Confederates the French could possibly come to ayd 'em. The Admiralls did
plainly perceive the loss they were at for want of intelligence; and ever after, they kept
scouts abroad, with the greatest care & exactness imaginable.*

The contention that the discovery of the Dutch would have prevented the division
of the fleet is debatable; the Irish invasion (of which the critic was unaware) would
probably have assumed the higher priority. But timely intelligence would at least have
made Albemarle's danger obvious. The fatal strategic flaw, his needless exposure in
the Downs, would surely have been recognized in time for him to reach a secure
concentration point before encountering de Ruyter. The King attempted to correct
the error by withdrawing the fleet into the river, but his intentions were foiled when
the Dutch appeared and Albemarle chose to attack them despite his inferior numbers.
Although many people admired the general's boldness, his decision was the one great
mistake that made all the others irreparable. It was also a decision for which the King
and the Duke of York bore some indirect responsibility. Albemarle had warned them
that he would not refuse battle unless ordered to do so; he had requested that order,
however cryptically, and they had declined to give it.

There was still another ruinous failing, one for which neither the Generals nor the
King and Council were at fault. It is seldom realized that the Royal Navy in May of
1666 had commissioned enough ships to deal with both the French and the Dutch
simultaneously. Even after deducting Rupert's twenty and the ten waiting for him off
the Lizard, ninety-eight still remained: eighty 'ships of force' and eighteen fifth-rates.
Albemarle had been given every reason to expect seventy of those ships for his part of
the task; why did he have but fifty-six when 'the day' came? Some absences were
unavoidable, such as the *Hampshire*'s late return with the Tangier silver, the *Kent*'s
scouting, and the operational accidents to the *Advice* and *Centurion*. Others were
deliberately excluded: the fourth-rate *Sapphire* was in Irish waters and the *Hope* on her
way to Barbados, while sixteen of the fifth-rates were needed for convoys, patrolling
foreign stations, and various miscellaneous duties. But the rest of the missing vessels
were simply idling in harbour because they had not been manned, victualled, or
equipped in time. At Portsmouth were the *Mary*, *Montagu*, and *Guinea*; in the Thames

---

*A possible author of this carefully considered account of the Four Days' Battle (quoted throughout this
book) is Major John Miller who had delivered Coventry's intelligence letter to the Generals on 27 May.
Also knwn as Captain Miller in the nautical sense, he was an important merchant shipowner.

the *Slothany*, *Sancta Maria*, *Convertine*, eleven hired merchantmen, and above all the *Royal Sovereign* which was worth a half-dozen of the rest. Her want of men had also caused the useless sacrifice of the *Charles V* and *Westfriesland*. Those twenty ships (every one of the fourth rate or larger) would have made all the difference to the Duke of Albemarle. Their unreadiness was in each case directly or indirectly attributable to the navy's scandalous financial starvation. There was not enough money to attract or keep the men, not enough to support the victualler, not enough for anything. None of this even takes into account the ships under construction. The *Loyal London*, *Warspite*, *Cambridge*, *Greenwich*, and *St. Patrick* would all have been launched and completed many weeks before had the Navy Board been able to supply the dockyards with the necessary materials, pay the workers, and give the private builders what was due them under their contracts.

It later became fashionable to say that the King had frittered away all the money on mistresses and idle pleasures. That was a gross distortion; his ladies were indeed well provided, but not from the navy's revenues. By the standards of his Continental counterparts Charles II maintained a very unostentatious court, his ramshackle firetrap of a palace being possibly the meanest royal abode in all Europe. In truth the navy was short of money partly because of uncontrollable corruption at its middle and lower levels of administration, but far more because a mistrustful and miserly Parliament had consistently voted too little. That body was dominated by the same commercial interests who had demanded the war in the first place, but they steadfastly refused to accept the necessary sacrifices. After the war a hostile committee of Parliament (the Brooke House Committee) spent nearly two years examining the navy's accounts. Many of its members fully expected to find that Charles and his ministers had stolen much of the wartime Parliamentary grants. To the opposition's scarcely concealed disappointment, the committee eventually found that nearly all of the £4,355,000 in special grants had been properly spent, and that the King in desperation had even diverted for war purposes large sums normally used for the administration of the kingdom. The committee did find Carteret, the wartime Treasurer of the Navy, unable to account for over £300,000; but subsequent investigation by the Privy Council traced the missing money to legitimate expenses. Carteret had even borrowed for the navy on his own credit and in extreme emergencies had paid bills directly from his own pocket.

None of the foregoing is meant to imply that the division of the fleet was anything other than a costly blunder. Although the reasoning of the King and his advisers may have been flawless, it is undeniable that all their decisions were governed from start to finish by abysmal intelligence failures, both in substance and interpretation. If any blame can be assigned for that (much of it was plain bad luck) the heaviest burden would have to be Arlington's, if only because foreign information was his express responsibility. This was not ignored by his contemporaries. Andrew Marvell, venomous as ever, wrote him up as '*The Secretary that had never yet / Intelligence but from his own Gazett*'. Yet it would be unfair to be too harsh with Arlington. After all, his network in the Netherlands was sophisticated, resourceful, and effective beyond any reasonable expectations. Williamson's star agents were bold enough to visit the

Dutch fleet on the very day it sailed. They gave ample warning of its preparedness, accurate accounts of its strength, and even details of the fighting tactics discussed in de Ruyter's councils-of-war. True, some of the reports conflicted, making possible the rejection of the crucial revelations of de Ruyter's intentions; but on the whole Arlington's Dutch agents served him well.

The failure was with the French. Predictions of their actions were in almost every instance totally, miserably, disastrously wrong. Arlington was able to glean little of value from within France itself; for the most part he had to rely on chance discoveries by English sea-officers and rumours overheard by the correspondents in the Netherlands. Sadly, these were seldom accurate. The French intelligence produced several ironies. Some of the rare authentic reports were completely misleading, while some of the false ones had just enough truth to make them plausible. Sir Edward Spragge's information on the location of Duquesne's flagship was quite accurate, and the Council's interpretation of it was in close accord with Louis' original plans. Likewise, the French did briefly contemplate sailing around Scotland, and they did request pilots from the Dutch in case the northern course became necessary. Louis, however, told his ambassador to the Netherlands that the Channel route was 'infinitely preferable' in that it would keep Beaufort within easy range of communication. Oddly, the most spurious canard of them all, Captain Talbot's inexcusable misidentification of the fleet at Lisbon, was among the least deceptive. Had his mission taken him just three days' sail nearer the Straits, he would have found the real French fleet somewhere between Cadiz and Cape St. Vincent. For Beaufort *was* in the Atlantic, having passed Gibraltar on 8 May.

Whether there was ever any validity to the Irish matter is less certain. Louis XIV unquestionably understood how useful Ireland could be. Later in the summer he paid the English arch-republican Algernon Sydney 20,000 *écus* to produce an uprising, and at another time he briefly considered landing a single battalion there as a diversion to cover a larger assault on the Isle of Wight. But that Louis would have planned anything so dangerous as a major invasion of Ireland seems most improbable. His *Mémoires*, which explain his intentions with only minor mendacity, give no indication of it; nor is it mentioned in his correspondence with d'Estrades, the French ambassador to The Hague. Yet Arlington had persuasive evidence for it, and he was not the only one; a Dutch newsletter written on 29 May insisted 'that ye french are to goe with ye fleet of ye Duke of Beaufort, & endeavor to land an army either in Scotland or in Ireland, & this is reported at Amsterdam for very certain'. Furthermore, on 6 June the Venetian ambassador to Spain, Marin Zorzi, saw letters signed by Beaufort himself discussing, among other things, plans 'to proceed towards Ireland to stir up commotions'. Perhaps Louis did at some point consider the idea, but a better explanation may be that English agents (and others) were taken in by a cunningly conceived deception. Throughout the naval campaign Louis was gathering armies for his eventual attack on Spain, but he did not want that revealed. In his *Mémoires* he describes how 'under the pretext of the English war' he amassed huge quantities of military stores and equipment along his coasts, 'so as to serve me for two purposes, that is, at sea against the English and on land against the Spanish, in case I should undertake an expedition against them towards the end of the campaign'. He added that subterfuges were devised 'in order to convince foreigners that this preparation was destined solely for the maritime war'. In addition, the French did intend to embark soldiers in their fleet, but only to alleviate the manning problems. It would, said Louis, give 'the double advantage of accustoming some of my troops to serving at sea and of saving the cost of feeding them in the provinces'. This deception, as will soon become apparent, was not the only trick in Louis' repertoire.

The reasons for the widely varying success of Arlington's intelligence efforts in the two enemy countries are not hard to find. The Dutch, with their quasi-democratic institutions, made no decisions without fractious debate in committees, councils, and assemblies which an enterprising spy could compromise with ease. This, added to a relatively open society, unfettered press, and non-existent postal regulations, made the Netherlands a paradise for a secret agent. By contrast, the France of Louis XIV was a proto-totalitarian state as repressive as any modern dictatorship. Louis was secretive by nature. He accepted no counsel except from the equally secretive Colbert, made his own decisions, and kept his intentions concealed, telling his admirals and ambassadors only what they needed to know to carry out their parts in his Byzantine machinations.

The actions and motives of the French remained a deep mystery in England long after the Four Days' Battle. Most people ultimately concluded, as have many modern authorities, that Louis had deliberately betrayed the Dutch. Things were actually not so simple. Although his behaviour was at times outrageously duplicitous, there is no evidence that he intended a betrayal. He certainly wanted the Dutch to win and gave them unwavering diplomatic support: he convinced the Elector of Brandenburg to lend 10,000 troops to the Netherlands; he forced the Bishop of Munster out of his quixotic alliance with the English; he pressured the Swedes not to interfere with the Danes; and the Danes themselves he heavily subsidized. For the one great miscarriage, the failure to unite the fleets, Louis placed the blame squarely on the Dutch. Indeed, he sincerely felt that *they* had betrayed *him*. Aside from that, his decisions were influenced by complex affairs of state of which the northern powers had only a vague understanding.

As the French plans stood in February, the duc de Beaufort was to leave Toulon as soon as he had mustered sufficient force, annihilate Smith, and then pass through the Straits to meet Duquesne. The only apparent impediment to a Franco-Dutch conjunction was the need for a satisfactory compromise on the nature of the joint command. This was a sensitive matter, but some precedent did exist. France and the Netherlands had been allied in 1635, and there had been a formal agreement on the management of the combined fleets. Under that agreement the French admiral would be the commander-in-chief, but all major decisions would be taken democratically in the full council-of-war. Each country was to have equal representation in the council, votes being cast one at a time beginning always with the senior French officer, followed by the senior Dutchman, then the second-ranking Frenchman and so forth in alternating fashion. In 1666 Louis proposed that the old treaty be adopted without alteration.

The Dutch accepted without demur that the duc de Beaufort as a member of the French royal house could not be denied the honours of the commander-in-chief. Nevertheless, the States-General demanded absolute control over discipline, promotions, and all other internal affairs of the Dutch fleet. They also noted that in battle, victory or defeat often hinged on the conduct of the flagship and the signals it made. They had grave doubts about the wisdom of entrusting such weighty responsibility to an officer so lacking in experience as Beaufort, regardless of his undoubted courage and good intentions. They further pointed out that, contrary to the circumstances of 1635, the fleets in 1666 would be unequal in size. A very large Dutch force with sixteen permanently appointed flag-officers would be operating with a French squadron having no more than six commanders of proper flag rank (Beaufort, Duquesne, and their respective vice- and rear-admirals). That meant that in the council-of-war French private captains would be voting on an equal basis with Dutch vice-admirals. This, they protested, would be intolerably demeaning.

In objecting to the 1635 treaty, the Dutch were not being fully consistent. Louis had ordered virtually his entire navy to the North Sea to ensure the greatest possible French role in the campaign. The Mediterranean would be stripped of warships, leaving only a few galleys to guard the whole area. He therefore asked that the Dutch make up the deficit by sending twelve of their own ships, which would temporarily be under Beaufort for the destruction of Jeremy Smith's squadron, and then remain behind to protect the allies' Mediterranean shipping – most of which was Dutch. Johan de Witt replied that he had already ordered Verburgh's eight ships from Cadiz to place themselves at Beaufort's disposal. If, however, twelve more were to be sent, the States-General would insist that the combined Mediterranean fleets be governed by the 1635 terms. This never became a major issue (the Dutch could not spare the twelve ships) but considering the double standard in de Witt's stance, Louis could have been forgiven had he chosen to press the French prerogatives under the treaty more forcefully.

In fact the King of France proved surprisingly accommodating. He cheerfully promised to respect the States-General's prerogatives, and he acknowledged that the Dutch had a valid complaint about the council-of-war. After many conferences between Louis and Dutch ambassador Van Beuningen, and between de Witt and French ambassador d'Estrades, it was agreed that decisions should be made by the mutual consent of de Ruyter and Beaufort; when a council-of-war was required it would be restricted to only four or five officers on each side. Louis did require every element of protocol to ensure recognition of his cousin's primacy as commander-in-chief. De Ruyter, for instance, would have to repair aboard the French flagship for conferences, and not the other way around. But Louis had no illusions as to Beaufort's fitness to direct a sea-fight. Even as the Dutch were discussing among themselves a tactful way of broaching this matter, the King suggested a solution. He requested that, in view of the 'default of experience' of Beaufort and the other French commanders, a volunteer be solicited from 'among the States' most tested Captains to lodge aboard the flagship of the Admiral of France, & to serve as Counselor to the aforesaid duc de Beaufort on all important occasions'. Greatly relieved, the Dutch selected Isaac Sweers, the respected Rear-Admiral of Amsterdam, for the honour.

At the end of March the negotiators were still haggling over a few minor points, notably the salute which the Dutch would render to the French commander and the exact composition of the council-of-war. But both sides had agreed in principle on all matters of consequence, and it appeared that the conjunction of the fleets could be accomplished within a few weeks. Then in April a seemingly trivial complication arose: the impending marriage of Louis' (and Beaufort's) niece, Marie-Françoise de Savoie, duchesse de Nemours et d'Aumâle, to King Alfonso VI of Portugal. This union had been under unhurried negotiation for two years, but for important political reasons both Louis and Alfonso now wanted it accomplished before France became too deeply embroiled against England. Since the Portuguese were at war with Spain, it was decided to send 'Mademoiselle d'Aumâle' to Lisbon by sea from La Rochelle under the protection of the French Atlantic fleet. The arrangements were not expected to affect the Dutch conjunction. The lady's proxy wedding and subsequent departure were scheduled for late April; if all went according to plan she would be in Lisbon by the middle of May, thereby freeing Duquesne's ships to join Beaufort's. In addition, Louis had obtained a guarantee of free passage from Charles II of England, who could not afford to jeopardize his fragile relations with Portugal. This meant that only a few ships would suffice for the escort, so that even if her departure were delayed the effect on the size of the combined French fleet would be slight.

Then everything began to go wrong. To understand what happened, it is necessary to realize that all of Louis' designs were based on the assumption that the Dutch fleet would keep the English fully diverted while his own much weaker forces were gathering. Through March he was confident that this all-important condition was being fulfilled. On 13 April, however, with the orders to his sea commanders already issued, Louis suddenly learned from d'Estrades that the Dutch were not yet prepared to oppose the English. He reacted to the ambassador's revelation with fury and dismay:

> I could not have received worse news than that which you have given me, that the States' Fleet will not be ready to sail until the end of May [the 21st, Old Style], in that a very great evil could come from this delay; for having taken my measures from the assurances of the Deputies of the States which they have often given me, that their Fleet would go to sea within the month of March, I have made no objection to giving orders to the duc de Beaufort to pass into the Atlantic as soon as he can, they having promised me that the States' Fleet would sufficiently occupy the Enemy, for without such fear they [the English] will be able to go with all their forces to encounter the aforesaid duc. Yet today I see that their business will be simplified if a way is not found to have the States' Fleet sail without delay: to that end I desire that you apply yourself effectively to see clearly what the matter requires, without my having to magnify its importance further.

A week later d'Estrades replied that de Ruyter had reiterated that he could promise nothing before 21 May. Johan de Witt had nevertheless assured the ambassador that if the English sent a detachment against the French, the Dutch would immediately sail to the Thames with all the ships that were already prepared. This was no comfort to the King of France. If the English were allowed the first move, his fleet would be doomed before the Dutch could react. Considering that this was exactly what Prince Rupert had in mind, Louis' concern was by no means unjustified.

While the couriers galloped back and forth between Paris and The Hague, there were several developments. The French fleet sailed from Toulon on 19 April, Smith's squadron was found to have returned to England, and the embarkation of Marie-Françoise was postponed until 5 June. That change was reluctantly approved on 23 April at the behest of the Marquis de Sande, the Portuguese envoy who had been sent to take charge of the new Queen's entourage. He claimed to be subject to seasickness; his constitution, he said, could never bear the usual storms of April and May, and he would not consent to embark before the quiet season arrived. On 30 April Louis advised Beaufort that the Dutch were not ready, though with some exaggeration:

> Inasmuch as the English fleet is not being opposed in the Channel by that of the States, which no matter how much I had urged them to do so will be at sea only by next June the 10th or 12th [New Style], I fear that they will seek out my fleet and do battle with it to their great advantage.

Louis' alarm cannot be overemphasized. Lowestoft had made him deeply respectful of the fighting prowess of the English, and Bergen had shown him how bold they could be. With the Dutch in port, all of his decisions were coloured by the knowledge that Rupert and Albemarle could destroy his nascent sea power in a single afternoon. To withstand the expected attack he at first hoped to concentrate all his ships as quickly as possible somewhere far from the English bases. The obvious choice was Lisbon, where a friendly reception could be expected and where Duquesne would be safely removed from the French coast. The Atlantic squadron had come under increased risk with the postponement of the wedding, for Charles II's gracious offer of free passage for the Queen's escort applied only when she was actually embarked. The Duke of York had specifically mentioned that fact in Rupert's instructions:

> You are to take notice that passes have bin granted by his Majesty & alsoe by mee for certaine ships of warr belonging to the French King for carrying the Queene of Portugall to Lisbonne, which passes are punctually to bee observed whilst the Q. of Port. shall bee on board, but are not to hinder your attempting any thing when the said Q. shall not bee on board, nor the taking or destroying any ship when separated from the fleet in which the said Q. is in person, however they may pretend to belong to that fleet.

Louis suspected as much. Accordingly, Beaufort was ordered to wait off the Tagus for Duquesne, who would sail there in a few days. Once united, the French fleet would be strong enough to venture north for further orders; by then the Dutch would presumably be at sea, and the royal wedding party ready for embarkation. But, stressed Louis, Beaufort was at all times to be very careful:

> I urge you to take every possible precaution in order to be forewarned in the event that all or the greater part of the English fleet might leave the Channel to seek you out, inasmuch as I consider at present nothing more consequential for the good of my

service than the preservation of my maritime forces which I have entrusted to you with such particular concern.

Louis' revised plans foundered on the protests of the Marquis de Sande, whose complaints were becoming increasingly tiresome for the French. He objected to the proposed departure of Duquesne's ships, which had been set aside for his use. Despite assurances that the fleet would return from Lisbon long before the new embarkation date, he remained adamant. Louis felt uneasy at the vulnerability of his divided squadrons, but to argue openly with the envoy might endanger the already delicate marriage agreement. There was no choice but to accede to the Portuguese demands. After this experience Louis prudently sent the prestigious Marquis de Ruvigny to take titular command of the Atlantic fleet so that Duquesne, a commoner, would not have to deal at a disadvantage with de Sande. Ruvigny was told not to interfere in the management of the fleet.

By this time the chances of the French joining the Dutch before the middle of June were decidedly slight. But now, even as de Sande's objection was being decided, the last hopes were dashed by the discovery of a new danger from an unexpected quarter: a third party had directly threatened the Portuguese wedding plans, and indeed the very person of Mademoiselle d'Aumâle.

The marriage agreement with King Alfonso was a machiavellian ploy typical of Louis XIV's diplomacy. The war which he intended to fight against the Spanish Habsburgs had been years in the planning, but now he could not allow that struggle to begin until he had finished the unwanted quarrel with the English. He also feared that Spain might be tempted to take advantage of his temporary preoccupation with the sea campaign to attack his flank. To prevent such mischief and to sap the Habsburg strength he felt it imperative to keep them fully occupied in their protracted hostilities with Portugal. As a first step he craftily encouraged the Spanish war effort by readily agreeing, at their insistence, to refrain from helping the Portuguese despite his growing friendship with Alfonso. But the English, seeing through his game, threatened to thwart his intentions by generously offering to have the Earl of Sandwich mediate a settlement between the Iberian powers. When Sandwich's negotiations showed signs of attaining their goal Louis played his trump: he hastily completed the marriage treaty, which, he calculated, would so enrage Madrid that peace with Portugal would be impossible. This succeeded far beyond his wishes. The Spanish government at this time was in the hands of a regency, the throne being occupied by a sickly and feeble-minded child, Carlos II. The thought of a Bourbon-Braganza union proved so repugnant to the Spanish regents that they resorted to an extreme measure: the blockading fleet under Mateo Maes (the same that Talbot found) was publicly instructed to prevent the arrival of the Queen and her retinue by any means possible; as Consul Westcombe put it, 'to surprise the French ladies'.

The unanticipated violence of the Spanish reaction placed the King of France in a most uncomfortable position. Duquesne's squadron was too small to fight its way through, but Beaufort could not be allowed to destroy Maes; that would bring on the Spanish war prematurely. Nor, ironically, did the Spanish desire war with France; ordinarily they would never have dared so provocative an action as they had just ordered. The explanation lay in a strange quirk in Louis' neutrality treaty with Spain which made it possible for Mateo Maes to attack Duquesne *without technically committing an act of war*! As Louis ruefully explained,

> I could have no doubt that my ships would be fair game for them whether going or returning; for if they considered them as carrying the wife of the King of Portugal, they had every right to take them, since this Prince was their open enemy, and if they regarded them as belonging to me, I had no grounds to reclaim them, since I had a special treaty with Spain by which, on their frequent complaints that the French were aiding Portugal, I had consented to their taking all the ships they might find within fifty miles of the coast of Portugal.

The obvious solution was for Beaufort to sail to La Rochelle and escort the wedding party with the whole fleet. But, even in this emergency, the possibility of an English attack precluded any such option. The only remaining alternative was to keep the Mediterranean fleet at Lisbon to overawe Mateo Maes, and this course was reluctantly adopted; the Dutch would have to wait. On 5 May revised instructions were issued to Beaufort requiring him not merely to lie off Lisbon, but to enter the Tagus itself. As justification Louis cited the uncertainty of the weather and the likelihood that even at Lisbon the English might descend upon the French fleet, 'which needs to be preserved for an infinite number of reasons'. Beaufort was to inform the King of Portugal

> that I have ordered you not to abandon his shores until my cousin arrives, in order to shelter her from the threats the Spanish have made to abduct her during her journey . . . . You will immediately make use of this authorization and will keep my vessels in the aforesaid river until my cousin is arrived.

The French fleet was thus eliminated from further participation in the campaign of the Four Days' Battle. That, however, was not quite true of Louis himself. One would have thought that Beaufort would be safe enough in the Tagus, but Louis insisted on one more precaution. In one of his more callous decisions, he chose not to inform the Dutch of the change in plans. To the contrary, on 11 May he instructed d'Estrades to tell Johan de Witt

> that the project which you have discussed with him of bringing his Majesty's fleet to Belle-Isle, is half completed, in that orders have been given to Monsieur de Beaufort to come there, & that the remaining part of the same project, for joining the fleets between Boulogne & Dieppe, seems advantageous to His Majesty provided that it can be executed.

This bald-faced lie was supported by a letter (also dated 11 May) which Louis had purportedly sent to Beaufort *at Belle-Île*. It began:

> My Cousin,
> Having no doubt that you are sailing with my naval forces to the road of Belle-Isle with all possible haste pursuant to my original orders, I thought it best to send this letter to the site of Belle-Isle to inform you of my intentions concerning the use of my naval forces that you are commanding . . . .

This message was undoubtedly a part of the deception, for Louis' *Mémoires* emphasize that there was never any question of allowing the French fleet to leave Lisbon before the new Queen arrived. His seemingly treacherous chicanery was purely a security measure. The Dutch were notoriously lax in protecting their secrets, and with the States' Fleet still in port Louis did not intend to allow some careless slip on the part of his ally to lead the English to Beaufort's anchorage. The subterfuge was undoubtedly instrumental in misleading Arlington's spies, but the Dutch were understandably indignant when the truth came out.

Although the King of France was unwilling to reveal the true situation, he did at least inform the Dutch that in view of Beaufort's last reported position (at Alicante on 28 April) the conjunction could not occur for some weeks. What de Ruyter might do in the meantime caused Louis considerable anxiety. It had occurred to the French early in their planning that it would be highly desirable for the English and Dutch to fight a major engagement just before Beaufort entered the Channel. As Duquesne put it, even if the Dutch lost, 'it will only have been after a great battle, in which the English will have been weakened'. The time required for the victorious fleet to refit would permit the French to pass the Channel unopposed. But if for some reason Beaufort could not take advantage of the opening before the English returned to sea, a Dutch defeat could have catastrophic consequences; the States' Fleet might be blockaded in its ports, rendering the conjunction all but impossible. When Beaufort's approach was postponed, Louis therefore ceased pressing the Dutch to hurry their fleet to sea and instead began to advise the opposite. His 11 May instructions to d'Estrades ordered the ambassador to remind de Witt that the English would surely exhaust themselves financially if the allies refused battle; this was the policy of delay that Coventry had so feared in 1665. Louis further urged that if the Dutch insisted on fighting, it would be of 'very great consequence' to enlist the aid of the Danish fleet first. This, he felt, could be brought about quite easily if the States-General would merely offer the King of Denmark 'some quantity of money of trifling importance'. In another memorandum written on the same day Louis propounded a plan that showed all too clearly his lack of understanding of naval strategy. He suggested that all the allies – French, Dutch, and Danes (whose cooperation he seemed to take for granted) – should keep their fleets in port until the English concentrated on one, and then the other two would combine and attack. That the allied fleets would be hundreds of miles apart did not seem to matter.

By then the Dutch already knew that it would take more than a small bribe to lure Frederik out of his shell. On the fundamental role of the States' Fleet, de Witt did confer with the Dutch sea commanders, and they understandably informed him that in view of Louis' assurances that Beaufort was under orders to join them, a passive policy made little sense. On the 17th d' Estrades reported the results of the conference:

> Admiral de Ruyter thinks, that the proper post to occupy is the one between Calais and Dover; because if he is at sea before the English, he will prevent those forces in the River of London from being able to join in the Downs; he will likewise interrupt in the same way the considerable traffic between the ports of Plymouth, Portsmouth, & others with the River of London, & he will be positioned between the English Fleet

and that of Your Majesty, which will be able to join with him without any opposition. But also if the English Fleet gets the start, it will be necessary to fight a battle immediately & to open the passage, so as not to lose the opportunity for the conjunction.

The King responded on the 24th with a desperate plea for the Dutch to reconsider their decision, pointing out

that there was no need for them to risk fighting the English fleet alone, since with the shortest wait they could be reinforced by my ships or by those of Denmark; that after their junction with both, our victory would be assured and that there was no point in taking unnecessary chances.

The trouble was that the 'shortest wait' acceptable to the Dutch was a matter of days, while the French were thinking of months.

Louis seemed incapable of comprehending the devastation to Dutch foreign trade that would result if their fleet stayed in port, or the extent to which Johan de Witt's political survival depended on the good will of the shipping, banking, and commercial interests of the Province of Holland, which stood to lose the most. On the 27th d'Estrades tried to explain the facts to his royal master:

They have strongly emphasized to me, that in a Republic it is not the same as in a Kingdom: that when a King wills something, it is done; but that in their State, when a Resolution is taken, & when it is with the consent of the Cities and of the Admiralties, no one can alter it, & then it is necessary to endure the consequences. There are also great considerations for the advances of money that the City of Amsterdam has made for getting the Fleet to Sea, in order to assure the safe arrival of the Fleet of the Indies, which is estimated at six millions, & which the East India Company expects in the month of June.

D'Estrades had used every argument to change their minds, but, he continued,

They replied to me that it would be impossible, for the reasons previously alleged, & that if their Fleet remained in their Ports, all the Bourses would close, & that would carry great risk of a general Revolt.

But when d'Estrades wrote this letter, the question was already settled; de Ruyter had sailed on the 22nd, only one day later than he had promised.

The subsequent events held little but frustration for the duc de Beaufort. Things went well enough when he arrived off Lisbon on 30 May, for Mateo Maes was un-questionably intimidated by the vast force before him; he saluted the French flag with many guns and obsequiously dipped his colours. Though the Spanish squadron resumed its operations on the Portuguese coast, it prudently stayed well south of the Tagus and made no further move to intercept Duquesne. This much assured, Beaufort anchored in the river to await his niece. But the time for her arrival came and went, and she did not appear. Unknown to Beaufort, her departure had been postponed again; at the last minute the duchesse had insisted on visiting her aunt, the abbesse de

Fontévrault, and de Sande had fallen ill. When the principals eventually arrived at La Rochelle, the local authorities found themselves totally unprepared for the incredible *impedimenta* for which transportation was demanded. Besides whole shiploads of furniture, the Marquis alone had forty horses and seven carriages. They finally sailed on 20 June, immediately encountering foul winds and unseasonably heavy seas; de Sande must have been miserably seasick.

Meanwhile Beaufort received no news from France, and the Portuguese petulantly denied him provisions because he would not attack the Spanish fleet. Whatever his failings as a commander, the duc de Beaufort was a courageous and honourable man. Mortified at his inability to help the Dutch, he became disgusted with the entire affair; with the Portuguese, with his niece, with Louis himself. When his victuals threatened to run out, he would wait no longer; on 19 July he weighed and sailed north without orders. The French fleets crossed without sighting each other and both had exceptionally long passages; Duquesne and Ruvigny arrived at Lisbon on 23 July, Beaufort at La Rochelle on 13 August. By then the duc de Beaufort was despondent at having missed the great North Sea actions. 'At present it cannot be dreamed', he wrote, 'that we have not given our allies cause to complain of us with justice'. Determined to play his part, he vowed never again to 'languish in sadness, while others triumph and receive acclamations from all the world'. But there was nothing he could do about it.

Both squadrons suffered further delays, the one because of the interminable celebrations at Lisbon and the other by the need to resupply. The victualling problem was no small matter. It had been decades since such a huge fleet had operated in the Atlantic, and the bureaucratic machinery necessary to support it was more than a little rusty. It was not until 5 September that the French squadrons at last united off Belle-Île. After a single attempt to join de Ruyter failed later that month, the French made no further contribution of any significance.

Chapter XII

The Morning of the First of June

Our fleet divides, and straight the Dutch appear,
In number, and a fam'd commander, bold:
The narrow seas can scarce their navy bear,
Or crowded vessels can their soldiers hold.

Prince Rupert's departure and the absence of so many other ships left the fleet in the Downs in need of reorganization. Allin and Myngs had gone with Rupert, leaving vacancies among the flag-officers, while the missing ships had left the squadrons and divisions unbalanced. Albemarle dealt with both problems during the council-of-war on the 30th, the Generals having predetermined the changes in the flag list. The original arrangement had been:

	Red	White	Blue
Admirals	Generals	Allin	Ayscue
Vice-Admirals	Myngs	Smith	Berkeley
Rear-Admirals	Jordan	Teddiman	Harman

As usual in the Restoration navy, little attention was paid to seniority and precedence. For the new organization the flag-officers of the White and Red rose one grade to fill Allin's and Myngs's places. The White and Blue then exchanged colours, and captains mutually acceptable to the Generals were appointed to the two available rear-admirals' positions. By this means the Prince's companion Sir Robert Holmes at last received his flag, as did one of Albemarle's former Commonwealth captains, Richard Utber. Sir Jeremy Smith was still included, since his arrival was expected shortly. The order then became:

	Red	White	Blue
Admirals	Albemarle	Ayscue	Smith (absent)
Vice-Admirals	Jordan	Berkeley	Teddiman
Rear-Admirals	Holmes	Harman	Utber

The new arrangement was temporary, it being understood that everyone would resume his original place when Rupert returned. The council-of-war also redistributed the ships remaining in the Downs and those still expected into squadrons and divisions. Albemarle's secretary Sir William Clarke forwarded the revised order to London on the 31st, noting that 'they are nott yett putt in the order of fighting'.

The strength of the fleet fluctuated so rapidly in the last days of May that Albemarle's actual force has never been established with certainty. Accounts and lists made up after the battle give the initial strength as anywhere from fifty-three to sixty ships, and the general's own reports were not consistent. Analysis of ship movements indicates that he probably had in the Downs fifty-three 'ships of force' and two fifth-rates, plus one fourth-rate scouting off the North Foreland, making fifty-six men-of-war in all. There were in addition four fireships and about sixteen ketches. According to the official establishments the fifty-six rated warships carried 3,058 guns and 14,335 men, though neither figure is very reliable. Ordnance Office records show that many of the English ships had more guns than the establishment allowed, and Albemarle's correspondence in the days before the battle shows that the fleet was about 200 men short of its complement.

The journal of Francis Digby, lieutenant of the *Royal Charles*, records that the fleet weighed at noon on the 31st. It beat out of the Downs on a southwest breeze, rounded the south head of the Goodwins, and anchored at nightfall with the North Foreland bearing N.W. by W. fifteen miles. At 4 o'clock the next morning the fleet headed north, making for the Swin. The English had little expectation of meeting the enemy. Clarke's letter of the 31st enclosing the order of battle repeated Captain Ewens's report that the Dutch had been at sea since the 21st, but with the comment, 'which I scarce beleeve'. On the evening of the day before, Albemarle's note sent with Ewens's original message had included the statement, 'Wee heere thunder and shooting towards ye West butt wee cannott thinke it is shooting being wee thinke the Enemy cannott bee soe neere'. The noise may well have been signalling or saluting by the Dutch fleet, carried and distorted in direction by stratospheric bounce. De Ruyter had been sailing southwest along the Zeeland coast, making for his intended station off the Downs. By the time of Clarke's letter the two fleets were very near indeed.

The Dutch approached the 1666 campaign with cautious optimism. The commanders were eager to try out the new ships and the new fighting methods, while the prospect of Louis XIV's assistance had changed the whole complexion of the war. Even so, de Ruyter regarded the arrival of Beaufort as 'too uncertain to allow one to judge'. The union of the fleets would obviously be desirable, but the Admiral-General was unwilling to rely too heavily on it. Nevertheless, Louis was given every opportunity to carry out his promises. Verburgh's squadron at Cadiz was ordered to cooperate with Beaufort, and in home waters it was resolved to keep the English occupied as fully as possible. As early as January a substantial squadron under Cornelis Evertsen boldly sailed to the mouth of the Thames, but the appearance of an unexpectedly large English 'winter guard' forced him to retire.

Unfortunately, repeating Evertsen's expedition with the whole fleet proved more difficult than anticipated. The trouble, as in England, was the shortage of seamen. With no conscription to fall back on, recruitment for the States' Fleet was largely dependent on patriotism, which could be carried only so far. Mariners naturally preferred the higher wages of the merchantmen and the chance of prize money held out by the privateers. To keep the men in port, the States-General in December renewed the merchant shipping embargo which had been in effect since the beginning of the war. The fishing and whaling fleets were forbidden to sail, and all outgoing foreign traffic was prohibited. Exceptions were allowed for small coasters and also for privateers, who were permitted to continue operations until April. Baltic traders were each authorized to carry out a single voyage for the purpose of procuring naval stores needed by the fleet. Extending the embargoes was unpopular. Loss of trade was already causing unemployment and deprivation among the urban working classes, and there was danger that another year's lost income would drive many commercial firms into bankruptcy. The only source of foreign wealth in view for 1666 was the annual East India convoy, due in June. If the Indiamen failed to get through, the Netherlands might be finished no matter what the French did.

The embargo accomplished its objective of leaving the seafaring people in need of employment, but the benefits to the fleet were slow in coming. On 26 January a newsletter reported from Rotterdam that

> The drumb does bate here continually for men, but gets so few that a man wold think it in vaine to cause bate any, and they begin now to have such a sencible feeling of the want of men that it is the saying of everyone: 'wee have ships enough if wee had but the men to them'.

In April the same source claimed

> that ther is here so great a scarcitie of seamen that they cannot attaine to half the number they stand in need of. At Hellevot ther are lying 5 of ther greattest men of warr which intend to goe to sea 8 days hence, ther are thrie of them which have not above 150 men each, and they doe require 400, being all ships of 70 and 60 guns the least.

On 18 March de Ruyter arrived in Rotterdam to join the *Zeven Provinciën*, but found her no better manned than the rest. Only half her complement was aboard. Two weeks later, still 175 men short, the flagship sailed to the designated fleet rendezvous at the Texel with four other Rotterdam ships. There de Ruyter was disappointed to find only two Noorderkwartier vessels and nineteen from Amsterdam. The Amsterdam contingent was under the command of Cornelis Tromp, who at his own request had been transferred from the Admiralty of the Maas to become Lieutenant-Admiral of Amsterdam. It quickly became apparent that the fleet would not be ready for many weeks. Ashore, de Witt was under constant goading from the French ambassador to send the fleet to sea. The Raadpensionaris worked wonders to hurry the dockyards and improve recruiting; drums beat in every town, French and Danish adventurers were actively sought, convicts pardoned, dollars offered to English prisoners-of-war. The situation was somewhat ameliorated by the arrival at the Texel of the Province of Holland's newly established marine regiment, which had easily filled its ranks from the multitudes of the nation's unemployed soldiers. The regiment's principal officers (Colonel Willem Joseph Baron van Ghent, Lt. Col. François Palm, and Major Johan Belgicus, Graaf van Hoorn) were each granted command of a major ship by the States of Holland. Despite all efforts, the number of men and ships at the Texel swelled very slowly. There was a regrettable setback when the States-General agreed, at the strident demand of Frederik of Denmark, to charter eight warships to the Danish service. De Ruyter did not mind losing the ships (they were old and small) but the requirement to provide fifty men per vessel was most unwelcome under the circumstances.

Preparations were difficult in other respects as well. Ordnance was still in short supply, as was ammunition, and the East India Company was able to cover the fitting-out costs of only eight men-of-war rather than the twenty requested. On the other hand, the big new ships made a stirring sight. Spirits were further uplifted when the fifteen-year-old Prince of Orange visited the Texel. Johan de Witt was behind this, and a shrewd move it was. Though mistrustful of William's ambitions, the Raadpensionaris knew how popular the young Prince was among the seamen, and how their morale would be raised by a show of unity among the nation's leaders. William arrived on 6 May, along with Frederick William, Elector of Brandenburg, and a host of other notables. To the accompaniment of booming salutes and constant cheering, the Prince spent two days touring the ships. He was undoubtedly flattered to find one of the newest vessels named in his own honour, the *Jonge Prins van Oranje* belonging to the Admiralty of the Noorderkwartier. The nobles made gifts of beer and silver coins to the common seamen, a mock battle was staged, and there was a grand banquet attended by all the officers. At the height of the festivities a sailor in one of the ships, acting on his own, suddenly scampered up the main shrouds and proceeded to perform a headstand on the topgallant cap. The humour of the acrobat's antics was lost on de Ruyter and the Prince, but the man was spared punishment by the Elector's good-natured intercession.

By the middle of May there were still only about fifty ships in the Texel anchorage. The Admiral-General was by then becoming increasingly impatient, for he had assured the French ambassador that he would come out on the 21st. Although Louis XIV had rather surprisingly ceased to urge the Dutch to sail, d'Estrades' earnest assurances that Beaufort was *en route* made de Ruyter more eager than ever to get to sea and open the Straits of Dover. De Witt was equally impatient for reasons of his own. Captain Clark's depredations on the Holland coast, beginning on the 14th, aroused angry clamours from the burghers. Indignant that an English squadron could ravage their coastal shipping almost in sight of the States' Fleet, they demanded that something be done. In addition, the East India Company was anxious for the safety of the spice convoy. Stung by these complaints, de Witt left The Hague on the 18th and arrived at the Texel the next day to hurry things along. On the 20th the council-of-war resolved to send out as many ships as possible the next day, for even though a number of vessels were not yet battle-worthy, their appearance in the North Sea would at least stifle the public criticism. On the 21st Clark sailed away and Cornelis Evertsen's Zeelanders, thirteen ships strong, hove in view off the Texel. Just as the fleet was about to weigh anchor, a change in the wind caused the movement to be postponed for one more day, but on the morning of the 22nd the ships at last came under sail and began to pick their way one by one through the Landsdiep passage. The shallow channel required careful navigation; the evolution took the better part of two days, but by the afternoon of the 23rd fifty-eight men-of-war had reached the open sea to join the Zeelanders. That was the same day, it might be remembered, that the English started down the Thames from the buoy of the Nore.

During the Dutch Fleet's assembly in the Texel, the ships were open to the public and the decks swarmed for weeks with nobles, curious burghers, women, children – and Sir Joseph Williamson's English spies. The Dutch made no effort to conceal their preparations. Williamson's agents were able to learn almost anything they wished to know by simply asking the commanders, and Arlington was kept abreast of every development. He knew the fleet's projected strength, was aware of its ordnance and manpower deficiencies, and read as early as the 24th of the decision to sail despite the adverse manning situation. Williamson's most daring spy, a shadowy figure known (among various aliases) as Johann Boeckell, was on the scene when the fleet began moving to sea on the 22nd. The news was rushed by secret courier to Boeckell's 'contact' in Antwerp, Hieronymus Nipho. Nipho transcribed the information into his French-language newsletter, which was then posted to Williamson on the 26th. Unfortunately, the Ostend packet boat was delayed, so the message took four days rather than the usual two to reach its destination. Read in Whitehall on the 30th, it was this intelligence that caused Prince Rupert's recall. Meanwhile, the industrious Boeckell remained with the Dutch fleet 'to see what resolutions were taken'. He continued to turn out startlingly accurate information about de Ruyter's intentions and tactics, but the messages did not get through in time. Thus, despite astounding carelessness on the part of the Dutch, their enemies did not hear of their sailing until eight valuable days had passed and discovered their whereabouts only on the day of battle.

Though de Ruyter was now at sea, his array was by no means ready for action. Manning was still unsatisfactory; the fleet was short over 2,000 men, the Noorderkwartier contingent being in almost hopeless straits. It was ultimately decided that the most poorly manned vessels should be sent home and their crews used to augment the rest. Three 46-gun ships and two 30-gun frigates, all from the Noorderkwartier, were accordingly dropped from the list along with a 40-gun ship from the Maas. The Friesland squadron, though in much better shape than the others, left behind the new 66-gun *Sneek*. The 500 or so seamen thereby made available reduced the shortage in the remaining ships to under 1,000, which was within an acceptable five per cent of the total complement. The sacrifice reduced the overall force from an expected strength of ninety-three men-of-war to the final total of eighty-six, though many were still absent when the fleet sailed. Among others, Tjerk Hiddes de Vries and most of his fellow Frisians were yet to appear, as was Jan Meppel, Lieutenant-Admiral of the Noorderkwartier.

While awaiting the tardy vessels and commanders, the flag-officers already present determined the fleet's organization and command structure. On the 23rd de Ruyter reluctantly agreed to accept the English three-squadron, nine-division order and dispense with the extra reserve squadron he and de Witt had preferred. On the next day the ships were distributed into their squadrons, and flag-officers assigned to their commands. The squadrons were composed as follows, the admiral of each centre division being the squadron commander:

	First Squadron (centre)		**Second Squadron** (van or right wing)
Van:	Aert van Nes, L.Adm. (M)	**Van:**	Tjerk Hiddes de Vries, L.Adm. (F)
		Extra:	Rudolf Coenders, V.Adm. (F)
			Hendrik Bruynsvelt, S.b.N (F)
Centre:	Michiel Adriaansz. de Ruyter, Adm.-Gen.	**Centre:**	Cornelis Evertsen, L.Adm. (Z)
Extra:	Jan van Nes, S.b.N. (M)	**Extra:**	Cornelis Evertsen the Younger, S.b.N. (Z)
Rear:	Jan de Liefde, V.Adm. (M)	**Rear:**	Adriaan Banckert, V.Adm (Z)

Admiralty	Ships	Frigates	3-mast Yacht	Admiralty	Ships	Frigates
Maas	10	5	1	Zeeland	9	4
Amsterdam	10			Friesland	10	
Noorderkw.	3	—	—	Amsterdam	5	—
	23	5	1		24	4

Third Squadron
(rear or left wing)

Van:	Jan Meppel, L.Adm. (N)
Extra:	Volckert Schram, V.Adm. (N)
	Frederik Stachouwer, S.b.N. (N)
Centre:	Cornelis Tromp, L.Adm. (A)
Extra:	Isaac Sweers, S.b.N. (A)
Rear:	Abraham van der Hulst, V.Adm. (A)

Admiralty	Ships	Frigates
Amsterdam	17	4
Noorderkw.	8	—
	25	4

As usual the senior Rotterdam officer, now Aert van Nes, was designated to assume the duties of the commander-in-chief if it became necessary. The Dutch gave the squadron commanders great latitude in arranging their order. The assignment of ships to divisions is known only for de Ruyter's squadron and for Tromp's own division of the Third Squadron. It seems reasonable to conjecture that Tjerk Hiddes's division of the Second Squadron was composed of Friesland ships, and that Meppel's division of the Third Squadron was mainly Noorderkwartier ships. One minor problem with the nine-division order was that it left seven junior flag-officers without any particular function. The disposition of these officers was left to the squadron commanders, and they apparently adopted differing solutions. De Ruyter is known to have set aside three ships and one frigate from his own division to form a sub-unit for *Schout-bij-Nacht* Jan van Nes. On the other hand, in the Third Squadron's centre division, the only one for which the stations of the individual ships are known, *Schout-bij-Nacht* Isaac Sweers was simply placed next to Tromp as one of his seconds in the line. The States' Fleet had a total of seventy-two ships, thirteen frigates, and one three-mast yacht bearing in all 4,581 guns and 21,144 men. There were in addition five advice-yachts and nine fireships.

The last of the missing vessels came out on the 26th. There was one final addition to the Dutch fleet the next day, when a sprightly middle-aged man in a fashionable broad-brimmed hat was rowed alongside one of the fleet's attending *galjoots*. With the dapper fellow watching every move, the boatmen handed aboard a seachest, an easel, a pencil case, and a thick sheaf of large-cut blank paper. The owner of this paraphernalia then climbed aboard and presented the *galjoot's* curious master a terse note bearing the signature of the great de Ruyter himself. It read:

> Captain Govert Pieterse is hereby ordered to receive and take on board the galjoot under his command the ship's draughtsman Willem Van de Velde and to go with him ahead or astern or with the fleet in such a manner as he shall judge expedient to make his drawings, without failing in any respect upon pain of severe punishment. From on board the States' ship the *Zeven Provinciën* under sail in the North Sea.

Born in Leiden in 1611, Willem van de Velde was a professional marine draughtsman. In his youth he had discovered an aptitude for making impeccably accurate portraits of ships and exceptionally rapid sketches of fleets at sea. He had exploited this unusual talent by carving a niche for himself as official war artist of the Dutch navy. He went with the fleet on many cruises, recording numerous battles. His son Willem the Younger, an equally skilful draughtsman and an even greater marine painter, sometimes came along as well, though not in 1666. Van de Velde the Elder was able to generate a fair amount of income from the sale of canvas grisailles (monochrome 'pen paintings') based on the eyewitness drawings. His authorization to accompany the fleet, however, was not granted merely for his own benefit. He was apparently regarded as a reliable unbiased observer, and after an action his testimony was sometimes sought to resolve disputed matters of fact. Van de Velde's drawings, flecked by salt spray, constitute a source more useful in many respects than the most detailed written accounts.

For two more days de Ruyter cruised off the Texel, allowing the crews to get their sea legs. On the 29th all was ready. Admiralty officials, observers from the States, and casual visitors returned to the shore in their yachts, whereupon the vast armada moved off down the coast to the southwest. Though at first retarded by light airs, the fleet passed Walcheren on the morning of the 31st and then headed W.S.W. along the Flemish coastline.

The Admiral-General's plan of action was quite simple: to seek out the enemy and give battle. As early as the 28th he had heard from a Zeeland privateer that the English had come out of the Thames, and this was confirmed by a Danzig trader. He further learned on the 30th from a Swedish merchantman that eighty men-of-war had been present in the Downs on the 27th. If de Ruyter was beginning to feel somewhat worried, it was easily understandable. Having heard nothing of the splitting of the English forces, he expected to encounter an enemy fleet equal in numbers to his own, with bigger ships and bigger guns. Furthermore, he must have had misgivings about the new tactical system which the other commanders had more or less forced upon him, especially since it demanded a greater degree of discipline than his captains had ever shown in the past. The chances of victory cannot have seemed very bright, but the strategic situation seemed to demand an immediate battle even if it could not be won. The only absolute requirements were that the States' Fleet survive the action intact, and that the English be battered sufficiently to force them into port and thereby leave an opening for the incoming East Indiamen and hopefully the French. Of his allies de Ruyter knew little. He had d'Estrades' unsubstantiated promises that Beaufort was on the way, but the Swedish vessel which the fleet met on the 30th had come from La Rochelle without sighting the Toulon squadron. Just in case, the Admiral-General prudently sent a message to the French authorities at Calais giving the Dutch fleet's intentions so that Beaufort could be notified. But no matter what, de Ruyter meant to fight.

At midday on the 31st the Dutch were about twenty miles north of Nieupoort. As this was less than a day's sail from the Downs, de Ruyter called his captains aboard for a final council-of-war. Always fond of oratory, he delivered an impassioned address reminding them of their duty. He also sternly pointed out that the States-General had granted him authority to hang any cowards from the nearest yardarm. When he finished, all the officers raised their hands and solemnly swore that they were prepared to lay down their lives for the fatherland. The captains returned to their ships, and the fleet cleared for action.

During the afternoon the Dutch advance was somewhat impeded when the wind gradually veered south and S.S.W. Since this made a direct course for the Straits of Dover impossible, de Ruyter steered close-hauled W. by S. and then west. In the evening he anchored about twenty-five miles north of Dunkirk and about thirty-five miles E. by N. of the North Foreland. The English were then anchored to the southwest, the nearest units of the two fleets lying no more than twenty-five miles apart – close enough for Captain Ralph Fell's Newcastle collier to have both in sight at once. Probably fearing the English fleet might press his crew, Fell neglected to warn Albemarle. Another vessel, the fifth-rate *Colchester*, also sighted the Dutch sometime on the 31st, but the *Colchester* was cruising independently and her captain did not know where to find the English fleet.

The 1st of June, 1666, dawned blustery. The wind whistled out of the southwest, whipping the seas into whitecaps and bringing creaks and groans from the heaving timbers of the anchored ships. At first light both fleets weighed and set sail. The English headed north to complete the necessary detour around Longsand Head on their way to the Swin. For the Dutch, the southwest wind was dead foul for the advance to the Straits of Dover, so de Ruyter accordingly moved off on the port tack to the W.N.W. on the first reach of an intended zig-zag beat into the Straits. This was soon frustrated by the tide; following slack water at around 5:30, the ebb hurrying through the Straits gradually built a current to the northeast of some two or three knots. Progress to windward eventually became impossible, and at 7 de Ruyter made the signal to anchor.

The position of the States' Fleet at that time is much in doubt. Contemporary reports vary widely, some erroneously placing the Dutch far to the south: 'off Dunkirk' according to the *London Gazette*, 'near Ostend' by Albemarle's reckoning, '7 leagues [twenty-one nautical miles] from Ostend' by the English official account, and 'near Nieupoort' according to Dutch Captain Ruth Maximiliaan. De Ruyter added to the confusion by vaguely noting in a letter to the States after the action that he had been anchored 'between Dunkirk and the North of these Provinces'; that is, between Dunkirk and the North Foreland. Actually, any of these southerly positions would have given the Dutch the weather gage, which they definitely did not have. Moreover, had they been anywhere near the Flemish coast, they could not have avoided discovery by the *Kent*, which was still patrolling 'between Blackness [Cap Blanc-Nez] & Ostend'.

Among the more reasonable accounts, de Ruyter's journal gives the position as seven miles E.N.E. of the North Foreland and nine miles N.N.W. of Dunkirk, while a letter from Hendrik Hondius, Tromp's flag-captain in the *Hollandia*, had it 'to the North-Westward, and at nine or ten miles distance from Ostend'. These two reports at first seem no better than the others – until it is realized that the old Dutch mile, or *mijl*, was equivalent to *four* English nautical miles. When the corrected ranges are plotted, the points fall in an area some ten to fifteen miles W.N.W. of the initial early morning anchorage. This is a reasonable distance for the fleet to have covered in the two to two-and-a-half hours it had been under sail, and is also in the right direction. In view of the geometry of the situation when the fleets met, the most probable position is the one reported by de Ruyter, twenty-eight nautical miles E.N.E. of the North Foreland.

The position of Albemarle's fleet was also variously reported. The official English account agrees with Lieutenant Digby's journal that Albemarle's fleet spent the night of the 31st with 'the North forland being 5 Leagues [fifteen miles] from us bearing N.W. & by W'. It continues, 'Ther being a fresh gale at S.W. on Friday the first of June at 4 in the morning wee weighed & stood Northward untill 6 in ye morne when the North forlands bore S.W. by S. 6 Leagues off'. This is absurd, since it made the fleet cover twenty-three nautical miles in only two hours. Other reports say that the English went north without event until 7, which implies three hours' sailing rather than two, while the *London Gazette* placed them four leagues (twelve nautical miles) from the North Foreland when the Dutch were discovered. Probably as good a way as any to determine the northernmost English position is simply to mark off three hours' sailing from the initial point, allowing a good pace of six or seven knots because of the strong breeze on the quarter. That would put the fleet about seventeen miles N.E. of the North Foreland, and in all probability about the same distance W. by N. of the Dutch. Seventeen miles is ordinarily within extreme visual range at sea, but the spray kicked up by the wind that morning would have kept the horizon well concealed.

The fourth-rate *Bristol*, Captain Phillip Bacon, had been scouting off the North Foreland since 28 May. Bacon had a watch station so precise that he could have maintained it at anchor. His orders required him to 'ply Northeast of ye Foreland so farr as you make just ye Land, and there to ply to discover what ships you can'. His lookouts, crouched on the crosstrees like gargoyles, had been wearily staring at the horizon for three days now. They had seen a few English vessels: the *Dover* and *Oxford*, latecomers to the fleet, hurrying down from Harwich; and the *Advice*, limping in the opposite direction with her headrails broken. Otherwise they had seen only the occasional dirty-hulled collier. This morning the churning seas sent the topmasts swaying dizzily so that the lookouts had to hold on to maintain their perches, but at least there had been some activity. Many ships were sighted soon after dawn, coming up from the south. They proved to be the English fleet, for some reason returning along the same path that had brought it out of the river the week before. At 7 o'clock the flagship was three miles to the west, passing inshore of the *Bristol*. At that moment a sharp-eyed seaman peering through the haze to the E.S.E. noticed ghostly shadows which soon resolved into ships. His hail brought officers clambering into the shrouds, and they soon realized that the enemy was at hand. Captain Bacon immediately signalled his discovery by loosing his fore topgallant sheets, 'and thereupon fired three guns, one after another' to attract attention. His orders included special provisions on what to do if the Dutch were sighted while his own fleet was also in view, and in accordance he hoisted his ensign. When the *Royal Charles* acknowledged by hoisting her own, Bacon tacked towards the Dutch to indicate their direction and began dipping the ensign over and over to show their number.

The English fleet wore to the southeast, heading for a position to windward of the Dutch. In mid-morning Sir William Clarke took time to compose a news-brief for Williamson in Whitehall. Datemarked, '*Royall Charles* 7 leagues off ye North Foreland 10 a Clock June 1 1666 in ye Morn', it read:

> This morning the *Bristol* plying about a league from ye Fleete discovered sevrall saile of shippes, & fired 3 guns one after another. About 8 of the Clock wee could perceive about 11 or 12 saile off the maine top masthead of the *Royall Charles*, other shippes discovered more about 20 or 30 saile towards the Coast of Flanders which wee apprehend to bee the Dutch Fleete, & are preparing to engage them. There being now about 40 saile in sight, I pray God give us success.

An hour later Clarke added a postscript. It includes a position report which, though inaccurate, confirms that the English had moved southeast: 'Wee have now Intelligence they are about 75 saile. Wee are halfway betw. ye Northforeland & Dunkirk 11 a Clock'.

At some point between the *Bristol*'s initial signal and the time Clarke completed his letter, Albemarle consulted his flag-officers in the great-cabin of the *Royal Charles*. The council-of-war decided to attack the Dutch. The timing and the issues involved in that decision were obviously important matters in view of the resulting catastrophes. This was not lost on Albemarle, who later sought to disperse the responsibility by implying that all of his actions including the initial southeasterly advance had been taken with the concurrence of the other commanders. The published 'True Narrative' which he and Rupert composed with Arlington's assistance a week or two after the battle reports that the council-of-war took place soon after the Dutch were sighted: '. . . at 7 a Councell of Flagg Officers aboard his Grace was called wherin was resolved to bear with them which wee did & at 10 wee discovered their fleet consisting of 84 sayle'. The general repeated this in much embellished form in his deposition to the House of Commons in 1667:

> I had but fifty-fower ships, when wee had sight of ye Dutch fleete, which wee discryed the first of June about eight in ye morning, lying att Anchor off ye North-foreland,

consisting of about 80 men of warr, besides fireships & ketches. Wee expected them not soe soon, having not heard before [that] they were out of theire harbour, or soe much as drawen to any Rendezvous, though it is well knowne they came out on ye 21st of May, as I had advice after ye fight [a bold string of lies!]. Considering ye condition I was in, most part of ye best saylers being gone with the Prince, that those with me were very heavy shipps, & many of them Merchantmen & Dutch prizes, I thought fitt to advise, if wee might not gett into ye River without fighting, & in order thereunto I called together all ye Flagg Officers & Capts. on board, who after some consideration unanimously agreed, that in regard most of our Fleete were heavy ships, wee could not avoid fighting, and thereupon ye Resolution was to fall upon them as they lay att anchor.

In both accounts the general carefully conveys the impression that things occurred in the following order: first, the *Bristol* sighted the Dutch; second, the council-of-war told a reluctant Albemarle he could not reach the safety of the Swin without fighting; and third, the fleet sailed towards the enemy. Although no one cross-examined him, his sequence of events appears to have been a deliberate distortion. That he could not have avoided battle is patently ridiculous. When first sighted, the Dutch were far to the E.S.E. De Ruyter could have deduced from the *Bristol*'s shooting that she was in sight of the English fleet, but not whether it was to the north, south, or west of her. Furthermore, had Albemarle continued north he would have had the wind on the quarter while de Ruyter would initially have had it off the bow; this would have given the speed advantage to the English despite their heavy sailers. It is inconceivable that the flag-officers would have told him otherwise had they been consulted immediately while the fleet was still W.N.W. of the Dutch. Afterwards, none of the participants in the council-of-war mentioned any discussion of a withdrawal to the river. The only explanation for this curious omission is that the meeting must have convened much later than Albemarle claimed, when the fleets were near each other and retreat was no longer an option. The truth was given away by the general himself, in an account released from the *Royal Charles* just four days after the fight – before his memory deserted him:

On friday being ye first of June ye fleete weighed Anchor from the north fore land with ye tyde of Flood standing away for the gunfleet, but about 7 of ye clocke our scout gave ye signall which was letting the topgallant sailes fly, and firing 2 or 3 gunns to let us know they discovered ye enemies fleete to the leeward which made us stand off to see how many they were, after 2 hours Chase wee discried them to bee the Duch. The Duke immediately called a Councell of war of his Flagg officers which being done ye signall was given to fall into a line of Batalia and soe bore away to the enemy.

Another of the general's reports, also written immediately after the battle, states that the commanders were called 'about ten a clock'.

The sequence now becomes clear. Following the initial sighting at 7 o'clock the English sailed southeast until they had attained a position almost directly to windward of the Dutch, and then the flag-officers were summoned. This removes all responsibility from the other commanders. Starting from a position of complete safety, Albemarle deliberately shifted to a station from which the Dutch could easily cut off the avenue of escape, and only then did he ingenuously ask his subordinates for advice. One can only conclude that he had resolved in advance to fight if he met the enemy, just as he had implied in his letters a few days before.

History has generally condemned Albemarle's decision to give battle, but one argument is sometimes advanced in his defence: if he had fled into the Thames, the Dutch might have sailed down the Channel to seek the French, placing Prince Rupert in mortal danger. This seems a valid point on the face of it, but Albemarle's correspondence gives no indication that it ever occurred to him. After all, he had received authoritative intelligence the previous Tuesday saying that the enemy meant to blockade the Thames, and furthermore, a voyage down the Channel would have been at odds with fundamental Dutch strategy. De Ruyter could not leave an English fleet unattended in the North Sea, for the harbours of the Netherlands, choked with shipping, would have been vulnerable to attacks like the raid Sir Robert Holmes carried out with devastating effect later in the summer. The Dutch also had the all-important East Indiamen to think about, their passage around Scotland being expected at any time.

It appears that Albemarle's wisest course would have been to send ketches to warn the ships in the Channel and then go straight into the Thames as the King wished. The general had already been told that powerful reinforcements were on the way. The *Slothany*, *Sancta Maria*, *Convertine*, *Advice*, *Centurion*, six of the merchantmen, and the matchless *Royal Sovereign* were all expected at the Swin within a few days. These twelve vessels would have brought his force to sixty-eight ships and given him a vastly better prospect of success. Why did he reject that option? At the time, nearly everyone put it down as a case of over-confidence brought on by the 'easy' victories of 1653. That was believed even by Andrew Marvell, otherwise one of the general's staunchest sympathizers:

> *But swoln with sense of former Glory won,*
> *Thought Monk must be by Albemarle outdon.*
> *Little he knew with the Same Arm and Sword,*
> *How far the Gentleman outcuts the Lord.*

But from all indications, the general seems to have had little confidence at all, much less over-confidence. He knew full well of the improvements in the Dutch fleet, and he had warned that it would take seventy ships to beat de Ruyter; he now had only fifty-six, twenty of them despised merchantmen and prizes. Almost certainly, he was driven to his decision by fundamental elements of his character: an exaggerated sense of honour, a fear of being thought a coward, the same fatalism that kept him in London during the Plague, and sheer fighting spirit. To someone unafraid of death, a battle against long odds brings a special kind of glory, and defeat no shame. His kinsman Sir Richard Grenville had shown the same attitude in the fabled defence of the *Revenge* in 1591, and the same attitude would carry later generations of

Englishmen through Albuera, Balaclava, and the Somme. Whether such ordeals were necessary or strategically sound was beside the point. The general had already explained it to Arlington in the bluntest of words: 'I should be loath to retreat from them being it goes against my stomach'.

When the council-of-war convened in the *Royal Charles*, the decision to fight was already a *fait accompli*. Still to be discussed, though, was the question of when the fight should begin. The weather gage gave the English the power to make that determination, and conditions were not favourable. Experienced tarpaulins knew that the strong southwest wind would heel the low-riding, over-armed English ships far enough to leeward to make the lower-deck ports too wet to use on the engaged side. Since the lower tier had the heaviest guns, the loss would amount to over half the fleet's firepower. The Dutch, engaged on their weather broadside with the ports heeled well clear of the water, would not be affected. It was one of the few circumstances in which Dutch warships had a significant advantage over the English. Most of the flag-officers consequently advised waiting until the next day in hopes the weather might settle down. This admittedly carried the risk that the wind might also change direction and thereby give the enemy the weather gage, but the commanders thought the wait well worth the risk. John Harman must have been among those who presented the argument, for he afterwards told Pepys

> that at the Council of War before the fight, it was against his reason to begin the fight then, and the reason of most sober men there, the wind being such and we to windward, that they could not use their lower tier of guns, which was a very sad thing for us to have the honour and weal of the nation ventured so foolishly.

Albemarle, however, apparently gave the impression that he regarded his officers' counsel of delay as merely a sign of faint-heartedness. Penn was later told by 'two-thirds of the commanders . . . that they durst not oppose it at the Council of War, for fear of being called cowards, though it was wholly against their judgement to fight that day'. The scene can easily be imagined: the Duke's huge frame facing them across the table, his jaws impatiently chomping his tobacco and his glaring eyes betraying his disapproval; they did not have the nerve to press their point. Full of foreboding, the flag-officers returned to their ships and cleared their decks.

Unknown to the commanders, their arguments had made a greater impression on the general than they knew; he was not a stupid man. At '11 in the Forenoone' he addressed a short note to Coventry:

> This Morning about 8 of the clock being sailing 7 or 8 leagues off the Northforeland wee discovered the Dutch Fleete towards the Coast of Flanders. Wee are sailing towards them & they towards us, butt the wind is soe high that I thinke wee shall not engage them this day; if any shippes bee ready hasten them to us, which is all att present.

This revealing note indicates that the general was indeed inclined to heed his officers' advice, and also shows that the English believed de Ruyter was under sail. Actually, the vessels Albemarle saw moving towards him were only the Dutch scouts, counting his ships and assessing his strength.

The English continued to edge towards the enemy, probably intending only to get close enough to recognize and foil any manoeuvres de Ruyter might initiate to gain the weather gage before the next morning. About noon, with the Dutch bearing E.N.E., the lookouts made the unexpected discovery that the enemy's main body was not under sail after all. Although the English had been under surveillance by de Ruyter's scouts for three or four hours his fleet was lying at anchor as though it were peacetime! To Albemarle's amazement the Dutch were arrayed in the most vulnerable attitude imaginable. In nothing approaching an organized line of battle, their squadrons were in an extended order stretching for miles to the N.N.E. This was nearly parallel to the wind direction, so the vessels nearest the English were almost directly to windward of those at the other end. The distant leeward ships were in much the same predicament Albemarle himself had faced at the Battle of Portland thirteen years before. As he knew from that experience, it would be hours before they could come to the assistance of their exposed windward friends.

This changed everything. The possibility of falling on a portion of a larger but obviously unprepared opponent was a once-in-a-lifetime opportunity that would disappear if not exploited immediately. Albemarle quickly decided to launch the attack. As it happened, his thrust did not succeed, so the flag-officers afterwards felt safe in disavowing it; but given that a battle sooner or later was unavoidable – and the general's southeasterly advance had made that a certainty – it is hard to fault him for beginning it when he did. Despite the adverse conditions, he could not have found a more inviting opening, for de Ruyter was unlikely to give a second chance.

As the English hurriedly arranged themselves in line-ahead, Willem van de Velde sketched them from his *galjoot*. Among other things, his drawings show that Albemarle did not make the normal signal for forming line of battle, which would have been the Union flag at the mizzen peak. Forming in the precise 'order of battailia prescrybed', as the Fighting Instructions required, often took an hour or more, and the general could not afford to give the Dutch time to correct their mistake. Instead he substituted a blue flag at the mizzen peak, which merely required every ship 'to beare up into his wake or graine upon paine of severe punishment'. This was the disciplinary Article Seven from his old 1653 fighting orders, still included in the current instructions. Sandwich had used it to mean 'follow me' when he broke through at Lowestoft, and now Albemarle used it to form line quickly without regard to station. The ships fell in wherever space was available, and the usual arrangement of divisions and flag-officers was ignored. Though Van de Velde was ill-informed on the identity of the English division and squadron commanders, the flags in his drawings give easy means to determine their positions. Harman, Rear-Admiral of the White in the *Henry*, was initially the foremost flag-officer, but Berkeley, Vice-Admiral of the White in the *Swiftsure*, passed in Harman's lee to take over the lead. Next came Jordan in the *Royal Oak*. As Vice-Admiral of the Red his proper station was considerably farther back, but he and several ships of his division fell in amongst the White. A little astern of Jordan was Admiral of the White Sir George Ayscue in the *Royal Prince*, and then Albemarle followed closely by Holmes, the Rear-Admiral of the Red in the new third-rate *Defiance*. In the rear came the *Royal Katherine*, flagship of the acting commander of the Blue Squadron, Vice-Admiral Sir Thomas Teddiman. The Rear-Admiral of the Blue, Utber in the new *Rupert*, was not indicated by Van de Velde but must have been near Teddiman.

At this point time was everything. It would have been a simple matter for the Dutch to roll back their exposed squadron and bring their fleet even on the wind. Each minute the English spent forming up gave the enemy that much more grace to act. No doubt stamping his feet with impatience, at about 12:30 the general would wait no longer even though the line was still ragged. With the blue flag still flying at the mizzen peak, he suddenly ordered the red 'bloody flag' hoisted to the fore. With that dramatic signal, every ship put over its helm; the English swept to the attack.

De Ruyter was taken completely by surprise. When he made the signal to anchor at 7 in the morning, his fleet was heading W.N.W. with the squadrons sailing abreast. Tromp's contingent formed the left wing to the S.S.W., de Ruyter's the centre, and Evertsen's the right wing to the N.N.E.; they anchored in that attitude. In the high winds and seas there was no thought of any real formation. Many vessels had trouble finding good ground and some dragged their anchors for considerable distances. The squadrons consequently overlapped, and individual ships and flagships were not in the stations intended for the order of battle. Van de Velde's drawing of the English approach also shows a panoramic view of the Dutch fleet at anchor, giving the division commanders' positions. In the Third Squadron Tromp's *Hollandia* was among the southernmost ships and the nearest flagship to the enemy. His third-in-command, Van der Hulst in the *Spiegel*, was fairly close by, but Meppel's *Westfriesland* was far to leeward, presumably having dragged his anchor. De Ruyter was near the southern end of his own squadron, well south of Meppel and only about one-third the way along the 'line' as the English would have viewed it. His second-in-command, Aert van Nes in the *Eendracht*, came next and then de Liefde in the *Ridderschap.* In the remaining squadron Evertsen's *Walcheren* was the southernmost flagship, lying next to and even slightly to windward of de Liefde. Well to the north were Banckert in the *Tholen* and finally de Vries in the *Groot Frisia.* This was the approximate order in which the Dutch flag-officers began the fight, for they had no opportunity to rearrange themselves. As de Vries was the only division commander who was where he belonged, it is safe to assume that the individual private ships were equally disarrayed.

At about the time the States' Fleet came to anchor, the *Bristol*'s cannon shots announced the proximity of the English. De Ruyter's frigates sailed out to investigate and kept him well informed of the enemy's motions during the morning. When the English finally came in view between 10 and 11 o'clock, the Admiral-General was surprised to find them in smaller numbers than expected. Seaman that he was, de Ruyter also realized that the force and direction of the wind would deny his opponents their lower-deck guns without affecting his own. That a heavily outnumbered enemy would deliberately choose to fight under such a handicap seemed madness. As if to emphasize just how bad conditions were, while the English were drawing up, an important ship of his own division was caught by a particularly violent gust which carried away both foremast and bowsprit. Distracted by the weather, secure in his numbers, and apparently oblivious to the glaring weakness in his fleet's deployment, de Ruyter concluded that the English would not attack that day. He accordingly did nothing. It was the worst mistake that illustrious commander ever made and one that could easily have resulted in disaster.

The ship damaged by the wind was the new 64-gun *Gelderland* belonging to the Admiralty of the Maas and commanded by Baron van Ghent, the Colonel of Marines. The disabled vessel left the fleet on de Ruyter's orders and slowly made her way to Hellevoetsluis, attended by a pair of *galjoots*. The Dutch had lost a ship without a shot being fired. Though mortified that the *Gelderland* would miss the fight, Van Ghent himself did not intend to be left out even if he could only be a spectator. Entrusting his ship to the lieutenant, he called away his boat and went aboard the nearby *Wapen van Utrecht* commanded by Hendrik Gotskens.

The English were in their final advance before the Dutch awakened. It was Cornelis Tromp, the nearest flag-officer, who first realized that Albemarle meant business. When an anxious glance at the *Zeven Provinciën* revealed no signs of instructions from that source, he acted on his own. As the English were already too close to allow time for weighing anchor properly, the *Hollandia* cut her cable and the rest of the squadron hastily followed suit. Tromp could have fallen back to the north or northeast to place himself even on the wind with the squadrons to leeward; but wholly in character, he stood his ground, leading off on the starboard tack to the southeast. The rest of the Dutch now came alive as well. The entire array cut its cables and stood in close-hauled to come to Tromp's assistance.

The Dutch had cleared for action the day before, so both sides had only to wait out the final minutes as the fleets drew near. The scene was the same in every ship. Decks, usually so cluttered, now lay open from end to end. Bulkheads and cabins had all been knocked down, hammocks unrigged, seachests and chicken coops stowed in the hold. When crews in both fleets had been fed and the cooks' fires extinguished, the men took their stations. Captain and lieutenant strode the poop, garbed in their finest; the thoughtful wore slippers and stockings in lieu of boots for less painful removal in case of injury. The topsides teemed with the rank and file, swaying together in the heavy swell. Marines with muskets at the ready lined the rails and knelt in the tops. Gun crews clustered around their pieces, linstocks smouldering, while seamen gathered near ranges and bitts to await the master's commands. In the foul-smelling hold beneath the waterline, the carpenter and his mates kept vigil, ready to staunch the rush of water should a shot intrude. The surgeon waited in the cockpit with the melancholy tools of his trade laid out before him. Below, in the gloom of the magazines, sober yeomen of the powder carefully filled cartridges and loaded carrying cases for the boys outside.

Seventeenth-century fleets did not go into battle in silence. The ships buzzed with excitement. Wizened veterans displayed their knowledge, their gnarly fingers pointing through the gunports at familiar opponents. As the range closed crews cheered each other and hurled coarse epithets at the enemy. Above it all trumpets' fanfares pierced the wind, and kettledrums rumbled and thumped.

Chapter XIII

The First Day

Straight to the Dutch he turns his dreadful prow,
More fierce th' important quarrel to decide:
Like swans, in long array his vessels show,
Whose crests, advancing, do the waves divide.

At approximately half past one o'clock on Friday, 1 June 1666 the range closed to point-blank. 'And then began', wrote Lieutenant Jeremy Roch of the *Antelope*, 'the most Terrible obstinate & bloodiest Batle that ever was fought on the Seas'. It is recorded that the first broadside was fired by a flagship in the Dutch van, probably Tromp's *Hollandia* or Van der Hulst's *Spiegel*, at the English ship *Clove Tree*. The *Clove Tree* was a member of Jordan's division of the Red which had fallen in amongst the White Squadron near the head of the line. In minutes greyish clouds of gunsmoke were billowing from all the leading ships, and the noise and fury gradually rose as the trailing vessels joined in. The artist Van de Velde also swung into action; he had wasted no time in hurrying off to the southeast during the English approach, and was rewarded with a fine head-on view as the fleets came together.

As the English hoped, the Zeelanders and Frisians had difficulty getting into the fight. Far to the north, they were helpless spectators for the first two or three hours. Many of de Ruyter's ships were also well to leeward, as was the commander of Tromp's van division, Meppel in the *Westfriesland*. Van de Velde shows that de Ruyter himself was in action quite early. Having been anchored at the windward end of his squadron, his position by chance brought the *Zeven Provinciën* opposite the *Royal Charles* right from the start; the two flagships were matched against each other for much of the afternoon, though not at close quarters. Except for the *Zeven Provinciën* and the southernmost vessels of the centre squadron, it was Tromp's three divisions that bore the initial brunt. His promptitude in getting under sail produced a running fight. Since he was able to keep pace with the White Squadron, moving off to the southeast ahead of most of the Red and Blue, he escaped the decisive concentration Albemarle intended.

The geometry of the situation produced an unusual effect. When Tromp slipped away to the southeast, the English centre and rear were temporarily left without opposition, because the rest of the Dutch were too far north and east to come into the wake of their windward close-hauled van. In order for Albemarle's and Teddiman's squadrons to reach the only available opponents in the Dutch centre, each vessel had to cross the wake of its next-ahead and fall in a little farther to leeward. The result was

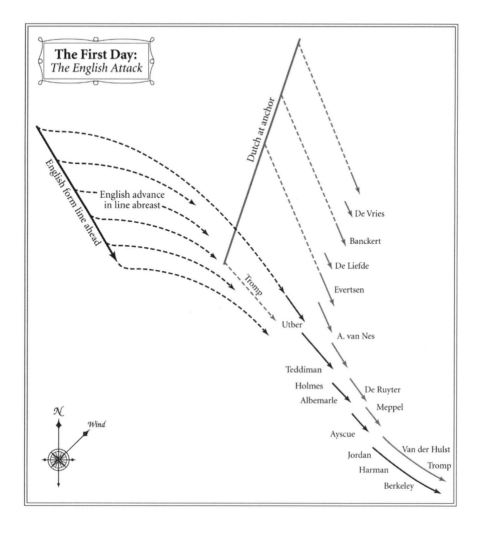

The First Day:
The English Attack

English form line ahead

English advance
in line abreast

Dutch at anchor

Tromp

Utber

De Vries

Banckert

De Liefde

Evertsen

A. van Nes

Teddiman

Holmes

Albemarle

De Ruyter

Meppel

Ayscue

Jordan

Harman

Berkeley

Van der Hulst

Tromp

N

Wind

that the early stages of the action were not fought in line-ahead at all, but with both fleets unavoidably arranged *en échelon*. Though not mentioned by any of the participants, this is clearly evident in Van de Velde's eyewitness drawings. The lines later straightened out when Tromp slyly fell off a little before the wind to draw the English farther north and thereby give the leeward divisions a more convergent angle of approach.

The Dutch felt themselves at something of a disadvantage in having to fight in inverse order with Evertsen in the rear. English fleets were meant to be reversible, and it never mattered whether the Blue or the White Squadron led. Not so the Dutch, for whom matters of precedence were involved. De Ruyter's council-of-war with the approval of representatives of the States and Admiralties had decreed that the Lieutenant-Admiral of Zeeland should command the van of the fleet as an established right, and the unplanned reversal at the Four Days' Battle seems to have made the commanders uncomfortable. Neither side was in anything approaching its intended order, reverse or otherwise. Surprisingly, the only officer who tried to sort things out was that reputed undisciplined hothead, Cornelis Tromp. One drawing shows his *Hollandia* briefly taking the port tack to the northwest, apparently for no reason other than to gain his proper station in the middle of the squadron.

There were no large-scale tactical manoeuvres for several hours, but a few captains attempted various moves on their own. Tromp's squadron initially overlapped the head of the English line to some extent, and at least one ship, the new 54-gun *Beschermer* under Captain Willem van der Zaan, put about to double on the White Squadron. A drawing of an early stage of the battle shows her on the port tack still to leeward of some of the English but to windward of others, firing with her lee guns at the *Prince* and *Royal Oak*. The Dutch captain and his crew soon found themselves in trouble. Sailing 'upstream' lengthwise through the English line, the *Beschermer* held on until she encountered a very large man-of-war with what Van der Zaan took to be two fireships in company. The big ship was presumably Ayscue's *Prince*, which should have been attended by the fireship *Providence* and an escorting light frigate of similar size, the fifth-rate *Oxford*. The two lesser vessels suddenly made for the *Beschermer*, which had already been roughly handled during her wild dash through the enemy. Her foremast and mizzenmast had both taken hits, her forestay and mainstay were holding by threads, and she had received dangerous large-calibre shot holes below the waterline which ultimately took two hours to stop. Van der Zaan quickly decided that discretion was the better part of valour. Setting his mainsail, he precipitously fled before the wind towards his own line. For a time it looked as though his pursuers might follow him right into the Dutch fleet, but at the last minute they luffed away. A little later the 34-gun frigate *IJlist* under Captain Jacob Boom also worked to windward of the English van and stood with them for some considerable time; for this initiative the little ship suffered heavily in masts and spars. Except for such isolated coups by individual vessels, the fleets simply sailed along side by side trading blows for over three hours.

Throughout the long first pass the Dutch had to endure all the usual disadvantages of the lee position. The English controlled the range and kept themselves well out of boarding distance. De Ruyter's substantial fireship advantage was negated, for the Dutch could not get them into action against the wind. In deep seas the windward fleet might have suffered from disabled vessels drifting into the enemy to leeward, but that did not apply in the shallow waters off the Thames. There, damaged English ships could (and did) haul their wind, anchor briefly and effect emergency repairs. That option was not available to the Dutch because ships anchored to leeward were vulnerable to fireships. De Ruyter's few injured vessels such as the *Beschermer* could repair safely only by falling off before the wind, and afterwards would lose much time beating back into the fight. Other normally unimportant effects were magnified by the high winds. In a deeply heeling ship of the leeward fleet, shot entering the hull near the water on the engaged windward side would leave holes below the normal waterline. The vessel consequently could not manoeuvre or change course in any way until the damage was repaired, since even a small reduction in the angle of heel could bring the holes underwater and cause dangerous flooding. In the windward fleet the effect was just the opposite. In that case the lowest damage on the lee side was usually above the normal waterline, and the ship could manoeuvre as desired without aggravating the situation. Gunhandling was also subtly affected. In the windward fleet the lee cannon ran out to the ports 'downhill', so the gun crews had an easy time of it and a high rate of fire could be maintained indefinitely. The gunners in the leeward fleet had to haul their massive pieces up the decks, which exhausted the men and slowed their fire.

In this action, however, all of the disadvantages of the lee gage were largely offset by the fact that Albemarle's ships were so laid over by the wind that they could not use their powerful lower-deck guns. Van de Velde observed that the English constantly stood in towards the Dutch, luffed, and then bore up again in a curious weaving motion. In all likelihood these odd manoeuvres represented the futile efforts of the English captains to find a course on which the lower ports could be safely opened. Seaman Barlow, still in the *Monck*, wrote ruefully that the enemy

> being to leeward of us, they could fire with their lower tier of guns to windward, but we could not fire our lower guns to leeward at them, it blowing so hard, which was a great disadvantage and weakening to us, for in two or three hours some of our fleet were very much torn and shattered in their masts and rigging.

Thus the thirty or forty Dutch vessels which received the initial onslaught could bring more guns to bear than the whole English fleet. Nearly every report from both sides made note of this, and because of it the Dutch – for a while at least – were quite content to accept the lee gage despite its many drawbacks.

Actually, in the early stages neither side could do much harm to the other. The violence of the wind and the roughness of the seas adversely affected all gunnery regardless of who had the weather gage. The English, trained to fire on the down roll, tended to throw their shot into the water short of the target; the Dutch, habitually firing on the up roll, had a high percentage of 'overs'. Captain John Aylett of the fourth-rate *Portland* recalled that 'the Dutch being on the leewards, their guns mounted so high, that they only shot our rigging, but did little execution on the men or hulls'. Even the damage to the rigging was largely superficial; ropes cut here and there and holes shot in the sails. Naturally, some ships were less fortunate than others. The *Monck* lost her fore topmast over the side which, said Barlow, 'was a great hindrance to us'. This occurred in sight of Van de Velde; one drawing shows the topmast falling, and another later in the day shows presumably the same ship with her main yard at least temporarily brought down as well. It is labelled, 'English frigate very much damaged'. The incident is specifically mentioned in Albemarle's account and also several others, which suggests that it was the *only* instance of heavy damage. For a single topmast to be shot away in three hours' pounding by over a hundred ships is hardly a devastating result.

When shot struck the hulls, the effects could be terrible. Roch of the *Antelope* related that as we began to fight this day one of our men, taking notice of my Sword which was but an ordinary or ammunition blade, he desired me to accept of a brave Scymetar which he said he would fetch to me if I pleased; I told him no, that which I had was fine enough to kill dutchmen. So taking ye fellow by ye hand & shaking it in token of Love for his good will, in the very action comes a Crossbar Shot from ye enemy & cuts him off by ye midle.

But such misfortunes were few in the early fighting. 'In this days worke', continued Roch, 'we came off indifferently on both sides with no considerable loss'. Aylett claimed his *Portland* was in hot action all day but had only one man killed. All in all, the furious firing seems to have done little more than waste a vast quantity of ammunition (which would be sorely missed later) and provide grand entertainment for the crews. What with the continual flashes from the muzzles of the guns, the churning clouds of smoke, the terrific din of the broadsides, and the whishing of shot through the air – all with few people getting hurt – the men in both fleets seem to have enjoyed themselves immensely. Aylett said that at one point the Dutch 'by accident' shot down Albemarle's standard, 'at which they made a great shout, but that being presently set up, the shout was returned by our men with advantage'. This festive atmosphere was to be shortlived.

If any of the English believed the indecisiveness of the fighting was to their advantage, they were sadly mistaken. The object of Albemarle's attack was to destroy the exposed Dutch divisions before the others could come to their aid, and in this he failed. The English would have been well-advised to force the issue by immediately coming to close action while Tromp was still unsupported, but English sea-officers of this period were trained to avoid yardarm-to-yardarm fights with the Dutch because of their prowess in boarding tactics; the best way to beat a Dutchman, they had always been told, was with the gun. The English captains consequently hesitated to close despite their initial advantage in numbers. Van de Velde indicates that most of the flagships and a few other vessels stood in quite near, but his drawings show the bulk of the English fleet drawn up at its customary distance several hundred yards to windward. The result of the indecisive action was that Tromp, Van der Hulst, and de Ruyter were able to buy time cheaply while the leeward divisions came up.

The number of Dutch ships in action swelled throughout the afternoon. Meppel with his powerful new *Westfriesland* joined Tromp in the van, and Aert van Nes, de Liefde, and the rest of de Ruyter's squadron came in contact with the English centre and rear; at about 3 o'clock, the numerical advantage swung to the Dutch. When the Zeelanders and Frisians at last came on the scene in the course of the next two hours, they found the enemy's lee side already fully occupied by the rest of the Dutch fleet. The resourceful Zeeland commander, Cornelis Evertsen the Elder, undoubtedly recognized that the Dutch could obtain nothing more than a draw despite their superior strength if the English kept the weather gage. He accordingly began to contest for the wind the moment he came up. With what must have been a brilliant piece of fighting seamanship, he, de Vries, and Banckert along with most of the ships of their divisions wrested the wind from the English Blue Squadron. How they did it is not certain. To Van de Velde far to the southeast it looked as though Evertsen's vessels simply sifted through the gaps in the disordered English line. One drawing showing both fleets still on the starboard tack is inscribed, 'The rest of the States' Fleet, namely the two squadrons of Zeelanders & Frisians, which on account of the preceding English ships being somewhat to leeward, broke through between their ships'. Another drawn slightly later says, 'They sailing along with us & there was a hard fight in the rear and I presume our ships break through, namely the wing of the Zeeland & Frisian squadrons'. Other vessels seem to have tacked across the wake of the Blue and then crowded sail to chase up the windward side in the classic 'doubling' manoeuvre. Albemarle's narrative explains that 'Wee Atacqu'd first the head of their fleete, but as soone as the reare saw us close ingag'd with them, they tackt & weather'd us with the greatest parte of their fleete'. The last phrase must mean the 'greatest part of their *squadron*'. Other accounts place the majority of the Dutch still to leeward, and Van de Velde agrees; the later of the two drawings mentioned above contains a second inscription over the scene in the van saying, 'Here the enemy keeps to windward of us in a running fight'. But whatever the number of ships, and however they accomplished it, many of the Zeelanders and Frisians gained the wind and placed the Blue Squadron and part of the Red between two fires.

From this point events began to unfold rapidly, with both sides meeting adversity. Among the Dutch, at about 5 o'clock a catastrophic fire broke out in a ship of Evertsen's squadron, the 58-gun *Hof van Zeeland* commanded by Simon Blok. The wind-fed flames quickly became an inferno, engulfing the hull from end to end and driving the desperate crew into the water, where they were doomed. Nearby vessels dared not approach the blazing hulk, and before the horrified eyes of both fleets Blok and nearly all of his 248 men drowned in the rough seas. The Zeelanders mourned both the men and the ship. From the time of her launching in 1653 until the building of bigger vessels in 1666, the *Hof van Zeeland* had been the pride of the Admiralty of Zeeland and had served as Jan Evertsen's flagship in many a battle.

Another fire more or less simultaneously claimed a vessel of the centre squadron, the 46-gun *Duivenvoorde* of Amsterdam. Her captain, Otto van Treslong, was one of the few members of the *Jonkheer* nobility to command a man-of-war in de Ruyter's fleet. With him as observers from the French government were three aristocratic young soldiers, Louis Grimaldi the Prince of Monaco, his brother-in-law Armand de Grammont, comte de Guiche, and the Sieur de Nointel. Having resolved to accompany the fleet, they naturally sought berthing in a ship with a captain of their own class. The flames erupted when the *Duivenvoorde* was a little to windward of the rest of her squadron. Her hull soon became a great floating torch and a mortal threat to all the nearby vessels. Searing heat drove the helmsman from his post; with sails still drawing, the ship swerved out of control into the body of the fleet and collided with the 54-gun *Klein Hollandia*. The two ships locked together. While the crew of the *Klein Hollandia* frantically chopped with axes at the binding wreckage, the men of the *Duivenvoorde* crowded to the beakhead hoping to clamber out on the bowsprit and drop to the deck of the *Klein Hollandia*. About thirty made it, including the three Frenchmen; Monaco, who had been wounded in both arms, fell into the water, but someone pulled him out 'by the hair'. Unfortunately for the rest, the ships then separated, and eight of the

French retinue were among those left behind. The stricken vessel drifted aimlessly for an hour or so – shunned by friend and foe alike – until the flames reached the magazine, whereupon she disappeared in a fearsome blast. Treslong and about 170 others drowned.

For a time it appeared that the *Duivenvoorde*'s survivors had only briefly cheated death, for the *Klein Hollandia* had herself been set afire in the collision. With much difficulty the ship was eventually saved, though the stubborn blaze twice flared up again after the crew thought they had put it out. When it was finally extinguished for good, a brief inspection of the charred timbers convinced the Frenchmen that their new ship was unlikely to accomplish anything further. Approaching the captain, de Ruyter's son-in-law Evert van Gelder, they asked to be taken to the *Zeven Provinciën* 'in order to show their conduct on such a great occasion and to demonstrate their courage at close quarters'. No doubt much amused at their bravado, Van Gelder duly delivered them to the flagship the next morning. De Guiche left a detailed if sometimes confused account of the battle which is one of the best sources for events as viewed from the *Zeven Provinciën*. As for the *Klein Hollandia*, her injuries were superficial; Van Gelder took her back into the fight on Saturday and was in the thick of it all four days.

Aside from the two ships destroyed, Tromp's *Hollandia* had 'much ado' to extinguish a dangerous conflagration in her starboard quarter-gallery. The origin of these fires was a great mystery. Survivors from the *Duivenvoorde* reported that they had been attacked by English 'artificial fires', as did the flag-captain of the *Hollandia*, Hendrik Hondius, who described the agent as 'a Fiery Bullet from the Enemies'. Dutch authorities subsequently found these claims incredible, concluding instead that the ships must have been victimised by flaming wads from their own guns, picked up by the wind and blown back aboard; this remains the generally accepted explanation. But the English fleet *was* equipped with incendiary projectiles in 1666. The Generals' order-book mentions '120 Brass fire shott' which were shared among eight ships in July. Such devices might well have been employed in the Four Days' Battle. The Prince of Monaco, in the only known eyewitness description of the objects that struck the *Duivenvoorde*, said that the enemy 'threw some rose-coloured balls and these, remaining on board, expanded and started an inextinguishable fire'. His wording fits cannon wads rather poorly but could be quite appropriate for fulminating 'Brass fire shott', so the possibility that Ordnance Office inventors were behind the conflagrations must be taken seriously.*

While the Dutch underwent their ordeal by fire, the English had their own troubles. The presence of enemy ships to windward of the Blue Squadron radically altered the tactical situation and demanded a reaction. Furthermore, though casualties were still light, the cumulative effects of four hours' fighting were beginning to tell on sails and rigging. Some of the flagships in particular needed to get clear of the action to make repairs before they were too disabled to do so. A change in course was going to be necessary sooner or later anyway, for the shallows of the Flemish coast lay ahead; the

---

*In 1689, fire-shot destroyed a French ship at the Battle of Bantry Bay. Those made in 1666 were sized for demi-cannon and culverins.

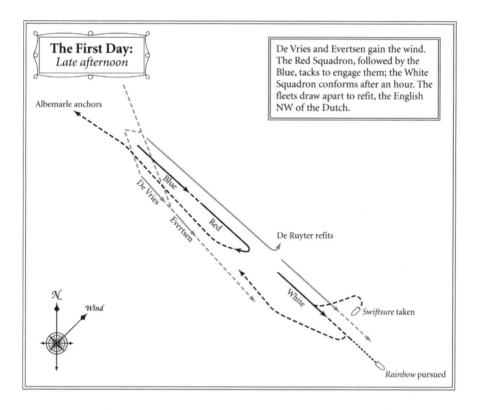

The First Day:
Late afternoon

De Vries and Evertsen gain the wind.
The Red Squadron, followed by the
Blue, tacks to engage them; the White
Squadron conforms after an hour. The
fleets draw apart to refit, the English
NW of the Dutch.

Albemarle anchors

Blue

De Vries

Evertsen

Red

De Ruyter refits

N.

Wind

White

Swiftsure taken

Rainbow pursued

leadsmen were already reporting fifteen fathoms. Coming about, however, presented a problem in that the present circumstances were not among those addressed by the Fighting Instructions. With the Blue Squadron under duress, tacking from the rear was obviously impractical, while tacking in succession from the van – miles ahead – would not give the Blue the timely assistance that it needed. Forced to improvise, Albemarle concluded that the flagship would have to initiate the manoeuvre, presumably relying on the blue flag at the mizzen peak to signal the conformance of the rest.

At about half past 5 the general gave Captain Kempthorne his orders. The *Royal Charles* swung ponderously into the wind and filled her sails on the port tack to the W.N.W. The ships of Albemarle's division followed him quickly, as did Holmes with the rear division of the Red. What Teddiman did with the Blue Squadron is unclear. Engaged on both sides, he probably waited until Albemarle and Holmes passed him going the other way, and then tacked in their wake. The White Squadron did not immediately participate in the movement. A crisis had developed in Berkeley's division at the head of the line, causing Ayscue, Harman, and also Jordan with the van division of the Red to continue their southeasterly heading to give support. These divisions, however, were in danger of being separated from the rest of the fleet, and 'after an houre' they reluctantly tacked towards Albemarle. By about 6:30 most of the English were on the port tack, though the proper order of squadrons and divisions had broken down. The General now led, followed by Holmes, Teddiman, and Utber, and then after a gap Ayscue, Jordan, and Harman. Berkeley did not tack at all, as will be related shortly.

When the English came about, the Dutch centre was temporarily left without opposition. De Ruyter gratefully accepted the respite, and the *Zeven Provinciën* and much of the rest of the centre squadron lay to for about an hour plugging shot holes and refitting rigging. Meanwhile, Albemarle's new course took him straight into the Zeelanders and Frisians. This Dutch squadron had been engaged for less than two hours, but had already seen violent action in forcing through and around the Blue Squadron. Now, as de Ruyter admiringly wrote, 'Admiral Evertsen and de Vries went on and charged them again, whilst we repaired our damages'. Few details of this encounter were recorded, but there was a heavy exchange of broadsides. The Dutch official account merely says that when the English tacked, 'That motion engaged the Squadron of Lieutenant Admiral Evertsen and Tjerk Hiddes de Vries in a Bloody Fight, in which the undaunted Valour and Courage of those two Generals were seen to shine with equal Lustre'. The *Royal Charles* met them almost head-on, the opponents passing each other on opposite courses at murderously close range with Evertsen keeping the weather gage. During this pass Albemarle was angered by the behaviour of some of his captains: 'Many of our ablest ships bore away to leeward of ye Dukes shipp when the enemy was to windward, & not only left us exposed to ye enemies Shot, but to their owne by fireing through and over us to ye enemy'.

After encountering Albemarle, Evertsen kept on the starboard tack until he had passed the rest of the English in turn, finally emerging far to the southeast. A Van de Velde drawing made at that time shows the Zeeland flagship still well to windward but even with Tromp's squadron. It is not impossible that Evertsen had every intention of leading his squadron past Tromp's to take over the van position, which he undoubtedly regarded as his prerogative. Such matters carried weight with the Dutch even in the heat of battle.

Even before Albemarle tacked, the English flagship's rigging had been 'very much shatterd'. The damage was further compounded by the clash with the Zeelanders and Frisians, in which 'the Dukes sailes were torne to the yards in peeces' and the ship rendered all but unmanageable. When the *Royal Charles* at last came clear of the action, she anchored to bend on a new suit of canvas. Being in like condition the *Monck* and Holmes's *Defiance* anchored as well, while the other ships in company stood by to await the next approach by the Dutch. Van de Velde noted, 'The English here luff up a little and remain more or less out of action, being considerably damaged'. Many of the Dutch were themselves refitting, and there was consequently a distinct lull in the fighting for about an hour. This lull did not extend over the whole of the scene. Far to the southeast, catastrophe had struck the English.

The commander of the van division of the White was the courtier Vice-Admiral Sir William Berkeley. His family had supported the Stuart cause in the Civil War and Interregnum, and Sir William was a particular favourite of the Duke of York. He had decided on a naval career in 1661. After a single year's apprenticeship as a lieutenant he was given command of a ship and in 1665, at the age of twenty-six, he was named Rear-Admiral of the Red before he had seen his first action. Berkeley's rise was generally regarded both within and without the service as indecently rapid. His performance was therefore subjected to closer-than-normal scrutiny by his less favoured colleagues and tended to be reported in a less-than-favourable light. His career had been particularly troubled in the year leading up to the Four Days' Battle. After Lowestoft the previous June many officers had denounced him as a coward. It appears that he had actually done nothing more than carry out the wishes of Penn and the Duke of York, and James had even singled him out for special praise. Nonetheless, such charges were hard to live down. Then came the looting of the East Indiamen in September, and Berkeley's part in it seemed especially deplorable to the public in view of his family's already considerable wealth. His tarnished reputation was further besmirched with the publication of Andrew Marvell's scurrilous account of the Battle of Lowestoft. Having described the gory demise of Sir William's brother Lord Fitzharding, Marvell set the indictments against the young admiral to biting verse:

> Barkley had heard it soon, and thought not good
> To venture more of Royall Harding's Blood.
> To be immortal he was not of Age
> (and did ev'n now the Indian Prize presage),
> But judg'd it safe and decent, cost what cost,
> To lose the Day, since his Dear Brother's lost.
> With his whole Squadron streight away he bore
> And, like good Boy, promist to fight no more.

Marvell's libellous epic is known to have circulated in the fleet, for Lieutenant Roch inserted lines from it in his journal. In light of all this, it should come as no surprise that Berkeley went into the Four Days' Battle with a grim determination to vindicate his name.

Unfortunately for Sir William, the Duke of Albemarle's instinctive mistrust for gentleman commanders made him suspect Berkeley's reliability from the start. When the English fleet was approaching the Dutch to begin the battle, it seemed from the *Royal Charles* that Berkeley might be holding back. The general disapprovingly reported that 'Sr. George Ayscue with the White Squadron leading the Vand, Sr. William Berkley the Vice Admirall of that Squadron ought to have borne in first, but he went to Windward with 6 or 7 of his Division'. Albemarle added a significant detail in a second account:

It was ordered that the Vice Admirall of the fleet of the White should fall in with the fleet upon a line; when the *Royall Charles* was in the middle of the Fleet and somewhat neare the Enemy, Sr. Wm. Berkley kept his loofe at which a gunn was fired to windward of him and then he bore up.

To a proud officer who had 'undergone the aspersion of a Coward' for all of the year preceding, the general's resounding rebuke before the whole fleet was a supreme insult.

Berkeley pressed towards the Dutch. In the course of the afternoon Van de Velde shows the *Swiftsure* matched first against Tromp's *Hollandia* and then more or less simultaneously against the 68-gun *Liefde* under Pieter Salomonszoon and the 70-gun *Calantsoog* commanded by Jan de Haan, the conqueror of the *Charity* at Lowestoft. Jordan in the *Royal Oak* was nearby most of the time, both he and Berkeley engaging more closely than the ships under them. About 5 o'clock the Dutch van was thrown into confusion when Salomonszoon inadvertently crossed Tromp's bow. The *Hollandia* rammed the *Liefde* with a sickening crash, whereupon the two ships lying foul of each other fell off to leeward. Berkeley must have seen this accident as a chance to redeem his reputation; with his state of mind and his youth conspiring to cloud his judgement, he bore straight through the Dutch fleet towards Tromp. The other, more experienced, flag-officers of the English van wisely declined to follow him amongst the enemy and could only watch in horror as the *Swiftsure* disappeared into the smoke.

Berkeley sailed up to the fouled ships and poured in a heavy raking broadside to which they were helpless to reply. But Tromp was quickly supported by his next astern, the 72-gun *Reiger* under Hendrik Adriaanszoon. As the *Reiger* came alongside, Tromp waved his hat at Adriaanszoon, pointed to the *Swiftsure*, and shouted, 'Keep that man away from me!' Adriaanszoon set his foresail and steered for the English ship, as did Berkeley's previous opponent, de Haan's *Calantsoog*. The English vice-admiral must have realized by this time that he had made a mistake. He tried to beat towards his own fleet; but before he could reach safety, a lucky shot from the *Calantsoog* brought down his main yard and carried away the topsail sheets, rendering escape impossible. By a Dutch account, 'seeing himself in such a pitiful condition he fired some Guns without Bullet to advertize his followers to come in to his Assistance; but they making as if they heard him not, betook themselves to flight and left him in danger'. That was not quite true; a rescue attempt was indeed mounted, but with disastrous results. In the meantime the *Calantsoog* and *Reiger* closed and administered broadside after broadside for at least an hour. Though Berkeley's situation was hopeless, he proved his courage by obstinately refusing to surrender. The final stages of this one-sided match were described by a young private of Marines aboard the *Reiger*, a Dane named Hans Svendsen:

> When my captain had been in the fight with Berkeley for 9 glasses, he [Berkeley] signalled with his hat and shouted, 'You dogs, You rogues, have ye the heart, so press on board!' As he said this he tacked and gave us his full starboard broadside; in one of these charges we had 13 dead and wounded. My captain saw that Berkeley meant to swing his rudder again and thus give us his larboard broadside; while he came about my captain called, 'Fire!', and we gave him our larboard broadside with grapeshot, and thereupon my captain ordered, 'Helmsman, put the helm over!', and then we gave him our starboard broadside; and then my captain dropped the foresail and laid him on board. Immediately the grapnels were heaved out, and my captain went on deck with a drawn sword in his hand and stirred up the people. Our First Lieutenant Swart was the first to jump over with drawn sword in his hand, and we leapt after him with 50 of us, and cut the enemy's shrouds to pieces, whereupon his foremast fell over the side.

This first wave of boarders found a nasty surprise waiting for them. Guns on the *Swiftsure*'s quarterdeck and in her coach had been swung around to point forward through ports in the quarterdeck bulkhead, which in the seventeenth century was a sturdy permanent structure. When the Dutch swarmed aboard, the English promptly retreated behind this barrier. Since the *Swiftsure* did not have a forecastle, the forward firing guns could spew case and grape over the whole length of the upper deck almost from the mizzen. Svendsen said that 'nobody could bear it on deck', and the Dutch beat a hasty retreat. But Adriaanszoon was not deterred. Before the guns could be reloaded he called away a second wave, this time preceded by a grenade which the gunner adroitly hurled among the English. In the confusion the boarding party quickly mastered the upper-works. The result was now a foregone conclusion, for the Dutch were without peer at this kind of fighting. When the defences were finally breached, the English 'began to beg for their lives and called, "Pardon! Pardon! Your servant with all my heart;" and kissed us and took off their weapons'.

Sir William Berkeley did not live to see his ship taken. He was shot down by a musket ball 'which went diagonally through his throat and exited through his neck, while standing next to his helmsman'. Someone carried him to the great cabin, where the Dutch found him lying dead across the table, arms outstretched and covered with blood. Svendsen added with a tinge of envy, 'They found a piece of diamond jewelry on him that was estimated at f.2000; it fell into the hands of a common seaman, who plundered the corpse'. The *Swiftsure*'s lieutenant was discovered in the magazine

> with a knife in his right hand with which he had cut his own throat. The reason was
> that he had promised the vice-admiral that in case the latter was killed in action, he
> would not surrender the ship, but set it afire. The other Englishmen who knew about
> this threw water on the powder, and when he touched it with the match, the powder
> did not explode, whereupon he said, 'Before the enemy takes me prisoner, I'd rather
> die'.

That, at least, was the story the English seamen told.

Svendsen avers that the hand-to-hand fighting in the *Swiftsure* was desperate to the very end. He claims that the *Reiger* had eighty men killed in the fight, the boarding party alone losing forty-eight dead and fifteen wounded. 'On the prize', he wrote, 'you could not move a foot because of the dead lying on and over each other'. This was a considerable embellishment, however, for the *Reiger*'s losses as returned by Captain Adriaanszoon amounted to four killed and eleven wounded for *the whole day*. The Dutch took aboard 300 unhurt English prisoners, the rest being killed and wounded. The *Swiftsure*'s complement was 380 men, so presumably eighty-odd or a little over a fifth were casualties. Many were undoubtedly hit during the long preceding cannonade, and thus it is evident that the final assault was not resisted with any great ferocity. The crew in all likelihood lost heart with the death of their commander.

Following the capture, Captain Adriaanszoon decided that the *Reiger* was unfit for further combat. Putting forty men aboard the *Swiftsure*, he caused a cable to be passed across and proudly towed her to Goeree. The prize was a famous veteran of forty-five years' service at the time of her capture. Rebuilt in 1653, she was generally regarded by the English as the best of the older second-rates. Though the ship was officially rated at 66 guns, the Dutch found 72, of which 60 were brass. She joined the States' Fleet as the *Oudshoorn* and fought against her former owners at the Battle of Solebay in 1672.

Most of the English attributed Berkeley's fall to the imputations against his courage. As one observer explained, 'the Disgrace, as was suppos'd, lay like a Load upon his mind; and his Valour, or his Rage, engaged him so far among the Enemy's, that neither his discretion nor his Friends knew how to bring him off'. Some were less charitable. The Duke of Albemarle for one could not bring himself to utter a single kindly word. Having previously humiliated the Vice-Admiral of the White before the whole fleet for not advancing rapidly enough, the general bluntly and gracelessly remarked in his report that 'The *Swiftsure* by not keepeing his Station fell into their Fleete'. Predictably, Marvell was moved to pen some of the most tasteless couplets of his career:

> *And if the thing were true, yet paint it not:*
> *How Barclay, as he long deserv'd, was shot.*
> *Though others, that surveyd the Corpse so clear,*
> *Say he was only petrify'd with Fear,*
> *And the hard Statue, mummy'd without Gumme,*
> *Might the Dutch Balm have spar'd and English Tombe.*

The last two lines belittled the disposition of Berkeley's remains. The Dutch, who knew he was no coward, treated him with the reverence they gave their own fallen heroes. Following a solemn procession, his embalmed body lay in state in the Groot Kerk at The Hague. The bier was eventually returned to England under flag of truce, accompanied by testimonials to the bravery of his last defence. He was finally laid to rest 'among the kings' beneath the north ambulatory of Westminster Abbey, where his monument still stands.

Two other English ships shared the *Swiftsure*'s fate. The luckless vessels, both belonging to Berkeley's division, were Captain James Jennifer's 54-gun fourth-rate *Seven Oaks* (formerly the *Zevenwolden* of the Admiralty of Friesland taken the previous September), and the hired 42-gun *Loyal George* under Captain John Earle. The Dutch reported that shortly before the English fleet tacked, Tromp's squadron 'got amongst them' and cut off these ships, but how that came about no one on either side seemed to know. The published English account attributed their loss to their 'staying a little behind' when the rest came about to the northwest. Others presumed they must have been too shattered aloft to follow the fleet's movement. There is ample evidence, however, that they were in fact under full press of sail with masts and yards intact almost to their final moments. That relatively undamaged ships would just haplessly 'fall to leeward' seems improbable. Dutch sources suggest that both vessels made straight for Berkeley, came near him a little before the *Swiftsure* was taken, and were then attacked by multiple opponents. From all this it would appear that Jennifer and Earle deliberately sailed through the Dutch with the intention of saving their chief. If such was the case it was surely a desperate, perhaps even foolhardy, foray – but gallant all the same. Unfortunately, the would-be rescuers were no sooner through the enemy line than the approach of Evertsen from windward forced the White Squadron to tack after Albemarle. With that, a large number of previously occupied men-of-war of Tromp's squadron became available to fall upon the intruders.

The plight of the *Seven Oaks* and *Loyal George* went almost unnoticed by the rest of the English. In the smoke and confusion of a great battle fought over many miles of ocean, flag-officers did well to keep track of their own divisions; with Berkeley dead there was no one to watch his vessels. Jordan alone observed in passing that 'some of our ships . . . were forced to leeward', but he was too busy himself to pay much attention. Amazingly, four days later the Duke of Albemarle had not even heard the two were missing!

One of the English ships fell to Van der Zaan's *Beschermer*. Van der Zaan was just completing the repairs following his previous adventures, when he noticed Berkeley's flagship at bay a short distance ahead of him. Making towards the scene, Van der Zaan arrived within musket shot just in time to witness the *Reiger*'s marines storming aboard the *Swiftsure*. As he watched the action, he was startled to find another English ship, which proved to be the *Seven Oaks*, rushing past him before the wind with Jan van Amstel's 60-gun *Vrijheid* in hot pursuit. Van der Zaan instantly joined the chase. The Dutch ships literally raced each other to overtake their prey, but the *Beschermer* with her freshly mended rigging gradually pulled ahead. Although it seemed for a while that the *Seven Oaks* might get away, Van der Zaan continually adjusted his sails and finally drew up to his opponent. There was a single exchange of broadsides, a volley with muskets and pistols, and the Dutch boarded and overran the ship in short order. The relative ease of the capture was undoubtedly influenced by the proximity of the *Vrijheid*.

Van der Zaan had much difficulty securing his prize. Jennifer and the other surviving officers were brought aboard the *Beschermer*; but before the 'people' could be taken out, the two ships, tethered by grapnels, began to drive together in the heavy swell. A particularly violent meeting broke off the head and bowsprit of the prize, whereupon Van der Zaan decided to cut her free and transfer the Englishmen by boat. But the ships were no sooner separated when it was discovered that the *Beschermer*'s longboat had been holed in the fight. It was almost nightfall before the carpenter could make it tight enough to put in the water; even then four men had to bail constantly to keep it afloat. After half the English had been brought over in two or three harrowing trips, the Dutch finally gave it up and Lieutenant de Wildt was ordered to sail the prize to the Texel. During the night Van der Zaan tried to beat back to the Dutch fleet, but he found that his foremast was shot halfway through and unable to bear sail safely. He accordingly put about and went to Goeree.

The *Loyal George* had even less chance than the *Seven Oaks*. As shown by Van de Velde, she was intercepted just short of the *Reiger* and *Swiftsure* by a whole cluster of Dutch warships bearing down from windward. They included two powerful Noorderkwartier flagships, Schram's *Pacificatie*, 73 guns, and Stachouwer's *Maagd van Enkhuizen*, 72, along with the 66-gun *Deventer* and two other substantial vessels. This tremendous concentration of force easily overwhelmed the merchantman. Her slender scantlings were battered to matchwood and her mainmast and mizzen mowed down close to the deck. She finally fell to boarders from the *Deventer*, an Amsterdam ship commanded by Jacob Andrieszoon Swart. Despite the impossible odds, Captain Earle afterwards defiantly swore to his captors that 'if his Lieutenant had not been killed hee had not lost his ship, for hee would not, but the people would have Quarter'. Earle himself never did give up: 'Hee was wounded after the ship was taken and was carryed by force out'. Like Adriaanszoon and Van der Zaan, Captain Swart decided that his own ship was unfit to keep the sea. She nevertheless proved fit enough to tow the *Loyal George* to Goeree. The departure from the fleet of the three victorious ships and their prizes was resented by other captains, especially those who stayed with the fleet despite heavy damage and casualties. The *Deventer* and *Reiger* each had four men killed, the *Beschermer* ten.

Aside from the ships captured, another English warship had a narrow escape. It was the ancient, twice-rebuilt second-rate *Rainbow*, some of whose timbers had shaken to the broadsides of the Spanish Armada. The *Rainbow* was Harman's second in the rear division of the White. She had fought near Harman all afternoon, but when the fleet tacked to the northwest she was unable to follow. Captain John Hart afterward explained that his ship 'was soe disabled in her masts, sailes, rigging & rudder, that she would neither stay nor beare up as the rest of the fleet did, but was forced to receive what 12 saile would bestow upon us, wherein I had about 25 men killed or wounded'. Hart fled on the starboard tack and was at least able to keep ahead of the vessels chasing him. Finally,

> about 7 at night they tackt & stood towards the rest of their fleet, which our fleet had engaged, onely one fireship which thought to have layd us on board, but it pleased God that shee did not stay soe well as to take the wind of us, but came a little to Leeward & left us, but I conceive not without some damage, soe this ship being in the Condition she was, I stood in toward Ostend, & coming to an Anchor 5 leagues short of it at 9 or 10 a clock lay that night mending our rigging what wee could.

At dawn he found that the twelve pursuers had come hunting him after all. As they were 'very neere us & as I conceive in pursuite of mee', he quickly cut his cable and fled into the harbour 'with a great deale of danger'. Placing his wounded in the care of the neutral Spanish authorities, Hart spent the whole of the day making repairs. The next morning he set sail for the Downs and, arriving there early on the 4th, wrote to Whitehall requesting orders. Lest anyone suspect his motives in leaving the fleet, he carefully added that 'ye ship is not able to doe any service till shee hath been in some dock'. On the 5th the *Rainbow* entered the river, Pepys confirming that she was 'maimed as the other ships are'.

The triumphs of the Amsterdam-Noorderkwartier squadron were achieved largely without the services of Cornelis Tromp. As described earlier, it was the collision between the *Hollandia* and the *Liefde* which lured Berkeley to his destruction. After the *Calantsoog* and *Reiger* drove away the *Swiftsure*, the Dutch flagship eventually came away from the *Liefde*. Tromp ordered Captain Hondius to take the *Hollandia* back into the fight, but her head and bowsprit had broken off at the stem in the

e *Zeven Provinciën* in 1666, a detail from a Van de Velde grisaille.

Willem v.d. Velde: Krijgsraad voor den 4daagschen zeeslag aan boord v/h Admiraal

A grisaille by Van de Velde the Elder showing a council-of-war in the Dutch fleet before the Four Days' Battle. At right is the *Zeven Provinciën* and at centre, the sterns of the *Wapen van Utrecht* commanded by Hendrik Gotskens and the *Eendracht* under Lt.-Adm. Aert van Nes. The 74-gun ship on the left bears flags and penda

H. de Ruyter, de Zeven Provincien: 10 Juni 1666. Geschenk van belangstellenden.

propriate for SbN. Jan van Nes in the *Delft*; but she was a much smaller vessel, so the scene apparently ntains a mistake.

The opening broadsides. Berkeley's *Swiftsure,* with a white flag at the fore, is at left. A little to the right Ayscue white flag is visible, but his ship is hidden by an English third-rate sailing large. In the centre, the nearest English vessel is Jordan's *Royal Oak,* and off his starboard quarter Teddiman's flag can be seen in the distance. Albemarle, with a union at the main and the red flag at the fore, lies astern of Jordan. The nearest Dutch ship

Sir William Berkeley, by Lely.

e Salomonszoon's *Liefde* (left) and Adriaanszoon's *Reiger*. Tromp is astern of Adriaanszoon with de Ruyter f his starboard quarter. Immediately to the left of de Ruyter are the flags of two English rear-admirals, Utber d Holmes.

Frescheville Holles (left) and Sir Robert Holmes, portrayed by Lely. Both distinguished themselves in the ur Days' Battle, in which Holles lost his left arm.

The drawings shown here are two parts of a panoramic view of the early fighting (a third part, which joins on to the right of the parts illustrated and which shows the remainder of the Dutch fleet not yet engaged, has been omitted). In the left-hand part (top), Van de Velde sketches furiously from his *galjoo* as the *Beschermer* manoeuvres to windward of the English. Off the *Beschermer*'s port bow is Berkeley's *Swiftsure* and off her starboard bow are Ayscue's *Prince* and Jordan's *Royal Oak* (Jordan's flag is marked

ue' but this is surely a mistake for red). Astern of Ayscue, Harman's *Henry* is in the distance, and
tween Ayscue and Jordan is another distant rear-admiral, probably Holmes. In the right-hand part
ottom) are mostly ships of the Dutch Third Squadron. Towards the left, Sweers in the *Gouda* (flag at
e mizzen) sails just ahead of Tromp, with Albemarle's Union flag visible between them. Farther to the
ht is Van der Hulst in the *Spiegel* (flag at the fore), with Teddiman's *Royal Katherine* in the distance.

Van de Velde (foreground) observes as disaster unfolds in the White Squadron. The *Swiftsure* (right, white fla at the fore) flees after having attacked the fouled *Hollandia* and *Liefde* (not shown), but her main yard is brought down by the pursuing *Calantsoog* and *Reiger*.

The captured *Swiftsure,* her foremast gone and Dutch boats coming alongside. To her left, Meppel's *Westfriesland* (flag at the main) sweeps past on the starboard tack. Ahead of the *Swiftsure* is Cornelis Evertser *Walcheren,* with erroneous ensign and jack. Many of the details and inscriptions on these drawings were evidently filled in later, as there are occasional references to events of the subsequent days.

he *Deventer*, which captured the *Loyal George*.

Sir John Harman, by Lely.

Cornelis Evertsen the Elder, by Nicolaes Maes.

After repairing, the fleets resume the action in the evening. The English sail from right to left on the starboard tack, led by Albemarle and a two-decker of the White Squadron. Of the rest, Jordan, Teddiman, a rear-admiral (Holmes or Utber), and Ayscue can be identified by their flags. Most of the Dutch cross ahead of the English t

...he frigate *Asperen*, which towed the *Hollandia* to Goeree.

...ke the wind, including Sweers (foreground) and a Lt.-Adm. (Tromp or Meppel). Some of the Dutch are ...rced to pass to leeward, among them Stachouwer in the *Maagd van Enkhuizen* (far right).

One of the few depictions of the fighting on the second day is this painting by Van de Velde the Younger showing the Westfriesland, flagship of the Lieutenant-Admiral of the Noorderkwartier, Jan Meppel. The artist, who was not present, should have given the ship a nine-striped ensign.

Vice-Admiral Sir Joseph Jordan, by Lely.

Sir Christopher Myngs, by Lely.

An engraving of the St. James's Day Fight. Neither Van de Velde was present, and pictorial representations of this tremendous engagement are quite rare.

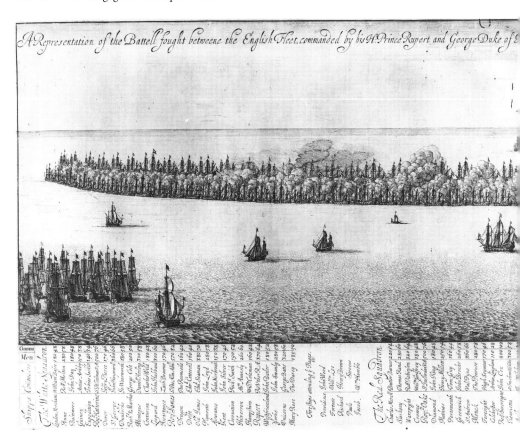

A Representation of the Battell fought betweene the English Fleet, commanded by his H. Prince Rupert and George Duke of [...]

ert van Nes, by Van de Helst.   Sir George Ayscue, by Lely.

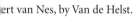

(OVERLEAF) The capture of the *Royal Prince*, a section of a grisaille produced by Van de Velde the Elder in 1672.
ke other works dating from long after the event, it contains minor mistakes. Off the *Prince*'s starboard bow is
e *Gouda*; Sweers's flag at the mizzen actually had only three stripes.

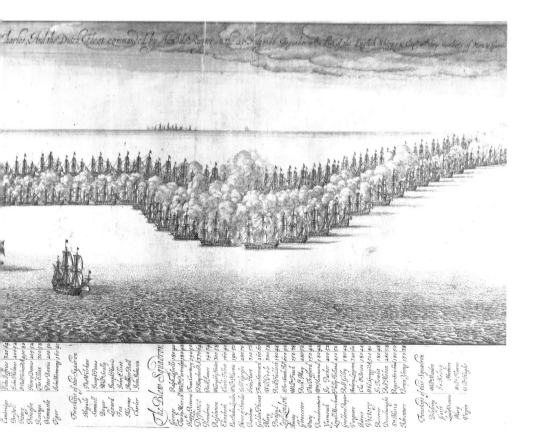

collision, leaving the forestay dangling uselessly. When Hondius tried to put the ship on the wind, the foremast, having no forward restraint, toppled into the mainmast; both went over the side in a monumental jumble. The great flagship was left wallowing in the trough of the sea while the battle raged around her. Not one to be content with a spectator's role, Tromp commandeered a *galjoot* which had come up to assist and ordered its master to take him to the nearest seaworthy man-of-war, which proved to be the 66-gun Noorderkwartier ship *Jonge Prins* commanded by Adriaan Houttuin. Tromp was presently back in action, though not in time to take part in the capture of the English ships. A disappointed Hendrik Hondius meanwhile remained in the *Hollandia*. After the tangled wreckage was at length cleared away, the second-largest warship in the Dutch fleet was ignominiously towed to Goeree by the frigate *Asperen*. A little later the 62-gun *Delft*, flagship of Rear-Admiral Jan van Nes of de Ruyter's division, lost her foremast. Van Nes shifted to Laurens van Convent's *Groot Hollandia*, while the *Delft* joined the growing procession of refugees to Goeree.

When Tromp shifted his flag the fleets had mostly drawn apart. The English gathered to the northwest where the *Royal Charles* and *Defiance* had lain at anchor refitting their rigging since about 6 o'clock. At 7 de Ruyter, having completed his repairs, stood towards the English, at which Albemarle and Holmes cut their cables and again came under sail. The English briefly 'cast to ye Westward' hoping to gain the weather gage and dress their line as well as circumstances allowed, and then tacked to the southeast. The fleets approached almost head to head on roughly opposite courses. As shown by Van de Velde, the *Royal Charles* was at the head of the line preceded only by a large two-decker of the White Squadron. This was perhaps the third-rate *Fairfax* commanded by Sir Thomas Chicheley, who was afterwards singled out by the general for having closely supported the flagship. Of the other flag-officers, Holmes and Harman are hidden in the smoke, but a little astern of Albemarle come Jordan and then Ayscue (these two having been near each other all day) with Teddiman and Utber sailing almost even with Ayscue. The English had evidently given up trying to sort themselves into squadrons and divisions. The Dutch too were somewhat disorganized; de Ruyter's squadron, having been nearest the English, was in the lead with Tromp's squadron following. The Zeelanders and Frisians had been somewhat fragmented in the preceding action, and circumstances again conspired to leave Evertsen towards the rear. Most of the Dutch succeeded in crossing the bows of the English to take the weather gage, but some who had been too far to leeward were unable to do so. The fleets passed with the Dutch on the port tack in two separate bodies, the English sailing between them on the starboard tack to the southeast. Winds and seas finally abated somewhat; both sides could now use the lower-deck guns, and the firing was heavy.

Of the few details recorded of this pass, Dutch sources report a memorable exchange between the *Royal Charles* and the new *Eendracht* of Lieutenant-Admiral Aert van Nes. None of the English commanders made any mention of the encounter, but two wounded men from the *Royal Charles* who were sent ashore with news on the 3rd recalled it as one of the most impressive events of the battle. They said that the Dutch ship made up boldly to board ye Admirall, & so neare as ye Yardarms to touch, but was received with so full a Broadside, besides a volley of small shot, that shee fell imediately to ye Sterne, & appeared no more, nor any other all that day to take her place; yet left dead & knocked downe in ye Admirall between 30 & 40 at that Salvo.

If nothing else, this brief duel emphatically demonstrated that the latest generation of Dutch warships was not to be taken lightly, even by the greatest English men-of-war. One of the casualties probably sustained in this encounter was the secretary and trusted confidant of the Duke of Albemarle, Sir William Clarke. Clarke was struck in the leg by a great shot. He underwent amputation the next morning 'and bore it bravely', but died two days later. The shower of debris from the shot that hit Clarke also slightly wounded Albemarle himself. A splinter bruised his hand, others 'having torne parts of his breeches away the last of which scratch't a very little his thigh'. This injury was to become a source of great embarrassment for the general.

The fleets drew apart at about 8 o'clock, and after a short pause both tacked and closed again, the English now standing northwest and the Dutch southeast. As before, heavy broadsides were exchanged along the full length of the lines with neither side gaining much advantage. The sun was already on the horizon when this pass began; by the time the rear divisions came up friend and foe could no longer be distinguished. The fleets at last separated, having engaged with few intermissions for over seven hours. Sometime in the course of the two final passes, Cornelis Tromp wore out his second flagship of the day. By the next morning he had shifted to the 54-gun *Provincie Utrecht* commanded by Jacob Corneliszoon Swart. The crippled *Jonge Prins* apparently stayed with the fleet, though she had thirteen killed including Captain Houttuin and thirty-five others wounded. The worst damage of the last passes on the English side was self-inflicted, when the fourth-rates *Jersey* and *Portland* somehow ran together; although the *Jersey* was not seriously harmed, the *Portland* was left crawling off towards Harwich with her head, foremast, and bowsprit 'unhappily' carried away.

The fleets settled in for the night, but there was little time for rest; parties of men were soon busy splicing ropes, patching sails, and fishing masts and yards. Gunners' mates retired to the magazines to fill cartridges, while other men pumped out the bilges and washed the blood from the decks. From time to time disquieting cries emanated from the cockpits where the surgeons were still at work. Aside from that and the occasional pounding of a carpenter's hammer, all was quiet. Then suddenly, at about 10 o'clock, the peace was shattered by a terrific eruption of broadsides from the Dutch fleet. As the English peered anxiously into the darkness to the southeast there were volleys of musketry and big fires could be seen. But though no one in Albemarle's fleet could tell what was happening, there was no doubt what it meant: an English crew was fighting for its life.

The ship was the *Henry*, and she was commanded by the redoubtable John Harman, Rear-Admiral of the White. Harman was a tarpaulin of long-established reputation, having commanded a ship with distinction at Portland and the Gabbard in the First Anglo-Dutch War, and again in the great victory over the Spaniards at Santa Cruz in 1657. Promoted to flag rank after Lowestoft for his service as flag-captain to the Duke

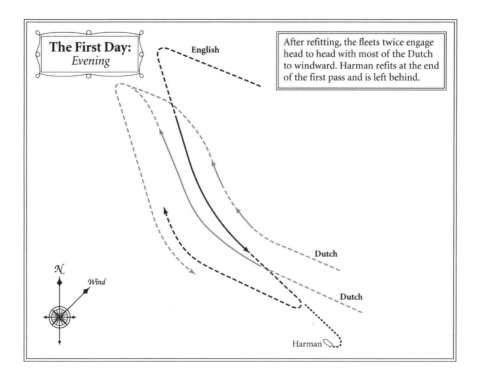

The First Day:
Evening

English

After refitting, the fleets twice engage head to head with most of the Dutch to windward. Harman refits at the end of the first pass and is left behind.

Dutch

Dutch

Harman

N

Wind

of York, he was held in universally high esteem. The *Henry* herself was a worthy adversary under any captain. She was a second-rate similar in design to the elderly *Rainbow* and *Swiftsure* (a three-decked two-tiered ship without a forecastle), but a larger 'modern' version built in 1656. Her ordnance nominally comprised 72 guns, but at the time of the Four Days' Battle she had 80 aboard, mostly of brass. The *Henry* was a powerful man-of-war; among the Dutch only the *Zeven Provinciën* could equal her broadside, and that just barely.

Harman had been in action all afternoon against Tromp's squadron. Although his precise motions thereafter were not recorded, the timing and circumstances of the *Henry*'s subsequent ordeal imply that she went with the rest of the fleet when it first tacked to the northwest and was still in company during the next pass, in which the English stood southeast. In that engagement the *Henry* suffered heavy damage. As Harman explained the next day, 'having her sailes shott away shee was unable to keepe company with our fleet'. Thus, when Albemarle tacked towards the sunset for the last pass of the day, Harman was left immobile to the southeast. The *Henry* lay to by herself for perhaps an hour changing her canvas. That completed, at a little before 10 she started out into the darkness to the northwest to rejoin the fleet. By unfortunate coincidence the Dutch were then standing southeast directly towards her following their final clash with Albemarle, and Harman unwittingly sailed into their midst.

From all indications de Ruyter was as surprised to find the *Henry* as Harman was to find the Dutch. The concealment of darkness gave the English ship a fighting chance, and Harman boldly decided to force his way through. After a short but spirited duel with the *Zeven Provinciën*, the *Henry* plunged into the middle of the Dutch. In the confusion she made it through de Ruyter's squadron and all the way to the rear, but there Cornelis Evertsen and nine of his Zeelanders threw themselves across her path. Harman grimly stood his ground. Broadsides were soon pouring in from every direction; guns were dismounted and many men were hit, slashed by splinters and dismembered by roundshot. The English fought bravely; gun crews, already near exhaustion, loaded and fired as fast as they could, but inevitably the *Henry*'s thunder eventually began to slacken. The English captain recounted the next day to Coventry that his vessel had withstood them all, but 'in doing which shee was very much disabled, soe that the Dutch thought it a good time to clap on their fireships; one of the Dutch admirall's came up and brought up a fireship . . . .' The flagship was Evertsen's *Walcheren*, 72 guns, the fireship the *Vrijheid* commanded by Engel Adriaanszoon. Before unleashing Adriaanszoon, Evertsen first ran alongside the *Henry* and shouted a final offer of quarter. Harman replied, 'It is not come to that yet!' And indeed it had not. Though much mauled, the *Henry*'s massive timbers could survive a lot more pounding than the likes of the *Seven Oaks* and *Loyal George*, or even the *Swiftsure*. Her masts were somehow still standing, her sails torn but still drawing, and many of her guns still in action. Her great demi-cannon roared in defiance, and the *Walcheren* sheered away.

Evertsen henceforth ceased his efforts to capture Harman, resolving instead to destroy him; the *Vrijheid* was sent in. Unknown to the Zeeland commander, de Ruyter had already assigned the same task to 'my fireship', as he put it; this must have been the *Gouden Ruiter* under Jan Broerszoon Vermeulen, the only fireship attached to the Admiral-General's division. These two smouldering, hellish apparitions came upon their prey within a few minutes of each other. Having approached under cover of night, they were not noticed until it was too late for the English ship to evade them. The *Gouden Ruiter* arrived alongside the *Henry* first and 'grapnailed her' on the starboard quarter. One of the English accounts said that 'The Dutch Fireships do not take Fire at first, as the English do, but first raise a Smoak incredibly stinking, and so thick as nothing can be seen at the least distance; so as it could not be seen where the Fireship's Grappling-Irons were fixed'. But just as the fire began to take hold, the *Henry* was saved by the heroic actions of Lieutenant Thomas Lamming, who 'swang himself into the Fireship, and by the light of the Fire found where the Grappling-Irons were fixed in the Fireship, and let them loose, and got on Board again

Lamming had no sooner returned when Adriaanszoon's *Vrijheid* 'clapped' on to the other side. This fireship being to windward could not be easily dislodged; the fire caught, and sheets of flame erupted from the *Henry*'s port quarter-gallery. For several minutes pandemonium reigned in the English ship. The chaplain, eyes wide with fright, dashed up to the boatswain and quaveringly shrieked, 'What shall we do?' The boatswain sarcastically recommended that he jump overboard, at which the 'parson' sprinted to the side, vaulted the rail, and disappeared never to be seen again. Fireships inspired an abject dread in the seventeenth-century mariner in any circumstances, and especially in the lurid glow at night. The collective wits of the *Henry*'s crew suddenly gave way; within seconds, scores of panic-stricken seamen followed the chaplain into the water, while others made off with the longboat. Harman immediately charged down from the quarterdeck and rushed among the men with his sword unsheathed. Vowing that he would cut down the next one that went for the rail, he herded them back to their stations. About fifty had already consigned themselves to the deep; the Dutch fished out a few, the rest drowned like rats. The chastened remainder aboard the *Henry* gathered aft where the flames were threatening to envelop the whole of the stern. Their nerve restored by their officers' example, they forced away the fireship 'with Oars and Iron Leavers' and eventually 'quencht' the fire. At one point a sail ignited, but the yard was immediately lowered to the deck, and Harman's quick-thinking cabin servant doused it with dampened cloths from the admiral's linen stores. The *Vrijheid* inflicted a final insult; as she drifted free, one of her yards tumbled into the *Henry*, felling Harman and breaking his ankle.

Evertsen, disappointed that the first two '*branders*' had not produced the desired result, now brought forth a third 'to repair the ill success of the others'. This was probably the one remaining Zeeland fireship, the *Hoop* under Willem Meerman. Harman did not intend to stay and receive it, though by this time he had given up all hope of rejoining his own forces. He afterwards told Coventry that the fires had just been extinguished when 'a 3d fireship came to lay him on board which hee had noe way to avoid but by putting before the wind, which shift carried him soe much farther from our fleet & the fireship following him within a stones throw at least an houre'. Fortunately for the men of the *Henry*, their injured captain kept his head. The four culverins in the stern were loaded with chain shot, and 'at last Harman had the Lucke from his sterne chass to shoote downe the fireships maine Yard, & soe freed himself'.

Paradoxically, the fireships were probably Harman's salvation. Their approach forced the rest of the Dutch to keep clear, which opened an avenue of escape and prevented any boarding attack from developing. The *Henry* would almost certainly have been taken had she been grappled by men-of-war rather than fireships. The whole incident was a graphic demonstration of how ineffectual incendiary craft were when confronted with a disciplined crew. As it was, most of the Dutch were sure the English vessel would never make it home. Ruth Maximiliaan of Bergen fame and now captain of the 56-gun *Wassenaar* wrote that 'There is reason to believe that [the] ship so shattered as she was sunk soon after, because she was never heard of since'. De Ruyter agreed, claiming flatly that 'In fine that English Rear-Admirals ship, called the *Injury* [an interesting phonetic confusion] sunk but we know not whether any of the rest of the men that staid on board her were saved or no'. The States-General's official report was somewhat more equivocal: 'The night then parted the Combatants, it being impossible for us to see, by reason of the darkness or the thick smoak, whether the aforesaid Rear-Admiral, being shrewdly battered scap'd away and saved himself, or whether he sunk to the bottom of the sea'.

All of them would have been amazed to learn that the *Henry*'s damages would not have prevented her from resuming the fight. One who saw her two days after described her as 'very much scorch't by a fire shipp, but not otherwayes disabl'd'. Harman's main problems were lack of men to work the guns (over a hundred were killed or drowned with another fifty wounded) and the fact that the Dutch lay between him and the English fleet. He accordingly proceeded to Aldborough Bay near Harwich, arriving the next day. There he found some colliers whose crews he pressed to man the ship, and then sailed to the Gunfleet on the 3rd, little suspecting the battle would still be in progress.

The Dutch could at least take satisfaction in having driven one of the largest English warships from the field. But the triumph had been bought at a price none would willingly have paid. The official account recorded that the last fireship advanced under the cover of the *Walcheren*'s guns. As Harman fled, a fateful Parthian shot from the *Henry* found the quarterdeck of the Zeeland flagship and, in the words of the deputies of the States, 'took away the life of the Illustrious Cornelis Evertsen, Lieutenant-Admiral, whose good Conduct and great Courage had made him to be Admired not only in that fight, but in many other encounters besides'. Cornelis Evertsen the Elder had been a cantankerous and argumentative officer, but respected throughout the States' Fleet. Charles II, who had known him well in the years of exile, was much distressed and sent heartfelt condolences. In the Netherlands the dead commander was mourned as no one had been since 'old' Tromp a decade before; the province of Zeeland was plunged into sadness even in victory.

Despite their rage at the loss of Evertsen, the Dutch to their credit were unstinting in their praise of Harman: 'According to the Testimony of all the Dutch Officers which were present, and were Spectators of that Glorious Action, the undaunted Bravery of that English Rear-Admiral cannot but be admired'. The escape of the *Henry* was celebrated in England as though it had been a major victory. Lamming, the fearless lieutenant, was rewarded with command of the fourth-rate *Ruby*. In addition, for some brave act which regrettably went unrecorded, the Generals' order-book contains an authorization 'to pay £15 to John Staunton seaman belonging to ye *Henry* as a reward for his good services done in ye same the last Engagement'. The rest of the officers and crewmen were everywhere lionized. Among them was Harman's division muster-master Balthasar St. Michel, whose post had been procured through the good offices of his brother-in-law Samuel Pepys. 'Balty' proudly regaled Pepys with the wondrous tale of his survival 'after the utmost imaginable danger he hath gone through in the *Henery*, being upon the quarterdeck with Harman all the time'. The greatest acclaim went to Harman himself, who was knighted. The affair had been 'as all say', wrote Pepys, 'the greatest hazard that ever any ship 'scaped and as bravely managed by him'. Though much flattered, Sir John was unable to enjoy the fruits of his fame as fully as he might have wished. The bones of his ankle never properly healed, forcing him to resign his commission and leaving him painfully crippled for the rest of his life. He eventually returned to the sea to take an honourable part in many battles, but he was mostly confined to a chair on the poop.

Chapter XIV

The Second Day

Now pass'd, on either side they nimbly tack;
Both strive to intercept and guide the wind:
And, in its eye, more closely they come back,
To finish all the deaths they left behind.

Saturday the 2nd of June dawned sunny and warm. The breeze was still from the S.W. and W.S.W., but now much lighter. The main bodies of the fleets had lain at anchor during the night, the Dutch to the southeast of the English with the nearest opposing vessels four or five miles apart. As soon as it was light enough to see, the commanders took stock of the situation. The English were missing six ships: The *Swiftsure*, *Seven Oaks*, and *Loyal George* had been captured and the *Henry*, *Rainbow*, and *Portland* driven away. At least two others were heavily damaged; the *Monck* was without her fore topmast and the second-rate *Vanguard* had been 'hardly besett' in the last pass the previous night. Their captains nevertheless meant to stay and fight, so Albemarle still had forty-eight 'ships of force' and two fifth-rates. The Dutch had permanently lost the *Hof van Zeeland* and *Duivenvoorde*; the *Gelderland*, *Hollandia*, *Delft*, *Reiger*, *Deventer*, *Beschermer*, and the frigate *Asperen* had all for one reason or another returned to the Netherlands. That left the States' Fleet with seventy-seven vessels including twelve frigates and one three-mast yacht.

The forces remaining were closely proportionate to the original numbers, so the English had not done too badly under the circumstances. At first it appeared that they had fared even better. On the morning of the 2nd de Ruyter was initially shocked to find only fifty-three warships in company, twenty-four others having somehow been separated. Twelve, including Tromp's latest flagship, the *Provincie Utrecht*, had missed the last tack in the darkness and had spent the night off to the west. They reappeared through the morning haze soon after dawn, much to de Ruyter's relief. Hurrying across south of the English, Tromp was just able to gain his station in the rear squadron before the fighting resumed. The other vessels absent were the twelve which had followed the *Rainbow* to Ostend. The identity of these ships is unknown, but they probably belonged to Tromp's squadron, with which the *Rainbow* had been engaged at the time of her flight. The captains of these twelve vessels had served de Ruyter poorly. Their futile chase had taken them many miles from the scene of the action and thereby denied their services to the fleet for all of the coming day's fighting, leaving de Ruyter with sixty-five men-of-war.

Albemarle was understandably encouraged to see his enemy in such diminished strength. Thinking English broadsides had been responsible, he eagerly signalled his squadrons back into line. The order of battle was unchanged except that Ayscue in the *Royal Prince*, the White Squadron's only remaining flagship, took station at the head of the line to give leadership at that important position.

The Dutch too fell into line. Once again they were in a different order from that originally established. De Guiche mentions in his *Mémoires* that Aert van Nes was at the head of the fleet on this day with de Liefde's division immediately astern; since both belonged to de Ruyter's squadron, the commander-in-chief himself was presumably in the next division. Other eyewitnesses noted that Tromp was still in the rear, which leads to the obvious conclusion that the Zeeland-Friesland squadron was now in the centre. The Admiral-General had called a full council-of-war at dawn, and the revised fighting order must have been the main subject of the discussion. Why the change was necessary is not certain. The previous day had given de Ruyter his first experience with the line-ahead in battle, and it may be that he had been impressed by the extent to which the line's performance depended on the manoeuvres of the leading squadron. At the same time, his decentralized signalling system made it difficult to exercise much direct tactical control over the other two squadron commanders. Consequently, if he wished to improve his management of the activities of the van, placing his own three divisions there would have been a good temporary solution. Having done that much, it would also have been logical to place his flagship in the squadron's aftermost division, from which he could still keep an eye on the rear some four or five miles astern. The arrangement must have been deemed satisfactory, for it appears to have been employed on the fourth day as well. Aside from the unusual fighting order, a peculiar situation existed in the Zeeland-Friesland squadron. In the course of the council-of-war de Ruyter undoubtedly learned of the death of Cornelis Evertsen. It had long been customary in the Dutch service to keep the flag of a dead commander flying throughout the remaining hours of the day of battle to avoid demoralizing the crews of the other ships. De Ruyter evidently decided that it would be best to observe this procedure for the present even though it was now a new day. The *Walcheren* accordingly kept the lieutenant-admiral's flag at the main, so that the Second Squadron was technically under the command of Captain Cornelis Evertsen the Youngest, the slain commander's 24-year-old son. Young Evertsen was an officer of some ability; even so, this decidedly odd state of affairs cannot have pleased the proper heir to the squadron, Vice-Admiral Adriaan Banckert of Zeeland.

As the fleets drew up, seamen on both sides steeled themselves for another test. Lieutenant Roch related that 'we began to rouse up preparing ourselves for a long days worke for now ye weather was fit for ye Sport'. His captain, Major Frescheville Holles, sent below for wine and 'all our Company being aloft, drinks a Glasse to all fore & aft, which having all pledged round, every man repaired to his Quarter'.

At 6 o'clock all was in readiness. Ayscue led the English off to the south, partly to gain the wind and also in hopes of isolating Tromp, who had come up from the southwest. Although the English failed in the second object, they did take the weather gage. The Dutch initially headed W.N.W. towards the English. When the English went south, de Ruyter answered by tacking to the south himself, which brought the fleets on parallel courses about two miles apart with the Dutch some distance ahead of the English. Brandt, de Ruyter's seventeenth-century biographer, believed that the

Admiral-General's move to the south was intended to offer Albemarle a classic duel with both fleets on the same tack. It seems improbable, however, that de Ruyter would willingly have allowed an inferior opponent to pin him to leeward and perhaps use fireships to even the odds. A better explanation is that his intention was the exact reciprocal of Albemarle's: to win the weather gage himself and also to keep the English from getting between him and the twelve Dutch ships to windward. Soon after Tromp's reunification was assured, de Ruyter must have realized that the weather gage could not be obtained on the southerly reach. Rather than waste time in useless manceuvre, he signalled his fleet to come about in succession and then beat northwest towards the enemy. The English, for their part, did not merely stand to receive his attack, but moved aggressively towards the Dutch. As Ruth Maximiliaan put it, 'they without waiting for us, advanced to meet us with much Resolution and Courage', and as de Ruyter wrote, 'came powring upon us'.

De Guiche reported that the English approached 'in an admirable order; they marched by the front as if they were an army on land, & when they drew near, they extended themselves & turned their broadsides for combat'. This presumably means that the English came down in line abreast until the range was within point-blank, when they suddenly wheeled together into line-ahead to present their broadsides. It was a relatively new manoeuvre specified by Article Fifteen of the Fighting Instructions, but originally devised by the Earl of Sandwich in February 1665. This was probably its first use in action; it must have been impressive to watch, the Frenchman obviously admiring the precision with which it was carried out.

The fleets 'fell to firing' at about 7:30. Roch claimed that the *Antelope* fired the first shot; she belonged to the Red Squadron, so the head of the Dutch line must have made its initial impact against the English centre. The fleets then went by and through each other at close range, establishing a pattern of head-on passes (as at Scheveningen) which were repeated over and over for the next ten hours. An anonymous English participant described the tactics with unusual clarity:

> The manner of fighting at that time was, that each Fleet lay in a line, and when the ships of one Fleet lay with their heads to the Northward, the heads of the other lay to the Southward; the headmost ships of our Fleet engaging first the headmost of theirs, so passing on by their Fleet in a line, fireing all the way, and as soon as the Rear of one Fleet was clear from the Rear of the other, then each Fleet tack'd in the Van, standing almost stem for stem one with another to engage again; by which meanes there was at least an hour's respit between every Encounter.

Each renewal of the action brought indescribable pandemonium. Friday's strong winds had at least blown away the smoke, but in Saturday's light airs it hung over the scene like a grey shroud. Its acrid, choking clouds became so thick that no one on the lee side of the battle could see anything beyond the nearest ships. The sultry weather added further misery. 'This day was very hot more ways then one', said Roch, 'for between ye flames of burning Ships, ye firey flashes from ye guns, with ye beams of ye Sun we seem'd to be in the fiery Region'. The fighting throughout was at such close quarters, and of such ferocity, that the participants lost all track of time. Things seemed to blur together, and everyone recalled the most fundamental details in different ways. Some remembered the fleets crossing on east–west headings; others thought it was north and south. With the wind S.W. and W.S.W., the true axis should have been something in between, roughly N.N.W.–S.S.E. Eyewitnesses could not even agree on the number of passes; some said four, some said five, others six or seven. By the best reconstruction there seem to have been at least seven. Passing tactics were common throughout the line-ahead era, but so many distinct engagements in one day was highly unusual. Of the morning's fighting especially, reports from both sides describe the fleets as repeatedly breaking each other's lines. The States-General's official account shows that this occurred from the very first pass:

> The two Fleets made a motion, viz. The Hollanders towards the North-West, and the English toward the South, with design to follow one the other; but the English having the Advantage of the Wind, disputed their Enemies passage, and without waiting any longer, advanced to them, and fell upon them. The Hollanders, without changing their Course or their Countenance, stood firm in luffing, so that the two Hostile Fleets broke through one another and began a most furious fight.

In the two subsequent passes the combatants met head to head sailing as close to the wind as possible. Each time, divisions and individual ships of both fleets passed through to windward whenever they could, and were forced to leeward at other times.

Assuming that both lines stretched five or six miles, and that the converging forces closed at a combined speed of around ten knots, each pass must have lasted some thirty to forty minutes. In that time a ship could get off perhaps four broadsides on its engaged side, and would receive a like number. It is also apparent that given equal conditions, damage in a passing action would not be as heavy as when fleets were on the same tack. This was partly because of the short duration of the encounters and partly because gunnery was less effective; a passing opponent was alongside for too short a time for the gunners to take careful aim. Consequently, except in those instances in which vessels were somehow cut off to leeward, a single pass in itself could not be expected to have decisive results. Nonetheless, repeated encounters eventually brought relentless, grinding attrition, the toll in shattered ships and mangled men building cumulatively over the course of the day. Albemarle's fleet, outnumbered sixty-four to fifty, inevitably received many more shot than the Dutch, but that was partly offset by the heavier English ordnance. 'Their Guns', said a Dutch account, 'made strange Havock: For the most part of the Ships of the two Fleets had their Masts, their Sails and Tackling either shot away, or shattered to pieces'.

At the end of each pass, commanders struggled to reorder their lines while the fleets tacked, and boatswains and carpenters did what they could to undo the effects of the previous clash. During the intervals men with no immediate duties crowded to the rail to cheer on their fleet's tiny yachts, ketches, and galliots, which pugnaciously sought out opponents of their own size among the enemy. One observer wrote that

> in the two fleets rallying to tack againe the small trade of each side must passe one the other as they were off aloofe from the fleet and when we were not loosing they usually were, which was a pleasant sight and I thinke a divertisment to both the fleets.

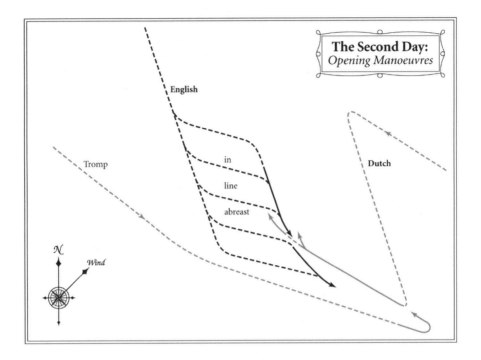

Comic though these lilliputian combats may have seemed, they were no doubt deadly enough for those who took part. They may also have sent Willem van de Velde ducking for cover, for the artist seems to have made few drawings of this day's events.

De Ruyter already had heavy responsibilities in directing his fleet in action, but from the second day on he had an extra cross to bear: the task of entertaining the French nobles from the *Duivenvoorde*, at least three of whom were now gathered on his quarterdeck. These worthies made quite a nuisance of themselves with their constant offers of advice. At one point, the Comte de Guiche began to berate de Ruyter for failing to immediately board and capture the *Royal Charles*. Fortunately, the admiral kept his sense of humour. Having patiently endured the Frenchman's criticism for some time, de Ruyter finally turned to him and, with a straight face, gravely told him that the Dutch had found it unwise to board the English, because when facing capture they usually blew themselves up along with their captors. That revelation ended de Guiche's ardour for boarding.

As to the course of the battle, the first two passes went badly for the English. The official 'True Narrative' admitted that '7 sail of good ships . . . were gone off disabled' before 10 o'clock. What ships they were is not recorded, but they must have included the third-rate *Anne* commanded by Robert Moulton, the hired *Baltimore* under Charles Wilde, and the fourth-rate *Bristol* in which Captain Phillip Bacon had been killed. These three were among the first to reach harbour, arriving off the Gunfleet some time Sunday afternoon (the *Portland* and *Henry* had come in the day before). At the end of the second pass, at about 10, the wind died just as the combatants drew clear, causing a longer-than-usual interval. The fleets lay becalmed in close proximity for about an hour. At 11 the breeze rose again; both sides immediately 'charged', the English on the starboard tack to the S.S.E. and the Dutch on the port tack to the N.N.W. The guns soon spoke again, but the third bout proved to be much different from the others. It marked the one notable break in the tactical pattern of the day, and also produced a major crisis.

Things started out much as before. Ayscue leading the English van met Van Nes with a terrific exchange of broadsides and there was a furious struggle for the wind as each side attempted to force the other to leeward. This time the Dutch van won out, and weathered the English. De Ruyter himself initially came up to leeward, but Maximiliaan said that the commander-in-chief 'broke through the Enemies Fleet' and 'got the Weather gage of them' with the whole of his squadron and probably the Zeelanders and Frisians as well. This was the first time the Dutch had gained the wind with enough force to make a difference. It was the chance de Ruyter had been awaiting, and he meant to make the most of it. According to Brandt he intended to abandon the line and launch a massive attack in the old style, which meant a grand mêlée with boarding and swordplay. Choosing his moment carefully, de Ruyter waited until the Zeven Provinciën was opposite the Red Squadron. He then ordered the flag-captain, Van Nijmegen, to hoist the signal for general attack. That much was done, but whether or not the English line could have withstood the onslaught will never be known. At that moment, the Admiral-General suddenly 'heard a most horrid noise of both great Guns and Muskets'. The clamour came from somewhere astern, and the musketry 'made him believe, that some of his Ships being surrounded by the Enemies, were making their last efforts'.

It was Tromp. No one knows exactly what happened; but it appears that, finding himself and his squadron to leeward, he attempted to follow the commander-in-chief's example by breaking through to windward – and did not make it. Some group of English vessels closed their intervals to block his path. Meppel's Westfriesland and the Gelderland of the Noorderkwartier under Van Hoorn found a way through, and other ships fell back to leeward; but Tromp's own Provincie Utrecht and seven or eight others were left squarely in the path of the enemy fleet. Tromp's three divisions at this time numbered no more than twelve or thirteen men-of-war in all, for the vessels missing at Ostend were almost certainly from his squadron. Since the remnant still in hand formed the rear of the fleet, there were no ships astern to give him support. The English swirled past, every ship as it went by hurling a devastating broadside at the hapless Dutchmen. In a matter of minutes the Provincie Utrecht, Van der Hulst's Spiegel, Schram's Pacificatie, Salomonszoon's Liefde, de Haan's Calantsoog, and Van Amstel's Vrijheid – all major vessels – suffered crippling damage to masts and spars, and seemed at their opponents' mercy; Tromp himself had a leg slashed open by a splinter.

The English were quick to exploit the situation with their fireships. When the Red Squadron came up, Albemarle called away the Spread Eagle commanded by William Seale. A little later Teddiman arrived on the scene and sent in the Blue Squadron's only fireship, William Bustow's Young Prince. Both made for the damaged ships and both found a target. Seale reportedly fell upon a vice-admiral's flagship, which could have been either the *Spiegel* under Abraham van der Hulst, Vice-Admiral of Amsterdam, or the *Pacificatie* under Volckert Schram, Vice-Admiral of the Noorderkwartier; both received major damage in this episode. Whichever it was, the ship was seen to be set afire; but much to Albemarle's chagrin, the Dutch crew succeeded in disentangling themselves and eventually extinguished the blaze. The *Young Prince* had better luck. Though Bustow did not, as he claimed, bag a rear-admiral, he did grapple an important man-of-war – Salomonszoon's *Liefde*, which had been in the thick of the fray throughout the battle. This time the prey could not shake free, and huge gouts of flame were soon shooting from her gunports.

Most of the English declined to break their order as they sailed by and were satisfied to pour in a blast of roundshot and case. However, as Tromp's vessels tried to crawl away to leeward, Jordan's *Royal Oak* and others of the Red Squadron including Holles's *Antelope* did peel out of line to chase them down. Jordan somewhat optimistically reported that 'there was two of their Vice Admiralls burnt, one of them this shipp boarded, and caused to be fired'. This may mean that Jordan directed the final advance of one of the fireships. The *Antelope* was also closely engaged at this time; by Roch's description,

> We borded a vize admiral & in 2 houres dispute [probably more like twenty minutes] sunk him by our side. It was a Ship of between 60 & 70 Guns & above 400 men of whom onely 30 sav'd themselves by swiming, the Capt. with all ye rest being kild or wounded.

The opponent in this case was probably Van der Hulst. Roch failed to mention that the unfortunate victim was under simultaneous attack by *three* English ships. The *Spiegel*, 68 guns, was reduced to wreckage, the mainmast over the side, thirty-five men killed and another sixty-six wounded. The dead included Van der Hulst himself, who was hit in the chest by a musket ball; the States-General 'extreamly regretted' his loss. Nevertheless, despite Roch's assurances the *Spiegel* stayed afloat. That the English did not notice her escape is perhaps understandable, for the *Antelope* and her companions were unexpectedly interrupted in their attack and suffered merciless retribution themselves:

> No sooner had we dispatcht him but we were ingaged with his whole Squadron of 18 sayle, yet having ye winde of them, tho now at a distance from our fleet, we receivd all their broadsides & would willingly have paid them again with double interest. But now alas our wings were clipt, our ship cruelly shattered, our Comanders Arme shot off, 55 of our men killed & neer so many more wounded, our masts, sayles & rigging all in totters our decks dyed with blood like a slaughter house! Yet I fought ye ship as well as I could in that condition till I had made my way into our fleet again.

The *Antelope*'s true casualties were twenty-one killed and thirty wounded, which was bad enough for a ship with a complement of 190. Credited with sinking a flagship, Holles was afterwards knighted. Roch obviously did not realize it, but the new opponents who so roughly handled his ship included de Ruyter himself. The officers on the quarterdeck of the *Zeven Provinciën* were at first unable to tell what was happening in the rear, though it soon became evident that a group of ships was trapped to leeward of the enemy. The Admiral-General's great attack was instantly called off, for the emergency demanded immediate attention. De Ruyter's reaction proved to be the most important manoeuvre of the day. In saving the rear squadron, he carried out a remarkable evolution, requiring unprecedented coordination with the other commanders, and accomplished in spite of a signalling system lamentably incapable of conveying his intentions. It also produced one of the more lively controversies of the battle. When de Ruyter first discovered the nature of the trouble, he undoubtedly realized that he was facing a daunting task. Whatever course of action he adopted, it would have to include a penetration to the other side of the English line, for that was where Tromp lay. Since it would be impossible to bring the whole fleet to leeward in good order in time to help the trapped vessels, the operation would have to be carried out by a relatively small number of ships. Unwilling to entrust such a dangerous mission to his subordinates, he resolved to head the relief expedition himself. But an important precaution was necessary before the attack could begin. If he was going to lead a daring foray to leeward of the enemy, it was imperative that a strong Dutch force be retained in a threatening posture to windward; otherwise, the English could simply swoop down and destroy him as soon as he appeared in their lee. Such a lack of windward support had contributed to the loss of the English *Seven Oaks* and *Loyal George* when they had tried to 'bring off' Berkeley in similar fashion the day before. As Maximiliaan explained,

> De Ruyter considering the danger in which Tromp was, resolved to disengage him, and for that effect, he ordered the greatest part of his fleet to make a tack to the South-ward, whilst himself with his Rear fell upon the Enemies main body, making directly towards Tromp, to assist him.

In other words, de Ruyter first directed the commanders lying ahead of him (Van Nes and de Liefde) to come about to the opposite tack, leaving them parallel to the English and still to windward.

Maximiliaan's clear and concise narrative would stand without further comment were it not for the Comte de Guiche, who left a drastically different version:

> The head of our line was led by Adraen van Essen [Aert van Nes], Lieutenant-Admiral of Rotterdam, & who was to succeed to the Flag after de Ruyter, in case he came to be killed or wounded. He was followed by de Liefde, Rear-Admiral of the same squadron. Both of them, seeing Tromp on the other side, flatly abandoned their proper course, & turned their sterns to the broadsides of the English. De Ruyter was surprised at this manoeuvre, & did what he could, in order to make known to other ships not to follow it; but, since it was already their inclination, in a moment it was imitated, & he in consequence was forced to conform to it, conserving nevertheless the best order he could, with three or four ships that followed, & let the others go.

This frequently quoted passage gives the impression that Van Nes and de Liefde fled in a disgraceful manner at the most decisive moment of the action. Though long

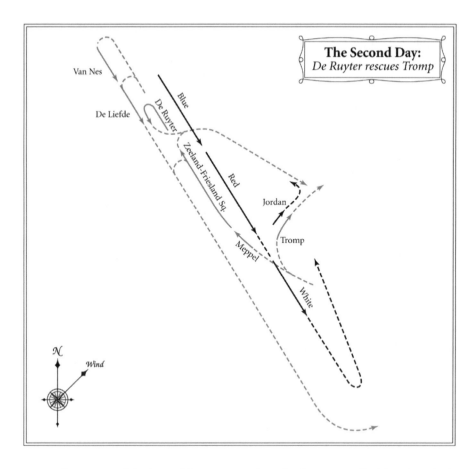

Van Nes

De Liefde

Blue

De Ruyter

Zeeland-Friesland Sq.

Red

Jordan

Tromp

Meppel

White

The Second Day:
De Ruyter rescues Tromp

N

Wind

accepted as a part of the lore of the Four Days' Battle, this is a totally false idea which appears to have arisen through a misunderstanding by the French observer. De Guiche's description of the motions of the ships is probably quite accurate (vessels to windward could not have tacked without temporarily presenting their sterns to the English) but he did not realize that the move was by de Ruyter's order. Brandt, writing some years later, obviously knew of de Guiche's confusion. The historian took particular (and otherwise inexplicable) care to dispel the misconception by emphasizing that the manoeuvres of the Lieutenant-Admiral of Rotterdam were on the direct instructions of the commander-in-chief – as Maximiliaan stated. De Ruyter's own activities in initially conforming to Van Nes's motions are probably explained by the inadequacies of the signalling system: it was not possible to order one part of his squadron to act differently from another. To accomplish his intentions the Admiral-General first had to order the whole squadron to tack, then come to the starboard tack himself, approach as many of the vessels coming up astern as he deemed necessary for the rescue effort, and send or personally shout instructions for them to follow the *Zeven Provinciën* rather than the *Eendracht*.

How many ships participated in the rescue is not recorded, but the number probably did not exceed the eighteen Lieutenant Roch reported having encountered in the *Antelope*. Maximiliaan's account implies that de Ruyter gathered his own division and perhaps some of the Zeelanders and Frisians who were immediately astern. At least two ships from the other squadrons are known to have joined, namely Van Hoorn's *Gelderland* of Tromp's squadron and the *Stad Gouda* under Captain Dirk Scheij. Scheij's vessel was one of five Amsterdam ships which had been assigned to the Zeelanders to make their divisions equal to the others.

It must have taken de Ruyter ten to fifteen minutes to make his signals and draw out his striking force, but with every passing second Tromp's situation became increasingly desperate. 'Without any longer hesitation', says the States-General's account, de Ruyter swung the head of the *Zeven Provinciën* towards the English. The Dutch van had been even with the Red Squadron when the emergency had first arisen, and the English had thereafter continued to sail south. Thus, de Ruyter's blow probably fell against the Blue Squadron, which seems confirmed in that the *Young Prince*, the Blue Squadron's fireship, reached Tromp's position before the Admiral-General did.

According to the official account, de Ruyter 'advanced with his Squadron, and falling upon that part of them, he forced a passage through the Storms of the Enemies shot and fire'. His ships must have crashed through in a compact mass; 'the English seeing him come, opened themselves', said Maximiliaan. Actually, there was little else they could do. Had the ships of Teddiman's rear-guard allowed themselves to be drawn into a mêlée, they might soon have been in an even worse predicament than Tromp's. The reasons for de Ruyter's careful precautions now became clear. Albemarle and Teddiman could not intervene, for Van Nes, de Liefde, and much of the Zeeland-Friesland squadron lay to windward sailing parallel with de Ruyter. The only English commander who could have stopped him was Ayscue, at the head of the line. Having passed to the south clear of the action, Ayscue did indeed bear up to leeward, but too late. The relief squadron at last came upon the scene of carnage in the rear. There de Ruyter

> found Lieutenant Admiral Tromp, whose flag was then hoisted in de Swart's Ship, in the last extremity, but yet fighting with all imaginable intrepidity, as likewise Vice Admiral Van der Hulst, and the Captains Salomonszoon, de Haan, and Van Amstel; their ships being surrounded on all sides by the English, were able to hold out no longer, and were at the point of being burnt or sunk, without the assistance of de Ruyter.

The rescuers soon mauled the *Antelope* and the other ships that were tormenting the damaged vessels. They then interposed themselves between Tromp and the English, and began shepherding the shattered squadron out of harm's way to leeward.

Cornelis Tromp, nursing his injured leg, left the *Provincie Utrecht* to find another flagship. On the way he visited the *Zeven Provinciën* to express his gratitude to the Admiral-General. When the seamen saw him they cheered his deliverance, but the commander-in-chief only muttered, 'It is not at this hour a time for rejoicing; it is a time for tears'. De Ruyter had ample cause for tears. Only a few minutes before, he had been on the verge of launching a grand attack which might have decided the war. Because of Tromp's troubles, the chance had been missed, good ships reduced to hulks, the weather gage lost, and the fleet left scattered in several fragments. On top of that, everyone on the flagship's quarterdeck now had a close-up view of the enormous prow of the *Royal Prince* bearing down on them with what looked to be two fireships sailing menacingly in her lee (one was actually the fifth-rate *Oxford*). Astern of the *Prince* came the White Squadron, and astern of the White Squadron came the rest of the English, wearing in succession in formidable array. 'Indeed', wrote de Guiche, 'our situation was awkward. The manoeuvre of each of our squadrons was found to be different; for, so far were our ships from being in line, they were all in flocks, & so tightly packed, that with their forty ships the English could have surrounded them all'.

As Ayscue drew near, the Dutch to leeward prepared themselves for what many feared might be the *coup de grâce*. But the axe never fell. 'Methinks', said Maximiliaan, the English 'committed then a strange fault; for it had been easy for them to have destroyed the few ships de Ruyter had with him, and Tromp's Squadron was able to make no more Resistance against them'. Instead, 'the English contented themselves with firing upon him at a distance with their Guns, without attempting to follow him'. De Guiche was equally mystified:

> It appears to me that the English did not press us closely enough at that advantageous moment, and that their idea was to increase our disorder, rather than to completely exploit it; whether due to the disproportion of their number, or for some other reason unknown, they declined to commit themselves more closely.

He added that if the English 'did not see themselves in a state to take full advantage of a success, they were very blameworthy for having preferred an obstinate battle to an honourable retreat, which they could have made the night before'.

Though de Guiche's observation was perhaps justified, the situation may not have seemed so advantageous to the English. Van Nes had by then advanced south of the point at which they were coming about. He was now duplicating their motion, wearing in a broad arc outside the radius of their own manoeuvre. He had only to bear north in order to rejoin de Ruyter, and the English could not interfere without dividing their own squadrons. The ships astern of Van Nes were still to windward, so the Dutch were actually well positioned to converge quickly if Albemarle's vessels 'broke ranks' to fall upon the enemy to leeward. It was probably for that reason that the English stayed in line. Ayscue led them to the north past de Ruyter and prepared to tack for the next pass; he had, at least, regained the weather gage. Van Nes in the meantime sailed towards de Ruyter, who in turn came south to meet him, and the Dutch fleet was soon reunited. The English were understandably disappointed. Their seemingly certain victory had been wrenched away by the Dutch commander's astonishing exploit, as they ruefully acknowledged: 'About 12 a clock wee thought wee had routed the Enemy, but De Ruyter with great courage & skill got them together again in good order'.

The Dutch had survived the crisis, though with staggering losses. Vice-Admiral Van der Hulst was dead; the *Spiegel*, *Calantsoog*, *Pacificatie*, *Vrijheid*, and *Provincie Utrecht* were all *hors de combat*, the five of them together having 349 casualties. The *Vrijheid* and *Provincie Utrecht* sailed for the Texel under jury rig, while Vice-Admiral Schram shifted to another ship and sent the *Pacificatie* to Vlissingen. The disabled *Calantsoog* and *Spiegel* were towed to the Texel, the *Calantsoog* probably by one of the other damaged vessels and the *Spiegel* by the 46-gun *Vrede*, a ship of de Ruyter's division which had perhaps received some injury of her own. Aside from Van der Hulst, Rear-Admiral Frederik Stachouwer of the Noorderkwartier was also killed on this day. Though the circumstances of his death are unknown, it seems reasonable to suppose that it occurred in the same incident. His *Maagd van Enkhuizen*, 72 guns, was as battered as the others and by the next day had departed for Vlissingen. All these ships could at least be repaired to fight another day. Not so the *Liefde*, for which de Ruyter's rescue came a few minutes too late: 'Captain Salomonszoon's Ship was already all on fire, which 'twas impossible to Quench'. The crew had taken to the water before help arrived, and most drowned. At the last instant Scheij in the *Stad Gouda* stood in as near as he dared and picked up some thirty-nine survivors including the captain. But for Pieter Salomonszoon the whole battle was fought under an unlucky star. He had collided with the *Hollandia* the day before, and now his own ship was burned; even his rescue was to no avail, for he was shot down and killed in the *Stad Gouda* during the next pass. The *Liefde* was the largest Dutch man-of-war to be lost in the Four Days' Battle. A fine 68-gun ship built in 1661, she had served in the past as flagship for both Tromp and de Ruyter.

While the fleets refitted during the interlude, the English received a reinforcement of sorts. It consisted of the 6-gun shallop *Young Rupert*, which came from Harwich bearing the diplomat Sir Thomas Clifford. He had been sent from Arlington's office with the latest news and intelligence. With him were two volunteers, William Cavendish (later Duke of Devonshire) and the soldier Thomas Butler, Earl of Ossory, a son of the Duke of Ormonde. The *Young Rupert* had come up towards the end of the previous pass. Weaving through the great ships, Ossory and Cavendish tried to insult de Ruyter with the shallop's puny broadside, which greatly amused the English and according to Clifford 'put some cheering among the men'. In a more practical vein, Clifford proudly remarked that the little vessel 'did noe small service in defence of our ketches and small trade'. When the fleets separated, the three gentlemen came aboard the *Royal Charles*, where they 'found all things well'. The packet of letters was promptly delivered, and it was from this source that Albemarle first learned of Prince Rupert's recall. The information was welcome, though the general must have noted with concern that no one knew where the Prince was, nor whether he had received the orders.

Off to the southeast, de Ruyter put his ships back into line. His own squadron placed itself in the van as before, the bedraggled remains of the Amsterdam-Noorderkwartier contingent resuming their post in the rear. While the Dutch fleet sorted itself out, a spate of unpleasantry arose among the flag-officers. As was so frequently the case, it involved Cornelis Tromp. He had stayed in the *Zeven Provinciën* until the squadrons were reunited, and then had begun to look around for a new flagship. Possibly at de Ruyter's suggestion, he first cast his eyes on the *Walcheren*, which was still wearing the more or less counterfeit flag of Cornelis Evertsen the Youngest. When Tromp went aboard the *Walcheren*, Evertsen quickly made it plain that the Zeeland flagship would not be turned over to the Lieutenant-Admiral of Amsterdam under any circumstances. The Holland commander departed angrily and proceeded to take over the 72-gun *Gouda*, which was already the flagship of his second, Rear-Admiral of Amsterdam Isaac Sweers. The *Gouda* now wore Tromp's flag at the main and Sweers's at the mizzen. Sweers had been without any particular command responsibility other than his own ship from the beginning, but that had not been blatantly obvious to the rest of the fleet. With Tromp aboard, the purely decorative nature of the rear-admiral's flag was pointedly demonstrated for all to see. It must have been a great humiliation for Sweers, though as Tromp's immediate subordinate he could not openly object. De Ruyter's fleet sailed back into action, its officers cursing and hating each other almost as intensely as they did the enemy.

The Dutch had either fifty-seven or fifty-eight ships remaining, depending on whether the *Maagd van Enkhuizen* was still available. The earlier departure of seven English vessels had left Albemarle with forty-three, of which the *Antelope* and possibly several others were no longer effective. The fleets were soon back in action, the English on the starboard tack to the S.S.E. and the Dutch to leeward on the opposite course. Though the results were less dramatic than in the previous encounter, the English did fire one shot of consequence. Just as the Dutch van was drawing clear of the English rear, a lucky hit from some ship in the Blue Squadron sent the main topmast of the *Zeven Provinciën* crashing over the side, the main yard and the commander-in-chief's flag going with it. Seeing this mishap, Aert van Nes quickly came about and drew near to render assistance. Van Nes's approach constituted a clear invitation for de Ruyter to join him in the *Eendracht*, as it would obviously take several hours to restore the *Zeven Provinciën* to fighting condition. Surprisingly, the commander-in-chief chose not to shift his flag. He instead sent a boat with a message ordering Van Nes to hoist the pendant of command himself and assume temporary control of the fleet. The Admiral-General would remain in the *Zeven Provinciën* to personally oversee the repairs.

De Ruyter's decision afterwards provoked considerable discussion. De Guiche, who did not know him well, suggested a sinister motive. He suspected that the Admiral-General was uncertain of the battle's eventual outcome, and wished to shift the blame on to Van Nes if things went badly. It would be hard to imagine a more distorted misreading of de Ruyter's character. Far more probable is the explanation given by Brandt: knowing what a psychological blow it was to the rest of the fleet to have the great flagship out of action, the commander-in-chief stayed aboard to ensure that she returned to the fight as soon as possible. Implicit in this are two further conclusions: first, that he was somewhat doubtful of the diligence of the *Zeven Provinciën*'s three captains; and second, that he had confidence in the ability of Aert van Nes to manage the battle. De Ruyter was undoubtedly influenced by his sheer fondness for the *Zeven Provinciën*. He never left his beloved flagship in any of her later actions either, although she often suffered heavy damage. The whole question of admirals shifting their flags was a matter of controversy in both English and Dutch navies. The Duke of Albemarle, for instance, would have approved of de Ruyter's decision, as he had already demonstrated when the *Royal Charles* was disabled the day before. On the other hand, Tromp and the Duke of York were never willing to relinquish tactical control for an instant if they could avoid it. Both changed ships without the slightest hesitation, often several times in the same battle.

De Ruyter and the *Zeven Provinciën* now drew off several miles to the east, while Van Nes tacked and again headed for the English. He directed the Dutch in three passes while the commander-in-chief refitted. Participants afterwards recorded few details of these encounters, which suggests that neither side attempted anything out of the ordinary. The elaborate manoeuvres of the great third pass had left the English well to windward of the Dutch. In that engagement and also in the earlier passes, Dutch squadrons to leeward had deliberately driven through the English line to gain the weather gage. The disaster to Tromp's squadron, however, had emphatically shown how dangerous such breakthroughs could be if part of the fleet could not get through. Nor were such risky tactics necessary. The great disparity in the numbers of the two fleets must have made it obvious by early afternoon that the Dutch would win a battle of attrition. If they avoided mistakes, they could not lose even from the lee position, which was a much less dangerous place now that the enemy was down to only two fireships. The English were much too weak to derive any real benefit from the weather gage other than mere survival, and could afford to take no risks whatsoever. Albemarle's only chances for victory were that Prince Rupert might suddenly appear, or that the Dutch might somehow become discouraged and go away. For all these reasons both fleets simply kept themselves in line as best they could and fought pass after pass with the English always keeping to windward.

Gunnery conditions were still excellent, and the broadsides produced fearsome results. The States-General's report said the fighting, 'especially afternoon', was 'terrible and Bloody . . . so that there were few Ships of either Fleet but sufficiently felt the effects of it by the loss of their Masts, Round-Tops, Top-Masts, Sails, and Rigging'. Both sides were in bad shape by late afternoon, but the English came off worst. At 5 o'clock the 56-gun merchantman *Loyal Subject* was towed out of action and sailed for the Gunfleet under jury rig. Another vessel, unidentified, departed at some point between the third and sixth pass, leaving only forty-one ships still in action. Dutch strength in the meantime remained undiminished despite considerable damage. By the time of Van Nes's third pass, fought at about 6 o'clock, Albemarle's forces were near collapse. As the fleets drew apart at the end of that encounter, an English ship began to fire guns without shot to attract attention, and then displayed a weft in her ensign and jack. The ship was the 48-gun *Black Eagle* commanded by John Silver, and the signal meant that she was *in extremis*. Utber's *Rupert* and other nearby vessels hurriedly sent boats to take out the crew, after which the ship sank. Captain Silver himself was badly wounded. Dutch accounts relate that his vessel had been trapped to leeward in much the same manner as the *Charity* and *John & Abigail* at Lowestoft. Silver had wisely held his course, but the ship took many shot in her windward side. On emerging from the Dutch rear he had tacked to rejoin the fleet, but in the process rolled the shot holes under water and the vessel quickly flooded.

There was much disagreement among the Dutch as to what ship was responsible for the sinking. Maximiliaan described the incident in a letter to the Admiralty of Rotterdam, modestly adding, 'to which I myself, without bragging, contributed the most'. Others had a different story. Both the States-General and Brandt, who had access to many eyewitnesses, gave the credit to a single tremendous broadside from Nicolaas Marrevelt's 68-gun Amsterdam ship *Geloof*. The *Black Eagle* was formerly the Friesland ship *Groningen* taken by Sandwich the previous autumn. The English name was derived from the two-headed black eagle which was the town of Groningen's armorial symbol. She is often confused in both modern and contemporary accounts with the fireship *Spread Eagle* which had been expended earlier the same day.

The sinking of Silver's ship was only one cloud in a veritable storm of bad tidings that assailed the Duke of Albemarle at the end of this pass. Clifford averred that up to then, matters had

> looked with a good aspect on our side for two or three houres, but then after another passe five of our better sort of ships of the 2d and 3d rates were so shatterd that they made some with leave and others without leave toward our owne ports which was a great disheartening to the rest.

Albemarle called his flag-officers for a council-of-war, but no one had anything encouraging to report. Most of the ships were severely battered and gunners were beginning to notice with concern their dwindling supplies of powder and shot. Casualties were heavy, crews were exhausted, and spirits were sagging; 'there was nothing to be heard among the common seamen but complaints against dividing our fleet and sending away Prince Rupert', said Clifford.

Then came a final, crushing blow: in the distance to the southeast, a fresh Dutch squadron was sighted sailing towards the scene. These were the twelve ships which had followed the *Rainbow* to Ostend; but the English knew nothing of that, and could only assume that they were fresh reinforcements sent out from the Netherlands. Actually, many English narratives report *two* Dutch reinforcements. The first, said to have arrived early in the morning, was merely Tromp rejoining at 7 a.m. after having been separated Friday night. The second was undoubtedly the Ostend ships, but there is some confusion over when they reached the scene. The only mention of them from the Dutch side is in a letter written by Tromp early on the 4th, and both Barlow and Roch say they came in on the morning of the 3rd. Other English eyewitnesses, however, unambiguously insist that this second 'recruit' appeared in the afternoon or evening of the 2nd. This is not the major discrepancy it seems, for it only means that the ships did not get up to the Dutch fleet before dark. They must have spent the night as a separate group, and thus did not physically join until the next morning. Nevertheless, they were very much in sight Saturday evening, and their effect on the morale of the English is easily imagined. It was 'some Discouriagement to our men, being alsoe soe over Powred with numbers' by one report, and enough 'to break ye hearts' according to another.

There was no question of resuming the action. The English had given their best, but there was nothing more to be done. Albemarle sadly gave orders to retreat towards the Gunfleet, directing that fourteen of the best-conditioned ships draw up with the *Royal Charles* in line abreast to form a rearguard, while the more damaged vessels went ahead as best they could. The intended destination lay nearly due west of the current position, but it would be necessary to steer about W.N.W. to ensure clearance of the Galloper Sand, which lay in the way. The fleet had fought the last pass on a northwesterly heading, so aside from drawing out the rearguard, no manoeuvres were required to begin the retreat; the fleet simply continued on the same tack, swinging slightly to the west. During the withdrawal another ship was lost. Sir Robert Holmes's second, the prize fourth-rate *St. Paul* commanded by the rear-admiral's brother John Holmes, had too much water in her hold to keep up with the rest. At Albemarle's orders the crew was taken out and the ship set afire to prevent capture. The loss of the *Black Eagle* and *St. Paul*, added to the departure of the five 'better sort of ships' in the last pass, left the fleet with only thirty-four men-of-war still in company. Of those, six were so badly damaged that they would have to be sent into port. There remained only twenty-eight which could be refitted at sea for further combat.

Van Nes did not anticipate the English retreat. His fleet fought the final encounter on the starboard tack to the southeast and was thus heading away from the enemy when the pass ended. Had the Dutch realized what was happening, they could have tacked together and begun their pursuit well within fighting range; many English ships would undoubtedly have been doomed. As it happened, Van Nes had already signalled to begin tacking in succession, and he apparently felt that countermanding the order would cause too much confusion. This regrettable decision gave Albemarle a good four- or five-mile head start, which was too much ground to make up before nightfall. As the sun was setting, the leading Dutch ships came near enough to try a few long-range shots, but 'to no purpose'. The wind abruptly died soon afterwards, leaving both fleets immobile for most of the night.

The English had fought as well as anyone could have expected. The Duke of Albemarle had kept his outnumbered fleet under good control, the line being well maintained throughout. De Guiche could not help but note the 'admirable order' of the English, and felt that their discipline had saved them from annihilation. As it was, they were badly beaten, and they knew it. One had only to glance around to see the evidence: guns dismounted, sails shredded, shrouds hanging uselessly. Hulls were pocked with jagged holes, broken frames showing through the openings. The slaughter among the crews had been terrible. Blood streamed from the scuppers in some cases, as if the ships themselves were bleeding. Despite the horrors of the ordeal, nearly every account made mention of the 'infinite courage and resolution' of the common seamen. In the *Royal Charles*, there were 'twelve they spoke of that with one member cutt off, imediately had themselves bound up, & to worke againe above deckes'.

The outlook for the wounded in a battle at sea was always grim. Some ships had thirty or forty men injured on this day alone, and their crowded cockpits must have seemed like charnel houses. Ghastly sights and nauseating smells and pitiful sounds assaulted all the senses, and the lurches of the hulls and the shudders of the timbers with the broadsides added further torture to men already in agony. The surgeons did all they could with the limited means available. Unfortunately, they were powerless to relieve the suffering, for the only pain-killers were shock, unconsciousness, and death. It is noteworthy that the English navy of the Restoration period was more responsive to the plight of its injured seamen than was ever the case in other eras of the age of sail. As soon as the situation permitted, ketches were sent alongside the worst-hit ships to take out the wounded for immediate transportation ashore. This thoughtful and eminently sensible gesture may well have saved many lives.

One of the more lightly hurt victims of the day's fighting was none other than seaman Barlow:

> We had not engaged above an hour but that an unlucky shot that came from the Holens, coming through our ship's side, hit me on the hollow of my ham on the right leg, it striking me lame for the present, but I praise the Lord it was spent before it hit me, or else it would have carried my leg away, but it did me no great harm; also I had a small hurt with splinters of the ship the day before, but not much.

Barlow's injury seems to have caused him more anger than pain, and inspired a furious tirade. He had tried to resume his duties,

> but my leg swelling so that I could not go, I was forced to go down amongst the wounded men, where one lay without a leg and another without an arm, one wounded to death and another groaning with pain and dying, and one wounded in one manner and another in another, which was a sad sight to see – poor men slaughtered by the treachery of our own nation and them who lived at home at ease and wanted nothing, but grudged to see their own nation flourish, striving what they could to bring in a papist power and sending the true-hearted subjects to fight against a trouble for to be devoured, we spending our dearest blood for our King and country's honour, not thinking it too much to spend our lives for the advance and liberty of our native country, whilst our traitorous countrymen lay at home eating and drinking the fat of the land, and rejoicing at our overthrow.

It had been a very hard day.

Chapter XV

The Third Day

Th' increasing sound is borne to either shore,
And for their stakes the throwing nations fear:
Their passion double with the cannons' roar,
And with warm wishes each man combats there.

Both sides spent the night of the 2nd fishing masts and splicing ropes. The fleets lay becalmed until 3 o'clock Sunday morning, when a light breeze from the northeast finally stirred the air. An hour later Albemarle called his flag-officers aboard, and it was decided to continue the retreat. As before, fifteen of the largest and best-conditioned vessels were drawn up in line abreast as a rearguard, while the remaining nineteen were to sail ahead, keeping in line as well as possible. The English moved off as soon as it was light enough to keep station, steering approximately west by north.

The Dutch also began the day with a council-of-war. Van Nes presided in the *Eendracht*, for the *Zeven Provinciën* was still many miles astern. In the absence of the commander-in-chief, Cornelis Tromp took the opportunity to gain some measure of revenge on the Zeelanders, who had injured his pride the day before in the altercation aboard the *Walcheren*. With the death of Cornelis Evertsen the Elder now publicly acknowledged, Tromp claimed primacy over Vice-Admiral Banckert, Evertsen's successor, and accordingly demanded that the Amsterdam-Noorderkwartier squadron no longer be relegated to the least prestigious post in the rear or left wing of the fleet. Van Nes evidently thought this reasonable. He directed that the Dutch carry out the pursuit arrayed abreast with Tromp's squadron forming the right wing to the north, his own Rotterdam squadron in the centre, and the Zeelanders and Frisians on the left. Tromp's 'victory' was rather meaningless, since his ships still wore a pendant at the mizzen signifying the Third Squadron, while the Zeelanders and Frisians kept the pendant of the Second Squadron at the fore.

The Dutch came under sail about the same time as the English, who were five or six miles ahead. Off to the east the *Zeven Provinciën* struggled to catch up under a jury main topmast, but it would be many hours before de Ruyter could be close enough to resume command. Throughout the morning the wind was variable but mostly easterly, and so light that neither side was able to cover much ground. Crews took advantage of the calm to continue their repairs. The *Monck* got up a new fore topmast, having fought without one for the better part of two days. Finally, about noon, the easterly wind freshened noticeably. With that, the Dutch commanders released their fastest ships to run down the enemy, and the pursuit began in earnest.

The sight of the English fleet flying for port under wetted stunsails was undoubtedly a bitter humiliation for the Duke of Albemarle. He had engaged at a disadvantage in hopes of avoiding just such an eventuality, and now his worst fears were realized. As if his discomfiture were not already enough, the calendar provided a cruel twist of the knife: it was exactly one year to the day since Lowestoft, when the English were chasing the Dutch. The flight undoubtedly went against his stomach, but ironically, nearly every observer including his most hostile critics had little but praise for his conduct of the retreat. Sir George Carteret, for instance, averred 'that the management in the late fight was bad from top to bottom', but had to concede that 'the fight on Sunday [was] a very honourable retreat, and that the Duke of Albemarle did do well in it'.

The effectiveness of the general's dispositions became apparent shortly before 2 o'clock, when 'the best saylors' of the Dutch 'came first in parties upon him but finding it too hot service to attacque him stayd for the rest of their fleet'. The ships of the English rearguard were exclusively large and powerful vessels. They included the six surviving flagships, and the rest were second- and third-rates.* Aside from the size of the ships, Albemarle's abreast arrangement took advantage of the fact that end-on fire in seventeenth-century warships was much better astern than ahead. The Dutch could make some limited use of their large lower-deck luff guns by veering the head several points to either side, but that cost valuable ground in the pursuit. Most ships could also bring a pair of medium-calibre upper-deck guns to bear forward through ports in the bulkhead, but those ports were meant for emergencies only; the blast from the muzzles was likely to damage the rather fragile headrails and the rigging secured there. The only guns which could freely fire directly ahead were the ones on the forecastle. In Dutch ships that meant 6-pounders at best, and usually smaller. By way of contrast, English first-rates and large second-rates each had eight to ten ports with clear arcs astern. In the *Royal Charles* and *Royal Prince*, the four great 'bower' stern chasers on the lower deck were demi-cannon. Third-rates and smaller second-rates had four to six stern ports, of which the two on the lower deck contained culverins. These chase pieces were special heavily fortified guns with abnormally long barrels. The great length was intended in part to ensure that the muzzles would protrude beyond the transom timbers and thus reduce self-inflicted blast damage, but also because the English mistakenly assumed that long guns had inherently greater range. Even in guns of normal length, the fast-burning powder employed in the seventeenth century was usually expended well before the shot reached the muzzle. This meant that extra length was actually detrimental to effective range. Chasers were nevertheless cast and bored with particular care, and on shipboard, calipers were used to select the smoothest, best sized, and most nearly spherical shot which were set aside and reserved for these guns. When firing in a deliberate manner, as was the case on the 3rd of June, the gunner himself personally aimed each piece. Consequently one could expect substantially better-than-normal accuracy.

What it all added up to was that the pursuers were confronted by upwards of eighty of the best guns in the English fleet, many of them large ones and all expertly served.

---

*The rearguard, as arrayed north to south: *St. Andrew, Rupert, Monck, Fairfax, Defiance, Old James, Royal Oak, Royal Charles, Royal Prince, Royal Katherine, Lion, Unicorn, Triumph, Golden Phoenix, St. George.*

As the Dutch came up, the leading ships were subjected to a galling concentration of fire to which they could make little reply. The bulk of the Dutch fleet was too slow or too damaged to overtake the English, while the few ships with enough speed had too little forward firepower among them to make an impression. The English were able to continue on their way essentially unmolested.

Even though the Dutch found it difficult to inflict further damage, they knew they had won the battle and were already celebrating. But in war things can change quickly. The shooting had gone on for a short time, perhaps only a half-hour, when the lookouts at the crosstrees of the leading English ships discovered masts and sails on the horizon to the southwest. These presently resolved themselves into a sizeable fleet which was standing northwards. A flurry of signal guns alerted the flagship, and the lookouts of the *Royal Charles* soon had the fleet in view as well. There must have been a few anxious minutes until the identity of the ships was established; but before long the Union could be made out at the mastheads of the flagships, leaving no doubt that Rupert had returned. With that, wrote Clifford, 'in our whole fleet there was such shouting and the English holloa that the Duch men that were all along firing at us were at a little pause, however kept on after us'.

The reason for the English cheering became apparent to the Dutch at about 3 o'clock. They knew quite well whose fleet it was, for they had learned from prisoners (presumably men of the *Henry*) of Rupert's detachment. Seeing a hard-earned victory about to vanish before his eyes, Van Nes mounted a concerted effort to bring the English to action before their fleets could unite. The *Eendracht* and de Liefde's *Ridderschap* pressed forward 'to within a saker shot' of the *Royal Charles*, but the rest of the Dutch could not get close enough to help. After enduring the hail of heavy shot from the English stern chasers for some considerable time, the two unsupported vessels finally fell back to a more respectful distance. Van Nes could only watch in dismay as the space between Rupert and Albemarle steadily narrowed.

The English sailed onwards. The general steered W.S.W. to hasten the union, Rupert keeping close-hauled to the N.N.E. for the same purpose. But even as the English exulted, fate had prepared a deadly stroke. Three days of constant tacking and confused fighting out of sight of land had, as one observer put it, 'amused all our Pylotts and put em out of their reckoning'. They now had a disastrously erroneous notion of the fleet's position. When Rupert came in sight, the pilots assumed that both his squadron and their own were somewhere north of the Galloper Sand – which in fact lurked unseen squarely between them. The Galloper is a linear rise oriented roughly N.N.E.–S.S.W., with the most dangerous section being some three miles long and very narrow, about three hundred yards. At approximately 5 o'clock, the English fleet unwittingly sailed headlong into the middle of it. As luck would have it, the disabled ships at the head of the fleet were all of small or middling size. These relatively shallow-draught vessels passed safely over the sand without even being aware of it, so the first warning for the big ships in the rear came when they hit the bottom. Actually, a fifth-rate sounding ahead had discovered the sand much earlier, but her cannon shots were mistaken as the signal for the sighting of Rupert's fleet. But foreknowledge might not have helped anyway; the English could not have gone around the sand without being brought to battle, so the only escape lay straight across it. Both the *Royal Charles* and the *Royal Katherine* grounded twice, but each time came free after a few harrowing moments. Many of the other great ships struck as well, and nearly all at least felt it; the *Monck*, a third-rate, 'ran just upon it'. These ships made it through none the worse for wear, but one was less fortunate. The huge *Royal Prince*, which drew more water than any of the others, buried her keel deeply in the sand and shuddered to a halt. The rest of the English did not dare to tack in the midst of the shoal to help. Horrified though they were, they swept on to the west.

What was a bad situation now very nearly became even worse. As the Dutch approached the sand, Banckert veered south with his Zeelanders and Frisians in an obvious challenge to Prince Rupert's squadron. Rupert, with Sir Thomas Allin at his side, at first steered towards them – on a course which led directly into the sandbank. The Dutch meant 'to trepan us', Allin afterwards explained,

> because the Galloper was betwixt them and us. They thought we should have gone to them, but that I had sent our shallop to my Lord Duke to know how causes stood, who sent us word to bear towards their shot, by reason the *Prince* had grounded upon them.

The *Royal James* bore away just in time. It seems likely that Banckert had indeed hoped to lure Rupert aground, for when the English squadron returned to its original course, the Zeelanders and Frisians wore again towards the rest of their fleet. The Dutch now closed in on the stranded first-rate.

In the *Prince*, Sir George Ayscue could only stamp about in helpless fury. His ship had come to rest on a steep slope, the leadsmen measuring four fathoms on one side and only two on the other. The afternoon flood had already begun, but as the *Prince* drew twenty-two feet it would obviously take hours for the water to rise high enough to float her off. That was much too long, for the Dutch needed only a few minutes to come swarming around her. Van Nes started towards her as soon as he saw her aground, but Tromp at the head of the Dutch right wing was the first on the scene. As he came on, two of his fireship captains eagerly crowded sail to take advantage of this once-in-a-lifetime opportunity. Ayscue and his men looked forlornly for help from the English fleet, but all they could see was an unimpressive group of five fourth-rates which were beating laboriously towards them. By then the Dutch were coming up in force. The two fireships, approaching from the vulnerable blind arc at the quarter, drew near enough to be recognized by the English. At that, terrified seamen crowded around Ayscue begging him to surrender, to which he angrily retorted that he would sooner burn the ship himself, and ordered them back to their stations.* But hysteria had conquered the crew much as it had in the *Henry*; ignoring the commander's wishes, a seamen identified as 'a waterman living at Lambeth, a yellow haired man' scrambled up the topgallant shrouds and took in the admiral's flag, while others hauled down the ensign, whereupon the 'people' began to shout for quarter. Amazed

---

*In the Court of Inquiry, two seamen testified that Ayscue responded, 'Do as you will', but this was emphatically denied by other witnesses.

at this development, Tromp quickly signalled the still unignited fireships to keep clear. A boat from one of the fireships then came alongside asking the Englishmen to confirm that they had surrendered, and the seamen replied that they had. It was not a proud moment in the history of the Royal Navy; hardly a shot had been fired.

A few miles away, Albemarle's rescue efforts were half-hearted at most. In the narrative forwarded to Coventry on 8 June, he claimed that he had 'resolved to tack & releive her, but before that could be done, or any of the lesser ships (sent to her rescue) could come up shee yeilded to severall Duch ships that came to her'. That made Ayscue look rather bad, and the wording seems to have been carefully constructed to mute possible public criticism that not enough had been done to help. Another report which the General submitted immediately after the action was much different:

> The *R. Charles* and *R. Katherine* gott off immediately but the *Prince* remained fast and wee durst not tack for fear of indangering all the rest of our *fleet*, soe eight Dutch ships came towards her drawing lesse water to whom she suddenly struck her flagg and ensigne before 5 frigates which I sent to fetch off her men and set her on fire could come up.

This shows that the general had resolved *not* to tack, and the last phrase indicates that he had already written off the *Prince* as lost. There was no realistic alternative, for it would have been idiotic to take the big ships back into the shoal. The five vessels which he sent to save the crew were a futile gesture. Aside from being hopelessly inadequate to deal with the Dutch fleet, they were able to make little progress towards their objective owing to the light contrary wind and strong leeward tide. The *Prince* would have floated free on her own before they could have arrived.

The Dutch now prepared to take possession of their magnificent prize. Before they could come aboard, Lieutenant John Pearce and about eighty of the crew leapt into the boats and successfully made their escape to the English fleet. That Ayscue elected to stay behind and face captivity with his men was perhaps a gallant decision; nonetheless, he could have saved his country a great deal of embarrassment had he gone with Pearce. A distinguished veteran of nearly all the battles of the First and Second Anglo-Dutch Wars, he was now to suffer the mortification of becoming the highest ranking English sea-officer ever to become a prisoner-of-war.

Jacob Philips, flag-captain of the *Gouda*, went aboard the *Prince* and had the honour of receiving Ayscue's formal surrender. The English commander was then transferred to the *Gouda* for presentation to Sweers and Tromp, who sent him aboard a *galjoot* the next day for immediate transportation to the Netherlands. For months thereafter, stories abounded in England of the ignominious abuse to which the admiral was supposedly subjected by the Dutch. One of the most outrageous said that he was made to parade through the streets painted up like a dog with a tail attached to him. But these were fabrications invented by Arlington's propagandists. In fact, aside from relieving Ayscue of his jewelry (which was allegedly appropriated by members of Tromp's retinue), the Dutch took exceptional care to treat their prisoner with the respect befitting his rank. Their official account, published throughout Europe, described his capture as 'a great misfortune for a General who had given signal proofs of his Courage all the whole time of the fight, and who was then retiring only by order of his Admiral'. On 6 June he underwent a scrupulously polite formal interrogation by the States-General at The Hague. This was a waste of time for everyone involved, for even fluent English-speakers among the *Hoogmogenden* found Ayscue's Lincolnshire burr – perhaps thickened by nervousness – virtually unintelligible. Two days later he was taken (quietly, in a closed state carriage) to Loevestein Castle, a rural estate where he and his personal servants were confined in relative comfort for the remainder of the war.

With the English officers removed from the *Prince*, the *Gouda*'s prize party swarmed over the ship. They must have marvelled at the power of her armament, the immensity of her scantlings, and the sumptuousness of her accommodations. Even more surprising was the discovery of several exceedingly lucky survivors of the *Duivenvoorde* who had been rescued on the first day. The Dutch now rounded up the *Prince*'s crew, of whom fewer than 500 remained out of an initial complement of 620, and began to herd them into small craft which had come alongside to take them off. This proved unexpectedly difficult. As soon as the Englishmen disembarked, they casually filed to the other end of the boat and slipped back aboard the *Prince* through open gunports. Their captors repeatedly had to hunt them down all over again. Eventually tiring of the game, the Dutch hauled in the guns, shut the port lids, and loudly announced that they were about to burn the ship. At that the English sullenly showed themselves and submitted to captivity.

The Dutch pause in the vicinity of the Galloper finally allowed the *Zeven Provinciën* to catch up with the fleet, whereupon Van Nes immediately yielded the pendant of command to de Ruyter. The wind gradually came more southerly as evening approached, so the Dutch fleet beat a short distance in that direction to keep to windward of the enemy, leaving the *Prince* in the custody of Rein Pieterszoon Mars, commander of the *Fortuin* fireship. At about 7:30 the rising tide at last lifted the ship free of the Galloper, with her head to the north. But when the prize crew tried to set sail, it was found that the rudder was disabled so that her head would not swing around. This disappointing news was dispatched to de Ruyter. Shortly afterwards the now-united English fleet began working northwards along the western side of the sand, making it clear that they meant to renew the battle. With that, de Ruyter made a prearranged signal to Captain Mars to burn the prize immediately.

The commander-in-chief must have known that the order to destroy the *Prince* would be a disappointment to Cornelis Tromp, who thereby lost the chance of triumphantly leading the great trophy into the Texel. According to de Guiche, the Lieutenant-Admiral of Amsterdam rather heatedly questioned the decision in the subsequent council-of-war. But de Ruyter must have given acceptable answers, for a letter which Tromp sent to the States the next day merely related the incident without protest; 'after we had taken her, we burnt her', he laconically wrote. De Ruyter had little to say about it either; only that 'The Admiral's Ship of the White being ready to sink, we burnt her'. The authors of the States-General's account repeated the Admiral-General's explanation with only slightly more elucidation, writing that 'tho' she was afterwards got off of the Bank, yet because she was so extreamly shattered that de Ruyter thought her not in a condition to be able to follow the main body of the Fleet, he Commanded her to be burnt'.

It may be that de Ruyter was misinformed as to the condition of the ship, which was in fact not sinking and indeed in no distress at all except for the rudder. Towing her to a safer position at which makeshift repairs might have been effected, or all the way to the Netherlands if necessary, would not have been unduly difficult. Still, there was ample justification for destroying her. As the situation stood, the English lay roughly W.S.W. of the *Prince*, the Dutch holding the weather gage a little farther south. With the tide by then high enough to float the *Prince*, the English could safely cut across the sand to retake her. The Dutch could easily move north to intervene, but only at the risk of surrendering their commanding windward position. For de Ruyter to have allowed any of his ships to be endangered (or even influenced in their motions, for that matter) in defence of a mere prize would have been highly irresponsible, for the only valid objective of the States' Fleet was the defeat of the rest of the English navy. That, one supposes, is what he told Tromp. There were yet other considerations that tact perhaps forbade mentioning. The commander-in-chief undoubtedly did not wish to see a repetition of the first day's fiasco, when three captains had taken good ships into port for no apparent purpose beyond the security of their prize money. That their prizes had been sent in without his permission was itself a violation of standing orders. Furthermore, though the *Prince*'s ninety-two guns would have been most welcome to the Admiralties, no ship drawing twenty-two feet of water would ever have been suitable for employment in the Dutch fleet.

Whatever de Ruyter's reasons, Captain Mars obediently took off the prize crew and put the ship to the torch. Her drifting pyre lit up the night sky until shortly before midnight, when a powder explosion sent her to the bottom. The *Royal Prince* had been a worthy adversary of the Dutch in many a battle. She had frequently served as flagship of the fleet and was one of the world's largest warships even after fifty-six years' service. Indeed, her gilded form had become almost synonymous with English sea power. Her loss, as Barlow mournfully recorded, 'was a great grief to all the rest of the fleet, for she did more good in a fight than five or six of some others'. The shock was also keenly felt by the public. Within three days after receiving the news, the nobles of the realm were moved to petition the King to 'allow them to rebuild ye *Prince* which was lost this battle, that they may have liberty to build a ship in her place, & by her name yet bigger', and so designed 'to beare 100 guns which his Majesty is only to furnish'. The Earl of Craven led the way with a subscription of £2,000. The new *Prince* went down the ways at Chatham four years later and had an even longer career than her namesake.

Sir George Ayscue was not blamed for the disaster. It was generally accepted that the crew had forced the surrender on him, and nearly everyone felt that the situation had been hopeless anyway. Seaman Barlow's brief description of the incident seems to have been typical of the public's assessment: 'Being encompassed about with them, she was forced to strike sail and yield to them, being all alone and aground and nobody to help her'. Even Andrew Marvell, who might have torn the admiral to pieces, this time chose to sheathe his claws. He settled for a single couplet: '*But in a dark cloud cover Askue when / He quit the* Prince *t'imbarke in Loovesten*'. The King and the Duke of York were also sympathetic; Charles graciously restored Ayscue's honours on his repatriation in 1667. It is widely held that the admiral declined further service, but that was not true. In the spring of 1668 a threatened resumption of hostilities with France found him back at sea in command of the second-rate *Triumph*. At the time of his unexpected death in April 1672 he had just been appointed to the new first-rate *St. Andrew* as Vice-Admiral of the Red (which would have been third-in-command after the Duke of York and the Earl of Sandwich, there being no Admiral of the White) of the huge fleet commissioned for the Third Anglo-Dutch War.

Inevitably there were a few who never forgave either Ayscue or his crew. A man-of-war of the size and obvious national importance of the Royal *Prince*, they said, should have been defended to the last gasp. Sir Thomas Clifford was especially bitter:

> . . . the Duch with theire small frigets imeadiately made toward her attended with a fireship or two and we sent fower or five of our frigets to defend her that drew least water and we ourselves would come as neer as we durst for the sands, but to the wounder of the whole fleet we saw the flag and auntient [i.e., ancient, or ensign] struck and she yeilded when she had not herselfe either shot ten guns in her defence or received ten shot from the enimy.

He went on to describe the burning of the ship,

> which was a sensible touch to every mans heart in our fleet especially since a little resistance would have preserved her and that she was so well able to stand it out. She was like a castle in the sea and I beleive the best ship that ever was built in the world to endure battering, but she is gon and this is an ill subject to be longer upon.

Clifford was unfair in belittling the Dutch force around the *Prince*. 'Theire small frigets' included the *Gouda* of 72 guns and the *Wapen van Utrecht* of 66, not to mention the *Eendracht*. Nevertheless, his criticism may have been justified. It seems fairly certain that the quick capitulation was induced mainly by the approach of the fireships. In that respect it was perhaps unfortunate for Ayscue's reputation that his crisis occurred in the same battle as Harman's defence of the *Henry*. Both were isolated among the enemy, and both were offered essentially the same choice: surrender or burn. Harman chose the fireships and was grappled by two of them, yet he and most of the men who stayed with him lived to tell about it. Only with that incident did it begin to be realized that fireships were an overrated threat. Had the *Prince* defeated the 'branders', she would arguably have had a fair chance of surviving long enough for the united English squadrons to sail around the Galloper. The Dutch would have had a hard time reducing such a stout-timbered vessel with gunfire alone, and her lofty sides would have made boarding a difficult proposition as well. No one knows what Ayscue might have done had the decision to fight been his alone, but no heroic defence was possible unless the crew cooperated; his apparently did not. Such collapses of morale in emergencies were not unique to the *Prince* in this battle. Other ships including the *Henry* were lost or nearly lost from the same cause. It revealed all too plainly that the Restoration navy's discipline was not what it should have been, and it was to remain an insidious and unpredictable weakness for many years to come.

In London, the first indication that trouble was brewing in the North Sea came before any message arrived. The battle could be *heard*. It was not very distinct, and at first most people shrugged it off as a distant storm; but a few remembered those same muffled thumps from the day of Lowestoft the year before. Aside from the fact that the guns were audible for over a hundred miles, the seemingly capricious behaviour of the sound was one of the most perplexing mysteries of the age. One who recognized the noise right away was John Evelyn, who happened to be strolling in the garden behind his house at Woolwich on the afternoon of the 1st. 'Hearing the Greate gunns go thick off', he immediately 'tooke horse' and rode towards the Downs to find out what was going on. Nearing Deal the next morning, he encountered Lieutenant Henry Clarke of the *Hampshire*, which had come into the Downs earlier that day; Clarke was probably on his way to report the disposition of the Tangier silver and to bring the news of Prince Rupert's imminent return. Amazingly, he professed to know nothing at all about a battle, 'there being no noise, nor appearance at Deale or that Coast of any engagement'. Evelyn took over the task of delivering the message, presumably to allow Clarke to go back to his ship. That evening, the King 'greatly rejoic'd' at the news of Prince Rupert; but he too, said Evelyn, 'was astonish'd when I assur'd him they heard nothing of the Gunns in the Downes, nor the Lieutennant who landed there by five that morning'.

Samuel Pepys had similar experiences. After hearing the guns off and on all day Saturday, he met Captain William Fazeby of the *Katherine* yacht, which had just returned from Flanders. Like Evelyn, Pepys was surprised to learn that Fazeby 'saw the Duch fleet on Thursdy and ran from them; but from that hour to this hath not heard one gun, nor any news of any fight'. Two days later, Pepys and some of his friends walked at St. James's, where they

> saw hundreds of people listening at the Gravell-pits, and to and again in the park to hear the guns. And I saw a letter, dated last night, from Strowd, Governor of Dover Castle, which says that the Prince came thither the night before with his fleet. But that for the guns which we writ that we heard, it is only a mistake for Thunder; and so far as to yesterday, it is a miraculous thing that we all Friday and Saturday and yesterday did hear everywhere most plainly the guns go off, and yet at Deale and Dover, to last night, they did not hear one word of a fight, nor think they heard one gun. This added to what I have set down before the other day about the *Katharine*, makes room for a great dispute in Philosophy: how we should hear it and not they, the same wind that brought it to us being the same that should bring it to them. But so it is.

The cause of this strange phenomenon remained unknown for over two-and-a-half centuries. It was only in the 1920s that physicists showed that it occurred because sound travels faster in warm air than in cold. As a sound wave moves away from its source, it expands both outward and upward. The upper parts slow down as they enter the colder air at high altitudes. The resulting velocity differential from top to bottom bends the entire wave bodily upward and away from the earth, leaving a ring-shaped 'zone of silence' which extends from a short distance beyond the horizon out to about sixty or seventy miles. As the sound wave passes over this zone, it continues to curve upward until it reaches the top of the stratosphere at a height of about thirty miles. There, the normal temperature gradient abruptly reverses itself, the air above becoming rapidly *hotter* with greater altitude. This causes the wave to be refracted back downwards at an angle steep enough to bring it all the way to the ground. In June of 1666, Deal and Dover happened to lie in the zone of silence, while London received the 'bounce'.

On Saturday the Londoners obtained definite evidence that their ears were not deceiving them, for that morning Williamson received Sir William Clarke's dispatch of 11 a.m. Friday announcing that the Dutch fleet was in sight. 'This', said Pepys in understated fashion, 'put us at the board into a Tosse'. The Navy Office now burst into a frenzy of activity as the Commissioners hurried to make arrangements for sending off the soldiers who would allow the six ships at Sheerness to join the fleet. This should have been done days before, but apparently no one had bothered to issue the orders, the matter having not seemed important at the time. In the afternoon the King and the Duke of York went to Greenwich in their barge and climbed the hill to listen to the guns. It must have been maddening to know that a battle was in progress, and even be able to hear it, but still have no knowledge of what was happening. For the time being, no news was forthcoming, not even rumours. One piece of welcome information from elsewhere did come in earlier in the day. As Pepys recorded that night,

> All our hopes now is that Prince Rupert with his fleet is coming back and will be with the fleet this noon – a message being sent to that purpose on Wednesday last. And a return is come from him this morning, that he did intend to sail from St. Ellens point [St. Helens] about 4 in the afternoon Wednesday [a mistake for Friday], which was yesterday; which gives us great hopes, the wind being very fair, that he is with them this noon; and the fresh going-off of the guns makes us believe the same.

This theory gained further credence when Evelyn brought Lieutenant Clarke's report from the Downs.

Eyewitness accounts of the fight began to trickle in on Sunday. Spirits repeatedly soared and sagged all day as good news alternated with bad. The first was from Captain John Aylett, whose collision-damaged *Portland* had put in at Harwich Saturday morning. Letters from there said that Aylett knew of no English ships lost, but 'confidently' affirmed

> that he saw one of their Dutch ships blown up, whether a flag or not he knows not, and that another of their great ships was fired in the cabin, which was at first quenched, but afterwards broke out again and burnt down; This he says he is sure of, he affirms moreover, that he saw two others on fire, which he believed were all Dutch.

This was soon all over London. Pepys was ecstatic: 'With this good news, I home by water again, and to church in the sermon time and with great joy told it my fellows in the pew'. Bad news followed soon after. It was said that Prince Rupert had only come to Dover at 10 o'clock the night before, 'so that we are defeated of all our hopes of his help to the fleet'. Before the day was out, Carteret was already spreading the rumour that Coventry had botched the recall orders, and that Rupert,

> instead of sailing presently, he stays till 4 in the evening, and that which is worst of all – the *Hampshire*, laden with merchants money come from the Streights, set out with or but just before the fleet and was in the Downes by 5 of the clock yesterday morning – and the Prince with his fleet came to Dover but at 10 of the clock at night. This is hard to answer, if it be true.

The charges were largely unfounded; the Prince had drawn near Dover by mid-morning, but had been becalmed thereafter. Nevertheless, the suggestion put 'great astonishment into the King and Duke and Court, everybody being out of countenance'. Pepys himself took a certain perverse pleasure in Rupert's supposed failings: 'But God knows, I am heartily sorry, for the sake of the whole nation; though if it were not for that, it would not be amisse to have these high blades find some check to their presumption'. Morale revived somewhat with the arrival of Harman's letter that afternoon. Aside from his own stirring tale, he was able to confirm Aylett's claim that at least two Dutch ships had been burned, while the English had lost none that he knew of.

Monday brought more of the same. The most exciting event of the day was the arrival in London of two participants in the fight. It so happens that one of Samuel Pepys's regular conquests that year (and one with whom he had spent a 'very pleasant' session just Saturday) was a Mrs. Daniel, whose husband was currently assigned to the *Royal Charles* as a reformado. Pepys was at home early Monday afternoon when a message came saying that two men from the fleet were waiting at the office to speak to him:

> So I down, and who should it be but Mr. Daniel, all muffled up, and his face as black as the chimney and covered with dirt, pitch and tar, and powder, and muffled with dirty clouts and his right eye stopped with Okum. He is come last night at 5 a-clock from the fleet, with a comrade of his that hath endangered another eye. They were set on shore at Harwich this morning at 2 a-clock in a ketch, with about twenty more wounded men from the *Royall Charles*. They being able to ride, took post about 3 this morning and was here between 11 and 12.

He immediately took them by water to the Privy Stairs at Whitehall, 'all the world gazing upon us and concluding it to be news from the fleet'. Temporarily leaving them at Coventry's lodgings (Coventry himself being out) Pepys found the King in the park and joyously announced the seamen's tidings: Prince Rupert had returned.

> The King was mightily pleased with this news and so took me by the hand and talked a little of it – I giving him the best account I could; and then he bid me to fetch the two seamen to him – he walking into the house. So I went and fetched the seamen into the Vane-room to him, and there he heard the whole account.

Daniel and his friend apparently thought it inadvisable to say anything that might put their sovereign out of humour. They admitted that the English had retreated all day Sunday, but stressed that the Dutch 'bore toward their own coast – and we with them' after Rupert's arrival. They cheerfully lied that the fleet had by then 'taken & fired 14 of ye Enemys'. As for English losses, they carefully neglected to mention the disaster to the *Prince* or any others except for an inaccurate description of the intentional abandonment of 'ye *St. Paul* & 2 other of Our Slugg Ships' during the retreat. Their forbearance paid off handsomely: 'The King did pull out of his pocket about twenty pieces in gold, and did give it Daniel for himself and his companion, and so parted, mightily pleased with the account he did give him of the fight and the success it ended with'.

The navy's representatives at Harwich and other observers at the Gunfleet were hearing the same wildly optimistic stories that were being told in London. But they could see with their own eyes the shocking condition of the ships which had already come in, and their horrendous casualties: the *Portland* partly dismasted; the *Henry* with her charred sides and quarters; the *Anne*, *Antelope*, and *Baltimore* all terribly mauled; the *Gloucester* 'lamed'; the *Bristol* 'much battered', her captain dead; the *Loyal Subject* 'torne to pieces the Commander Capt. Fortiscue hurt in the legg & face'. The *House of Sweeds* had staggered in at Landguard Point to put ashore her wounded. Her captain, Jeffrey Dare, was himself 'very weake by cannon shott' and died soon after. The number of vessels driven into port began to reach alarming proportions early Monday morning. John Knight, a Commissioner for Sick and Wounded, sailed down the King's Channel at that time and counted twenty ships either already in the river or entering it on the flood, 'all which pretend themselves soe disabled as not to keep the sea'.

News of the carnage began to filter through to Whitehall Monday afternoon. After several such reports, an excessively cheerful letter came in from Captain Clark of the *Gloucester* reiterating that the Dutch had taken flight at Rupert's approach the previous evening. Pepys sceptically remarked, 'but all this day they have been fighting [the guns could still be heard], therefore, they did face again, to be sure'. The latest stories of shattered ships and dead captains had had a depressing effect on the Clerk of the Acts. He and a colleague

walked into the park till 9 or 10 at night, it being fine moonshine – discoursing of the unhappiness of our fleet. What it would have been if the Prince had not come in. How much the Duke [of Albemarle] hath failed of what he was so presumtuous of. How little we deserve of God Almighty to give us better fortune. How much this excuse all that was imputed to my Lord Sandwich; and how much more he is a man fit to be trusted with all these matters then these that now command, who act by nor with any advice, but rashly and without any order. How bad we are at intelligence, that should give the Prince no sooner notice of anything, but let him come to Dover without notice of any fight, or where the fleet were, or anything else; nor give the Duke any notice that he might depend upon the Prince's reserve. And lastly, of how good use all may be to check our pride and presumtion in adventuring upon hazards upon unequal force, against a people that can fight, it seems now, as well as we, and that will not be discouraged by any losses, but that they will rise again.

Following the grounding of the *Prince* and the near entrapment of Rupert's squadron, the English fleets united without further incident. Albemarle 'with some gentlemen' repaired aboard the *Royal James* to report the events of the preceding days. Rupert had already summoned his flag-officers, and the Generals now convened a council-of-war which was attended only by Allin, Myngs, Spragge, the Earl of Ossory, and possibly Clifford and Cavendish.

The council carefully considered the fleet's strength. The Duke had carried out his retreat with thirty-four ships, which the loss of the *Prince* had reduced to thirty-three. Six of the worst-damaged vessels continued on into port, the *Antelope, Gloucester,* and probably the *House of Sweeds* being among them. Only twenty-seven remained, but Prince Rupert brought a substantial force. One of his secretaries had noted in a dispatch the night before that the reinforcements would number '26 sayles of the swiftest saylors in the fleet'. These were the original twenty men-of-war and four fireships, along with the *Kent* and probably the *Hampshire*. Just before joining Albemarle, the squadron was further augmented by three fourth-rates which had sortied from the Thames: the freshly-repaired *Centurion,* along with the *Convertine* and *Sancta Maria*. The latter two were a rather odd pair in the Royal Navy. The *Convertine* was taken from Portugal during that country's brief war with England in 1650. The *Sancta Maria* was a great Venetian merchantman which Allin had taken in the Mediterranean in late 1664. Though she had had proper Venetian flags and papers, Allin had kept her because the officers and crew were all Dutch. The Venetian Senate had protested vociferously ever since, but to no avail. The various 'recruits' restored the English fleet to about fifty-two men-of-war (nearly half of them undamaged) and six fireships. This was still weaker than the Dutch, who now had some sixty-nine warships and six or seven fireships. Even so, it seemed enough to justify a final effort. As Barlow put it, the council resolved 'to set upon the Holens fleet again the next day to see what fortune would befall them, being very loath that the groat-headed Flemings should go home victorious'.

Before the action could resume, the reinforcements necessitated a reorganization of the fleet. It was agreed that the Prince's ships should form the van, since all were fast sailers and still in good condition. They would now become the White Squadron, shifting accordingly to white ensigns and vanes. Rupert then announced that he would not be rejoining Albemarle in the *Royal Charles*, but would instead personally direct the new White Squadron from the *Royal James* with a Union at the main to signify his equality with the Duke. Although the Prince had openly preferred such an arrangement all along, it must have disappointed Sir Thomas Allin, who was once more denied a squadron command. The ships were to be arrayed for battle with Myngs in charge of the van division, Rupert the centre, and Spragge the rear.

Albemarle's own squadrons also needed reorganization. The most important deficiency was settled with 'an order to Sr. Robt. Holmes to comand the squadron lately comanded by Sr. George Ayscue'. The former White Squadron had lost its last flag-officer with the capture of the *Prince*. The selection of Holmes was a high compliment, but the post was not a particularly great plum; no more than ten of Ayscue's original twenty ships were still in condition to fight and possibly as few as seven or eight. Barlow confirms that Sir Robert's *Defiance* 'wore the white flag on the Monday', though the ships may have worn red ensigns to avoid confusion with Rupert's vessels. Where the squadron was placed in the line is unknown. Another adjustment is suggested by at least two references in Dutch accounts to the presence of an English 'Admiral of the Blue' on the fourth day. Teddiman had to this point commanded the Blue Squadron with his flag at the fore because Smith, the intended Admiral of the Blue, had been expected at any moment. Prince Rupert would now have been able to report that Smith could not arrive for some days yet. In view of that, it seems likely that the Generals allowed Teddiman to temporarily fly his flag at the main, where it would be more easily visible to the rest of his squadron.

Besides the reorganization, the Generals also took the opportunity to fill (or rather attempt to fill) two vacancies among the captains. One was for the famous old second-rate *St. George*, in which Captain John Coppin had been killed. Both Rupert and Albemarle thought highly of the Earl of Ossory, 'who had a mind to doe a brave action upon Monday', and so they inquired as to whether he might be interested in becoming a sea-captain. Though Ossory accepted with alacrity, the appointment did not turn out as well as either he or the Generals had hoped. According to Clifford, who accompanied the young soldier to the *St. George*,

> he tooke possession of her sunday night but we found her in a condition totally unserviceable. She could not make saile either with foremast or mainemast and therefore my lord intinding by the command to doe more than ordinary, finding it impossible to doe so much as others in ships better conditioned, prudently declind goeing in her in the great fight and so returns to the R. C. She was also leakey in her powder roome and had very few rounds left in her. My Lord was the most pleasd man with the command that ever I saw in my life upon the first view of the ship before her defects and wants were seen.

The other vacancy resulted from a disciplinary action. Captain Henry Teddiman, elder brother (or perhaps cousin) of Vice-Admiral Teddiman and until then the respected commander of the second-rate *Unicorn*, had inexplicably misbehaved in some way during the fight. The Generals sacked him on the spot. He was peremptorily ordered to go aboard the *Victory* and place himself in the custody of Sir Christopher Myngs. For his replacement Albemarle selected Mark Harrison, an experienced former Commonwealth officer who had been serving without command as a reformado in one of the flagships. Samuel Pepys commented a few days later that 'Old Teddiman . . . did deserve to be turned out this fight'; but Pepys also 'heard Sir W. Coventry say that the Duke of Albemarle put in one as bad as he in his room – and one that did as little'. This was all too true; Harrison lasted less than a week. His performance on the last day of the battle being disapproved, he was sent ashore in favour of George Batts from the *Hampshire*. The *Unicorn* seems to have been a graveyard for reputations that summer. Batts himself was put out in disgrace after the St. James's Day Fight in July, though the Duke of York vainly defended him as 'a very stout man, all the world knew'.

It was nearly dusk when the council-of-war adjourned. By then the wind was mostly south. Although the tide had probably risen high enough for the English to have crossed the Galloper without touching, the Generals wanted nothing more to do with it. They took the only available alternative, heading N.N.E. against the flood to round the north head of the sand, 'by which meanes', wrote Jordan, 'ye Enemy gott ye wind'. De Ruyter led the States' Fleet to the east soon afterwards. He too needed to gain sea room, for low water early the next morning would make the Galloper dangerous even for the Dutch. Both sides continued to repair their damages long into the night; it was obvious to everyone that the morrow's contest would resolve the issue once and for all.

Chapter XVI

The Fourth Day

Borne each by other in a distant line,
The sea-built forts in dreadful order move:
So vast the noise, as if not fleets did join,
But lands unfix'd and floating nations strove.

Monday the 4th of June was a cloudy, misty day, with a brisk wind between S.W. and S.S.W. The fleets had stood east during the night under easy sail, leaving the Galloper about twenty miles astern. Their courses had diverged slightly so that by dawn they had temporarily lost contact with each other. Rupert and Albemarle altered course to the southeast, and their scouts soon found the Dutch to the south.

When the English came in sight, de Ruyter called his flag-officers aboard to discuss yet another rearrangement of the fighting order. According to an eyewitness,

> The L. Admiral Banckert formed, with the Zeelanders and Frisians, the left wing of the fleet; L. Admiral Van Nes and Vice-Admiral de Liefde sailed forward on the right wing; the L. Admiral-General de Ruyter was in the middle; and the L. Admirals Tromp and Meppel had the rearguard.

This rather ambiguous description may mean that Tromp was actually in the centre instead of the rear, though it seems more likely that de Ruyter was between Van Nes and Banckert, Van Nes in the van and Banckert in the centre as *de Ruyter's* left wing, with Tromp as the proper rearguard. This was the order de Ruyter had installed on Saturday, and English narratives contain evidence that it was also used on Monday. At one point early in the fight Albemarle launched a heavy assault against what he said was 'part of their Reare'; the one vessel destroyed in the attack belonged to Tromp's squadron and Tromp himself along with many of his ships was driven out of line. If this interpretation is correct, then the order of divisions and commanders would have been thus: Van Nes, de Liefde, and then de Ruyter; the Zeeland-Friesland squadron in the centre with De Vries leading and then Banckert followed by the rear division now under Rear-Admiral Cornelis Evertsen the Younger; and Tromp's squadron in the rear with Meppel's Noorderkwartier division leading, Tromp's own Amsterdam division next, and the Amsterdam division formerly commanded by Van der Hulst at the tail end of the line. Reinstatement of this order must have been yet another disappointment to Tromp, who was thereby relegated to his original position after having usurped the right wing in the Admiral-General's absence on Sunday.

After the meeting with the flag-officers all of the captains were called aboard to hear an impassioned oration from de Ruyter, who exhorted them with both solicitous encouragement and the direst threats. It undoubtedly made a deep impression, for various versions and excerpts were recorded in several accounts. The officers now returned to their ships to put the fleet in order. At some point in the morning, probably immediately after the council-of-war, Cornelis Tromp removed himself from the *Gouda* into the 66-gun *Wapen van Utrecht* commanded by Hendrik Gotskens, who had already taken in Colonel Van Ghent on the first day. The timing of Tromp's change of ships is a minor controversy. Both Brandt and the States-General's account say that he was with Sweers until late in the fight, but the dateline of a letter of the morning of the 4th which Tromp wrote to the States 'in haste' just before the fighting began proves that he was already in the *Wapen van Utrecht*. Though the letter gives no explanation for the shift, a good reason is readily available: Isaac Sweers was the natural successor to the division formerly led by the now-deceased Van der Hulst, and he could hardly exercise that function with the squadron commander aboard the *Gouda*. One supposes that Tromp arranged for his new flagship during the council-of-war. His squadron had no suitably large Amsterdam ships left, and he could not have taken over the *Wapen van Utrecht* (a member of de Ruyter's division) without the commander-in-chief's permission.

While the Dutch completed their preparations, the English were rapidly approaching. Allin's journal records that

> By the light of the morning the Dutch fleet was got out of sight. We standing off to find them spied them about 5 leagues off from us, the wind at S.S.W. We made their whole body upon our weather bow and by 8 oclock we came up nigh and they having the weather gage put their fleet into order and came into a line all to the windward of us. Our frigates that were then ahead lay by to stay for our fleet to come up the Dutch that thought they were in good order. Next Sir Chris. Myngs put himself and his division into a line and led the van, next the Prince in the *R. James* with his division followed and next Sir Edward Spragge, and so the rest of the fleet, which came up in very good order.

The Dutch now filled on the port tack and stood in to begin the engagement. Allin continued, 'We made sail close by a wind having our starboard tacks aboard, the wind S.W., and the enemy bore up presently to fall into the middle of our line with part of their fleet'. As might be gathered from Allin's wording most of the Dutch did not get very near at this time. They had probably intended to bear down abreast, but they had started too late and the opposing lines were perhaps not quite parallel, so the advance became somewhat oblique. Consequently only a small portion, presumably the rear, was able to get in range. The fleets otherwise very nearly missed each other completely the first time by. Albemarle related that 'At the first encounter, wee being to leeward of them standing to the Eastward at the first passe, wee could not come in to fire a gunn being too much to leeward'. He said that it was only on the second pass that the English 'got close to the Dutch'. This was confirmed by Clifford: 'we made what hast we could to them and they stayed for us till we came at a convenient distance and then made toward us; they having the wind kept at a greater post from us then we would have bin willingly at'.

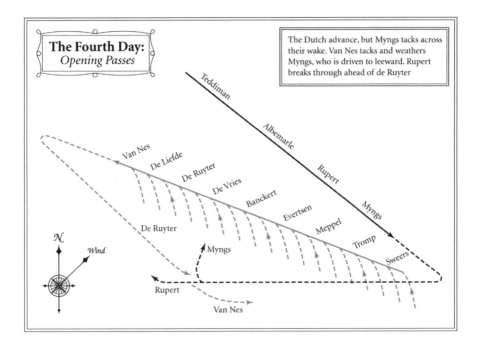

The Fourth Day: *Opening Passes*

The Dutch advance, but Myngs tacks across their wake. Van Nes tacks and weathers Myngs, who is driven to leeward. Rupert breaks through ahead of de Ruyter

Teddiman

Albemarle

Rupert

Van Nes

De Liefde

De Ruyter

De Vries

Banckert

Evertsen

Myngs

Meppel

Tromp

De Ruyter

Sweers

Myngs

N

Wind

Rupert

Van Nes

The rather wide approach of the Dutch gave the English an opportunity to steal the initiative 'and therefore', Clifford went on, 'our braver commanders impatient of it bore in upon them'. One could easily get the impression that this was a precipitous and even rash action, but it seems to have been an organized manoeuvre which Prince Rupert may well have prearranged with his subordinates. In the passes on Saturday the English had usually waited until the fleets were entirely clear of each other before tacking to renew the fight. This time the head of the line came around immediately after the Dutch rear had gone by. The 'True Narrative', based in part on Allin's report, says that the Dutch bore up 'to fall into ye middle of our line with part of their fleet, at which as soon as Sr. Chr. Mings had their wake hee tacked & stood in & then the whole line tacked in ye Wake of him & stood in'.

The English attack was led by one of the best officers in the fleet. Sir Christopher Myngs was a former Cromwellian tarpaulin, one of the few who was a favourite of both Rupert and Albemarle. He enjoyed telling people that he came from humble origins, that his mother was a hoyman's daughter and his father a shoemaker. Actually, 'shipowner's daughter' and 'prosperous shoe merchant' may have been better descriptions. Despite being short and rather slight of build, Myngs was a magnetic and inspiring leader. He displayed a humanitarian attitude in his approach to discipline which was almost unique among his contemporaries. He was one of a tiny handful of officers (Kempthorne being another) who voted for clemency in the Nixon court-martial in 1665, and was himself subjected to ridicule for refusing to hang deserters. Not surprisingly, his own men were among the most loyal in the fleet, following him faithfully from ship to ship. Myngs acquired much of his 'great renown' between 1655 and 1664 in a series of expeditions to the Spanish West Indies. By sheer force of character he moulded a seemingly ungovernable rabble of planters, pirates, and cutthroat soldiers of fortune into a formidable weapon of seaborne guerrilla warfare. It was he who taught Henry Morgan and the Jamaica buccaneers the hit-and-run amphibious tactics that eventually made them the scourge of the Caribbean. Now, in the culminating – and final – act of his career, Myngs led the English fleet into battle from the quarterdeck of the *Victory*.

After tacking, Myngs probably got off a few broadsides at the Dutch rear as he went by. However, his objective was to gain the wind by passing to the south of the whole of the Dutch, and their rear merely happened to be in range when he crossed under their sterns. Leaving them to continue on their way, he beat to the west close to the wind. But the Dutch soon recognized the threat; Van Nes leading the van tacked to the S.E. to head off the English and the fleets raced for the weather gage head to head, both straining to windward. When they met, the result was a wild and violent clash. The States-General's account said that 'the Hollanders came powring with the Three Squadrons of their Fleet upon the Enemies Navy, in three several Places, forcing a Passage through them by which means some English ships were separated from the rest'. Their opponents at the same time were making directly opposite claims in similar language. The English, said Clifford, 'bore in upon them to goe throu and throu of which were Sr. Chris. Minns and Sr. Rob. Holmes in severall places that had each many brave seconds and they had successe enough, for by it we divided theire fleet and did them much mischiefe'.

Participants recalled many details of this incredible pass. Myngs had won a similar race for the wind to begin the fighting at Lowestoft, but this time he failed. Van Nes cut across his bow, and the *Victory* came up against a crashing wave of broadsides from the lee side of the next Dutch division. When Myngs tried to force a passage through them he found his way blocked by de Liefde's sturdy *Ridderschap*, a new ship of 66 guns. The Dutch reported that the two passed so close 'that the yardarms were only just clear of each other'. Each loosed a mighty salvo of roundshot, chain, and case, and a rattling volley of musketry from the massed marines. The men crowding the decks were mowed down in both ships; Myngs himself was shot through the cheeks with a musket ball. The *Victory* staggered on past several more opponents, receiving the first broadside from each ship within pistol range. Myngs stayed on deck, using his hands to hold his mangled face together, until a second musket ball pierced his neck and lodged in his shoulder. With that the seamen insisted on carrying him below despite his protests. His place was immediately taken by Lieutenant John Narbrough, but by then the ship was disabled. Narbrough sheered away to the north to refit the rigging, accompanied by several other ships of the van division that gathered around to protect their flagship.

Jordan sourly noted that the sight of the *Victory* and her companions falling off to leeward 'gave ye Enemy noe small encouragement'. The Dutch had in fact suffered severely as well, for the *Victory*'s cannon-of-seven had ruined the *Ridderschap*. Partially dismasted, completely unmanageable, and drifting helplessly to leeward, she was nakedly vulnerable when the *Royal James* drew up with two fireships under her lee. Prince Rupert was at that point intent on breaking through the Dutch line. Neither he nor the other captains left their stations to engage the damaged flagship, but he did unleash one of the fireships. This vessel successfully rammed the *Ridderschap*. With flames threatening to envelop the ship, the two light frigates of de Liefde's division came rushing down to assist. In what must have been a superb display of seamanship, the 34-gun *Nijmegen* under Willem Boudewijnsz. van Eyk towed the fireship away. In the process a Dutch fireship somehow got in the way and collided with the now-blazing English vessel; their rigging entwined by grapnels, both fireships were soon 'reduced to ashes'. The only fireship attached to de Liefde's division, and thus the likely victim of the accident, was the *Rotterdam* under the eventually much celebrated Jan van Brakel. His 'opponent' was either John Kelsey's *Little Unicorn* or the *Greyhound* under William Flawes; these were the two which had followed the *Royal James* into action. The *Ridderschap* now departed the scene without delay, probably under tow by the other attending frigate, the 36-gun *Wapen van Utrecht* commanded by Eland du Bois. When the ship was out of danger, de Liefde sent her to the Netherlands under jury rig and shifted his flag to the *Wapen van Utrecht*. In this diminutive flagship he soon returned to the fight, though he had ended up so far to leeward that he never regained his station in the main body.

Meanwhile Prince Rupert came into action against the rest of de Liefde's ships and the leading units of de Ruyter's division. The Prince had hardly dispatched the fireship towards the *Ridderschap* when a Dutch *brander* suddenly emerged from the smoke

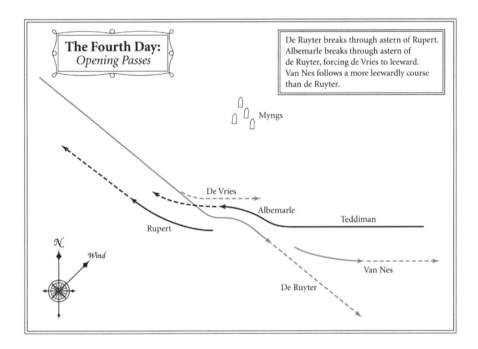

making for the *Royal James* herself. At the last instant Rupert's remaining fireship adroitly 'got betwixt that danger and us', and sacrificed herself to the flames to save the flagship. Thus the seldom-seen spectacle of fireship burning fireship occurred twice in the same battle, simultaneously and only a few hundred yards apart. The Dutch claimed that an English warship became entangled with the pair nearest the *Royal James*. If so she must have broken free, for no English men-of-war were burned this day.

Prince Rupert now plunged into the Dutch fleet seeking a way through. He met fierce resistance, being 'in this Passe . . . environed with as many dangers as the enemy could apply unto him'. Aside from the fireship attack,

> they raked him fore & aft, plyed him on both sides . . . & tho his Highness received very considerable prejudice in that difficult passage in his Masts & rigging yet hee answered the shot they powered on him with as many close returns which the enemy felt & carried away with them.

Despite inflicting heavy damage the Dutch gave way before the greater bulk of the *Royal James*. Once the gate was open the ships astern of Rupert began to pour through. According to the English official account, 'the Prince thought fit to keep the Wind & soe led the whole Line through the middle of the enemy, the Generall with the rest of the fleet following in good order'. Actually, the breakthrough was by no means as surgically precise as the 'True Narrative' would have it. Clifford's statement that the penetrations occurred 'in severall places' shows that the Dutch repeatedly closed the gap, only to have the English find other openings farther along the line.

The initial break must have come ahead of de Ruyter, for the *Zeven Provinciën* was reportedly to leeward for a brief period. The Admiral-General quickly fought back through to windward, but then a major break occurred a little astern of him. Spragge, Jordan, Albemarle, and Holmes all swarmed through more or less together. The next Dutch division, the Frisians under Tjerk Hiddes de Vries, were forced to bear up to leeward of all the English. Soon afterwards the tables were turned when Banckert and his Zeelanders found an opening towards the end of the Red Squadron and promptly drove through to windward. They were followed by Meppel's Noorderkwartier contingent, which formed the leading division of Tromp's squadron. This left Teddiman's and Utber's ships piling up against the lee side of the Dutch line, and the whole of the Blue Squadron was thrown into confusion.

This was a dangerous moment for the English, for Tromp's two remaining divisions were now coming up. The advantage was soon reversed, however, by a remarkable manoeuvre which Rupert and Albemarle carried out, each acting independently. As Rupert explained it, 'As soone as the Prince came on the other side and stood out soe as hee would weather the end of their fleete hee tacked and ye Generall tacked at the same tyme and bore up to the ships to Leeward, and the Prince followed him'. How this came about has never been very clear. Prince Rupert, who always preferred to lead the line, probably tacked from the van (in succession) as soon as he was clear of the Dutch rear. Simultaneously, Albemarle must have recognized that the Blue Squadron was in trouble, and also saw an opportunity to do great harm to the isolated enemy divisions to leeward of him. If Rupert's wording is accurate, Albemarle apparently tacked from

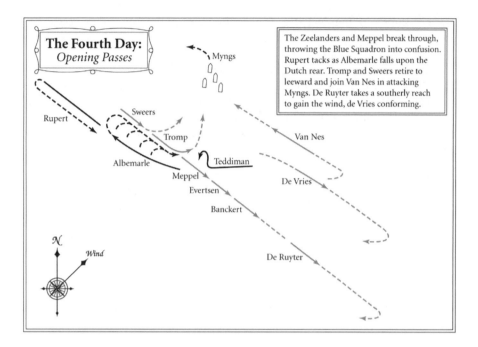

The Fourth Day: *Opening Passes*

The Zeelanders and Meppel break through, throwing the Blue Squadron into confusion. Rupert tacks as Albemarle falls upon the Dutch rear. Tromp and Sweers retire to leeward and join Van Nes in attacking Myngs. De Ruyter takes a southerly reach to gain the wind, de Vries conforming.

Myngs

Rupert

Sweers

Tromp

Van Nes

Albemarle

Teddiman

Meppel

De Vries

Evertsen

Banckert

N

Wind

De Ruyter

the rear (that is, together, as Penn had done at Lowestoft) and subsequently bore up to attack the Dutch in his lee. Alternatively, it may be that he simply wore to the other tack, inducing the rest to conform by means of the blue flag at the mizzen – Article Seven of the Fighting Instructions, the ubiquitous 'beare up into his wake or graine' provision. Albemarle himself gave no information other than that he 'fell upon part of their Reare'. However it happened, the Red Squadron came about in a body and now 'stood along' on the same tack as the Dutch to leeward, while Rupert's squadron trailed behind a little more to windward in a good position to deter the rest of the Dutch from tacking to support their rear.

As soon as the Red Squadron came about, the English sent in a fireship, probably James Coleman's *Hound* of Jordan's division. Albemarle reported that she fired two enemy ships, they presumably having fallen foul of each other. One was the 46-gun *Landman* commanded by Pieter Uyttenhout of Amsterdam; the ship burned and blew up, killing about 180 men out of 230 aboard, including Uyttenhout. That another vessel was involved is confirmed by the Comte de Guiche, who assumed that both were destroyed; in fact, only the *Landman* succumbed. The more fortunate second vessel may have been Sweer's *Gouda*, for it is known that Sweers was forced to shift his flag to the 50-gun *Gouden Leeuwen* during the fight. The *Gouda* afterwards had to have all her spars replaced, and some of the damage might well have been caused by fire.

With the Red Squadron sailing alongside, Tromp had no hope of following Meppel to windward. The Blue Squadron must have been directly ahead of him. Having been separated from the Noorderkwartier division he can have had no more than twelve to fourteen ships with him including frigates, for many of the Amsterdam vessels had gone into port on the previous days. Overwhelmingly outnumbered, he had no choice but to fall away to leeward.

Although both sides gained notable successes during the opening engagement, the English clearly had the better of it. Rupert and Albemarle were so proud of themselves for the breakthroughs and the subsequent manoeuvre (however fortuitously it may have happened) that they afterwards inserted a new article in the Fighting Instructions making it the preferred method for attacking an enemy to windward. Dated 18 July, it specified what amounted to a re-enactment of the whole pass:

> In case ye Enemy hath ye winde of us, and wee have Searoom, then wee are to keep ye wind as close as wee can ly untill such time as wee see an opportunity by gaining their wake to divide their Fleet; And if ye vann of our Fleet finde they have ye wake of any part of them, then they are to tack and stand in to strive to divide ye Enemy's body; And that Squadron that shall pass first being come to ye other side are to tack again, & ye midle Squadron is to bear up [wear] upon that part of ye Enemy so divided, which ye last is to second either by bearing down to ye Enemy, or by endeavouring to keep off those that are to windward, and shall be lost for ye service.

When Tromp and Sweers withdrew to leeward, the guns briefly fell silent with both fleets lying in great disorder. The Comte de Guiche felt that the English

> were very fortunate in that our fireships were so mismanaged that they burned themselves without harming them, while on their side they burned two of our ships in passing through our line, which they did with all their fleet, except four or five separated ships [the *Victory* and her companions] of which we gained the wind by the head, by crowding sail. This movement gave a very bizarre face to affairs; for all were found to be separated. The English were like us, on one side and the other.

The opponents now struggled to put themselves back in order for the next bout. 'In a little', continues de Guiche,

> the English were rallied: for, at whatever distance & whatever difficulty the spacing of our divided squadrons may have posed for their rallying, in less than an hour they were together, & reformed their line with the same order and the same discipline as if they had not yet fought.

The main difficulty for the English would have been getting the Blue Squadron back into line. The Dutch had greater problems:

> Our general could have had near him or of those which conformed to his manoeuvre, 35 to 40 ships. The rest were far away, with M. Tromp and the admiral of the Frisians, de Vries, who had a great part in all our success, and with Van Nes, who could have kept with us, but who had taken the decision, with 14 or 15 sail, to pursue those 3 or 4 ships of the white flag that I have told you we had passed by the head, instead of keeping with his admiral against the greater of the enemies. M. Tromp had lost the wind, and therefore he had been forced to fall back towards Van Nes.

Why Van Nes decided to chase Myngs to leeward is nowhere explained, but it is not hard to imagine how it happened. After weathering the White Squadron he must have tried to keep in range of the rest of the English, steering due east along their line. At the same time de Ruyter, Banckert, and Meppel had followed a different course. That much is apparent from the report of the States-General, which said that after the great breakthroughs, 'De Ruyter caused a motion to be made to the Southward, with design to charge the Enemy again, who did the same on their side'. In other words, the opposing main bodies (both now on the starboard tack, the English a few miles astern of de Ruyter) kept as southerly a course as they could, hoping to gain the weather gage for the next pass. That left Van Nes well to leeward of the rest of the fleet. Having thus inadvertently taken himself practically out of the fight, he obviously decided to make the best of the situation by going after the only enemies immediately available – the *Victory* and her loyal consorts. Very shortly afterwards or perhaps even simultaneously, Tromp's retreat from the Red Squadron carried the Amsterdam divisions to the same area.

The result was that Lieutenant Narbrough found himself with plenty of unwanted company on the lee side of the battle. Van Nes and Tromp together must have numbered upwards of twenty-five ships; but much to the amazement of the Dutch, the little cluster of English vessels steadfastly refused to flee and instead manoeuvred gamely to rejoin their own forces. This they could not do because the rest of their fleet kept close to the wind. Even so, they did survive the battle, and their constant twists and turns kept a major portion of the Dutch fleet occupied for many hours. Narbrough (phonetically spelled 'Norbrook' by most of his contemporaries) was enthusiastically applauded for his performance. The Generals rewarded him with command of the fourth-rate *Assurance* after the battle and marked him up for greater things in the future. Seven years later he was a knighted admiral with a successful career still ahead of him. The conjunction of Van Nes with the Amsterdam divisions, incidentally, gives a ready explanation for one of the minor oddities of the action: how Isaac Sweers was able to shift his flag from the damaged *Gouda* to the *Gouden Leeuwen* – a ship that belonged to Van Nes's division, originally at the opposite end of the line.

Another group of Dutch ships had also been separated. Tjerk Hiddes de Vries and the Friesland division had been forced to leeward in the initial breakthroughs. Left in an even more northerly position than Van Nes, de Vries reacted differently. Ignoring the sideshow around the *Victory*, he devoted his efforts to rejoining de Ruyter in the main body and thus beat to windward at every opportunity. Eyewitnesses stated that de Ruyter himself had no more than thirty-five to forty ships still in company, and that was probably optimistic. He had parts of all three squadrons: a few ships from his own and de Liefde's divisions and most of the Noorderkwartier and Zeeland contingents. Of the Zeelanders, the States-General's account says that Rear-Admiral Cornelis Evertsen the Younger (the son of Jan Evertsen) was among the flag-officers left to leeward. On the other hand, a report from Zeeland after the fight placed him to windward with Banckert and de Ruyter, which seems more probable. Even with Evertsen present, the commander-in-chief may well have had as few as thirty-two or thirty-three ships at this time, while the English line still numbered about forty-eight.

But the Dutch retained one notable advantage. As de Guiche explained, 'fortune willed that our greatest body, which followed our admiral, kept to windward; & that the greatest body of the English ships, who were in the same way attached to the suite of their admiral, remained to leeward'. This had probably come about because part of the English had briefly veered north in attacking Tromp, and the rest would have had to bear up to the leewardmost ships in order to re-form the line. De Ruyter at the same time had steadily pushed southeast close-hauled. By that means the Admiral-General had regained the weather gage, and he did not intend to give it up again. 'This', de Guiche rightly added, 'was the origin of our salvation, and their ruin'.

De Ruyter now came to the port tack and made towards the English, who were already following the starboard tack. The main bodies soon converged again to begin a series of sweeping end-to-end passes that consumed all of the late morning and early afternoon hours. Albemarle claimed that in the first of them, the English again 'divided them into three or four parts'; but this is not supported by other accounts. The Dutch squadrons had already been separated in the initial engagement, and it is fairly clear that the English now did nothing more than sail between two of the parts, de Ruyter on one side and de Vries on the other. The Frisians worked to windward as best they could while the fleets were tacking in the intervals, and after the second or third of the midday passes they succeeded in rejoining de Ruyter.

Sir Joseph Jordan's account of this stage of the action mentions that 'Sometimes wee had ye wind apart of them [presumably meaning de Vries], other whiles they fought, and wee ye like, in a halfe moone'. The half moon would have occurred when the two close-hauled fleets met not on reciprocal courses, but at a shallow angle. The leading ships of both forces had a natural tendency to swing slightly to leeward after the initial contact to bring their broadsides to bear on the nearest opponents, producing a broad curve in the lines. Jordan also noted rather cryptically that he 'supposed we lamed them most when they had ye wind of us'. It is known that the breeze was fresh enough to heel the ships considerably, and he may have meant that it sometimes interfered with the leeward broadsides, as it had on Friday.

Neither side accomplished anything of consequence during the midday passes. De Ruyter had no intention of becoming involved in a close engagement while his strength was so seriously depleted. It was one thing for an English fleet with its massive ordnance to fight against numbers, but another entirely for his own much lighter vessels. De Guiche says of the main body that 'we kept at a considerable distance. The English, on their side, kept as near as was possible for them; but we tacked about continually, & took the same care to stay apart from them as they did to approach us'. The English said much the same thing. By the 'True Narrative',

> wee stood along backward & forward, the enemy being some to Leeward & some to Windward of us; which course was 4 times repeated, the enemy always keeping the greatest part of their fleet to ye Windward, but still at so much distance as to bee able to reach our sayles & rigging with their shot & to keep themselves out of the reach of our guns, the only advantage they thought fit to take upon us at that time.

Allin wrote that at one point the Dutch to windward 'having passed us by with firing their guns at such distance as not to prejudice us, we scorned to fire at them'.

Some of the English had another reason for holding their fire: magazines and shot-lockers were badly depleted after so many days' fighting, and the shortage of ammunition was becoming serious. The English had originally been supplied with a standard allotment of forty rounds per gun, or enough for only eighty broadsides. Shortly before the fleet sailed the Generals had ordered the allowance increased to fifty rounds per gun, but many ships including the *Royal Charles* were found to have too little magazine space to safely accommodate the additional powder. Those vessels were now severely handicapped. The Dutch do not seem to have complained of this problem, so perhaps they carried more.

During the long-range passes de Ruyter displayed remarkable patience and for-bearance. From what later transpired it is clear that he was waiting, no doubt with growing irritation, for the Dutch divisions to leeward to rejoin the main action, which they finally did. De Guiche, showing his usual contempt for Van Nes, cynically professed that he did not know whether the Rotterdam commander was brought back by Tromp, or whether the two of them were drawn back fortuitously in their efforts to prevent Narbrough from rejoining the English. By whatever means, about twenty-five ships under Tromp, Van Nes, de Liefde, Jan van Nes, and Sweers began to come into action against the lee side of the English line during the third of the indecisive passes sometime around 3 o'clock. The English soon split into two separate bodies. Albemarle, Holmes, and Teddiman, along with Spragge's division of the White, together comprising thirty-seven ships or thereabouts, concentrated on the enemies to leeward. Rupert kept a little to windward with about ten ships of the White Squadron to ward off de Ruyter, who was still more to windward and who seemed to the English to have no interest in further close combat. In this the English mis-construed their enemy's intentions, but some among the Dutch were guilty of the same error. De Guiche, for instance, believed the English were concerned only to preserve their order and tire their opponents. That was anything but true, for the Duke of Albemarle was in fact impatient to conclude the action once and for all – before both time and his ammunition ran out.

The fleets drew apart and 'rallied' again, the English coming to the starboard tack and their opponents to the port. Now Albemarle launched what he hoped would be the decisive blow. He closed to within musket distance of Tromp and Van Nes, 'plying them very sharply with our Leeward guns in passing'. Caught by the English line at close range, the outnumbered and outgunned Dutch divisions to leeward were soon in disarray. As he had earlier in the day, Albemarle preceded his advance with a fireship, this time Andrew Ball's *Happy Entrance* which had just arrived from Harwich. According to the English, Ball had the good fortune 'to fire a Holland ship of 70 peices of Ordnance', but in fact his intended target, Van Nes's *Eendracht*, narrowly escaped. Nevertheless, the *Happy Entrance* undoubtedly increased the confusion among the Dutch. Albemarle's men-of-war followed her in and, said Clifford, 'fell so after them in the reare that in plaine terms those that were to Leeward of us in dividing of their fleet set all the saile they could and began to run', the English giving chase 'and picking up some of theire lame geese'.

Teddiman's *Royal Katherine* had a major role, 'having given Trump himself such a broadside as was hardly ever given to any ship'. The States-General's narrative admitted that Tromp

> and some others of his Squadron, after he had maintained a long and furious Fight, found himself reduced into so pitiful a Condition, that he was forced to retire out of the Fray, to refit and repair his Damages, with Design to return again, as soon as was possible to the Charge.

Tromp never did get back into action. Another Amsterdam ship, the 46-gun *Dom van Utrecht* commanded by Jacob Willemsz. Broeder, lost her mainmast over the side and could not escape. When the fearsome batteries of the *Royal Charles* loomed alongside, Broeder's crew meekly hauled down their colours. Dutch reports do not admit to any other vessels surrendering, though the English insisted that 'several' of them 'struck their Ensignes, & came by the Lee in token of submitting themselves to ours'. Clifford even avers that a Dutch captain was taken prisoner, but this seems impossible since Broeder never left the *Dom van Utrecht* and the Dutch afterwards found no captains missing except those killed. The truth of the various claims may never be established; still, there is no doubt that a number of disabled vessels were left wallowing under the guns of the English. As was his usual policy Albemarle had no intention of taking possession of them, but he complained afterwards that 'our Captaines that comanded the nimblest frigots did not doe their duty in destroying them'. Despite this failure, Albemarle's attack had overwhelmed the leeward portions of the Dutch fleet; an English victory seemed certain.

Three miles to windward, de Ruyter looked on with dismay. He had been waiting hours for Tromp and Van Nes to get back into action, but he could hardly have anticipated that they would be so utterly routed in a matter of minutes. He later 'confessed that at this point he thought the battle was lost'. Uncertain whether emergency action would help or merely make things worse, he consulted Banckert, whose ship happened to be nearby. The doughty Zeelander instantly shouted back that they must attack at once with everything they had. Thus encouraged, de Ruyter waited only long enough for the White Squadron to pass on to the east and then wore across Rupert's wake, making straight for Albemarle.

When the Duke saw this force bear down from windward, he ceased chasing Tromp and Van Nes and tacked to the west in the belief that de Ruyter would pass head to head to reunite with the shattered leeward divisions. It is apparent that the English thought their 'defeated' opponents were trying to escape. It is also apparent that Albemarle's exhausted forces were quite prepared to let them go. It consequently came as a great surprise when, in Clifford's words, the Dutch 'gave the Duke of Albemarle's Squadron noe breath at all but tack[ed] immeadiately againe upon us'. De Ruyter thereby declined the head-on pass and instead bore in on the same reach as the English to very close range, broadsides roaring. Only then did the English realize that they were facing a serious attack.

The unexpected onslaught must have had a daunting psychological effect, for some of Albemarle's captains lost their nerve. As Clifford indignantly noted, most of our owne frigets to avoyed the shock runs to leeward and shelter themselves under the *Royall Charles*; scarce any but the *Defiance* [Holmes] diverted the enimy from powring theire whole broadsides upon us, but we bore it well enough though at this tyme very much disabled in our rigging and masts which indeed was the only ayme of the Duch for the most part placing theire shot above our hulls.

Although many captains may well have performed poorly at this juncture, there were others besides Holmes who stood by the flagship. Jennings of the *Ruby*, Sanders of the *Sweepstakes*, and Chicheley of the *Fairfax* certainly did so, for all three were praised afterwards for their support. A brave act was also committed possibly at this time by John Wilmot, Earl of Rochester, a volunteer in Spragge's *Dreadnought*. One of the few courtiers tolerated in Rupert's and Albemarle's fleet, Rochester's presence was permitted by the Generals because of the courage he had shown at Bergen. Now he made himself useful again:

> Sir Edward Spragge not being satisfied with the behaviour of one of the captains, could not easily find a person that would cheerfully venture through so much danger, to carry his commands to the captain. This Lord [Rochester] offered himself to the service, and went in a little boat through all the shot, and delivered his message, and returned back to Sir Edward, which was much commended by all that saw it.

But it was Holmes who drew most of the acclaim during the crisis. His seconding of the *Royal Charles* was all the more remarkable in that his own ship was practically out of ammunition. It was said that

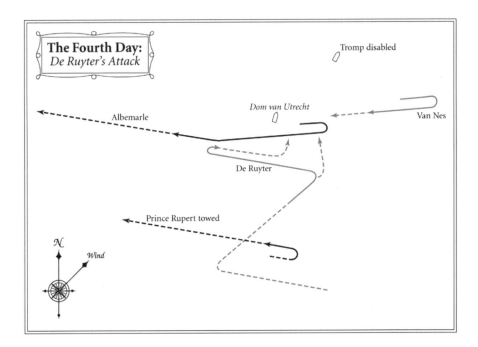

The Fourth Day: De Ruyter's Attack

when Holmes his powder grown low, & he was forced to husband it a bold Dutchman came up close to him asking him where his powder was now, at which Sr. Robert tooke up his skrewd gun [a pistol with a long screw-on barrel extension], & fairly shotte ye Capt. dead upon ye quarter decke.

Despite the heroics of the steadier commanders, fortunes had turned around with astonishing suddenness. From this point on nothing went right for the English.

At the time de Ruyter began his advance, the *Royal James* and '8 to 10 ships' of the White Squadron had been standing to the eastward under his lee. When the Dutch wore across their stern, Rupert and Allin assumed like the rest of the English that the enemy was breaking off the action: 'they bearing up, as we conceive, to run away', said Allin. Thinking the battle was over, the Prince and the captains with him thankfully luffed up to begin repairing their rigging, the masts of the *Royal James* in particular having been 'terribly shaken'. When it was discovered that the enemy was not retreating after all, the English instantly cut short their repairs to resume the fight. Now holding the weather gage, Rupert was in a strong position. The Dutch had left themselves open to a counterstroke from windward, and there seemed a good chance that the Prince could trap de Ruyter between himself and Albemarle, with possibly dire consequences for the future of the States' Fleet. Then disaster struck. 'Just as we thought to break into the Holland fleet we were prevented', lamented Allin, for 'in the time of bearing up our main topmast, mizzen mast, main yard, and mizzen yard came down about our ears'. This was catastrophic. The captains of the other ships with Rupert showed no inclination to go in without him, so the potentially decisive counterattack was ruined as if by the intervention of the gods before it ever started.

De Ruyter had taken a daring risk in leaving an English force to windward. He surely expected an attack from that quarter, and how he could have dealt with it no one can say. What is certain is that the instant he saw the masts of the *Royal James* inexplicably falling down, he knew the day was his. Throwing caution to the winds, he made 'againe a sudden tack' and, in a dramatic flourish, the *Zeven Provinciën* broke out the red flag at the fore – the signal for all-out attack, close action, and boarding. With that, according to the States-General, 'the Lieutenant-Admirals van Meppelen and de Vries, as also the Vice-Admirals Banckert, Schram, and Koenders, and Rear-Admiral Bruinsveld broke in among the Enemies with all imaginable undauntedness'.

The Dutch hurled all their strength against the English rear, whose unfortunate vessels were left to fend for themselves. By Clifford's account,

My Ld. Generall as ill as his ship was gives order for tacking likewayes to preserve our lam'd frigets, but having receivd in the passe before two shots in his powder roome betweene wind and water they could not be stopd but by standing upon the same course, besides our maine topmast was so disabled by a shot through him that we were faine to lower our maine topsaile and our foremast had receivd so many shots that it was the generall opinion there was danger of bringing her by the board in tacking, and noe signes for any of the rest to tack would prevaile any thing with them so that we were forcd to see them fall upon our frigets in the reare without being able to rescue them.

Albemarle gave the same story, except that he said the two shot holes on the windward side were 'in the gunroom' rather than the powder room. The holes were most likely *beneath* the gunroom, in the breadroom or the steward room on the orlop. The danger in tacking was not that the ship would sink, but that flooding would spoil the powder in the magazine – and ammunition was by then a precious commodity.

There is no reason to doubt the Generals' claims that their flagships were disabled. The question nevertheless remains: if they wished to stay in the fight, what was to keep them from simply changing ships? For Albemarle, entering a small boat in rough seas might have been a physical impossibility owing to his age, obesity, infirmities, and a painful wound he had received on Friday; but Rupert had no such excuses. The Prince said only that 'I was once in a posture to have strake a greate stroak, but having not soe many shippes to change as my Spitsbroder Drump [Tromp] whoe was faine to change three besides that [which] hee came in first, I was forced off'. That no ships were available cannot be taken seriously, and this did not go unnoticed. An anonymous eyewitness felt that one of the 'greater' mistakes of the battle was committed

> on Munday afternoon . . . when Prince Rupert, being on board the *Royall James*, had the wind of the Enemy; and the Generall in good Order to leeward of em. The *Royall James* being disabled, the Prince steer'd away, and all his squadron after him. Whereas, if he had gone aboard another ship, and put up his Flag, he might have pursued the Advantage he had gotten; and the Enemy being in bad condition & between both the English Fleets, would in all likelyhood have been utterly ruined.

Later in the summer the Prince tacitly acknowledged the error by issuing a belated revision to the Fighting Instructions directing flag-officers to change ships when their own were disabled.

The new instruction came much too late to benefit the ships of the English rear on the 4th of June. Seeing only the sterns of the flagships, the captains and crews of the trailing vessels found themselves facing the wrath of the whole Dutch fleet without hope of assistance. Their opponents triumphantly swarmed through and around them in crushing numbers. The previously dispirited Amsterdam divisions and those under Van Nes took heart, regrouping to leeward to prevent escape in that direction. The *Dom van Utrecht* quickly raised her colours again; rescuers in a boat from the Friesland ship *Oostergo* reported that most of the crew appeared to be drunk, having presumably broken into the spirit room for a final fling in expectation of a long captivity. The English now fought desperately to avoid such a fate themselves. The proper fighting order had as usual broken down somewhat in the course of the day; Teddiman and Utber had ships from all three squadrons under their wings. Most of the captains evidently had wits enough to stay in line and were somehow able to follow Albemarle to the west, their escape no doubt much aided by the exhaustion and injuries the Dutch themselves had suffered in four days of fighting. Even so, there was a great deal of confusion among the English. Some fled on their own, and others were damaged and fell behind. Utber, the Rear-Admiral of the Blue, narrowly avoided capture. His *Rupert* had the misfortune to lose her mainmast over the side, forcing him to run before the wind with two enemy men-of-war following close astern. It is hard to imagine that the

Dutch could have failed to overtake a vessel thus handicapped, but catching such a ship was not the same as taking her. The pride of the later-famous shipwright Anthony Deane, the *Rupert* was a brand-new third-rate mounting full tiers of demi-cannon and culverins. Utber fought off his pursuers and eventually got into Harwich.

Four others did not escape. Three of the English losses were accounted for by the Frisian sub-commanders, Vice-Admiral Rudolf Coenders and *Schout-bij-Nacht* Hendrik Bruynsvelt. Coenders, in the new 72-gun *Groningen*, boarded and carried the 62-gun third-rate *Clove Tree* (formerly the Dutch East Indiaman *Nagelboom* taken at Lowestoft). The *Clove Tree*'s captain, a steady old tarpaulin named John Chappell, had been killed earlier in the fight. Coenders had thus done well enough, but it was Bruynsvelt who scored the greatest coup of the day. His 72-gun *Prins Hendrik Casimir* happened upon two English ships which had become entangled in a collision, the 56-gun third-rate *Essex* under Captain William Reeves of the White Squadron and the 40-gun *Black Bull* (the ex-Dutch *Wapen van Edam*) commanded by the Lowestoft fireship hero John Gethings of the Blue Squadron. The two ships being completely helpless, Bruynsvelt's men boarded and took them both.

The *Essex* was a more important ship than her mere 56 guns would indicate. Many of the English saw the capture from a distance, but none of them knew how it happened. Both Clifford and Albemarle initially thought that Captain Reeves had 'most indiscreetly and unskillfully' fouled a Dutch ship which had previously surrendered, probably meaning the *Dom van Utrecht*. Others knew the *Essex* had run into the *Black Bull*, but assumed it had occurred 'when shee bore up bravely to her rescue'. Another observer turned the whole thing around, saying that the two English vessels 'had taken a Dutch flagship, and were board & board of one another, when our retreat gave de Ruyter opportunity to seize them all three together'. A more probable explanation, said to be based on an account by Reeves himself, is given in Charnock's *Biographia Navalis* of 1794. This describes how Reeves had

> received, towards the conclusion of the action, in which he had eminently distinguished himself, a musket shot a little below his right temple, which passing diagonally, lodged in his throat on the left side, and occasioned such an internal effusion of blood as deprived him of his speech. He himself was, consequently, rendered incapable of command; most of his officers were wounded, and those on whom, in this distressed situation, the command devolved, were obliged to bring the ship upon the heel to stop some shot-holes which she had received under water. In this perilous state the *Bull*, another English man of war, which was nearly as much disabled as the *Essex*, fell on board her. The Dutch taking advantage of this accumulated distress, boarded and took possession of her.

Charnock also reported the more dubious anecdote

> that captain Reeves, when he had a little recovered himself [from a musket ball in the throat, remember], endeavoured, in conjunction with his gunner, to have blown the ship up, but found the powder-room in the enemy's possession, who had wisely taken the proper precautions for its security.

Whatever precautions Bruynsvelt took, they proved insufficient to secure the prizes. The Dutch recounted that after subduing the ships he left a few of his men aboard and then sailed away to hunt other game. The *Prins Hendrik Casimir* had no sooner departed when the English successfully rose against their guards, but this gained them only temporary freedom. Before the still-entangled vessels could make their escape, an alert Captain Jacob Pauw of the 46-gun *Stavoren* (an Amsterdam ship attached to the Zeeland-Friesland squadron) somehow discovered what had happened. He immediately laid his ship alongside and sent in another wave of boarders who quickly regained the upper hand, this time permanently. Soon thereafter the *Bull* suddenly sank. Captain Gethings, evidently still aboard, was drowned along with many others.

Reeves afterward complained bitterly of maltreatment at the hands of the Dutch. He alleged

> that they led him to the deck, and seeing him wounded immediately stripped him to his skin; that he was then conveyed into a Dutch boat and brought on board a man of war, whose captain refused to give him the assistance of his chirurgeon, and in which ship he was forced to lay several hours covered only with a rug: the next day he was sent to Flushing without any care taken of him, or allowance made to him, during the passage. He, certainly in consequence of his ill-treatment, flung himself overboard, but was again recovered by the men's boat-hooks, and, notwithstanding his ill condition, put in irons. For the space of three days he received no sustenance, till at last, being nearly perishing, he was removed to a provost's house, where by the care of the chirurgeon, he, contrary to all expectations, recovered; but still was kept almost naked and in chains!!!

The Dutch themselves ('those monsters of cruelty', wrote Charnock, his pen fairly quivering with outrage) gave another story which suggested that Reeves may have had to be restrained for his own protection:

> We cannot but admire the courage of the English, particularly of captain Reeves, our prisoner, who, though much wounded, when he saw his vessel must inevitably fall into our hands, threw himself twice overboard, to avoid being taken, but was recovered by our men.

Reeves was knighted on his repatriation and performed creditably in many subsequent actions. The *Essex* was repaired and taken into the Dutch service, but was wrecked off Vlieland with great loss of life in October 1667.

A fourth English ship was taken late in the action by a member of de Liefde's division. The 56-gun *Convertine*, which had only joined the fleet the evening before, tried to escape by herself. Chased down by two opponents, she struck her flag to Maximiliaan's *Wassenaar* after what most observers described as a decidedly ignoble defence. Maximiliaan added that she 'yielded in sight of Prince Robert, he not daring to come to her Assistance, but contented himself with killing me one Seaman and shooting off the Arm of another'. Maximiliaan appears to have confused the English commanders, a common mistake in the Dutch accounts. The flagship that fired on him was surely the *Royal Charles* and not the *Royal James*. Rupert's ship was miles to windward and in no condition to influence events. Jordan, who was in Albemarle's line, stated that the capture took place 'to leeward'. The *Royal James* thus could not have interfered, which is further confirmed in that neither the Prince nor Allin gave any indication that they were even aware of the incident, whereas those in the *Royal Charles* left descriptions of it. Clifford most definitely saw it; he wrote in disgust that the *Convertine*

> beeing an old Duch ship [actually Portuguese] and a slow sailer was overtaken by two of theire little frigets and without shooting a gun or making any resistance she struck her auntient and yeelded; we might else have brought her off with some of our frigets but Capt. Perce [Pearce] the commander was the more to be blamd for that he had scarce engagd the whole day.

Fortunately for Pearce's reputation, a newsletter from Rotterdam came to his rescue soon after the battle. It announced that 'Capt. John Pearsie and his company are prisoners at Delft; the men revolted and struck their flag by force, being persuaded by some bold fellows that if they did not give up the ship, they would have no quarter'. Probably on the strength of that, Pearce was given a second chance after his release. Regrettably, when he later faced another test he again was found wanting. In command of the fourth-rate *Sapphire* off Sicily in 1671, he ran his ship ashore rather than engage what he thought was a squadron of Algerine corsairs. The squadron turned out to be English and Pearce paid for his mistake before a firing squad.

Aside from the four vessels known to have been captured, there is evidence that another was briefly in the hands of the Dutch. Maximiliaan insisted that he saw *five* ships taken. The States-General's account agreed, explaining that one was by some means retaken and got away. An anonymous observer in the *Royal Charles* also claimed to have seen a surrendered ship recaptured, but wrongly thought it was the *Convertine*. If another vessel did give up, as seems probable, a prime suspect is the fourth-rate *Kent*, from which Captain Ewens was afterwards dismissed for cowardice.

De Ruyter's charge had decided the battle. The very success of his great attack tends to obscure what a courageous, desperate, and dangerous gamble it was. While still to windward he could easily have broken off the fight with no loss of honour. He had already accomplished his strategic objective; the English would obviously be many weeks in port repairing their damages, leaving the way open for the East Indiamen and the French. A retreat by de Ruyter might have cost Tromp and Van Nes three or four ships, but probably no more than that since four days of fighting had left the enemy in no condition to chase them. When he made the decision to attack, the Admiral-General had no assurance that the battered leeward divisions would have the means to assist. Furthermore, in falling upon Albemarle (whose broadsides if not numbers were little inferior to his own, considering the ever-present firepower disparity) de Ruyter could not avoid surrendering the weather gage to the White Squadron. Entirely in character, he nevertheless accepted the risks rather than leave a portion of his fleet in distress. He was rewarded for his loyalty with what was surely one of the most satisfying victories of his career.

As soon as it was clear that the Dutch had the situation well in hand, de Ruyter led most of his fleet after the English main body hoping to keep Rupert and Albemarle from joining. The English for their part held on steadily westward towards the King's Channel in full retreat. Those in both the *Royal James* and the *Royal Charles* were excessively defensive in describing this course, the Generals and their supporters going to considerable lengths to justify it as something other than an outright flight. Clifford, for instance, wrote that

> Our business was now to beare away before a wind to joyne with the Princes Squadron and this cannot be called even by the Hollanders a running away but the proper course to joyne which was the most justifyable working, and when we were joynd the Duch made noe farther after us, but by this tyme it was sun set and most of our ships in an ill condition as I have told yr. Lordship our two admiralls were, otherwayes we might have steerd to have met with them this morning againe for by all that we can guesse by the working of the Enemy they were as glad to be quit of us as we of them.

Albemarle's initial report on the 5th was actually fairly truthful:

> Prince Rupert being a league and a halfe to windward of us, wee made what way we could to joyne with him and soe they followed us till night. The Prince, haveing received many shott in his ship's masts and rigging was not able to come and joyne with us, which kept us asunder the longer; soe, night comeing on, the Dutch sayled towards Holland, and wee finding our powder and shott near spent (that part of the Fleet with me haveing fought neare four days) wee stood homewards.

Three days later he submitted a second narrative with a slight embellishment:

> In ye night wee mended our sailes & rigging. But upon inquiry wee found our Amunition almost spent, whereby wee could not renew the fight, & the enemy made soe fast away that they prevented us. Never were men more willing than ours to engage againe, nor enemies in a worse condition to receive us. They left us in ye night & went homewards, haveing a much greater loss than ours.

Prince Rupert did not so much embellish as simply leave out a few details. After describing the disaster to his rigging, he merely said that

> The Generall then with that parte of the fleete which was to Leeward with him got their Larboard tacks aboard keepeing their wynd cloose to make up towards ye Prince and wee bore downe to them seeing the Enimy makeing what saile they could to come betwixt us, and when they saw that could not bee, they boore away before the wynd for their owne Port. This is the plaine matter of fact without descending to many particulars.

The 'particulars' were that the Prince 'had much ado to get from them', as Allin unabashedly put it. The *Royal James* had to be *towed* away by the fourth-rate *Breda*, and Rupert was fortunate to be far enough to windward that de Ruyter could not get to him. Other English flag-officers and private captains were more forward than their seniors in describing the fleet's motions. Jordan unhesitatingly called it 'our retreat', and Captain Thomas Page of the *Newcastle* bluntly reported 'that the Duch did pursue us two hours before they left us; and then they suffered us to go on homewards, and they retreated toward their coast'.

According to the Dutch, de Ruyter's pursuit was cut short only by the intervention of the weather:

> For the shattered Remainder of them miraculously escaped by the Favour of a thick Fog, about 7 a Clock at Night. However, the Dutch fleet being victorious and triumphant, continued to chace them a long time after their being routed, and would have pursued them into their very Ports, if they had not been afraid their Ships would have lost themselves, and have been scattered. And therefore de Ruiter having fired some Guns for a Signal to advertise all the Ships of his Fleet to veer back towards their Admiral, and the whole Dutch Fleet thereupon assembling together, they sailed away all Night leisurely, and with little Sail homewards.

It seems improbable that the Dutch would have been deterred merely by the fog, which persisted only briefly. It is more likely that de Ruyter realized that he could accomplish nothing more without unacceptable risk. His own fleet was badly scattered; some ships were disabled and already headed for the Netherlands, others were chasing Utber or following Narbrough's contingent, and still more were swarming around the prizes. The divisions in pursuit of the English main body had fewer than forty vessels, while Albemarle still had nearly that number together, including most of the big ships. The fogbank nevertheless seemed providential to many of the English, and Andrew Marvell found good use for it:

> *As firy Rupert, with revengefull Joy,*
> *Does on the Dutch his hungry Courage cloy,*
> *But, soon unrigg'd, lay like an uselesse Board,*
> *As wounded in the wrist men drop the Sword;*
> *When a propitious Clowd betwixt us stept*
> *And in our aid did Ruyter intercept.*
> *Old Homer yet did never introduce,*
> *To save his heroes, Mist of better use.*
> *Worship the Sun, who dwell where he does rise:*
> *This Mist does more deserve our Sacrifice.*

Whether or not the fogbank played a significant role, its descent did ring down the curtain on the Four Days' Battle. With seamen on both sides dropping to their knees with exhaustion, the ordeal was over. Joseph Jordan spoke for all his countrymen when he wrote the next day to his friend Sir William Penn that he thought the English would have won had the whole fleet been together from the start,

> but wee must submit to ye Allseeing Providence, who knows what is best for us; its my part to praise my God that hath delivered mee, and this Shipp wonderfully after soe many dayes battle, ye greatest passes I think that ever was fought att Sea.

Chapter XVII

Aftermath

Amidst these toils succeeds the balmy night;
Now hissing waters the quench'd guns restore;
And weary waves, withdrawing from the fight,
Lie lull'd and panting on the silent shore.

When the combatants separated, both sides made for their own ports. During the night confused pilots *again* led the English on to the Galloper, but fortunately near high water so that none of the ships touched. The fleet entered the King's Channel on the evening of the 5th, finding the newly arrived *Royal Sovereign* along with the damaged *Henry, Gloucester, Anne, Bristol*, and one or two more; the other disabled vessels had already gone on to Sheerness. As soon as the anchors were dropped in the Swin, the Generals and other participants sent off the letters and narratives they had composed during the day.

As fate would have it, the earliest messages to reach the capital were spectacularly inaccurate. The first originated with Captain Thomas Blackman of the fifth-rate *Little Victory*. His ship was sent out from Harwich on the 4th to join the battle, but had come up just as the Dutch turned back. Quickly gathering what information he could, mostly from Captain John Hayward of the *Dunkirk*, Blackman sped back to Harwich and arrived there about the same time the fleet was entering the river. His news was received by the Storekeeper of Harwich Dockyard, Silas Taylor, who wrote it down and relayed it to Coventry with the breathless endorsement, 'Hast Hast Hast post Hast, by expresse'. It announced a glorious, smashing victory of unprecedented proportions: on Monday 'at 4 of the clocke or there abouts', the Dutch

> layd downe the Bucklers & betooke themselves to a plaine flight after they had soe long & soe pertinaciously maintain'd the fight from Friday; soe that this proves a deare victory yett it is a great one; & such a one as I hope England may have occasion for many ages hereafter to rejoyce in, for it is affirm'd that of all their Fleet & those 2 additionall recruits (I mentioned in my last) to them there have been soe many sunke & burnt that there is not neare fifty (as they are accounted) gott backe & escaped by flight; & it is very remarkable that all or the most of their Flaggs suffered in these renowned incounters, for particulars I can say nothing . . . .

Taylor's express reached Whitehall the next day, with predictable results. 'We were all so overtaken', wrote Pepys, that the Duke of York 'ran with it to the King, who was gone to chapel; and there all the Court was in a hubbub, being rejoiced over head and ears in this good news'. Evelyn recorded that when James burst into the chapel, the

King 'made a suddaine Stop, to heare the relation, which being with much advantage on our side, his Majestie commanded that Publique Thanks should immediately be given as for a Victory'. The service, which had begun in keeping with a solemn fast day, was promptly altered in mid-course, instructions for the same effect being sent to St. Paul's and Westminster Abbey.

Another fantastic report was soon brought in person by Sir Daniel Harvey of Albemarle's entourage in the *Royal Charles*. He had hurried ashore and galloped to London spreading the word that there were 'but 36 in all of the Duch fleet left at the end of the voyage when they run home'. This produced delirious excitement; orders were given 'for bone-fires and bells', and courtiers dashed about repeating inflated rumours. By the end of the day the news had spread all over London. Fireworks were set off, women danced around the bonfires, and crowds swarmed through the streets giving 'volleys of their Musquetts' and drinking to the fleet. 'The joy of the City was this night exceeding great', wrote Pepys.

But even as London celebrated, sobering reports began to come in. It was learned, said Evelyn, 'that our losse was very greate both in ships & men'; that the mighty *Royal Prince* had been burned and Ayscue captured, 'which exceedingly abated our former jolitie'. Pepys arose the next morning and went happily to the office

> with the same expectation of congratulating ourselfs with the victory that I had yesterday. But my Lord Brounker and Sir T. Harvey, that came from Court, tell me quite contrary news, which astonishes me. That is to say, that we are beaten – lost many ships and good commanders – have not taken one ship of the enemy's, and so can only report ourselfs a victory; nor is it certain that we were left maisters of the field.

Even though letters from the fleet insisted that the Dutch had suffered heavily, the public was disappointed at the lack of prizes and regarded the destruction of the *Royal Prince* as outweighing the supposed Dutch losses. Accounts of the battle's closing act were also telling. Pierce, the Surgeon-General, came to London saying openly that 'all the fleet confess their being chased home by the Dutch; and yet the body of the Dutch that did it was not above 40 sail at most'. The gloom in the capital deepened when the full extent of the English loss became known. That was not evident at first; the *Seven Oaks* and *Loyal George* were not missed until the fleet returned to port, while some thought that they had seen the *Swiftsure* getting away and still others were sure the *Essex* had escaped as well. In point of fact, what had been taken for the *Swiftsure* was the *Rainbow* running to Ostend, and the *Essex* had been confused with the *Rupert*. By the 9th, when there was no longer any hope for the missing ships, Pepys found that 'all give over the thoughts of it as a victory, and to reckon it a great overthrow'.

Those who went downstream to view the fleet in person found a scene of astounding destruction. Evelyn's inveterate curiosity led him to Chatham and Sheerness, where he

> beheld that sad spectacle, namely more than halfe of that gallant bulwark of the Kingdome miserably shatterd, hardly a Vessell intire, but appearing rather so many wracks & hulls, so cruely had the Dutch mangled us: when the losse of the Prince

(that gallant Vessell) had ben a losse to be universaly deplor'd, none knowing for what reason we first ingagd in this ungratefull warr.

The whole of the Medway was filled with battered men-of-war waiting to take their turns before the masthouses and in the drydocks. Everywhere were jagged stumps of masts and broken heads and splintered rails and hulls pierced like sieves. Barlow said that the *Monck* needed a new mainmast, mizzen, fore topmast, and bowsprit, 'all being shot through and through, having shot sticking in them'. Ten ships were gone forever: the *Prince* taken and burned; the *Black Bull* taken and sunk; the *Swiftsure, Essex, Clove Tree, Convertine, Seven Oaks*, and *Loyal George* carried into Holland; the *Black Eagle* sunk in action; and the *St. Paul* deliberately burned to prevent capture. Another vessel, the hired *Loyal Subject*, survived the battle but was afterwards written off by the surveyors as a total loss, at least as far as the navy was concerned. She lay in port, unrepaired, for the remainder of her hire, which expired in September. The capture of the hired *Loyal George* indirectly caused yet a further loss when her desolated owner, Thomas Gould, secured the release of his brand-new 48-gun *Albemarle* which the navy had recently hired.

Casualties were heavy. Over 1,000 were killed including those in the captured ships, and there were in England about 1,450 wounded. Another 1,800 were prisoners in the Netherlands, hundreds of them wounded. The total loss was about 4,250 men, or over one-fifth of those engaged. Despite the staggering scale of the casualties, the wounded found Evelyn, Knight, and the other Commissioners for Sick and Wounded well prepared to receive them. Harwich accommodated between three hundred and four hundred, Aldborough one hundred, Yarmouth one hundred, and Southwark two hundred, while three hundred of the most 'miserably dismembred' were brought to London and housed in Savoy Palace. Barlow and most of his forty 'lamed' shipmates from the *Monck* were treated at Rochester, where

we were sent some to one house and some to another, His Majesty paying seven shillings a week for every man for his diate and looking after, there being a kind of an hospital where they lay that were worst wounded, and a doctor to dress them, which we went to every day from the other places when we wanted any dressing.

Some men preferred their own ships' surgeons. The *Bristol*, for instance, sent twenty-eight victims ashore, but still had thirty more 'which the Chirurgion under takes to cure aboard'. The English people responded to the needs of the wounded with noteworthy generosity, 'many merchants & others giving considerable gratuities . . . as an encouragement to ye maimed seamen'. Among others, 'Charitable people at Oxford' donated £50 and the Canary Company £100.

If the public was distressed at the casualty list, the officials of the government and Navy Board were positively horrified at the carnage among the commanders; nearly everyone lost friends. Of the flag-officers and 'Great Persons', Berkeley and Albemarle's secretary Sir William Clarke were dead, Ayscue a prisoner in Holland, and Rear-Admirals Harman and Utber 'ill-wounded'. Hope was at first held out that Sir Christopher Myngs might survive his gruesome injuries, but he lasted less than a week. Many thought his death the worst disaster of the battle. Pepys mourned him as 'a very stout man, and a man of great parts and most excellent tongue among ordinary men; and as Sir W. Coventry says, could have been the most useful man in the world at such a pinch of time as this'.

Ten captains were killed outright or died within a few days: John Coppin, Henry Terne, John Whitty, Jeffrey Dare, Walter Wood, Peter Mootham, John Chappell, Roger Miller, Phillip Bacon, and John Gethings. The death of these officers was a heavy blow to the Royal Navy. Most of them were the Duchess of Albemarle's 'old plain sea captains' – fighting tarpaulins of irreplaceable judgement and experience. There was also a long list of wounded captains: Frescheville Holles, John Holmes, William Jennings, John Fortesque, Thomas Page, John Silver, William Reeves, and John Earle. Reeves and Earle were also prisoners-of-war, along with the unhurt John Pearce and James Jennifer. Twenty-five commanders in all, nearly a third of those engaged, were killed, wounded, or captured. This was the greatest loss of senior officers ever suffered by the Royal Navy in a single action.

Albemarle himself did not emerge unbloodied, though it was his pride that was hurt the most. Reports from the flagship mentioned that the general had sustained a bruised hand and a scratch in the thigh on the evening of the 1st. But when authoritative (and unauthorized) details of the 'thigh' wound were revealed, many could not help but smile. Andrew Marvell, grinning fiendishly behind the security of his pseudonym, set aside his usual sympathy for the Duke to loose a ribald broadside:

> But most with story of his Hand or Thum,
> Conceale, as honour would, his Grace's Bum.
> When the rude bullet a large Collop tore
> Out of that Buttock, never turn'd before.
> Fortune it seem'd would give him, by that lash,
> Gentle correction for his Fight so rash.
> But should the Rump* perceive't, they'd say that Mars
> Had now reveng'd them upon Aumarle's Arse.

Williamson too was overtaken by the possibilities. The *London Gazette* reported with uncharacteristic light heart that 'The Duke had all his tackle taken off by chain shot, and his breeches to the skin were shot off, but he rigged again with jury masts, and fell into the body of the Dutch fleet . . .'. This elicited a further effort from Marvell, who rendered the friendly advice, '*Guard thy posteriour left, lest all be gone: / Though Jury-masts, th' hast Jury-buttocks none*'. Everyone else had sense enough to keep quiet, at least in public.

The Dutch knew they had won, though one might have thought otherwise from the state of the fleet. Four ships had been destroyed by fire: the *Hof van Zeeland*, *Duivenvoorde*, *Liefde*, and *Landman*. Most of the surviving vessels showed plainly the effects of the broadsides, and some such as the *Hollandia*, *Spiegel*, and *Pacificatie* were little more than floating masses of charred and splintered wreckage. Over 1,550 men

---

*The Protectorate Parliament dissolved by Monck.

were killed. This was an even greater death toll than the English suffered, and was largely due to the horrific losses in the four ships burned; the rest of the fleet had fewer than 700 dead. There were also slightly under 1,300 wounded, so Dutch casualties amounted to about 2,850 in all. Like the English, the Dutch lost many commanders. Cornelis Evertsen the Elder, Vice-Admiral Van der Hulst, and Rear-Admiral Stachouwer were dead, along with six captains: Otto van Treslong, Pieter Salomonszoon, Pieter Janszoon Uyttenhout, Wouter Wijngaarden, Adriaan Houttuin, and Simon Blok. A wounded captain, Cornelis Victol, died ashore.

Despite their losses the Dutch at least had something to show for their sacrifices. Some of the prizes arrived before the battle was over, and flotillas of *jachts* bearing spectators from the shore were already on hand when the fleet returned. The *Swiftsure*, *Loyal George*, and *Convertine* were brought to the Goeree entrance of the Maas (where Van de Velde the Younger came out to record them) and the *Essex*, *Clove Tree*, and *Seven Oaks* to the Texel. Not since the Battle of the Downs a generation before had Dutch harbours seen such processions of captive warships.

The celebrations were on an unprecedented scale. There were bonfires and fireworks displays in the humblest villages and prayers of thanks in every church. Banquets were given, medals struck, songs and poems composed, paintings commissioned; the Van de Veldes, Abraham Storck, and other marine artists received enough orders to keep them busy for years. State funerals were staged for the dead commanders. A marble monument was erected in Middelburg for Cornelis Evertsen, and another for Van der Hulst in Amsterdam. The States-General appointed 20 June (the 30th by the Continental calendar) a special day of rejoicing both at home and in Dutch embassies abroad. This caused a riot in Brussels, where England was favoured. Prevented by force from tearing down the fireworks scaffolding, a mob stormed the Dutch residency and had to be dispersed by a troop of horse. Elsewhere the festivities were well-received; the Danish fleet fired three full broadsides, and nearly every European government offered formal congratulations. As could only be expected, the grand public display in Amsterdam surpassed all others. An English-language newsletter described the scene:

> . . . on wednesday last wee had a Thanksgiveing much more strickt then any Sunday, & at night so many Bonfires as if the Citty had been of one entire fire, & because none came from Heaven, wee sett them up as high as wee could – on the peers of all our Churches & all steeples full of Lanthornes, & as many pitch Barrells burn'd as are not to bee numbred.

Elaborate effigies of the King and Queen, the Duke of York, Rupert, Albemarle, and Clarendon were set in pitch tubs 'that you may see our Ingenuity to burne our Enemies as well as to gett the victory over them'. The King 'was made like a Dogg with a Crowne on his head', and the Generals were each equipped with a long tail.

> When all this was sett in Exquisite manner, then was the Fire kindled, & small gunns like Chambers discharg'd, & many Fireworks & some more then was desired, for the fire flying over the walls was by the wind so caryed that it burned 2 houses & a barne, many Children killd & many hurt, however wee kept at it till 5 the next day, till most

people wanted bedds, for their heads was too heavy for their Bodyes, and now I leave you to Judge of the acceptablenesse of this sacrifice.

The commanders of the fleet were greeted by adoring throngs everywhere they went. The same newsletter-writer reported that 'About 8 days [ago] Mine heer Trump went by my dore in a Coach with more people admireing his valour then I ever saw goe after the Bears to the Beargarden, though the Ape was there also'. De Ruyter was showered with honours and public triumphs that would have satisfied a general of imperial Rome. The States-General praised him to the heavens, and on medals and in verse he was immortalized as an 'unshakable Atlas' and the 'pillar of the Fatherland'. Unlike Tromp, the Admiral-General was ill-at-ease with the attention. He stayed aboard his flagship as much as possible and kept away from crowds when he could not avoid coming ashore. As always he maintained his simple habits; the day after the battle de Guiche had found the great commander sweeping out his own cabin and feeding his chickens.

It was only later realized that the celebrations were far out of proportion to what had been accomplished. The States' Fleet had been hard-pressed to overcome a much weaker opponent and had been within a hair's-breadth of disaster on both the second and the fourth day. Excessive rejoicing was perhaps to be expected from a public so long starved of victory, but the soaring elation within the fleet had a further explanation: all the participants from the admirals to the powder boys believed that they had permanently ruined the English.

A tendency to magnify an enemy's suffering is to be found in warfare of every age. Men find it difficult to admit that their herculean efforts, made at such great hazard and often at terrible cost, could have been without important result. The confusion of battle in the age of sail brought ample opportunity for error. One usually could not focus attention on a damaged opponent long enough to see the final outcome, for too many things were happening at once. A briefly glimpsed vessel which had taken water and was temporarily listing would often be counted as sunk. Another seen to be afire would be reported as destroyed 'for certain', while a fireship burning out in the distance could easily be transformed by the mind into an enemy flagship. When a vessel really did sink or burn, observers might recall it as having happened at different times, and it would then become two victims – or three, four, or even more. The Dutch carried such mistakes to remarkable extremes after the Four Days' Battle.

When Johan de Witt and four other deputies of the States-General charged with composing the official account of the fight finished interviewing the admirals and captains, and carefully reviewed all the testimony, they concluded that the English had lost no fewer than twenty-three men-of-war 'without counting in those Ships of the Enemies that were burnt or sunk of which the Dutch Officers had no Knowledge'. English casualties were placed at above six thousand dead (high by a factor of six!) plus an unknown number of wounded. The prisoners had not yet been counted, but de Witt supposed there must have been about three thousand.

The final report enumerated the six prizes brought in, two more taken but destroyed, ten sunk in action, two burned by fireships, and three intentionally burned by the English during their flight on the second day. De Witt and his colleagues regarded the list as quite conservative. They did not count the *Henry* among the ships destroyed despite the opinions of most eyewitnesses including de Ruyter. They rejected many other claims as well, conceding only

> that 'tis not to be doubted, that some English Ships were burnt, which yet we could not be absolutely assured of; because fire being set to several Fire-Ships at divers times, we cannot positively say whether the Ships they grapled were destroyed, or whether they escaped, except only two that we are sure were burnt to Ashes during the fight, because the Officers and Seamen that served on board the said Fire-Ships are now actually soliciting for the reward allotted by the States for such Service, by producing good Certificates of their performance of it.

The deputies insisted that they had accepted only claims which seemed incontrovertible, such as two ships of the Blue Squadron 'known' to have gone down on the first day: 'The two aforesaid English Ships sinking in the view of the Officers and Sea men of the whole Dutch Fleet, I think there is no reason to doubt it'. Special care was also taken in verifying two of the many reported sinkings of the second day:

> And absolutely to convince the World, that the two abovesaid Ships of the White Squadron were two different Ships, it is to be observ'd that several Officers and other Sea-faring men saw both of them sink, that is to say, that the same persons that saw one perish, saw the other undergo the same fate a little after; for we have so carefully distinguisht things in our Examination, that there is no reason to fear we have mistaken 2 Ships for one.

In fact *six* had been mistaken for one that day.

The wording of the States-General's account gives the impression, no doubt intentionally, that the estimates of English losses were actually much too modest. That was certainly the conclusion drawn by the public. Ambassadors and consuls from France, Denmark, Venice, and elsewhere reported privately to their governments that the English had probably lost between thirty and forty ships and as many as eleven thousand men killed or captured. This version was generally believed in foreign capitals in preference to the official claims from both sides, much to the chagrin of Charles II. But of much greater import, the larger figures were also readily accepted by the States, the Admiralties, and the officers and seamen of the Dutch fleet – who should have known better. The next cruise was planned under the assumption that the weakened English would be incapable of resistance. This was a foolish and inexcusable mistake, for it is a cardinal sin of warfare to believe one's own lies.

In England, despite the all-too-visible evidence of defeat, the government outwardly kept a brave face. This was not entirely dishonest, for the Dutch were not the only ones who could miscalculate their opponent's losses. Both sides were subject to such errors, and when the States-General reported only four ships missing, English seamen scoffed loudly. One eyewitness writing some years later commented on the Dutch admissions that 'by the Observations I could make from the Poop of the *Royall Charles*, where I stood all the Fight, I thought their losse much more considerable, and so did other men that were far better Judges than I'. Barlow acknowledged the English loss of ten ships, but insisted that 'neither could they brag of losing little less than that number; though we took none of them yet we sent them where they were never seen more'. Ironically, the most conservative estimate of the Dutch loss was Albemarle's. He initially claimed only seven ships destroyed, though this grew in a later narrative to seven burned and two sunk 'that we know of'.

The government accepted these exaggerated figures and enlarged them further. When Arlington published the Generals' 'True Narrative . . . to contradict false reports of the enemies . . . hitherto most disingeniously & artificially dissembled by them', the Four Days' Battle was officially proclaimed a glorious success for the Royal Navy. It was grudgingly admitted that the English had lost four good men-of-war

> & 5 or 6 small ships more . . . which makes 10 in number small & greate; whereas we are confidently assured from our Owne Observation, & from letters, that ye Enemy lost as many more, three of which new Flagg ships, their men all sunk & burnt with them. And it is certaine they must every where have suffered a much greater losse of men than we from ye Difference in ye manner of fighting, for they shooting high & att greate distance, damaged us most in ye Rigging, & we on ye other hand forbearing to shoote but when we came neare & then levelling most att ye Hulls must needs have done more Execution upon their men, the particulars whereof we shall quickly learne. In ye meane tyme we know they went much shattered & torne into their first ports they could make, & concluded themselves beaten, till from ye Hague they were told ye Contrary by those who could know it lesse.

In July the government's claims of massive Dutch losses were seemingly confirmed when a discontented Rotterdam captain named Laurens van Heemskerck defected to the English. Heemskerck, who was later knighted by Charles II, brought with him an official-looking document naming fifteen States' ships purportedly destroyed in the battle and twenty-one commanders killed. It was widely disseminated at Coventry's urging to cure what he saw as 'great dejectedness' in the fleet. But few minds were changed; the seamen already believed that they had inflicted great damage, but in their eyes it still did not add up to an English triumph. As the unknown observer from the *Royal Charles* explained,

> whatever their Losses were, they had all the marks of a Victory on their side; they carryed away as Prize six of our Ships of Warr, an Admirall a Prisoner alive, a Vice Admirall dead of his wounds, five Captains, & near 1800 men Prisoners, while the English had no such Tokens to shew, and all that can be said to make it seem a Drawn-Battell is that the two Fleets parted in the Channell half seas over, both sides sufficiently shattered & almost beaten to pieces.

Captain Thomas Guy of the *Assurance* candidly told Pepys that the English had been 'beaten home', adding 'that the whole fleet was ashamed to hear of our Bone-fires'.

While the men of the fleet were quietly acknowledging defeat, the dejection of which Coventry spoke was to be found mainly at Whitehall, where the government was officially trumpeting victory. To judge from journals and letters in the weeks following the action, the mariners were best described as angry; officers and common seamen alike were in a decidedly foul humour. Lieutenant Roch recounted that when the *Antelope* came to the buoy of the Nore, some men in a victualler's boat

> passing by us in ye evening & not perceiving our Case, in a jeering way bid us pull ye Tomkins out of our Guns, as if we had made no use of them in ye fight, which affront I could not put up, but presently comanded them aborde. Then showing them ye Ship, on ye starbord side full of holes like a sieve, on ye larborde a breach that a Coach might enter, 12 of our Guns broken, every mast yard & rope with 2 suits of sayles spoyled, ye Platforme full of wounded or dismembred men & lastly Holles show'd them his Arm at which they shook their heads & would have excused their rash abuse; but that was not enough for such sawcy impudent Rascalls that sleeping in whole skin & not daring to look an Enemy in ye face themselves yet dare be so bold to censure others that doe; therefore tying their hands to ye Capstern bar, I showing ye way, commanded all that were able to give them 3 Lashes a piece on ye naked back with a Cat of nine tayls, which correction they took very impatiently & like litle boys cryd they would do so no more &c.

Much of the anger was directed at the obvious errors of the campaign. The men knew they had not been outfought, only outnumbered. Many felt betrayed in having been left to fight at a disadvantage when so many more good ships could have been with them. Aside from their outrage over the division of the fleet, the seamen must have been infuriated that the *Royal Sovereign* and other powerful vessels in the river had lain idle merely for want of men. Their feelings undoubtedly intensified when Jeremy Smith's *Mary*, *Montagu*, and *Guinea* at last joined from Portsmouth on the 7th, and even more so a week later with the arrival of the *Resolution*, *Foresight*, *Tiger*, *Elizabeth*, *Adventure*, *Sorlings*, *Richmond*, *Garland*, and *Nightingale*. These nine ships, along with the fifth-rate *Orange*, had sailed from Plymouth on the 3rd to join Prince Rupert's expedition. They had waited off the Lizard for day after day, battling storms and mountainous seas, until someone finally thought to recall them. They had seen no enemies and fired no guns in anger, their broadsides totally wasted. The seamen's bitterness over all that might have been was bluntly expressed in Barlow's defiant summation of the battle:

> But if it had pleased God that we had had our whole fleet together we had made an end in half the time, for we should have had them to have showed us their butter-box arses and run from us the first day, for they are nothing if they have no more ships than we have, but we may thank our own traitors-born countrymen or else we had not come to this.

Fortunately for England, the 'lower deck' was quite willing to take out its frustrations on the Dutch if given the chance. Pepys and Coventry attended Myngs's funeral at St. Mary's Whitechapel on 13 June. As they entered their coach after the service, 'there happened', as Pepys related, this extraordinary case – one of the most Romantique that ever I heard of in my life, and could not have believed but that I did see it – which was this. About a Dozen able, lusty, proper men came to the coach-side with tears in their eyes, and one of them, that spoke for the rest, begun and says to Sir W. Coventry – 'We are here a Dozen of us that have long known and loved and served our dead commander, Sir Chr. Mings, and have now done the last office of laying him in the ground. We would be glad we had any other to offer after him, and in revenge of him – all we have is our lives. If you will please to get his Royal Highness to give us a Fireshipp among us all, here is a Dozen of us, out of all which choose you one to be commander, and the rest of us, whoever he is, will serve him, and, if possible, do that that shall show our memory of our dead commander and our revenge'. Sir W. Coventry was herewith much moved (as well as I, who could hardly abstain from weeping) and took their names; . . . .

Regrettably, there is no record of further action on their request, though one supposes it must have been granted.

June and July of 1666 were difficult times for Prince Rupert and the Duke of Albemarle. As the defeated commanders they were inevitably subjected to criticism. Rupert was widely held to have been at least partly responsible for the division of the fleet and was also blamed for his seemingly dilatory response to the recall orders. Albemarle was attacked both from London and from within the fleet. Surgeon-General Pierce, apparently no friend, averred

that all the commanders, officers, and even the common seamen, do condemn every part of the late conduct of the Duke of Albemarle. Both in his fighting at all – in his manner of fighting, running among them – in his retreat, and running the ships on ground – so as nothing can be worse spoken of . . . [and] that even Smith himself, one of his creatures, did him himself condemn the late conduct from beginning to end.

Why Smith would have been so outspoken is unclear, since his absence had itself contributed to his patron's defeat. The other flag-officers were careful to evade responsibility by claiming that they had been against fighting all along, thereby leaving the general to face the public by himself.

Albemarle's most dangerous detractors were the members of the Navy Board, particularly Coventry, Carteret, and Penn, all of whom had important influence. Coventry and Carteret at first spoke openly of the overall mismanagement of the fleet, but Penn was more specific. A month after the battle Pepys recorded a lengthy conversation with him:

And in the evening Sir W Pen came to me, and we walked together and talked of the late fight. I find him very plain that the whole conduct of the late fight was ill, and that that of truth's all, and he tells me that it is not he, but two-thirds of the commanders of the whole fleet have told him so – they all saying that they durst not oppose it at the council of war, for fear of being called Cowards, though it was wholly against their judgment to fight that day with that disproportion of force; and then we not being able to use one gun of our lower tire, which was a greater disproportion then the other. Besides, we might very well have stayed in the Downs without fighting, or anywhere else, till the Prince could have come up to them – or at least till the weather was fair, that we might have the benefit of our whole force in the ships that we had. He says three things must [be] remedied, or else we shall be undone, by this fleet.

1. That we must fight in a line, whereas we fight promiscuously, to our utter and demonstrable ruine – the Duch fighting otherwise – and we, whenever we beat them.
2. We must not desert ships of our own in distress as we did, for that makes a captain desperate, and will fling away his ship when there is no hopes left him of succour.
3. That ships, when they are a little shattered, must not take the liberty to come in of themselfs; but refit themselfs the best they can, and stay out – many of our ships coming in with very small disablings.

He told me that our very commanders, nay, our very flag-officers, do stand in need of exercizing among themselfs and discoursing the business of commanding a fleet – he telling me that one of our flag-men in the fleet did not know which Tacke lost the wind or which kept it in the last engagement. He says it was pure dismaying and fear that made them all run upon the Galloper, not having their wits about them; and that it was a miracle they were not all lost. . . . He did talk very rationally to me, insomuch that I took more pleasure this night in hearing him discourse then I ever did in my life in anything that he said.

Because of Penn's proven expertise as a tactician, his frequently quoted observations have been accorded greater weight over the years than they deserved. One must always consider the relationship of critic to criticized; Penn had never forgiven Albemarle for having denied him a sea command, so it is likely that Sir William was not entirely displeased at the turn of events. His jealousy is particularly transparent in the implication that *he* would not have run the fleet on the Galloper. Other points were indisputable, at least in retrospect. To have engaged in adverse circumstances was clearly a mistake, for the battle was lost. That captains had gone into port without permission was another clear failing, and one at which Albemarle was equally infuriated. But most of Penn's arguments were simply unfounded. It would have been suicidal to stay in the Downs, and Albemarle had left there on the King's orders. Furthermore, the English *had* fought in line, and abandoning the line to assist ships in distress was strictly forbidden by the Fighting Instructions for sound reasons, as Penn knew perfectly well. Finally, the lack of exercising was unavoidable, for de Ruyter appeared before the English were ready; it in any event had no significant effect on the outcome, the Dutch themselves expressing the highest admiration for the smartness of the English manoeuvres.

The Generals' supporters fought hard to protect the reputations of their chiefs. When accounts of the action appeared in the *London Gazette*, Prince Rupert's secretary John Hayes lost no time in complaining to Williamson that the Prince's heroics had not been adequately described. Hayes suggested that since in ye Dutch Gazzet those lying wretches speake dishonourably of ye Prince it will offer the occasion of a word or two in yours more to his merit, who did indeed discover so extraordinary Courage Conduct & presence of mind in ye middest of ye showers of Cannon bullet, that higher I thinke cannot be imagin'd of any man that ever fought. I observed him with astonishment all the day.

Williamson obligingly responded in the next issue with unrestrained panegyrics, whereupon Hayes wrote to thank him: 'You have done a right to a very Brave Prince whose worth will endure praise, though I must needs say I find his Eares are too modest to heare his own'.

Modest or not, Prince Rupert and the Duke of Albemarle were not inclined to acknowledge faults pointed out by 'ordinary men'. They mounted an offensive of their own against the Navy Board, berating the Commissioners for having failed to send the promised reinforcements out of the river and for inadequate impressment efforts. Albemarle also had a direct confrontation with Coventry at which 'high words' were passed. What was said is unknown, but it may be surmised that the Duke advised Sir William to mind his tongue when discussing the battle with others. This had some effect, for a few days later Pepys encountered Coventry and found that 'He doth, I perceive, with some violence forbear saying anything to the reproach of the Duke of Albemarle, but, contrarily, speaks much of his courage; but I do as plainly see that he doth not like the Duke of Albemarle's proceedings, but, contrarily, is displeased therewith'.

Alone among the commanders, Albemarle stubbornly denied defeat. Pierce reported 'that the Duke of Albemarle is as high almost as ever, and pleases himself to think that he hath given the Dutch their bellies full – without sense of what he hath lost us – and talks how he knows now the way to beat them'. Major James Halsey, Scoutmaster-General of the Army and 'a great creature of the Duke of Albemarle's', heard the general 'say that this is a victory we have had, having, as he was sure, killed them 8000 men, and sunk about 14 of their ships; . . . He lays much of the little success we had, however, upon the fleet's being divided by order from above and the want of spirit in the commanders'.

This alleged 'want of spirit in the commanders' was to cause long-standing bitterness and controversy. On the fleet's return Albemarle was very gracious in thanking those officers whose performance he admired. His narratives praised all the flag-officers (excepting Berkeley and Ayscue) along with Captains Kempthorne, Penrose (Barlow's commander), Dare, Terne, Miller, Holles, Jennings, Moulton, Chicheley, Mootham, Wood, and Bacon, 'with other brave men whose names I know not'. His recommendations resulted in knighthood for Harman, Holles, and Jennings, and a flag appointment for Kempthorne. He was also careful to note that 'The Prince had in his Squadron twenty picked ships who all acquitted themselves well'. Although fireship captains were not mentioned in the initial report, they too were deemed to have shown courage, commanders and crews of five of the six fireships expended being granted bounties for successful service. The sixth, William Seale, was employed again and later promoted. But for the fleet's remaining captains the general showed utter contempt. 'I assure you I never fought with worse Officers than now in my life', he wrote to Coventry, 'for not above 20 of them behaved themselves like men'. And to Arlington: 'I had not above two or three & twenty that stucke to me in the hottest of the engagement before the Prince came in so that I hope the King will not be displeas'd if I displace many Captaines'.

The Duke of Albemarle's condemnation of his officers had an unavoidably self-serving ring to it. Pepys's friend Captain Cocke was not alone in pointing out that the Generals, having 'the sense of our ill-success upon them, . . . must either let the world think it was the miscarriage of the captains, or their own conduct'. This has generally been the verdict of history and it was probably true to some extent. Albemarle was definitely guilty (whether deliberately or not one cannot say) of understating the number of men who fought well. He partly belied his own accusations by giving twenty-three commanders from his own portion of the fleet clear marks of favour after the fight, either by direct praise or by immediate promotion to better ships, and there were seven others who were beyond reproach by reason of death or dangerous wounds. That makes at least thirty who can be presumed to have discharged their duty bravely. Indeed, from what is known of the casualty lists, most of those thirty had made their ships 'swim with blood' enough to satisfy even the gore-minded Duchess.

But thirty of Albemarle's ships and twenty of Rupert's did not make the whole fleet. There is damning evidence that many of the rest did not cover themselves with glory, and the general's charges were confirmed by other observers who had nothing to gain from slander. Sir Thomas Clifford seemed even more outraged than Albemarle:

> . . . if the Kinge doe not cause some of the Capts. to be hangd he will never be well servd. We heare of two good Ships that were coming out of the Swing [Swin] to put to sea when they heard shooting they went back. We have this relation from a Ketch. By this backwardness in some of the Captaines the Kinge still looses the stoutest, for when they engage frankely and are not seconded the enemy hath advantage upon them and often cuts them off, when the cowardly ones still remaine to omit theire dutys another tyme. If a severe course be not taken in this matter this is alone enough to ruine any great action of our fleet.

Clifford had not been on hand for the fight on Friday, but the anonymous eyewitness so frequently quoted in these pages had seen it all too well. 'There was a want of Courage in some, and of Conduct in others, during all the first days Engagement', he wrote, adding that 'some of the Captains had the Tampions in their Gunn's the next morning'. Then there is Van de Velde, whose drawings of the action on the 1st plainly show many English ships keeping out of danger far to windward.

Casualties are also revealing. At least seventeen of Albemarle's original fifty-six ships (figures are unknown for nine vessels) had less than ten per cent of their complement killed or wounded, despite four days of supposedly savage fighting. These ships cannot have been heavily engaged. Intelligence from the Netherlands indicated similar 'want of spirit' in the prizes, one of Williamson's agents noting that 'the boarded vessels yielded without much resistance'. This is borne out by the rather light casualties among the captors: the *Wassenaar* had six men killed, the *Stavoren* three, the *Deventer* and

Reiger four each (a notable exception was the captor of the *Clove Tree*, the *Groningen*, which sustained thirty killed and twenty-four wounded). It seems clear from all of this that the Duke of Albemarle's accusations were not entirely without substance.

Within a few days of the action six captains had been discharged. Henry Teddiman of the *Unicorn* was put out during the battle. On the fleet's return his replacement Mark Harrison followed him ashore, along with Thomas Ewens of the *Kent*, Henry Cuttance of the *Happy Return*, John Aylett of the *Portland*, and Jean-Baptiste du Tiel of the *Jersey*.

Du Tiel's case required special handling. The Duke of York, who all his life seemed to keep (at least) one foot in France, had several young French companions, and the captain of the *Jersey* was among them. Rupert and Albemarle consequently exercised singular tact and circumspection in explaining his shortcomings:

> We kept a very strict eye in ye late Engagement upon ye several Comanders in ye Fleet that we might be able to place just characters upon those who were intrusted & to esteem of all according to their qualifications for his Majs. service. And amongst ye rest there was particular reason to take notice of Mons. du Tiel, whom tho' we repute a Gentleman worthy of respect & imployment otherwise, yet of his great insufficiency in ye English tongue, we judge him not fully qualify'd for a Comand of a Ship of warr, and could not but remark some great miscarryages & disorders in ye late Engagement, which might possibly arise from ye difference of Language 'twixt ye said Capt. du Tiel, & those who ought to have been comanded by him. And that we might not seem to place any marks of favour, but to proceed in every thing with an equall care of his Majs. concerns without respect to any person, we have thought fit to recomend that Capt. to your R. H. that by your favour he may be received to some other Imployment wherein he may doe his Maj. better service. This being our duty we present it to your H. in all humility.

About a year later Pepys heard a different story when Albemarle, a little in his cups, gave the details during a private dinner with some old Army cronies. The general's 'nasty wife' brought up the subject, saying that she understood du Tiel had

> fired more shot into the Prince's ship, and others of the King's ships, then of the enemy. And the Duke of Albemarle did confirm it, and that somebody in the fight did cry out that a little Dutchman by his ship did plague him more then any other; upon which they were going to order him to be sunk, when they looked and found it was Du Tell, who, as the Duke of Albemarle says, had killed several men in several of our ships. He said, but for his interest which he knew he had at Court, he had hanged him at the Yard's-arm without staying for a Court Martiall.

The *Jersey* had also disabled the *Portland* in a collision.

The attempt to soften du Tiel's disgrace had little effect. The affair caused 'great Jarrs' with the Lord High Admiral, who 'mightily defended' his protégé. James himself had earlier sent word that any actions against the captains would have the full backing of the Crown and Admiralty; unfortunately, he had neglected to explain that this would not apply to his own favourites. He made a point of taking the Frenchman into his household as Cupbearer, which evoked a typical Marvellian response:

> *Ah, rather than transmit our scorn to Fame*
> *Draw Curtains, gentle Artist, o'er this Shame.*
> *Cashiere the Mem'ry of Dutell, raisd up*
> *To taste in stead of Death's, his Highnesse' Cup.*

Du Tiel prospered under James's protection and was eventually knighted. He also obtained another captain's post in 1671, but luckily of a galley at Tangier which never went to sea.

The removal of the other captains proved hardly less troublesome. It seemed that everyone either had friends among the accused or knew of others more guilty. The officers of the *Providence* reviled Swanley of the *York* for having 'basely' deserted them; Coventry defended Aylett but 'found fault with Steward [of the *Golden Phoenix*], whom the Duke keeps in, though as much in fault as any commander in the fleet' (Steward would go a few weeks later). The only universally applauded dismissal was Henry Teddiman's, and even that caused unhappiness. An early report of the battle had regrettably mentioned that 'They condemn mightily Sir Thomas Teddiman for a Coward', which quickly became common gossip. The vice-admiral had of course been confused with his erring kinsman, and when word of what was being said reached his ears he took predictable umbrage. The King and the Duke of York hastened to assure everyone that Sir Thomas had 'behaved himself most eminently brave all the fight'; even so he was 'mightily discontented, as being wholly slighted', and for weeks afterwards wore a duelling sword at his hip.

In view of the storms of unpleasantry that arose over the displacement of those whom the Generals regarded as the worst of the lot, it is perhaps understandable that Rupert and Albemarle thought better of proceeding against the lesser offenders. There was only one further disciplinary action. Captain George Chapple of the *Crown* was replaced in early July, but his fall seems to have been related more to some 'mutiny or disorder' in the ship than misconduct in action. The Generals did seek to prevent repetitions of du Tiel's offence: the Fighting Instructions were amended to make firing over one's own ships a capital crime.

Perhaps the greatest irony of the Four Days' Battle is that England would almost certainly have fared better had Prince Rupert been allowed to continue his expedition as planned. He might well have found and destroyed Duquesne, which would undoubtedly have diminished Louis XIV's enthusiasm for further naval adventures. Meanwhile, Albemarle's defeated but still-proud fleet could have continued its retreat into the Thames on the third day without having to undergo the calamities of the fourth. From the Dutch point of view the action as fought could have been decisive had the duc de Beaufort been poised for a Channel dash or had the East Indiamen arrived on time. Since neither of those events came to pass, the great battle had remarkably few results. The confidence of one side was shaken and the confidence of the other raised beyond reason, but the strategic situation essentially reverted to the *status quo ante*. The Dutch still needed to cover the spice convoy and the possible approach of the French, though the eventual discovery of Beaufort's idleness reduced the priority of that issue. The one important new twist was that the Dutch, emboldened by the belief that they had broken their opponent's strength beyond recovery, began to think in terms of a knockout blow: a daring penetration of the Thames with landings ashore which would speedily bring England to her knees.

Among the English, no one knew what to make of Beaufort's absence. Talbot's error was discovered on the 13th, when letters of 29 May came from Lisbon reporting that the Toulon fleet had not yet arrived. But the same correspondence also said that Beaufort was then 'daily expected' and would soon rendezvous with Mademoiselle d'Aumâle's escort, so the threat seemed undiminished. Rupert and Albemarle were still anxious at the prospect of facing the united enemy forces, and Hayes expressed the Generals' concerns to Williamson on 21 June: 'Tis strange you have no better notice of ye French fleet, I wish it doth not prove that they are making theyre silent passage round about Ireland in order to a Conjunction'. But the strategists at Whitehall were tormented even more by their former nightmare: the Irish invasion was 'on' again. As Arlington reported to Sandwich on the 14th, 'We have yet no News of Monsieur de Beaufort, the common Opinion is, he is to take Land-men in at Rochelle, to make a Descent into Ireland'. Intelligence from the Netherlands was full of this throughout the month of June, some sources even saying the invasion was already in progress. The English felt helpless, for there was now no hope of intervention by the fleet. The Duke of Ormonde had finally reached agreement with the rebellious Carrickfergus garrison and was trying to repair his fortresses, but the attitude of the 'discontented Irish' was ominous. Williamson's spies had also learned of the ambitious intentions of the Dutch. Rupert and Albemarle no longer had time or strength to oppose two possible invasions simultaneously, so it seemed that the mistakes of May might bring severe penalties.

For most of June Arlington dreaded every dispatch. But on the 27th the terrors suddenly evaporated, for a letter from Falmouth at last brought long-sought 'notice' of the French fleet. The vital intelligence had been gleaned by the alert master of an English collier captured by a French 'picaroon' and interned at La Rochelle, but subsequently released by corrupt officials on payment of ransom. The collierman revealed that Beaufort had halted at Lisbon and was under orders to stay there until Duquesne's twelve ships delivered the Queen of Portugal (whose wedding post-ponement had been reported earlier). The news meant that the Royal Navy could at least temporarily focus all its attentions on the Dutch without fear from the flank. England had been granted an ill-deserved reprieve; the mistakes would carry no penalty beyond the ships and men already lost.

Chapter XVIII

Sequel

At length the adverse admirals appear;
(The two bold champions of each country's right:)
Their eyes describe the lists as they come near,
And draw the lines of death before they fight.

The States' Fleet had only fifty days to enjoy its ascendancy. A confident de Ruyter emerged from the Maas on 25 June and eight days later anchored with his full array in the mouth of the Thames. The plan of action as drawn up by Johan de Witt called for de Ruyter to drive straight up the King's Channel and deliver the *coup de grâce* to the English fleet at its moorings. In addition, 2,700 infantry embarked in flyboats were to be landed in Essex or Kent to complete the enemy's demoralization. The English, however, easily countered these threats. A flotilla under Banckert and de Liefde did probe the King's Channel, but found no buoys or navigation aids except false ones cunningly laid out in the sands. They also found a squadron of English men-of-war and fireships waiting in the East Swin to contest the passage. Since de Ruyter lacked trained pilots anyway, he abandoned all thoughts of penetrating the river. As for the landings, wherever the Dutch reconnoitred the shore English troops were observed marching in the fields. These were mostly ill-equipped 'Train-Bands' (local militia), but from the sea they looked like regular regiments. There being no hope of putting Dutch soldiers ashore without stiff opposition, the transports were sent home. De Ruyter now put into operation his own uncomplicated though still overly optimistic plan: he would blockade the Thames until the English either sued for peace or sent out the decimated remains of their fleet to be destroyed.

In England, the dockyards completed the necessary repairs expeditiously. At first it was feared that it would be more difficult to find men to make up for the casualties and the wave of desertions that always occurred when the fleet was in port. Impressment was consequently carried to unusual extremes. Sea-borne press gangs staged surprise raids on coastal towns, while London, previously left alone for fear of civil unrest, was subjected to a sudden massive sweep. The usual niceties were ignored. Pepys was 'mightily troubled' on 30 June to find that citizens had been 'pressed in the City out of houses – the persons wholly unfit for sea, and many of them people of very good fashion – which is a shame to think of; and carried to Bridewell they are, yet without being impressed with money legally, as they ought to be'. London's riverine transportation system was disrupted; all the watermen who were not carried away went into hiding. In a particularly idiotic excess, men were taken even from victualling ships and Ordnance Office boats. Though illegal and unpopular, the 'irregular impress' did send some 2,750 men to the fleet from the capital alone. When these were added to the hundreds more brought in from the coastal towns and another 2,000 soldiers rushed to sea by the King, the navy eventually had more men on hand than ever before.

The English could have sailed in numbers equal to the Dutch as early as the first week of July. But even though the enemy was 'vapouring off the Gunfleet', Rupert and Albemarle took their time. Satisfied that the Train-Bands on the coast and the absence of buoys in the river would defeat de Witt's intentions, and now knowing that the French were not a threat, the Generals refused to sail until the dockyards had fitted out the long-delayed *Loyal London*, *Warspite*, *Cambridge*, and *Greenwich*. When all was ready, the massed strength of the Royal Navy filed through the King's Channel on 22 July in a line nearly ten miles long. The Dutch were waiting in the Sledway off Harwich. De Ruyter, unwilling to fight in shoals known only to his enemy, beat into open water against a light easterly breeze for two days. On the night of the 24th the fleets anchored about twelve miles apart with the Dutch S.E. by S. of the English. Though position reports vary, de Ruyter probably lay ten to fifteen miles east of the Galloper – roughly on or near the 'battleground' of the 4th of June.

At dawn on 25 July, St. James's Day in the English liturgical calendar, the fleets prepared for action. The opponents were almost identical in numbers, but (unknown to the Dutch) size and firepower tipped the scales heavily in favour of the English. De Ruyter had seventy-two ships, seventeen frigates, and two three-mast yachts with 4,645 guns and 22,234 seamen and marines. He also had twenty fireships and seven small advice-yachts. The Royal Navy had deployed eighty-seven ships of the fourth rate or larger along with two of the fifth rate, one of the sixth, and sixteen fireships. Ten of the fourth-rates were merchantmen, but mostly bigger and better than those formerly employed; the *Charles Merchant* even boasted a few demi-cannon. The English had an understated nominal strength of 4,854 guns and 23,142 men, excluding fireships. Uncounted small ordnance and supernumerary crewmen would have swelled the totals to about 5,100 guns and not less than 24,000 men. The disparity in calibres was as wide as ever.

The English did have a weakness: the scarcity of fifth-rates. This want had also been felt in the Four Days' Battle, and the Generals had subsequently advised the Duke of York that it would be 'very advantageous' to have at least one light frigate for each division. James had accordingly spared eight from other pressing duties, but in the end Rupert and Albemarle took only two after all. This came about because of the manning situation. Although the intensive press left the navy in excellent condition in sheer numbers of men, there was still a shortage of proper mariners. When the four large new ships joined the fleet in mid-July with only landsmen aboard, crews were found for them by transferring all the topmen from the three weakest merchantmen, three elderly prize fourth-rates – and six of the long-sought fifth-rates.* Some such expedient was undoubtedly warranted, since the four new men-of-war had half again

---

*The fourth-rates *Marmaduke*, *Welcome*, and *Zealand*; the hired *Katherine*, *East India Merchant*, and *Castle Frigate*; and the fifth-rates *Norwich*, *Pearl*, *Oxford*, *Garland*, *Nightingale*, and *Sorlings*. The hired *East India Merchant* was not the same ship as the *East India London*, which remained with the fleet.

the firepower of the twelve vessels deleted. Still, it might have been better to have sacrificed a few more small fourth-rates instead of the frigates; their absence seriously hampered English capabilities in scouting, pursuit, and both offensive and defensive fireship tactics.

Both sides had adjusted their flag-lists since the previous battle. The English had confirmed Spragge, Holmes, and Utber in their originally temporary flags, while Kempthorne stood in for the convalescent Harman. Among the Dutch, Jan Evertsen had come out of retirement to replace his brother as Lieutenant-Admiral of Zeeland over de Witt's protests. Lesser vacancies were filled by Van der Zaan of Amsterdam and Govert 't Hoen of the Noorderkwartier. Both English and Dutch reverted to the basic fighting order drawn up in May, though with command assignments revised:

English		Dutch	
White Squadron (van)		**Second Squadron (van)**	
Van:	Teddiman, V.Adm.	**Van:**	De Vries, L.Adm. (F)
		Extra:	Coenders, V.Adm. (F)
			Bruynsvelt, SbN. (F)
Centre:	Allin, Adm.	**Centre:**	J. Evertsen, L.Adm. (Z)
		Extra	C. Evertsen, SbN. (Z)
Rear:	Utber, R.Adm.	**Rear:**	Banckert, V.Adm. (Z)
Red Squadron (centre)		**First Squadron (centre)**	
Van:	Jordan, V.Adm.	**Van:**	A. van Nes, L.Adm. (M)
Centre:	Generals	**Centre:**	De Ruyter, Adm.-Gen.
		Extra:	J. van Nes, SbN. (M)
Rear:	Holmes, R.Adm.	**Rear:**	De Liefde, V.Adm. (M)
Blue Squadron (rear)		**Third Squadron (rear)**	
Van:	Kempthorne, R.Adm.	**Van:**	Meppel, L.Adm. (N)
		Extra:	Schram, V.Adm. (N)
			't Hoen, SbN. (N)
Centre:	Smith, Adm.	**Centre:**	Tromp, L.Adm. (A)
		Extra	Van der Zaan, SbN. (A)
Rear:	Spragge, V.Adm.	**Rear:**	Sweers, V.Adm. (A)

The weather was warm and hazy with a barely perceptible breeze from the north, giving the English the weather gage. The protagonists formed in roughly parallel lines, heads to the east. When the English seemed suitably dressed, the Generals made the signal to advance. As the Fighting Instructions required, the leading ship steered for the headmost of the enemy with the rest of the fleet attempting to keep station in line abreast. Meanwhile, all was not well with the Dutch. Their line was poorly formed, de Ruyter's squadron lying to leeward of the other two. The resultant 'halfe moone' might have been a manifestation of the *slangvormige* line, the formation designed to preserve the commander-in-chief; but if so, de Ruyter violated its spirit by keeping the *Zeven*

Provinciën and a few seconds in an exposed position to windward of the rest of their squadron. The Dutch also failed to coordinate their motions. Evertsen came under sail before de Ruyter was ready, which produced a gap between van and centre. When de Ruyter did follow, several of his ships were intermingled with the Third Squadron. Waiting for these vessels to draw clear (which they never did), Tromp's divisions continued 'to ly with their foretop sayles to the mast' so that another gap appeared between centre and rear. Even more surprising than the disordered line was de Ruyter's passive acquiescence in the lee gage. Attempting no manoeuvres, he seemed content with a broadside gunnery contest on the same tack as the enemy; 'to try who were the best men', as seaman Barlow put it. This uncharacteristic inactivity was explained by the fatal Dutch delusion that their own fleet was the stronger. Prisoners-of-war afterwards admitted that they thought the Four Days' Battle had cost the Royal Navy thirty-five ships and at least ten thousand men. When the English reappeared in unexpected numbers, it was merely supposed that the lost ships had been replaced by contemptible merchantmen, and the whole fleet 'very ill mann'd'.

The English attack did not come off quite as planned. Rupert and Albemarle had intended to bring the whole fleet into action together, but owing to the calm weather the van made contact long before the centre and rear. The first shots were fired at about 9:30 when the Frisians opened up on the leading units of the White Squadron at rather long range. The English continued to close with kettledrums beating but guns silent for another half-hour. At 10 the third-rate *Anne* finally replied with a rolling salvo of roundshot, and the violence thereafter rose steadily over the next three hours. When the rear division of the Blue was at last engaged about 1 o'clock, there were nearly five thousand guns in continuous service. The fighting was then 'extremely hot and fierce', wrote Barlow, 'the noise of the cannon roaring in the seas like claps of thunder, which were heard in England all over Kent'.

The English expected great things from their fireships. But these, as Allin lamented, were 'lost very foolishly; they going on without order were torn a-pieces and then forced to burn themselves without doing any execution'. Six were expended in vain and others driven off disabled. These fruitless efforts were much influenced by the lack of fifth-rates, unescorted fireships being approached and towed away with impunity by the enemy's frigates and even longboats. The light wind also contributed by slowing the advance; the Dutch were able to train their broadsides on the attackers for much longer than usual, and ignition had to be delayed until so near the targets that the incendiary crews could have little chance of rescue. Most of the fireships expended were reportedly abandoned too early, some before they were even clear of their own fleet. This one English failure, however, could not turn the fortunes of the day; the St. James's Day Fight was decided by the gun.

The gaps between the Dutch squadrons caused the battle to develop into three separate actions. In the van, the White Squadron proved to be much stronger than the Zeeland-Friesland squadron, the weakest of the Dutch. Even so, Allin reported that 'The fight continued nigh 5 howers before there was any appearance of advantage on either side'. The English flagships suffered severely; and both Utber's *Rupert* and Teddiman's *Royal Katherine* were forced to 'come out of the line and lay by to mend ther hurts'. Allin was also displeased with many of his officers, charging that

> our people were very awk to get into a line and some never did, as Day [of the
> *Baltimore*], Sackler [of the *Expedition*] and some others, but those shot through
> several of our ships contrary to a strict order. . . . Sir Tho Teddeman fought bravely
> upon his party, although the *St. George* and *Anne* did him no service and the *Old
> James* did us as little. The *Rich. & Martha* went away from us. The Rear Admiral's
> division did us little help.

Allin may have been a little too hard on some of the captains; at least two of the
criticized ships had received quite legitimate damage. The hardest fighting apparently
fell to the four vessels lying immediately astern of the *Royal Katherine* (the *Dover, St.
George, Dunkirk*, and *Richard & Martha*), all of which were among the few requiring
dockyard repairs after the action. Nevertheless, the White Squadron had the upper
hand throughout. A Dutch account frankly admitted that 'Upon the first brunt the
English wounded and killed abundance of the Zeelanders and Fries'. The Frisians were
particularly hard pressed. They gradually fell back before Teddiman's division so that
the heads of the fleets began to bend around to the southeast, threatening the line of
retreat of the whole Dutch van. The defeat of the hapless squadron was finally sealed
by a series of calamitous casualties among the commanders. The first was Jan Evertsen,
who was killed about 1 o'clock when a great shot carried away both his legs. Soon
afterwards the Frisians suffered a double blow: the beloved Tjerk Hiddes de Vries was
severely wounded and Vice-Admiral Rudolf Coenders was killed outright. De Vries still
clung to life three days later, but a newsletter from Vlissingen reported that he had
been 'shot in one leg even up to his belly', adding with resigned (and accurate) finality,
'soe hee must dye'. The flagships of the stricken commanders maintained the fight
much to the credit of their captains, but at 3 o'clock Evertsen's *Walcheren* had her
main topsail yard 'shot a-pieces' and fell off to leeward. With that the Dutch van
seemed to lose heart. The whole squadron bore away before the wind, 'being come to
fire only their stern guns', as Allin exultantly wrote.

The action in the centre opened at 11. There the English divisions under Jordan, the
Generals, and Holmes enjoyed a decisive firepower superiority over their corresponding opponents under Van Nes, de Ruyter, and de Liefde. Jordan and Holmes
acquitted themselves well as usual, but it was the Generals' division that carried the
day. Rupert and Albemarle had appropriated for their own command a disproportionate concentration of major warships including eight of the third rate or
larger. The captains of this division were the picked elite: John Cox, Sir William
Jennings, Sir Frescheville Holles, Robert Clark, Thomas Penrose, Richard Beach, and
Thomas Lamming, to name only a few. De Ruyter's division was rather modestly
equipped, and four hours of sustained bombardment gradually reduced his ships to
wreckage, with great loss of life. Three of his best captains were killed: Hugo van
Nieuwenhof of the *Stad en Lande*, Cornelis van Hogenhoeck of the *Zuiderhuis*, and the
recklessly courageous Ruth Maximiliaan of the *Wassenaar*.

It was nevertheless a hard fight. The most notable event, one remembered with
pride by the Dutch even in defeat, was the Olympian struggle between the fleet

flagships. According to a second-hand account related by Coventry, the Duke of Albemarle was smugly confident when the ships first came together: '"Now", says he (chawing of Tobacco the while), "will this fellow come and give me two broadsides, and then he will run."' But after two hours it was the English flagship that 'ran'; the *Royal Charles* tacked to repair her rigging and was out of action for nearly an hour. When she resumed the duel and was received as rudely as before, an officer tactlessly remarked to the Duke, 'Sir, methinks De Ruyter hath given us more than two broadsides'. Albemarle grimly muttered, 'Well, but you shall find him run by and by'. Yet after another hour the *Zeven Provinciën* still stood proudly while the *Royal Charles*, as Sir Thomas Clifford admitted, 'was againe soe much shattered that wee had not a rope to help ourselves, and could not steer, soe that wee were towed out of the line by boates'.

This time the *Zeven Provinciën* gained little respite. She had no sooner driven off the *Royal Charles* when the gilded form of the *Royal Sovereign* came looming alongside. Commanded by John Cox as a private ship distinguished only by a special 'blood-red pennant' at the main, the *Sovereign* was a mighty force in the English centre. Her original station had been several places ahead of the *Royal Charles*, but during the approach the flagship had shifted forward of her to bring the Generals opposite the *Zeven Provinciën*. Cox had been left to engage de Ruyter's trailing seconds, among them Van Ghent's *Gelderland*, Van Gelder's *Klein Hollandia*, and Maximiliaan's *Wassenaar*. These vessels suffered terrible mauling from the great ship, the *Gelderland* in particular being 'rendered uncapable of Action'. A little before 3 o'clock the *Sovereign* herself was attacked by a Dutch fireship which she sank alongside with her guns. It was shortly after this incident that Cox's leviathan, having disposed of all other immediate opposition, challenged the *Zeven Provinciën*. De Ruyter's dauntless crew manned their guns once more. But not even they could stand against the hated 'Golden Devil'; overwhelmed by the awesome fifty-gun salvoes, the Dutch flagship reeled away with her main topmast shot down and the timbers of her sides bashed and broken. This marked the end for the Dutch centre; by 4 o'clock the whole squadron was streaming south in full retreat.

The fight in the rear went differently. Tromp, Meppel, and Sweers had the strongest of the Dutch squadrons, with substantially more men and guns than Smith, Spragge, and Kempthorne. Tromp's advantage was further enhanced by four or five wayward vessels from de Ruyter's squadron. But beyond the sheer strength of the Dutch, the Blue Squadron contributed to its own troubles. Smith's fireships were so deplorably mismanaged that one observer thought them more of a menace to their own side than to the enemy; three were expended without result. Of greater consequence, much of the Blue Squadron was somewhat tardy in forming line. Although the fighting here began at noon, the leading division under Kempthorne at first had to shoulder more than its share because of straggling by the rest. As the junior rear-admiral, Kempthorne had been given a rather weak assemblage of ships: two of the third rate, three of the fourth, and three merchantmen. These vessels met a hot reception – too hot, as it predictably turned out, for the ever-incompetent Charles Talbot of the *Elizabeth*. Pleading 'eight or nine dangerous shots', Talbot departed for Harwich sometime in mid-afternoon. His reports of the success of the Red and White Squadrons thrilled the London public, though Pepys and Coventry heard correctly 'that this gallant is come away a little too soon, having lost never a mast nor sail'. Talbot was cashiered.* But others of Kempthorne's ships experienced real carnage. Captain William Martin's hired *East India London* was practically torn apart and Martin killed. A greater disaster occurred shortly before 3 o'clock when the third-rate *Resolution*, having lost her fore topmast, drifted into the enemy. The rest of the division loyally bore up to assist, but a Dutch fireship took advantage of her distress, and the English could do nothing more than rescue Captain Willoughby Hannam and about one hundred of his crew. Some two hundred drowned.

Kempthorne's unavailing efforts on behalf of the *Resolution* led to further difficulties for the Blue Squadron. His temporary reversal of heading forced Smith's division to take over the van and also left the leading division of the Dutch rear unattended. Led by Meppel, these mostly Noorderkwartier vessels gradually forged into the gap vacated by Kempthorne and then tacked at about 5 o'clock to weather Smith by the head. In the process they nearly trapped an English flagship. The *Henry*, carrying Rear-Admiral of the Red Sir Robert Holmes, had luffed out of the line at 4 o'clock after sustaining damage to both fore and main topmasts during the long engagement in the centre. When Meppel's ships tacked to the west the *Henry* lay squarely in their path. Holmes barely completed his makeshift repairs in time to flee into the Blue Squadron, with which he kept company for the remainder of the action. The new third-rate *Cambridge* of Holmes's division also joined the Blue, perhaps in similar circumstances.

The Dutch manoeuvre threw the already disordered English into further confusion. Smith's division tacked (towing around with boats) to engage the westerly-headed Meppel, who now held the weather gage. The rest of the Blue Squadron kept on the original port tack holding the wind over Tromp and Sweers for another hour, but gradually fell back to the northeast under pressure from superior numbers. At 6 o'clock Spragge and Kempthorne tacked to follow Smith, their opponents tacking with them. The change in course took the two rear squadrons almost directly away from their southeasterly sailing main bodies. Apparently oblivious to events elsewhere, Tromp with about thirty-five ships and Smith with twenty-eight went off towards the Galloper firing furiously until long after dark. What passed between them no one knows. From the distant viewpoint of the *Royal Charles*, observers could discern only 'a great part of that squadron very far to the leeward and the Flag with many of his division all in a smoke intermixed with the Dutch colours, which confused fighting could not well please'. Smith afterwards claimed to have put the Dutch to flight, while Tromp vehemently insisted that the English gave way steadily and that he broke off the 'pursuit' only when he learned by advice-boat of de Ruyter's defeat. At some point the newly appointed Rear-Admiral Govert 't Hoen was killed in the *Jozua*, though no ships were lost other than the *Resolution*. Smith's *Loyal London* had 147 killed and wounded,

---

*Despite his consistently poor performance, Talbot with the help of powerful family and friends obtained another captain's commission in 1678 and again in 1685.

most of them probably by the guns of Meppel's *Westfriesland* which lost over 100 men herself.

While the rear squadrons fought their private battle, the rest of the States' Fleet raced for the Weilings. The English pursued vigorously but with little success. The difference in gunnery practice probably had much to do with this, the English having fired mostly into the hulls with roundshot and the Dutch high with bar and chain. It was consequently the victors rather than the vanquished who had suffered worst in sails and rigging. In the centre de Ruyter personally covered the withdrawal despite the damage to his flagship. 'With great gallantry', said Clifford, the Dutch commander made 'severall tacks to fetch off his maimed ships, and once endangered himselfe very much for the rescue of his second, who at last was soe disabled that hee could not gett off'. The maimed second was Van Ghent's *Gelderland*. But de Ruyter need not have worried; Van Ghent was saved by his own wits. As the *Royal Sovereign*, *Fairfax*, *Lion*, and *Triumph* closed in to summon his surrender, the colonel of marines 'like a very knowing seaman' suddenly 'chopt to an anchor', whereupon the powerful ebb rushing from the Thames swept the surprised English past him to leeward. The current made it impossible to beat back to him in the light airs. A serious attempt was mounted by the weatherly fireship *Abigail*, Thomas Wilshaw commanding; but a Dutch fireship under tow by a longboat intercepted the *Abigail* and turned her aside. The *Gelderland* later crept home safely under jury rig. In the remaining hours of daylight only two vessels were caught, both by the White Squadron. At 6 o'clock the new 65-gun Friesland ship *Sneek* commanded by Ruyrt Hillebrantszoon yielded to the *Royal James*, and about an hour later the *Warspite* captured Banckert's flagship, the 60-gun *Tholen*. To the great disappointment of the captors Banckert had earlier shifted his flag to the 50-gun *Kampveere*. The prizes would have required more seamen than the English were willing to spare, so both were burned on Allin's orders.

The fleets continued their southeasterly progress during the night. Early in the morning the still gentle breeze swung to the southwest, giving the Dutch the weather gage. The English were dismayed to find that the despised 'butterboxes' were markedly superior sailors in light winds; most of the Dutch easily pulled away. But one matchless prize seemed within reach: the battered *Zeven Provinciën* with a few loyal escorts was left far behind the others. At dawn Allin with part of the White Squadron was slightly ahead of this group, though some distance to the east. On finding that he could not approach closely from his leeward position, Allin tacked to engage de Ruyter in a distant head-to-head pass in hopes of inflicting some disabling injury; but he merely succeeded in losing all the ground he had gained (and also in getting himself wounded in the face with splinters, to his 'great dolour'). His manoeuvre proved to be a major mistake, for none of the larger warships was able to make up the distance again. Rupert and Albemarle now came to regret having left behind the nimble fifth-rates which had been so useful in the chase at Lowestoft. De Ruyter did suffer an embarrassing if inconsequential indignity when a fast pleasure-boat belonging to Prince Rupert, the *Fanfan*, impudently peppered the *Zeven Provinciën*'s stern with two tiny guns. The fireship *Land of Promise* posed a greater threat but was towed away by Dutch longboats. The rest of the English were left to engage mainly with their bow chasers which eventually caused enough damage to bring de Ruyter to the point of despair; but in the end Banckert put together a hastily improvised line which distracted the English vanguard long enough for the flagship to be towed out of danger. By late morning the Dutch were safely behind the sandbanks.

Having failed to catch the enemy's main body, the English now missed an even better opportunity to entrap the remaining squadron. The wind veered to the northeast during the day. At about 3 p.m. the Dutch rear was sighted in the distance sailing towards the Netherlands with the Blue Squadron following. The Generals worked inshore and by the end of the day were positioned to intercept off the entrance to de Ruyter's anchorage. In the middle of the night they anchored hoping that the leeward tide would bring Tromp towards them. That much succeeded; the Dutch were indeed carried within reach. But at dawn it was discovered that only the *Triumph* and one or two other vessels had noticed the signal to anchor. The rest had fallen downwind to the southwest and, inexplicably, the Blue Squadron was nowhere to be seen. Themselves endangered, Rupert and Albemarle could only move aside as Tromp gained the Weilings unopposed. When the Blue Squadron rejoined at 4 o'clock, it was learned that during the night Sir Jeremy Smith had called off the pursuit after being erroneously advised by his pilot that the Dutch had led him into the shoals.

Thus ended the St. James's Day Fight. It was a clear-cut if not very satisfactory English victory. The Dutch had escaped with the loss of only two ships, and those partly offset by the burning of the *Resolution*. English casualties amounted to between 1,000 and 1,200 according to the Generals. Five captains were killed or fatally wounded: Martin of the *East India London*, Hugh Seymour of the *Foresight*, John Parker of the *Yarmouth*, Joseph Sanders of the *Breda*, and Arthur Ashby of the *Guinea*. The Dutch had suffered more, though not as severely as the English supposed; the totals of killed and wounded probably did not exceed 2,500.

The battle produced the usual round of quarrels among the English, chief of which was the great feud between Robert Holmes and Jeremy Smith. The already strained relations between these two natural rivals broke completely with Smith's decision to cut short his pursuit of Tromp. This so incensed Holmes that he fired shots to windward of the *Loyal London* and afterwards loudly denounced the Admiral of the Blue as an outright coward. The Generals wisely maintained an outward neutrality, but did express private opinions to the King and Duke of York. Albemarle defended Sir Jeremy without reservation as 'most falsely accused'. Rupert supported Holmes to the extent of accusing Smith of 'gross errors', though carefully adding, 'not in point of courage but want of conduct'. In October Holmes brought official charges so that the King found it necessary to conduct a formal inquiry. He ultimately declared Smith guilty of an error in judgement by 'having too easily yielded to the single opinion of his pilote without consulting the Masters or Pilotes of any other ships'. On the other hand, Charles with his usual good sense found the accusation of cowardice a little ridiculous in view of the fact that the *Loyal London* had the worst casualties in the fleet; Holmes had lost only two or three men.

The Smith–Holmes dispute was the most sensational controversy, but not the only one. Richard Utber, the Rear-Admiral of the White whose division had been criticized by Allin, was 'turned out for cowardice' immediately after the action, being 'sent from the *Rupert* into a ketch of three guns' to await trial. His ship was turned over to Captain Francis Sanders of the *Sweepstakes*. But Utber (Allin's brother-in-law) was evidently able to explain his behaviour, for within two days his flag was again flying from the *Rupert*. Retribution for his division's failures was instead visited on the captains, of whom George Batts of the *Unicorn* and Abraham Ansley of the *Helverston* were dismissed. Several captains from other divisions also incurred the Generals' wrath. Those displaced included Tobias Sackler of the *Expedition*, Francis Steward of the *Golden Phoenix*, and Robert Gilby of the *Golden Ruyter*, along with the afore-mentioned Charles Talbot.

If the winning side was less than pleased with the outcome, the losers were utterly demoralized. The arguments among the English were mere ripples on the surface compared with the storms of recrimination among the Dutch. The Zeelanders and Frisians were angry at de Ruyter, who in turn blamed everything on the commanders of the rear squadron. When Tromp went aboard the *Zeven Provinciën* on his return, the commander-in-chief greeted him with torrents of reproachful invective. The Admiral-General accused him in the most abusive language – before the ears of all the seamen – of having deliberately failed to support the centre squadron in its hour of need. Tromp was incredulous. Having expected to be received as a hero for his successful action against Smith, he responded with insults of his own. The long-standing enmity between the two soon became a seemingly irreconcilable breach, which was resolved by the States-General in the only way possible: Tromp was dismissed from the service. For good measure his rear-admiral, Van der Zaan, was stripped of his flag. The other rear squadron division commanders, Meppel and Sweers, were also attacked by de Ruyter but were allowed to remain. Both were, however, passed over for the coveted post of Lieutenant-Admiral of Amsterdam, the States of Holland instead appointing Colonel Van Ghent.

As indecisive as the St. James's Day Fight was in material terms, it soon produced important benefits for the victors. Seven damaged English warships including the *Royal Charles* were sent into port between the 29th and the 1st, joining four others which had gone in during or immediately after the battle. All the rest were able to remain at sea, where they were reinforced by the belated arrival of nine freshly manned fifth-rates. Casting about for ways to exploit the victory, the Generals on the 7th decided to mount a descent on the Dutch coast: the traitor Laurens van Heemskerck would guide a landing party through the shallows to the islands of Vlieland and Terschelling where, according to Heemskerck, the States and the East India Company kept well-stocked storehouses. The expedition was entrusted to Sir Robert Holmes, who was assigned five fourth-rates with the *Tiger* as flagship, four fifth-rates, five fireships, and Rupert's yacht *Fanfan*. The landing force consisted of 1,170 marines, seamen, and gentlemen volunteers embarked in ketches and longboats.

Holmes's detachment left the fleet on 8 August. On his arrival off the Terschelling coast in rather dirty weather that afternoon, a hitch developed when it was found that Heemskerck's knowledge of the shoals had been woefully exaggerated. Fortunately, the fifth-rate *Garland* happened to capture a Danish merchantman whose captain was well acquainted with the channel. The Dane agreed to take over the pilotage in return for freedom for himself and his ship and cargo. When the weather cleared the next morning, the English discovered that the Vlie roads was packed from end to end with merchantmen – over 160 of them, with only a few small warships in attendance. Holmes instantly postponed the landing, since the shipping was far more important than anything he might find ashore. Shifting with his Danish pilot to the *Fanfan*, Sir Robert advanced towards the anchorage accompanied by the fireships and a flotilla of ketches and longboats escorted by the fifth-rate *Pembroke.* At Holmes's approach two frigates sallied forth to engage him. These were quickly dispatched by the fireships *Richard* commanded by Henry Brown and the *Bryar* under Joseph Paine. Actually, the *Bryar* ran aground short of her target; but the terror-stricken Dutch crew had already taken to their boats, so Paine's men simply rowed over in their own boat, fired the ship by hand, and then returned to float the *Bryar* free. By this time the Dutch merchantmen had been mostly abandoned. The fireships *Samuel*, *Lizard*, and *Fox* destroyed the three largest, after which English longboats rowed from ship to ship until over 150 vessels were afire. About ten escaped ('to tell the news on the Change of Amsterdam', said Allin) by sheltering in a narrow channel under the protection of a 24-gun privateer. The next morning Holmes successfully landed his companies on Terschelling, but found little of value. After plundering and burning to the ground the small town of West Terschelling, the invaders re-embarked and returned to enjoy the accolades of the fleet. Holmes's Bonfire, as it came to be known, cost the Netherlands an estimated £1,000,000 in ships and cargo. There were ugly riots in Amsterdam; de Ruyter's house was stoned. But the Dutch were even more furious at the English for the senseless destruction of a harmless fishing village. They vowed revenge.

The English returned to Solebay on 15 August to replenish ammunition and obtain new fireships. There were high hopes for another cruise on the Dutch coast, but that was not to be. The Royal Navy was instead thrown on the defensive by the re-appearance of the duc de Beaufort, whose arrival at La Rochelle on the 13th was soon discovered by Williamson. By this time it was too late in the year for the French to attempt anything against Ireland. Thus, when scouts reported on the 27th that de Ruyter had gone to sea with eighty sail the day before, the Generals could confidently 'conclude them designed for as speedy a Conjunction as they can with ye French Fleet'. The English were still in doubt whether the conjunction would be attempted by the Scottish route or the Channel, and plans were drawn up for both contingencies. De Ruyter soon settled the question by sailing towards the Straits of Dover, whereupon the Generals weighed and moved south to intercept.

On the 31st the English sighted the Dutch off Long Sand Head. Rupert and Albemarle made towards them, but (for the third time in the war) the pilots led the fleet onto the Galloper. The *Royal Charles* and *Royal Katherine* ran aground, 'contrary to all our imagination and to our great surprisal'. Though both were refloated, the delay prevented an engagement that day. During the night de Ruyter tacked north in high winds and seas, and part of his fleet encountered the Blue Squadron. In the confused action that resulted the English lost the 54-gun *Charles Merchant*, which had her foremast shot down and drifted among the Dutch to be captured and the next day set afire. She was the best of the hired ships, larger than most fourth-rates. Morning brought a violent easterly gale. De Ruyter, having tacked again, passed through the straits keeping close under the French shore between Cap Gris-Nez and Boulogne. This gave shelter from the worst of the storm, for the coastline there runs north and south. The Generals tried to weather the Dutch by tacking even closer inshore. Holmes's division of the Red succeeded, but had to be recalled when rough seas prevented the rest of the fleet from following. Left well offshore, the English were exposed to the full fury of the elements. When sails and rigging began to carry away, the Generals gave up all thoughts of a battle and retreated down the Channel to the safety of St. Helens. The storm disabled many ships; the veteran second-rate *St. Andrew* was wrecked, breaking her back on the Varne Sand.

The English were obliged to lie off Portsmouth for nearly two weeks while the damaged vessels refitted. During this interval came the sad news of the Great Fire, which over three days burned out many of the most prosperous districts of London. On 5 September the Duke of Albemarle received urgent orders from the King to return to the capital to deal with the crisis. The next day the general departed 'with tears in his eyes', his service at sea never to be resumed. Prince Rupert now assumed sole command.

During the enforced idleness of the English, the Dutch and French missed their chance for an unopposed conjunction. This time, contrary to common belief, it was the Dutch who backed out and not Louis XIV. After the unfought battle of 1 September, de Ruyter anchored in the Channel near Étaples, a few miles south of Boulogne. At that time the States' Fleet could easily have sailed to meet the French at Belle-Île, as Louis hoped it would. De Ruyter was unaware, however, that the English had been incapacitated by the storm, and assumed that Rupert and Albemarle were at sea somewhere to the west. The Dutch were unwilling to fight in the Channel owing to the lack of harbours to which disabled ships could retire, and de Ruyter consequently concluded that the conjunction should be postponed until the English could be lured away. On 8 September the States' Fleet withdrew through the straits to the flats off Dunkirk. That day the Dutch council-of-war wrote to the duc de Beaufort, warning him of his danger and urging him to seek safety in the nearest harbour.

With almost perfect bad timing, the French had already begun their one and only serious attempt to join the Dutch. Having victualled at La Rochelle, Beaufort met Duquesne's ships at Belle-Île on 5 September and set sail a few days later with some forty men-of-war and fifteen fireships. On the 13th he anchored off Dieppe to embark six hundred soldiers sent there to augment his crews, and also to await fourteen ships which had been separated in storms during the passage. He was still there the next day when he received the unexpectedly discouraging letter from his allies, with its implication that the unopposed English were seeking him. Understandably dismayed, he promptly called off the expedition and made his way back to Brest. That was probably a fortunate decision, for by then the French *were* in danger. Prince Rupert had hurried to sea on the 13th on receiving intelligence that Beaufort had been off Ushant two days before. The English were lurking in wait south of Dungeness on the

14th and might well have destroyed the French fleet had it pressed on.

Seven of Beaufort's missing vessels never got the word to turn back. On the 18th they blundered into the White Squadron, mistaking Allin's white command flag for their own colours. On discovering their mistake the French scattered in every direction. The *Mazarin, Bourbon*, and *Mercoeur* fled to Le Havre and the *Dragon* to Dieppe, while the *Ville de Rouen* and a fireship somehow slipped past the English and eventually reached Zeeland. But the largest ship, the new 60-gun *Rubis* under Duquesne's third-in-command Louis de la Roche, surrendered after a hard three-hour fight with the *Adventure, Foresight, Monck*, and Allin's *Royal James* (which lost more men than she had in the Four Days' Battle). De la Roche was a friend and former comrade-in-arms of several of the English commanders, having served with Rupert's Royalist squadron in the Civil War. Marvell quipped that *'our whole Fleet, angling, has catcht a Roach'*.

Operations in the second half of September were increasingly hampered by bad weather. De Ruyter had been sick for much of the cruise and finally went ashore on the 23rd. His place was taken by Van Nes, but only under the watchful eye of Johan de Witt, who thought fit to oversee affairs in person. As soon as it was certain that the French had retired, Prince Rupert decided to bring the fleet into port for the winter. While passing by the Downs on the way to the King's Channel on the 25th, his scouts sighted the Dutch. Both sides prepared for action, but yet another storm built up before they could engage. The English anchored, but the Dutch did not and were soon blown out of sight. When the weather cleared Rupert continued on into the river, reaching the Nore on 3 October. As for the Dutch, they received welcome news that the East India Company's long-delayed *retourvloot* had slipped around Scotland undetected. With this the States' Fleet also returned to port.

The campaign of 1666 appeared to have gone reasonably well for the Royal Navy. It had rebounded impressively from its initial defeat. It had reaffirmed its dominance in battle on St. James's Day, had wreaked havoc with the enemy's merchant marine in the Bonfire, and had driven back the French. But all of that was deceptive; the war was lost. England might have won it by capturing the East India convoy or more surely by defeating the States' Fleet severely enough to keep it permanently in its harbours. Opportunities for the second alternative had been missed with the division of the fleet before the Four Days' Battle and then with the Dutch escape in the St. James's Day Fight. That was to be the last chance. As Coventry had feared, the Netherlands needed only to survive long enough, and England would inevitably tire. And now the moment of exhaustion was at hand: the treasury was bare.

By September the government was living from hand to mouth by borrowing at staggering rates from City merchants and bankers. With the fire many of those last sources of credit literally went up in smoke. The Navy Board's debts had topped £900,000, and more bills flooded in every day. The administration could not afford to keep the whole fleet in pay over the winter, so the men began to be discharged from all first-rates, second-rates, and prize third- and fourth-rates as soon as the ships were moored – and before the cash to back their tickets was in hand. This desperate step was taken in the hope that speedy relief could be obtained from Parliament. But the Houses, angered by alleged 'Mal-administracion' of previous revenues, voted the King only £1,800,000; 'a great sum', said Coventry, 'were it not for his debts'. Furthermore, Lords and Commons disagreed over the nature of the new taxes, so that although the amount was settled in October, the final bill was not passed until January. It would be still more months before the money began to flow in, and by then all of it would be consumed by existing obligations anyway. In the meantime discharged seamen had to wait many weeks to get their pay. Destitute, they rioted daily at the Ticket Office and threatened mayhem against the officers of the Navy Board; the Duke of Albemarle was forced to lead troops against his own shipmates. The navy's morale plummeted. Dockyard workers and crews of ships still in commission mutinied with depressing frequency throughout the winter. In the spring, press gangs met such fierce resistance that a small squadron destined for the West Indies had to be manned partly with soldiers. It was 'a sad consideration', commented Pepys, 'that at the very beginning of the year, and few ships abroad, we should be in such want of men; but they do hide themselfs and swear they will not go to be killed and have no pay'.

The King and Council soon realized that it would be impossible to send out a major fleet in 1667. They concluded in February that if the war were to continue, operations would have to be confined to squadrons of commerce-raiders, with the great ships left unmanned in the Medway. This strategy was hesitantly adopted on the advice of Coventry and Arlington over the objections of Prince Rupert and the Duke of Albemarle. That it was a dangerous policy no one could deny. Peace seemed a much better alternative, and negotiations with the Dutch had already opened in the fall through Swedish mediation. But when formal talks commenced at Breda in March, the discussions went badly for England. The Dutch, aware that their enemy no longer had the means to enforce its previously imperious demands, now saw no reason to make concessions. In retrospect it is painfully clear that Charles should at this point have accepted the best terms he could get. But, unwilling to capitulate, he instead gambled on a daring diplomatic subterfuge.

By early 1667 the French build-up on the borders of Spanish Flanders had proceeded too far for concealment. This presented England a way out of the dilemma. On Arlington's urging Charles opened secret negotiations with Louis, and in April the two monarchs struck a bargain: they would for the time being remain at war (because of the French treaty obligations), but the King of France would intercede with the Dutch to make peace on reasonable terms and would also keep his fleet in home waters if England did not obstruct his Flemish designs. Charles recognized that French domination of the southern Low Countries would be a grave menace to the Netherlands, and that the Dutch would therefore offer England an acceptable compromise in order to free their hands to deal with the greater threat. This actually succeeded. In May French armies stormed across the frontier without a declaration of war. Just as Charles hoped, Dutch negotiators moderated their terms. By the Treaty of Breda, signed on 21 July, England gave up all rights in West Africa and Indonesia, while the Dutch abandoned their claims in North America and acknowledged a somewhat weakened version of the Navigation Act. But unfortunately for Charles, the process of diplomacy was too slow. Before obtaining the settlement, England had to endure its worst humiliation since Hastings.

In an 'audacious enterprise' conceived by Johan de Witt, overseen by de Witt's brother Cornelis, and reluctantly but brilliantly executed by de Ruyter and his subordinates, the Royal Navy was mauled in its own lair. On the 8th and 9th of June renegade English pilots guided the Dutch fleet into the Thames, reconnoitring as far as Gravesend. On the evening of the 10th a landing force supported by a special squadron under Van Ghent captured with ease an unfinished fort at Sheerness guarding the mouth of the river Medway. Emboldened by this surprising success, Van Ghent entered the Medway itself the next day. Ahead of him lay most of the Royal Navy's greatest warships, moored peacefully off Gillingham and Chatham with neither crews nor guns aboard.

The English had known all along that the Medway anchorages were vulnerable. The Ordnance Board was attempting to improve the defences; but with no money to buy materials and the unpaid work-force surly and unresponsive, the fortifications were incomplete except for a heavy chain stretched across the river. The Duke of Albemarle rushed to the scene when the Dutch appeared. He issued intelligent orders, but he might as well have saved his breath. The terrified dockyard labourers, green militia-men, and demoralized seamen at his disposal seemed incapable of carrying out the simplest assignments. Confusion reigned throughout.

Sailing upstream, the Dutch were held up for a day clearing a passage through a barrier of sunken ships with which the English had blocked the channel. On the 12th Van Ghent's fireships rammed and easily broke the chain, the main line of defence. Three fourth-rates deployed for its protection made inglorious resistance, many of their men jumping overboard at the first shots. The *Charles V* and *Matthias* were destroyed by the fireships while the *Unity* surrendered to the 46-gun *Vrede* commanded by Captain Jan van Brakel. The Dutch now had only one obstacle to overcome. Albemarle, not trusting the chain, had on the previous evening ordered three large ships sunk in the narrow fairway just above it. The fireship *Norway Merchant* and the fourth-rate *Marmaduke* (a 'good shipp' which could not afterwards be salvaged) were accordingly emplaced; but the fourth-rate *Sancta Maria* never arrived, her incompetent dockyard crew having run her aground in Cockham Wood Reach. The gap that she should have occupied proved just wide enough to admit Van Ghent's men-of-war, which triumphantly swarmed through into Gillingham Reach. There, to their amazement the Dutch came upon the mighty *Royal Charles*, the principal flagship of the Royal Navy, lying in stately majesty with not a soul aboard. Albemarle had ordered her removed, but in the confusion everyone seems to have thought someone else had taken care of it. After possessing themselves of the great prize the Dutch ended their day's work by burning the stranded *Sancta Maria*.

From the beginning of the attack dockyard commissioner Peter Pett had been frantically shifting as many men-of-war as possible to the relative safety of the river's upper reaches. Unfortunately, he could not find enough men and pilots to move them all. When the chain failed, Albemarle sought to save the vessels still at Chatham by ordering them temporarily sunk in shallow water. This task too was bungled by the dockyard workers. The second-rate *Vanguard* was holed and then stupidly allowed to drift on the tide almost to the bridge at Rochester, where she went down in water so deep that she could never be recovered. The others were duly scuttled – the *Victory*, *St. George*, and *Royal Katherine* along Dockyard Reach, and near Upnor Castle the *Royal James*, *Royal Oak*, and *Loyal London* – but these were foolishly sunk in water *too* shallow, so that they were exposed almost to their normal waterlines.

On the 13th Dutch fireships advanced through heavy cannon fire from the castle and dockyard to fall upon the sunken vessels at Upnor. De Ruyter and Cornelis de Witt personally directed the attack from a longboat, disdainfully ignoring the English shot. Thus exhorted and encouraged, the fireship crews performed their duty bravely: the Duke of Albemarle could only look on in hapless misery as the famous *Royal Oak*, Rupert's beloved *Royal James*, and the *Loyal London*, the City's magnificent gift, all burned to water's edge amid billowing clouds of smoke. The Dutch then withdrew to the Thames, taking the *Royal Charles* and *Unity* to be displayed as trophies in the Maas.

The Royal Navy suffered 'incredible mischiefe' even beyond that inflicted by the Dutch. In the Thames, Prince Rupert had with rather undue haste blocked the channels leading to Woolwich and Blackwall by sinking the big prize third-rates *Golden Phoenix* and *House of Sweeds*, along with the fourth-rate *Welcome* and the fifth-rate *Leicester*. This proved to be a needless waste of perfectly good men-of-war, for the Dutch never ventured beyond Gravesend. A less avoidable self-inflicted calamity occurred at Chatham a week after the action: the third-rate *Helverston* foundered after staving in her bottom on the sunken *Norway Merchant*. The total loss from all causes was two ships of the first rate, three of the second, three of the third, six of the fourth, and one of the fifth. Aside from the debilitating psychological effects of the debacle, the physical losses were crushing. The sudden deletion of four of the five most powerful ships in the fleet (the *Royal Sovereign* was mercifully at Portsmouth) was to have strategic ramifications lasting years after the war.

For the present, English naval power was utterly broken. The Dutch ruled the lower Thames for the rest of the war, their presence in Evelyn's estimation 'a Dreadfull Spectacle as ever any English men saw, & a dishonour never to be wiped off'. De Ruyter divided his fleet into several independent squadrons, which roamed the British seas at will and threatened so many places simultaneously that Commissioner Batten was driven to exclaim, 'By God! I think the Devil shits Dutchmen'. The English forces at sea were too weak to offer battle, though there were two minor skirmishes in the Thames in late July. On the 24th a fireship attack engineered by Sir Edward Spragge inflicted no damage, but did drive back a Dutch squadron under Van Nes which had probed into the Hope. On the 26th (a year and a day after the St. James's Day Fight) Van Nes's fleet was the object of an unsuccessful fireship attack directed by Jordan, who sallied from Harwich with a few frigates. The English were ignominiously chased into the Thames in what was inevitably christened the St. James's Day *Flight*. Charles II's neglected land forces did better, routing a Dutch invasion force at Harwich on 2 July and deterring other landings elsewhere. But that did nothing to help English merchant shipping, which remained blockaded in its harbours right up to the designated cease-fire date of 26 August.

It was left to Sir John Harman, who had brightened the gloom of the Four Days' Battle, to restore some measure of English self-respect. He took a squadron to the Caribbean in April to counter a French fleet commanded by the Viceroy of the French West Indies, Le Fèvre de La Barre. The English found La Barre anchored in the roads at Fort St. Pierre, Martinique. Harman's command comprised nine men-of-war, two ketches, and two fireships.* La Barre had seven ships mounting from 30 guns to over 50 along with fourteen smaller men-of-war and three fireships. The French were moreover supported by strong batteries ashore. Undaunted, Harman attacked them at their moorings on 25 June and, in a remarkable feat of arms, annihilated them. Only two small hired merchantmen escaped. Harman had been in such pain from his unhealed ankle that he had seldom ventured out of his bunk since leaving port. At the prospect of action he not only appeared on deck, but bounded about like a powder boy until the fight was over. He then promptly returned to his cabin and was hardly seen again for the rest of the voyage. His exploit, news of which reached England in September, was the Royal Navy's only major success for the whole of 1667.

*Third-rate: *Lion* (flag); fourth-rates *Jersey, Crown, Newcastle, Dover, Bonaventure, Assistance, Assurance*; fifth-rate *Norwich*; ketches *Portsmouth, Roe*; fireships *Joseph, Prosperous.*

Chapter XIX

Epilogue

In fortune's empire blindly thus we go,
And wander after pathless destiny;
Whose dark resorts since prudence cannot know,
In vain it would provide for what shall be.

The Four Days' Battle had long passed from the stage when the war ended. But a final act remained to be played, for the English government had to face the fury of the nation for three years' wasted efforts. It could not be denied that the commanders had directed the great battles skilfully, that the seamen had fought bravely, and that the fleet had been demonstrably superior to the Dutch in nearly every respect. Yet the war had been lost in the most dismal circumstances. Many concluded that such an unexpected outcome could have resulted only from unconscionable mistakes by the King's advisers and the navy's administrators. Among the perceived mistakes the division of the fleet stood out with particular prominence. Few even in the higher echelons of government fully understood it, and those outside of government, kept in profound ignorance, harboured suspicions of treachery and betrayal. There were demands that those responsible for this and other errors be called to account. Sensing that the administration's detractors might bring down even his own house, Charles II sought to keep the wolves at bay by tossing them a bone: Clarendon, blamed for almost everything by the public though in fact long without influence, was dismissed from his Chancellor's post following intrigues by Arlington and Coventry. But that was not enough. In October a still-dissatisfied Parliament appointed an unprecedented tribunal to investigate 'the miscarriages of the late warr'. In four months of sensational testimony the 'Committee of Miscarriages' delved into the division of the fleet and almost every other imaginable failing: Bergen, the Medway raid, the pursuit at Lowestoft, and the 'Indian Prize' scandal, along with general deficiencies such as the ticket pay system, 'Want of Intelligence', and 'the ill choice of officers in the fleete'.

The committee encountered fierce resistance. Those suspected of misdeeds fought back stoutly, and since most of them had allies in the Commons to protect them from danger, the hearings resulted in disgrace for very few. Henry Brouncker (the villain of the Lowestoft pursuit) was impeached, and Commissioner Pett became the administration's sacrificial lamb for the Medway raid; he was expelled from the Navy Board and even briefly locked up in the Tower. The rest of the politicians, commanders, and senior bureaucrats all by one means or another avoided significant censure. The proceedings nevertheless embarrassed the navy and the government. Hidden details of most of the unsuccessful operations came out; numerous instances of incompetence, lack of foresight, corruption, and cowardice were laid bare for all the world to see, often exaggerated and twisted to the worst advantage by hostile questioners. Few modern governments could withstand such an inquisition.

But with the division of the fleet, the committee met a wall of silence. The detachment had come about through miscalculations at the highest levels, and everyone involved from the King on down apparently agreed that the full truth should not come out. The investigation faltered from the beginning when the committee allowed itself to be intimidated by Prince Rupert and the Duke of Albemarle. They had emerged from the war with such popularity that the examiners simply did not have the nerve to risk antagonizing them. The Generals were merely asked (with ingratiating tact) if they would deign to submit their observations on the various failures. They graciously responded on 31 October with unabashedly self-serving depositions. Albemarle recounted in minute detail Commissioner Pett's shortcomings in the Medway raid. Both commanders also went out of their way to cite damning examples of the 'great negligence of the Commissioners of the Navy . . . in fitting out our shipps' and the 'intollerable neglect in the supplying provisions during the whole summers expedicion'. But when it came to the division of the fleet they became vague and evasive. Both perjured themselves freely. Albemarle lied that he had never heard of it before Carteret and Coventry visited the fleet on 14 May, adding the further falsehoods that he was 'much surprised at the proposicion' and that he agreed to it only on positive assurance 'that the Dutch fleete would not be out in six weekes'. Rupert stressed that his squadron had sailed only on direct orders from above. That he had himself been an enthusiastic participant in the planning he did not mention. As for the objectives, he seemed able to recall only that it 'was founded upon the intelligence of some shipps of the French Kings being at Belle-Isle and that some others were expected there . . . .'

The committee learned little more, because the other parties to the decision were not talking either. The exasperated members finally ventured into uncharted constitutional waters by ordering the Secretaries of State to turn over all their intelligence papers. With the King's permission (and careful instructions) Morrice and Arlington made a show of compliance, but withheld anything that might have been enlightening – such as the embarrassingly inaccurate Irish invasion intelligence. Coventry's testimony corrected some of the Generals' more outrageous lapses of memory, particularly concerning their professed ignorance of the Dutch preparedness. But otherwise Coventry too kept quiet, omitting all mention of Ireland even in his private notes. The committee was left to draw its own conclusions. It had heard only that the Prince's voyage had been ordered from Whitehall on the advice of persons unknown. The expedition had apparently been based solely on unsubstantiated rumours of a French fleet at the mouth of the Channel, and had been permitted to continue even after de Ruyter was known to be ready for sea. It seemed incomprehensible.

On 14 February 1668 the division of the fleet was officially voted a miscarriage by the full Commons. The open debate produced 'great high words' over the committee's inability to assign blame, and there was angry talk of interrogating the Privy

Councillors to find out who among them had advocated the expedition. Coventry (who held a seat in both Parliament and Council) fought desperately to avert that potentially inflammatory constitutional confrontation by observing that men would never agree to counsel the sovereign if they were to be held accountable merely for their opinions. His arguments finally won out. The very obduracy with which the secrets had been defended undoubtedly convinced the more perceptive members of the Commons that continued investigation would inevitably lead perilously near the throne. Enjoyable as it was to bait the King's ministers, baiting the King himself could be dangerous sport. The matter was quietly closed.

The mysteries of the division of the fleet were thus left unsolved, and those who knew the truth took it with them to their graves. Chief among them was Charles himself. The King spent the years following the war in painstakingly rebuilding his fleet. In 1672, in concert with France, he again attacked the Netherlands. But he never obtained the revenge he sought, for the untrustworthiness of Louis XIV forced him to make a separate peace after two summers of profitless campaigning. Charles afterwards devoted himself to the intricacies of Restoration politics and diplomacy, though always taking special care of his navy. To the end of his reign in 1685 he never gained the full trust of his subjects, but then neither did he lose their affections. The Duke of York continued for some years as an exceptionally active Lord High Admiral. He personally led the Anglo-French fleet at the Battle of Solebay in 1672, displaying commendable courage and leadership in difficult circumstances. The next year his openly professed Catholicism led to his ousting with the passage of the Test Act, though he later returned for his ill-starred reign as King James II. His former secretary, Coventry, left the Navy Board in early 1667, transferring his talents to the beleaguered Treasury. His role in Clarendon's downfall, however, cost him James's friendship. Shortly afterwards he lost all his official posts when the Earl of Arlington, his former ally, turned on him. Coventry nevertheless remained a force to reckon with in Parliament until his retirement in 1679. With Clarendon out of the way, Arlington himself scaled the heights as a leading member of the 'Cabal' quintumverate that ran the English government until 1674. In that year he fell from prominence through intrigues not unlike those he had earlier devised for his own rivals. Despite his defeat he lived on in wealth and ease until 1685. Arlington's rise to power also brought prosperity for his principal protégés. Sir Thomas Clifford ascended to a peerage, a place in the Cabal, and eventual installation as Lord Treasurer. A Catholic, he resigned under the Test Act in 1673 and died soon afterwards, by suicide according to rumour. Sir Joseph Williamson had more lasting luck; he went on to earn universal renown as an incorruptible, dedicated, and quietly efficient public servant, constantly active in both administration and Parliament up to his death in 1702. At the height of his career in the late 1670s, Sir Joseph was simultaneously Secretary of State, Admiralty Commissioner, and President of the Royal Society.

As the Four Days' Battle receded into history, those who had taken part in it met varying fortunes. The Duke of Albemarle was past his prime by the war's end. He served for a year at the head of the Treasury Commission, but in 1668 failing health forced his permanent retirement. He died on 3 January 1670, 'like a Roman general and soldier, standing almost up in his chair, his chamber like a tent open, and all his officers about him'. Pepys never understood 'how that blockhead Albemarle hath strange luck to be beloved, though he be, and every man must know, the heaviest man in the world'; but Pepys himself had to add, 'but stout and honest to his country'. The old general, despite his faults, had been one of England's greatest leaders. His colleague Prince Rupert was to be an important figure in the Royal Navy almost to his death in 1682. In the Third Anglo-Dutch War he led the fleet in three indecisive but hard-fought battles against de Ruyter, afterwards serving creditably for seven years as senior member of the Admiralty Commission created on the fall of the Duke of York. Never a truly great admiral, the Prince was nevertheless revered (if not always liked) throughout his career. Both he and Albemarle found final resting places in Westminster Abbey (as did Berkeley, Spragge, and Holles, along with Sandwich and the Earl of Marlborough of Lowestoft fame).

Most of the older flag-officers of the Four Days' Battle were nearing the end of their sea careers in 1666. Teddiman, Utber, and Ayscue died peacefully ashore within six years, while Allin retired from the fleet in 1668 to join the Navy Board, on which he served usefully for seventeen years. He lived until 1685, obtaining a baronetcy and amassing a substantial fortune from landed wealth. Spragge, Harman, Jordan, and Holmes saw further action in the Third Anglo-Dutch War. Spragge was killed at the Battle of the Texel in 1673, and Harman died that same year, apparently of sheer exhaustion. Jordan thrived on in comfortable retirement until 1685, supported to the end of his eighty-two years on a generous pension. Holmes continued in public life; he gained great wealth through a permanent appointment as Bashaw (governor) of the Isle of Wight, but spent much of the time until his death in 1692 as a vocal if rather ineffectual member of Parliament. Sir Jeremy Smith, who had taken an important part in the campaign though not the battle itself, joined Allin on the Navy Board in 1668 and was an active Commissioner until his death in 1675.

For a defeat, the Four Days' Battle was unusual in the number of men who made or increased their reputations from it. Kempthorne, Narbrough, Chicheley, Beach, and John Holmes all attained flag rank within a few years, as did the Earl of Ossory (who had turned down command of the *St. George*). Sir William Jennings, who won his knighthood in the great fight, afterwards proved too headstrong and quarrelsome to ever merit consideration for a flag. He nevertheless had an action-filled career, commanding important ships almost continuously throughout the reigns of both Charles II and James II. In 1689 he followed James into exile in France and served the French fleet against his countrymen at the Battle of Beachy Head. Several officers who drew praise in the Four Days' Battle later had promising careers cut short by untimely death. John Hayward of the *Dunkirk* and Sir William Reeves of the captured *Essex* would certainly have been granted flags sooner or later, but both were killed commanding first-rates at the Battle of the Texel in 1673. Two others marked for greatness, Sir Frescheville Holles and Francis Digby (who had been lieutenant of the *Royal Charles*) fell in heroic circumstances at Solebay in 1672. That action also claimed the Earl of Sandwich and Sir John Cox.

Many of the victors of the Four Days' Battle went on to further glory in the years following. De Ruyter led the States' Fleet in four great battles against the combined forces of England and France in 1672–73. All were tactical draws, but in each the outnumbered Dutch earned further respect from their opponents. Though weary from relentless responsibilities, de Ruyter afterwards mounted campaigns against the French in the West Indies in 1674 and then in 1675–76 in the Mediterranean. There he twice engaged a French fleet ably commanded by Abraham Duquesne. In the second action, fought off Augusta on the coast of Sicily on 12 April 1676, de Ruyter was directing the battle from an armchair aboard his flagship, the *Eendracht*, when a cannonball suddenly carried away part of his left foot. The force of the blow hurled him from the quarterdeck into the waist, the fall breaking his right leg above the ankle and inflicting a gash to his head. The injuries were obviously serious but appeared survivable. A few days later, however, he became feverish and thereafter weakened rapidly. On 19 April, lying 'on the bed of honour' in the great cabin of the *Eendracht*, he died. After many months of preparation, his remains were interred in the Nieuwekerk in Amsterdam amid solemn pomp attended by the largest crowd ever seen in the Netherlands.

De Ruyter's friend Johan de Witt had died earlier in less inspiring circumstances. The attack on the United Provinces by England and France in 1672 caused terrible hardship in the Netherlands. In the emergency the nation turned to William of Orange for leadership, rejecting de Witt. The transfer of power was accompanied by violent civil disturbances. On 10 August 1672, Johan and his brother Cornelis fell into the hands of a mob at The Hague and were tortured to death with barbarous cruelty.

One who fared well from the Orange resurrection was Cornelis Tromp. In 1673 William mediated a delicate reconciliation between Tromp and de Ruyter, and then repaid Tromp's loyalty to the Orange cause by restoring him to the fleet with strict orders to obey the Admiral-General. The two commanders were wary of each other to the end, but together they made the Dutch fleet an invincible weapon. Their conduct in action won such admiration from Charles II that he later invited both of them to visit England. De Ruyter declined, but Tromp accepted in 1675. His journey up the Thames became a triumphal progress; in London he was received like a brother by the English admirals, the Duke of York, and especially by Charles, who knighted him and conferred a hereditary baronetcy complete with estates and income. Afterwards, Tromp accepted a commission to command the navy of Denmark, leading the Danes to a resounding victory over the Swedes at the Battle of Öland in 1676. Danish service was followed by brilliant if smaller-scale success in command of the lilliputian navy of the Elector of Brandenburg. At home, de Ruyter's death at last led to Tromp's appointment as Lieutenant-Admiral of Holland and Westfriesland, though his abilities at sea were not again required. His remaining years were spent in peace and content-ment, entertaining throngs of adoring visitors at his appropriately ship-shaped mansion of Trompenburg. He died in 1691 and was buried at Delft in the tomb of his great father.

Of the other Dutch flag-officers of the Four Days' Battle, Meppel died ashore in about 1671. Schram was shot down in the First Battle of Schooneveld in 1673, Sweers and de Liefde following him to glory a few weeks later at the Battle of the Texel. Banckert, Cornelis Evertsen the Younger, Bruynsvelt, and the Van Nes brothers all fought through these great actions to live out their days in honoured retirement. Many of their captains from June 1666 went on to flag rank, including David Vlugh (killed at Schooneveld), Jan de Haan, Enno Doedes Star, Jan Mathijszoon, and Philips van Almonde. Cornelis Evertsen the Youngest eventually rose to become Tromp's successor as Lieutenant-Admiral of Holland and Westfriesland, surviving many battles to die peacefully in 1706; but Baron Van Ghent, who might have surpassed them all, fell at Solebay.

The French, who had influenced the Four Days' Battle without firing a shot, gained nothing. The Spanish army in Flanders turned out to be more than the hollow shell Louis thought it would be. After initial successes, his invasion stalled in the muddy siegeworks below the Spanish fortresses. Then the English and Dutch, having made peace, temporarily aligned themselves against him. When Sweden joined them, Louis sullenly withdrew within his borders. But his project of conquering the Low Countries was by no means dead; indeed, he was to devote almost another half-century of war and deceitful diplomacy to the same goal, and would exhaust his kingdom without attaining it. Of his admirals of 1666, only Abraham Duquesne went on to greatness. The duc de Beaufort continued in command of the French fleet for three more years, but the acclamations of the world that he so ardently desired came only in death. He met his end on Crete in 1669, in a gallant but futile attempt to raise the Turkish siege of Candia.

The ships that fought in the Four Days' Battle included many of the most famous vessels ever to serve England or the Netherlands. Several important English flagships were gone within a few years: the *Royal James* and *Royal Oak* destroyed in the Medway and Holmes's *Defiance* burned by accident soon after. The captured *Royal Charles*, useless to the Dutch fleet because of her draught, was dismantled in 1673 after six years as a popular tourist attraction at Rotterdam. Another vessel that met an early – and spectacular – end was the smallest English participant in the battle, the fifth-rate *Oxford*. In 1668 Charles II gave her to the governor of Jamaica, who in turn assigned her to Sir Henry Morgan as flagship for one of the great buccaneer's patented raids on the Spanish Main. One day in 1669 Morgan called his captains to the *Oxford* for a council-of-war, in the course of which everyone got roaring drunk. At the height of the bacchanal one of the inebriates entered the magazine to obtain saluting charges, and in a moment of carelessness let flame touch powder. It was his last second on Earth; the *Oxford* disappeared with a terrific blast, launching masts, cannon, and buccaneers into the heavens. Amazingly, the bemused Morgan and a few others somehow came out alive.

Eventually, the floating veterans of the battle fell by the wayside one by one: sunk, burned, blown up, wrecked, or broken up due to old age. But before meeting their fate, many of them sailed the seas for fifty years or more and compiled records that few of their officers and seamen could match. Some were already worthy campaigners even before 1666; the *Triumph* and *Vanguard* had each taken part in seven great battles by then, the *Dunkirk* eight even though she had only been built in 1651. Unlike regiments ashore, English warships have never displayed 'battle honours' on their colours. If they did, no fewer than twenty of the vessels that were present for the Four Days' Battle could have listed ten or more major actions by the end of their 'lifetimes'. Between 1652 and 1702 the fourth-rate *Ruby* took part in sixteen, her sister ship *Diamond* fifteen, the *Dunkirk* and *Lion* fourteen each. (The third-rate *Mary*, the grand champion of the Royal Navy to this day with eighteen major actions to her credit, ironically missed the Four Days' Battle.) None of this includes the Elizabethan honours amassed by the *Rainbow, Vanguard,* and *Lion* before their seventeenth-century reconstructions, nor the innumerable single-ship duels fought by some of the smaller fourth-rates.

No Dutch men-of-war saw as much action, but many nevertheless built impressive records. The *Amsterdam, Wapen van Nassau, Kampveere,* and Van Ghent's *Gelderland* all took part in at least seven battles. Van Nes's *Eendracht* fought in eight, but also had the sad distinction of becoming the second ship of her name to carry a commander-in-chief to his death. The *Reiger*, conqueror of the *Swiftsure*, was last engaged in 1690 at Beachy Head where the *Wapen van Utrecht* (Tromp's flagship of the fourth day) was sunk. Tjerk Hiddes de Vries's *Groot Frisia* and Bruynsvelt's *Prins Hendrik Casimir* also had long careers. Both were present for the victory over the French at Barfleur in 1692, as was the *Gelderland*. The most renowned of all Dutch men-of-war, though not the most frequently engaged, was the mighty *Zeven Provinciën*. She proudly bore de Ruyter's flag in all the great actions of 1672–73 and was still afloat to take an honourable part at Barfleur. Her fame could not save her from the ship-breakers two years later, but since then the Dutch navy has seldom been without a *Zeven Provinciën*.

Dutch warships had shorter combat records than their most active English counterparts mainly because the Admiralties in the Netherlands rarely kept ships in service longer than about twenty-five years. The last Dutch veteran of the Four Days' Battle was the *Provincie Utrecht* (another of Tromp's flagships) which was broken up in 1696. Many English ships lasted much longer. Fourteen which had been in action in June 1666 were still employed at the turn of the century and some long after: the *Assistance* until 1745, the *Dunkirk* until 1749, and Utber's *Rupert* until 1769. This is actually somewhat deceptive, for such long-lived vessels were in most cases two or three times 'rebuilt'; that is, broken up and their 'serviceable timbers' incorporated in otherwise entirely new ships. There were a few exceptionally well-built men-of-war, however, which were maintained for decades through less radical repairs. The last intact English veteran of the battle was probably Teddiman's *Royal Katherine*. She was made into a conventional three-decker at Portsmouth in 1673, when a forecastle was erected and her waist bulwarks raised to accommodate a full upper tier of gunports. Then in 1702 she was officially rebuilt, but apparently not entirely taken apart as most others were. Renamed *Ramillies* in 1704, she survived with at least some of her original structure until 1749 (when she *was* broken up and rebuilt, only to be wrecked in 1760).

Today, only a few relics remain from the proud fleets of 1666; the Stuart arms from the stern of the *Royal Charles* in the Rijksmuseum in Amsterdam, here and there a ship's bell or a rusty cannon. But some vessels were wrecked or sank in more or less accessible locations, where archaeologists may someday find them. The *York* rests in the sands of the Shipwash where she went down in 1703, while the bones of the *Rainbow* and the *Leopard* lie somewhere in the foundations and breakwaters of Sheerness. One wreck which has already drawn attention is the giant *Royal Prince*, whose charred remains were discovered on the Galloper a few years ago. Even if nothing is ever recovered from these vessels, we can be thankful that most of the greatest ships of 1666 still live on in the magnificent paintings and drawings of the Van de Veldes.

The Four Days' Battle obviously was not a turning point of history. After all, the losing side returned the favour a few weeks later. Even that made little difference, for the Second Anglo-Dutch War was decided not by arms, but by default when one side went bankrupt. Although the battle involved an enormous number of ships (eighty-five Dutch and eighty-one English, excluding yachts and fireships), it was not unusual in that respect. About the same number fought at the Texel in 1673, and that was exceeded at both Lowestoft and the St. James's Day Fight. More were also present at the Gabbard, Scheveningen, and the Battle of the Downs in 1639; but in those three most of the ships were relatively small. Barfleur probably involved more men and guns than any other. The Four Days' Battle was unquestionably hard-fought, but again not unusually so. De Ruyter thought Solebay the most intense engagement he ever saw, and casualties suggest that St. James's Day must have been almost as violent as Solebay.

The Four Days' Battle does stand out sharply in the sophistication of its tactics. Aside from a duel of courage, strength, and will, it was very much a duel of wits orchestrated by experts who thoroughly understood their business – Albemarle and Rupert, applying theoretical doctrines which they had themselves helped to devise, and de Ruyter working mainly from instinct and a lifetime of experience. Certainly no sea-fight ever had so many organized thrusts and parries, all carried out despite clumsy ships and sometimes uncomprehending captains. The level of generalship in this battle is seldom fully appreciated. For example, Rodney's breaking of the French line in a head-to-head pass at the Saintes in 1782 is often hailed as a triumph of daring and ingenuity; yet the English and the Dutch in the Four Days' Battle perpetrated the very same deed on each other again and again with no one ever thinking it particularly revolutionary. The commanders at times showed striking originality; de Ruyter's rescue of Tromp on the second day was never equalled in its audacity except perhaps by Nelson at Cape St. Vincent, while the evolutions executed by Rupert and Albemarle in the early passes of the fourth day had no later parallels. This does not mean that the commanders of 1666 were towering geniuses, or their successors mere dullards; it was just that by the eighteenth century the line-ahead and the Fighting Instructions had gradually become Sacred Cows – hallowed ends in themselves in ways that their seventeenth-century authors never intended. Unconstrained by hidebound tradition, admirals of the Restoration period felt perfectly free to break rules and improvise whenever the need or opportunity arose.

But tactics, however remarkable, were still not what made the Four Days' Battle special. Aside from Albemarle's much-extolled retreat on the third day, neither the

English nor the Dutch public took the slightest notice of formations and manoeuvres. What did set the battle apart was the astonishing tenacity with which it was fought; the stubborn unwillingness of the English to accept defeat, and the implacable resolution of the Dutch. True, several other great actions were multi-day affairs: the Gabbard, Lowestoft, and St. James's Day all took place over two days, Portland three. But in all these the winner was known at the end of the first day, and everything else was one side running and the other chasing. No one before or after in all the age of sail ever saw another sea-fight that raged on for *four days* before being resolved, and that left both sides so exhausted that neither could stay at sea. It caught the imagination of all Europe. The Dutch forever after remembered it in song and verse as one of their proudest triumphs, the English as a noble effort in defiance of odds. After three centuries it has naturally faded from consciousness, though historians still debate the manoeuvres and puzzle over the intricacies of the campaign. But to those who lived through it, it was an inconceivably terrible and unforgettable experience. Because of the seasonal nature of sea warfare in the seventeenth century, many of the greatest engagements of the age occurred in the month of June: the Gabbard, Lowestoft, one of the Schooneveld actions, Beachy Head, and (by the Continental calendar) Solebay. Yet as late as the mid-1700s, when someone wrote or spoke of the 'Great June Fight', everyone knew it meant the Four Days' Battle.

Appendix A

Instructions for the Division of the Fleet

Three important documents concerning instructions for the division of the fleet are preserved in Longleat Coventry MSS 95 in the collection of the Marquis of Bath. The first (ff. 200–201) gives the instructions themselves in Sir William Coventry's hand in a working draft dated 22 May 1666. Coventry transcribed the unpreserved official draft early the next morning and delivered it to Sir Edward Spragge before 11 a.m. It was dated 23 May, as noted in Albemarle's deposition to the House of Commons.

22 5 66   Instructions to Prince Rupert

Whereas his Maj. upon intelligence received of the French King's fleet putting to sea from Toulon & intending to come into the ocean seas & joyne with other ships of the French Kings, hath resolved to send a fleet to attend their motions & endeavor to destroy them. Of which fleet upon your owne desire whereof his Majesty hath thought fitt that the chiefe command bee given to you.

You are therefore by advice with the Duke of Albemarle to choose out of the body of the fleet under your joynt command 20 ships whereof two to bee of the 2nd rate, or else one of the 1st & one of ye 2d, 5 of the 3d rate, 13 of the 4th rate together with 5 or 6 fireships, to which shall bee joyned a considerable number of other ships (which now are or shall suddainly bee sent to the western station) out of those ships reserved for the guard of the Coast.

Having thus chosen out your fleet you are to embarke your selfe upon one of the said ships & taking upon you the charge & command of the said fleet as an admirall. The officers & seamen belonging to the same are required to bee obedient to you. You are to use all possible diligence to saile towards ye Lizzard, there to gather together such other ships as shall bee ordered to you or as many of them as order shall reach timely enough to meet you there; & when your fleet shall bee soe strengthened as you shall judge sufficient for ye worke you goe about, you shall endeavor to find out & destroy the French fleet, especially that under the command of the duke of Beaufort if it shall bee come into these seas; & if you shall not have any good intelligence of their being in some other place, you are to saile directly for Belle Isle or to the Isle of Rhee & Rochelle where it is most probable their rendezvous will bee & where his Maj. hath been informed that some of the French Kings ships of warre were already some time since.

In case you shall not find the french fleet there, nor have intelligence to lead you to some considerable designe, you shall not continue there above eight dayes but shall return with your fleet to the Coast of England sending into Falmouth for intelligence or new orders.

During your stay on the French Coast you are to bee carefull to keepe your fleet in a body, excepting such of the smaller ships as you shall find necessary to send out to scout, lest otherwise the French take you at an advantage.

You are to endeavor by all meanes you can to get intelligence from the French Coast what numbers of soldiers are in any places there, & what preparations they make for embarquing them, & if any thing considerable of that nature come to your knowledge you are to give notice by ketches or small vessells to his Maj. & likewise to the Lord Lt. of Ireland that soe in case of any attempt both kingdomes may bee in readiness to oppose them.

In case the French shall ship any Land Forces in any port you are to use your utmost endeavors to keepe them from going out, or to intercept them in their passage, but if that cannot bee done you are to follow them, & endeavor to destroy them in their landing either their men or other necessities, & alsoe to hinder all recruits to come to them after their landing.

In case the french fleet shall [sail] without any Land army embarqued or them get the start of you & saile about by the North of Scotland, you shall then returne into the Channell the sooner to joyne his Majs. fleet that soe it may bee in a condition to encounter the united forces both of Dutch & French.

You are not to goe in search of the French fleet beyond the mouth of ye River of Bordeaux but wherever you shall meet any ships belonging either to the French King, the King of Denmarke or States of the United Provinces or any other vessels of their subjects you are to take or destroy [them]. You are to take notice that passes have bin granted by his Majesty & alsoe by mee for certaine ships of warr belonging to the French King for carrying the Queene of Portugall to Lisbonne, which passes are punctually to bee observed whilst the Q. of Port. shall bee on board, but are not to hinder your attempting any thing when the said Q. shall not bee on board, nor the taking or destroying any ship when separated from the fleet in which the said Q. is in person, however they may pretend to belong to that fleet.

As soon as you shall have passed the Lands end you are to give order that the fleet under your command goe to short allowance of victualls for [which] satisfaction shall bee given to the Seamen in money.

For the defraying such contingent charges as shall bee found necessary you are to take with you 1000 of the contingent money now in the fleet which shall be supplied againe from heere.

In all things not mentioned in these instructions you are to doe as you shall judge most for his Majesties service. Given under my hand & seale at Whitehall this 22 of May 1666.

[In the margin:] Draught Instructions for P. Rupert May 22nd

The second document is an explanatory letter to the Generals written by the Duke of York on 22 May and enclosed with the instructions. There are two copies, ff. 198 and 202. The spellings and punctuation used here are from f. 202; it is in a clerk's hand except that the part of the endorsement beginning with the word 'shewing' was added by Coventry.

22 May 1666   His R.H.s lr to Pr. Rupert & D. of Albemarle accompanieing Pr. Ruperts Instructions/ shewing the dividing ye fleet was pursuant to their resolution taken when Sr G. Carterett & my selfe were with them.

Most Deare & most intirely Beloved Cousin & my Lord Duke of Albemarle, you will perceive by the Instructions sent by this conveyance to my Cousin Prince Rupert that the King hath intirely approved of the Resolutions taken by you, when Sr George Carterett & Sr William Coventry were with you, the Instructions being for the most part pursuant to the Report, which they made to His Majty. and in pursuance of all that alsoe, I intend that the Resolution & Foresight which I have ordered to victuall att Plimouth, shall saile to joine with that Fleet for the farther strengthening it. By the Report which they made, I perceive my Cousin Pr. Rupert was very desirous to have the R. James, if that bee agreed on betwixt you (for which latitude is left in the Instructions), I suppose the best way wilbee to remove Sr Thomas Allin into the Triumph if my Cousin Pr. Rupert shall approve Sr Edward Spragg to bee Capt. of the James, all which I leave to yr determination with the same liberty, as if it had not been mentioned to you.

The third document (ff. 216–217) is a copy in Coventry's hand of a letter of 28 May 1666 from the Duke of York to Prince Rupert, modifying the instructions in light of new intelligence and answering the Prince's queries of the 26th about the original orders (for the queries see Bath Coventry Appendix I, f. 13). The 28 May letter has caused much confusion, for its rather loosely edited transcription in Navy Records Society vol.112 (*The Rupert and Monck Letterbook, 1666*) was erroneously dated the 24th.

Letter to P. Rupert   May 28th '66   Worded yesterday & this day approved by his Maj. in Councell relating to his H's voyage against the French & reporting debates about it.

His Maj. having received certaine intelligence that the Duke of Beaufort was come to this side of the Straights, did againe enter into consideration of the designe on which you are about to goe, & although the debate did not produce any alteration in the maine designe, yet I judge it may bee of use to acquaint you (as very much as may bee at this distance) with some such considerations as arose upon the debate. It was by some suggested that possibly the Duke of Beaufort (who was seene at Lisbon on the 14th instant) might saile directly to the North of Scotland soe to endeavor a conjunction with the Dutch, in which case his Majesty would encline not to send you from the fleet, if there should bee any certainty of it; that which seemed to induce the beleef of it was only an intelligence that the Dutch had provided ye D. of Beaufort with pilots (which they would not want of their owne for the Channell), but this advertisement not being very certaine, was over balanced by the probability of his touching in France to joyne with the Vandosme & other ships provided for him, which it was judged hee could not with certainty meet at sea, & very improbable hee would goe without them. Upon supposition that hee would touch in France the places most probable seemed Belle Isle or Rochelle, & upon that supposition the next consideration was what probability there might bee of your finding him there, for that supposing him to have already been there some days, if hee had no other businesse but to joyne the Vandosme & not to stay, it is probable hee may bee gone before you get thither, & then you will bee wanting from the body of the fleet, whilst they joyne the Dutch, and the rather because of the depth of the Bay into which you goe.

On the other hand, in case the D. of Beaufort have any army to embarque in order to an invasion (which if intended must bee for Ireland) it is conceived that soe much time will bee required for his embarquing as may give you opportunity of falling upon him, which would bee most desirable. Therefore since the service of this businesse & successe of the summers expedition depends soe much upon taking right measures of the station of the Duke of Beaufort, which it will not bee possible to receive from France & send to you, it was thought very advisable that if you could not meet with other intelligence before you engage into the Bay, that you should send into Conquet Roads & endeavor to take some ships there to gain intelligence, which nevertheless having bin there mentioned to you & the importance of it stated, must bee left to your judgement & done with as you shall see fitt.

When you shall find cause to conclude the D. of Beaufort sailes from the Coast of France without a land army & other necessaries for invasion, his Maj. would have you make all possible haste to the Body of the fleet by returning into the Channell, but if there bee ground to believe in invasion, then to follow him as farr as the Blasquets on ye west of Ireland, but not past them, which if hee passes without endeavoring landing there will bee noe danger of it & therefore the businesse of the sea is wholly to bee intended by uniting his Majs. fleets againe. Whilst you shall bee on the Coast of Ireland you will doe well to send frequently on shoare for intelligence & when you shall return into the Channell I desire you to leave the frigats which joyne you in the west (except the Resolution & Foresight) to ply on the Western Station as formerly. When you leave the Coast of England & as often as you can afterwards with convenience, I desire to heare from you with the best directions you can give for sending to you in case any thing of moment shall happen.

Having seene your letter to my Secretary I spake with his Maj. about the flaggs to bee carried of your fleet, for which his Majesty approoved Sir Edward Spragge, in which I desire you to give orders accordingly. The list of ships intended to joyne you in the west is in the Margens,* the Eagle & Guernsey are now in the Downes ordered to convoy some ships for Masts through the Soundings which is a worke soe necessary that it cannot bee dispensed with, otherwise they alsoe should have gone with you.

*[In the margin:] *Resolution, Tyger, Elizabeth, Foresight, Adventure, Sorlings, Nightingale, Garland.*

Appendix B

The English Fleet at Lowestoft, 3 June 1665

Documentary sources contain no known lists of the English fleet at Lowestoft. The list of probable participants given here and the accompanying fleet distribution list are based on reconstructed ship movements in the weeks preceding the fight. The starting point was a fleet list of about 10 May in the Public Record Office (SP29/127, f. 264 or dup. f. 268). It gives squadron assignments for 109 men-of-war of the sixth rate and above. Of those, nineteen can be shown to have been detached prior to the battle, while five previously unlisted vessels arrived. The fleet should thus have had ninety-five ships when the Dutch were sighted, and this is the number given by Commissioner Sir William Batten in a report from Harwich on 2 June (Cal. SP Dom.). In addition, five of the previously detached vessels rejoined during the fight: the *Leopard* and the hired *Katherine*, both from Harwich; and the *Amity* and two other previously detached small frigates, names unrecorded, from Lowestoft. The probable final total was thus an even one hundred.

Stations in the line are from the order of battle of 20 April as recorded in the Earl of Sandwich's journal. It gives only ninety-two of the eventual participants. For the other eight (distinguished below by asterisks), squadron and division assignments are known for all except the *Charity*, but not stations in the line. The *Charity*, which was a late addition to the fleet, is arbitrarily inserted below in the admiral's division of the Red. Note that fifth- and sixth-rates were not in the line itself, but were to lie on the disengaged side of the fleet opposite their appointed stations.

The number of fireships present for the action is uncertain. Surviving accounts mention only the *Dolphin*, *Fame*, and *Bramble* (all expended), plus the *Bryar* disabled. But the *Hound* belonging to the White Squadron apparently took part also, for she was among the vessels listed in Sandwich's journal as having been sent into the Thames for repairs afterwards.

The small craft listed after each squadron are those assigned to the fleet as of 10 April. It is virtually impossible to trace their movements, but most were probably on hand for the battle. The *Hind*, *Roe*, *Eaglet*, and *Nonsuch* were ketches belonging to the navy; the rest were hired. The numbers given for men and guns are merely official allowances, and are undoubtedly understated. Complements were reportedly augmented by upwards of 2,000 supernumeraries, most of them soldiers. As for armament, a fleet list of 29 March notes that the Red Squadron alone had 'some 100 guns not reckoned'.

In this and the following English fleet lists, ships acquired as prizes are denoted by **P** in the Rate column, hired merchantmen by **M** and fireships by **fs**. Flagships are in **bold** type.

WHITE SQUADRON – Prince Rupert (*Royal James*)

Rate	Ship	Guns	Men	Captain
5	*Colchester*	28	145	Daniel Helling
2	***Triumph***	66	380	V.A. Christopher Myngs
3	*Monck*	54	260	Thomas Penrose
4	*Newcastle*	48	200	Thomas Page
3	*Lion*	52	260	Edward Spragge
4	*Ruby*	46	180	William Jennings
4	*Expedition*	30	140	Tobias Sackler
M	*John & Abigail*	40	160	Joseph Sanders
M	*Return*	40	190	John Hubbard
M	*Katherine*	36	160	Thomas Elliott
M	*John & Katherine**	32	150	John Whately
4	*Reserve*	46	170	John Tyrwhit
2	*Rainbow*	56	320	Willoughby Hannam
M	*Exchange*	36	170	Samuel Wentworth
3	*Revenge*	58	280	Robert Holmes
1	***Royal James***	78	500	John Kempthorne
5	*Garland*	28	145	Charles Talbot
fs	*Hound*	8	45	James Coleman
fs	*Dolphin*	4	45	William Gregory
4	*Assurance*	32	150	John Jeffries
4	*Mary Rose*	48	190	William Reeves
3	*Henrietta*	58	300	Walter Wood
M	*Bendish*	42	180	Robert Taylor
4	*Portland*	46	180	John Aylett
M	*East India Merchant*	44	180	John Wilgresse
2	*St. Andrew*	60	360	Valentine Pine
4	*Advice*	40	170	William Poole
4P	*Bear*	42	170	John Waterworth
M	*Constant Catherine*	40	180	Francis Sanders
4	*Kent*	46	180	Thomas Ewens
3	*Anne*	58	280	Arnold Brown
3	***Resolution***	58	290	R.A. Robert Sansum
5	*Milford*	28	155	John Seale

Ketches, Smacks, and Hoys

Hind		8	55	John Withers
Sea Venture				
James				
Desire				
Little Sampson				
William & Mary				

RED SQUADRON – Duke of York (*Royal Charles*)

Rate	Ship	Guns	Men	Captain
4	*Bristol*	48	200	John Hart
3	*Gloucester*	58	280	Robert Clark
M	*Royal Exchange*	46	220	Giles Shelley
4	*Diamond*	46	180	John King
6	*Martin Galley*	14	65	Richard White
2	**Royal Oak**	76	450	V.A. Sir John Lawson
5	*Norwich*	24	135	John Wetwang
4P	*Guinea*	36	150	John Abelson
2	*St. George*	60	360	Joseph Jordan
M	*Coast Frigate*	34	150	Thomas Lawson
4	*Dover*	46	170	Jeffery Pearse
M	*King Ferdinando**	36	180	Francis Johnson
3	*Plymouth*	56	280	Thomas Allin
5P	*Fountain*	30	150	Jean Baptiste du Tiel
M	*Blackamore*	38	170	Richard Neales
3	*Mary*	58	300	Jeremy Smith
4	*Happy Return*	50	190	James Lambert
6	*Drake*	12	85	Richard Poole
1	**Royal Charles**	78	550	Sir Wm. Penn/John Harman
5	*Mermaid*	28	145	Jasper Grant
fs	*Fame*	12	45	John Gethings
fs	*Bramble*	8	35	Nepthali Ball
4	*Antelope*	46	180	John Chicheley
2	*Old James*	68	380	Earl of Marlborough
M	*Loyal George*	42	190	John Earle
4	*Yarmouth*	52	190	Thomas Ayliffe
2	*Vanguard**	56	320	Jonas Poole
4P	*Convertine**	48	180	John Pearce
4P	*Charity**	46	170	Robert Wilkinson
M	*Eagle*	44	220	Thomas Hendra
4	*Amity*	36	150	John Parker
M	*Satisfaction*	46	180	Richard May
3	*Fairfax*	58	300	Robert Salmon
2	**Swiftsure**	60	380	R.A. Sir William Berkeley
4	*Bonaventure*	40	160	Arthur Laughorne
4	*Portsmouth*	38	160	Robert Mohun
M	*George*	40	180	Robert Hatubb
4	*Leopard*	54	240	Richard Beach
4	*Sapphire*	38	160	Henry Hyde
M	*Loyal Merchant**	44	210	Robert Sanders

Ketches, Smacks, and Hoys

	Ship	Guns	Men	Captain
	Roe	8	55	James Lock
	Eaglet	8	55	William Berry
	St. George			
	Bachelor			
	Isabella			
	Hopeful Margaret			
	Seaflower			
	Edward & Eve			

BLUE SQUADRON – Earl of Sandwich (*Prince*)

Rate	Ship	Guns	Men	Captain
5	*Forester*	28	145	Edward Cotterell
2	***Royal Katherine***	70	450	R.A. Thomas Teddiman
3	*Essex*	52	260	Richard Utber
4P	*Marmaduke*	38	150	John Best
4	*Princess*	52	220	George Swanley
M	*Golden Phoenix*	36	160	Samuel Dickenson
4	*Adventure*	36	150	Benjamin Young
M	*Society*	36	160	Ralph Lascelles
3	*Dreadnought*	58	280	Henry Terne
M	*Prudent Mary**	36	160	Thomas Haward
4	*Dragon*	38	160	John Lloyd
4	*Centurion*	46	180	Robert Moulton
3	*Montagu*	58	300	Henry Fenne
5	*Oxford*	24	135	Phillip Bacon
1	***Prince***	86	700	Roger Cuttance
5	*Pembroke*	28	145	Thomas Darcy
fs	*Bryar*	12	45	Richard Cotton
3	*Dunkirk*	54	260	John Hayward
4	*Breda*	46	180	Robert Kirby
M	*John & Thomas*	44	200	Henry Dawes
4	*Swallow*	46	180	Richard Hodges
M	*Madras**	42	180	John Norbrook
4	*Jersey*	48	190	Hugh Hide
M	*Hambro' Merchant*	36	170	James Cadman
4	*Hampshire*	40	160	George Batts
M	*Castle Frigate*	36	160	Philip Euatt
4	*Assistance*	40	170	Zachary Brown
2	*Unicorn*	56	320	Henry Teddiman
4	*Providence*	30	140	Richard James
3	*York*	58	280	John Swanley
2	***Henry***	70	430	V.A. Sir George Ayscue
5	*Guernsey*	28	145	Humphrey Connisby

Ketches, Smacks, and Hoys

Nonsuch	8	55	Robert Crossman
Thomas & Rebecca			
Hopewell			
John smack			
John hoy			
Two Sisters			

The reconstructed fleet distribution for 3 June 1665 includes all ship-rigged men-of-war which did not participate in the action. Vessels distinguished by asterisks appear on the 10 May fleet list.

THAMES AND MEDWAY

Rate	Ship	Captain	Status or Location
1	Royal Sovereign	—	Ordinary
2	Victory	—	Rebuilding
4P	Unity	Thomas Trafford	Under repair
4P	Welcome	—	Ordinary
4P	Golden Lion	William Dale	Fitting out
M	Loyal Subject	John Fortescue	Fitting out
M	Baltimore	Charles Wilde	Fitting out
6	Merlin*	Charles Howard	Ready for sea
6P	Fox	Henry Osgood	Fitting out
6	Cygnet	Roger Jones	Fitting out

CHANNEL (all at sea or ready for sea except as noted)

4	Tiger	Phineas Pett	Portsmouth
4P	Matthias	John Hubbert	Portsmouth
4	Constant Warwick	—	Portsmouth, rebuilding
4	Foresight	Packington Brooks	Plymouth
4	Elizabeth	Robert Robinson	Plymouth
4P	Sancta Maria	—	Plymouth, fitting out
5P	Coventry*	William Hill	Portsmouth
5P	Lizard*	John Andrews	Portsmouth
5P	Happy Entrance	Francis Steward	Portsmouth, fitting out
5	Eagle	John Stanesby	Plymouth
5P	Sorlings	Jonathan Waltham	Plymouth
5P	Orange	—	Rye, needing repair
5P	Greyhound	Richard Country	Dover
6	Lily	Amos Beare	Dover
6P	Little Mary*	Abraham Blackleach	Plymouth
6P	Paradox*	Leonard Guy	Scilly

OTHER STATIONS (all at sea or ready for sea except as noted)

4	Crown	Charles Wager	Tangier
M	Good Hope*	Anthony Archer	Taken by Dutch 20 May
M	Maryland*	Abraham Ansley	Harwich, 'defective'
M	John & Margaret	George Chapple	South Atlantic
M	William	William Basse	South Atlantic
M	Pearl	Walter Morgan	Bristol, fitting out
M	George of Bristol	William Davis	Bristol Channel
M	Barbados Merchant	John Heath	Guinea
5P	Great Gift	Jacob Reynolds	Guinea
5	Success*	Edward Grove	Lowestoft
5	Speedwell*	John Lightfoot	Newcastle
5P	Paul*	Peter Foot	Scouting Calais–Winterton
5P	Hector*	John Cuttle	Scouting Flamborough–Tynemouth
5P	Sophia	—	Ordinary, location unknown
5P	Westergate	Samuel Titsell	Overdue from Jamaica, presumed lost
5P	Little Unicorn	William Davies	Fitting out, location unknown
5	Pearl	Hugh Seymour	Ireland

[cont.]

[*cont.*]

5	*Nightingale*	Richard Long	Ireland
5	*Richmond*	Thomas Knevett	Ireland
5	*Dartmouth*	Richard Rooth	Ireland
6	*Harp*	James Sharland	Ireland
6P	*Little Gift**	John Johnson	Ireland
6P	*Truelove**	William Peach	Downs
6P	*Francis*	Robert Turner	Fishery patrol
6	*Blackamoor* pink*	John Barton	Scouting Winterton–Flamborough
6	*Chestnut* pink	John Stephens	India
6	*Hart* pink	—	Ordinary, location unknown

Appendix C

The Dutch Fleet at Lowestoft, 3 June 1665

The list of the Dutch fleet at Lowestoft is drawn mainly from de Jonge, *Geschiedenis van het Nederlandsche Zeewezen*. Some details are from a list in Penn, *Memorials of Sir William Penn*, and two lists from English intelligence sources in Sandwich's journal. De Jonge gives the fleet as it stood at its departure from the Texel on 13–14 May. The only known adjustments thereafter were the addition of the late-arriving *Zwanenburg* and *Visscher*, and the deletion of the 30-gun Noorderkwartier frigate *Kasteel van Medemblik* which was sent home due to weather damage.

The Dutch had not yet adopted the line-ahead, so the ships had no assigned stations. The squadrons are listed not in order of fighting, but in order of precedence. Within each squadron, the commanders of the first three ships served as admiral, vice-admiral, and rear-admiral. Of the VOC ships, the *Oranje*, *Sphera Mundi*, and *Agatha* were from the Zeeland chapter, the *Nieuw Batavia* from Rotterdam, the *Nagelboom* from Hoorn, the *Delfland* from Delft, and the rest from Amsterdam.

FIRST SQUADRON (pendant at the main)

Admty.	Ship	Guns	Men	Captain
M	*Eendracht*	76	409	Gen. Jacob van Wassenaer, Baron Obdam
A	*Amsterdam*	68	290	V.A.(A) Abraham van der Hulst
A	*Huis Tijdverdijf*	58	258	Albert Klaasz. Graef
A	*Huis te Kruiningen*	58	255	Jacob Swart
A	*Vrijheid*	56	254	Jan van Amstel
A	*Landman*	48	200	Hugo van Nieuwenhof
A	*Vrede*	48	205	Hendrik Gotskens
A	*Stad Gouda*	48	205	Otto van Treslong
A	*Dom van Utrecht*	48	195	Jacob Willemsz. Broeder
A	*Harderwijk*	46	200	Jacob Wiltschut
A	*Haarlem*	46	180	Adam van Brederode
A	*Zeelandia*	38	151	Balthazar van de Voorde
A	*Star*	36	144	Herman Egbertsz. Wolff
A	*Brak*	18	75	Gerrit Polanen
VOC	*Maarseveen*	78	330	Jacob de Reus
	2 fireships			
	2 galjoots			

SECOND SQUADRON (pendant at the fore)

Admty.	Ship	Guns	Men	Captain
Z	*Hof van Zeeland*	58	373	L.A.(Z) Jan Evertsen
M	*Klein Hollandia*	57	264	SbN.(M) Jan de Liefde
Z	*Utrecht*	50	236	Cornelis Evertsen the Younger
Z	*Middleburg*	46	210	Jacob Adriaansz. Pens
Z	*Wapen van Zeeland*	36	178	Bastiaan Tuyneman
Z	*Delft*	34	181	Jan Banckert
Z	*Zeelandia*	34	174	Simon Blok
Z	*Schakerlo*	29	125	Jan Krijnssen
M	*Prins Maurits*	53	201	Marinus de Clercq
M	*Dordrecht*	46	208	Jacob Cleydyck
M	*Wapen van Utrecht*	36	163	Christiaan Eldertsen
M	*Delft*	36	150	Jacob van Boshuisen
M	*Schiedam*	25	95	Adriaan Solderwagen
VOC	*Oranje*	76	383	Bastiaan Senten
M	*Lopende Hert* yacht	8	26	Pieter Wijnbergen
Z	*Dieshouk* yacht	6	20	Jan Pietersz. Tant
	2 fireships			
	2 galjoots			

THIRD SQUADRON (pendant at the mizzen)

Admty.	Ship	Guns	Men	Captain
M	*Groot Hollandia*	68	350	L.A.(M) Eghert Cortenaer
A	*Oosterwijk*	68	290	Dirk Scheij
A	*Stavoren*	48	200	Nicolaas Marrevelt
A	*Hilversum*	58	258	Albert Mathijszoon
A	*Zuiderhuis*	50	214	Joost Verschuur
A	*Doesburg*	48	200	Ysbrandt de Vries
A	*Vereenigte Provinciën*	48	205	Cornelis van Hogenhoeck
A	*Duivenvoorde*	48	205	Hendrik van Tholl
A	*Wakende Boei*	48	205	Anthony de Marre
A	*Ter Goes*	46	185	Gerbrant Boes
A	*Harderin*	38	148	Lieuwe van Hasevelt
A	*Maagd van Enkhuizen*	38	146	Johannes van der Mars
A	*Overijssel*	36	116	Jan van Blankenburch
VOC	*Delfland*	70	340	Juriaan Poel
VOC	*Sphera Mundi*	41	200	Apolonia Poel
	1 fireship			
	1 galjoot			

FOURTH SQUADRON (yellow vanes)

Admty.	Ship	Guns	Men	Captain
F	*Zevenwolden*	58	253	L.A.(F) Auke Stellingwerf
F	*Groningen*	40	199	V.A.(F) Rudolf Coenders
F	*Prinses Albertina*	52	248	SbN.(F) Hendrik Bruynsvelt
F	*Oostergo*	68	289	Allart Piersen de Boer
F	*Elf Steden*	54	253	Tjerk Hiddes de Vries
F	*Westergo*	52	236	Jan Jansz. Vijselaar
F	*Omlandia*	44	205	Cornelis Allartsz. Oostrum
F	*Klein Frisia*	40	205	Wytse Beyma
F	*Postillon van Smirna*	40	205	Barend Hiddes de Vries
F	*Hollandia*	40	186	Joost Michielszoon
A	*Phesant*	38	150	Jacob Pieteys
A	*IJlst*	36	121	Willem Codde van der Burgh
VOC	*Huis te Zwieten*	70	300	Cornelis de Rechter
VOC	*Mars*	50	200	Kat
VOC	*Ruiter*	18	65	Vogel
	1 fireship			
	2 galjoots			

FIFTH SQUADRON (red vanes with white stripe)

Admty.	Ship	Guns	Men	Captain
A	*Liefde*	70	340	V.A.(A) Cornelis Tromp
A	*Koevorden*	56	265	Gilles Thijssen Campen
A	*Kampen*	48	205	Pieter Salomonszoon
A	*Luipaard*	58	280	Kommer Gerritszoon
A	*Stad en Lande*	56	265	Jan de Haan
A	*Tromp*	48	205	Adriaan van Rheede
A	*Huis te Jaarsveld*	48	200	Thomas Fabritius
A	*Raadh. van Haarlem*	48	200	Jan Adelaar
A	*Groningen*	48	200	Pieter Jansz. Uyttenhout
A	*Zon*	48	195	Hendrik van Vollenhoven
A	*Wapen van Edam*	38	140	Cornelis Gerritsz. Burger
A	*Schager Roos*	38	140	Joosten Smient
A	*Asperen*	36	108	Adriaan van Veen
A	*Vollenhoven*	30	110	Hendrik Haeckroy
A	*Fortuin*	14	61	Laurens Bruyn
N	*Prinses Roijaal*	40	196	Adriaan Teding van Berkhout
VOC	*Nieuw Batavia*	50	206	Jan Pietersz. Onclaer
	1 fireship			
	1 galjoot			

SIXTH SQUADRON (white vanes with red stripe)

Admty.	Ship	Guns	Men	Captain
Z	*Vlissingen*	46	241	V.A.(Z) Cornelis Evertsen the Elder
Z	*Kampveere*	46	226	SbN.(Z) Adriaan Banckert
N	*Drie Helden Davids*	50	200	Pieter Bronsaart
Z	Dordrecht	46	150	Adriaan de Haaze
Z	Zeeridder	34	154	Willem Marinissen
Z	Goes	30	140	Adriaan van Cruiningen
Z	Zwanenburg	30	120	Cornelis Cuyper
Z	Visschers Harder	26	105	Jan Adriaansz. Blanckert
Z	Westcappel	24	119	Marinus Loncke
Z	Visscher	16	c.60	Simon Loncke
M	Stad Utrecht	48	200	Jacob Oudart
M	Rotterdam	46	202	Cryn Cerckhoven
M	Vrede	40	156	Laurens van Heemskerck
M	Gorinchem	36	158	Jacob van der Cam
M	Briel	21	86	Frans van Nijdek
M	Swol	20	68	Jacob Simonsz. de Witt
Z	Zouteland yacht	4	18	Willem Hendriksz. van der Veere
M	Hasewinthont yacht	3	12	Andries Pietersen
	2 fireships			
	2 galjoots			

SEVENTH SQUADRON (blue vanes with yellow stripe)

Admty.	Ship	Guns	Men	Captain
N	*Wapen van Nassau*	60	300	V.A.(N) Volckert Schram
N	*Eendracht*	44	239	SbN.(N) Frederik Stachouwer
N	*Wapen van Medemblik*	46	238	Adriaan Houttuin
N	Gelderland	56	264	Cornelis Jacobsz. de Boer
N	Hollandse Tuin	56	237	Bebberen
N	Jozua	50	260	Cornelis Slordt
N	Westfriesland	50	260	Jacob Bruynings
N	Jupiter	44	222	Huysman
N	Jonge Prins	36	134	Halfhoorn
N	Eenhoorn	30	150	Cornelis Victol
N	Hoorn	30	154	Klaas Valehen
VOC	Carolus Quintus	54	200	Joris Kuiten
VOC	Nagelboom	52	225	Boon
VOC	Beurs van Amsterdam	52	213	Cornelis Muts
VOC	Agatha	32	105	Gerrit Klaasz. Posthoorn
	2 fireships			
	2 galjoots			

Appendix D

The English Fleet at Bergen, 2 August 1665

A list of the English fleet at Bergen, including casualties, is in the collection of the Marquis of Bath and printed in Navy Records Society vol. 64, *The Journal of the Earl of Sandwich*. The list below is mainly from that source, but expanded to include armament, complements, and captains. Note that Captain James Cadman of the *Hambro' Merchant* was killed in the action aboard the *Revenge*, to which he had been temporarily assigned probably as a special pilot. The *Hambro' Merchant* was presumably under the command of her lieutenant, Roger Strickland, who was subsequently confirmed as Captain.

ENGAGED AT BERGEN

Rate	Ship	Guns	Men	Captain	Casualties K	W
3	*Revenge*	58	280	R.A. Sir Thomas Teddiman	4	7
4	*Happy Return*	50	190	James Lambert	14	48
4	*Breda*	46	180	Thomas Seale	29	55
4	*Foresight*	46	180	Packington Brooks	14	54
4P	*Golden Lion*	42	200	William Dale	0	6
4	*Sapphire*	38	160	Thomas Elliot	15	41
4P	*Guinea*	36	150	Thomas Room Coyle	0	7
M	*Bendish*	42	180	Robert Taylor	14	38
M	*Society*	36	160	Ralph Lascelles	2	0
M	*Prudent Mary*	36	160	Thomas Haward	7	13
M	*Coast Frigate*	34	150	William Lawson	2	0
5	*Guernsey*	28	145	John Utber	2	9
5	*Pembroke*	28	145	Richard Cotton	0	6
5	*Norwich*	24	135	John Wetwang	7	24
6	*Martin Galley*	14	65	William Kempthorne	1	1
fs	*Bryar*	12	45	Vincent Pierse	1	0
fs	*Hound*	8	45	James Coleman	0	0
					112	309

NOT ENGAGED; SEPARATED BY WEATHER

4	*Mary Rose*	48	190	Thomas Darcy		
4	*Bonaventure*	40	160	Arthur Laughorne		
4	*Expedition*	30	140	Tobias Sackler		
M	*John & Thomas*	44	200	Henry Dawes		
M	*Constant Catherine*	40	180	Francis Sanders		
M	*Exchange*	36	170	Samuel Wentworth		
M	*Hambro' Merchant*	36	170	Roger Strickland, acting		

Appendix E

Smith at Tangier,
December 1665–March 1666

Sir Jeremy Smith's Tangier fleet is recorded in the journal of Jeremy Roch, lieutenant of the *Antelope* (National Maritime Museum MSS IGR/17, f.11). Smith sailed from Plymouth on 18–19 December 1665 with thirteen men-of-war, two fireships, and a ketch, being joined at sea by a fourteenth man-of-war, the *Crown*. During the outward passage the squadron encountered a powerful storm, as a result of which the *Crown*, *Lion*, *Swallow*, and *Antelope* returned to England on 6 January with severe damage. Two fresh ships, the *Reserve* and *Dragon*, arrived in the Straits in late January after escorting ambassador Sir Robert Southwell to Lisbon. Of the four storm-damaged vessels, the *Crown* remained in England, but the other three at last reached Tangier in March (the *Antelope* on the 1st, the *Lion* and *Swallow* on the 14th).

Roch's list, drawn up on 9 March, shows a fully reversible order of battle. He notes that the *Montagu* was to lead if an engagement occurred on the starboard tack, the *Dragon* if on the larboard. Having too little space on his paper to properly insert the later-arriving *Lion* and *Swallow*, Roch entered them to the side as shown:

	Montagu	*Swallow*
	Guinea	
	Kent	
	Reserve	
	Bristol	
	Antelope	
	Bryar fireship	
Ketch	*Mary* Admiral	
	Greyhound fireship	
	Newcastle	
	Portland	
	Eagle	
	Assistance	
	Portsmouth	
	Dragon	*Lion*

Nominal ordnance and manning allowances for Smith's ships (using data from September 1665), along with their captains, were as follows:

Rate	Ship	Guns	Men	Captain
3	*Mary*	58	300	Sir Jeremy Smith
3	*Montagu*	58	300	Henry Fenne
3	*Lion*	52	260	John Hubbard
4	*Newcastle*	48	200	Thomas Page
4	*Bristol*	48	200	Phillip Bacon
4	*Antelope*	46	180	Frescheville Holles
4	*Swallow*	46	180	Richard Hodges
4	*Portland*	46	180	John Aylett
4	*Kent*	46	180	Thomas Ewens
4	*Reserve*	46	170	John Tyrwhit
4	*Assistance*	40	170	Zachary Brown
4	*Portsmouth*	38	160	Robert Mohun
4	*Dragon*	38	160	Daniel Helling
4P	*Guinea*	36	150	Thomas Room Coyle
5	*Eagle*	26	135	John Crabb
6	*Portsmouth* ketch	10	45	Thomas Willoughby
fs	*Bryar*	12	45	Joseph Paine
fs	*Greyhound*	16	70	William Flawes

Appendix F

The English Fleet in the Four Days' Battle

As with Lowestoft, no satisfactory list of the English fleet in the Four Days' Battle has come to light. Two documents appear at first glance to be authoritative sources, but both contain demonstrable inaccuracies. A particularly misleading list in the Public Record Office (SP29/158, ff. 8–9) is endorsed, 'Ld. Genll's fleet when he engaged June 1 66'. It names sixty men-of-war, including three known to have been elsewhere and another which was actually a fireship. A more useful list is in the British Library (Additional MSS 9336, ff. 85v–86). It gives important information, but omits three participants and does not distinguish several vessels which arrived after the start of the fight. The lists in this appendix giving the order of battle and the distribution of the remaining major warships are reconstructions drawn from fleet and dockyard correspondence, casualty reports, accounts of the action, ship-movements noted in the *London Gazette*, and several fleet lists drawn up a few days before the engagement.

The Duke of Albemarle's original forces are derived from a list in the British Library (Additional MSS 32094, f. 116) giving Prince Rupert's squadron and the distribution of the remaining ships after the Prince's departure on 29 May. It names fifty-two men-of-war and four fireships present in the Downs. There were no known subsequent detachments from the Downs, so in order to obtain the fleet which engaged on 1 June it should be necessary only to add four vessels which joined on or after the 29th: the *Dover* and *Oxford*, both from Harwich, and the scouting *Sweepstakes* and *Bristol*. That makes a total of fifty-six warships and four fireships, which agrees with most contemporary reports.

Aside from Prince Rupert's twenty men-of-war and four fireships, five vessels reinforced the fleet on 3 June: the *Centurion*, *Convertine* and *Sancta Maria* came from the Thames, while the *Kent* and probably the *Hampshire* had met the Prince's squadron off the Downs. The *Hampshire*'s participation is undocumented, but her presence (and indeed good service) is implied by the promotion of both her captain and lieutenant to second-rates immediately afterwards. One additional vessel, the fireship *Happy Entrance*, arrived from Harwich during the fighting on the 4th.

The divisions of Prince Rupert's squadron are given in the ship-list in British Library Additional MSS 9336 (except for the omitted *Portsmouth*, which probably belonged to Spragge's division). The divisions of Albemarle's fleet are from the order of battle of 29 May (British Library Additional MSS 32094, f. 118), which included the ships present in the Downs and all those which were expected to be on hand within two or three weeks. The unanticipated absence of Sir Jeremy Smith left the Blue Squadron's centre division without a flagship; how these ships were disposed is unknown. There are further uncertainties concerning the six vessels which reinforced the fleet on the 3rd and 4th. All appear on the 29 May order of battle, but some may have been reassigned on arrival. The *Kent, Hampshire,* and *Happy Entrance* were to have been in Harman's division, the *Convertine* in Ayscue's, the *Centurion* in Jordan's, and the *Sancta Maria* in Teddiman's. The ships in the list below are not in order of fighting. Stations in the line, at least for Albemarle's squadrons, had not been assigned as of the 31st and possibly never were.

Complements of the men-of-war are from the establishment of 22 April in the Generals' order-book (subsequently altered by an addition of 20 men for the *Fairfax*), and from various sources for the merchantmen. On 12 May, the Generals ordered artificial increases of 50 men for the *Royal Charles* and 12 men each for the *Prince, Royal James, Royal Oak, Victory, Royal Katherine, Henry, Swiftsure, Triumph,* and *Defiance.* These were the crews of the hired ketches, and were carried on the ships' books for victualling purposes only; they are excluded from the complements in the list below. Aside from the special allowances for ketch crews, all other ships contributed two or three men from their own complements for the same purpose. Owing to a general want of men, supernumeraries were temporarily forbidden and most ships were thus slightly undermanned. Correspondence from the Generals on 23 May (Bath Longleat Coventry MSS 95, f. 204) indicates an overall shortage of about 200 men.

Casualties for forty ships are from a list in Bath Longleat Coventry MSS 98, ff. 185–186, giving the names of the killed and wounded. The fleet list in British Library Additional MSS 9336 gives casualty figures for the same forty ships along with twenty-five others, while the losses of the *Henry* and *Loyal Subject* are from separate reports. Regrettably, the two principal casualty sources disagree for many vessels. Some conflicts may be simple transcription errors in the British Library document – consistent confusion of certain numerals; these are arbitrarily resolved here in favour of the very detailed Bath source. One group of discrepancies has another explanation: as the Bath list makes obvious, the British Library document has all the casualties for Ayscue's division of the White lined up with the wrong ships; each set of killed and wounded should have been given for the next ship down. This systematic error probably applies also to the vice-admiral's division of the White; it is hard to see how the captured *Swiftsure* could have submitted a casualty report, and heavy losses for the *Happy Return* seem improbable since her captain was dismissed for having avoided close engagement. The figures here are accordingly adjusted, with the ships of Berkeley's division arranged in the same order as in the British Library document. Incidentally, the Bath paper notes that the list of slain for the *Rupert* included one man from the ship's attending ketch and four rescued from the sunken *Black Eagle* on the second day who were subsequently killed aboard the *Rupert.*

Fireships expended in the action are indicated by asterisks. As an aside, note that the Captain Thomas Elliott who commanded the hired *Katherine* throughout the war was not the Thomas Elliot who commanded the *Sapphire* in 1665 and the *Revenge* in 1666 (Pepys's 'Register of Sea-Officers' treats them as one person).

WHITE SQUADRON

Rate	Ship	Guns	Men	Captain	Casualties K	W
2	*Swiftsure*	66	380	V.A. Sir William Berkeley	–	–
3	*Fairfax*	60	320	Sir John Chicheley	19	25
4	*Yarmouth*	52	200	John Lloyd	7	40
4	*Happy Return*	52	190	Henry Cuttance	–	–
M	*John & Thomas*	48	200	Henry Dawes	16	17
M	*Loyal George*	42	190	John Earle	–	–
4P	*Seven Oaks*	54	190	James Jennifer	–	–
1	*Prince*	92	620	Adm. Sir George Ayscue	–	–
2	*Triumph*	72	430	Henry Terne	9	15
3P	*Helverston*	60	260	Richard May	6	15
3	*Gloucester*	58	280	Robert Clark	18	27
4	*Crown*	48	180	George Chapple	8	15
4	*Portland*	48	180	John Aylett	1	4
4P	*Unity*	42	150	Thomas Trafford	0	9
5	*Oxford*	26	100	James Carteret	–	–
fs	*Providence*	10	45	John Wood	–	–
2	*Henry*	72	440	R.A. John Harman	100+	50+
2	*Rainbow*	56	310	John Hart	5	22
3	*Anne*	58	280	Robert Moulton	10	30
4P	*Zealand*	40	160	John Whatley	1	4
4P	*Welcome*	36	150	Michael Lindsey	7	13

RED SQUADRON

Rate	Ship	Guns	Men	Captain	Casualties K	W
2	*Royal Oak*	76	450	V.A. Sir Joseph Jordan	31	60
2	*Old James*	70	380	Edmund Seaman	14	30
3P	*Clove Tree*	62	250	Thomas Chappell	–	–
3	*Dunkirk*	58	280	John Hayward	11	31
4P	*Matthias*	54	200	Peter Bowen	2	0
4P	*Marmaduke*	42	160	William Godfrey	10	31
fs	*Hound**	8	45	James Coleman	–	–
I	*Royal Charles*	82	650	Albemarle/John Kempthorne	32	55
3P	*House of Sweeds*	70	280	Jeffrey Dare	14	29
4	*Antelope*	52	190	Frescheville Holles	21	30
4P	*Golden Ruyter*	48	180	Francis Courtney	3	10
4	*Ruby*	46	170	William Jennings	10	32
5	*Sweepstakes*	36	130	Francis Sanders	7	16
3	*Defiance*	64	320	R.A. Sir Robert Holmes	40	73
2	*St. Andrew*	66	360	Valentine Pine	12	17
3	*Monck*	58	280	Thomas Penrose	16	41
4	*Bristol*	52	200	Phillip Bacon	12	58
4P	*Black Eagle*	48	180	John Silver	–	–
4	*Dover*	46	170	Jeffrey Pearse	3	12
4P	*St. Paul*	40	160	John Holmes	–	–
fs	*Spread Eagle**	10	40	William Seale	–	–

BLUE SQUADRON

Rate	Ship	Guns	Men	Captain	Casualties	
					K	W
2	*Royal Katherine*	76	450	V.A. Sir Thomas Teddiman	13	39
2	*Unicorn*	60	320	Henry Teddiman	4	24
3	*Lion*	58	280	John Hubbard	8	20
M	*Loyal Subject*	56	200	John Fortesque (killed & wounded)	34	
4	*Assistance*	46	170	Zachary Brown	4	18
4	*Providence*	34	140	Richard James	2	6
2	*St. George*	66	360	John Coppin	17	23
3	*York*	58	280	John Swanley	8	14
4	*Newcastle*	50	200	Thomas Page	1	5
4P	*Delft*	40	160	Abraham Ansley	2	11
4P	*Black Bull*	40	150	John Gethings	–	–
fs	*Young Prince**	8	50	William Bustow	–	–
3	*Rupert*	64	320	RA. Richard Utber	17	46
2	*Vanguard*	60	320	John Whitty	27	35
3P	*Golden Phoenix*	60	260	Francis Steward	5	12
4	*Jersey*	50	185	Jean Baptiste du Tiel	7	9
M	*Baltimore*	48	180	Charles Wilde	3	5
M	*Katherine*	40	160	Thomas Elliott	1	0

JOINED 3–4 JUNE

Rate	Ship	Guns	Men	Captain	Casualties	
					K	W
4P	*Convertine*	52	190	John Pearce	–	–
4P	*Sancta Maria*	50	180	Roger Strickland	3	7
4	*Centurion*	48	180	John Hubbert	3	5
4	*Kent*	46	170	Thomas Ewens	5	8
4	*Hampshire*	42	160	George Batts	–	–
fs	*Happy Entrance**	8	35	Andrew Ball	–	–

[*cont.*]

[*cont.*]

PRINCE RUPERT'S SQUADRON

Rate	Ship	Guns	Men	Captain	Casualties K	W
2	*Victory*	76	450	V.A. Sir Christopher Myngs	28	87
3	*Revenge*	58	300	Thomas Elliot	11	8
4	*Swallow*	48	180	Richard Hodges	1	10
4	*Bonaventure*	48	180	John Waterworth	2	8
4	*Dragon*	40	160	Daniel Helling	1	6
4	*Assurance*	38	150	Thomas Guy	3	4
4	*Expedition*	34	140	Tobias Sackler	2	3
1	*Royal James*	82	520	Rupert/Sir Thomas Allin	21	21
3	*Henrietta*	58	300	Walter Wood	2	10
3	*Essex*	56	260	William Reeves	–	–
4	*Leopard*	56	250	Richard Beach	2	21
4	*Princess*	52	205	Peter Mootham	3	4
4	*Diamond*	48	180	John King	2	2
4	*Breda*	48	180	Joseph Sanders	3	0
3	*Dreadnought*	58	280	R.A. Sir Edward Spragge	6	30
3	*Plymouth*	58	280	Roger Miller	5	20
4	*Mary Rose*	48	185	Thomas Darcy	6	3
4	*Reserve*	48	180	John Tyrwhit	1	2
4	*Portsmouth*	44	160	Robert Mohun	–	–
4	*Amity*	38	150	John Parker	2	2
fs	*Bryar*	12	45	Joseph Paine	–	–
fs	*Little Unicorn**	8	35	John Kelsey	–	–
fs	*Greyhound**	6	35	William Flawes	–	–
fs	*Fortune*	6	35	William Lee	–	–

The fleet distribution for 1 June 1666 includes all ships above the sixth rate which were not with Rupert's or Albemarle's forces when the battle began. It proved impossible to trace the movements of sixth-rates, but only the *Lily* seems to have been near the action; she was in sight of the fighting on the first day but did not take part. Vessels distinguished by asterisks appear on the 29 May order of battle.

THAMES AND MEDWAY

Rate	Ship	Captain	Status or Location
1	*Royal Sovereign**	John Cox	Wanting men
2	*Loyal London*	—	New, not yet launched
3	*Cambridge*	John Jeffries	New, not yet launched
3	*Warspite**	Robert Robinson	New, fitting out
3P	*Slothany**	Thomas Rand	Wanting men
4	*Greenwich*	John Brooks	New, not yet launched
4	*Advice**	William Poole	Under repair
4	*Centurion**	John Hubbert	Under repair
4P	*Convertine**	John Pearce	Ready for sea
4P	*Sancta Maria**	Roger Strickland	Ready for sea
4P	*Charles V*	Gerard White	Unmanned by order
4P	*Westfriesland*	Charles O'Bryan	Unmanned by order
M	*Society*		Ordered discarded
M	*East India Merchant**	William Treherne	Wanting men
M	*Turkey Merchant**	William Partridge	Wanting men
M	*Castle Frigate**	Henry Ady	Wanting men
M	*Coronation**	Richard Smith	Wanting men
M	*Richard & Martha**	George Colt	Fitting out
M	*George**	Ralph Lascelles	Fitting out
M	*Loyal Merchant**	Phillip Holland	Fitting out
M	*East India London**	William Dale	Fitting out
M	*Albemarle**	Jonathan Hide	Fitting out
M	*London Merchant**	Amos Beare	Fitting out
M	*Charles Merchant**	Butler Barnes	Fitting out
5	*Falcon*	—	New, not yet launched
fs	*Paul**	Charles Juxon	Fitting out
fs	*Lizard*	—	Fitting out
fs	*Great Gift*	—	Fitting out

PORTSMOUTH

Rate	Ship	Captain	Status or Location
3	*Mary**	Sir Jeremy Smith	Victualling
3	*Montagu**	Henry Fenne	Victualling
4P	*Guinea**	Thomas Room Coyle	Victualling
4	*Hampshire**	George Batts	Sailed for Downs, 1 June
4	*Constant Warwick*	Robert Ensom	Rebuilding, not yet launched
4P	*Mars*	—	Ordinary, needing repair
4P	*Golden Lion*	—	Ordinary, needing repair

[*cont.*]

[*cont.*]

WESTERN STATION (all at sea or ready for sea except as noted)

Rate	Ship	Captain	Status or Location
3	*Resolution*	Willoughby Hannam	Plymouth
4	*Foresight*	Hugh Seymour	Plymouth
4	*Adventure*	Benjamin Young	Plymouth
4	*Tiger*	John Wetwang	Plymouth
4	*Elizabeth*	Charles Talbot	Falmouth 22 May
5	*Nightingale*	Richard Long	Plymouth
5	*Garland*	Charles Howard	Plymouth
5	*Richmond*	Thomas Knevett	Plymouth
5P	*Sorlings*	Stephen Akarman	Plymouth
5P	*French Victory*	Thomas Scott	Fitting out at Plymouth
5P	*Orange*	Christopher Gunman	Guernsey; Plymouth 3 June
5P	*Fountain*	Thomas Leggatt	Jersey
5	*Eagle*	John Crabb	Westward convoy
5	*Guernsey*	John Moore	Westward convoy
5	*Success*	Nepthali Ball	With *Milford*, mission unknown
5	*Milford*	Richard White	With *Success*, mission unknown

OTHER STATIONS (all at sea or ready for sea except as noted)

Rate	Ship	Captain	Status or Location
4	*Kent**	Thomas Ewens	Scouting near Calais
4	*St. Patrick*	Robert Sanders	New, fitting out at Bristol
4	*Sapphire*	Jasper Grant	Ireland
4P	*Hope*	Jacob Reynolds	Convoy to Barbados
5P	*Coventry*	William Hill	Convoy to Barbados
5	*Forester*	Richard Country	Ireland
5	*Dartmouth*	Richard Rooth	Ireland
5	*Mermaid*	George Watson	Ireland
5	*Norwich*	Robert Warden	Northern Station
5	*Pearl*	Benjamin Carteret	Gothenburg
5P	*Sophia*	John Anderson	Scotland
5	*Little Victory*	Thomas Blackman	Convoy, Newcastle to Harwich
5	*Pembroke*	Richard Goodlad	Convoy, Newcastle to Harwich
5	*Colchester*	William Hammond	North Sea
5	*Speedwell*	John Lightfoot	Home waters, station unknown
fs	*Happy Entrance**	Andrew Ball	Harwich, under repair

Appendix G

The Dutch Fleet in the Four Days' Battle

The ships and captains of the Dutch fleet in the Four Days' Battle are known with reasonable confidence from lists in Brandt's *Leven van de Ruiter* and the anonymous *Life of Tromp*. Additional information on manning, casualties, and some details of the fighting order was graciously supplied by Dr R.E.J. Weber from data which he and the late R.A. van Foreest compiled for their book, *De Vierdaagse Zeeslag 11–14 Juni 1666*.

The three squadrons are known in varying degrees of detail. Records of divisional organization have not been found for the Second (van) Squadron. It seems probable, however, that the ten Frisian ships formed the van division, so they are listed first.

In the First (centre) Squadron, the assignment of ships to divisions is known, but not stations in the line. Note that the centre division had separate sub-groups under de Ruyter and *Schout-bij-Nacht* Jan van Nes. Van Nes's group was stationed ahead of de Ruyter's in the St. James's Day Fight and was probably so placed in the Four Days' Battle as well.

In the Third (rear) Squadron, the ships (but not frigates) of Tromp's own centre division are given in fighting order. The composition of the other divisions is uncertain, but it seems reasonable to suppose that the van division consisted of Noorderkwartier ships, perhaps reinforced by one or two of the remaining Amsterdam vessels; the rear division probably had Amsterdam ships exclusively.

The command flag used by all flag-officers was the national tricolour or Prince's flag. As usual it was flown at the main by lieutenant-admirals, at the fore by vice-admirals, and at the mizzen by *schout-bij-nachts*. Ships displayed their admiralty affiliation by differing combinations of jacks and ensigns using three flags: the Prince, the nine-striped Triple Prince, and the Vlissingen ewer standard. They were worn as follows:

Admiralty	Jack	Ensign
Maas	Prince	Prince
Amsterdam	Triple Prince	Triple Prince
Noorderkwartier	Prince	Triple Prince
Zeeland	Vlissingen	Prince
Friesland	Prince	Prince

Friesland and the Maas used the same combination, but the ships of those admiralties were in different squadrons and could thus be distinguished by their squadron masthead pendants. Ships of the First Squadron wore a pendant at the main, those of the Second Squadron a pendant at the fore, and those of the Third Squadron a pendant at the mizzen. There was an exception in the First Squadron: Lt.-Adm. Aert van Nes omitted the masthead pendant in the *Eendracht* to avoid confusion with the pendant of command flown beneath de Ruyter's flag in the *Zeven Provinciën*.

SECOND SQUADRON (van or right wing) – Evertsen

Admty	Ship	Guns	Men	Captain	Casualties K	W
F	*Groot Frisia*	72	393	L.A.(F) Tjerk Hiddes de Vries	24	15
F	*Groningen*	72	306	V.A.(F) Rudolf Coenders	30	24
F	*Prins Hendrik Casimir*	72	370	SbN.(F) Hendrik Bruynsvelt	–	–
F	*Oostergo*	60	265	Jan Jansz. Vijselaar	6	2
F	*Westergo*	56	237	Wytse Beyma	11	4
F	*Elf Steden*	54	238	Barend Hiddes de Vries	9	14
F	*Stad en Lande*	52	228	Joost Hermansz. Clant	3	6
F	*Prinses Albertina*	50	224	Joost Michielsz. Cuyk	8	6
F	*Omlandia*	48	186	Christiaan Ebelsz. Uma	10	12
F	*Klein Frisia*	38	177	Jan Pietersz. Vinckelbos	–	–
Z	*Walcheren*	70	380	L.A.(Z) Cornelis Evertsen	7	13
Z	*Tholen*	60	290	V.A.(Z) Adriaan Banckert	7	4
Z	*Zierikzee*	60	300	SbN.(Z) C. Evertsen the Younger	14	30
Z	*Hof van Zeeland*	58	248	Simon Blok	c.240	–
Z	*Middelburg*	50	208	Jacob Adriaansz. Pens	3	9
Z	*Vlissingen*	50	200	Jan Matthijszoon	3	4
Z	*Kampveere*	50	215	Adriaan de Haaze	4	7
Z	*Utrecht*	50	216	Jan Pietersz. Tant	4	6
Z	*Dordrecht*	50	200	Adriaan van Cruiningen	5	9
A	*Stad Gouda*	46	222	Dirk Scheij	3	6
A	*Huis te Jaarsveld*	46	216	Joost Verschuur	10	20
A	*Stavoren*	46	213	Jacob Pauw	3	7
A	*Wakende Boei*	46	222	Hendrik Vroom	9	11
A	*Harderwijk*	44	218	Thomas Tobias	6	14
	Frigates					
Z	*Zeeridder*	36	158	Willem Marinissen	3	1
Z	*Delft*	36	167	Dirk Jacobsz. Kiela	8	12
Z	*Zeelandia*	36	155	Abraham Crijnssen	4	7
Z	*Schakerlo*	30	135	Jan Krijnssen	5	10
	Advice-Yachts					
Z	*Dishoek*	6	21?	Gilles Geleynszoon	–	–
Z	*Zouteland*	6	29?	Klaas Reinierszoon	–	–
Z	*West-Souburg*	6	13	Frans Roys	–	–
Z	*Oost-Souburg*	6	13	Daniel Verdiest	–	–
	Fireships					
Z	*Vrijheid*	2	14	Engel Adriaanszoon	–	–
Z	*Hoop*	6	15	Willem Meerman	–	–
F	*Rob*	2	14	Roelof Jansz. de Rob	–	–

FIRST SQUADRON (centre) – de Ruyter

Admty	Ship	Guns	Men	Captain	Casualties K	W
Van Division						
M	*Eendracht*	76	380	L.A.(M) Aert van Nes	5	32
M	*Groot Hollandia*	64	280	Laurens Davidsz. van Convent	17	41
M	*Prinses Louise*	34	180	Frans van Nijdek	2	20
A	*Geloof*	68	380	Nicolaas Marrevelt	14	27
A	*Zuiderhuis*	50	237	Cornelis van Hogenhoeck	5	–
A	*Gouden Leeuwen*	50	238	Enno Doedes Star	12	22
N	*Wapen van Nassau*	60	250	David Vlugh	5	14
N	*Jozua*	54	228	Govert 'tHoen	4	–
M	*Harderwijk*	32	135	Nicolaas Naalhout	4	8
M	*Swol* 3-mast yacht	18	41	Pieter Wijnbergen	11	4
M	*St. Paulus* fs	?	19	Barend Volkertszoon	–	–
Centre Division						
M	*Delft*	62	279	SbN.(M) Jan Jansz. van Nes	0	2
A	*Amsterdam*	60	269	Jacob van Meeuwen	2	6
A	*Duivenvoorde*	46	207	Otto van Treslong	c.170	–
M	*Gorinchem*	34	136	Huybert Jacobsz. Huygen	4	7
M	*Zeven Provinciën*	80	450	Adm.-Gen. de Ruyter	19	25
M	*Gelderland*	64	335	Col.Willem Jos, Baron van Ghent	0	0
M	*Klein Hollandia*	54	230	Evert van Gelder	4	11
A	*Wapen van Utrecht*	66	290	Hendrik Gotskens	5	30
A	*Vrede*	46	224	Jan du Bois	0	1
M	*Schiedam*	22	70	Jacob Pietersz. Swart	2	11
M	*Gouden Ruiter* fs	2	12	Jan Broersz. Vermeulen	–	–
Rear Division						
M	*Ridderschap*	66	345	V.A.(M) Jan de Liefde	17	30
M	*Wassenaar*	56	230	Ruth Maximiliaan	6	34
M	*Dordrecht*	44	186	Philips van Almonde	2	21
A	*Provincie Utrecht*	64	283	Jacob Cornelisz. Swart	22	54
A	*Stad en Lande*	60	273	Hugo van Nieuwenhof	8	27
A	*Raadhuis van Haarlem*	46	209	Jan de Jong	6	11
N	*Hollandse Tuin*	56	239	Jan Crook	2	4
M	*Wapen van Utrecht*	36	139	Eland du Bois	5	14
M	*Nijmegen*	34	125	Willem Boudewijnsz. van Eyk	11	14
M	*Lopende Hert* yacht	8	20	Dirk de Munnik	–	–
M	*Rotterdam* fs	6	22	Jan van Brakel	–	–

THIRD SQUADRON (rear or left wing) – Tromp

Admty	Ship	Guns	Men	Captain	Casualties K	W
Van Division – One or two Amsterdam ships probably should be included						
N	*Westfriesland*	78	394	L.A.(N) Jan Cornelisz. Meppel	14	24
N	*Pacificatie*	73	326	V.A.(N) Volckert Schram	10	16
N	*Maagd van Enkhuizen*	72	311	SbN.(N) Frederik Stachouwer	19	8
N	*Jonge Prins*	66	286	Adriaan Houttuin	13	35
N	*Noorderkwartier*	60	294	Pieter Klaasz. Wijnbergen	11	9
N	*Caleb*	50	237	Cornelis Victol	5	11
N	*Drie Helden Davids*	48	228	Adriaan Teding van Berkhout	8	4
Centre Division – in fighting order						
N	*Gelderland*	56	281	Maj. Jo. Belgicus, Graaf van Hoorn	7	4
A	*Beschermer*	54	280	Willem van der Zaan	10	20
A	*Vrijheid*	60	266	Jan van Amstel	14	41
A	*Gouda*	72	370	SbN.(A) Isaac Sweers	14	22
A	*Hollandia*	80	450	L.A.(A) Cornelis Tromp	14	23
A	*Calantsoog*	70	313	Jan de Haan	21	70
A	*Huis te Kruiningen*	60	286	Lt. Col. François Palm	–	–
A	*Deventer*	66	273	Jacob Andriesz. Swart	4	18
Rear Division – One or two were probably in the van division						
A	*Spiegel*	68	397	V.A.(A) Abraham van der Hulst	35	66
A	*Reiger*	72	345	Hendrik Andriaanszoon	4	11
A	*Liefde*	68	320	Pieter Salomonszoon	c.280	–
A	*Huis Tijdverdrijf*	60	277	Thomas Fabritius	9	13
A	*Dom van Utrecht*	46	218	Jacob Willemsz. Broeder	6	14
A	*Tromp*	46	215	Hendrik van Vollenhoven	17	24
A	*Kampen*	46	220	Michiel Suis	6	15
A	*Landman*	46	230	Pieter Jansz. Uyttenhout	c.180	–
A	*Zon*	44	205	Floris Florisz. Bloem	12	32
A	*Haarlem*	44	209	Wouter Wijngaarden	12	7
Frigates – divisions unknown						
A	*Harder*	34	134	Jan Davidsz. Bont	1	0
A	*Overijssel*	34	130	Arend Symonsz. Vader	1	5
A	*Asperen*	34	130	Jan Gijselsz. van Lier	1	5
A	*IJlst*	34	136	Jacob Dirksz. Boom	5	11
Fireships – divisions unknown						
A	*Fortuin*	0	19	Rein Pietersz. Mars	–	–
A	*Kat*	?	19	Hendrik Dirksz. Boekhoven	–	–
A	*Wapen van Engeland*	?	19	Hendrik Hendrikszoon		

Appendix H

The English Fleet in the St. James's Day Fight

The English fleet in the St. James's Day Fight is listed, in reverse order, in a manuscript in the British Library (Additional MSS 9336, ff. 87–88r). Evidently adapted from the order of battle drawn up about ten days before the action, it includes (but clearly identifies) a number of vessels which were deleted prior to the engagement. A closely related list is printed on an engraving of the action in the National Maritime Museum. The engraving gives the fleet in normal order and lists only the ships that took part in the fight. It erroneously transposes two of the fireship commanders, but otherwise agrees with the British Library document in all details – including several minor mistakes. Both wrongly list the fireship *Mary* and omit the sixth-rate *Little Mary*. The fireship (which belonged to the Blue Squadron) was sent to Harwich after being disabled by lightning the night before the battle, while the sixth-rate was present throughout. Both lists also give Richard Smith as captain of the hired *Coronation*. The Generals' order-book shows that Smith was transferred to the *Zealand* and replaced in the *Coronation* by William Davies on 16 July. Although both lists give the stations in the line, neither shows boundaries between divisions. That want is supplied by a fleet list of 22 August in Charnock's *History of Marine Architecture*, confirmed by an early version of the order of battle dating from about 10 July in the Public Record Office (SP29/164, ff. 183–184 – wrongly endorsed in the heading as the fleet which engaged on the 25th).

Manning figures are drawn from the Generals' order-book. In early July, 50 men were added to the complements of all flagships and the fourth-rates *Leopard* and *Matthias*. Because of increased armament, 80 supernumeraries were allowed for the *Loyal London* (beyond the 50 men already approved), and 100 for the *Royal Sovereign*. In mid-July at least thirty-nine ships were assigned from 10 to 40 landsmen 'above their complements' to compensate for inadequate proportions of trained seamen among their crews. These 'temporary' supernumeraries (they were authorized only 'till the next engagement be over' but were still aboard in October) are indicated below, though the numbers of men added are unknown for many vessels. As in the list for the previous battle, ketch crews carried on the ships' books for victualling purposes are excluded; these were already deducted in the two principal source lists except for 50 men from the *Royal Charles* and 12 from the *Triumph*. One late adjustment in manning is not reflected below. On the morning of the battle, Captain Francis Digby's 50-gun fourth-rate *Jersey* (stationed in the Generals' division between the *Lion* and *Triumph*) was ordered to Sheerness because of lightning damage. Before her departure 100 of her 185-man crew were transferred to other ships.

Fireships expended in the action are indicated by asterisks. In the order of battle, the three light frigates were not in the line but did have specific duties. The *Colchester* was to assist the *Royal Sovereign* and above all protect her from fireships, the *Sweepstakes* was to perform the same services for the *Royal Charles*, and the *Little Mary* was to act as flagship for the fleet's auxiliaries. Aside from the usual flotilla of ketches, smacks, and hoys, the auxiliaries on this occasion included hospital ships and ammunition ships, both types accompanying the fleet to sea for the first time as the result of experience in the Four Days' Battle. One final note: the owner of the hired *Turkey Merchant* was none other than Rear-Admiral John Kempthorne, so it was probably no coincidence that she was assigned to Kempthorne's division.

WHITE SQUADRON

Rate	Ship	Guns	Men Comp.	+ Sup.	Captain
M	London Merchant	48	180	+ 30	Amos Beare
3	Anne	58	280	+ 30	Robert Moulton
M	Baltimore	48	180		John Day
4P	Guinea	38	150	+ ?	Arthur Ashby
4	Expedition	34	140		Tobias Sackler
2	**Royal Katherine**	76	500		V.A. Sir Thomas Teddiman
4	Dover	46	170		Jeffery Pearse
2	St. George	66	360	+ 40	John Hayward
3	Dunkirk	58	280		John Waterworth
M	Richard & Martha	50	200		George Colt
3	Montagu	58	300		Daniel Helling
4	Centurion	48	180		Charles Wilde
4	Leopard	60	300		John Hubbert
4	Assistance	46	170	+ ?	Zachary Brown
1	**Royal James**	82	570		Adm. Sir Thomas Allin
4	Dragon	40	160		Thomas Room Coyle
4P	Delft	40	160		Edward Cotterell
2	Old James	70	380		Edmund Seaman
3	Plymouth	58	280	+ ?	John Lloyd
4	Assurance	38	150		John Narbrough
4	Kent	46	170		John Silver
M	Coronation	52	190	+ ?	William Davies
3P	Helverston	60	260		Abraham Ansley
4	Hampshire	42	160		William Coleman
3	**Rupert**	64	370		R.A. Richard Utber
4P	Westfriesland	52	180		John Butler
3	York	58	280		John Swanley
2	Unicorn	60	320	+ ?	George Batts
4	Mary Rose	50	185	+ 20	Thomas Darcy
	Fireships				
	Providence*	10	45		John Wood
	Fortune*	6	35		William Lee
	Richard	4	45		Henry Brown
	Paul	4	50		Daniel Stephens
	Jacob	4	40		William Humble

RED SQUADRON

Rate	Ship	Guns	Comp.	+ Sup.	Captain
			Men		
M	*Charles Merchant*	54	220	+ ?	Butler Barnes
3P	*Slothany*	60	280		Thomas Rand
3	*Warspite*	64	320		Robert Robinson
4	*Crown*	48	180		William Godfrey
2	**Royal Oak**	76	500		V.A. Sir Joseph Jordan
4	*Diamond*	48	180		John King
4P	*Matthias*	54	250	+ ?	Henry Millett
4	*Portsmonth*	44	160	+ ?	Thomas Guy
4	*Greenwich*	58	260		John Brooks
2	*St. Andrew*	66	360		Valentine Pine
3	*Monck*	58	280	+ ?	Thomas Penrose
4	*Foresight*	46	170	+30	Hugh Seymour
5	*Colchester*	28	110		Arthur Laughorne
1	*Royal Sovereign*	102	700	+100	John Cox
3	*Henrietta*	58	300		Sir Frescheville Holles
4	*Antelope*	52	190	+25	Francis Wilshaw
5	*Sweepstakes*	36	140		Francis Sanders
1	**Royal Charles**	82	700		Generals/John Hubbard
6	*Little Mary*	12	60		John Berry
4	*Swallow*	48	180		Bernard Ludman
3	*Fairfax*	60	320	+ ?	Richard Beach
4	*Ruby*	46	170	+30	Thomas Lamming
2	*Triumph*	72	430	+30	Robert Clark
3	*Lion*	58	280	+20	Sir William Jennings
4	*Breda*	48	180		Joseph Sanders
M	*John & Thomas*	48	200		Levi Greene
3	*Cambridge*	64	320		John Jeffries
4	*Bristol*	52	200	+ 30	John Holmes
2	**Henry**	80	490	+ ?	R.A. Sir Robert Holmes
4	*Princess*	52	205	+ ?	Henry Dawes
3	*Revenge*	58	300	+ ?	Thomas Elliot
4	*Newcastle*	50	200		Peter Bowen
4	*Tiger*	40	160	+ 20	John Wetwang
	Fireships				
	*Abigail**	4	35		Thomas Wilshaw
	Samuel	4	35		William Seale
	Bryar	12	45		Joseph Paine
	Lizard	6	45		Joseph Harris
	Fox	6	35		John Elliot
	Alepine	6	40		Andrew Ball
	Charles	6	40		John Johnson
	Yacht				
	Fanfan	2	30		William Harris

BLUE SQUADRON

Rate	Ship	Guns	Men Comp.	+ Sup.	Captain
M	*George*	40	180		Ralph Lascelles
M	*Turkey Merchant*	48	180		William Partridge
4	*Happy Return*	52	190	+ ?	Francis Courtney
3	**Defiance**	64	370		R.A. John Kempthorne
4	*Providence*	34	140		Richard James
3	*Resolution*	58	300		Willoughby Hannam
4	*Elizabeth*	40	160	+ 20	Charles Talbot
M	*East India London*	50	190		William Martin
3P	*House of Sweeds*	70	280		John Wilgresse
2	*Rainbow*	56	310	+ ?	John Hart
3P	*Golden Phoenix*	60	260	+40	Francis Steward
3	*Mary*	58	300	+ ?	William Poole
4	*Portland*	48	180	+ ?	Richard Haddock
2	**Loyal London**	92	520	+80	Adm. Sir Jeremy Smith
4	*Amity*	38	150	+ ?	William Finch
3	*Gloucester*	58	280	+ ?	Richard May
4P	*Unity*	42	150		Thomas Trafford
4	*Bonaventure*	48	180	+ ?	William Hammond
4	*Yarmouth*	52	200	+ ?	John Parker
M	*Loyal Merchant*	50	210		Phillip Holland
4P	*Golden Ruyter*	48	180	+ 20	Robert Gilby
2	*Vanguard*	60	320		Anthony Langston
4	*Advice*	48	180	+ ?	Charles O'Bryan
2	**Victory**	80	500	+ ?	V.A. Sir Edward Spragge
4	*Reserve*	48	180		John Tyrwhit
3	*Dreadnought*	58	280	+40	Robert Mohun
4P	*Sancta Maria*	50	180		Roger Strickland
4	*Adventure*	38	150	+ ?	Benjamin Young
	Fireships				
	*Blessing**	4	20		William Maiden
	*Great Gift**	4	50		John Kelsey
	*Land of Promise**	4	45		William Minterne
	Virgin	4	30		William Hughs

The fleet distribution for 25 July 1666 omits sixth-rates, the activities of which are poorly documented. It is reasonably certain, however, that no ships of that class other than the *Little Mary* took part in the St. James's Day Fight.

THAMES AND MEDWAY

Rate	Ship	Captain	Status or Location
4	*Jersey*	Francis Digby	Needing repair
4P	*Charles V*	Gerard White	Under repair
4P	*Marmaduke*	Richard Trevanion	Wanting men
4P	*Welcome*	Michael Lindsey	Wanting men
4P	*Zealand*	Richard Smith	Wanting men
M	*East India Merchant*	William Treherne	Wanting men
M	*Katherine*	Thomas Elliott	Wanting men
M	*Castle Frigate*	Henry Ady	Wanting men
M	*Albemarle*	Jonathan Hide	Released to owner
M	*Loyal Subject*	John Fortescue	Needing repair
5	*Oxford*	James Carteret	Wanting men
5P	*Sorlings*	Stephen Akarman	Wanting men
5	*Pearl*	Benjamin Carteret	Wanting men
5	*Nightingale*	Richard Long	Wanting men
5	*Garland*	Charles Howard	Wanting men
5	*Norwich*	Robert Warden	Wanting men
5	*Falcon*	Robert Sheppard	New, not yet launched

HARWICH

5	*Pembroke*	Richard Goodlad	Ready for sea
5	*Richmond*	Thomas Knevett	Ready for sea
5	*Speedwell*	John Lightfoot	Ready for sea
5P	*Fountain*	Thomas Leggatt	Ready for sea
fs	*Mary*	William Flawes	Needing repair

CHANNEL

4P	*Mars*	—	Portsmouth, needing repair
4P	*Golden Lion*	—	Portsmouth, under repair
4	*Constant Warwick*	Robert Ensom	At sea
5	*Success*	Nepthali Ball	At sea
5	*Milford*	Richard White	At sea
5P	*Orange*	Christopher Gunman	At sea
5P	*French Victory*	Thomas Scott	At sea
5	*Eagle*	John Crabb	Falmouth
5	*Guernsey*	John Moore	Falmouth

OTHER STATIONS

4	*St. Patrick*	Robert Sanders	Bristol, fitting out
4P	*Hope*	Jacob Reynolds	Barbados
4	*Sapphire*	Jasper Grant	Ireland
5	*Forester*	Richard Country	Ireland
5	*Dartmouth*	Richard Rooth	Ireland
5	*Mermaid*	George Watson	Ireland
5P	*Coventry*	William Hill	Barbados
5P	*Sophia*	John Anderson	Scotland
5	*Little Victory*	Thomas Blackman	Unknown; probably Newcastle

Appendix I

The Dutch Fleet in the St. James's Day Fight

A complete list of the Dutch fleet in the St. James's Day Fight appears in Brandt's *Leven van de Ruiter*, from which most of the information below is drawn. The assignment of ships to divisions is known only for the First (centre) Squadron, and stations in the line only for the ships of de Ruiter's division. Members of other divisions and squadrons are simply listed by admiralty. In the Second (van) Squadron, the Frisians probably formed the van division and are accordingly listed first. Similarly, the Noorderkwartier ships are listed first in the Third Squadron, since most of them were probably in the van division. Flags and pendants were worn as in the previous battle.

SECOND SQUADRON (van or right wing) – Evertsen

Admty.	Ship	Guns	Men	Captain
F	*Groot Frisia*	72	413	L.A.(F) Tjerk Hiddes de Vries
F	*Groningen*	70	341	V.A.(F) Rudolf Coenders
F	*Prins Hendrik Casimir*	70	392	SbN.(F) Hendrik Bruynsvelt
F	*Sneek*	65	326	Ruyrt Hillebrantszoon
F	*Oostergo*	60	275	Jan Jansz. Vijselaar
F	*Westergo*	56	230	Wytse Beyma
F	*Elf Steden*	54	236	Barend Hiddes de Vries
F	*Prinses Albertina*	50	213	Pieter Feykesz. Eykema
F	*Omlandia*	48	206	Christiaan Ebelszoon
F	*Klein Frisia*	38	191	Jan Pietersz. Vinckelbos
Z	*Walcheren*	70	380	L.A.(Z) Jan Evertsen
Z	*Tholen*	60	296	V.A.(Z) Adriaan Banckert
Z	*Zierikzee*	58	317	SbN.(Z) Cornelis Evertsen the Younger
Z	*Middelburg*	50	217	Jacob Adriaansz. Pens
Z	*Vlissingen*	50	210	Jan Matthijszoon
Z	*Kampveere*	50	218	Adriaan de Haaze
Z	*Utrecht*	50	220	Jan Pietersz. Tant
Z	*Dordrecht*	49	200	Adriaan van Cruiningen
A	*Stad Gouda*	46	230	Dirk Scheij
A	*Dom van Utrecht*	46	228	Jacob Willemsz. Broeder
A	*Stavoren*	46	230	Jacob Pauw
A	*Wakende Boei*	46	229	Hendrik Vroom
A	*Zon*	44	198	Floris Florisz. Bloem

Frigates

Z	*Zeeridder*	34	175	Willem Marinissen
Z	*Delft*	34	169	Dirk Jacobsz. Kiela
Z	*Zeelandia*	34	173	Abraham Crijnssen
Z	*Schakerlo*	29	147	Cornelis Evertsen the Youngest
Z	*Visschers Harder*	26	105	Jan Adriaansz. Blanckert

Three-Mast Yacht

Z	*Prins te Paard*	14	75	Willem Hendriksz. van der Veere

Advice-Yachts

Z	*Zouteland*	6	29	Klaas Reinierszoon
Z	*Dishoek*	6	21	Gilles Geleynszoon
Z	*West-Souburg*	6	13	Frans Roys
Z	*Oost-Souburg*	6	13	Daniel Verdiest

Fireships

Z	*Eendracht*	2	8	Willem Meerman
Z	*Hoop*	4	14	Engel Andriaanszoon
F	*Prinses*	3	16	Meindert Jentjes
M	*Fortuin*	2	9	Jan Danielsz. van den Rijn
M	*Schiedam*	4	?	Gerrit Andriesz. Mak
M	*Erasmus*	?	?	Bartel Evertsz. Licht

FIRST SQUADRON (centre) – de Ruyter

Van Division – not in fighting order

Admty.	Ship	Guns	Men	Captain
M	*Eendracht*	71	402	L.A.(M) Aert van Nes
M	*Groot Hollandia*	65	311	Laurens Davidsz. van Convent
M	*Prinses Louise*	40	200	Frans van Nijdek
A	*Provincie Utrecht*	64	273	Jacob Cornelisz. Swart
A	*Gouden Leeuwen*	52	251	Enno Doedes Star
A	*Tromp*	46	245	Hendrik van Vollenhoven
A	*Harderwijk*	44	220	Thomas Tobias
M	*Wapen van Utrecht*	36	149	Eland du Bois
M	*Nijmegen*	34	130	Willem Boudewijnsz. van Eyk
M	*Swol* 3-mast yacht	16	58	Pieter Wijnbergen
M	*Lijdzaamheid* fs	2	10	Cornelis Jacobsz. van der Horven
M	*Helena* fs	2	10	Jan Broersz. Vermeulen
M	*Delft* fs	4	?	Willem Pauluszoon

Centre Division – ships (but not frigates) in fighting order

Admty.	Ship	Guns	Men	Captain
M	*Delft*	62	304	SbN.(M) Jan Jansz. van Nes
A	*Wapen van Utrecht*	66	290	Hendrik Gotskens
A	*Stad en Lande*	58	280	Hugo van Nieuwenhof
A	*Zuiderhuis*	50	243	Cornelis van Hogenhoeck
M	*Zeven Provinciën*	80	492	Adm.-Gen. de Ruyter
M	*Gelderland*	66	360	Col. Willem Joseph Baron van Ghent
M	*Klein Hollandia*	54	244	Evert van Gelder
M	*Wassenaar*	58	254	Ruth Maximiliaan
A	*Vrede*	46	230	Jan du Bois
M	*Gorinchem*	34	130	Huybert Jacobsz. Huygen
M	*Schiedam*	22	80	Jacob Pietersz. Swart
M	*Lopende Hert* yacht	8	20	Dirk de Munnik
M	*Lammertje Kweek* fs	2	11	Jan van Brakel
M	*Rotterdam* fs	?	?	Gysbert Jacobsz. de Hay
F?	*Ekster* fs	2	11	Reiner de Vos

Rear Division – not in fighting order

Admty.	Ship	Guns	Men	Captain
M	*Ridderschap*	66	364	V.A.(M) Jan de Liefde
M	*Dordrecht*	46	200	Philips van Almonde
A	*Geloof*	64	335	Nicolaas Marrevelt
A	*Amsterdam*	62	294	Jacob van Meeuwen
A	*Raadhuis van Haarlem*	46	232	Jan de Jong
A	*Huis te Jaarsveld*	44	216	Joost Verschuur
N	*Wapen van Nassau*	60	285	David Vlugh
N	*Hollandse Tuin*	56	244	Jan Crook
M	*Vrede*	34	118	Juriaan Juriaansz. Poel
M	*Harderwijk*	32	141	Nicolaas Naalhout
M?	*Goede Hoop* fs	2	12	Pieter Lievenszoon

THIRD SQUADRON (rear or left wing) – Tromp

Admty.	Ship	Guns	Men	Captain
N	*Westfriesland*	78	398	L.A.(N) Jan Cornelisz. Meppel
N	*Pacificatie*	73	354	V.A.(N) Volckert Schram
N	*Jozua*	54	242	SbN.(N) Govert 't Hoen
N	*Maagd van Enkhuizen*	72	312	Pieter Kerseboom
N	*Gelderland*	64	288	Maj. Johan Belgicus, Graaf van Hoorn
N	*Jonge Prins*	62	274	Hendrik Visscher
N	*Noorderkwartier*	58	275	Pieter Klaasz. Wijnbergen
N	*Wapen van Holland*	48	226	Cornelis Jacobsz. de Boer
N	*Drie Helden Davids*	48	224	Adriaan Teding van Berkhout
N	*Caleb*	47	304	Jan Hek
N	*Wapen van Medemblik*	46	200	Klaas Valchen
N	*Eendracht*	44	188	Klaas Anker
A	*Hollandia*	80	450	L.A.(A) Cornelis Tromp
A	*Gouda*	71	368	V.A.(A) Isaac Sweers
A	*Beschermer*	52	284	SbN.(A) Willem van der Zaan
A	*Reiger*	72	346	Hendrik Adriaanszoon
A	*Calantsoog*	72	305	Jan de Haan
A	*Oosterwijk*	68	313	Lt. Col. François Palm
A	*Deventer*	66	289	Jacob Andriesz. Swart
A	*Vrijheid*	58	258	Jan van Amstel
A	*Huis Tijdverdrijf*	56	291	Thomas Fabritius
A	*Vereenigde Provinciën*	48	230	Jacob Binckes
A	*Kampen*	46	231	Michiel Suis
A	*Haarlem*	42	209	Pieter van Middelland
A	*Edam*	37	147	Pieter Magnussen
	Frigates			
N	*Wapen van Hoorn*	30	150	Gerrit Klaasz. Posthoorn
N	*Kasteel van Medemblik*	30	127	Jan Mauw
A	*Asperen*	34	140	Jan Gijselsz. van Lier
A	*Harder*	34	136	Jan Davidsz. Bont
A	*IJlst*	32	140	Jacob Dirksz. Boom
A	*Overijssel*	30	120	Arend Symonsz. Vader
	Advice-Yachts			
A	?	?	?	Jan Jansz. Verboekelt
A	?	?	?	Pieter Martenszoon
	Fireships			
A	*Bristol*	4	14	Hendrik Dirksz. Boekhoven
A	*Eenhoorn*	4	14	Rein Pietersz. Mars
A	*Brak*	4	14	Henricus Roseus
A	*Wapen van London*	4	14	Gerrit Floriszoon
M	*Pro Patria*	?	?	Joost Gilleszoon
M	*Reus*	?	?	Jacob Maartsz. de Haas

Appendix J

Holmes in the Vlie, 9–10 August 1666

Of the men-of-war given below as supporting Sir Robert Holmes's descent on the Dutch coast, all but the *Fountain* were named in accounts in the *London Gazette* and elsewhere. The *Fountain* appears in Wenceslaus Hollar's engraving of the action, and her assignment to the squadron is confirmed by instructions to her captain in the Generals' order-book.

Fireships expended are indicated by asterisks. Note that the numbers of men listed for the fireships were those who actually participated in the operation. These vessels had complements of 35 to 50 men for watches and routine maintenance, but in attacks everyone except the special volunteers disembarked in advance.

Rate	Ship	Guns	Men	Captain
4	*Tiger*	40	180	Holmes/John Wetwang
4	*Advice*	48	180+	Charles O'Bryan
4	*Hampshire*	42	160	William Coleman
4	*Dragon*	40	160	Thomas Room Coyle
4	*Assurance*	38	150	John Narbrough
5	*Sweepstakes*	36	140	Francis Sanders
5P	*Fountain*	36	130	Thomas Leggatt
5	*Garland*	28	110	Charles Howard
5	*Pembroke*	28	110	Richard Goodlad
6	*Fanfan* yacht	2	30	William Harris
	Fireships			
	Bryar	12	16	Joseph Paine
	*Richard**	4	16	Henry Brown
	*Lizard**	6	14	Joseph Harris
	*Fox**	6	12	John Elliot
	*Samuel**	4	12	William Seale

Appendix K

The French Fleet, 1666

A list of the duc de Beaufort's squadron when it sailed from Toulon on 19 April 1666 is preserved in French archives and printed in Colenbrander, *Bescheiden uit Vreemde Archieven*. Duquesne's squadron is from a list in Clowes, *The Royal Navy*. It gives all the vessels commissioned in the Atlantic in 1666, though Duquesne seems to have had no more than about twelve together at any one time. *La Victoire* was captured off Portugal on 3 May by the English *Resolution* and *Oxford*, while *Le Bourbon* was a new ship completed during the summer.

Manning of both squadrons is from Clowes except for *L'Anna*, *Le St. Sauveur*, *La Ville de Rouen*, and *La Perle* (all omitted in Clowes) for which the figures are from an English intelligence list in the sea-book of Sir Edward Spragge (National Maritime Museum MSS DAR/2). Both armament and manning data are generally unreliable, for the various sources disagree. The English found *La Victoire* to have had 26 guns and 207 men aboard, while *Le Rubis* when captured in September had 412 men with 40 guns of brass and 14 of iron in addition to 6 pedreros.

A list of the French captains of 1666 probably exists, but was not found. Beaufort was in *Le St. Philippe* (with Mathurin Gabaret as flag-captain), his second-in-command the Chevalier Paul in *La Royale*, and Duquesne in *Le Vendôme*. *Le Rubis* was commanded by Louis de la Roche, *La Ste. Anne* by the Comte de Chateau-Renault, and *La Ville de Rouen* by the Chevalier de Buoux.

BEAUFORT	Guns	Men
Le St. Philippe (Adm.)	74	600
La Royale (V. Adm.)	56	400
Le Dauphin (R. Adm.)	56	350
La Thérèse	60	350
Le St. Louis	56	400
La Reyne	56	400
Le César	52	350
Le Jules	40	250
L'Hercule	40	300
L'Anna	40	280
Le Lion Rouge	40	–
Le St. Sauveur	40	230
La Ville de Rouen	38	230
La Perle	36	230
Le Dragon	36	250
Le Palmier	36	230
L'Escureuil	36	230
L'Étoile de Diane	36	250
La Françoise	36	230
La Notre Dame	36	230
Le Croissant d'Afrique	36	230
Le Soleil d'Afrique	34	230
Le St. Joseph	34	230
Le Soleil	34	230
La Vierge	34	200
Le Lion d'Or	30	250
Le St. Antoine	30	200
L'Elbeuf	24	230
Le Ligournois	24	250
La Petite Infante	22	80
La Ste. Anne	16	120
Le Postillon	8	80

9 fireships

DUQUESNE	Guns	Men
Le Vendôme (Adm.)	72	600
Le Diamant (V. Adm.)	60	400
Le Rubis (R. Adm.)	50	400
Le Bourbon	50	400
Le Triomphe	40	300
Le Mazarin	40	300
Le Mercoeur	36	230
Le Beaufort	36	230
Le St. Charles	34	130
L'Infant	30	200
L'Hermine	30	200
L'Hirondelle	30	220
La Victoire	30	230
Le Dunquerquois	24	200
La Notre Dame des Anges	16	150

6 fireships

Appendix L

Ordnance and Manning – English

This appendix includes only the vessels in commission in 1666. Complements are from the manning establishment of 22 April 1666 recorded in the Generals' order-book (National Maritime Museum MSS DAR/3), except for men-of-war acquired subsequently and for hired merchantmen, for which complements are extracted from various fleet lists. For changes in complements after 22 April, see Appendices F and H.

In April 1666 an establishment of guns for each ship (draft copy in British Library Add. MSS 9302, ff. 181v–182r) was approved and taken as the nominal armament in official fleet lists. However, Ordnance Office 'returns' (gunners' inventories, preserved for 1666–7 in Public Record Office WO55, vols. 1652 and 1653) and 'Issues of stores and guns' to a few, mostly smaller, vessels in 1664 (Public Record Office PRO 30/37/7) show that the armament actually aboard the ships usually differed somewhat from the establishment, in a few cases drastically. After the Four Days' Battle, establishments were updated for several vessels to reflect the true armament (including the *Royal Sovereign*, *Loyal London*, *Victory* and *Henry*), but variances were ignored in other ships. The detailed data in the table below are from returns or issues for as many ships as possible (identified by asterisks in the 'Guns Aboard' column). For vessels for which returns or issues are unavailable (identified by asterisks in the 'Guns Est.' column), the detailed data are from the less reliable establishment. For some of these, the number of guns aboard (but not calibres) is known from Dutch reports of captured ships or from wharfingers' bills recording ordnance transported to or from the ships (Public Record Office WO51, vols. 6 and 7). No detailed data were found for the fourth-rates *Unity* or *Welcome*, the fifth-rate *Orange*, or for many of the sixth-rates, pinks, and ketches. A numerical discrepancy in the establishment for the third-rate *House of Sweeds* appears in the manuscript source.

The third-rates *Lion* and *Gloucester* each had only 19 demi-cannon aboard at the time their gunners submitted their Charges and Returns (October 1666), but it is clear that each originally had 20 demi-cannon, of which one had been broken and off-loaded but not yet replaced. The list here has been adjusted accordingly.

Hired ships are not included in the British Library establishment, but armament schemes 'agreed upon' for many of them appear in Public Record Office SP29, vols. 111, 112, 156, and 158. Merchant owners typically supplied about half the guns and the Ordnance Office made up the rest. The detailed data given for the *Charles*, *Loyal Merchant*, *Richard & Martha*, and *East India Merchant* are the owners' contributions, while the calibres of the King's guns are unknown. It might be noted that in those merchantmen in which both the establishment and the actual armament are known, the Ordnance Office often substituted 12-pounders for requested culverins. This may have applied as well to at least some of those ships for which only the intended armament is known.

In the traditional nomenclature for English guns, cannon-of-seven were 42-pounders, demi-cannon 32-pounders, culverins 18-pounders, demi-culverins 9-pounders, sakers 5¼-pounders, minions 4-pounders, and falcons 2½-pounders. No attempt is made here to distinguish drakes and cuts. Drakes came in most calibres, but cuts were generally limited to demi-culverins, sakers, and minions. The shot weight totals are merely approximations in some cases, since the nominal calibres included captured weapons of non-standard bore, firing similarly non-standard captured ammunition or sub-calibre English shot. The many captured Dutch 8-pounders, for instance, were designed for shot weighing almost 9 English pounds, while the culverins of the prize *French Victory* were 16-pounders which no standard English ball would fit properly.

Omitted from the table are swivel-mounted 'bases' and 'murderers', of which a few were carried in several ships. These were short-range breech-loaders, typically ½-pounders, with removable chambers. Firing shrapnel ammunition for defence against boarding, the guns were supplied with multiple chambers (up to eight) which were loaded before going into action. After firing, the expended chamber could be replaced in a few seconds by a loaded one, giving the closest approximation in the seventeenth century to a quick-firing gun.

	Men	Guns Est.	Guns Aboard	Shot Weight	Cannon-of-7	Demi-Cannon	24-Pounder	Culverin	12-Pounder	Demi-Culverin	8-Pounder	6-Pounder	Saker	Minion	3-Pounder	Falcon
First-Rates																
Royal Sovereign	700	92	102*	1888	13	13	–	36	–	18	–	–	22	–	–	–
Royal Prince	620	92*	92	1944	22	6	–	28	–	36	–	–	–	–	–	–
Royal Charles	650	82	82*	1770	20	6	–	26	–	30	–	–	–	–	–	–
Royal James	520	82	82*	1524	–	24	–	26	–	32	–	–	–	–	–	–
Second-Rates																
Loyal London	470	80	92*	1826	7	19	–	28	26	12	–	–	–	–	–	–
Victory	450	76	80*	1704	20	–	6	26	–	28	–	–	–	–	–	–
Royal Oak	450	76	79*	1538	6	16	–	30	–	24	–	3	–	–	–	–
Royal Katherine	450	76	76*	1554	10	12	–	30	–	22	–	2	–	–	–	–
Henry	440	72	80*	1331	–	22	–	4	28	22	–	–	4	–	–	–
Triumph	430	72	74*	1312	–	20	–	24	–	22	–	–	8	–	–	–
Old James	380	70	72*	1310	–	22	–	24	–	10	–	–	16	–	–	–
Swiftsure	380	66*	72	1352	–	22	–	28	–	16	–	–	–	–	–	–
St. Andrew	360	66	66*	1204	–	20	–	20	–	18	–	–	8	–	–	–
St. George	360	66	72*	1123	–	20	–	14	–	12	–	–	20	–	6	–
Unicorn	320	60	63*	1132	–	16	–	26	–	11	–	–	10	–	–	–
Vanguard	320	60	60*	991	–	20	–	4	–	24	–	–	12	–	–	–
Rainbow	310	56	56*	917	–	18	–	4	–	24	–	–	10	–	–	–
Third-Rates																
House of Sweeds	280	70*	68	1249	–	26	–	–	26	–	–	–	20	–	–	–
Defiance	320	64	65*	1352	–	22	–	29	–	14	–	–	–	–	–	–
Rupert	320	64	67*	1370	–	22	–	30	–	12	–	3	–	–	–	–
Warspite	320	64	66*	1172	–	22	–	2	26	12	–	–	–	–	4	–
Cambridge	320	64	68*	1434	–	24	–	30	–	14	–	–	–	–	–	–
Clove Tree	250	62*	–	1065	–	24	–	–	–	26	–	–	12	–	–	–
Golden Phoenix	260	60*	60	1182	–	24	–	2	24	10	–	–	–	–	–	–
Slothany	280	60	60*	1135	–	22	–	2	24	12	–	–	–	–	–	–
Helverston	260	60	60*	720	–	–	8	16	2	2	18	–	–	12	2	–
Fairfax	300	60	66*	1162	–	22	–	4	26	–	–	–	14	–	–	–
Henrietta	300	58	65*	1120	–	22	–	4	–	37	–	–	2	–	–	–
Mary	300	58	63*	1106	–	18	–	6	33	–	–	–	4	–	–	2
Montagu	300	58	58*	1005	–	20	–	4	–	32	–	–	–	–	–	2
Resolution	300	58*	–	1096	–	20	–	4	26	8	–	–	–	–	–	–
Revenge	300	58	69*	1107	–	22	–	4	–	30	–	–	10	–	2	1
Anne	280	58	58*	1039	–	22	–	2	–	32	–	–	2	–	–	–
Dreadnought	280	58	66*	1142	–	22	–	6	–	36	–	–	–	–	2	–
Gloucester	280	58	58*	1018	–	20	–	4	–	34	–	–	–	–	–	–
Plymouth	280	58	60*	1051	–	22	–	2	–	34	–	–	–	–	–	2
York	280	58	58*	1011	–	20	–	4	–	32	–	–	2	–	–	–
Dunkirk	280	58	58*	962	–	16	–	8	–	34	–	–	–	–	–	–
Lion	280	58	60*	1024	–	20	–	4	–	34	–	–	–	–	2	–
Monck	280	58	58*	1006	–	20	–	2	2	34	–	–	–	–	–	–
Essex	260	56*	–	873	–	12	–	12	–	28	–	–	4	–	–	–

	Men	Guns Est.	Guns Aboard	Shot Weight	Cannon-of-7	Demi-Cannon	24-Pounder	Culverin	12-Pounder	Demi-Culverin	8-Pounder	6-Pounder	Saker	Minion	3-Pounder	Falcon
Fourth-Rates																
Greenwich	260	58	61*	822	–	–	20	2	–	27	–	–	12	–	–	–
Leopard	250	56*	–	998	–	22	–	2	–	24	–	–	8	–	–	–
Seven Oaks	190	54*	–	962	–	22	–	–	–	24	–	–	8	–	–	–
Matthias	200	54	52*	783	–	–	22	2	–	6	18	–	4	–	–	–
Charles V	200	54*	–	654	–	–	–	22	–	24	–	–	8	–	–	–
Princess	205	52	56*	768	–	10	–	11	–	2	24	–	5	2	2	–
Yarmouth	200	52	54*	663	–	–	–	22	2	24	–	–	4	–	2	–
Bristol	200	52	48*	641	–	–	–	24	–	22	–	–	2	–	–	–
Mars	180	52*	–	644	–	–	–	22	–	24	–	–	6	–	–	–
Happy Return	190	52	52*	644	–	–	–	22	–	24	–	–	6	–	–	–
Antelope	190	52	52*	509	–	–	–	–	22	24	–	–	4	2	–	–
Convertine	190	52*	–	644	–	–	–	24	–	–	20	–	8	–	–	–
Newcastle	200	50	50*	767	–	10	–	12	–	22	–	2	4	–	–	–
Westfriesland	180	50*	54	758	–	–	22	–	–	22	–	–	6	–	–	–
Sancta Maria	180	50*	48	626	–	–	–	22	–	22	–	–	6	–	–	–
Jersey	185	50	48*	608	–	–	–	22	–	20	–	–	6	–	–	–
Mary Rose	185	50	52*	636	–	–	–	22	–	22	–	–	8	–	–	–
St. Patrick	200	48	48*	730	–	–	20	2	–	22	–	–	–	4	–	–
Portland	180	48*	–	623	–	–	–	22	–	24	–	–	2	–	–	–
Breda	180	48	46*	597	–	–	–	22	–	20	–	–	4	–	–	–
Centurion	180	48	48*	591	–	–	–	20	–	22	–	2	4	–	–	–
Diamond	180	48	46*	597	–	–	–	22	–	20	–	–	4	–	–	–
Reserve	180	48	49*	618	–	–	–	22	–	22	–	–	4	–	1	–
Swallow	180	48*	46	608	–	–	–	22	–	20	–	–	6	–	–	–
Crown	180	48	48*	603	–	–	–	22	–	20	–	–	4	–	2	–
Black Eagle	180	48*	–	600	–	–	–	22	–	18	–	–	8	–	–	–
Golden Ruyter	180	48*	–	600	–	–	–	22	–	18	–	–	8	–	–	–
Advice	180	48	50*	600	–	–	–	23	–	12	4	–	6	–	3	2
Bonaventure	180	48	50*	587	–	–	–	20	–	20	–	4	2	–	4	–
Assistance	170	46*	48	597	–	–	–	22	–	20	–	–	4	–	–	–
Dover	170	46	52*	651	–	–	–	22	–	26	–	–	4	–	–	–
Foresight	170	46*	–	597	–	–	–	22	–	20	–	–	4	–	–	–
Kent	170	46	50*	655	–	2	–	20	–	22	–	2	4	–	–	–
Ruby	170	46	48*	615	–	–	–	22	–	22	–	–	4	–	–	–
Portsmouth	160	44	51*	630	–	–	–	23	–	22	–	–	–	–	6	–
Marmaduke	160	42	42*	456	–	–	–	12	–	22	–	–	8	–	–	–
Elizabeth	160	42	40*	438	–	–	–	12	–	20	–	–	8	–	–	–
Hampshire	160	42	40*	419	–	–	–	12	–	16	–	–	10	–	2	–
Golden Lion	170	42	42*	304	–	–	–	–	6	–	14	18	–	–	4	–
Unity	150	42*	–	–	–	–	–	–	–	–	–	–	–	–	–	–
St. Paul	160	40*	48	558	–	–	–	22	–	18	–	–	–	–	–	–
Hope	170	40*	44	491	–	–	–	22	–	–	–	–	18	–	–	–
Dragon	160	40	46*	541	–	–	–	18	–	20	–	–	6	–	–	2
Tiger	160	40	46*	449	–	–	–	12	–	16	–	–	16	–	–	2
Sapphire	160	40	44*	359	–	–	–	6	–	16	–	–	18	–	4	–
Black Ball	150	40	36*	324	–	–	–	–	20	–	–	12	–	–	4	–
Delft	160	40*	–	359	–	–	–	–	22	–	–	–	18	–	–	–

	Men	Guns Est.	Guns Aboard	Shot Weight	Cannon-of-7	Demi-Cannon	24-Pounder	Culverin	12-Pounder	Demi-Culverin	8-Pounder	6-Pounder	Saker	Minion	3-Pounder	Falcon	
Fourth-Rates (Contd)																	
Zealand	160	40*	–	359	–	–	–	–	22	–	–	–	18	–	–	–	
Assurance	150	38	42*	437	–	–	–	10	–	26	–	–	2	–	4	–	
Amity	150	38	38*	405	–	–	–	12	–	14	–	–	12	–	–	–	
Adventure	150	38	38*	377	–	–	–	10	–	14	–	–	12	2	–	–	
Guinea	150	38*	38	365	–	–	–	10	–	10	–	–	18	–	–	–	
Welcome	150	36*	36	–	–	–	–	–	–	–	–	–	–	–	–	–	
Constant Warwick	150	34	34*	377	–	–	–	12	–	12	–	–	10	–	–	–	
Providence	140	34*	–	308	–	–	–	6	–	14	–	–	14	–	–	–	
Expedition	140	34	38*	338	–	–	–	7	–	13	–	6	10	–	2	–	
Hired Fourth-Rates																	
Loyal Subject	200	–	56*	647	–	–	–	22	–	18	–	6	10	–	–	–	
Charles Merchant	220	54*	–	–	–	4	–	7	–	–	–	–	12	4	–	–	+27 unknown
Loyal Merchant	210	50*	–	–	–	–	–	6	–	22	–	–	4	–	–	–	+18 unknown
Richard & Martha	200	50*	–	–	–	–	2	6	4	–	–	–	12	–	–	–	+26 unknown
Coronation	190	50*	–	588	–	–	–	22	–	14	–	–	10	2	–	2	
London Merchant	180	48	48*	457	–	–	–	–	20	20	–	–	4	4	–	–	
Turkey Merchant	180	48*	–	576+	–	–	–	22	–	20	–	–	–	–	–	–	+6 'small'
Albemarle	180	48*	–	552	–	–	–	20	–	12	–	–	16	–	–	–	
East India London	190	46	46*	455	–	–	–	3	12	25	–	–	6	–	–	–	
John & Thomas	200	46	46*	393	–	–	–	–	20	5	–	6	9	6	–	–	
East India Merchant	180	44*	–	–	–	–	–	–	20	–	–	–	6	–	–	–	+18 unknown
Loyal George	190	42	49*	455	–	–	–	–	18	20	–	1	10	–	–	–	
Baltimore	180	42	42*	381	–	–	–	10	–	10	–	–	18	4	–	–	
George	180	40*	–	381	–	–	–	12	–	6	–	–	18	4	–	–	
Castle Frigate	160	36*	–	404	–	–	–	10	–	24	–	–	–	2	–	–	
Society	160	36	36*	298	–	–	–	–	8	16	–	–	8	4	–	–	
Katherine	160	–	36*	252	–	–	–	–	5	3	10	–	14	–	2	2	
Fifth-Rates																	
Falcon	140	36	44*	380	–	–	–	22	–	–	–	–	22	–	–	–	
Fountain	130	36*	–	342	–	–	–	20	2	–	14	–	–	–	–	–	
Sweepstakes	130	36	36*	338	–	–	–	22	–	–	–	–	14	–	–	–	
Great Gift	130	34	40*	378	–	–	–	16	–	18	–	–	–	6	–	–	
French Victory	140	–	34*	258	–	–	–	2	6	–	6	8	10	–	–	2	
Sorling	130	34	34*	250	–	–	–	–	2	22	8	–	2	–	–	–	
Sophia	130	34*	30	251	–	–	–	–	–	20	–	–	12	2	–	–	
Paul	90	32	28*	198	–	–	–	–	–	–	18	8	–	–	2	–	
Success	120	30*	–	323	–	–	–	10	–	10	–	–	10	–	–	–	
Orange	90	30*	–	–	–	–	–	–	–	–	–	–	–	–	–	–	
Mermaid	110	28	33*	251	–	–	–	–	–	22	–	–	9	–	2	–	
Pembroke	110	28*	–	222	–	–	–	–	–	20	–	–	8	–	–	–	
Nightingale	110	28	30*	221	–	–	–	–	–	18	–	–	10	–	2	–	
Colchester	110	28*	–	215	–	–	–	–	–	18	–	–	10	–	–	–	
Dartmouth	110	28*	–	215	–	–	–	–	–	18	–	–	10	–	–	–	
Forester	110	28	32*	243	–	–	–	–	–	20	–	–	12	–	–	–	
Guernsey	110	28	28*	213	–	–	–	–	–	16	–	8	4	–	–	–	

	Men	Guns Est.	Guns Aboard	Shot Weight	Cannon-of-7	Demi-Cannon	24-Pounder	Culverin	12-Pounder	Demi-Culverin	8-Pounder	6-Pounder	Saker	Minion	3-Pounder	Falcon
Fifth-Rates (Contd)																
Garland	110	28	28*	207	–	–	–	–	–	16	–	–	12	–	–	–
Milford	110	28	30*	207	–	–	–	–	–	14	–	2	12	–	2	–
Eagle	100	26	26*	197	–	–	–	–	–	16	–	–	10	–	–	–
Norwich	100	26	26*	200	–	–	–	–	–	18	–	–	6	–	2	–
Oxford	100	26	34*	238	–	–	–	–	–	21	–	–	2	5	6	–
Pearl	100	26	24*	184	–	–	–	–	–	16	–	–	6	2	–	–
Speedwell	100	26	26*	197	–	–	–	–	–	16	–	–	10	–	–	–
Little Victory	90	26	26*	175	–	–	–	–	–	12	–	2	8	2	–	2
Richmond	100	24*	–	186	–	–	–	–	–	16	–	–	8	–	–	–
Coventry	90	22	24*	162	–	–	–	–	–	6	–	18	–	–	–	–
Lizard	75	20	20*	96	–	–	–	–	–	–	–	10	–	6	4	–
Sixth-Rates																
Fox	60	14	16*	84	–	–	–	–	–	–	–	–	16	–	–	–
Little Gift	80	12	20*	111	–	–	–	–	–	–	6	–	8	–	–	6
Drake	70	12	10*	68	–	–	–	–	–	–	4	2	–	4	–	–
Paradox	70	12	14*	79	–	–	–	–	–	–	4	–	6	–	2	2
Little Mary	60	12*	–	–	–	–	–	–	–	–	–	–	–	–	–	–
Martin Galley	60	12	14*	88	–	–	–	–	–	–	6	–	4	2	–	2
Truelove	60	12*	–	–	–	–	–	–	–	–	–	–	–	–	–	–
Francis	50	10	10*	30	–	–	–	–	–	–	–	–	–	–	10	–
Young Lion	50	10*	–	–	–	–	–	–	–	–	–	–	–	–	–	–
Cygnet	50	8	8*	29	–	–	–	–	–	–	–	–	2	–	6	–
Lily	35	6	6*	32	–	–	–	–	–	–	–	–	6	–	–	–
Harp	35	6*	–	–	–	–	–	–	–	–	–	–	–	–	–	–
Ketches & Pinks																
Blackamoor	50	12	14*	96	–	–	–	–	–	–	6	–	8	–	–	–
Deptford	45	10	10*	53	–	–	–	–	–	–	10	–	–	–	–	–
Portsmouth	45	10*	–	–	–	–	–	–	–	–	–	–	–	–	–	–
Colchester	45	8	8*	40	–	–	–	–	–	–	–	–	6	2	–	–
Roe	45	8*	8	–	–	–	–	–	–	–	–	–	–	–	–	–
Wivenhoe	45	8*	8	–	–	–	–	–	–	–	–	–	–	–	–	–
Eaglet	40	8*	–	–	–	–	–	–	–	–	–	–	–	–	–	–
Hawk	40	8	8*	37	–	–	–	–	–	–	–	–	4	4	–	–
Hind	35	8*	–	–	–	–	–	–	–	–	–	–	–	–	–	–
Nonsuch	35	8	6*	24	–	–	–	–	–	–	–	–	–	–	–	–
Swallow	35	6	8*	33	–	–	–	–	–	–	–	–	4	–	4	–
Giles	20	4*	–	–	–	–	–	–	–	–	–	–	–	–	–	–

Appendix M

Ordnance and Manning – Dutch

The Dutch ordnance and manning lists below include only the vessels present for the Four Days' Battle. Manning figures are the intended complements. Armament data for ships of the Maas, Amsterdam, and Zeeland are from 1666, but details from that year are unavailable for vessels of Friesland and the Noorderkwartier. The Frisian ships are given as armed in 1665; nothing is known for most beyond the calibres carried (indicated by asterisks), and nothing at all for the *Groningen* (completed in 1666). For the Noorderkwartier, the first five ships listed are given as armed in 1669, while the remaining six ships are given as armed in 1665; five of these last six carried additional armament in 1666, the difference accounting for the guns in the 'Unknown' column.

The total shot weight for each ship is calculated in Amsterdam pounds of 0.4941 kg., but then converted and entered in the table in English pounds of 0.4536 kg. for ease of comparison with the English fleet. For several ships the available sources grouped some guns of two calibres together. Such guns are here assigned average values for the weight of shot calculation; for instance, 4- and 5-pounders grouped together are counted as 4½-pounders. As with English ships, the shot weight totals will seldom be precisely accurate anyway owing to the high proportion of foreign guns manufactured to different standards of measure.

The two guns of unknown calibre listed for the Zeeland ship *Utrecht* were swivel-mounted *bassen* (bases). Such pieces varied, but were typically ½-pounders. The *draakjes* carried by three Amsterdam ships were small thin-walled short-range shrapnel guns, often with flared muzzles. They could not safely fire solid balls and are therefore not counted in the weight of shot calculations. The *klokswijs* (bell-bored) guns listed for some Maas and Amsterdam ships had conically taper-bored chambers using small charges and were analogous to English drakes. The 12-pounder *kamerstukken* (chamber pieces) carried by the *Groot Hollandia* of the Maas were narrow-chambered sixteenth-century guns originally intended for stone shot. In the mid-seventeenth century they were commonly loaded with grape and case-shot rather than stones.

The sources of these tables were the appendices in de Jonge, *Geschiedenis van het Nederlandsche Zeewezen*; and, through the generosity of Dr R.E.J. Weber, the extensive data compiled by Van Foreest and Weber for their *De Vierdaagse Zeeslag 11–14 Juni 1666*.

MASS

	Men	Guns	Shot Weight	36-pdr	24-pdr	18-pdr	15-pdr	12-pdr	8-pdr	6-pdr	5-pdr	4-pdr	3-pdr
Zeven Provinciën	475	80	1490	12	16	14	–	12	–	26	–	–	–
Eendracht	400	76	1172	–	14	26	–	12	–	16	–	8	–
Ridderschap	350	66	963	–	12	12	–	24	–	10	–	–	–
Gelderland	350	64	863	–	6	16	–	24	–	–	–	18	–
Groot Hollandia	300	64	876	–	4	20	–	22[1]	–	6[2]	–	12	–
Delft	300	62	902	–	8	16	–	22	–	10	–	6	–
Wassenaar	250	56	745	–	–	22	–	16	6	–	–	12	–
Klein Hollandia	250	54	745	–	–	22	–	20[2]	–	2	–	12	–
Dordrecht	200	44	541	–	–	10	–	18	10	–	–	–	6[3]
Prinses Louise	200	34	383	–	–	–	–	24	6	–	–	4	–
Wapen van Utrecht	150	36	370	–	–	–	–	18	14	–	–	–	4
Gorinchem	150	34	325	–	–	–	2	16	–	4	8	–	4
Nijmegen	130	34	349	–	–	–	–	16	14	–	–	4	–
Harderwijk	150	32	305	–	–	–	–	16	–	12	–	4	–
Schiedam	80	22	157	–	–	–	–	–	14	–	–	8	–
Swol	50	18	113	–	–	–	–	–	–	16	–	2	–

[1] including 6 *kamerstukken*. [2] including 6 *klokswijs* guns. [3] 3- and 4-pdrs.

AMSTERDAM

	Men	Guns	Shot Weight	24-pdr	18-pdr	12-pdr	8-pdr	6-pdr	5-pdr	4-pdr	3-pdr	2pdr	Draakjes
Hollandia	450	80	1137	10	18	28	–	–	24	–	–	–	–
Gouda	370	72	924	–	26	–	26	–	20[1]	–	–	–	–
Reiger	345	72	976	6	20	26	–	–	–	20[2]	–	–	–
Calantsoog	320	70	863	6	20	8	–	16	–	4[2]	16	–	–
Spiegel	400	68	967	8	16	24	–	–	20[2]	–	–	–	–
Liefde	320	68	819	6	18	8	–	16	–	–	20[2]	–	–
Geloof	320	68	819	6	18	8	–	16	–	–	20[2]	–	–
Deventer	290	66	780	6	18	6	–	16	–	–	16	–	4
Wapen van Utrecht	290	66	780	6	18	6	–	16	–	–	16	–	4
Provincie Utrecht	290	64	741	6	16	6	–	16	–	–	16	–	4
Amsterdam	290	60	675	–	22	–	–	22	–	–	16	–	–
Huis te Kruiningen	290	60	675	–	22	–	–	22	–	–	16	–	–
Huis Tijdverdriff	290	60	675	–	22	–	–	22	–	–	16	–	–
Stad en Lande	290	60	675	–	22	–	–	22	–	–	16	–	–
Vrijheid	290	60	675	–	22	–	–	22	–	–	16	–	–
Beschermer	290	54	741	–	24	8	–	16	–	6	–	–	–
Gouden Leeuwen	255	50	521	–	8	12	–	20	–	–	10	–	–
Zuiderhuis	245	50	521	–	8	12	–	20	–	–	10	–	–
Dom van Utrecht	230	46	497	–	8	12	–	18	–	–	8	–	–
Duivenvoorde	230	46	497	–	8	12	–	18	–	–	8	–	–
Stad Gouda	230	46	497	–	8	12	–	18	–	–	8	–	–
Huis te Jaarsveld	230	46	497	–	8	12	–	18	–	–	8	–	–
Kampen	230	46	497	–	8	12	–	18	–	–	8	–	–
Landman	230	46	497	–	8	12	–	18	–	–	8	–	–
Radhuis van Haarlem	230	46	497	–	8	12	–	18	–	–	8	–	–
Stavoren	230	46	497	–	8	12	–	18	–	–	8	–	–
Tromp	230	46	497	–	8	12	–	18	–	–	8	–	–
Vrede	230	46	497	–	8	12	–	18	–	–	8	–	–
Wakende Boei	230	46	497	–	8	12	–	18	–	–	8	–	–
Harderwijk	230	44	497	–	8	12	–	18	–	6	–	–	–

AMSTERDAM (Contd)

	Men	Guns	Shot Weight	24-pdr	18-pdr	12-pdr	8-pdr	6-pdr	5-pdr	4-pdr	3-pdr	2pdr	Draakjes
Haarlem	215	44	405	–	4	14	–	–	18	–	8	–	–
Zon	215	44	405	–	4	14	–	–	18	–	8	–	–
Asperen	140	34	270	–	–	6	–	12	12	–	–	4	–
IJlst	140	34	270	–	–	6	–	12	12	–	–	4	–
Harder	140	34	270	–	–	6	–	12	12	–	–	4	–
Overijssel	140	34	270	–	–	6	–	12	12	–	–	4	–

[1] including 10 *klokswijs* guns.   [2] including 4 *klokswijs* guns.

NOORDERKWARTIER

	Men	Guns	Shot Weight	36-pdr	24-pdr	18-pdr	12-pdr	8-pdr	6-pdr	4-pdr	3-pdr	2pdr	1-pdr	Unknown
Westfriesland	400	78	1111	4	2	20	28	–	18	6	–	–	–	–
Pacificatie	380	73	955	–	–	22	30	–	20	–	–	–	1	–
Maagd v. Enkhuizen	360	72	1007	–	4	22	26	–	20	–	–	–	–	–
Jonge Prins	300	66	928	2	–	22	24	–	12	6	–	–	–	–
Noorderkwartier	300	60	793	–	–	24	12	10	8	6	–	–	–	–
Wapen van Nassau	260	60	802+	–	4	20	12	14	–	6	–	–	–	4
Gelderland	300	56	732+	–	–	24	10	8	4	8	–	–	–	2
Hollandse Tuin	250	56	671	–	–	20	2	22	4	8	–	–	–	–
Jozua	260	54	634+	–	–	20	8	10	2	6	2	2	–	4
Caleb	240	50	519+	–	–	6	18	16	4	–	–	–	–	6[1]
Drie Helden Davids	240	48	519+	–	–	6	18	16	4	–	–	–	–	4

[1] At least some were 3-pdrs.

ZEELAND

	Men	Guns	Shot Weight	36-pdr	24-pdr	18-pdr	16-pdr	14-pdr	12-pdr	8-pdr	6-pdr	5-pdr	4pdr	3-pdr	Unknown
Walcheren	380	70	1054	–	16	14	–	–	20	–	6	–	14	–	–
Tholen	310	60	963	–	8	20	–	2	22	–	4	–	4	–	–
Zierikzee	300	60	889	–	12	14	–	–	16	–	6	–	12	–	–
Hof van Zeeland	256	58	930	2	4	18	8	–	14	–	6	6	–	–	–
Middelburg	210	50	569	–	4	2	–	–	24	–	14	–	–	6	–
Dordrecht	210	50	549	–	2	4	–	–	16	12	16	–	–	–	–
Utrecht	220	50	549+	–	2	6	–	–	18	–	22	–	–	–	2
Vlissingen	220	50	562+	–	2	4	–	–	26	–	12	–	–	4	2
Kampveere	220	50	527+	–	2	4	–	–	16	10[1]	6	7[2]	3	–	2
Delft	170	36	314+	–	–	–	–	–	16	–	12	–	6	–	2
Zeeridder	170	36	337	–	–	2	–	–	14	–	14	–	–	6[3]	–
Zeelandia	180	36	321	–	–	–	–	–	16	–	10	6[4]	4	–	–
Schakerlo	160	30	200	–	–	–	–	–	–	8	17	–	3	2	–

[1] 9- and 8-pdrs.   [2] 6- and 5-pdrs.   [3] 4- and 3-pdrs.   [4] 5- and 4-pdrs.

FRIESLAND

	Men	Guns	Shot Weight	24-pdr	18-pdr	12-pdr	8-pdr	6-pdr	4-pdr	3pdr	2-pdr	Unknown
Groot Frisia	400	72	–	*	*	*	*	*	–	*	*	–
Groningen	306	72	–	–	–	–	–	–	–	–	–	–
Pr. Hendrik Casimir	380	72	–	*	*	*	–	*	*	–	–	–
Oostergo	265	60	–	–	*	*	*	–	*	–	–	–
Westergo	240	56	–	–	–	*	*	*	–	–	–	–
Elf Steden	240	54	662	–	18	14	10	–	6	–	6	–
Stad en Lande	230	52	593+	–	12	16	14	4	–	–	–	6
Prinses Albertina	224	50	–	–	*	*	*	–	*	*	–	–
Omlandia	190	48	540+	–	12	12	14	4	–	–	–	6
Klein Frisia	180	38	–	–	–	*	–	*	–	*	*	–

Notes

References and notes are listed by page number and are indicated by the opening words of quotations or by brief descriptions of subjects. Titles are abbreviated; full titles are given separately in the list of sources. Entries shown as simply 'Pepys', 'Evelyn', 'Barlow', 'Teonge', 'Sandwich', and 'Allin' refer to their published journals and diaries except as otherwise noted. Other abbreviations are as follows:

BL	British Library
Add.	Additional Manuscripts
Bath	Marquis of Bath, Longleat Coventry Manuscripts
CSP	Calendar of State Papers
Dom.	Domestic Series, Charles II
HMC	Historical Manuscripts Commission
NMM	National Maritime Museum, London
PRO	Public Record Office

All the documents listed from the Public Record Office are at present housed in the old office in Chancery Lane, except for the War Office papers which are in the new office at Kew. The State Papers in the Chancery Lane office usually bear two separate numbers: one in the upper right-hand corner corresponding to the document number in the *Calendar of State Papers*, and a proper folio number in the lower margin. They do not coincide, because some documents have more than one page. Since there seems to be no convention as to which should be listed, I have arbitrarily chosen to use the folio numbers.

Page

PREFACE

ix   'Ye particulars': BL Add. 17484, f. 9.

I. THE GENERALS

1   'Whereas ye King': NMM DAR/3, f. 4.
2   'Knew the architecture': Burnet, *History of His Own Time* i, 170.
3   'Always very sparkish': *Dict. Natl. Biog.*
4   'A man': Pepys, 25 June 1665.
4   'Prince Rupert do nothing': *Ibid.*, 3 June 1664.
4   'Swearing bloodily': *Ibid.*, 4 June 1664.
6   'God damn me': *Ibid.*, 5 Sept. 1664.
6   'If a sober': *Ibid.*, 20 Oct. 1666.
7   'He had no fumes': Clarendon, *History of the Rebellion* vi, 154.

7   'Immoderate lover': Clarendon, *Life* i, 366.
7   'The sole pillar': *Ibid.*, 365.
8   'Ever a plain', *et seq.*: Pepys. 8 Mar. 1661, 9 Dec. 1665, and 25 Feb. 1666.
8   'A dull heavy man': *Ibid.*, 14 Mar. 1660.
8   'A thick-skulled fool': *Ibid.*, 3 May 1666.
8   'Your honest': Fraser, *Cromwell, the Lord Protector*, 635.
10 'That each ship': Corbett, *Fighting Instructions*, 89.
11 'That it intended': *Ibid.*, 63–64.
11 'Ships which': *Monson's Tracts* iv, 97–98.
11 'Instructions for the better': Corbett, *Fighting Instructions*, 99–104.
12 'They stayed': *The First Dutch War* v, 109.
13 'Our fleet': *Ibid.*, 83–84.
13 'By reason divers': Gumble, *The Life of General Monck*, 64.
13 'Still battered': *The First Dutch War* v, 109.
13 'The harvest': Penn, *Memorials* i, 498.
13 'In a lamentable': *The First Dutch War* v, 86.
14 'Leaving part': *Ibid.*, 367.
14 'Almost at push': *Ibid.*, 368.

II. THE ROYAL NAVY

16 'Resembling some villa': Evelyn, 2 Aug. 1663.
16 Pepys worth £40: Pepys, 29 Jan. 1660.
17 Pepys worth £6,200: *Ibid.*, 31 Dec. 1666.
17 'That he was a fool': Pepys, *Tangier Papers*, 182.
19 'Disobedience, unruliness': Sandwich, 173.
20 Bitts ordered removed: Pepys, *Tangier Papers*, 119.
21 'That no commander': *Ibid.*, 218.
21 'While you live': *Ibid.*
21 'Swear, drink': *Ibid.*, 96.
22 Teonge's invective: Teonge (1927 ed.), 226–227, 3 Nov. 1678.
22 'Those who': *CSP Dom.* iv, 62, 11 Nov. 1664.
23 'Refractory': NMM DAR/3, f. 36.
23 'Lately sent in': *CSP Dom.* iv, 92, 28 Nov. 1664.
23 'Clothed with rags': *Ibid.*, 103, 5 Dec. 1664.
24 'For the Regulating': Rodger, *Articles of War*, 13.
24 'A parcel': Allin ii, 206.
24 Allin's punishments: *Ibid.* i, 6, 60, 102, 121, 122; ii, 35 and 183.
24 'This day': Teonge (1825 ed.), 18, 24 June 1675; see also 1927 ed., 39, 79, 124–125, 196, 219, and 220.
25 Barlow welcomed back: Barlow i, 94–97.
25 'This little stick': Teonge (1927 ed.), 271, n. 148.
25 'Commonly this execution': *Boteler's Dialogues*, 19.
25 'Black Mondays': Teonge (1927 ed.), 55, 26 July 1675.
25 'God damn me': Pepys, 2 Jan. 1668.
26 Mrs. Penrose at sea: Barlow 1, 133.
26 'Hither many': Teonge (1825 ed.), 5, 1 June 1675. The sentences after 'had there been occasion' are in modern spellings and are taken from the 1927 edition, p. 29. They were omitted from the 1825 edition, the anonymous editor having evidently found them unsuitable for his gentle readers.
26 'Weeping eys': Teonge (1825 ed.), 14, 21 June 1675.
26 'Turn all ye women': NMM DAR/3, f. 2.
26 Plague in the *Princess*: *Ibid.*, f. 32.
26 'A studdy': PRO SP29/143, f. 191.

26 'Walnut tree': Laughton, *Old Ships*, 264.
26 'Very curiously': *Ibid.*, 245.
27 'Thirty-four foot': PRO SP29/137, f. 114 *et seq.*
27 Pett's canvas cabins: PRO SP29/144, f. 47.
27 'A thing much like': Barlow i, 32.
28 'This day': Teonge (1825 ed.), 27, 10 July 1675.
28 'Wee had': *Ibid.*, 269, 25 Dec. 1678.
28 'We had nothing': Barlow i, 68.
28 'Englishmen': Pepys, *Naval Minutes*, 250.
29 'One pound': *Cat. of Pepysian MSS* i, 166; for the earlier list see *Hollond's Discourses*, 153.
29 'Our steward': Barlow i, 51.
29 'A purser': Pepys, 22 Nov. 1665.
30 'The difficulty': *Boteler's Dialogues*, 65.
30 'We had some': Barlow i, 112.
30 'No fleete': PRO SP29/121, f. 128.
31 Slops rates: Tedder, *The Navy of the Restoration*, 69, citing Adm. Libr. MSS 23, 2 Mar. 1663.
     Rates for white shirts had not been set.
31 'Apothecaries': *CSP Dom.* iv, 36, 18 Oct. 1664.
32 Pay tables: flag-officers' rates from *Cat. of Pepysian MSS* i, 140; others from NMM DAR/3,
     f. 178.
34 Chatham Chest annuities: *Cat. of Pepysian MSS* i, 139.
34 'For fear': Barlow i, 115; see also Allin i, 262; and NMM DAR/3, f. 35.
34 'Whosoever putteth': Barlow i, 90.
35 'The hardships': *Ibid.*, 61.

III. THE SHIPS

37 'The little room': Pepys, *Naval Minutes*, 217.
39 'Cost his Majestie': Evelyn, 19 July 1641.
39 Carvings of the *Charles*: PRO SP46/137, f. 114, a complete manifest.
40 'Because in the midship': *The Jacobean Commissions*, 289. Some authorities disapproved:
     Life and Works of Sir Henry Mainwaring ii, 131.
40 *Speaker* specifications: PRO SP46/1 36, f. 227.
40 *Tiger's* chimney: *CSP Dom.* iv, 376, 21 May 1665.
43 Rates for hired ships: see *CSP Dom.* iv, 117, 20 Dec. 1664 and 346, 4 May 1665; also six
     contracts in PRO SP29/108.
48 'At such convenient': *The Jacobean Commissions*, 289.
48 Charles personally directed: *CSP Dom.* iv, 165,9 Jan. 1665.
48 Guns of *Defiance*: PRO SP29/110, f. 104 for intended weight; Lavery, *Deane's Doctrine*,
     106, for actual.
49 Original guns of *Huis te Zwieten*: De Jonge, *Geschiedenis van het Nederlandsche Zeewezen*
     i, 780.
49 Percentages of brass guns: for typical examples see PRO WO55/1650.

IV. GUNS, FLAGS, AND THE RIVER THAMES

51 Tudor and Elizabethan ordnance development: Caruana, *The History of English Sea
     Ordnance, 1523–1875*, i.
54 'We finde': NMM DAR/3, f. 14.
55 'To lay': Clarke, *Life of James II* ii, 413.
55 'A principal thing': *Monson's Tracts* iv, 33.
56 'He that shooteth': *Ibid.*, 43.
56 'For the first month': Tedder, *The Navy of the Restoration*, 68, citing Adm. Libr. MS 23.
57 'Good to ply': *Life and Works of Sir Henry Mainwaring* ii, 225.
57 'Munitions': PRO WO55/1650.

58 Rewards for fireship crews: BL Harleian MSS 1247, f. 53; NMM Wyn/14/10.
59 'Would much countenance': NMM DAR/3, f. 43.
59 'To know': NMM DAR/2.
59 'Show themselves': *Ibid.*
59 'Besides the preferrment': BL Harleian MSS 1247, f. 53; NMM Wyn/14/10.
61 English fighting signals, 1665–66: most are published in Corbett, *Fighting Instructions*, 108–109 and 122–129. For sailing instructions, see NMM Wyn/14/11.
62 Private ships' signs: for examples see NMM DAR/3, f. 33.
62 Thames sandbanks: for past configurations see four articles by H. Muir Evans in *The Mariner's Mirror* 1929, 1930, and 1932.
64 'Answered that': Pepys, *Naval Minutes*, 112.
65 'That the whole': *Ibid.*, 138.

V. PREPARATIONS

67 'Grievances': *Journals of the House of Commons* viii, 547.
67 'The King's design': Pepys, 30 Mar. 1664.
68 'The trade': *Ibid.*, 2 Feb. 1664.
68 'What we want': Boxer, *The Anglo-Dutch Wars*, 23.
68 Coventry's reservations: BL Add. 32094, ff. 50–51.
70 'Held up': Pepys, 12 Apr. 1665.
70 'Unless the King': *Ibid.*, 7 Apr. 1665.
71 'The enemy': *CSP Dom.* iv, 351,5 May 1665.
72 Opinions of Penn: Pepys, 7 Mar. 1663, 29 Dec. 1663, and 6 Nov. 1665.
72 Penn's royalist overture: Clarendon, *History of the Rebellion* iii, 576; Penn, *Memorials* ii, 14–15.
73 'Oliver on horseback': Evelyn, 9 Apr. 1665; see also Pepys, 14 Dec. 1663.
74 'A company of 40': *CSP Dom.* iv, 40, 24 Oct. 1664.
74 'Throngs': *Ibid.*, 44, 26 Oct. 1664.
74 'And so it fell': Barlow i, 93.
74 'That seamen': *CSP Dom.* iv, 46, 28 Oct. 1664.
74 'To order': *Ibid.*, 205, 17 Feb. 1665.
75 'Fitter': *Ibid.*, 38, 21 Oct. 1664.
75 'Those pitiful': *Ibid.*, 100, 1 Dec. 1664.
75 'Men utterly unfit': *Ibid.*, 240, 6 Mar. 1665.
75 'The only remedy': *Ibid.*, 192, 6 Feb. 1665.
75 'Too much': PRO SP29/132,f. 10.
76 Firepoles too heavy: *CSP Dom.* iv, 273, 25 Mar. 1665.
76 'Would severely': Sandwich, 173.
76 'Not in the esteem': *CSP Dom.* iv, 301, 11 Apr. 1665.
76 'To show': *Ibid.*, 320, 20 Apr. 1665.
76 'Little satisfaction': *Ibid.*, 368, 16 May 1665.
76 'Make people': *Ibid.*, 373, 19 May 1665.
76 'Hates': *Ibid.*
77 Nixon court-martial: Sandwich, 214–215.
77 Fighting Instructions: NMM DAR/2; BL Sloane MSS 3232, f. 83.
78 'By which means': Sandwich, 222.
78 'There are only': *CSP Dom.* iv, 395, 31 May 1665.
78 'There never': *Ibid.*, 321, 20 Apr. 1665.
79 'Would not': PRO SP Foreign, Holland 84/176, f. 71.
79 Dutch squadrons: De Jonge, *Geschiedenis van het Nederlandsche Zeewezen* i, 776–779.
80 Dutch order of fighting: from archives of the States-General dated 3 and 5 May 1665 (New Style), according to information furnished by Dr. R.E.J. Weber of the Commissie voor Zeegeschiedenis of the Koninklijke Nederlandse Akademie van Wetenschappen;

confirmed in a letter from Downing to Arlington in PRO SP Foreign, Holland 84/176, 12/22 May 1665 (The Hague).

80 Dutch tactics: see Weber, 'Een Beschouwing over het Invoeren van de Linie van Bataille bij de Nederlandse Oorlogsvloot 1665–1666' in *Marineblad* 1980, 331–342; for use of a line at Tamandare see Robinson, *Van de Velde Drawings* i, 119.
81 'The Lord Wassenaer': Sandwich, 186.
81 Boasting by English and Dutch: *CSP Venetian* xxxiv, 100, 105, 114, 122, and 130.

VI. LOWESTOFT

83 'Mr. Gauden': Bodleian, Rawlinson MSS A.174, f. 458.
83 'So overtaken': Colenbrander, *Bescheiden uit Vreemde Archieven* i, 206.
83 'Orders': Sandwich, 221.
83 'Notwithstanding': *Ibid.*, 222–223; see also Allin i, 234.
84 'Our General': Barlow i, 102.
84 Dutch fleet: De Jonge, *Geschiedenis van het Nederlandsche Zeewezen* i, 776–782; see also Penn, *Memorials* ii, 318.
85 'They loved': Barlow i, 102.
85 'God Almighty': quoted in Howarth, *The Men-of-War*, 126; and in slightly different form in Sandwich, intro., li.
85 'By the imprudence': *Life of Tromp*, 269.
85 'Drawn up': *CSP Venetian* xxxiv, 139.
85 'Both fleets': Sandwich, 224.
86 'In the last': Boxer, *The Anglo-Dutch Wars*, 26.
86 'Whereas': Sandwich, 224.
87 'Wounded and well': *CSP Dom.* iv, 412, 6 June 1666; see also PRO SP Foreign, Holland 84/77, Downing to Arlington, 14/24 July 1665 (The Hague).
87 'That he never': Colenbrander, *Bescheiden uit Vreemde Archieven* i, 238.
87 'Old and rotten': Barlow i, 106.
87 'To little': Allin i, 234.
87 'The sailor': Penn, *Memorials* ii, 344.
88 'Prince Rupert': Sandwich, 225.
88 'How poorly': Pepys, 23 June 1665.
89 'Upon this tack': Penn, *Memorials* ii, 328.
89 'His Royal Highness': Sandwich, 225.
90 'Because the Duke': *Life of Tromp*, 270.
91 'Some of them': Sandwich, 225.
91 'Above eighty': Clarke, *Life of James II* ii, 410.
91 'So near': *Ibid.*, 411; see also *CSP Dom.* iv, 407, 4 June 1665.
91 'Sir John Lawson': Sandwich, 226.
91 'One of the best': PRO SP Foreign, Holland 84/176, Downing to Arlington, 12/22 May 1665 (The Hague).
92 'Sometimes at great': Sandwich, 225.
92 'The very heavens': *The First Dutch War* v, 368.
92 Evelyn heard the noise: Evelyn, 3 June 1665.
92 'While it is true': *CSP Venetian* xxxiv, 147; see also *CSP Dom.* iv, 2 June 1665.
93 English reinforcements: *CSP Dom.* iv, 403, 407–408, 2–4 June 1665.
93 'Ran into': *Ibid.*, 408, 5 June 1665.
93 *Royal Oak's* adventures: Sandwich, 226; Pepys, 8 June 1665.
93 'That the most': Pepys, 23 June 1665.
93 'Fought very far': Allin i, 234.
93 'This little accident': Penn, *Memorials* ii, 344.
93 'But these': Marvell, 'The Second Advice to a Painter', lines 87–88.
93 'His Royal Highness' Penn *Memorials* ii, 328–329.

94 'The continual smoke': *Ibid.*, 329.
94 'His Highness sent': Allin i, 234.
94 'About 2 oclock': Sandwich, 226.
94 *Montagu* vs. *Oranje*: Lediard *Naval History of England*, 577.
94 'His Royal Highness stretched': Sandwich, 226.
95 'When his Royal Highness': *Ibid.*, 226–227.
95 'Into whom': *Ibid.*, 227.
95 'Endeavored': *Ibid.*
95 'Have a bout': Penn, *Memorials* ii, 329.
95 'Falmouth was there': Marvell, 'The Second Advice to a Painter', Lines 177–184.
95 'Carried away': *CSP Venetian* xxxiv, 145. Another report said Obdam had been dead three hours: PRO SP Foreign, Holland 84/176, Downing to Arlington, 6/16 June 1665 (The Hague).
96 'An Englishman': *CSP Venetian* xxxiv, 145.
96 'Began to turn': Barlow i, 106.
96 'Made them': Sandwich, 227–228.
96 Berkeley chased: *CSP Dom.* iv, 408, 5 June 1665.
96 'They would quickly': Clarke, *Life of James II* ii, 413.
97 'And actually was': *CSP Venetian* xxxiv, 150.
97 'Brandishing': Clarke, *Life of James II* ii, 413.
97 'Abundance': Sandwich, 226.
97 'The Dutch Urania': Marvell, 'The Second Advice to a Painter', lines 193–210.
97 'For having not': Clarendon, *Life* ii, 387.
97 'To the great trouble': *Ibid.*
98 'And after some': Sandwich, 228.
98 'His Royal Highness': *Ibid.*, 227.
99 Brouncker's treachery: Clarendon, *Life* ii, 396–397.
99 Prizes and captors: PRO SP29/123, f. 47; Allin i, 234; for the *Bramble*'s exploit see Clarke, *Life of James II* ii, 418.
100 'Lett goe': Colenbrander, *Bescheiden uit Vreemde Archieven* i, 228; see also *CSP Dom.* iv, 491 and 570, 26 July and 22 Sept. 1665.
100 English casualties: Sandwich, 229.
100 'He led': Marvell, 'The Second Advice to a Painter', lines 171–174.
100 'Marleburgh': *Ibid.*, lines 211–216.
101 'And found her': Allin i, 235.
101 Norway squadron: Bodleian, Rawlinson MSS A.252, ff. 121–123; *CSP Dom.* iv, 393 and 407.
101 'A prating coxcombe': Pepys, 16 June 1665.

VII. THE INDIAN PRIZE

102 'Saying': Pepys, 5 July 1665.
102 'Expressed more': Sandwich, 236.
103 'Did ruminate': Sandwich, 237.
103 'Without hesitation': *Ibid.*, 239.
103 Council-of-war, 17 July: *Ibid.*, 244.
104 'He wanted strength', *et seq.*: BL Harleian MSS 6859, f. 46.
104 'All is now well': Bodleian, Rawlinson MSS A.252, ff. 139–140.
104 D. of York's orders: Bodleian, Rawlinson MSS A.468.
104 'That Sir Gilbert': *Ibid.*
105 'For his honors sake', *et seq.*: BL Harleian MSS 6859, f. 48. A copy of the letter to be 'slipt' is in Bodleian, Rawlinson MSS A.252, ff. 152–153.
105 Undelivered messages of 20th and 26th: Bodleian, Rawlinson MSS A.252, ff. 150 and 158; see BL Harleian MSS 6859, f. 47 for the adventures of the first messenger.

106 'Full of hopes': Warnsinck, *De Retourvloot van Pieter de Bitter*, 125, citing *Wordsworth's Ecclesiastical Biography* iv, 4th ed., 611.

106 Clifford's account: Bodleian, Rawlinson MSS A.256; folios are unnumbered, but the events of July–September 1665 occupy the first twenty folios.

106 'That blockhead': Pepys, 18 Sept. 1665.

107 'To use all': BL Harleian MSS 6859, f. 48. Sir Gilbert's claims therein that he knew in advance of the certain failure of the plot and that he tried to halt the operation are shown to have been lies by one of his own letters preserved in Bodleian, Rawlinson MSS A.252. ff 154–155 (to Arlington, 29 July 1665).

107 Montagu's negotiations (incl. all quotations): Bodleian, Rawlinson MSS A.256.

108 'Lying one on another': *CSP Dom.* iv, 528, 21 Aug. 1665.

108 Dutch order of battle: Warnsinck, *De Retourvloot van Pieter de Bitter*, 45; also drawings by Van de Velde the Elder in Museum Boymans-van Beuningen, Rotterdam, nos. MB1866/T56, T58, T59a, T59b, and T60b; and by Van de Velde the Younger in NMM, Nº 289 (all based on interviews with participants). See Robinson, *Van de Velde Drawings . . . in the National Maritime Museum* i, 66–67, 127, and 308; also Robinson and Weber, *The Willem Van de Velde Drawings in the Boymans-van Beuningen Museum, Rotterdam* i, 36–39, and ii, 98–114.

109 English order of battle: Eyewitness drawing by Charles Harbord with labelled key, BL K.Top.CXI, 86.

109 'For a little': Bodleian, Rawlinson MSS A.256.

109 'Being constantly': *Ibid.*

110 'They had': extract from Sandwich's journal reproduced in Warnsinck, *De Retourvloot van Pieter de Bitter*, facing p.122 and transcribed p. 123; or see Sandwich, 262–263 for edited version in modern spellings.

110 Cadman aboard *Revenge*: Bodleian, Rawlinson MSS A.256.

110 Dutch losses: Warnsinck, *De Retourvloot van Pieter de Bitter*, 122.

110 'Beate the towne': *Ibid.*, 126, citing *Wordsworth's Ecclesiastical Biography* iv, 4th ed., 611.

110 'Such rules': Bodleian, Rawlinson MSS A.256.

111 'So afflicted': BL Harleian MSS 6859, f. 54.

111 'A treasure': Pepys, 18 Sept. 1665.

111 'Divers high': Sandwich, 258.

112 Prizes of 3–4 Sept.: *CSP Venetian* xxxiv, 205–206; Penn, *Memorials* ii, 364; Sandwich's account, BL Egerton MSS 2618, f. 119; and Bodleian, Rawlinson MSS A.256.

113 Action of 9 Sept.: Sandwich, 280–281; PRO SP29/132, ff. 83 and 85; and Bodleian, Rawlinson MSS A.468.

113 'To engage': Bodleian, Rawlinson MSS A.468.

114 'The greatest wealth': Pepys, 16 Nov. 1665.

114 'Easier to keepe': *Ibid.*, 23 Sept. 1665.

114 'They did toss': *Ibid.*, 12 Oct. 1665.

115 'A very honest': *CSP Dom.* iv, 324, 22 Apr. 1665.

115 'The chief hand': Pepys, 12 Oct. 1665.

116 'Had great confidence': Clarendon, *Life* ii,485.

116 Clarendon's interview with Rupert: *Ibid.* ii, 483; and iii, 69.

116 Clarendon's interview with Albemarle: *Ibid.* ii, 486–487.

117 'upon putting': Pepys, 27 Nov. 1665.

117 'Was all storm', *et seq.*: Clarendon, *Life* iii, 36–37.

117 'If my Lord': Pepys, 9 Dec. 1665.

118 'United Gen'ralls!': Marvell, 'The Third Advice to a Painter', lines 17–20.

118 'There appeared': Clarendon, *Life* iii, 69.

118 'The two Generals': Gumble, *The Life of General Monck*, 427.

118 'Holmes commanded': Pepys, 20 Oct. 1666.

118 'The Generall thinks': PRO SP29/167, f. 164.

119 'Do less agree': Pepys, 8 Oct. 1666.

VIII. THE OTHER SIDE OF THE HILL

123 Van Beuningen admitted: *CSP Venetian* xxxiv, 145.
124 'Admiral Everson': *Ibid.*
124 'Feeble harangue': *Ibid.*, 141.
125 'Superintendence': Blok, *De Ruyter*, 201.
125 'A business': *CSP Venetian* xxxiv, 176.
126 'A parcel': Liefde, *The Great Dutch Admirals*, 312.
126 'Not wish': *CSP Venetian* xxxiv, 158.
126 Sentences of court-martial: Aitzema, *Saken van Staet en Oorlogh* v, 460–462.
127 Dutch tactics: the sequence of events presented here generally follows Weber, '. . . Invoeren van de Linie van Bataille bij de Nederlandse Oorlogsvloot 1665–1666', *Marineblad* 1980, 331–342.
127 'The greatest advantage': Aitzema, *Saken van Staet en Oorlogh* v, 455.
127 'Directed so': *Ibid.*, 457.
128 'Everyone shall': Weber, '. . . Invoeren van de Linie van Bataille bij de Nederlandse Oorlogsvloot 1665–1666', *Marineblad* 1980, 335.
128 'Lying on': Allin i, 234.
129 Sandwich's proposed reserve squadron: Sandwich, 222.
129 De Ruyter's reserve squadron: Blok, *De Ruyter*, 196.
130 Charters: Dik, 'De Zeven Provinciën', *De Model Bouwer* 1983, nos. 1 and 2; also see Elias, *De Vlootbouw in Nederland 1596–1655*.
131 Dutch naval shipbuilding: for list and dimensions see Vreugdenhil, *Ships of the United Netherlands 1648–1702*.
133 'We have made': PRO SP Foreign Newsletters 101/48, 7/17 Apr. 1666 (The Hague).
133 Cannons from town walls: BL Add. 32094, ff. 71–72; also *London Gazette* Nº 54.
134 'The clothes', *et seq.*: Blok, *De Ruyter*, 293 and 296.
134 'Tore out': *Ibid.*, 139.
134 'Uttering threats': *Ibid.*, 192.

IX. THE DIVISION OF THE FLEET

137 'It hardly': Colenbrander, *Bescheiden uit Vreemde Archieven* i, 294–295.
137 'Use all': *Ibid.*, 298.
138 'Sir Jer. Smith': Pepys, *Tangier Papers*, 131; for the other explanation see NMM IGR/17, ff. 2–7.
139 'The English fleet': Colenbrander, *Bescheiden uit Vreemde Archieven* i, 299–301.
139 'Ships that came': HMC *Heathcote MSS*, 251.
139 'Admiral Beaufort': *CSP Dom.* v, 465.
140 Concern over Danes: NMM DAR/3, f. 18.
141 King's visit: Allin i, 264–265.
141 'Yr Highness': Bath 95, f. 188.
141 'Bee well': PRO SP29/155, f. 184; copy, Bath 95, f. 190.
141 Council meeting: Clarendon, *Life* iii, 69–70; Coventry's account, Bath 95, f. 214.
142 English intelligence methods: see Fraser, *The Intelligence of the Secretaries of State*.
142 'Brought to': PRO SP29/156, f. 63.
142 Arlington's intelligence: BL Add. 32094, ff. 71–73 (memoranda).
142 'The Duke of Beaufort': Clarendon, *Life* iii, 37.
143 'The Vandosme': Bath 95, f. 190.
143 'Must be well': Clarendon, *Life* iii, 37.
143 Beaufort's departure reported: *London Gazette* Nº 51.
143 'It seemed': Bath 95, f. 214.
143 Meeting in the *Royal Charles*: *Ibid.*, ff. 214–215.

143   Fleet lists: 16 Mar., NMM DAR/3, f. 4; 21 May, BL Add. 32094, f. 102.

143   Ships deleted: NMM DAR/3, ff. 28 and 36.

144   'Confirmed': Clarendon, *Life* iii, 71.

144   Approval on 16th: Bath 95, ff. 194 and 214 show that Coventry advised the Generals of the decision on the 17th, but PRO SP29/157, f. 16 (Arlington to Generals, abstract) shows that the decision itself was made on the 16th.

144   'Wee have heard': Bath 95, f. 204.

145   'The [French] King': *London Gazette* N⁰ 53.

145   'There are 15,000': *CSP Ireland* vii, 113.

145   'That M. Beaufort': *Ibid.*, 121.

145   'The army': *Ibid.*

146   'Att present': PRO SP29/156, f. 176.

146   'To hasten': Allin i, 266.

146   'At the Tennis Court': Bath 95, f. 215. Though often stated in modern sources to have occurred on the 24th, the transfer of the orders must in fact have taken place on the 23rd. Allin's journal shows that Spragge left the fleet at the Nore on the 22nd; the preserved draft of the instructions is also dated the 22nd, and Coventry's 'Recollections' (*op. cit.*) state unequivocally that Spragge received the orders the same morning he appeared at Whitehall. In view of the urgency of the errand, it is inconceivable that Spragge would have taken two days to reach London from the Nore, or that Coventry would have taken two days to copy the document. The final version was undoubtedly dated 23 May, for Albemarle referred to it as 'yours of the 23rd instant' (Bath 95, f. 210) and confirmed that date in his deposition to the House of Commons (BL Add. 32094, f. 197).

146   'He flew': All Souls College MSS 256, f. 144.

146   *Elizabeth's* voyage: *Ibid.*; also PRO SP29/155, f. 30; and *London Gazette* N⁰ 57.

147   Arrival at Falmouth on the 22nd: *London Gazette* N⁰ 57; confirmed by a letter from Plymouth, PRO SP29/157, f. 27.

147   Arrival of Talbot's express on the 25th: Bath 96, f. 152.

147   'Since those': All Souls College MSS 256, f. 143.

147   'You will perceive': Bath 95, f. 198; f. 202 is a more legible copy.

148   Rupert's instructions: *Ibid.*, ff. 200–201.

149   'They report': HMC *Heathcote MSS*, 249.

149   Ships missing and command flags: Bath Coventry App. I, f. 13.

149   Only two western ships named: *Ibid.*

149   List of western ships wanted: Bath 95, f. 210.

149   Torbay preferred: *Ibid.*, f. 212; for conditional approval see BL Add. 32094, f. 112; also NMM DAR/2.332

149   Missing ships found: BL Add. 32094, f. 109.

149   Covering letter: Bath 95, f. 198 or 202 (duplicates).

149   Spragge appointed: Bath 1, f. 53; copy Bath 95, f. 208.

150   'I went aboard': Allin i, 267.

150   'In August': *CSP Ireland* vii, 113; Arlington's warning of the 15th (apparently not preserved) is acknowledged therein. See also HMC *Ormonde MSS. New Series* iii, 198–199, 223, and 229–231.

150   'Our intelligence': Brown, *Miscellanea Aulica*, 402.

150   'Severall Dutch': PRO SP29/156, f. 64.

150   Confirmation from Paris: PRO SP Foreign 78/122, f. 190; also *London Gazette* N⁰ 57.

151   Norwood's news: *London Gazette* N⁰ 57.

151   Copy to Portsmouth: BL Add. 32094, f. 111.

151   'His Maj. having received': Bath 95, ff. 216–217. *The Rupert and Monck Letterbook, 1666*, 216–217, gives the date of this letter as the 24th, but the date on the document is clearly the 28th.

152   'Which you': Barlow i, 116.

152   Fast day: *CSP Dom.* v, 415, 28 May 1666; Pepys, 31 May 1666.

X. RUPERT'S EXPEDITION

153   'The two Seymours': BL Add. 32094, f. 120; see also ff. 109 and 111; also *CSP Dom.* v, 418, 28 May 1666, Coventry to Arlington, Rupert to Arlington, and especially Seymour to Arlington, all in PRO SP29/157.
153   'The English': *CSP Venetian* xxxv, 7.
153   'The King of England': d'Estrades, *Lettres* iv, 308–309.
153   'The letters': Bath 96, f. 152.
154   Arlington's letter of 24th: PRO SP29/157, f. 16 (memorandum).
154   'For ye Danes': *Ibid.*, f. 89.
154   Clark's cruise: NMM DAR/3, f. 22; Bath 95, f. 206; BL Add. 32094, f. 105; and *London Gazette* Nº 55.
154   'The expedition': Bath 99, f. 88.
154   'Though I suppose': BL Add. 32094, f. 107.
154   21 May fleet list: *Ibid.*, f. 102.
155   *Guinea*'s return from Lisbon: *London Gazette* Nº 53.
155   *Westfriesland* and *Charles V*, sacrificed: NMM DAR/3. f. 28.
155   *Centurion* and *Happy Entrance* leaky: Bath 95, f. 206; BL Add. 32094, f. 107.
155   Albemarle's earlier agreement: Bath 95, f. 194.
155   'Wee had': BL Add. 32094, f. 120.
155   *Eagle* and *Guernsey* detached: Bath 95, ff. 217–218; see also *CSP Dom.* v, 464, 27 June 1666, for their eventual return to Falmouth.
155   *Fountain* detached: BL Add. 32094, ff. 109 and 116; she returned 13 June, as shown by NMM DAR/3, f. 44.
156   'Bee with you': BL Add. 32094, f. 127; see also Middleton to Pepys, *CSP Dom.* v, 430, 5 June 1666, for their actual departure.
156   'If the Captains': Bath 95, f. 210.
156   'Shall all saile': BL Add. 32094, f. 127.
156   'By Saturday', *et seq.*: *Ibid.*, f. 131; *The Rupert and Monck Letterbook, 1666*, 229, erroneously gives this as 'more ships' rather than the correct 'these ships'.
156   'Down to Blackewall': Pepys, 2 June 1666.
157   'To get': PRO SP29/158, f. 29.
157   'Very poorly', *et seq.*: PRO SP29/157, f. 16 (memoranda).
157   'Design will': BL Add. 32094, f. 80; for the original (in French), see PRO SP Foreign Newsletters 101/49, 18/28 May 1666 (The Hague).
157   'To go find': *Ibid.*, 25 May/4 June 1666 (Haarlem).
157   'Goe & venture': BL Add. 32094, f. 87.
158   'The discourse': *London Gazette* Nº 57.
158   'I cannot think': BL Add. 32094, ff. 127–128.
158   Conference on the 28th: *Ibid.*, f. 202.
158   'Where ye Prince': Bath 95, f. 220.
158   *Advice–Bonaventure* collision: *Ibid.*; also BL Add. 32094, f. 125.
159   'I doubt': BL Add. 32094, f. 107.
159   'In my opinion': *Ibid.*, f. 109.
159   'I have received': PRO SP29/157, f. 89.
159   Shovell's troubles: Pepys, *Tangier Papers*, intro, xlviii–xlix.
159   'To be very careful': NMM DAR/3, f. 22.
160   'The King': Pepys, 10 Jan. 1666.
160   'My secretary': BL Add. 32094, f. 113; f. 114 is a more legible copy.
161   Penn's opinion: Pepys, 4 July 1666.
161   'That if there should': BL Add. 32094, f. 120; also f. 125.
162   'May it please': *Ibid.*, f. 123.

162 'Wee had': *Ibid.*, f. 121.
162 'From the D.': *Ibid.*, f. 209.
162 'If . . . the Dutch': *Ibid.*, f. 120.
162 'Wee should': *Ibid.*, f. 125.
163 'Told [the] Ld. Gen.': part of a marginal note on a letter of 28 May from Albemarle to Coventry, Bath 95, f. 218. The marginal note begins, 'My letter of 26th wch this acknowledges (receaved, went by Major Miller), it told Ld. Gen. the Dutch would very suddainly bee out, . . .' In *The Rupert and Monck Letterbook, 1666*, 224, the opening phrase is mistakenly transcribed as 'Your letter . . .' and is attributed in the introduction (pp. 187–188) to Sir William Clarke, Albemarle's secretary. The actual phraseology (and the handwriting) shows that the marginal note was in fact Coventry's own, probably entered in 1667 in preparation for his testimony before the Parliamentary 'Committee of Miscarriages'. Oddly, Coventry had confused his own letters. The important intelligence message carried to the Generals by Major Miller (partial copy, Bath 96, f. 192) was dated the 25th and had been acknowledged by Albemarle on the 27th (BL Add. 32094, f. 109). Coventry's letter of the 26th, which Bath 95, f. 218 acknowledged, actually dealt with administrative matters.
163 '51 great shipps': BL Add. 32094, f. 131; see ff. 86–87 for an English-language copy of the actual newsletter.
163 Scarborough incident: *London Gazette* Nº 57. The item, referring to the incident as 'yesterday', is datelined 8 May; however, the context makes it clear that this was a misprint for 28 May. For confirmation see BL Add. 32094, f. 131.
163 'Because it was': BL Add. 32094, f. 209. *The Rupert and Monck Letterbook, 1666*, 205, erroneously shows this as '*not* so intended' (my italics).
164 'Might be some': BL Add. 32094, f. 131.
164 Rupert's recall orders: Bath 1, f. 34.366
164 East wind in London: BL Add. 32094, ff. 127 and 131.
165 'A tenderness': Clarendon, *Life* iii, 70.
165 'Under the lash': Pepys, 24 June 1666.
165 'About five': Honeywood's deposition, Bath 95, f. 389; Allin's deposition (*Ibid.*, ff. 228 and 391) consisted of extracts from his journal.
166 Rupert's return voyage: Allin i, 269–270.

XI. THE FRENCH

168 Choisin innocent: *CSP Dom.*, 341, 12 Dec. 1666.
168 Spanish fleet: *London Gazette* Nº 61 also Fernandez Duro, *Armada Española* v, 90; and HMC *Heathcote MSS*, 253–254.
168 'Walking the deck': *CSP Dom.* v, 591, 30 July 1666.
169 'Papists': Barlow i, 116.
169 'Some said': All Souls College MSS 256, f. 143.
170 'Upon [Clark's]': *Ibid.*, ff. 144–145.
171 'The Secretary': Marvell, 'The Third Advice to a Painter', lines 283–284.
172 Intelligence of fighting tactics: BL Add. 32094, ff. 78 and 82.
172 'Infinitely': d'Estrades, *Lettres* iv, 93.
172 Beaufort at Gibraltar: HMC *Heathcote MSS*, 253–254.
172 'That ye french': BL Add. 32094, f. 89.
172 'To proceed': *CSP Venetian* xxxv, 12.
172 Irish plans and military subterfuges: Louis XIV, *Mémoires*, 181, 197–198, and 213–214.
173 Franco-Dutch negotiations: Rauws, 'De Mislukte Vereeniging', *Marineblad* 1937, 883–901; for pertinent extracts from the 1635 treaty see d'Estrades, *Lettres* iv, 293–294.
174 Twelve Dutch ships: d'Estrades, *Lettres* iv, 94–95, 97–98, 126.
174 French concessions: *Ibid.*, 189, 293–294.
174 'Among the States': *Ibid.*, 156.

175 'I could not': *Ibid.*, 246–247.
175 D'Estrades' reply: *Ibid.*, 257–258.
176 'Inasmuch': Colenbrander, *Bescheiden uit Vreemde Archieven* i, 306.
176 'You are': Bath 95, f. 201.
176 'I urge': Colenbrander, *Bescheiden uit Vreemde Archieven* i, 307.
177 'To surprise': HMC *Heathcote MSS*, 249; see also Fernandez Duro, *Armada Española* v, 90–91.
178 'I could have': Louis XIV, *Mémoires*, 174–1 75.
178 5 May instructions: Colenbrander, *Bescheiden uit Vreemde Archieven* i, 307.
178 'That the project': d'Estrades, *Lettres* iv, 288–289.
178 'My Cousin': Colenbrander, *Bescheiden uit Vreemde Archieven* i, 311–312.
179 Beaufort not to leave Lisbon: Louis XIV, *Mémoires*, 203.
179 'It will only': Colenbrander, *Beschciden uit Vreemde Archieven* i, 300.
179 'Some quantity': d'Estrades, *Lettres* iv, 291.
179 Second 11 May memorandum: *Ibid.*, 297–301.
179 'Admiral de Ruyter': *Ibid.*, 292–293.
180 'That there was': as paraphrased in Louis XIV, *Mémoires*, 175; for the actual letter of the 24th see d'Estrades, *Lettres* iv, 301–303.
180 'They have strongly': *Ibid.*, 308–309.
180 Spanish salute: Louis XIV, *Mémoires*, 202; Fernandez Duro, *Armada Española* v, 225.
180 Beaufort and the delayed wedding: Rauws, 'De Mislukte Vereeniging', *Marineblad* 1937, 885–891.
181 'At present': Colenbrander, *Bescheiden uit Vreemde Archieven* i, 487.

XII. THE MORNING OF THE FIRST OF JUNE

182 'Nott yett putt': Bath 95, f. 222.
183 200 men short: *Ibid.*, f. 204.
183 Digby's account: BL Add. 17484, f. 9.
183 'Scarce beleeve': Bath 95, f. 222.
183 'Wee heere': BL Add. 32094, f. 121.
183 'Too uncertain': Blok, *De Ruyter*, 225.
183 Embargoes: *Ibid.*, 221–222.
184 'The drumb': PRO SP Foreign Newslctters 101/48,26 Jan./5 Feb. 1666 (Rotterdam).
184 'That ther': *Ibid.*, 20/30 Apr. 1666 (Rotterdam).
185 William's visit: Blok, *De Ruyter*, 224–225; Liefde, *The Great Dutch Admirals*, 204–205.
186 'To see': PRO SP Foreign, Holland 84/180, f. 52.
187 Dutch organization: Brandt, *Leven van de Ruiter*, 468–470; Van Foreest and Weber, *De Vierdaagse Zeeslag*, 42–44.
188 'Captain Govert Pieterse': Robinson and Weber, *The Willem Van de Velde Drawings in the Boymans-van Beuningen Museum, Rotterdam* i, 40.
188 Intelligence from shipping: Van Foreest and Weber, *De Vierdaagse Zeeslag*, 26.
189 'Off Dunkirk': *London Gazette* Nº 58.
189 'Near Ostend': BL Add. 32094, f. 137.
189 '7 leagues': PRO SP29/158, f. 178.
189 'Near Nieupoort': *Life of Tromp*, 343.
190 'Between Dunkirk': *Ibid.*, 340.
190 'Between Blackness': NMM DAR/3, f. 37.
190 De Ruyter's journal: quoted by Anderson in Allin ii, intro., xx.
190 'To the North-Westward': *Life of Tromp*, 337.
190 'The North forland': PRO SP29/158, f. 77.
190 Twenty-three n.m. in two hours: noted by Anderson in Allin ii, intro., xx.
190 English reports of time and position: BL Add. 32094, f. 137; Jordan's account, NMM Wyn/14/1; and *London Gazette* Nº 58.

190 'Ply Northeast': NMM DAR/3, f. 37.
191 'And thereupon fired': *London Gazette* № 58.
191 'This morning': PRO SP29/158, f. 3.
191 '. . . at 7': *Ibid.*, f. 77.
191 'I had': BL Add. 32094, f. 197.
192 'On friday': *Ibid.*, f. 137.
192 'About ten': NMM CLU/2.
193 'But swoln': Marvell, 'The Third Advice to a Painter', lines 39–42.
194 'That at the Council': Pepys, 11 June 1666.
194 'Two-thirds': *Ibid.*, 4 July 1666.
194 'This Morning about 8': BL Add. 32094, f. 133.
195 Van de Velde's drawing: Museum Boymans-van Beuningen, Rotterdam, MB. 1866/T80.
195 Fighting Instructions: BL Harleian MSS 1247, ff. 51–52; or NMM DAR/2; see BL Sloane MSS 3232, f. 83 for 'Additional Instructions'.

XIII. THE FIRST DAY

198 'And then began': NMM 1GR/17, f. 27.
198 First broadside: PRO SP29/158, f. 77.
200 Tromp tacked: Boymans drawing MB1866/T82b.
200 *Beschermer* to windward: Boymans drawing MB1866/T81a.
200 *Beschermer*'s adventures: Brandt, *Leven van de Ruiter*, 480; Van der Zaan's report is printed in Van Foreest and Weber, *De Vierdaagse Zeeslag*, 170.
200 *IJlst* to windward: Boymans drawing MB1866/T83.
201 'Being to leeward': Barlow i, 117.
201 'The Dutch being': *London Gazette* № 58.
201 'Great hindrance': Barlow i, 118; see also Albemarle's account, NMM CLU/2.
201 'English frigate': Boymans drawing MB1866/T87a; see also MB1866/T83.
202 'As we began': NMM IGR/2.
202 Aylett claimed: *London Gazette* № 58.
202 'At which they': *Ibid.*
203 'The rest': Boymans drawing MB1866/T84b.
203 'They sailing': Boymans drawing MB1866/T83.
203 'Wee Atacqu'd': BL Add. 32094, f. 137; also PRO SP29/158, f. 152; and Bodleian, Carte MSS 72, f. 37, all with slightly different wording.
203 'Here the enemy': Boymans drawing MB1866/T84b.
204 'In order': Brandt, *Leven van de Ruiter*, 482; see also de Guiche, *Mémoires*, 234–264.
204 'Much ado': *Life of Tromp*, 338.
204 'Artificial fires': *CSP Venetian* xxxv, 28; see also d'Estrades, *Lettres* iv, 324.
204 'A Fiery Bullet': *Life of Tromp*, 338.
204 'Threw some rose-coloured': *CSP Venetian* xxxv, 28.
204 '120 Brass fire shott': NMM DAR/3, f.60. In *The Rupert and Monck Letterbook 1666*, 99, this is erroneously given as 'brassshot'.
205 Fifteen fathoms: PRO SP29/158, f. 77.
205 'After an houre': NMM Wyn/14/1.
206 'Admiral Evertsen': *Life of Tromp*, 341.
206 'That motion': *Ibid.*, 351.
206 'Many of our ablest': BL Add. 32094, f. 137; PRO SP29/158, f. 152; and Bodleian, Carte MSS 72, f. 37.
206 Evertsen even with Tromp: Boymans drawing MB1866/T87b.
206 'Very much shatterd': PRO SP29/158, f. 78.
206 'The Dukes sailes': *Ibid.*, f. 152.
206 'The English here luff': Boymans drawing MB1866/T86a.
207 'Barkley had heard': Marvell, 'The Second Advice to a Painter', lines 185–192.

207 'Sr. George Ayscue': BL Add. 32094, f. 137; PRO SP29/158, f. 152; Bodleian, Carte MSS 72, f. 37.

207 'It was ordered': NMM CLU/2.

208 *Swiftsure*'s opponents: Boymans drawings MB1866/T82a, T82b, and T83.

208 'Keep that man': Svendsen's account, Colenbrander, *Bescheiden uit Vreemde Archieven* i, 364.

208 *Swiftsure* loses main yard: Boymans drawing MB1866/T86a; confirmed by Jordan, NMM Wyn/14/1.

208 'Seeing himself': *Life of Tromp*, 338 (Hondius).

208 'When my captain', *et seq.*: Colenbrander, *Bescheiden uit Vreemde Archieven* i, 364; see also Brandt, *Leven van de Ruiter*, 480.

209 *Reiger*'s casualties: Van Foreest and Weber, *De Vierdaagse Zeeslag*, 190.

210 'The Disgrace': All Souls College MSS 256, f. 146.

210 'The *Swiftsure*': PRO SP29/158, f. 152.

210 'And if': Marvell, 'The Third Advice to a Painter', lines 109–114.

210 'Staying a little': PRO SP29/158, f. 77.

210 English ships undamaged, near *Swiftsure*: Boymans drawing MB1866/T87c; Brandt, *Leven van de Ruiter*, 480.

211 Capture of *Seven Oaks*: *Ibid.*, also Van der Zaan's report, Van Foreest and Weber, *De Vierdaagse Zeeslag*, 170.

211 *Loyal George* attacked: Boymans drawing MB1866/T87c.

212 'If his Lieutenant', *et seq.*: PRO SP Foreign Newsletters 101/49, 22 June/2 July 1666 (Amsterdam).

212 Casualties in Dutch captors: Van Foreest and Weber, *De Vierdaagse Zeeslag*, 175, 177, and 190.

212 'Was soe disabled', *et seq.*: PRO SP29/158, f. 71.

212 'Maimed': Pepys, 5 June 1666.

213 Tromp in *Jonge Prins*: Boymans drawing MB1866/T86c.

213 'Cast to': PRO SP29/158, f. 78.

213 *Royal Charles* leading: Boymans drawing MB1866/T560 and T561.

213 *Eendracht* vs. *Royal Charles*: Brandt, *Leven van de Ruiter*, 483.

214 'Made up': PRO SP29/158, f. 73. One of the witnesses was probably John Daniel; see Pepys, 4 June 1666.

214 'And bore': Pepys, 4 June 1666.

214 'Having torne': PRO SP29/158, f. 100.

214 Damage to *Portland*: *Ibid.*, ff. 47 and 94.

215 'Having her sailes': *Ibid.*, f. 47, as related by Coventry after a letter (apparently not preserved) from Harman at Aldborough; Pepys paraphrased the same letter in the *Diary* on 3 June.

216 'In doing which': PRO SP29/158, f. 47.

216 *Vrijheid*: the only Zeeland fireship expended, so it could have been no other.

216 'It is not': Kennet, *Complete History of England* iii, 281; said to be Harman's words, but more likely second-hand.

216 'Grapnailed': PRO SP29/158, f. 94.

216 'The Dutch Fireships': Kennet, *Complete History of England* iii, 281.

216 'Swang himself': *Ibid.*

216 Chaplain's panic: reported by Prince Rupert, PRO SP29/158, f. 156; see also Pepys, 3 June 1666.

217 'With Oars': *Life of Tromp*, 342 (de Ruyter's account).

217 Harman's servant: Kennet, *Complete History of England* iii, 281.

217 'To repair': *Life of Tromp*, 353.

217 'A 3d fireship': PRO SP29/158, f. 47.

217 'At last': *Ibid.*; see also Kennet, *Complete History of England* iii, 281.

217 'There is reason': *Life of Tromp*, 344.
217 'In fine': *Ibid.*, 342.
217 'The night': *Ibid.*, 354.
217 'Very much': PRO SP29/158, f. 100.
218 Colliermen pressed: *Ibid.*, f. 94.
218 *Walcheren* covered fireship: *Life of Tromp*, 353.
218 'Took away': *Ibid.* Contrary to some English sources, Dutch accounts consistently place Evertsen's death at the end of the action; see *Ibid.*, 342 and 354.
218 'According': *Ibid.*, 353.
218 'To pay £15': NMM DAR/3, f. 54.
218 'After the utmost': Pepys, 8 June 1666.
218 'As all say': *Ibid.*, 3 June 1666.

XIV. THE SECOND DAY

219 'Hardly besett': PRO SP29/158, f. 94.
219 *Rainbow* engaged against Tromp's squadron: Hart actually thought Tromp's ships were Zeelanders, as did most of the English; see *Ibid.*, f. 71.
220 Van Nes at the head: de Guiche, *Mémoires*, 250; confirmed by Brandt, *Leven van de Ruiter*, 484.
220 *Walcheren*'s flag: Van Foreest and Weber, *De Vierdaagse Zeeslag*, 67.
220 'We began': NMM IGR/17, V.28.
220 Brandt . . . believed: Brandt, *Leven van de Ruiter*, 484.
221 'They without waiting': *Life of Tromp*, 344.
221 'Came powring': *Ibid.*, 342.
221 'In an admirable': de Guiche, *Mémoirés*, 248–249.
221 *Antelope* fired first: NMM 1GR/17, f. 28.
221 'The manner': All Souls College MSS 256, V.138.
221 'This day': NMM IGR/17, f. 29.
222 'The two Fleets': *Life of Tromp*, 354.
222 'Their Guns': *Ibid.*, 354–355.
222 'In the two': PRO SP29/158, f. 115 (Clifford's account). In *The Rupert and Monck Letterbook, 1666*, 252, the paragraph containing this passage erroneously appears as a part of Jordan's account.
223 The English . . . blew themselves up: related by Monaco to the Venetian ambassador to France a week after the battle; *CSP Venetian* xxxv, 16.
223 '7 sail': PRO SP29/158, f. 78.
223 Early arrivals at the Gunfleet: *London Gazette* № 59; PRO SP29/158, f. 100.
224 'Broke through': *Life of Tromp*, 345.
224 De Ruyter's intended attack: Brandt, *Leven van de Ruiter*, 484.
224 'Heard a most horrid': *Life of Tromp*, 355.
225 'There was two': NMM Wyn/14/1.
225 'We borded': NMM IGR/17, f. 29.
225 *Spiegel*'s casualties: Van Foreest and Weber, *De Vierdaagse Zeeslag*, 192.
225 'Extreamly': *Life of Tromp*, 356.
225 'No sooner': *Ibid.*
225 *Antelope*'s casualties: Bath 98, f. 185.
226 'De Ruyter considering': *Life of Tromp*, 345.
226 'The head': de Guiche, *Mémoires*, 250.
227 Van Nes acted on de Ruyter's orders: Brandt, *Leven van de Ruiter*, 485.
228 'Without': *Life of Tromp*, 355.
228 'Advanced': *Ibid.*
228 'The English seeing': *Ibid.*, 345.
228 'Found Lieutenant Admiral Tromp': *Ibid.*, 355.

228   'It is not': de Guiche, *Mémoires*, 253.
229   'Indeed': *Ibid.*, 253–254.
229   'Methinks': *Life of Tromp*, 345.
229   'It appears': de Guiche, *Mémoires*, 254.
229   'About 12 a clock': All Souls College MSS 256, f. 138.
230   'Captain Salomonszoon's': *Life of Tromp*, 355.
230   'Put some cheering': PRO SP29/158, ff. 111 and 115. In *The Rupert and Monck Letterbook, 1666*, 252, the paragraph containing this passage erroneously appears as a part of Jordan's account.
230   'Found all things': PRO SP29/158, f. 111.
230   Letters from Whitehall: probably those in BL Add. 32094, ff. 127–131.
230   Tromp's disputes: Van Foreest and Weber, *De Vierdaagse Zeeslag*, 70–71.
231   De Guiche's opinion: de Guiche, *Mémoires*, 255–256.
231   Brandt's explanation: Brandt, *Leven van de Ruiter*, 486.
232   'Especially afternoon', *et seq.*: *Life of Tromp*, 357.
232   *Loyal Subject* towed: PRO SP29/158, f. 102.
232   Loss of *Black Eagle*: *Life of Tromp*, 345–346 and 357; also Brandt, *Leven van de Ruiter*, 486. All the sinkings described therein were obviously a single incident. The *Rupert* was one of the rescuers, for her casualty list included men from the sunken ship; see Bath 98, f. 185.
233   'Looked with': PRO SP29/158, f. 111.
233   'There was nothing': *Ibid.*
233   Ostend ships joined on or after the 3rd: *Life of Tromp*, 399; Barlow i, 119; and Roch, NMM IGR/17, f. 30.
233   Ostend ships appeared on the 2nd: Jordan, NMM Wyn/14/1; and PRO SP29/158, ff. 73, 94, and 125; in addition, PRO SP29/158, f. 78 ('True Narrative') and Brandt, *Leven van de Ruiter*, 487, both say that the Dutch pursued in the evening of the 2nd with sixty-six ships, a number which could not have been attained without the Ostend ships.
233   'Some Discouriagement': PRO SP29/158, f. 94.
233   'To break': *Ibid.*, f. 125.
234   English strength at end of second day: All Souls College MSS 256, f. 139; and PRO SP29/158, f. 111. PRO SP29/158, f. 78 says '28 sayle of fighting ships'. Brandt, *Leven van de Ruiter*, 487, says that the States' Fleet pursued thirty-eight or thirty-nine English ships, but the vessels which had departed during the final pass would not have been out of sight.
234   'Infinite courage': *London Gazette* № 59.
234   'Twelve they spoke of': PRO SP29/158, f. 73.
235   'We had not', *et seq.*: Barlow i, 118–119.

XV. THE THIRD DAY

236   Dutch council-of-war: Van Foreest and Weber, *De Vierdaagse Zeeslag*, 73.
236   *Monck's* new topmast: Barlow i, 119.
237   'That the management': Pepys, 10 June 1666.
237   'The best saylors': PRO SP29/158, f. 78.
238   'In our whole': *Ibid.*, f. 111.
238   'To within': Brandt, *Leven van de Ruiter*, 488.
238   'Amused all': All Souls College MSS 256, f. 139.
239   'Ran just': Barlow i, 120.
239   'To trepan us': Allin i, 270.
239   'A waterman': Bodleian, Rawlinson MSS A.195, f. 53v; ff. 51–54 are testimony from the Court of Inquiry into the loss of the *Prince* and constitute the main English source for this episode.
240   'Resolved to tack': BL Add. 32094, f. 137.
240   'The *R. Charles*': NMM CLU/2.
240   Ayscue abused: *CSP Dom.* v, 518, 10 July 1666.

240 Jewelry stolen: Svendsen's journal, Colenbrander, *Bescheiden uit Vreemde Archieven* i, 365–366.
241 'A great misfortune': *Life of Tromp*, 359.
241 Ayscue in Holland: Van Foreest and Weber, *De Vierdaagse Zeeslag*, 75–76.
241 'After we had': *Life of Tromp*, 339.
241 'The Admiral's Ship': *Ibid.*, 343.
241 'Tho' she was': *Ibid.*, 359.
242 'Was a great grief': Barlow i, 120.
242 'Allow them': PRO SP29/158, f. 125.
242 Craven's subscription: HMC *12th Rep., App. Part VII* (Le Fleming MSS), 40.
242 'Being encompassed': Barlow i, 120.
243 'But in a dark': Marvell, 'The Third Advice to a Painter', lines 119–120.
243 Ayscue at sea, 1668 and 1672: Pepys's 'Register of Sea-Officers', *Catalogue of Pepysian MSS* i, 313 and 320. Counterclaims in Penn, *Memorials* ii, 521, are based on an unsubstantiated assumption that the *Triumph* was not in commission; BL Add. 32094, f. 212 shows that she was indeed fitted for sea, and that Ayscue was her captain. The *St. Andrew* was definitely in commission in 1672, since she fought at Solebay a few weeks after Ayscue died.
243 'The Duch': PRO SP29/158, f. 112.
244 'Hearing the Greate', *et seq.*: Evelyn, 1–2 June 1666.
244 'Saw the Duch': Pepys, 2 June 1666.
244 'Saw hundreds': *Ibid.*, 4 June 1666.
245 'Put us at': *Ibid.*, 2 June 1666.
245 'All our hopes': *Ibid.*
245 'That he saw': *London Gazette* N° 58.
245 'With this': Pepys, 3 June 1666.
246 'So that we': *Ibid.*
246 'Instead of sailing', *et seq.*: *Ibid.*
246 Harman's letter: described by Coventry, PRO SP29/158, f. 47.
246 Daniel in London: Pepys, 4 June 1666. Though often described as lieutenant of the *Royal Charles*, John Daniel was actually a reformado as shown by NMM DAR/3, f. 34.
247 Daniel's account: PRO SP29/158, f. 73.
247 Damaged ships: *Ibid.*, ff. 73, 95, and especially 100; also *CSP Dom.* v, 480 30 June 1666.
247 'All which pretend': PRO SP29/158, f. 100.
247 'But all this day': Pepys, 4 June 1666.
247 'Walked into': *Ibid.*
248 'With some gentlemen': Allin i, 270.
248 Ossory present: PRO SP29/158, f. 115.
248 '26 sayles': *Ibid.*, f. 42.
248 Three ships from the Thames: *Life of Tromp*, 360; Brandt, *Leven van de Ruiter*, 489.
248 Capture of *Sancta Maria*: Allin i, 191–206 and ii, 221–223; Venetian diplomatic protests are mentioned throughout *CSP Venetian* xxxiv.
248 'To set upon': Barlow i, 120.
248 'An order': NMM DAR/3, f. 179.
249 'Wore the white': Barlow i, 124.
249 English 'Admiral of the Blue': *Life of Tromp*, 362; Brandt, *Leven van de Ruiter*, 493.
249 'Who had a mind': PRO SP29/158, f. 114.
249 'He tooke': *Ibid.*; see also NMM DAR/3, f. 179.
249 Harrison's appointment: *Ibid.* The generals' secretary erroneously gave the ship as the *Vanguard*, in which deceased Captain John Whitty was actually replaced by his own lieutenant, Anthony Langston. The *Unicorn* and *Vanguard* were often confused by secretaries, possibly because of the frequent similarity in the handwritten forms of the names. Another example is in *CSP Dom.* v, 439, 13 June 1666. All of these are corrected by the entries for Harrison, Langston, and Teddiman in Pepys's 'Register of Sea-Officers',

Catalogue of Pepysian MSS i. For further confirmation see Bath 98, f. 192 and other entries in NMM DAR/3, f. 179.

249   'Old Teddiman': Pepys, 13 June 1666.
249   'A very stout man': *Ibid.*, 2 Jan. 1668.
250   'By which meanes': NMM Wyn/14/1.

XVI. THE FOURTH DAY

251   'The L. Admiral': Brandt, *Leven van de Ruiter*, 493.
251   De Ruyter's speech: *Ibid.*
252   *Gouda-Wapen van Utrecht* controversy: *Life of Tromp*, 339 and 361; Brandt, *Leven van de Ruiter*, 491.
252   'By the light': Allin i, 270–271.
252   'At the first': NMM CLU/2.
252   'We made': PRO SP29/158, f. 112.
253   'To fall': *Ibid.*, f. 79.
253   Nixon court-martial: Sandwich, 215.
254   'Great renown': Pepys, 13 June 1666.
254   Van Nes tacked: Brandt, *Leven van de Ruiter*, 491.
254   'The Hollanders': *Life of Tromp*, 360–361.
254   'Bore in': PRO SP29/158, f. 112.
254   'That the yardarms': Brandt, *Leven van de Ruiter*, 491.
254   'Gave ye enemy': NMM Wyn/14/1.
255   'Reduced to ashes': *Life of Tromp*, 361; see also Brandt, *Leven van de Ruiter*, 491.
256   'Got betwixt': PRO SP29/158, f. 79.
256   English ship entangled: *Life of Tromp*, 361.
256   'In this Passe': PRO SP29/158, f. 79.
256   'The Prince thought': *Ibid.*
256   'As soone': NMM AGC/R2.
257   'Fell upon': NMM CLU/2.
257   Two ships fired: *Ibid.*
258   'In case ye Enemy': NMM DAR/3, f. 63.
258   'Were very fortunate': de Guiche, *Mémoires*, 261. This quite clear passage, which is fully compatible with other accounts, is preceeded by one which has caused great confusion:
      'The wind was Southwest, & we having it over the English, who kept towards us to gain it, but in a very daring manner. For, instead of advancing on us for passing from poop to prow, the confidence which they had in the speed of their ships made them take the same course as our Fleet, thinking they could overtake us on that course. We were thus for three hours' duration broadside to broadside, which is extremely hard; for when one passes from ship to ship, & when the prows are opposed, the headings that one and the other take separates them quickly enough, & it is the same for all the line: but, when one is accompanied broadside to broadside, one does have the time and the means to see more clearly & more accurately.'
      This passage gave some nineteenth- and early twentieth-century historians (notably Mahan and Sir Arthur Tedder) the impression that the English began the action by chasing up the windward side of the Dutch line and then engaged on the same tack for three hours, a reconstruction which disagrees violently with other narratives. The context, however, shows that de Guiche's troublesome passage is not a chronological description of the action at all, but merely a preface in which the eyewitness set forth what he took to be the intentions of the enemy. In the early stages of the battle he saw two apparent attempts by the English to fall upon the Dutch rear from windward on the same course. The first was when Myngs initially came to the port tack across the wake of the Dutch rear, which could easily have been mistaken for an effort to overtake from astern. The second came when Albemarle did get on the same tack with the Dutch rear, leaving Rupert a little behind

and again in the position of overtaking from astern. The third sentence of the passage probably should be interpreted as, '[In the course of the battle] we were thus for three hours' duration'. De Guiche was only trying to convey that the English wanted to engage the rear on the same tack from windward, and that it meant hard fighting when they did so. His actual chronological narrative opens with the sentence cited by this note, and which immediately follows the disputed passage. Although the narrative begins without warning, a definite break is indicated in that the English are brought back where they started, to the north of the Dutch: 'The English, who were still to leeward, were very fortunate in that our fireships . . .'

258   'Our general': This is not from de Guiche's *Mémoires*, but from a similarly worded account in a letter of 20 June 1666 (N.S.) said to be from a Dutch captain to a friend in France (published in *Revue Maritime et Coloniale* lxxxii, 1884, 137–148). Rightly or wrongly, some modern authorities regard this letter as nothing more than a plagiarism from de Guiche, and for that reason I have generally refrained from using it. The quotation in question has been substituted here because the corresponding passage in the *Mémoires* contains a major mistake:

> 'Van Essen [Van Nes], who could well have kept with us, had taken the diversion, with fourteen or fifteen sail, to follow those three or four ships of the White Flag, that I have mentioned having passed to *windward* [my italics] of our Fleet, instead of supporting his Admiral against the greater part of the enemy fleet. In the course of the division, Tromp, having lost the wind, had been forced to fall back towards Van Essen.'

The isolated ships of the White Squadron (Myngs) had of course been driven to *leeward*, as the succeeding sentence makes clear. It may be that the eighteenth-century editor of the *Mémoires* simply mistranscribed de Guiche's term for leeward (*au dessous*) as that for windward (*au dessus*). However the mistake may have arisen, the suspect 20 June letter appears in this case to be the more accurate rendering of events.

259   'De Ruyter caused': *Life of Tromp*, 361.

259   Narbrough's manoeuvres: de Guiche, *Mémoires*, 262.

259   Report from Zeeland: Colenbrander, *Bescheiden uit Vreemde Archieven* i, 377–378.

260   'Fortune willed': de Guiche, *Mémoires*, 261.

260   'Divided them': NMM CLU/2.

260   'Sometimes wee': NMM Wyn/14/1.

260   'Supposed we': *Ibid.*

260   'We kept': de Guiche, *Mémoires*, 262.

260   'Wee stood': PRO SP29/158, f. 80.

260   'Having passed': Allin i, 271.

261   English ammunition allowances: NMM DAR/3, ff. 14–15, 17, 19–20, and 23.

261   Van Nes and Tromp return: de Guiche, *Mémoires*, 263.

261   'Plying them': PRO SP29/158, f. 80.

261   'To fire': BL Add. 32094, f. 135.

261   *Eendracht* nearly burned: Brandt, *Leven van de Ruiter*, 494.

261   'Fell so': PRO SP29/158, f. 112.

262   'Having given': Pepys, 8 June 1666.

262   'And some others': *Life of Tromp*, 361.

262   Surrender of *Dom van Utrecht*: Brandt, *Leven van de Ruiter*, 492.

262   'Struck their Ensignes': All Souls College MSS 256, f. 140.

262   Dutch captain captured: PRO SP29/158, f. 113.

262   'Our Captaines': BL Add. 32094, f. 137.

262   'Confessed': Colenbrander, *Bescheiden uit Vreemde Archieven* i, 377.

262   Banckert's advice: *Ibid.*

262   'Gave the Duke': PRO SP29/158, f. 112.

263   'Most of our owne': *Ibid.*, f. 113.

263   'Sir Edward Spragge': Greene, *Lord Rochester's Monkey*, 58.

264 'When Holmes': PRO SP29/158, ff. 125–126.
264 'They bearing up': Allin i, 271.
264 'Terribly shaken': PRO SP29/158, f. 80.
264 'Just as': Allin i, 271.
264 'Againe': PRO SP29/158, f. 113.
264 'The Lieutenant-Admirals': *Life of Tromp*, 361–362.
264 'My Ld. Generall': PRO SP29/158, f. 113.
265 'In the gunroom': NMM CLU/2.
265 'I was once': PRO SP29/158, f. 156.
265 'On Munday': All Souls College MSS 256, ff. 146–147.
265 Belated instruction: NMM DAR/2 (Spragge's seabook). The instruction is addressed to Spragge as Vice-Admiral of the Blue and is signed only by Rupert, so it was probably issued in September after Albemarle's return to London.
265 *Dom van Utrecht*'s drunken crew: Van Foreest and Weber, *De Vierdaagse Zeeslag*, 83.
266 'Most indiscreetly': PRO SP29/158, f. 113; see also NMM CLU/2.
266 'When shee': PRO SP29/158, f. 81.
266 'Had taken': All Souls College MSS 256, f. 141.
266 'Received, towards': Charnock, *Biographia Navalis* i, 122–123.
267 'That they led': *Ibid.*
267 'We cannot': *Ibid.*, said to be an extract from a letter from The Hague of 29 June 1666, whether Old Style or New is not specified.
267 *Essex* wrecked: *CSP Dom.* vii, 527, 15 Oct. 1667.
267 'Yielded in sight': *Life of Tromp*, 347.
268 'To leeward': NMM Wyn/14/1.
268 'Being an old': PRO SP29/158, f. 113.
268 'Captain John Pearsie': *CSP Dom.* v, 442, 15/25 June 1666.
268 Five ships taken: *Life of Tromp*, 347–362.
268 Observer in the *Royal Charles*: All Souls College MSS 256, f. 141.
269 'Our business': PRO SP29/158, f. 113.
269 'Prince Rupert being': NMM CLU/2.
269 'In ye night': BL Add. 32094, f. 137.
269 'The Generall then': NMM AGC/R2.
269 'Had much ado': Allin i, 271.
269 *Royal James* towed: *Ibid.*
269 'Our retreat': NMM Wyn/14/1.
270 'That the Duch': Pepys, 7 June 1666.
270 'For the shattered': *Life of Tromp*, 363.
270 'As firy Rupert': Marvell, 'The Third Advice to a Painter', lines 153–162.
270 'But wee must': NMM Wyn/14/1.

XVII. AFTERMATH

271 'Hast Hast Hast': BL Add. 32094, f. 135.
271 'We were all': Pepys, 6 June 1666.
272 'Made a suddaine': Evelyn, 6 June 1666.
272 'But 36': Pepys, 6 June 1666.
272 'For bone-fires': Evelyn, 6 June 1666.
272 'Volleys', *et seq.*': Pepys, 6–7 June 1666.
272 'All the fleet': *Ibid.*, 10 June 1666.
272 'All give over': *Ibid.*, 9 June 1666.
272 'Beheld': Evelyn, 17 June 1666.
273 'All being shot': Barlow i, 122.
273 *Loyal Subject*: PRO SP29/158, f. 227.
273 Housing of wounded: *Ibid.*, f. 96.

273   'We were sent': Barlow i, 122.
273   'Which the Chirurgion': Bath 98, f. 186, which shows a similar entry for the *Rupert.*
273   'Many merchants': PRO SP29/158, f. 126.
273   'Charitable people': Evelyn, 4 July 1666.
273   'A very stout man': Pepys, 13 June 1666.
274   Commanders killed: Bodleian, Rawlinson MSS A.191, f. 198.
274   'But most': Marvell, 'The Third Advice to a Painter', lines 123–130.
274   'The Duke': *London Gazette* № 59.
274   'Guard thy posteriour': Marvell, 'The Third Advice to a Painter', lines 375–376.
275   Dutch commanders killed: Brandt, *Leven van de Ruiter*, 496; *Life of Tromp*, 366.
275   Prizes to Goeree and Texel: Brandt, *Leven van de Ruiter*, 480–482; *Life of Tromp*, 362–363.
275   Riot in Brussels: *Life of Tromp*, 371.
275   'On wednesday', *et seq.*: PRO SP Foreign Newsletters 101/49, 22 June 12 July 1666 (Amsterdam).
276   De Ruyter's honours: Blok, *De Ruyter*, 238.
276   'Without counting', *et seq.*: *Life of Tromp*, 356–357 and 364.
277   Foreign estimates: Colenbrander, *Bescheiden uit Vreemde Archieven* i, 371–379.
277   'By the Observations': All Souls College MSS 256, f. 142.
278   'Neither could they': Barlow i, 121.
278   Albemarle's claims: NMM CLU/2 and NMM HSR/1/2.
278   'True Narrative': PRO SP29/158, ff. 77–81.
278   Heemskerck's list: described in All Souls College MSS 256, f. 142; and PRO SP29/164, f. 125. The list itself has not been found.
278   'Great dejectedness': Pepys, 18 July 1666.
278   'Whatever their': All Souls College MSS 256, f. 142.
278   'Beaten home': Pepys, 28 Oct. 1666.
279   'Passing by us': NMM IGR/17, ff. 32–33.
279   Smith's arrival: inferred from NMM DAR/3, f. 38; Blue Squadron orders were addressed to Teddiman on the 6th, Smith on the 7th. *CSP Dom.* v, 430, 5 June 1666, Middleton to Pepys, shows that Smith had sailed from Portsmouth on the 5th.
279   Plymouth squadron: PRO SP29/158, f. 52 for departure from Plymouth on the 3rd; see NMM DAR/3, ff. 43–44 for arrival in the Thames. The *Elizabeth* was initially not with the others, but probably joined them off the Lizard from Falmouth.
279   'But if': Barlow i, 122.
280   'This extraordinary': Pepys, 13 June 1666.
280   'That all': *Ibid.*, 10 June 1666.
280   'And in the evening': *Ibid.*, 4 July 1666.
282   'That since': PRO SP29/159, f. 4.
282   'You have done': *Ibid.*, f. 92.
282   'High words': Pepys, 19 June 1666.
282   'He doth': *Ibid.*, 24 June 1666.
282   'That the Duke': *Ibid.*, 10 June 1666.
282   'A great creature': *Ibid.*, 24 June 1666.
282   'With other brave': PRO SP29/158, f. 153; also a similar list, omitting Allin and Kempthorne, in BL Add. 32094, f. 137.
282   Fireship bounties paid: NMM DAR/3, ff. 43 and 46.
283   'I assure you': Bodleian, Rawlinson MSS A.194, f. 209; see also Pepys, 7 June 1666.
283   'I had not': PRO SP29/158, f. 157.
283   'The sense': Pepys, 27 July 1666.
283   Promotions: NMM DAR/3, ff. 179–180; Bath 98, f. 192.
283   'If the Kinge': PRO SP29/158, f. 114.
283   'There was': All Souls College MSS 256, f. 146.
283   Van de Velde: Boymans drawings MB1866/T82–T86.

283 Casualty lists: Bath 98, ff. 185–186; BL Add. 9336, ff. 85v–86v.
283 'The boarded vessels': *CSP Dom.* v, 449, 20 June 1666.
283 Dutch casualties: Van Foreest and Weber, *De Vierdaagse Zeeslag*, 174–200.
284 Captains dismissed: Bath 98, f. 190. Harrison was not listed since he had never received a formal commission. He was nevertheless not employed again until 1672; see Pepys's 'Register of Sea-Officers', *Catalogue of Pepysian MSS* i, 361.
284 'We kept': NMM DAR/3, ff 46–47.
284 'Fired more shot': Pepys, 4 Apr. 1667.
284 'Great Jarrs': *Ibid.*, 13 June 1666.
285 'Ah, rather': Marvell, 'The Third Advice to a Painter', lines 105–108.
285 Swanley reviled: Pepys, 23 June 1666.
285 'Found fault': *Ibid.*, 21 June 1666.
285 'They condemn': *Ibid.*, 4 June 1666.
285 'Behaved himself': *Ibid.*, 8 June 1666.
285 'Mightily discontented': *Ibid.*, 10 June 1666.
285 'Mutiny or disorder': NMM DAR/3, f. 54; see f. 180 for Chapple's replacement.
286 'Daily expected': *London Gazette* № 61.
286 ''Tis strange': PRO SP29/159, f. 92.
286 'We have yet': Arlington, *Letters* ii, 180.
286 Intelligence of Irish invasion: for examples, see BL Add. 32094, ff. 88–89; and PRO SP Foreign Newsletters 101/49, 22 June/2 July 1666 (Amsterdam).
286 Collierman's intelligence: *CSP Dom.* v, 455–456, 24 June 1666.

XVIII. SEQUEL

287 'Mightily troubled': Pepys, 30 June 1666.
288 'Vapouring': All Souls College MSS 256, f. 148.
288 Position reports: reviewed by R. C. Anderson in Allin ii, intro., xxvii–xxviii.
288 'Very advantageous': NMM DAR/3, ff. 41 and 43.
288 Twelve ships deleted: NMM DAR/3, ff. 60–64.
289 'Halfe moone': Bodleian, Rawlinson MSS A.195, f. 204.
290 'To ly': *Ibid.*
290 'To try': Barlow i, 124.
290 'Very ill mann'd': PRO SP29/165, f. 6.
290 'Extremely hot': Barlow i, 125.
290 'Lost very foolishly': Allin i, 278.
290 'The fight': PRO SP29/165, f. 10.
290 'Come out': *Ibid.*, f. 1.
291 'Our people': Allin i, 277–278.
291 'Upon the first': PRO SP Foreign Newsletters 101/50, 28 July/7 Aug. 1666 (Vlissingen).
291 'Shot in one': *Ibid.*
291 'Shot a-pieces', *et seq.*: Allin i, 278.
292 ' "Now", says he': Pepys, 30 July 1666.
292 'Was againe': PRO SP29/165, f. 4.
292 'Blood-red pennant': Barlow i, 124.
292 'Rendered uncapable': Lediard, *Naval History of England*, 585.
292 Smith's fireships: Pepys, 27 July 1666; the source was Talbot.
292 'Eight or nine': *Ibid.*
293 'That this gallant': *Ibid.*
293 'A great part': *The Naval Miscellany* iii, 12. This is an anonymous account entitled 'The Daily Motion and Public Transactions of His Majesty's Fleet from their setting out of the Buoy in the Nore the 19th of July 1666 till their return thither the 3rd of October, . . .'
294 'With great gallantry', *et seq.*: PRO SP29/165, f. 4. 'The Daily Motion' in *The Naval Miscellany* iii, 10–11, adds details but differs somewhat in chronology; see also Lediard,

Naval History of England, 585.

294 Allin's mistake: PRO SP29/165, f. 5; and Allin i, 279.

294 *Fanfan's* exploit: 'The Daily Motion' in *The Naval Miscellany* iii, 10, places this incident on the 25th; but Clifford (PRO SP29/165, f. 4) and *London Gazette* Nº 75 both describe it in detail as occurring during the chase on the 26th.

294 *Land of Promise*: *The Naval Miscellany* iii, 13.

295 English casualties: NMM DAR/3, f. 68. For captains killed see Bodleian, Rawlinson MSS A. 191, f. 198; the confusion therein over Joseph Sanders is settled by *CSP Dom.* vi, 1, 1 Aug. 1666 (Browne to Williamson), which shows that Sanders was indeed a casualty of the St. James's Day Fight.

295 'Most falsely': *CSP Dom.* vi, 14 Aug. 1666 (Albemarle to Charles II).

295 'Gross errors': BL Add. 32094, f. 158.

295 'Having too easily': PRO SP44/23, f. 264.

296 'Turned out': *CSP Dom.* vi, 1 Aug. 1666 (Bowen to Williamson, Scrivner to Hickes, and Carlisle to Williamson).

296 Captains displaced: inferred from NMM DAR/3, f. 180 (Generals' commission list). Captains not killed, wounded, or transferred to other ships who were replaced after the battle were presumably relieved for cause.

296 Holmes in the Vlie: *London Gazette* Nº 79; NMM DAR/3, f. 76; and *The Naval Miscellany* iii, 18–24. The operation is thoroughly described in Ollard, *Man of War*, 148–161.

297 'To tell': Allin i, 283.

297 'Conclude them': NMM DAR/3, f. 87.

297 'Contrary': *The Naval Miscellany* iii, 31.

298 'With tears': Allin i, 288.

298 Beaufort in the Channel: Rauws, 'De Mislukte Vereeniging', *Marineblad* 1937, 890–899. That Beaufort withdrew without orders from Paris is confirmed in Louis XIV, *Mémoires*, 202–207.

299 Capture of *Rubis*: Allin i, 290–292; Barlow i, 125–126. Two Dutch ships often mentioned as having been destroyed in this incident had actually been run ashore on the 15th; see Allin i, 289–290.

299 'Our whole Fleet': Marvell, 'The Third Advice to a Painter', line 434.

300 'A great sum': Pepys, 13 Oct. 1666.

300 'A sad consideration': *Ibid.*, 4 Apr. 1667.

301 'Audacious enterprise': Evelyn, 11 June 1667.

301 Medway raid: Bodleian, Rawlinson MSS A.195, ff. 78, 106–107, 129–131, 159, and 163; Albemarle's deposition, BL Add. 32094, ff. 196–200 (another copy in All Souls College MSS 123); Rogers, *The Dutch in the Medway*, is an excellent modern account.

302 'A Dreadfull': Evelyn, 28 June 1667.

302 'By God!': Pepys, 19 July 1667.

303 Harman at Martinique: *CSP Colonial, America and West Indies* v, 481 (Nº 1524) and 495–496 (Nº 1568); *CSP Dom.* vii, 447–448.

XIX. EPILOGUE

304 'The miscarriages': Bodleian, Rawlinson MSS A. 195, f. 6, which lists the subjects to be investigated.

305 'Great negligence': Albemarle's deposition, BL Add. 32094, ff. 196–200; another copy in All Souls College MSS 123.

305 'Intollerable neglect': Rupert's deposition, BL Add. 32094, ff. 202–205.

305 Coventry's testimony: Bath 95, f. 214; his notes are in BL Add. 32094, ff. 206–208.

305 'Great high words': Pepys, 17 Feb. 1668.

307 'Like a Roman': *Dict. Natl. Biog.*, citing *Moncton Papers*, ed. Peacock, 1885, 94.

307 'How that blockhead': Pepys, 23 Oct. 1667.

308 'On the bed': Blok, *De Ruyter*, 383.

309 *Oxford* blown up: Pope, *The Buccaneer King*, 165–166.

310 Fates of warships: Vreugdenhil, *Ships of the United Netherlands, 1648–1702*; and Colledge, *Ships of the Royal Navy* i.

310 *Royal Katherine*'s 1673 modifications: *CSP Dom.* Addenda, 375, 20 Feb. 1673 (Beach to Navy Commissioners).

Manuscript Sources

Codrington Library, All Souls College, Oxford

MSS 123:   Albemarle's deposition to the Committee of Miscarriages.
MSS 256:   Anonymous account of the Four Days' Battle, ff. 136–147.

Bodleian Library, Oxford

Carte Papers
Vol. 72:   Albemarle's narrative of the Four Days' Battle, f. 37.
Rawlinson MSS
A.174:   Letter, Coventry to Pepys, 21 Apr. 1665, f. 458.
A.191:   List of captains killed during the war, f. 198.
A.194:   Letter, Albemarle to Coventry, 16 June 1666, f. 209.
A.195:   Pepys Papers, correspondence and narratives.
A.252:   Sir Gilbert Talbot's correspondence as ambassador to Denmark.
A.256:   Sir Thomas Clifford's narratives, July–Sept. 1665.
A.468:   Sandwich's narratives, 1665.

British Library

Additional MSS
9302:   Fleet ordnance list, Apr. 1666, ff. 181v.–182r.
9336:   Ship Lists, ff. 85–88.
17484:   Journal of Francis Digby.
32094:   Naval affairs, 1664–1668.
Egerton MSS
2618:   Sandwich's narrative, Sept. 1665.
Harleian MSS
1247:   Sea-book of Capt. Robert Moulton.
6859:   Sir Gilbert Talbot's narrative of the Bergen affair, ff. 43–61.
Sloane MSS
3232:   Additional Instructions for Fighting, f. 83.

Marquis of Bath, Longleat House, Wiltshire – Longleat Coventry MSS

Vol. 1:   Fleet correspondence, May 1666, including Rupert's recall orders.
Vol. 95:   Correspondence concerning the division of the fleet.
Vol. 96:   Intelligence letter, Coventry to Generals, 25 May 1666, f. 152.
Vol. 98:   Casualty lists, ff. 185–186; Officers replaced, ff. 190–192.
Vol. 99:   Notes for Coventry's testimony to the Committee of Miscarriages, f. 88.
App. I: Letter, Rupert to Coventry, 26 May 1666, f. 13.

National Maritime Museum

AGC/R2:	Prince Rupert's narrative of the Four Days' Battle.
CLU/2:	Albemarle's narrative of the Four Days' Battle.
DAR/2:	Sea-book of Sir Edward Spragge.
DAR/3:	Letter-book of Prince Rupert and the Duke of Albemarle, 1666.
HSR/l/2:	Letter, Generals to Charles II, 5 June 1666.
IGR/17:	Journal of Jeremy Roch.
Wyn/14/1:	Letter, Jordan to Penn, 5 June 1666.
Wyn/14/10:	Fighting Instructions, 1665.
Wyn/14/11:	Sailing Instructions, 1665.

Public Record Office

PRO 30/37:	Journal, Issues of Stores and Arms, vol. 7.
SP29:	State Papers Domestic, Charles II: vols. 108–167.
SP44:	State Papers Domestic, Supplementary: vol. 23.
SP46:	State Papers Domestic, Supplementary: vols. 136–137.
SP78:	State Papers Foreign, France: vol. 122.
SP84:	State Papers Foreign, Holland: vols. 176, 177, and 180.
SP101:	State Papers Foreign Newsletters: vols. 48–50.
WO51:	War Office Bill-Books, vols. 6 and 7.
WO55:	War Office Miscellanea: vols. 1652 and 1653.

Printed Sources

Aitzema, Lieuwe van: *Saken van Staet en Oorlogh in ende Omtrent de Vereenigde Nederlanden*, Vol. V., 's-Gravenhage, 1670.

(Allard, Carel): *L'Art de Batir les Vaisseaux . . .* , Amsterdam, 1719.

Allin, Sir Thomas: *The Journals of Sir Thomas Allin, 1660–1678*, ed. R.C. Anderson. 2 vols., Navy Records Society, London, 1939–1940.

Arlington, Henry Bennet, Earl of: *The Right Honourable the Earl of Arlington's Letters*. 2 vols., London, 1701.

Barlow, Edward: *Barlow's Journal of his Life at Sea in King's Ships, East & West Indiamen & Other Merchantmen from 1659 to 1703*, ed. Basil Lubbock. 2 vols., London, 1934.

Blok, P.: *The Life of Admiral de Ruyter*, translated by G.J. Renier. London, 1933.

Boteler (Butler), Nathaniel: *Boteler's Dialogues*, ed. W.G. Perrin. Navy Records Society, London, 1929.

Boxer, C.R.: *The Anglo-Dutch Wars of the 17th Century, 1652–1674*. London, 1974.

Brandt, G.: *Het Leven en Bedrijf van den Heere Michiel de Ruiter*. Amsterdam, 1687.

Brown, Thomas: *Miscellanea Aulica*. London, 1702.

Burnet, Gilbert: *Bishop Burnet's History of His Own Time*. Second edition, 6 vols., Oxford, 1833.

Calendar of State Papers, Colonial Series: America and West Indies, ed. W. Sainsbury. Vol. V (1661–1668), London, 1880.

Calendar of State Papers and Manuscripts Relating to English Affairs Existing in the Archives and Collections of Venice, ed. A.B. Hinds. Vols. XXXIV–XXXV, London, 1933.

Calendar of State Papers, Domestic Series, Charles II. Vols. IV–VII and XXVIII, London, 1860–1939.

Calendar of State Papers Relating to Ireland, ed. R.P. Mahaffy. Vol. VII, London, 1908.

Caruana, Adrian B.: *The History of English Sea Ordnance.* Vol. I, *The Age of Evolution, 1523–1715.* Jean Boudriot Publications, Rotherfield, 1994.

Charnock, John: *Biographia Navalis.* 6 vols., London, 1794–1798.

Charnock, John: *An History of Marine Architecture.* 3 vols., London, 1800–1802.

Clarendon, Edward Hyde, Earl of: *The History of the Rebellion and Civil Wars in England*, ed. W.D. Macray. 6 vols., Oxford, 1888.

Clarendon, Edward Hyde, Earl of: *The Life of Edward Earl of Clarendon, Written by Himself.* New edition, 3 vols., Oxford, 1827.

Clarke, J.S.: *The Life of James II.* 2 vols., London, 1816.

Clowes, William Laird: *The Royal Navy, a History from the Earliest Times to the Present.* 7 vols., London, 1897–1903.

Colenbrander, H.T.: *Bescheiden uit Vreemde Archieven Omtrent de Groote Nederlandsche Zeeoorlogen, 1652–1676.* 2 vols., The Hague, 1919.

Colledge, J.J.: *Ships of the Royal Navy, an Historical Index.* 2 vols., New York, 1969–1970.

'Combat Naval entre les Hollandais et les Anglais, les 11, 12, 13 et 14 Juin 1666', *Revue Maritime et Coloniale*, LXXXII (1884), 137–148.

Corbett, Julian S.: *Fighting Instructions 1530–1816.* Navy Records Society, London, 1905.

Dictionary of National Biography.

Dik, G.C.: 'De Zeven Provinciën', *De Model Bouwer*, 1983, nº. 1, 16–26, and nº. 2, 60–64.

Dryden, John: *The Poetical Works of Dryden*, ed. George R. Noyes. Second edition, Cambridge, Mass., 1937.

Elias, Johan E.: *De Vlootbouw in Nederland in de Eerste Helft der Zeventiende Eeuw, 1596–1655.* Amsterdam, 1933.

Estrades, Godefroi Comte d': *Lettres, Mémoires et Négociations de Monsieur le Comte d'Estrades.* Second edition, 9 vols., London, 1743.

Evans, H. Muir: 'The Kentish Flats and Southern Channels', *The Mariner's Mirror*, XVI (1930), 319–342.

Evans, H. Muir: 'The Long Sand and Southern Channels', *The Mariner's Mirror*, XVIII, (1932), 45–63.

Evans, H. Muir: 'The Sandbanks of Yarmouth and Lowestoft', *The Mariner's Mirror*, XV (1929), 251–270.

Evans, H. Muir: 'Sands, Gats and Swatchways between Harwich and the Nore', *The Mariner's Mirror*, XVI (1930), 68–84.

Evelyn, John: *The Diary of John Evelyn*, ed. E.S. de Beer. London, 1959.

Fernandez Duro, Cesareo: *Armada Española desde la Union de los Reinos de Castilla y de Leon.* 9 vols., Madrid, 1895–1903.

Fraser, Antonia: *Cromwell, the Lord Protector.* New York, 1973.

Fraser, Peter D.: *The Intelligence of the Secretaries of State and Their Monopoly of Licensed News, 1660–1688.* Cambridge, 1956.

Greene, Graham: *Lord Rochester's Monkey.* New York, 1974.

Guiche, Armand de Gramont, Comte de: *Mémoires du Comte de Guiche Concernant les Provinces-Unies des Païs-Bas.* London, 1744.

Gumble, Thomas: *The Life of General Monck.* London, 1671.

Historical Manuscripts Commission:
  The Manuscripts of J.M. Heathcote. 1889.
  The Manuscripts of the Marquess of Ormonde, New Series. Vol. III, 1904.
  The Manuscripts of S.H. Le Fleming, 12th Report, Appendix VII. 1890.

Hollond, John: *Two Discourses of the Navy, 1638 and 1659*, ed. J.R. Tanner. Navy Records Society, London, 1896.

Howarth, David: *The Men-of-War*. Alexandria, Virginia, 1978.

The Jacobean Commissions of Enquiry, 1608 and 1618, ed. A.P. McGowan. Navy Records Society, London, 1971.

Jonge, J.C. de: *Geschiedenis van het Nederlandsche Zeewezen*. 5 vols., Haarlem, 1858–1862.

Journals of the House of Commons. Vol. VIII (1660–1667).

Kennet, White: *Complete History of England*. Vol. III, second edition, London, 1719.

Laughton, L.G. Carr: *Old Ship Figure-Heads & Sterns*. London, 1925.

Lavery, Brian: *Deane's Doctrine of Naval Architecture, 1670*. London, 1981.

Lediard, Thomas: *The Naval History of England*. London, 1735.

Letters and Papers Relating to the First Dutch War, 1652–1654, ed. C.T. Atkinson. Vols. IV–V, Navy Records Society, London, 1909 and 1911.

Liefde, Jacob de: *The Great Dutch Admirals*. London, 1873.

The Life of Cornelis Tromp. English edition, London, 1697.

London Gazette, nos. 51–80, May–Aug. 1666.

Louis XIV: *Mémoires for the Instruction of the Dauphin*, ed. and trans. Paul Sonnino, New York, 1970.

Mainwaring, Sir Henry: *The Life and Works of Sir Henry Mainwaring*, ed. G.E. Manwaring and W.G. Perrin. 2 vols., Navy Records Society, London, 1920–1921.

Marvell, Andrew: *Andrew Marvell: Complete Poetry*, ed. George de F. Lord. New York, 1968.

Monson, Sir William: *The Naval Tracts of Sir William Monson*, ed. M. Oppenheim. 5 vols., Navy Records Society, London, 1902–1914.

'Naval Operations in the Latter Part of the Year 1666: "The Daily Motion and Public Transactions of His Majesty's Fleet . . .",' ed. R.C. Anderson, in *The Naval Miscellany*, vol. III, ed. W.G. Perrin. Navy Records Society, London, 1928 (pp. 5–47).

Ollard, Richard: *Man of War, Sir Robert Holmes and the Restoration Navy*. London, 1969.

Penn, Granville: *Memorials of the Professional Life and Times of Sir William Penn, Knt.* 2 vols., London, 1833.

Pepys, Samuel: *The Diary of Samuel Pepys*, ed. Robert Latham and William Matthews. 11 vols., Berkeley, 1970.

Pepys, Samuel: *Samuel Pepys's Naval Minutes*, ed. J.R. Tanner. Navy Records Society, London, 1926.

Pepys, Samuel: *The Tangier Papers of Samuel Pepys*, ed. Edwin Chappell. Navy Records Society, London, 1935.

Pope, Dudley: *The Buccaneer King, the Biography of Sir Henry Morgan, 1635–1688*. New York, 1978.

Rauws, H.: 'De Mislukte Vereeniging der Fransche en Staatsche Vloten in het Najaar van 1666', *Marineblad*, 52 (1937), 883–901.

Robinson, M.S.: *Van de Velde Drawings, a Catalogue of Drawings in the National Maritime Museum Made by the Elder and the Younger Willem Van de Velde*. 2 vols., Cambridge, 1973.

Robinson, M.S., and Weber, R.E.J.: *The Willem Van de Velde Drawings in the Boymans-van Beuningen Museum, Rotterdam*. 3 vols., Rotterdam, 1979.

Rodger, N.A.M.: *Articles of War, the Statutes which Governed our Fighting Navies, 1661, 1749, and 1886*. Homewell, Havant, Hampshire, 1982.

Rogers, P.G.: *The Dutch in the Medway*. London, 1970.

The Rupert and Monck Letterbook, 1666, ed. J.R. Powell and E.K. Timings. Navy Records Society, London, 1969.

Sandwich, Edward Montagu, Earl of: *The Journal of Edward Mountagu, First Earl of Sandwich*, ed. R.C. Anderson. Navy Records Society, London, 1929.

Sutherland, William: *The Ship-builder's Assistant . . .* London, 1711. Facs. Jean Boudriot Publications, Rotherfield, 1989.

Tanner, J.R.: *A Descriptive Catalogue of the Naval Manuscripts in the Pepysian Library at Magdalene College, Cambridge*. Vol. I, Navy Records Society, London, 1903.

Tedder, Arthur W.: *The Navy of the Restoration*. Cambridge, 1916.

Teonge, Henry: *The Diary of Henry Teonge, Chaplain on Board H.M.'s Ships* Assistance, Bristol *and* Royal Oak, *anno. 1673 to 1679*, (a) ed. anon., London, 1825; (b) ed. G.E. Manwaring, London, 1927.

Van Foreest, H.A., and Weber, R.E.J.: *De Vierdaagse Zeeslag, 11–14 Juni 1666*. Amsterdam, 1984.

Van IJk, Cornelis: *De Nederlandsche Scheeps-bouw-konst open Gestelt . . .* Ian ten Hoorn, Amsterdam, 1697.

Vreugdenhil, A.: *Ships of the United Netherlands, 1648–1702*. London, 1938.

Warnsinck, J.C.M.: *De Retourvloot van Pieter de Bitter*. 's-Gravenhage, 1929.

Weber, R.E.J.: 'Een Beschouwing over het Invoeren van de Linie van Bataille bij de Nederlandse Oorlogsvloot, 1665–1666', *Marineblad*, 90 (1980), 331–342.

Woodall, John: *The Surgeon's Mate*. London, 1639.

Witsen, Nicolaes: *Aeloude en Hedendaegsche Scheeps-Bouw en Bestier . . .* , Amsterdam, 1671. Repr. Canaletto, Alpen a/d Rijn, 1979.

Index

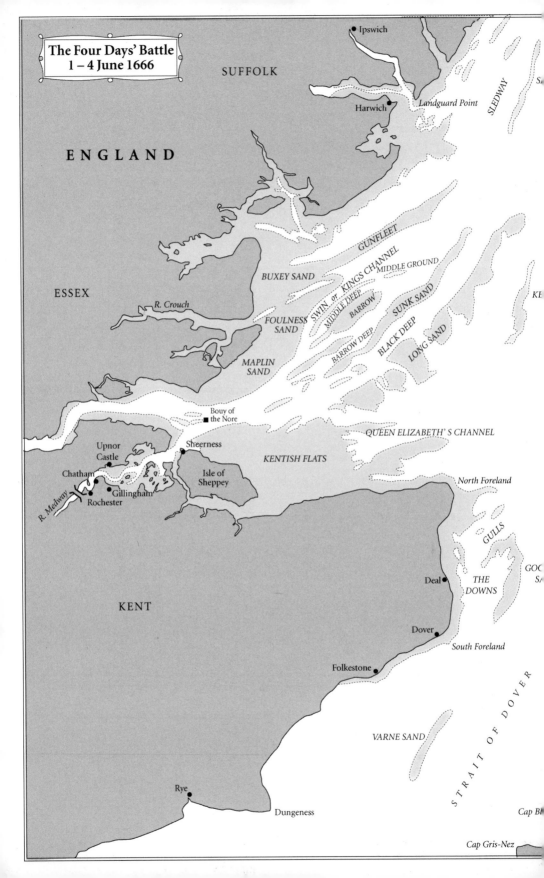

**The Four Days' Battle
1 – 4 June 1666**

ENGLAND

SUFFOLK

● Ipswich

Landguard Point

Harwich ●

SLEDWAY

ESSEX

R. Crouch

BUXEY SAND

FOULNESS
SAND

MAPLIN
SAND

GUNFLEET

SWIN or KINGS CHANNEL

MIDDLE DEEP

BARROW

BARROW DEEP

MIDDLE GROUND

SUNK SAND

BLACK DEEP

LONG SAND

KE

■ Bouy of
the Nore

Upnor
Castle

Chatham ●

Sheerness ●

Gillingham

Rochester

R. Medway

Isle of
Sheppey

KENTISH FLATS

QUEEN ELIZABETH'S CHANNEL

North Foreland

GULLS

GOO
S/

KENT

Deal ●

THE
DOWNS

Dover ●

South Foreland

Folkestone ●

VARNE SAND

S T R A I T   O F   D O V E R

Rye ●

Dungeness

Cap Bl

Cap Gris-Nez